Toy Cars & Trucks

Identification and Value Guide

2nd Edition

Richard O'Brien

© 1997 by

Richard O'Brien

Published by

krause publications

700 E. State Street • Iola, WI 54990-0001
Telephone: 715/445-2214

Please call or write for our free catalog. Our toll-free number to place an order or obtain a free catalog is 800-258-0929 or please use our regular business telephone 715-445-2214 for editorial comment and further information.

ISBN: 0-89689-128-3

Printed in the United States of America

CONTENTS

Introduction 5
Condition & Pricing 6
Fakes 7

A.C. Gilbert 9
A.S. (Adolf Schumann) 9
Acme 9
Acme Plastic Toys, Inc. 10
Aerocar 14
Al Otto 14
Al Toy 14
All-American (Los Angeles) 14
All American Toy Company
    (Oregon) 15
All-Nu 18
Allied Molding Corporation 18
American Metal Toys 19
American National 20
American Precision Co. 21
AMF 22
AMT (Aluminum Model Toys):
    See Promotionals
Andy Gard 22
Animate Toy Co. 22
Arcade 23
Archer Plastic 41
Archer Non-Space 41
Argo 41
Arnold 42
Astra Pharos 43
Auburn Rubber 43
Auburn Rubber Vinyl 52
Aurora 53
Automatic Toy Company 53
B-Line Toys 54
Banner 54
Banthrico: See Promotionals
Barclay 56
Barr Rubber 72
Beaut Mfg. Co. 72
Benbros 72
Best Toy & Novelty Factory 73
Bico 76
Big Bang 76
Big Boy: See Kelmet
Bing Toy Works 76
BMC 79
Bonnie Bilt 79
Boycraft 80
Breslin 80
Brimtoy 80
Brinks 81
Britains 81

Britains Farm 85
Britains Lilliput 86
Brooklin Models 87
Buckeye 99
Buddy L 99
Buffalo Toys 112
Built-Rite 112
Burdette Murray 113
Burnett Ltd. 113
BW Molded Plastics 114
C.A.W. Novelty Company 114
C.R. (Charles Rossignol) 118
Carette, Georges 119
Cass Toys 120
Chad Valley 121
Champion 121
Chein 122
Chein Hercules "C" Cab
    Mack Trucks 123
CIJ 128
Citroen 128
Clark, D.P. 128
Cleveland Toy 132
Cohn 133
Comet-Authenticast 133
Converse 135
Conway 135
Cor-Cor 136
Corgi 137
Courtland 139
Cox 151
Craftoys 151
Cragstan 153
D&L Plastics 153
Daisy 153
Daytime Lines 154
Dayton Friction Toy Works 154
Deluxe 155
Dent Hardware Company 156
Dinky (Civilian) 158
Dinky (Military) 160
Distler 173
Doepke "Model Toys" 174
Doll & Co. 179
Dooling Brothers 179
Druge 179
Dunwell 180
Dyna-Model Products Company . 181
EBO 182
Elastolin (Hausser) 182
Eldon 187
Elmar Products 188

Empire Forces (Gardel) 188
Erie 188
Ertl 189
Erwin 192
F&F Cereal Premiums 192
Fallows Toys 193
Firestone 193
Fischer, Heinrich & Co. 194
Fisher-Price 195
Freidag 196
"Futuristic" 197
G&K 197
Gama 197
Garland 201
Garrett 201
Garton 201
Gay Plastics 201
Gendron 201
General Toy of Canada 203
Gibbs 203
Giftcraft 203
Gilbert: See A.C. Gilbert
Gilmark 203
Girard 203
Glass 204
Globe Co. 205
Gong Bell 205
Goodee 205
Grey Iron 206
Grimland 206
Gunthermann 207
Gyro 208
Hafner 209
Halsam 209
Handi-Craft Co. 211
Happy Sam 211
Harris 211
Hauser: See Elastolin
Henry, M.A. 211
Hess Promotional Toys 212
Hess Toy Co. 217
Highway Patrol (TV) 218
Hill Climber 218
Hiller 218
Hoge 218
Holgate 219
Holmes Coal 219
Hot Wheels: See Mattel
Hubley 219
Ideal 238
Ingap 243
Irwin Toy Corporation 243

Ives 244
J&S 244
Jane Francis 244
Japanese Battery-Operated Toys . 246
Japanese (etc.) Tin Cars ... 258
JEP 284
Jo Han: See Promotionals
Jones & Bixler 285
Judy Company, The 285
Kahn 285
Kansas Toy & Novelty Company 286
Kansas Toy
    Transitional Vehicles 295
Karl Bub 295
Kelmet 296
Kenton 297
Keystone 303
Kilgore 324
Kingsbury 328
Kingston Producers 332
Knapp 332
Laketoy 333
Lansing Slik-Toys 333
Lapin 334
Lee Stokes Industries 335
Lehigh Bitsi-Toys 335
Lehmann, Ernst Paul 336
Lido 339
Limousine 340
Lincoln Logs 340
Lincoln Toys 341
Lincoln White Metal Works 341
Lindstrom 345
Linemar: See Marx
Lineol 346
Lionel 349
Lledo Models 349
Londontoy 350
Lumar: See Marx
Lupor Metal Products 351
M&L Toy Co., Inc. 352
Manoil 353
Marklin 357
Marx 363
Mason & Parker 391
Matchbox 391
Mattel's Hot Wheels 401
Meccano Cars 409
Metal Cast Products Company ... 415
Metal Masters 418
Metalcraft 418
Metalgraf Company 422
Mettoy 422
Midgetoy 422
Mid-West Metal Novelty
    Manufacturing Company 424
Military Vehicles
    (IDs and miscellaneous) 427
Miniature Vehicle Castings, Inc. 433
Minic 434
Mitten 447
Modern Toys 447
Mohawk Toy 447
Moko Toys 448
Mormac 448
"Moxie" 449
MPC (Model Products Corp.) 449
Murray 449

National Products:
    See "Promotionals"
Neff-Moon Toy Company 449
Nifty 451
Noma 451
North & Judd 451
Nosco 452
Nylint 453
Oh Boy 457
Ohio Art 459
Ohlson & Rice 460
Orobr Toy Works 460
Pagco 461
Parker Bros. 461
Paya (Spain) 461
Payton 461
Perfect Rubber Co. 463
Peter-Mar Toys 463
Pinard 464
Plas-Tex: See Aerocar
Plasticraft 465
Plasticville 465
Playboy 465
Playwood Plastics 465
Precision Plastics 466
Premier (Brooklyn) 466
Premier (Japan) 466
Pressman 466
Processed Plastic 466
Product Miniatures:
    See Promotionals
Promotionals 467
Pyro 476
Rainbow 479
Ralstoy 480
Ranger Steel Co. 482
Ranlite 482
Realistic 485
Rehrberger 486
Reliable 486
Reliance Molded Plastics, Inc. ... 487
Remco 488
Renwal 488
Republic Tool Products Co. 495
Reuhl Products, Inc. 496
Revell 497
Rich Toy 498
Richard Appel 499
Richard Toys 499
Richmond 499
Rico Co. 499
Roberts 499
"Rocket" 499
Roi-Tan 499
Ross Tool and
    Manufacturing Co. 500
RSA 500
Rubber Vehicles
    (unknown manufacturers) 501
Saunders 503
Savoye 504
Scale Model Products:
    See Promotionals
Schieble Toy & Novelty Co. 507
Schoenhut 508
Schuco 508
Scientific 510
Seiberling Rubber 510

Sharron 510
Sherwood Toy Co. 511
Skippy 511
Skoglund & Olson 511
Slik-Toys: See Lansing
Smith-Miller (Smitty) 512
Solido 520
Sonicon 521
Sonny 521
Stanley & Cox 522
Stanley Works 522
Star Brand 522
Steelcraft 523
Steer O Toys 526
Strauss 526
Strombecker 528
Structo 528
Sturdi-Bilt 537
Sturditoy 537
Sun Rubber 539
Superior 542
TCO 542
Technofix 543
Ted Toys 543
Thimble Drome 543
Thomas Toys 545
Timmee 561
Timpo 561
Tip Top 561
Tipp (Tipp & Co., Tippco) 564
Tipper 564
Toledo Metal Wheel Company ... 568
Tommy Toy 568
Tonka 570
Tootsietoy 576
Toy Founders 584
Trailer Co. 584
Tru-Scale International Trucks ... 585
Tru-Toy 588
Trumodel: See Kelmet
Turner, John C. 588
Unique Art. Mfg. Co. 590
Unknowns 591
Varney 594
Viceroy 594
Viking 595
Vindex 595
Walker & Stewart 596
Wannatoy 596
Warren 597
Weeden 597
Wellmade Doll & Toy Co. 598
Wells 598
Wen-Mac 598
Western Toy Co. 598
Wilkins Toy Company 598
Williams, A.C. 599
Wolverine 603
Wood Commodities Corp. 603
Wood Products Corp. 604
Woodhaven 604
Wyandotte 604
Yone 629

Toy Shows 631
Toy Publications 631
Toy Repairers 631
Some Leading
    Collectors & Dealers 633

INTRODUCTION AND ACKNOWLEDGMENTS

When I began work on the first edition of this book, it was because I thought there would be considerable interest by collectors; vehicles seemed to be the most popular toy, with the possible exception of trains.

It turned out I was right. Sales of the first edition were very strong, thus resulting in this updated and expanded version. Last time, more than 250 manufacturers were represented; this edition has over 300. More than 1,500 listings have been added, and nearly 900 black-and-white photos are new. All new is the color section, which has also been expanded.

This book would be nothing without its contributors. Pitching in this time with whole sections (and sometimes considerably more) were: Ron Smith, Bob Smith, Thomas G. Nefos, Vincent Rosa, Jack Matthews, John Gibson, Mark McManus, Don DeSalle, Gates Willard, Joe and Sharon Freed, William H. Kilborn, Don Hultzman, Brian Seligman, Ed Poole, Kent M. Comstock, Dave Leopard, Terry Sells, Mary Gaeta, Fred Maxwell and Ray Funk.

Photos are the lifeblood of a book like this. In addition to most of the above-mentioned, providers of visual material include Ron Fink, Stan Alekna, Perry Eichor, Al Lane, Dick MacNary, Bill Holt, Bill Bertoia, Jeffrey L. Hubbard, Scott Smiles, John Monteleone, Tim Oei, Joe Lechleider, Don Patman, Patrick O'Neil, Roy Bonjour, Chic Gast, Rod Carnahan, Harvey K. Rainess, Mary Gaeta, Christie's East, and Sotheby's New York.

Thanks to all, and to Dan Alexander, my former publisher, who gave me the chance to do this book.

Richard O'Brien
May, 1997

CONDITION AND PRICING

When it comes to toys, condition is paramount. Prices are based on condition, so it's important to understand what condition means to a collector or dealer. Here are some terms and general guidelines (note that Mint-in-Box commands a higher price, and condition below C6 brings considerably lower prices):

C6: Good. Evident overall wear, well-played with, but acceptable to many collectors.
C8: Very Good. Minor wear overall, very clean.
C10: Mint (like new).

It's also important to remember that this book is a guide. It is not the absolute last word on the price of a toy. Nothing could be. Prices may inflate or deflate in the months it takes to compile and publish a book. Even on the same day, a toy can vary in price, depending on the dealer, the buyer, the geographical area, and whether it's being offered in the first moments of a toy show or in the last, draggy minutes, (when the dealer finds himself having to pack up all that stuff again).

"Auction fever" can drive a toy to a ridiculous new height; or establish it as the new height. Employed by itself, *Collecting Toy Cars & Trucks* should at least prevent very serious mistakes from being made when buying or selling. Used with the assistance of a few current prices found on lists or on dealer tables, it can get the prospective buyer or seller much nearer to the current market price.

Concerning the notation *No Price Found*. This means that I or my contributors haven't found a price. It could mean the toy is rare. It could even mean it is rare and valuable (the two don't always go together). But so many toys were produced and so many bought and sold that often even a common toy doesn't surface on the lists or at shows for months or even years.

Finally, for those who wish to consider this field as an investment, and it can be a good one, it should be stressed that mint or near-mint condition provides considerably more financial safety than any of the other conditions, as this is the only condition certain to attract all collectors and dealers of any particular toy.

FAKES

by Rod Carnahan

Like any other field of collecting, fakes can be a problem in toy collecting. Cast-iron fakes have a thick cast, and pieces often don't fit together properly or evenly. The bottoms of many fake iron castings have break marks. When old toy makers took toys from the molds, they filed or machined-away those marks; this doesn't happen on most fakes, because it could increase the cost of labor for a cheap product (many iron copies are made in countries like Taiwan and are meant to be sold as copies, but often aren't).

Cast-iron fakes also have a rougher feel, a blurring of details, and a coarse and gritty look. Spot-welds also hold many fake castings together (rather than with the steel rivet rod that has been peened on one end). Fake wheels are thicker and often don't have enough spokes (as little as four where there should be nine). Some reproductions also have hollow-rolled tubing for the axles and screws to hold the castings together. Some people actually bury the fakes to "age" them; rust can be a giveaway, when combined with some or all of the other aspects already mentioned. A too-cheap price can be another indication the toy isn't original.

The best protection is knowledge. Go to shops and shows to help develop an "eye" for originals and fakes. Research via books and collector publications. Know the measurements of an original—reproductions are almost invariably a bit smaller. In the case of lead alloy toys, a heavier-than-expected weight suggests a recent casting, as the people who legitimately cast from the old molds usually make the toys heavier to keep them from breaking when shipped.

Many plastic toys are being reproduced. In this case, know what the original plastic looked like and what its color was. Reproductions, in general, try to use a different color. Also, plastics today look different, because (due to the danger of some of the original components) a different plastic must be used.

Final tips: For insurance purposes, it helps to videotape your collection. A computer software program can aid in keeping up with your investment.

A. C. GILBERT

Alfred Carlton Gilbert (1884-1961) is best known as the creator of the Erector set. However, Gilbert also produced some very attractive vehicles c. the early 1920s.

	C6	C8	C10
A.C. Gilbert Gilmotor Windup Truck, early, 10-1/2" long	250	375	500
A.C. Gilbert Racer, 9" long, windup	300	500	700
A.C. Gilbert Stutz	500	800	1200
A.C. Gilbert "U.S. Mail" Truck, copyright 1920, 8" long	375	565	750

A.C. Gilbert Gilmotor windup truck. Courtesy Joe and Sharon Freed.

A.S.

(Adolf Schumann, Nuremberg, Germany, 1910-1930s)

By Bob Smith

Schumann was making toys for about 20 years, but like many German toy companies, his went out of business in the mid-1930s. Not much is known about this small company, and its toys are considered rare. The A.S. trademark is usually on the door of the car.

A.S. (Germany) Racer, driver, c.1908. tin litho. "6," 7" long	500	750	1100
A.S. Touring Car, red/black, c/w motor, glass windshield 9" long, c.1915	1100	1350	1850

A.S. (Germany) Racer, driver, c.1908, tin litho. Courtesy Bill Bertoia Auctions. Photo by Jeanne Bertoia.

A.S. Touring Car, c.1915, 9" long. Photo by Bob Smith.

ACME

Acme seems to have produced only two toy vehicles, both in clockwork: a 1903 curved-dash Oldsmobile roadster and a delivery truck with a pressed-steel canopied roof. In 1905, Jacob Lauth, the owner of the Chicago firm, turned to production of the real thing under the name Lauth-Juergens, Co.

Acme Curved Dash Olds, 11" long, clockwork, c.1905	500	750	1000

Acme Curved Dash Olds, 11" long. Courtesy Wilkinson Collection, Detroit Antique Toy Museum.

ACME PLASTIC TOYS, INC.

Many, perhaps all, Acme vehicles are exactly like Thomas Toys. The reason is that Acme's Ben Shapiro was a financial partner in Thomas Toys. Thomas Toys' Islyn Thomas made up toys for Shapiro at his request, with the Acme imprint substituted for that of Thomas. Acme's order sheets sometimes show the name Acme Plastic Toys, Inc. and at other times, B.H. Shapiro & Co. In both cases the address was the same: 121 East 24th Street in New York City. Dates in parentheses indicate the year (where known) the items appeared in the firm's order sheets. Acme also made other toys including helicopters, planes, baby carriages and strollers, wagons, etc.

	C6	C8	C10
No. 16 Truck & Trailer, 9" long (1947)	14	16	18
No. 17 Jeep, 4-1/2" long, movable windshield (1947)	23	25	27

No. 16 Truck & Trailer

No. 17 Jeep

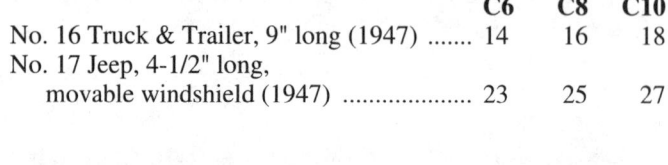

Acme No. 17 with original box. Photo by Terry Sells.

Acme Plastic Toys, Inc.

No. 18 Streamlined Truck

No. 19 Jeep & Trailer

No. 27 Sedan

No. 26 Truck Wrecker

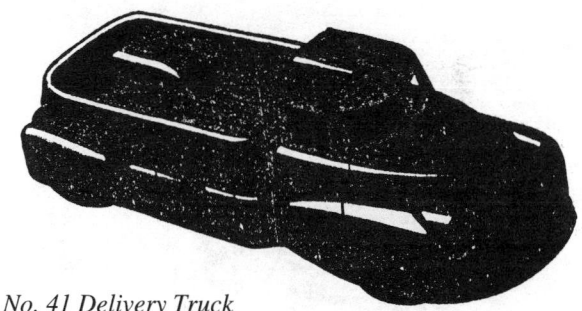

No. 30 Coupe & House Trailer

No. 29 Airline Limousine

No. 41 Delivery Truck

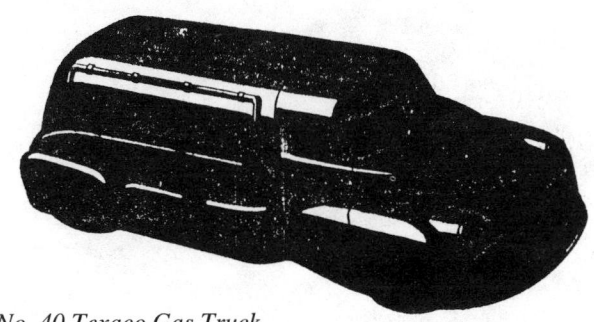

No. 40 Texaco Gas Truck

No. 42 Dump Truck

Acme Plastic Toys, Inc.  11

	C6	C8	C10
No. 18 Truck, Streamlined, 5" long (1947)	10	12	14
No. 19 Jeep & Trailer, 8-1/2" long (1947)	14	16	18
No. 26 Truck Wrecker, 5" long	35	40	45
No. 27 Sedan, 4-5/16" long (1947)	18	20	22
No. 29 Airline Limousine, 4-1/2" long (1947)	23	25	27
No. 30 Coupe & House Trailer, 8-1/4" long (1947)	20	22	24
No. 40 Texaco Gas Truck, 4" long (1947)	21	23	25
No. 41 Delivery Truck, 4" long (1947)	16	18	20
No. 42 Dump Truck, 5" long (1947)	12	14	16
No. 43 Esso Gas Truck (1947)	No Price Found		
No. 48 Streamlined Utility Trailer, "fits items 27-29-40-41," 2-1/2" long	6	8	10

	C6	C8	C10
No. 55 Limousine and Trailer, 6-3/4" long	26	31	36
No. 67 Police-Fire Chief Radio Car, each 4-1/2" long, price per each	23	25	27
No. 72 Plastic Motorcycle & Rider, 4" long	45	50	55
No. 74 Merry-Go-Round Truck, 4-3/4" long	20	25	30
No. 77 Streamlined Sedan, 4-1/2" long	11	13	15
No. 77 Streamlined Convertible Coupe, 4-1/2" long (Acme used the same number for these toys on the same order sheet)	9	11	13
No. 90 Service Motorcycle & Rider, 4-7/16" long	25	30	35
No. 125 Plated Motorcycle, 4" long	20	25	30

No. 43 Esso Gas Truck

No. 48 Streamlined Utility Trailer

No. 55 Limousine & Trailer

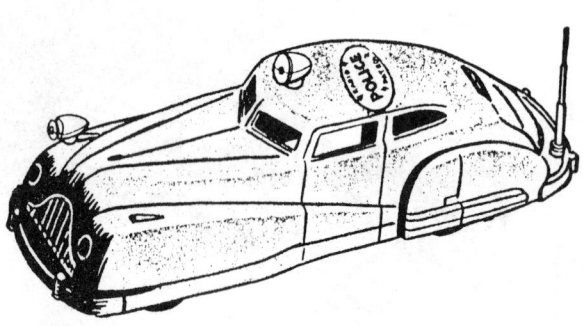

No. 67 Police-Fire Chief Radio Car

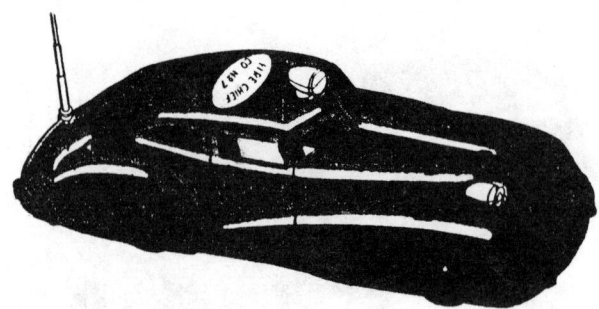

  Acme Plastic Toys, Inc.

No. 72 Plastic Motorcycle & Rider

No. 74 Merry-Go-Round Truck

No. 77 Streamlined Sedan

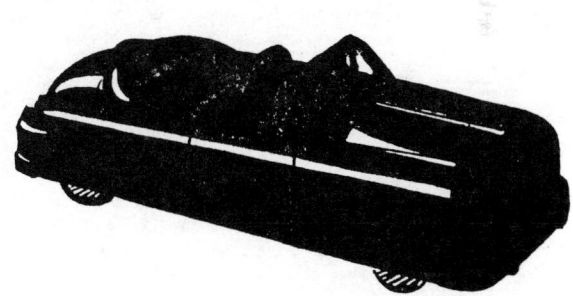

No. 77 Streamlined Convertible Coupe

No. 90 Service Motorcycle & Rider

No. 125 Plated Motorcycle

AEROCAR

	C6	C8	C10
Aerocar PT 560 Made in U.S.A. "Plas-Tex," 7-1/2", plastic	125	175	200

"Aerocar PT560 Made in U.S.A. Plas-Tex." Courtesy James S. Maxwell/Virginia Caputo. Photo by Virginia Caputo.

AL OTTO

(Chicago, 1940s-1950s)

	C6	C8	C10
Al Otto Stock Car Racer, 4-1/2" long, early plastic	4	10	25

Al Otto Stock Car Racers, made since 1949, are still sold at some racetracks in dull modern plastic. The old ones are very smooth and very shiny, as shown. Photo and caption courtesy Bob and Alice Wagner.

AL TOY

	C6	C8	C10		C6	C8	C10
Al Toy "Jeep" Fire Truck	1000	1700	2500	Al Toy Jeepster	1100	1850	2700
Al Toy Jeep Pickup Truck	400	750	1100	Al Toy Woody Station Wagon	600	950	1500

ALL-AMERICAN

(Los Angeles, California)

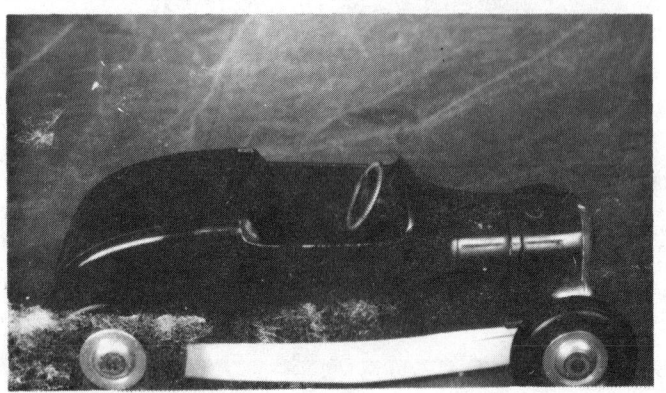

	C6	C8	C10
"All American Hot-Rod," 9" long, sold in 1949	210	315	420

"All American Hot-Rod," 1949, 9" long. Photo by Roger E. Canup.

ALL AMERICAN TOY COMPANY

All American was founded by Clay Steinke in Salem, Oregon, c. 1948. It continued until 1955, with its location the Jorgenson Building on Ferry Street. At its peak, it employed 42 people. In total, it sold 26,000 toys. Its most popular toy was the Timber Toter, despite its formidable 1950 price of $20. Bill Hellie purchased the defunct company—molds, dies, and parts. All American now sells parts and is producing new limited editions (see Leading Collectors and Dealers).

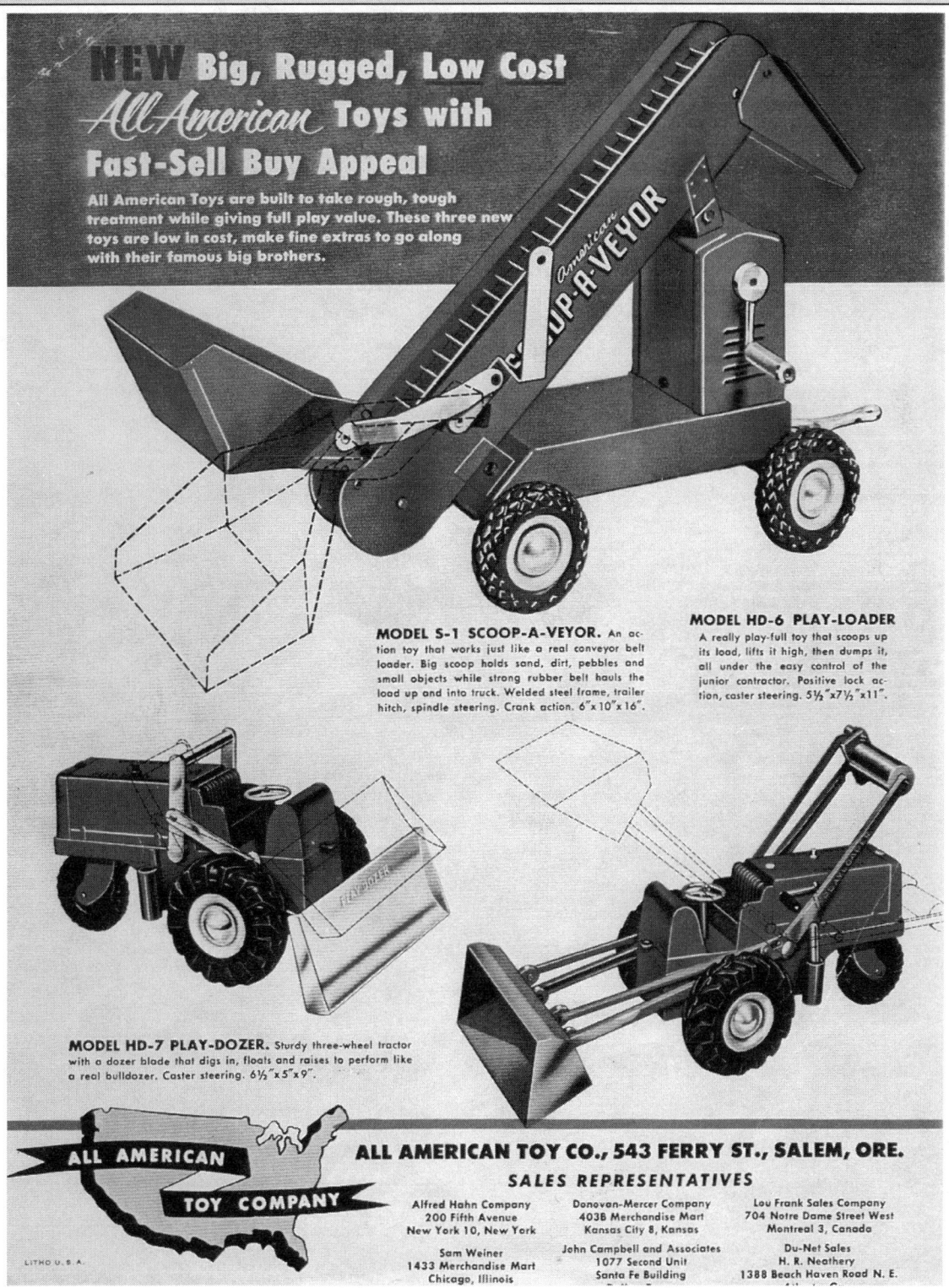

All American Catalog

AIR HORN STEERING

**MODEL CL-8
CARGO-LINER**
. . . top-selling "ride 'em"
truck and semi. Easy Air
Horn Steering for full
maneuverability. Hauls
just about anything a child
can think of. 8"x8"x38".

**MODEL L-2
TIMBER TOTER**
...a rugged, adjustable-bed
truck built just like the
mammoth logging trucks
that roar through West-
ern mountains. Air Horn
Steering. Truck 8"x8"x20".
Combination truck and
trailer adjustable to full
38". Logs are available at
slight extra cost.

**MODEL C-5
CATTLE-LINER**
Open-top truck and semi
is newest of big, tough
"ride-'em" trucks. Strong
steel sides are latticed. Air
Horn Steering. 8"x8"x38".

ALL AMERICAN TOY COMPANY

ALL AMERICAN TOY C

All American Toy Company

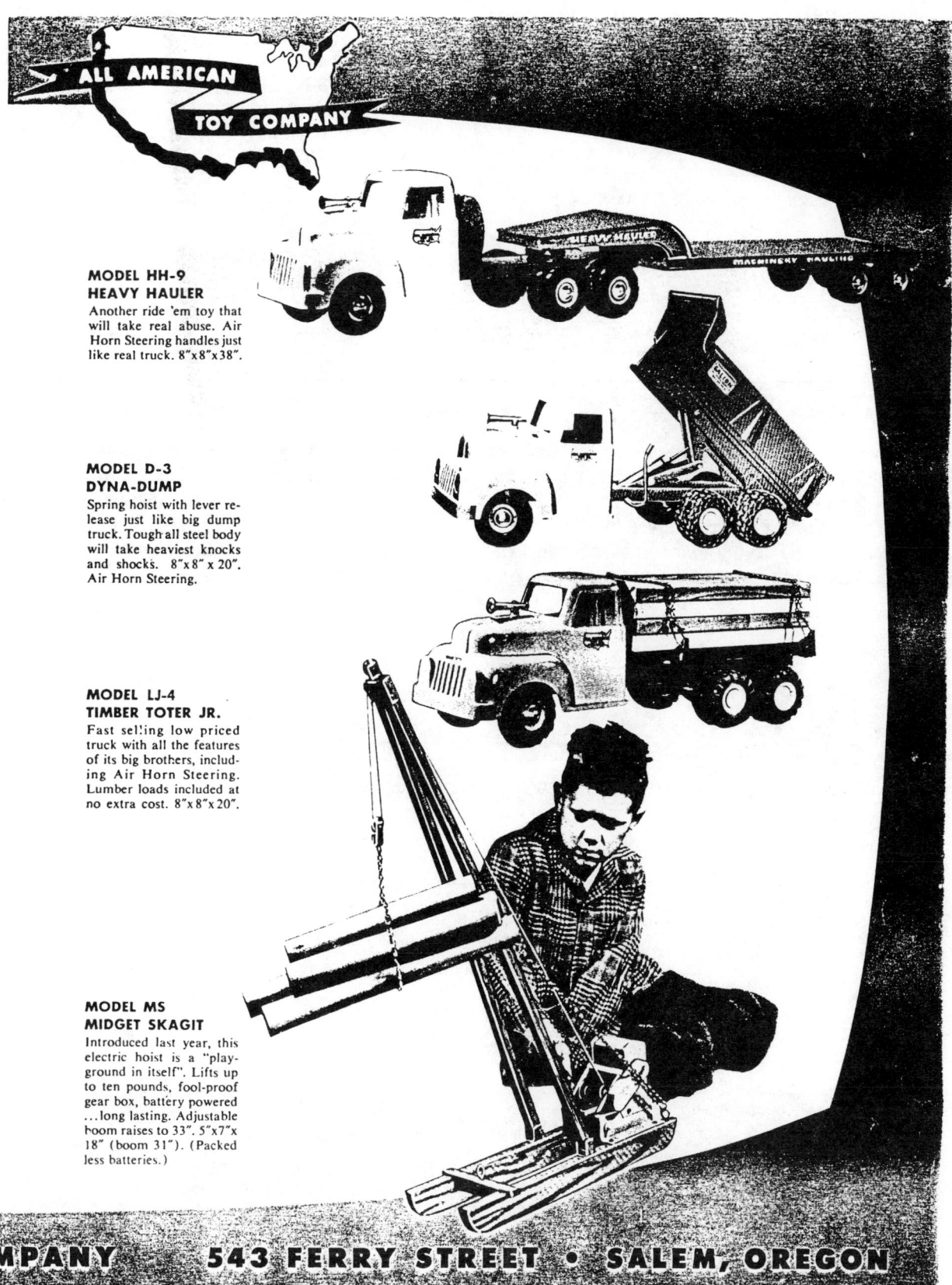

ALL AMERICAN TOY COMPANY

**MODEL HH-9
HEAVY HAULER**

Another ride 'em toy that will take real abuse. Air Horn Steering handles just like real truck. 8"x8"x38".

**MODEL D-3
DYNA-DUMP**

Spring hoist with lever release just like big dump truck. Tough all steel body will take heaviest knocks and shocks. 8"x 8" x 20". Air Horn Steering.

**MODEL LJ-4
TIMBER TOTER JR.**

Fast selling low priced truck with all the features of its big brothers, including Air Horn Steering. Lumber loads included at no extra cost. 8"x 8"x 20".

**MODEL MS
MIDGET SKAGIT**

Introduced last year, this electric hoist is a "playground in itself". Lifts up to ten pounds, fool-proof gear box, battery powered ...long lasting. Adjustable boom raises to 33". 5"x7"x 18" (boom 31"). (Packed less batteries.)

MPANY   543 FERRY STREET • SALEM, OREGON

	C6	C8	C10
All American C-5 Cattle Liner, 38" long	400	650	925
All American CL-8 Cargo Liner, 38" long	275	400	600
All American D-3 Dyna-Dump, 20" long	250	400	550
All American HD-6 Play-Loader, 11" long	300	500	700
All American HD-7 Play-Dozer, 9" long	300	500	700
All American HH-9 Heavy Hauler, 38" long	300	475	750

	C6	C8	C10
All American L-2 Timber Toter, with logs, 38" extended length	260	400	585
All American L J-4 Timber Toter, Jr., 20" long, with lumber	200	300	550
All American MS Midget Skagit, 18" long, battery-powered	250	450	600
All American S-I Scoop-A-Veyor, 16" long	240	360	480
All American U-1 Utility Truck	No Price Found		
All American W/T-6 Trailer	No Price Found		

ALL-NU

All-Nu was founded by former Barclay sculptor Frank Krupp in 1937 or 1938 (incorporation was Feb. 16, 1938). The original address was 55-58 Main Street, Yonkers, New York. The firm moved by the summer or fall of 1941 to 67 Irving Place in Manhattan. All-Nu's main products were soldiers and novelties. All-Nu's four lead vehicles are known only from the collection of Krupp's daughter. They would presumably be valuable if any reached the market (which seems likely, as the four examples seem to have come from finished molds), because All-Nu's very rare soldiers bring high prices.

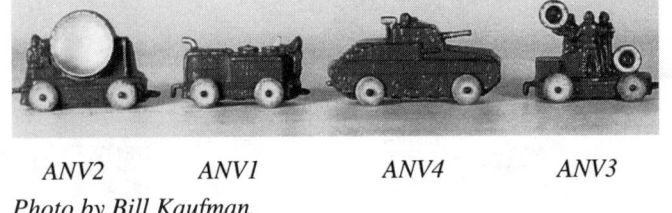

ANV2   ANV1   ANV4   ANV3

Photo by Bill Kaufman.

ANV 1 All-Nu "Field Kitchen," approx.
2-1/2" long,"Made in USA," lead .... No Price Found
ANV 2 All-Nu Searchlight, approx.
2-3/4" long, "Made in USA," lead .... No Price Found

		C6	C8	C10
ANV 3 All-Nu Sound Detector, approx. 2-3/4" long, "Made in USA," lead	No Price Found			
ANV 4 All-Nu Tank "USA," 3" long, "Made in USA," lead	No Price Found			
All-Nu cardboard vehicles:				
All-Nu 150 Jeep		3	5	7
All-Nu 151 Cannon		3	5	7
All-Nu 152 Wheeled AA Gun		3	5	7
All-Nu 153 Tank		3	5	7
All-Nu 154 Ambulance, Military		3	5	7
All-Nu 155 Army Troop Carrier		3	5	7

ALLIED MOLDING CORPORATION

Allied, of 126-02 Northern Blvd., Corona, New York, seems to have made only plastic toys. It made a variety, including vehicles, pistols, boats, animals, a Ferris Wheel, and a baby carriage.

	C6	C8	C10
Allied Auto Sales & Station, 5 vehicles	65	100	130
Allied Cement Mixer, No. 197, 4" long	No Price Found		
Allied Delivery Service Truck	35	52	70
Allied Dump Truck, Large, No. 174, 5-1/2" long	No Price Found		

	C6	C8	C10
Allied Dump Truck, Small, No. 191, 4-1/2" long	10	15	20
Allied Emergency Truck, 7" long, No. 129	No Price Found		
Allied Enclosed Van, 6" long	10	15	20

Allied Tractor, No. 30

Allied Haulaway Truck and Trailer, No. 122. Courtesy Bob and Alice Wagner.

Allied Fire Engine, No. 125

Allied Emergency Truck, No. 129

Allied Stake Truck with Animals, No. 193

Allied Old Fashioned Car, No. 218

Allied Furniture Moving Van. Photo by Dave Leopard.

	C6	C8	C10
Allied Fire Engine No. 125, 6-1/2" long .... No Price Found			
Allied Furniture Moving Van, Large, 5-1/2" long, No. 208, clear trailer ("Viso Box"), price without original ten pieces of furniture	10	15	20
Allied Haulaway Truck & Trailer, No. 122, 10" long, 2 small cars, one large car	15	25	38
Allied Old Fashioned Car, 4-1/2" long, No. 218 .... No Price Found			
Allied Pickup Truck, 3-1/2" long	8	10	15
Allied Racer No. 130, 4-5/8" long	15	25	33
Allied Stake Truck, 4-1/2" long	10	15	20

	C6	C8	C10
Allied Stake Truck with Animals, No. 193, 9-1/2" long, removable racks, 8 assorted farm animals .... No Price Found			
Allied Station Wagon, 3-1/2" long	8	10	15
Allied Steam Shovel Truck No. 134, 6" long .... No Price Found			
Allied Taxi, 3-1/2" long	8	10	15
Allied Tractor No. 30, 3" long .... No Price Found			
Allied Wrecker, 4-3/8"	15	20	25
Allied Construction Set No. 620: Dump Truck, Cement Truck, Emergency Truck with ladder, 15" long box .... No Price Found			

AMERICAN METAL TOYS

This was essentially a toy soldier company, in business in Chicago from 1937 to early 1942. Its toys were composed of a lead-zinc alloy.

	C6	C8	C10
(AMV1) Tank, throwing flame, flame touching hull	40	60	80
(AMV2) Tank, throwing flame, flame not touching hull	45	68	90

	C6	C8	C10
(AMV3) Tank, throwing flame, "25"	60	90	120
(AMV4) Tank, "22" on side	50	75	100

L to R: AMV3, AMV4, AMV2. Photo by Ed Poole.

L to R: AMV2, AMV1

AMERICAN NATIONAL

American National, of Toledo, Ohio, produced a huge number of pedal cars in the 1920s and 1930s. It also had a line of pressed-steel toy trucks from the late 1920s until the early 1930s. It was founded by the Diemer brothers—William, Walter, and Harry—about 1894.

American National "American Railway Express," 27" long. Courtesy Bill Bertoia Auctions. Photo by Jeanne Bertoia.

	C6	C8	C10
American National "American Railway Express," 27" long	1000	1600	2400
American National Army Truck, Mack "Giant," 26-1/2" long	800	1400	2000
American National Chemical Fire Truck, 28" long	2000	3200	4500
American National Circus Truck, 27" long	800	1400	2000
American National Coal Truck	1500	2500	4200
American National Duesenberg Bobtail Pedal Car, late 1920s	3000	5500	7000
American National Dump Truck, 28" long	800	1400	2000
American National "Fire Chief" Pedal Truck, 66" long	3000	5000	7900
American National Fire Pedal truck, c.late 1920s	4000	7500	13,000
American National Jordan Pedal Car, 40" long	1000	1700	2400
American National "Juvenile Auto" Dump Truck Pedal Car, 57" long	2000	3500	5000
American National Lincoln, Dual Cowl Pedal Car	4000	7500	12,000

American National Packard Coupe pedal car, 1928, 56" long. Courtesy Bill Bertoia Auctions. Photo by Jeanne Bertoia.

American National Packard, 1923 pedal car, 70" long. Courtesy Bill Bertoia Auctions. Photo by Jeanne Bertoia.

	C6	C8	C10
American National			
Moving Van, 28" long	800	1400	2000
American National Open			
Bed Truck, 29" long	700	1150	1700
American National Packard			
Coupe Pedal Car, 1928, 56" long	2000	3200	4600
American National Packard Coupe,			
54" long, steerable front wheels	1500	2500	3400
American National Packard,			
1923 Pedal Car, 70" long	3000	5500	10,000

	C6	C8	C10
American National Packard			
Fire Chief Car, 27" long	3000	5500	10,000
American National Racing Car, 1927	2000	3200	4500
American National "Richfield"			
Gasoline Truck, 27" long	1500	2250	3100
American National Screenside Truck	1500	2500	3600
American National Sprinkler Truck	1400	2500	3500
American National Tanker	1400	2500	3500

The premier line....exactingly modeled after the real cars....lustrous enamel finishes in flashy color combinations. Each with adjustable pedals

"WHIPPET"—Extreme length 32 in., American red enameled, blue & yellow trim, yellow number, 8 in. red enameled double spoke wire wheels, ⅜ in. rubber tires. EQUIPMENT—Cast steering wheel, gas lever, motor-meter, steel pedals. 1F820—1 in carton, 22 lbs...........Each $3.75

"DODGE"—Extreme length 35 in., American red enameled, chrome yellow trim, 10 in. wheels, ⅝ in. rubber tires. EQUIPMENT—Cast steering wheel, gas lever, motor-meter, steel pedals. 1F824—1 in carton, 26 lbs.........Each $4.50

"CYCLONE"—Extreme length 35 in., dk. blue enameled, tangerine trim, 10 in. double disc wheels. ½ in. rubber tires. EQUIPMENT—Gas lever, motor-meter, rubber pedals. 1F822 — 1 in carton. 33 lbs.........Each $5.50

"VELIE"—Extreme length 35 in., Falcon tan enameled, blue & yellow trim and stripes, spring chassis, 10 in. red enameled double disc wheels. ½ in. rubber tires. EQUIPMENT—Cast steering wheel, gas lever, nickeled motor-meter, metal headlights, horn, bumper, rubber pedals, oil can, oil. 1F833 — 1 in carton. 35 lbs.........Each $6.75

"ESSEX"—Extreme length 41 in. Chinese blue enameled, red, black & yellow trim, spring chassis, 10 in. red enameled disc wheels, 1 in. rubber tires. EQUIPMENT—Cast steering wheel, gas lever, nickeled motor-meter, horn, license plate, rubber pedals, oil can, oil. 1F835—1 in carton. 40 lbs.........Each $7.95

"OAKLAND" — Extreme length 38½ in., Chrysler blue enameled, dk. blue & yellow trim and stripes, spring chassis, 10 in. red enameled disc wheels, ½ in. rubber tires. EQUIPMENT — Cast steering wheel, gas lever, adjustable windshield, motor-meter, metal headlights, license plate, rubber pedals, oil can. 1F837—1 in carton, 45 lbs. Each $9.75

"JEWETT"—Extreme length 41 in., Bolera cream enameled, blue & red trim, spring chassis, 10 in. blue enameled balloon type disc wheels, ¾ in. rubber tires. EQUIPMENT — Cast steering wheel, gas lever, horn, instrument board, adjustable windshield, nickeled motor-meter, metal headlights, license plate, gear shift, rubber pedals, oil can. 1F848—1 in carton, 50 lbs. Each $12.00

"MARMON" — Extreme length 41¼ in., Drake blue enameled, tangerine, yellow & aluminum trim, spring chassis, 10 in. tangerine balloon type disc wheels, 1 in. rubber tires. EQUIPMENT—Composition steering wheel, gas lever, horn, instrument board, adjustable windshield, nickeled motor-meter, metal headlights, license plate, gear shift, rubber pedals, oil can, oil. 1F849—1 in carton, 56 lbs. Each $12.95

"REO"—Extreme length 44½ in., Ottawa tan enameled, amber, black, white & aluminum trim, Ottawa tan fenders, spring chassis, 10 in. cream enameled auto type heavy wire wheels, 1¼ in. rubber tires. EQUIPMENT — Composition steering wheel, French horn, instrument board, adjustable windshield, nickeled motor meter, metal headlights, gear shift, rubber pedals. 1F850—1 in wire bound box, 85 lbs...............Each $14.75

"AMERICAN-NATIONAL" DUMP TRUCKS

End gate automatically opens and closes when box is raised or lowered by steel lever. Each with adjustable pedals. Sturdy trucks that are finding a tremendous and fast-growing market. And, in this field, it pays to sell the line children prefer....the name "American-National" is that line.

"JUNIOR"—Extreme length 44 in., American red enameled body, black & yellow trim, black enameled dump box, 10 in. red enameled double disc wheels, ½ in. rubber tires. EQUIPMENT — Gas lever, license plate, horn, rubber pedals. 1F857—1 in wire bound box, 80 lbs.................Each $8.25

"SPEED"—Extreme length 44 in., Larchmont blue enameled body, red, black & yellow trim, black enameled dump box, 10 in. red enameled disc wheels, 1 in. rubber tires. EQUIPMENT — Composition steering wheel, gas lever, horn, radiator cap, rubber pedals. 1F858—1 in crate, 65 lbs. Each $10.75

"BUICK"—Extreme length 46 in., deep maroon enameled, green, tangerine and yellow trim, aluminum bead, full spring chassis, 10 in. maroon enameled balloon type disc wheels, 1 in. rubber tires. EQUIPMENT—Composition steering wheel, gas lever, French horn, instrument board, nickeled adjustable windshield, spotlight, nickeled motor-meter and radiator, metal headlights, license plate, gear shift, upholstered seat, rear trunk, rubber pedals, motor buzzer, oil can, oil. 1F853—1 in wire bound box, 79 lbs........Each $19.75

"STUDEBAKER"—Extreme length 53 in., russet brown enameled, green, tangerine & yellow trim, aluminum bead on hood, black enameled fenders, full spring chassis, 12 in. green enameled roller bearing balloon type disc wheels, 1 in. rubber tires. EQUIPMENT—Composition steering rod, gas lever, French horn, instrument board, nickeled adjustable windshield, spotlight, nickeled motor-meter, metal lamps, license plate, gear shift, stationary hood, round bumper, heavy "die-form" fenders, rubber pedals, motor buzzer, oil can, oil. 1F854—1 in crate, 125 lbs. Each $23.00

American National pedal cars, as shown in a 1929 Butler Bros. Christmas catalog

AMERICAN PRECISION CO.

American Precision Co. Allis-Chalmers
"C" Model Tractor, die-cast, 1950 150   225   300

AMF

	C6	C8	C10
AMF Pontiac Pedal Car, 1930, 37-1/2" long	1500	2500	3500
AMF Rebel Racer Pedal Car, 1965	200	300	400

AMF Pontiac Pedal Car, 1930, 37-1/2" long. Courtesy Bill Bertoia Auctions. Photo by Jeanne Bertoia.

AMT (Aluminum Model Toys): See "Promotionals"

ANDY GARD

	C6	C8	C10
Andy Gard Bell Telephone Truck	22	33	45
Andy Gard Brink's Armored Car, battery-operated	30	45	60
Andy Gard Crane, magnetic, battery-operated	62	93	125
Andy Gard Fire Engine, battery-operated	37	56	75
Andy Gard "Gee I Jeep," battery-operated	20	30	40
Andy Gard MG, motor-powered cable steering	100	150	200
Andy Gard Pickup Truck, 6" long, soft plastic	7	11	15
Andy Gard Telephone Truck	30	45	60
Andy Gard Touring Sedan, 19" long	37	56	75

ANIMATE TOY CO.

In 1918, this firm was located at East 17th St., in New York City, and its president was L.T. Savage. By 1931, it had moved to 30 North 15th Street, East Orange, New Jersey, and employed 10 men and 40 women. In 1934, the president-vice president was George V. Turnbull, and the secretary-treasurer was George H. Webb. Five men and 11 women made up the work force. See also "Woodhaven."

	C6	C8	C10
Animate Toy Co. "Baby Haymaker," 1916 tin push toy playset	100	150	200
Animate Toy "Baby Tractor," friction, "patented June 20, 1916"	85	130	175
Animate Toy "Climbing Tractor," 9" long, 1929, windup	110	165	225
Animate Toy "U.S. Baby Tank," pat. 6/20/16, 2-1/2" long, new in 1918, windup	37	56	75

Animate Toy "Baby Tractor"

Animate Toy "U.S. Baby Tank." Photo by Ed Poole.

	C6	C8	C10

Animate Toy Tractor and Dump
  Trailer, 15-1/2" long, windup .... No Price Found
Animate Toy Tractor with
  Snow Plow, 13" long, windup .... No Price Found
Animate Toy Tractor with
  Sweeper, 12-1/2" long, windup .... No Price Found
Animate Toy Tractor, windup, 8-1/2" long .... No Price Found

*Animate Toy
Tractor & Dump
Trailer, from a
c.1940-41 L.
Gould catalog*

*Animate Toy
Tractor with
Snow Plow,
from a
c.1940-41
M.S. Young
& Co. catalog*

*Animate Toy
Tractor with
Sweeper, from
a c.1940-41
M.S. Young
& Co. catalog*

ARCADE

Arcade is one of the great names in cast-iron toys; perhaps the most highly regarded of all. It was founded in 1868 as the Novelty Iron Works and was located from first to last in Freeport, Illinois. In 1884, when the firm was known as Arcade, it began to produce toy coffee mills from the left-over scraps of the "adult" mills it sold. However, it wasn't until 1921, when the firm struck a deal to produce Yellow Cabs, that it made its mark in the toy world. The cab was an instant, overwhelming success and led to a continuing line of cast-iron toy vehicles, as well as other toys. The firm's heyday was the 1920s, both financially and esthetically, but it continued to produce toys until the advent of WWII.

Arcade AR1. Courtesy Sotheby's New York.

Arcade AR4

(AR1) A.C.F. Bus, 1927, 11-1/2" long 1700 2700 4000
(AR2) Allis-Chalmers Tractor and Trailer,
  1936, No. 2650, 13" long total length..... 230 345 460
(AR3) Allis-Chalmers Tractor and Dump
  Trailer, 1937, No. 2657, 12-3/4" long
  with trailer.............................. 130 195 260
(AR3A) Allis-Chalmers Tractor and Dump
  Trailer, 1937, No. 2660, 8-1/4" long 80 120 160

(AR4) Allis-Chalmers Tractor Trailer,
  1937, No. 2650, 13" long with trailer 225 338 450
(AR5) Allis-Chalmers "WC" Tractor,
  1941, 7-3/4" long 450 675 900
(AR6) Ambulance, 1932,
  No. 187, 7-3/4" long 375 562 750
(AR7) Ambulance, 1932,
  No. 188, 6" long, blue............................ 350 525 700
(AR7A) Ambulance, 1932,
  No. 188, 6" long, white.......................... 300 450 600

Arcade AR3A

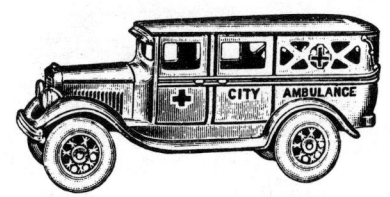

Arcade AR6

Arcade, L to R: AR6, AR6 (different wheels), AR7, AR7A. Courtesy Bill Bertoia Auctions. Photo by Jeanne Bertoia.

Arcade AR10. Courtesy David W. Mapes Auctions.

Arcade AR14. Courtesy Bill Bertoia Auctions. Photo by Jeanne Bertoia.

Arcade AR15. Photo by Rod Carnahan.

Arcade AR20. Courtesy Bill Bertoia Auctions. Photo by Jeanne Bertoia.

Arcade AR17. Photo by Orville C. Britton.

Arcade, L to R: AR20A, AR20B. Courtesy Bill Bertoia Auctions. Photo by Jeanne Bertoia.

Arcade, L to R: AR21, AR22. Courtesy Bill Bertoia Auctions. Photo by Jeanne Bertoia.

Arcade AR23. Courtesy Bill Bertoia Auctions. Photo by Jeanne Bertoia.

Arcade AR24. Courtesy Sotheby's New York.

Arcade AR26

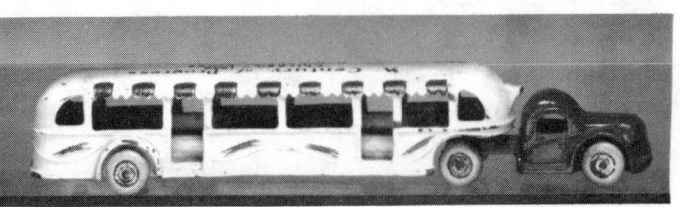

Arcade AR36. Courtesy Sotheby's NY.

  Arcade

	C6	C8	C10
(AR8) Ambulance, 1936, 4" long, (white-painted version) of No. 2620X Chevrolet Panel Delivery Truck	370	555	740
(AR9) Anthony Dump Truck, 1927, 8-1/8" long	1100	1700	2400
(AR10) Austin Autocrat Road Roller, 1928, No. 291, 7" long	312	468	625
(AR11) Austin Delivery Truck, 1932, No. 173, 3-3/4" long	50	75	100
(AR12) Austin Racer, 1932, No. 175X, 3-3/4" long	48	72	95
(AR13) Austin Roadster, 1932, No. 174, 3-3/4" long	137	205	275
(AR14) Austin "Roll-A-Plane," 7-1/2" long	550	900	1300
(AR15) Austin Stake Truck, 1932, No. 176X, 3-3/4" long	150	225	300
(AR16) Austin Wrecker, 1932, No. 177X, 3-3/4" long	150	225	300
(AR17) Avery Tractor, 1923, 4-1/2" long, stack, no hood	30	45	60
(AR18) Avery Tractor, 1926, 4-1/2" long, has hood, no stack	125	188	250
(AR19) Borden's Milk Bottle Truck, 1936, 6-1/4" long, No. 2640X	1000	1500	2500
(AR20) Brinks Express Truck, 1932, 11-3/4" long, auctioned in 1994 in excellent condition for $20,000.			
(AR20A) Brown & White Cab, 1923, 9" long	1800	3000	4500
(AR20B) Brown & White Cab, 1923, 8" long	2200	3700	5500
(AR21) Buick Coupe, 1927, 8-1/2" long	2800	4500	6000
(AR22) Buick Sedan, 1927, 8-1/2" long	1500	2500	4000
(AR23) Bus, Double-Decker, 1929, No. 316X, 8-1/2" long	400	600	800
(AR24) Bus, Double-Decker, 1936, No. 317, "Chicago Motor Coach" stamp, 8-1/4" long	450	675	900
(AR25) Car Carrier, 1931, No. 238, 24-1/2" long, cargo has 4- 25¢ cars or 3-50¢ cars	1500	2500	3900
(AR26) Car Carrier, 1932, No. 296, carries either 2 No. 114 Ford sedans and 1 113X Ford Coupe, or one No. 213 Ford Stake Truck and one each of the others, 24-1/2" long	1400	2250	3400
(AR27) Car Transport, 1937, No. 3107, came with 2 No. 1501 Sedans, No. 1502 Stake Truck and No. 1503 wrecker, 18-1/2" long	900	1350	1800
(AR28) Car Transport, 1937, No. 2977, holds 2 Sedans, 2 Trucks, 11-1/4" long	427	640	855
(AR29) Carry Car Truck and Trailer Set. 1934, No. 2970, 14-1/4" long, carries Austin Coupe, Delivery and Stake	650	1000	1500
(AR30) Caterpillar Tractor, 1930, No. 271, 7-1/2" long	322	488	645
(AR31) Caterpillar Tractor, 1931, No. 269X, 6-7/8" long	650	1100	1550

Arcade AR30

	C6	C8	C10
(AR31A) Caterpillar Tractor, 1931, No. 268X 5-5/8" long	550	900	1250
(AR32) Caterpillar Tractor, 1931, No. 267X, 3-7/8" long	250	375	500
(AR33) Caterpillar Tractor, 1931, No. 266X, 3" long	25	38	50
(AR34) Caterpillar Tractor, 1936, No. 270Y, later 2700Y, 7-3/4" long	800	1300	1750
(AR35) Century of Progress Bus, 1933, No. 3200, later No. 3250 (1934), 14-1/2" long	275	415	550
(AR36) Century of Progress Bus, 1933, No. 3210, 12" long	232	348	465
(AR37) Century of Progress Bus, 1933, No. 3220, 10-1/2" long	225	338	450
(AR38) Century of Progress Bus, 933, No. 3230, 7-5/8" long	115	172	230
(AR38A) Century of Progress Bus, 1933, approx. 5-1/2" long, won't pivot or detach	187	280	375

Arcade AR37. Courtesy Sotheby's NY.

Arcade AR38. Courtesy Sotheby's NY.

	C6	C8	C10
(AR38B) Century of Progress Yellow Cab, 6-1/2" long	1200	2200	3000
(AR39) Checker Cab, 1923, 9" long, paint variation of No. 1 Yellow Cab	2500	4200	6250
(AR40) Checker Cab, 1932, No. 157, 9-1/4" long (came with and without "Checker" on visor). With "Checker" auctioned in 1994 in near-mint condition with Arcade tag for $62,000.			

Arcade AR39. Courtesy Bill Bertoia Auctions. Photo by Jeanne Bertoia.

Arcade AR40. Courtesy Bill Bertoia Auctions. Photo by Jeanne Bertoia.

Arcade AR41. Courtesy James S. Maxwell/Virginia Caputo. Photo by Virginia Caputo.

Arcade, L to R: AR44A, AR44. Courtesy Bill Bertoia Auctions. Photo by Jeanne Bertoia.

Arcade, L to R: AR45, AR42. Photo by Chic Gast.

Arcade AR48. Courtesy Bill Bertoia Auctions. Photo by Jeanne Bertoia.

Arcade AR49. Courtesy Bill Bertoia Auctions. Photo by Jeanne Bertoia.

Arcade AR50. Courtesy Bill Bertoia Auctions. Photo by Jeanne Bertoia.

Arcade AR51. Courtesy Bill Bertoia Auctions. Photo by Jeanne Bertoia.

Arcade AR53. Courtesy Bill Bertoia Auctions. Photo by Jeanne Bertoia.

Arcade AR60 (both). Courtesy Bill Bertoia Auctions. Photo by Jeanne Bertoia.

Arcade AR63. Courtesy Bill Bertoia Auctions. Photo by Jeanne Bertoia.

At right: Arcade AR64. The Mack Stake Truck is a Hubley, about 5" long.

Arcade AR64. Courtesy Bill Bertoia Auctions. Photo by Jeanne Bertoia.

	C6	C8	C10
(AR41) Chevrolet Coupe, 1929, No. 121X, 8-1/4" long	700	1150	1700
(AR42) Chevrolet Coupe, 1934, rumble seat, No. 1150X, 4-3/8" long	155	232	310
(AR43) Chevrolet Panel Delivery Truck, 1936, No. 2620X, 4" long	125	188	250
(AR44) Chevrolet Sedan, 1929, No. 122X, 1929, 8-1/4" long, single stripe	1000	1600	2200
(AR44A) As above, double stripe, 1930	1400	2300	3200
(AR45) Chevrolet Sedan, 1934, No. 1170X, 4-1/4" long	50	75	100
(AR46) Chevrolet Stake Truck, 1925, 9" long	1050	1700	2300
(AR47) Chevrolet Stake Truck, 1936, No. 2610, 4-1/4" long	No Price Found		
(AR48) Chevrolet Superior Roadster, 1925, 7" long	1100	1800	2500
(AR49) Chevrolet Superior Sedan, 1925, 7" long	500	750	1050
(AR50) Chevrolet Superior Touring Car, 1925, 7" long	800	1400	2000
(AR51) Chevrolet Utility Coupe, 1925, 7" long	800	1400	1870
(AR52) Chevrolet Wrecker Truck, 1936, No. 2630X, 4-1/4" long	150	225	300
(AR53) "Chief" Fire Chief Coupe, 1934, No. 1230, 6-3/4" long	1500	2500	3400
(AR54) "Chief" Fire Chief Coupe, 1934, No. 1240, 5" long	500	800	1100
(AR55) "Coast To Coast GMC" Transcontinental Bus, 1937, No. 4378X, 9" long	215	325	430
(AR56) Corn Harvester, 1939, No. 702, 6-1/2" long	200	300	400
(AR57) Corn Harvester, 1939, No. 4180, 5" long	150	225	300
(AR58) Corn Planter, 1939, 4-1/2" long	62	93	125
(AR59) Coupe, "1922" on spare tire, 9" long	1500	2500	4000
(AR60) Coupe, like above, no 1922 date on spare	850	1275	1700
(AR61) Coupe, 1932, No. 109, 6" long, no Arcade markings, rumble seat opens	262	395	525
(AR62) Deluxe Sedan, 1941, No. 1590X, same as Yellow Cab No. 1590Y, but with top lights and sun roof ground off. 8-1/2" long	500	825	1200
(AR63) DeSoto Sedan, 1936, No. 1460X, 4" long	150	225	300
(AR64) Double Decker Bus, 1939, No. 3180, 8" long	438	657	875
(AR65) Dump Truck, 1936, No. 2320, 4-1/2" long	55	82	110
(AR66) Dump Truck, 1941, No. 3910X, 7" long	300	450	600
(AR66A) Dump Truck, transitional, 1940s, lighter metal, 11-1/4" long	300	450	600
(AR67) Dump Truck Trailer, 1931, No. 234, 12-7/8" long	900	1500	2200

	C6	C8	C10
(AR68) Dump Wagon, 1917, 7" long, driver, no cab	425	638	850
(AR69) Express Truck, 1929, No. 270X, 8" long	500	750	1000
(AR70) Express Truck, 1929, No. 209X, 6" long	No Price Found		
(AR71) Express Truck, 1929, No. 214X, 5" long	No Price Found		
(AR72) Fageol Bus, 1925, 12" long	385	575	770
(AR73) Fageol Bus, 12-1/2" long	480	720	960
(AR74) Fageol Bus, 8" long	350	555	740
(AR74A) Fageol Bus, 5" long	162	243	325

Arcade AR66A. Courtesy Bill Bertoia Auctions. Photo by Jeanne Bertoia.

Arcade AR68 as seen in Arcade catalog No. 26; found in the archives of a rival company. The catalog is hand-stamped "Received March 19, 1917."

Arcade AR69. Courtesy Bill Bertoia Auctions. Photo by Jeanne Bertoia.

Arcade AR72

	C6	C8	C10
(AR75) Farm Mower, 1939, No. 4210X, 4" long	60	90	120
(AR76) Farmall "A" Tractor, 1941, No. 7050, 7-1/2" long	600	1050	1440
(AR77) Farmall "M" Tractor, 1941, No. 7070, 7-1/4" long	240	360	480
(AR78) Farmall Tractor, 1929, No. 279, 6" long	500	750	1045
(AR78A) Fire Chief Car, 1941, 5-5/8" long	160	240	320
(AR79) Fire Engine, 1923, pumper, 7-1/2" long	250	375	500
(AR80) Fire Engine, 1936, No. 1740, pumper, 9" long	500	785	1150

	C6	C8	C10
(AR81) Fire Engine, 1936, No. 1810, 6-1/4" long	No Price Found		
(AR82) Fire Engine, 1936, No. 2340, 4-1/2" long	90	135	180
(AR83) Fire Engine, 1941, No. 6990, 13-1/2" long	700	1150	1525
(AR84) Fire Ladder Truck, 1936, No. 1820, 7" long	200	300	400
(AR85) Fire Trailer Truck, 1934, No. 1940, Ladder Truck, 16-1/4" long	475	715	950
(AR86) Ford Carry Car Truck and Trailer, 1934, No. 2400	No Price Found		
(AR87) Ford Coupe, 1923, 6" long	175	265	350

Arcade AR78, late wheels. Photo by Perry R. Eichor.

An unlisted fire engine, as seen in Arcade catalog No. 26; found in the archives of a rival company. The catalog is hand-stamped "Received March 19, 1917." No price found.

Arcade AR80 (with original box). Courtesy Bill Bertoia Auctions. Photo by Jeanne Bertoia.

Arcade AR83. Courtesy Bill Bertoia Auctions. Photo by Jeanne Bertoia.

Arcade AR85. Courtesy Bill Bertoia Auctions. Photo by Jeanne Bertoia.

Arcade AR88. Courtesy Bill Bertoia Auctions. Photo by Jeanne Bertoia.

Arcade AR91. Courtesy Bill Bertoia Auctions. Photo by Jeanne Bertoia.

Arcade AR92. Courtesy Bill Bertoia Auctions. Photo by Jeanne Bertoia.

Arcade AR94. Courtesy Bill Bertoia Auctions. Photo by Jeanne Bertoia.

	C6	C8	C10
(AR88) Ford Coupe, 1924, 6-1/2" long	290	435	580
(AR89) Ford Coupe, 1934, No. 1610X, 6-3/4" long, rumble seat opens	175	262	350
(AR90) Ford Coupe, 1930s, No. 1190X, 4-3/4" long	125	188	250
(AR91) Ford Dump Truck, 1929, No. 219X, 7-1/2" long	285	425	570
(AR92) Ford Express Truck, 1929, No. 210X, 8-1/4" long	1000	1650	2400
(AR93) Ford Fordor Sedan, 1924, 6-1/2" long, removable chauffeur	250	375	500

Arcade AR93 color variations in blue, red, and green. Courtesy Bill Bertoia Auctions. Photo by Jeanne Bertoia.

	C6	C8	C10
(AR94) Ford Sedan, 1923, 6-1/2" long, "Center Door"	338	407	675
(AR95) Ford Sedan, 1934, No. 1620X, 6-7/8" long	No Price Found		
(AR96) Ford Sedan, 1934, "Century of Progress," 6-7/8" long	1000	1700	2400
(AR97) Ford Sedan, 1930s, No. 1200, 4-3/4" long	190	285	380
(AR97A) Ford Sedan, 1934, "Century of Progress," 4-3/4" long	No Price Found		
(AR98) Ford Sedan with Trailer, 1937, No. 1970, 12" long (trailer 5-1/2" long)	650	1100	1500
(AR99) Ford Stake Truck, 1925, 8-3/4" long	700	1250	1600
(AR100) Ford Stake Truck, 1927, 9" long	1000	1700	2250

	C6	C8	C10
(AR101) Ford Stake Truck, 1934, No. 2010X, 4-3/4" long	No Price Found		
(AR102) Ford Touring Car, 1923, 6-1/2" long	450	675	900
(AR103) Ford Touring Car Bank, 1923, 6-1/2" long	1100	1800	2700
(AR104) Ford Tractor and Plow, 1941, No. 7220, tractor 6-1/2" long, overall length 8-3/4"	438	657	875
(AR105) Ford Truck, One-Ton Pickup, 1923, 8-1/2" long, C-Cab	900	1400	2200
(AR106) Ford Wrecker, 1929, No. 215, 8-1/4" length to end of hoist	500	750	1000
(AR106A) Ford Wrecker, 1929, No. 217	300	450	600
(AR107) Ford Wrecker, 1930, No. 218, 4-1/2" long	125	188	250
(AR108) Fordson Tractor, 1923, 5-3/8" long	165	248	330
(AR108A) Fordson Tractor, No. 275, 1928, 6" long	133	200	265
(AR109) Fordson Tractor, 1928, No. 274, 4-3/4" long	112	168	225
(AR110) Fordson Tractor, 1928, 3-7/8" long, No. 273	55	82	110
(AR111) Fordson Tractor, 1934, rubber wheels, No. 2730X, 3-1/2" long	75	112	150
(AR111A) Green & White Cab, c.1923, 9" long	1200	2000	3200
(AR112) Greyhound Cruiser Coach bus, 1941, No. 4400, 9-1/8" long	200	300	400

Arcade AR98

Arcade, top to bottom: AR96, AR97A. Photo by John M. Ianuzzi.

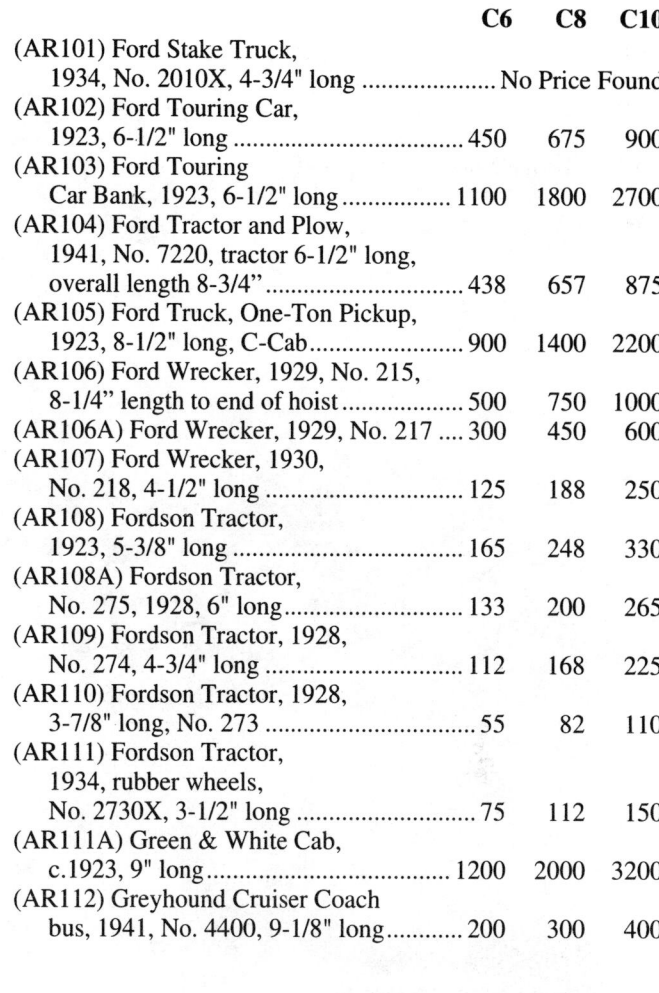

Arcade AR102. Courtesy Bill Bertoia Auctions. Photo by Jeanne Bertoia.

Arcade AR103. Courtesy Bill Bertoia Auctions. Photo by Jeanne Bertoia.

Arcade AR106

Arcade AR108-110

Arcade AR108A

Arcade AR110. Courtesy Mapes Auctioneers.

Arcade AR111A. Courtesy Bill Bertoia Auctions. Photo by Jeanne Bertoia.

Arcade AR112. Courtesy Sotheby's NY.

Arcade, L to R: AR113, AR113 color variation, AR113A, AR113B. Courtesy Bill Bertoia Auctions. Photo by Jeanne Bertoia.

AR116. Courtesy Sotheby's NY.

Arcade AR117. Courtesy Bill Bertoia Auctions. Photo by Jeanne Bertoia.

	C6	C8	C10
(AR112A) As above, but "Coast To Coast"	250	375	500
(AR113) "Greyhound Lines" Bus, 1937, No. 3850 SP, 7-3/4" long	150	225	300
(AR113A) As above, but marked "Coast To Coast," No. 3850K	262	395	525
(AR113B) As above, but marked "The Shortline"	1000	1650	2400
(AR114) "Greyhound Lines Great Lakes Exposition," 1936, No. 437, 11" long	475	710	950
(AR115) "Greyhound Lines Great Lakes Exposition," 1936, No. 436, 6-3/4" long	362	493	725
(AR116) Greyhound Super Coach, 1937, No. 4380, 9" long	282	425	565
(AR117) "Ice" Truck, c.1941, No. 1933, 6-3/4" long	275	362	550
(AR118) International Delivery Truck, 1932, No. 226, 9-3/4" long	500	800	1260
(AR119) International Delivery Truck, 1936, No. 3020, 9-1/2" long	1800	2900	4200
(AR120) International Dump Truck, 1931, No. 236-0, 10-3/4" long	750	1200	1750

	C6	C8	C10
(AR121) International Dump Truck, 1936, No. 3030, 10-1/2" long	1000	1600	2200
(AR122) International Dump Truck, 1937, No. 3710, 9-1/2" long	462	695	925
(AR123) International Dump Truck, 1940, No. 1670, chassis and dump box are steel, 11-5/8" long	700	1150	1650
(AR124) International Dump Truck, 1941, No. 7100, 11-1/8" long	600	900	1200
(AR125) International Harvester Company Public Utility Truck, 1932, No. 197, 11-1/4" long	No Price Found		
(AR126) International Pickup Truck, 1941, No. 7000, 9-1/2" long	500	750	1000
(AR127) International Stake Truck, 1931, No. 237-0, 12" long	700	1100	1600
(AR127A) International Stake Truck, 1935, 12" long	900	1500	2200
(AR128) International Stake Truck, 1936, No. 3090, 12" long	1000	1550	2300
(AR129) International Stake Truck, 1937, No. 2600, 9-1/2" long	1000	1600	2250
(AR130) International Stake Truck, 1941, No. 7090, 11-1/2" long	1000	1500	2000

Arcade AR118. Courtesy James S. Maxwell/Virginia Caputo. Photo by Virginia Caputo.

Arcade, L to R: AR118, AR119, AR118 "Hathaway's Bread Cake" variation, value in mint $2,000. Courtesy Bill Bertoia Auctions. Photo by Jeanne Bertoia.

Arcade AR121. Courtesy Bill Bertoia Auctions. Photo by Jeanne Bertoia.

Arcade AR122. Courtesy Bill Bertoia Auctions. Photo by Jeanne Bertoia.

Arcade AR124. Photo by Tim Oei.

Arcade AR126. Courtesy Bill Bertoia Auctions. Photo by Jeanne Bertoia.

Arcade, L to R: AR128, AR130, AR127A. Courtesy Bill Bertoia Auctions. Photo by Jeanne Bertoia.

Arcade AR129. Courtesy Bill Bertoia Auctions. Photo by Jeanne Bertoia.

Arcade AR132. Courtesy Bill Bertoia Auctions. Photo by Jeanne Bertoia.

	C6	C8	C10
(AR131) International Wrecker, 1940, No. 1650, 13" long, wrecker crane body and crane are steel	500	800	1100
(AR132) Ladder Truck, 1936, No. 1700, length with ladders, 12-1/2" long	475	715	950
(AR133) Ladder Truck, 1936, No. 2350, 4-3/4" long	75	112	150
(AR134) "Mack 6" Bus, 1929, No. 318, 13-1/4" long, auctioned 1996, near-mint for $24,200.			
(AR135) Mack Cement Mixer, 1931, 6-11/16" long, drum revolves			No Price Found

Arcade AR134. Courtesy Bill Bertoia Auctions. Photo by Jeanne Bertoia.

Arcade AR136. Courtesy Bill Bertoia Auctions. Photo by Jeanne Bertoia.

Arcade AR138. Courtesy Bill Bertoia Auctions. Photo by Jeanne Bertoia.

Arcade AR139

Arcade AR141. Courtesy Bill Bertoia Auctions. Photo by Jeanne Bertoia.

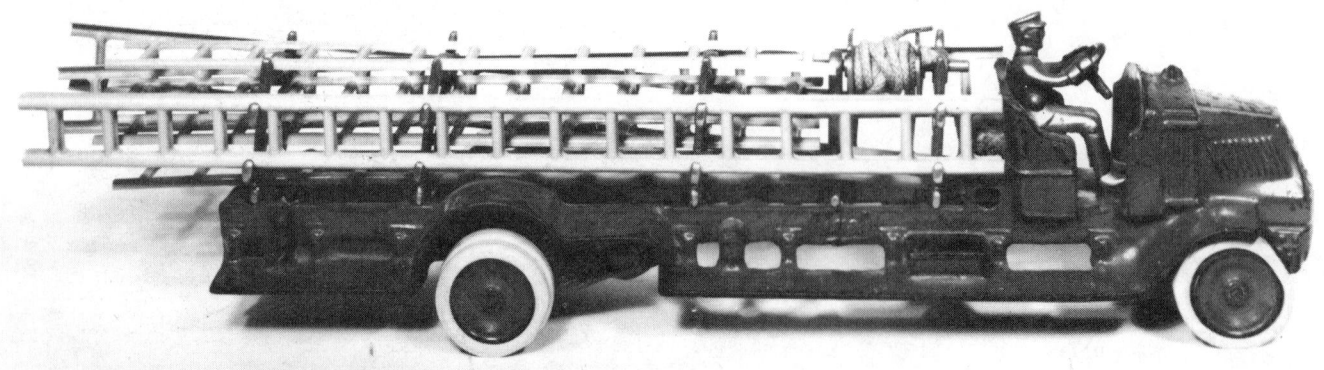

Arcade AR143. Courtesy Phillips NY.

	C6	C8	C10
(AR136) Mack Chemical Truck, 1928, fire engine No. 245R, 15" long, has ladders	2000	3500	5500
(AR137) Mack Chemical Truck, 1929, fire ladder truck, 15" long	800	1300	1800
(AR138) Mack Chemical Truck, 1929, fire engine with ladders, 10" long	430	645	860
(AR139) Mack Dump Truck, 1925, 12" long	1000	1700	2700
(AR140) Mack Dump Truck, 1929, No. 248X, 8-1/2" long	600	950	1350
(AR141) Mack High Dump Truck, "Coal," 1931, No. 244X, 12-3/8" long	1000	1600	2140
(AR142) Mack High Dump Truck, 1931, No. 259X, 8-1/2" long	700	1150	1550
(AR143) Mack Fire Apparatus Truck, 1929, No. 242, 21" long, ladder truck	600	1000	1500
(AR144) Mack Hoist Truck, 1932, No. 198, body 8" long	900	1500	2130

	C6	C8	C10
(AR145) Mack Ice Truck, 1930, No. 257, 10-5/8" long	375	562	750
(AR146) Mack Ice Truck, 1931, No. 226, 8-1/2" long	450	675	900
(AR147) Mack Ice Truck, 1932, No. 257, 10-3/4", with driver, glass "ice" and tongs	1700	2800	4000
(AR147A) Mack Ladder Truck, c.1928, 17-3/4" long	1200	2000	3000
(AR148) Mack Side Dump Truck, 1932, No. 1960, 9" long	1200	2000	2800
(AR149) Mack Stake Truck, 1929, 12" long, No. 246X	1200	2000	2750
(AR150) Mack Stake Truck, 1929, 8-3/4" long, No. 253	1000	1600	2200
(AR151) Mack Tank Truck 1925, 13-1/4" long	1000	1600	2200
(AR151A) As above, "Webaco Fuel Co."	1100	1900	2800
(AR151B) As above, "Pennsylvania"	1200	2000	3000
(AR152) Mack Tank Truck, 1925, 13-1/4" long, "American Gasoline"	1200	1850	2500

Arcade AR144

Arcade, L to R: AR147, AR145. Courtesy Bill Bertoia Auctions. Photo by Jeanne Bertoia.

Arcade AR147

Arcade AR147A. Courtesy Bill Bertoia Auctions. Photo by Jeanne Bertoia.

Arcade AR148

Arcade AR151. Courtesy David W. Mapes Auctions.

Arcade, L to R: AR151A, AR151B, AR153. Courtesy Bill Bertoia Auctions. Photo by Jeanne Bertoia.

Arcade AR153. Courtesy Bill Bertoia Auctions. Photo by Jeanne Bertoia.

Arcade AR154

Arcade AR155. Courtesy James S. Maxwell/Virginia Caputo. Photo by Virginia Caputo.

Arcade AR156. Photo by Perry R. Eichor.

	C6	C8	C10
(AR153) Mack Tank Truck, 1925, 13-1/4" long, "Lubrite"	1200	2000	3000
(AR154) Mack Tank Truck, 1930, No. 241, sheet metal tank, "Gasoline," "Mack,"13" long	1200	2000	2775
(AR155) Mack Wrecker No. 255, 1930, 12-1/2" long	2000	3300	4600
(AR156) McCormick-Deering Farmall Tractor, 1937, 6-1/4" long	350	525	700
(AR157) McCormick-Deering Thresher, 1927, 12" long	305	458	610
(AR157A) McCormick-Deering Thresher, 11" long	210	315	420
(AR158) McCormick-Deering Thresher, 1930, 9-1/2" long	192	285	385
(AR159) McCormick-Deering Tractor, 10-20, 1925, 7-1/4" long	412	618	825
(AR160) Milk Truck, 1931, No. 256, 13-5/8" long, box is wood	No Price Found		
(AR161) Model A Coupe, 1928, No. 116X, 5" long, rumble seat	220	330	440
(AR162) Model A Coupe, 1928, No. 106, 6-3/4" long, rumble seat	550	875	1250
(AR163) Model A Coupe, 1928, No. 113X, 4-1/8" long	125	188	250
(AR164) Model A Fordor, 1928, No. 207, 6-3/4" long	325	488	650
(AR165) Model A Tudor, 1928, No. 108, 6-3/4" long	500	750	1100
(AR166) Model T Stake Truck, 1927, 9" long	600	925	1250
(AR167) Model T Stake Truck, 1927, 5-3/4" long	130	185	260
(AR168) Model T Wrecker, 1927, 11" long	700	1200	1600

Arcade AR157

Arcade AR162. Courtesy Bill Bertoia Auctions. Photo by Jeanne Bertoia.

Arcade AR165. Courtesy Bill Bertoia Auctions. Photo by Jeanne Bertoia.

Arcade AR170. Photo by Bob Smith.

	C6	C8	C10
(AR168A) "Mullins Red Cap" auto trailer	225	338	450
(AR169) Nash Wrecker, 1936, 4-1/2" long	250	375	500
(AR170) National Trailways Bus, 1937, No. 3870, 9-1/4" long	750	1300	1700
(AR171) New York World's Fair Bus, 1939, No. 3780, 10-1/2" long	450	675	900
(AR172) New York World's Fair Bus, 1939, No. 3770, 8-1/2" long	332	500	665
(AR173) New York World's Fair Bus, 1939, No. 3750, 7" long	140	210	280
(AR174) New York World's Fair Tractor-Train, 1939, No. 7270, tractor and one car, tractor 3-1/4" long, car 4-1/4" long	245	368	490
(AR175) New York World's Fair Tractor-Train, 1939, No. 7290, same as above with three cars	438	655	875
(AR176) Oliver Plow, 1923, 6-1/2" long	250	375	500
(AR177) Oliver Plow, 1941, No. 4230X, 6-1/4" long	138	208	275
(AR178) Oliver Superior Spreader, No. 7140, 1941, 9-1/2" long	600	950	1300
(AR179) Oliver Tractor, 1937, No. 356, 7-1/2" long	338	505	675
(AR179A) Oliver Tractor, 1937, No. 359, 5-1/2" long	88	132	175
(AR180) Oliver Tractor, 1941, No. 3560, 7-1/2" long	500	800	1100
(AR180A) Panel Delivery Truck, 1925, 8-1/8" long	No Price Found		
(AR181) "Plymouth" Coupe, 1934, No. 1340X, 4-1/2" long	500	800	1100
(AR182) "Plymouth" Sedan, 1934, No. 1330X, 4-3/4" long	375	563	750
(AR183) "Plymouth" Stake Truck, 1934, No. 1840X, 4-3/4" long	No Price Found		
(AR184) "Plymouth" Wrecker, 1934, No. 1830X, 4-3/4" long	125	188	250
(AR184A) Pontiac Fire Pumper, 4-1/2" long	55	82	110
(AR185) Pontiac Sedan, 1934, No. 1350X, 4-1/4" long	162	245	325
(AR186) Pontiac Sedan, 1935, 6-1/2" long	350	525	700
(AR187) Pontiac Stake Truck, 1935, No. 2390X, 6-1/4" long	300	450	600
(AR188) Pontiac Stake Truck, 1936, 2780X, 4-1/4" long	No Price Found		
(AR189) Pontiac Wrecker, 1936, No. 2000X, 4-1/4" long	125	188	250
(AR190) Racer, pre-1923, 7-3/4" long	400	600	800

Arcade AR171. Courtesy Sotheby's NY.

Arcade AR172. Courtesy Sotheby's NY.

Arcade AR173. Courtesy Sotheby's NY.

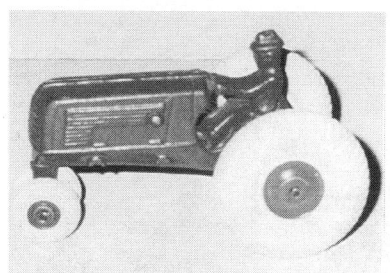

Arcade AR179A. Photo by Rod Carnahan.

Arcade AR180A. Courtesy Bill Bertoia Auctions. Photo by Jeanne Bertoia.

L to R: Two early Arcade cars, AR190 and ARA, as seen in Arcade catalog No. 26; found in the archives of a rival firm. The catalog is hand-stamped "Received March 19, 1917." ARA was auctioned in 1995 in very good condition (with a replacement driver) for $440. It is 8-1/2" long.

Arcade AR191

Arcade AR196

Arcade AR197. Courtesy Sotheby's New York.

	C6	C8	C10
(AR191) Racer, Bullet Racer, 1931, No. 139X, 7-5/8" long	900	1400	2200
(AR192) Racer, 1931, No. 138X, 6-3/4" long	150	225	300
(AR193) Racer, 1932, No. 140X, 10-1/2" long, plastic or celluloid windshield, auctioned in 1994, excellent condition, for $11,500.			
(AR194) Racer, 1932, No. 137X, 5-5/8" long	120	180	240
(AR195) Racer, 1937, No. 1440X, 8" long			No Price Found
(AR196) Racer, 1937, No. 1457, 5-3/4" long	62	93	125
(AR197) Red Baby Dump Truck, 1923, No. 2, 10-3/8" long	490	735	980
(AR198) Red Baby Truck, 1923, No. 1, 10-3/4" long	475	700	950
(AR199) Red Baby "Weaver" Wrecker, 1929, 12" long	900	1400	2000
(AR200) Red Coupe, 1931, No. 1247, 9-3/8" long	1000	1700	2500
(AR201) Red Coupe, 1931, smaller size	1000	1700	2300
(AR202) Sand Loading Shovel, 1932, No. 298 (later No. 299)	500	800	1200
(AR203) Scraper, 1929, No. 287, 8-1/4" long	42	63	85
(AR204) Sedan, 1937, No. 1501X, 4-3/4" long	90	135	180

Arcade AR198. Courtesy James S. Maxwell/Virginia Caputo. Photo by Virginia Caputo.

Arcade AR199. Courtesy Bill Bertoia Auctions. Photo by Jeanne Bertoia.

Arcade AR202

Arcade AR200. Courtesy Bill Bertoia Auctions. Photo by Jeanne Bertoia.

	C6	C8	C10
(AR205) Sedan and Mullins Red Cap Trailer, 1937, No. 1497X, car 5-5/8" long, trailer 2-1/2" long	375	562	750
(AR205A) Service Station "Arcade Service"	500	750	1030
(AR206) Side Dump Trailer, 1932, No. 290, 7" long, fastens to trucks or tractors	No Price Found		
(AR207) "Silver Arrow," 1934, 7-1/4" long	275	363	550
(AR208) Stake Trailer Truck, 1931, No. 233, 11-5/16" long	350	525	700
(AR208A) Stake Truck No. 206, 7-1/4" long	1100	1700	2500
(AR209) Stake Truck, 1929, No. 208X, 6" long	220	330	440
(AR209A) Stake Truck, 1932, approx. 6" long	200	300	400
(AR210) Stake Truck, 1929, No. 213X, 5" long	125	188	250
(AR210A) Stake Truck, 1929, 7-1/2" long	325	488	650
(AR211) Stake Truck, 1932, No. 208, 6" long, no Arcade markings	290	435	580

	C6	C8	C10
(AR212) Stake Truck, 1937, No. 1502X, 4-1/4" long	125	188	250
(AR213) Steam Shovel, 1932, No. 292 Industrial Derrick, body 6" long	750	1125	1500
(AR214) Tandem Disc Harrow, 1939, No. 704, 6-3/4" long	60	90	120
(AR215) Tank, Army, 1937, No. 400, 8" long	600	950	1325
(AR216) Tank, Army, 1941, No. 3960, 4" long, shoots	200	300	400
(AR217) Texas Centennial Bus, 1936, 10-3/4" long (Extremely Rare)	1300	2200	3000
(AR218) "Trac-Tractor," International Harvester, 1937, No. 277, 8-1/4" long	800	1300	1680
(AR219) Trac Tractor, 1941, No. 7120, 7-1/2" long	1500	2500	3500
(AR220) Unused			
(AR221) Unused			
(AR222) Tractor, 1941, No. 7200, 6-1/2" long	180	270	360
(AR223) Tractor, 1941, No. 4060X, 6-1/4" long, black rubber wheels	338	510	675
(AR224) Tractor, 1941, No. 7341X, 6-1/4" long, wood wheels	425	638	850
(AR225) Tractor, 1941, No. 7321X, 4-1/4" long	No Price Found		

AR207

Arcade AR205A. Courtesy Bill Bertoia Auctions. Photo by Jeanne Bertoia.

Arcade AR208. Courtesy Bill Bertoia Auctions. Photo by Jeanne Bertoia.

Arcade AR209. Courtesy Bill Bertoia Auctions. Photo by Jeanne Bertoia.

Arcade AR210A. Courtesy Bill Bertoia Auctions. Photo by Jeanne Bertoia.

Arcade AR216. Photo by Ed Poole.

Arcade AR219. Courtesy Thomas G. Nefos, National Toy Connection.

	C6	C8	C10
(AR226) Tractor, 1941, No. 7260X, 3-1/8" long, wooden wheels	No Price Found		
(AR227) Tractor, 1941, No. 7240X, 3-1/8" long, rubber wheels	100	150	200
(AR228) Tractor and Dump Trailer, 1941, No. 7300, 15-1/2" long	600	950	1300
(AR229) Trailer, farm, 1929, No. 286, 6-3/8" long	155	233	310
(AR230) Trailer, farm, 1929, No. 288, 4-5/8" long	35	52	70
(AR231) Trailer, farm, 1929, No. 289, 3-3/4" long	30	45	60
(AR232) Transport Trailer Truck, 1934, No. 1800, 7-1/2" long	385	580	770

	C6	C8	C10
(AR233) W&K Truck Trailer, 1923, 8-1/2" long	100	150	200
(AR234) Two-wheeled Jack, 1932, No. 216, 5-1/2" long	30	45	60
(AR234A) "Webaco Oil Co." Truck, 13-1/4" long, see AR151A.			
(AR235) White Bus No. 319, 1928, 13-1/4" long	2700	5000	7500
(AR236) White Delivery Truck, 1929, No. 252X, 8-1/4" long	2000	3800	6000
(AR236A) As above, side mounts	1500	2800	4000
(AR237) White Moving Van, 1929, No. 251, 13-1/2" long, auctioned 1994, excellent for $13,200.			
(AR238) White Dump Truck, 1929, No. 249, 11-1/2" long, auctioned 1994, excellent, for $23,000.			
(AR239) White Dump Truck, 1931, No. 258X, 13-1/2" long	No Price Found		
(AR240) White Tank Truck, 1931, No. 254X, 14-1/8" long, "Gasoline"	1000	1500	2000
(AR240A) Whitehead & Kales Tractor, 1923, 5-3/4" long	160	240	320
(AR241) Wrecker, 1929, No. 217, 1928, body 8" long	500	750	1000
(AR242) Wrecker, 1932, No. 225, no Arcade markings	600	950	1350
(AR243) Wrecker, 1934, No. 2020X, 7" long	600	950	1350

Arcade AR234A. Photo by Bob Smith.

Arcade AR235. Courtesy Sotheby's New York.

Arcade AR236A. Courtesy Bill Bertoia Auctions. Photo by Jeanne Bertoia.

Arcade AR236. Courtesy James S. Maxwell/Virginia Caputo. Photo by Virginia Caputo.

Arcade AR237. Courtesy James S. Maxwell/Virginia Caputo. Photo by Virginia Caputo.

Arcade AR237 "David" variant; four known. This was auctioned, in near-mint condition in 1994, for $22,000. Courtesy Bill Bertoia Auctions. Photo by Jeanne Bertoia.

Arcade AR238. Courtesy Bill Bertoia Auctions. Photo by Jeanne Bertoia.

Arcade AR248. Courtesy Bill Bertoia Auctions. Photo by Jeanne Bertoia.

Arcade AR249. Courtesy Bill Bertoia Auctions. Photo by Jeanne Bertoia.

Arcade AR250. Courtesy Sotheby's New York.

Arcade AR256. Courtesy Sotheby's New York.

Arcade AR257. Courtesy Bill Bertoia Auctions. Photo by Jeanne Bertoia.

Arcade AR258. Courtesy Chic Gast.

Arcade, L to R: AR258, AR258A. Courtesy Bill Bertoia Auctions. Photo by Jeanne Bertoia.

Arcade AR260. Courtesy Sotheby's New York.

Arcade AR259, side-mounted tire; original tires missing Courtesy James S. Maxwell/Virginia Caputo. Photo by Virginia Caputo.

Arcade AR261 variation as Pennsylvania Rapid Transit. It was auctioned in very good condition 1994 for $3,500. Courtesy Bill Bertoia Auctions. Photo by Jeanne Bertoia.

	C6	C8	C10
(AR244) Wrecker, 1937, No. 1493X, 6-1/2" long	150	225	300
(AR245) Wrecker, 1937, No. 1503X, 4-3/4" long	85	128	170
(AR246) Wrecker, 1941, No. 3900X, 8-1/2" long	90	135	180
(AR246A) Yellow Baby Dump Truck, 1923, 10-1/2" long	600	1050	1450
(AR247) Yellow Baby Wrecker, 1929, 12" long	650	1100	1600
(AR248) Yellow Cab, 1922, No. 1, 9-1/4" long	600	900	1400
(AR249) Yellow Cab, 1923, No. 2, 8" long	500	800	1200
(AR250) Yellow Cab, 1927, No. 1, 9" long	600	900	1400
(AR251) Yellow Cab, 1927, No. 05, 8-1/2" long	425	638	850
(AR252) Yellow Cab, 1927, No. 2, 8" long	550	850	1300
(AR253) Yellow Cab, 1927, No. 3, 5-1/4" long	500	800	1200
(AR254) Yellow Cab, 1934 Ford Sedan, 6-7/8" long	1300	2000	3000

	C6	C8	C10
(AR255) Yellow Cab, 1936, No. 1580Y, 8-1/4" long	1800	3000	4100
(AR256) Yellow Cab, 1941, No. 1590Y, 8-1/2" long	175	263	350
(AR257) Yellow Cab Bank, 1923, 8" long	750	1300	1800
(AR258) Yellow Cab Bank, 1927, 8-1/2" long, auctioned 1994, near mint, for $9200.			
(AR258A) As above, Green Cab version, value similar.			
(AR259) Yellow Cab Panel Delivery Truck, 1925, 8-1/4" long, with driver	1100	1800	2500
(AR260) Yellow Coach Double-Decker Bus, 1925, 14" long	2000	3400	4800
(AR261) Yellow Parlor Coach Bus, 1926, 13" long	800	1400	1900
(AR262) Yellow Parlor Coach Bus, 1926, 9-1/2" long	325	488	650
(AR263) Andy Gump Car, 1920s, 7-1/4" long	1500	2500	3500

Arcade AR259. Courtesy Sotheby's New York.

Arcade AR262. Courtesy Sotheby's New York.

Arcade AR263. Courtesy Christie's NY.

Arcade set; no price found. Photo by Bob Smith.

Arcade "Gasoline-Motor Oils," value with gas pumps, without car, $1,450 in mint. Courtesy Bill Bertoia Auctions. Photo by Jeanne Bertoia.

ARCHER PLASTIC

(New York, NY)

Archer produced a number of space toys, beginning at least as early as 1949.

	C6	C8	C10
Archer A21 Rocket, Red, Yellow and Black, 13"	75	112	150
Archer A22 Futuristic Convertible, 10"	42	63	85
Archer A23 Futuristic Truck, 10"	55	83	110
Archer A24 Futuristic Coupe, 10"	42	63	85
Archer A25 Futuristic Coupe, 5"	18	27	36
Archer A26 Futuristic Sedan, 5"	18	27	36
Archer A27 Futuristic Truck, 5"	18	27	36
Archer A28 Futuristic Convertible, 5"	18	27	36
Archer A29 Raymobile	37	56	75
Archer A30 Scopemobile	No Price Found		
Archer A31 Searchmobile	No Price Found		
Archer A31A Gasoline Truck, 10"	No Price Found		
Archer A32A Futuristic Auto Carrier, 14" long, No. 349, contains 4 of the 5" futuristic vehicles	No Price Found		

Archer, Top L to R: A22, A23, A24. Bottom L to R: A28, A26, A27. Photo by Bill Hanlon.

ARCHER NON-SPACE

	C6	C8	C10
Steam Roller	32	48	65

Archer, A25, A26, A27, A31A. Photo by Bill Hanlon.

Archer A30. Photo by Terry Sells.

ARGO

by David M. Leopard

Argo produced a number of variations of a 4-inch tin vehicle based roughly on a late 1940s Hudson sedan. Each vehicle has some distinctive movement that makes it special. Similar toys were also produced in Canada by General Metal Toys.

	C6	C8	C10
(AR1) Ambulance, bell rings	12	15	20
(AR2) Chief Car, bell rings	12	15	20
(AR3) Police Car, gun moves	12	15	20
(AR4) Taxi, meter in roof moves	12	15	20
(AR5) Taxi, meter in windshield moves	12	15	20
(AR6) Sedan, windshield wipers work	12	15	20
(AR7) Sedan, windows roll up and down	12	15	20
(AR8) Armored Car, Army, gun shoots	12	15	20

Argo, L to R: AR1, AR2. Photo by Dave Leopard.

Argo, L to R: AR5, AR4. Photo by Dave Leopard.

Argo, L to R: AR8, AR3. Photo by Dave Leopard.

ARNOLD

(German)

	C6	C8	C10
Arnold Fire Chief Car, tin litho, battery siren, friction, 10" long	150	225	300
Arnold A754 Military Rider w/rifle Motorcycle	388	582	775
Arnold A63 Motorcycle, windup, 8" long, orange	200	325	450
Arnold A560 Motorcycle, windup, 7-3/4" long, green	200	325	450
Arnold Mac 700 Motorcycle, windup, black	325	488	650
Arnold Packard Convertible, 10" long	90	135	180
Arnold Police Car, friction, 10" long	250	375	500
Arnold Sparkling Fire Truck, 4-1/2" windup, U.S. Zone	238	355	475

Arnold, L to R: A63, A560. Courtesy Kent M. Comstock.

Arnold Mac 700. Courtesy Kent M. Comstock.

Arnold postwar jeep with U.S. MP crew; value as shown $300. Photo by Jack Matthews.

Arnold postwar white MP jeep (rare) with remote control; value as shown $550. Photo by Jack Matthews.

ASTRA PHAROS

This British company dates to before WWII; many of its toys are particularly attractive to military collectors. Prices range from a few dollars to $100 or more for its large AA Gun. Its number 12 Mobile Unit would presumably run near that price.

Astra Pharos (U.K.) Ordnance. Various Scales. L to R - Back Row: Pom-Pom, small searchlight, large AA gun, AA gun on pedestal. Middle: AA gun and searchlight on trailer, AA gun on Y-mount, searchlight on large mount, searchlight small mount. Front Row: AT gun with split trails, three versions of multiple barrel mortar (dual and single wheeled box trail and split trail), tandem wheeled AT gun with box trail. Not shown: Pillboxes with cannons, at least two variants. Photo by Ed Poole.

AUBURN RUBBER

by Dave Leopard

For about 20 years (roughly 1935 to 1955), American kids enjoyed playing with rubber toys. Moms were told that these toys would not mar the furniture or floors. Then, almost as suddenly as they came on the market, they disappeared again, but left a rich legacy for toy collectors.

The Auburn Rubber Company of Auburn, Indiana, was not the first to introduce rubber toys to the American market, but it was no doubt the largest and had the greatest impact on the toy field. After introducing toy soldiers in 1935, Auburn brought out its first vehicle in 1936—a beautiful coffin-nosed Cord sedan. Today, the Auburn Cord is one of the most highly prized rubber toys and is seldom seen for sale.

Auburn followed the Cord with a wealth of vehicles, including trucks, farm tractors and implements, motorcycles, racers, fire engines, military vehicles, aircraft, ships, and trains. In all, I have catalogued about

90 different varieties of Auburn rubber vehicles, and I'm sure there are more than that. To my knowledge, 1952 was Auburn's last year of marketing rubber toys exclusively. The 1953 Auburn catalog contained a vinyl motorcycle, which I believe was its first vinyl toy. By 1955, its toy line was mostly vinyl, with a few rubber varieties hanging on. The 1956 catalog was exclusively vinyl except for two rubber fire engines, which were no doubt the last rubber toys to be marketed by Auburn. Auburn continued in the toy business in Auburn, Indiana, and later in Deming, New Mexico, until it went out of business in 1969.

Dave Leopard is a retired U.S. Air Force Colonel, now employed by the State of South Carolina. Leopard is a collector of small, American-made toy cars and trucks and is an authority on rubber toys. He has published a book entitled *Rubber Toy Vehicles*, which is the definitive work in this field.

NOTE: Because Leopard changed some codes when he did his own book, his book's codes, where they differ, are shown in parentheses in the photo captions.

Dave Leopard

	C6	C8	C10
AA01 '36 Cord, 4- door coffin-nose Sedan 6" long	65	98	130
AA02 '37 Olds, 4-door Sedan, 4-1/2" long	22	33	45
AA03 '38 Olds, 4-door Sedan, 5-3/4" long	30	45	60

	C6	C8	C10
AA04 '40 Olds, 4-door Sedan, open fenders, 6" long	27	41	55
AA05 '40 Olds, 4-door Sedan, fender skirts, 6" long	25	38	50
AA06 '48 Buick, 2-door Sedanette, fastback, 7-1/4" long	40	60	80

Auburn AA01. Photo by Max Heiss.

Auburn AA02. Courtesy Dave Leopard, from his book Rubber Toy Vehicles.

Auburn AA03. Courtesy Dave Leopard, from his book Rubber Toy Vehicles.

Auburn, L to R: AA05, AA04. Courtesy Dave Leopard, from his book Rubber Toy Vehicles.

	C6	C8	C10
AA07 '39 Buick, Y Job			
Experimental Roadster, 9-3/4" long	No Price Found		
AA08 '35 Ford Coupe, 4" long	27	41	55
AA09 '35 Ford 2- door			
Slantback Sedan, 4" long	27	41	55
AA10 '50 Cadillac,			
4-door Sedan, 7-1/4" long	40	60	80
AA11 Unused			

	C6	C8	C10
AA12 '39 Plymouth, 2-door			
Trunkback Sedan, 4-1/4" long	22	33	45
AA13 '46 Lincoln convertible,			
2-door, square headlights, 4-1/2" long	20	30	40
AA14 '46 Lincoln convertible,			
2-door, round headlights, 4-1/2" long	20	30	40
AA15 Late 40s Futuristic			
Sedan, fin down back, 5" long	20	30	40

Auburn AA07; from a 1941 Butler Bros. catalog

Auburn AA06. Photo by Dave Leopard.

Auburn AA10. Courtesy Dave Leopard, from his book Rubber Toy Vehicles.

Auburn AA12 (AA11 in Leopard's book); from a 1940 Butler Bros. catalog

Auburn, L to R: AA13, AA14 (AA12, AA13 in Leopard's book). Courtesy Dave Leopard, from his book Rubber Toy Vehicles.

Auburn AA15 (Leopard's AA14). Courtesy Dave Leopard, from his book Rubber Toy Vehicles.

Auburn AA17; from a 1941 Butler Bros. catalog

Auburn AA16. Photo by Tim O'Callaghan.

Auburn AT01. Courtesy Dave Leopard, from his book Rubber Toy Vehicles.

Auburn AT01A. Photo by Ed Poole.

AT01A in two colors. Photo by Tim O'Callaghan.

	C6	C8	C10
AA16 Army Staff Car (AA04 in Khaki), "U.S. Army" label	25	38	50
AA17 Taxi, 6" long	No Price Found		
AT01 '37 International Cabover Stake Truck, 5-3/8" long	22	33	45
AT01A '37 Same as above, "U.S. Army" decal, khaki	22	33	45
AT02 Same as above with rounded bumper, minor variations	22	33	45
AT03 '37 International Cabover Stake Truck, 4-1/4" long	20	30	40
AT03A Same as above, Khaki	20	30	40
AT04 Same as above with rounded bumper, minor variations	20	30	40

	C6	C8	C10
AT05 '37 International Cabover Stake Truck, 3-3/4" long	20	30	40
AT06 Unused			
AT07 '37 International Cabover Stake Truck, milk version, 4-1/4" long	60	80	100
AT08 '37 International Cabover Stake Truck, ambulance version	No Price Found		
AT09 Cab-Forward Box Truck, smooth sides, futuristic, 5-1/2" long	22	33	45
AT10 Cabover Box Truck, smooth sides, futuristic, 4-1/8" long	20	30	40
AT10A Army Truck, as above	20	30	40
AT11 '47 Chevy Cab Forward Box Truck, 5-3/4" long	22	33	45

Auburn, L to R: AT01, AT03, AT05. Courtesy Dave Leopard, from his book Rubber Toy Vehicles.

Auburn AT07 (Leopard's AT06). Courtesy Dave Leopard, from his book Rubber Toy Vehicles.

Auburn AT08 (Leopard's AT07); top not original. Courtesy Dave Leopard, from his book Rubber Toy Vehicles.

Auburn AT09 (Leopard's AT08). Courtesy Dave Leopard, from his book Rubber Toy Vehicles.

Auburn AT10 (Leopard's AT09). Courtesy Dave Leopard, from his book Rubber Toy Vehicles.

Auburn AT11 (Leopard's AT10). Photo by Dave Leopard.

	C6	C8	C10
AT12 c.'50 Pickup Truck, wheels outside fenders, 4-1/2" long	20	30	40
AT13 c.'50 Pickup Truck, wheels inside fenders, 4-1/2" long	20	30	40
AT14 '38 GMC "Carry Car" Auto Transport, 11-1/2" long (no top).....	42	63	85
AT14A Same as above, with rubber on top to carry cars	42	63	85
AT15 '38 GMC Cab/Open Squared-off Trailer, 9" long	42	63	85
AT16 Updated Carry Car Transport, cab changed, trailer same, 11-3/4" long	42	63	85

	C6	C8	C10
AT17 Unused			
AE01 Ahrens-Fox Fire Engine, 5-1/2" long	75	112	150
AE02 c.40s Fire Engine, hose and ladders, 7-3/4" long	35	52	70
AE03 c.40s Pumper, boiler, 7-1/4" long	35	52	70
AE04 c.40s Fire Engine, ladders, no hose, 7-3/4" long	35	52	70
AR01 Open racer, V-6, high fin, 10-1/2" long	55	82	110

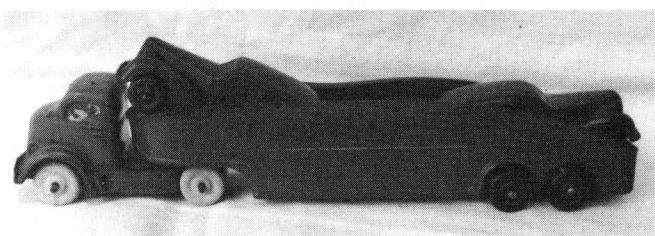

Auburn AT14. Photo by Dave Leopard.

Auburn AT14A; from a 1940-41 L. Gould & Co. catalog

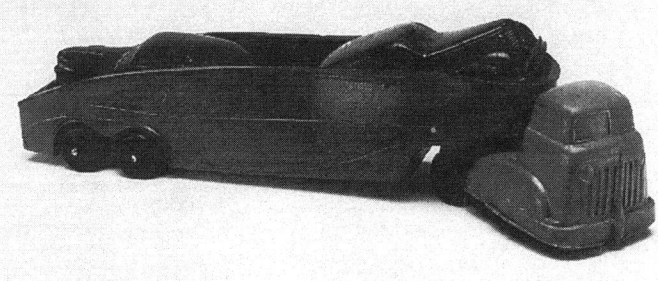

Auburn AT16 (Leopard's AT17). Courtesy Dave Leopard, from his book Rubber Toy Vehicles.

Auburn AT15. Courtesy Dave Leopard, from his book Rubber Toy Vehicles.

Auburn AE01; from a 1940-41 L. Gould catalog

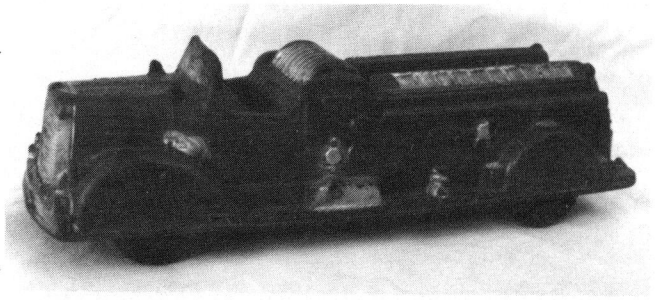

Auburn AE02. Photo by Dave Leopard.

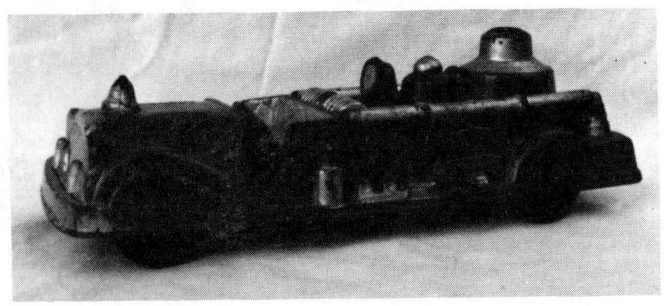

Auburn AE03. Photo by Dave Leopard.

	C6	C8	C10
AR02 Open racer,			
V-6, low fin, 10-1/2" long	40	60	80
AR03 Open racer, short,			
tapered tail, large tires, 10-1/2" long	37	56	75

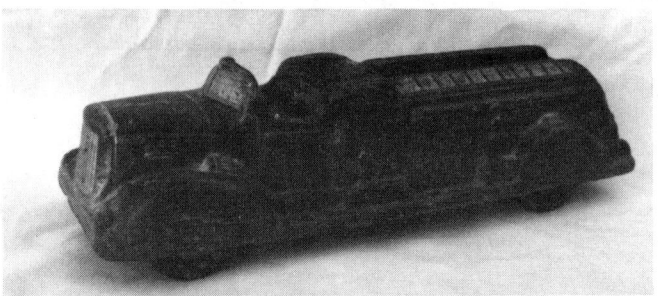

Auburn AE04. Photo by Dave Leopard.

Auburn AR02. Courtesy Dave Leopard, from his book Rubber Toy Vehicles.

Auburn AR04; from a c.1940-41 M.S. Young & Co. catalog

	C6	C8	C10
AR04 Open racer,			
short, boat tail, 6-1/2" long	27	41	55
AR05 Open racer, boat tail, 4-3/4" long	22	33	45
AR06 Open racer, small fin, 6-1/4" long	22	33	45
AR07 Open racer short,			
boat tail, early, 6-1/2" long	35	52	70
AR08 Open racer, no fenders,			
low fin, long back, 5-1/4" long	20	30	40
AR09 Open racer,			
boat tail, no side pipes, 4-3/4" long	22	33	45
AR10 Open racer,			
midget type, early, 5" long	No Price Found		
AF01 Farm Tractor,			
John Deere "A," 5" long	22	33	45
AF02 Unused			
AF03 Farm Tractor,			
Minneapolis-Moline "Z," 4" long	22	33	45
AF04 Farm Tractor, Minneapolis-Moline			
"R," early style, 7-1/2" long	37	56	75

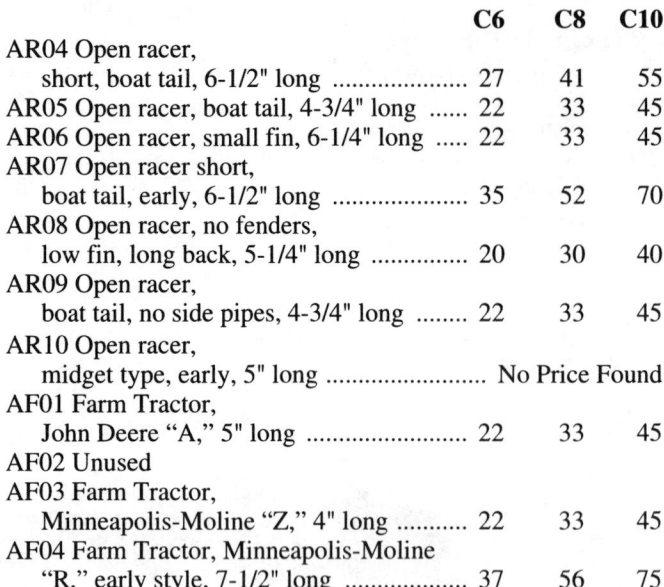

Auburn AR01. Courtesy David Mapes Auctions.

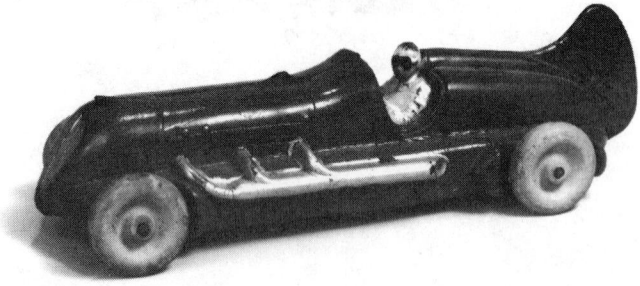

Auburn AR03. Photo by Dave Leopard.

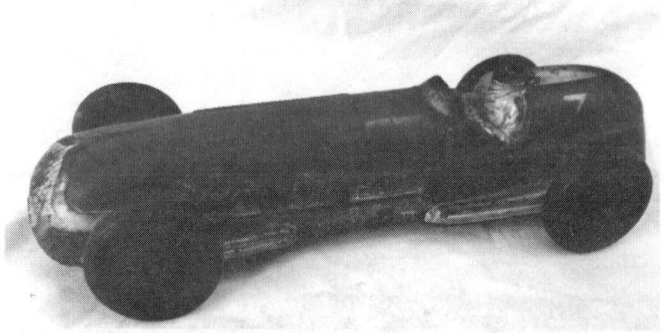

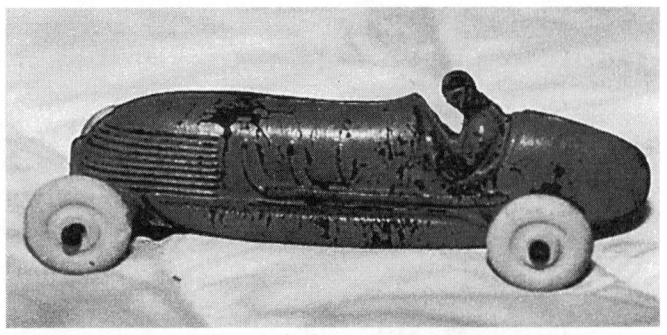

Auburn AR05. Courtesy Dave Leopard, from his book Rubber Toy Vehicles.

	C6	C8	C10
AF05 Farm Tractor, Minneapolis-Moline "R," later style, 7-1/4" long	37	56	75
AF06 Farm Tractor, Oliver Row Crop "70," 8" long	37	56	75
AF07 Unused			
AF08 Farm Tractor, McCormick-Deering IH Farmall "M," 4" long	22	33	45
AF09 Farm Tractor, Graham-Bradley, 4-1/4" long	25	38	50

	C6	C8	C10
AI01 Trailer, 2-wheel, Graham-Bradley, 5-3/4" long	22	33	45
AI02 Trailer, 4-wheel, Graham-Bradley, 4-3/4" long	22	33	45
AI03 Harvester, open top, 5-1/2" long	27	41	55
AI04 Manure Spreader, David Bradley, 4-3/4" long	20	30	40
AI05 Reliable Front-Lift Seeder, 5" long	22	33	45
A105A Spreader, 4-3/4"	20	30	40

Auburn AR06. Courtesy Dave Leopard, from his book Rubber Toy Vehicles.

Auburn AR07. Courtesy Dave Leopard, from his book Rubber Toy Vehicles.

Auburn AR08. Courtesy Dave Leopard, from his book Rubber Toy Vehicles.

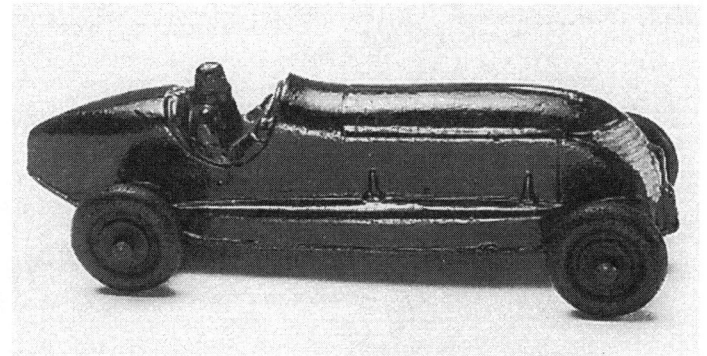

Auburn AR09. Courtesy Dave Leopard, from his book Rubber Toy Vehicles.

Auburn AR10

Auburn AF01. Courtesy Dave Leopard, from his book Rubber Toy Vehicles.

Auburn AF03 (Leopard's AF02). Courtesy Dave Leopard, from his book Rubber Toy Vehicles.

Auburn Rubber  49

Auburn AF04 (Leopard's AF03). Courtesy Dave Leopard, from his book Rubber Toy Vehicles.

Auburn AF05 (Leopard's AF04). Courtesy Dave Leopard, from his book Rubber Toy Vehicles.

Auburn AF07 (Leopard's AF05). Courtesy Dave Leopard, from his book Rubber Toy Vehicles.

Auburn AF08 (Leopard's AF06). Courtesy Dave Leopard, from his book Rubber Toy Vehicles.

Auburn AF09 (Leopard's AF07). Courtesy Dave Leopard, from his book Rubber Toy Vehicles.

Auburn AI01. Courtesy Dave Leopard, from his book Rubber Toy Vehicles.

Auburn AI02. Courtesy Dave Leopard, from his book Rubber Toy Vehicles.

Auburn AI03. Courtesy Dave Leopard, from his book Rubber Toy Vehicles.

Auburn, top to bottom: AI04, AI05A (Leopard's AI05). Courtesy Dave Leopard, from his book Rubber Toy Vehicles.

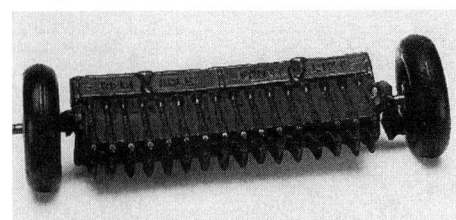

Auburn AI05 (Leopard's AI06), yoke missing. Courtesy Dave Leopard, from his book Rubber Toy Vehicles.

Auburn, top to bottom: AI08, AI09 (Leopard's AI10). Courtesy Dave Leopard, from his book Rubber Toy Vehicles.

Auburn AI09 (Leopard's AI10). Courtesy Dave Leopard, from his book Rubber Toy Vehicles.

	C6	C8	C10
AI06 Plow Seeder, 3-1/2" long ...... No Price Found			
AI07 Side-Cutter Sickle Bar			
Mower, David Bradley, 3-3/4" long	20	30	40
AI08 Two Furrow			
Plow, David Bradley, 4-3/4" long	20	30	40
AI09 Cultipacker (Disc Harrows?),			
David Bradley, 4-3/8" long	22	33	45
AI10 Harrow, 4-1/2" long	20	30	40
AI11 Disc Harrows, 4-1/2" long	22	33	45
AI12 Plow with riding farmer .... No Price Found			
AI13 Unused			
AI14 Blade, 2-3/4",			
fits Graham-Bradley tractor ...... No Price Found			

	C6	C8	C10
AM01 Tank,			
Marmon-Harrington, 4-1/2" long	22	33	45
AM02 Tank,			
Marmon-Harrington, 3-1/4" long	17	26	35
AM03 Tractor			
and Cannon, 11-1/2" long, olive green ...	50	75	100
AAM1 Ambulance, insert top	22	33	45
AMC1 Motorcycle Cop, 5" long	25	38	50
AMC2 As above, in khaki	25	38	50
AMC3 Motorcycle soldiers with sidecar	25	38	50
AMC4 Army Motor Scout on motorcycle	22	33	45
AMC5 Motorcycle Cop, large, 5" high	25	38	50

Auburn AI11 (Leopard's AI12). Courtesy Dave Leopard, from his book Rubber Toy Vehicles.

Auburn AI12 (Leopard's AI13). Courtesy Dave Leopard, from his book Rubber Toy Vehicles.

Auburn AI14 (blade for Graham-Bradley tractor). Courtesy Dave Leopard, from his book Rubber Toy Vehicles.

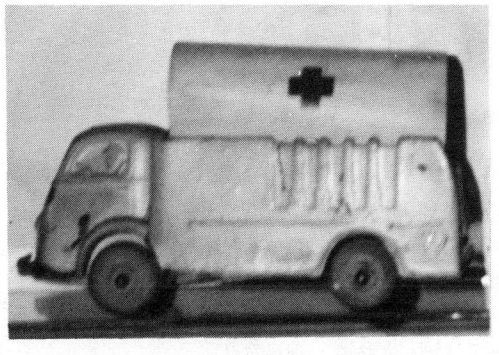

Auburn AAM1. Courtesy K. Warren Mitchell.

Auburn AMC1; from a 1941 Butler Bros. catalog

Auburn Rubber  51

	C6	C8	C10
Airport Limousine No. 504, 7-1/2" long	10	15	20
Army Recon Car No. 652	8	12	16
Army Truck No. 656	8	12	16
Bulldozer No. 348, 8" long	30	45	60
Cadillac Convertible, 3-1/2" long	6	9	12
Cadillac Convertible, 5" long	12	18	25
Crane Shovel No. 356	50	75	100
Delivery Truck	10	15	20
Dump Truck No. 352, 10-1/2" long	35	52	70
Fire Truck No. 614	10	15	20
Fire Truck Pumper No. 500, 7-1/2" long	10	15	20

	C6	C8	C10
Fork Lift w/driver No. 538, 5" long	35	52	70
Hot Rod No. 612, 4-1/4" long	10	15	20
Hot Rod Take-A-Part Kit, w/box	50	75	100
Jeep	7	11	15
Jeep w/Cannon No. 654	16	24	33
Krazy Tow Set, Hot Rod & Tow Truck	55	82	110
Motorcycle	32	48	65
Motorcycle Cop No. 530, 6-1/4" long	35	52	70
Motorcycle Cop No. 520, 3-7/8" long	25	38	50
Motorcycle Cop No. 521, 3-wheel, 4" long	15	22	30

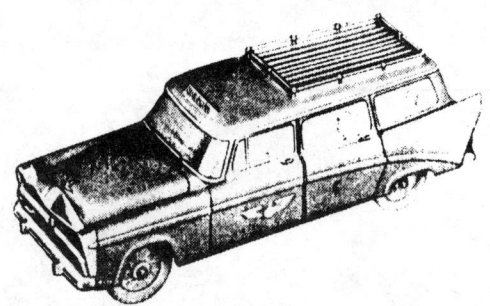

Auburn Vinyl Airport Limousine No. 504

Auburn Vinyl Fork Lift w/driver, No. 538

Auburn Vinyl Motorcycle Cop, 3-wheel. Photo by Gary Linden.

Auburn Rubber Vinyl Police Set No. 9 with original box. Photo by Kent M. Comstock.

Auburn Vinyl, L to R - Top to Bottom: Tank, Army Recon Car, Jeep with Cannon, Army Truck

Auburn Vinyl Telephone Truck

	C6	C8	C10
Police Set No. 9 w/original box	150	225	300
Racer No. 556, 10-1/2" long	27	41	55
Racer, 7" long	37	56	75
Ranchero No. 610, 4-3/4" long	10	15	20
Road Scraper No. 350, 10-1/2" long	30	45	60
Sedan	20	30	40
Stake Bed Truck No. 354, 10-5/8" long	10	15	20
Station Wagon No. 577, 4-5/8" long	12	18	25
Steamroller No. 362	17	25	35
Streetsweeper No. 360, 9" long	75	112	150
Take-Apart Hot Rod	32	48	65
Tank, Army No. 650	7	11	15
Telephone Truck No. 503, 7" long	15	22	30
Tractor w/Plow, 8" overall	16	24	32
Truck No. 518, 5-1/2" long	14	21	28
Utility Truck No. 508	12	18	25

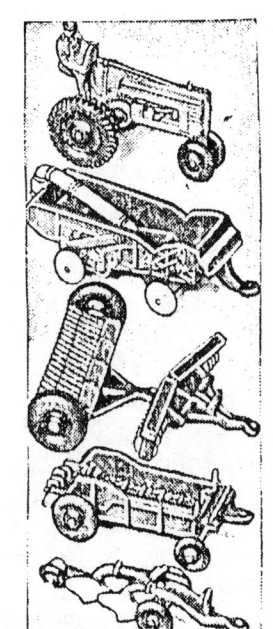

Auburn Rubber tractor and farm implements as seen in a 1940 Butler Bros. catalog

AURORA

	C6	C8	C10
Aurora T-Jet HO scale Mack Stake Truck	25	38	50
Aurora Vibrator 1962 Ford Sunliner, Convertible or Hardtop ...	40	60	80

AUTOMATIC TOY COMPANY

Around the early 1950s, Automatic Toy Company was at 77 Alaska St., Staten Island, New York.

Automatic Toy Company "Auto Speedway," c.1930 windup 85   128   170

Automatic Toy Company "Cop 'N Car," 4" long motorcycle, 8-1/2" car, plastic with motor, siren, c.1953 .... No Price Found

Automatic Toy Company "Magic Crossroads" track, 2-windup cars, c.1950 85   125   170

Automatic Toy Company "Auto Speedway." Courtesy Don Hultzman.

Automatic Toy Company "Cop 'N Car." From a 1953-54 Toy Yearbook.

	C6	C8	C10
Tow Truck, plastic, 9-3/4" long	60	90	120

BANNER

Banner was begun by Emanuel M. Pressner (8/4/99 to 1/1/74) and Bernard Schiller in 1944, probably at 150 Bruckner Blvd., in the Bronx, New York. Pressner had been a toy importer before the war. About 1938 he bought an interest in Columbia Protektosite, which, among other things, cast Beton's plastic toy soldiers. (Though his family has no recollection of this, in 1942 Pressner was noted in a toy trade magazine as being secretary of Beton). Schiller was eventually edged out. Banner moved to 80 Beckwith Ave., Paterson, New Jersey, in 1950, where it remained. The firm's original toys seem to have been small plastic cars and trucks, with the leading items for years being tea sets and metalicized plastic forks, knives, and spoons. Other items included plastic sand molds. The stamped steel Banner used was made up of "off-falls" (blanks formed when holes were cut in steel to allow for car windows and television tubes).

The company, which at its peak periods had as many as 200 employees, went into Chapter 11 bankruptcy in 1965, came out of it, and then was sold in 1967 to Tal-Cap, a toy conglomerate in Minnesota. During its heyday, Banner produced at least tens of thousands of toys a week, according to former vice-president Joseph Stern. Banner got its name, according to Stern, because Pressner (his father-in-law) wanted a company with a name "high up in the alphabet."

	C6	C8	C10
Banner "Ambulance" (Army), 6" long, tin & plastic	12	25	40
Banner American Express Truck, tin, 11-1/2" long	70	105	140
Banner American Express Truck, tin, 11-1/4" long	142	213	285
Banner American Express Truck, tin, 10"	100	200	350
Banner Army Truck, 12" long	37	56	75
Banner Buick Sedan, 4-1/2" long	7	11	14
Banner Circus Train, pulled by tractor, c.1949	No Price Found		

Banner American Express truck, 10" long. Photo by Bob Smith.

Banner American Express truck, 10" long, same size and value as other shown (only detailing varies). Photo by Bob Smith.

Banner Circus Train, pulled by Tractor. Photo by Terry Sells.

	C6	C8	C10
Banner Clown Van, 4-1/2" long, 1950s	12	25	40
Banner "Coronation Milk" Van	162	243	325
Banner "Delivery" Van, 4-1/4" long	8	12	25
Banner Dodge, 1950, 4" plastic	8	15	25
Banner Dump Truck, plastic, 4-1/2" long	9	14	19
Banner Dump Truck, plastic, 5-1/4" long	10	15	20
Banner Dump Truck, metal, 9" long	100	150	200
Banner Express Truck, plastic, 7" long	22	33	45
Banner Garbage			
Truck, Ford, plastic, 1954, 4" long	8	12	25
Banner Garbage Truck, 5-1/2" long	15	22	30
Banner "Grocery			
Service" Truck, 10" long	100	200	350
Banner International Harvester			
Metro 1950 Van, plastic, 4"	8	12	25
Banner Jewel Tea Van	182	273	375
Banner LaFrance			
Fire Truck, plastic, 4", 1950	8	12	25
Banner Livestock Truck, 5-1/2" long	12	18	25
Banner Livestock Truck, plastic, 7" long......	22	33	45
Banner North American			
Van Lines Truck & Trailer, 15" long ...	110	130	200
Banner Oil Truck, 4-3/8" long, plastic	9	14	18
Banner Sand & Gravel			
Truck, plastic, 7" long	25	38	50
Banner Sedan, 4-1/2" long, plastic, 1950s	7	11	15

Banner Clown Van. Courtesy Bob and Alice Wagner.

Banner "Delivery" Van. Photo by Terry Sells.

Banner Garbage Truck, 5-1/2" long. Photo by Terry Sells.

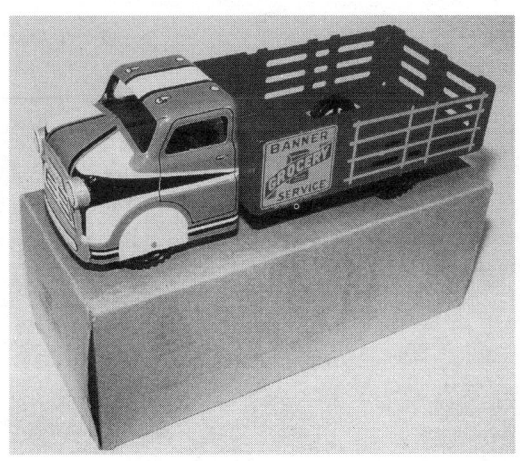

Banner "Grocery Service" truck. Photo by Bob Smith.

Banner Trailer Steamshovel. Photo by Terry Sells.

	C6	C8	C10
Banner Service Station (cardboard) with 3 plastic trucks, c.late 40s - early 50s	22	35	50
Banner Side Dump Truck, 5-1/4" long, plastic, 1950s	10	20	30
Banner Stake Truck, 4-1/2" long	9	14	19
Banner Stake Truck, plastic, 8" long	25	38	50
Banner Station Wagon, 1948 Oldsmobile, plastic, 4"	16	24	32
Banner Steamroller, 4" long, plastic	10	15	20
Banner Steamshovel, 4" long, plastic	10	15	20
Banner Tanker, plastic, 7" long	15	22	30

	C6	C8	C10
Banner Trailer Steamshovel, 6-3/4" long	15	25	35
Banner "Toy Truck" Van, 9" long	75	112	150
Banner Tractor, Wheelhorse, 3" plastic	12	18	25
Banner "U.S. Army" Truck, plastic & tin, 6" long	22	33	45
Banner U.S. Mail Truck, 11" long	35	52	70
Banner "Whelan's" Steel Truck, c.1930s	No Price Found		
Banner Wonder Bread Truck, c.1950s 11" long, tin litho	80	120	160

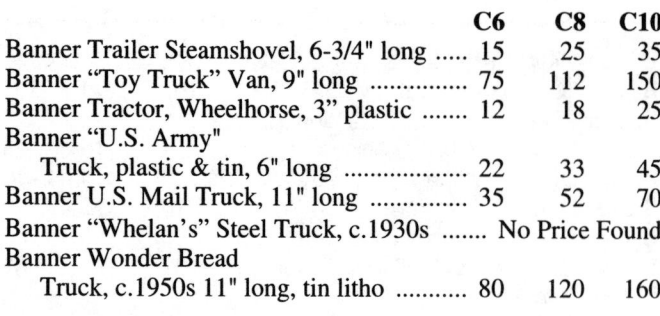

Banner, L to R: "US Army" truck; "Ambulance." Courtesy Roger Johnson & Charles Breslow.

Banner "Whelan's" steel truck, c. 1930s. Photo by Calvin L. Chaussee.

BANTHRICO: See "Promotionals"

BARCLAY

In the 1930s and early 1940s, Barclay was the largest producer of lead-alloy vehicles. The firm was in business in New Jersey as early as—and probably not before—1924. It is best known for its toy soldiers, but in the early 1930s, its largest seller was its tiny No. 53 racer (BV53). Barclay was originally co-owned by Leon Donze and Michael Levy; Levy bought out Donze about 1928. The firm closed in 1971. It was located variously in West Hoboken, Union City, and North Bergen.

	C6	C8	C10
(BV 1) Ambulance, No. 194, 3-1/2" long, small cross	12	18	25
(BV 2) Ambulance, No. 194, 3-1/2" long, large cross	20	30	40
(BV 3) Ambulance, No. 50, 5" long	70	105	140

	C6	C8	C10
(BV 4) No. 151 Army Truck with Gun, 2-3/4" long	10	15	20
(BV 5) No. 151 Army Truck with Anti-Aircraft Gun, 2-1/2" long	12	18	25

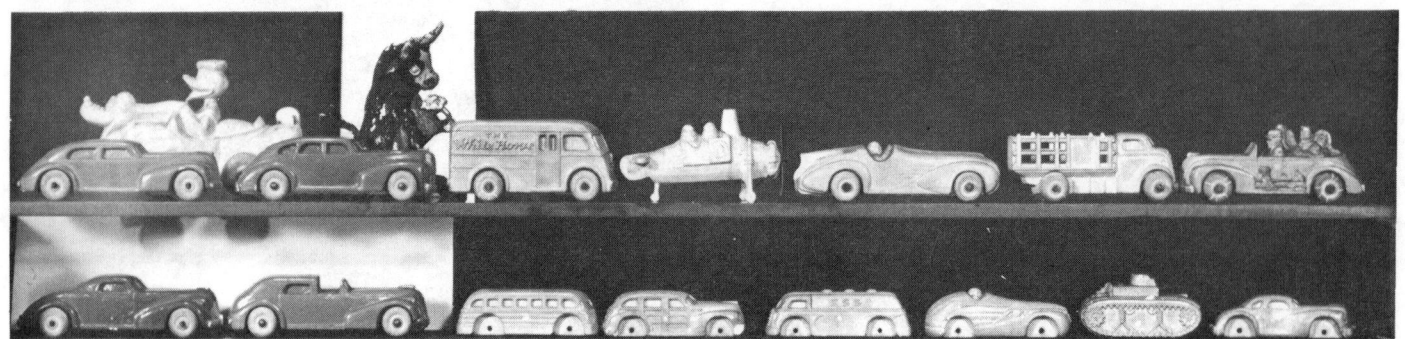

In 1984, 45 plaster castings retained by Barclay's chief of maintenance when he cleaned out the shut-down factory in 1971 were shown to the author in the course of his research. Included were soldiers, Disney figures, vehicles and an autogiro; many were never produced.

The earliest catalog appearance yet found for illustrated Barclay vehicles: This is from the September, 1931 Butler Bros. catalog. Note the metal wheels.

BV1   BV2   BV3

Photo by Craig A. Clark

	C6	C8	C10
(BV 6) No. 152 Armored Army Truck, 2-7/8" long	9	13	18
(BV 6A) Same as above, with variations	10	15	20
(BV 7) No. 197 Army tank truck, c.1935-36, 3-1/8" long	15	22	30
(BV 8) Army Car with two silver bullhorns, approx. 2-1/2" long (this may be same as BV86).	22	33	44
(BV 9) Army Tractor (Minneapolis-Moline "Jeep"), 2-3/4" long	15	22	30
(BV 10) Austin Coupe, c.1931, 2" long, No. 43	30	45	60
(BV 11) No. 330 Auto Transport Set, 4-1/2" long, 2 50s cars	50	75	100

Barclay BV8. Photo by Stan Alekna.

BV6A   BV6

BV6A has larger windows, no rivets up center, smaller front gun, no headlights, etc. Photo by Stan Alekna.

BV10

	C6	C8	C10
(BV 12) "Beer" truck, c.1940, No. 376, 4" long, wood barrels	26	39	52
(BV 13) Beer Truck No. 377, with barrels	35	52	70
(BV 14) Bus, futuristic, "Made U.S.A.," 3" long	34	51	68
(BV 15) Cannon Car, 3-5/16" long, gunner low	14	21	28
(BV 16) No. 198, Anti-Aircraft Gun Truck, in 1931 Barclay catalog, 3-1/8" long	20	30	40
(BV 17) Cannon Car, 3-1/4" long, slight casting differences from headlight version	25	38	55
(BV 18) Cannon Car, battery powered headlight, 3-1/2" long, in 1935 catalog	80	130	225
(BV 18A) Same as above, but no fitting for bulb	22	33	44
(BV 19) No. 48 Anti-Aircraft Gun Truck, 4" long, one man	22	33	45
(BV 20) No. 48 Anti-Aircraft Gun Truck, 4" long, two men	16	24	32
(BV 21) Cannon Truck, 4" long, with moveable cannon	20	30	40
(BV 22) Unused			
(BV 23) Chrysler Airflow, 4" long, c.1936	30	45	60
(BV 24) "Coast To Coast" 2-7/8" long die-cast bus, "Barclay Toy," two-piece, No.405	40	50	85
(BV 25) Coupe, 1930s, "Made in U.S.A." 3" long	10	20	25
(BV 26) Coupe, 2-1/2" long, c.1935 XXX	40	70	100
(BV 27) Coupe, 1934, 4-1/2" long, XXX	40	60	80
(BV 28) Coupe, 2-piece, 1930s, 2-7/8" long, "Barclay Toy"	40	50	85
(BV 29) Unused			
(BV 30) Coupe, 1934, 4-1/2" long, XXX	40	60	80
(BV 31) No. 40 Cord Front Drive Coupe, c.1931, 3-5/8" long	25	38	50
(BV 32) No. 302, Streamline Car, c.1936, 3-1/8" long?	45	68	90
(BV 33) "Delivery" Truck, No. 309, 2-15/16" long, XXX	14	21	28
(BV 34) Double Decker Bus, 4"	60	90	120
(BV 35) (Unused)			
(BV 36) (Unused)			
(BV 37) "Express" Stake Truck, 1930s, 2-15/16" long	30	45	60
(BV 38) Fire Engine No. 390?, moveable ladder, c.1950s	15	22	30
(BV 39) Field Kitchen, 2-1/4" long	10	15	20
(BV 40) Fire Engine, 2 firemen, black metal wheels, 1930s, No. 41, 2-3/4"	17	26	35
(BV 41) Fire Engine, 4" long, French-looking (Barclay often copied foreign toys), XXX	17	26	35
(BV 42) Ford, 1931, 2-1/4"	15	22	30

BV11　　　BV49　　　BV14　　　BV13

BV82　　　BV61 sedan　　　BV47

Barclay, L to R: BV12, BV13. Photo by Craig A. Clark.

BV15　　　BV6　　　BV4　　　BV9

BV56　　　BV19　　　BV20

Photo by Ed Poole

BV24

BV28

	C6	C8	C10
(BV 43) "Golden Arrow Racer," 4-1/2" long, X?X	20	30	40
(BV 44) Mack Pick Up Truck, 3-1/2"	15	22	30
(BV 45) "Milk & Cream" Truck, stamped No. 377, 3-5/8" long, white rubber tires	32	48	65
(BV 45A) Milk Truck, No. 377, 3-5/8" long, black rubber tires	22	33	45
(BV 46) Motorcycle with flat rider, full-dimensioned sidecar, No. 55, 2-3/4"	48	72	95

	C6	C8	C10
(BV 47) "Oil-Fuel" Truck, c.1936, 3-9/16" long	12	18	25
(BV 48) "Parcel Delivery," 3-5/8" long, slush lead, No. 45, c.1931	100	150	200
(BV 49) "Police" Car No. 317, slush mold, approx. 3-5/8" long, c.1930s (Radio Police), 1939 Packard	34	51	68
(BV 49A) Police Car No. 317, die-cast, 3-5/8" long	17	26	35
(BV 50) Race Car, 3"	12	18	24
(BV 51) Racer, 5-1/2", closed cockpit	17	26	35

BV31

BV32   *BV33*   *BV41*

BV32

BV40

Barclay BV34 (tires in photo not correct). Photo by James Apthorpe.

BV45. Photo from the Barclay files. Courtesy Toy Soldier Review.

BV47

BV48

Barclay BV51. Photo by Craig A. Clark.

	C6	**C8**	**C10**
(BV 52) Racer, closed cockpit, 7" long, c.1939	30	45	60
(BV 53) Racer, No. 53, early slush lead, 1920s-30s approx. 2" long	40	60	80

	C6	**C8**	**C10**
(BV 54) Racer, two passengers, 4-1/4" long, XXX	55	83	110
(BV 55) Racer with tail fin, "Made U.S.A.," 3-1/2" long	25	38	50
(BV 56) Renault Tank, c.1937, No. 47, 4" long	22	33	45
(BV 57) Searchlight Truck, white rubber tires, c.1940, 4-1/16" long	87	130	175
(BV 57A) Searchlight Truck, second version	87	130	175
(BV 58) Sedan, 4-door, approx. 5" long, maybe Chrysler, c.1936	17	26	35
(BV 59) Sedan, 2-door, 3-1/8" long, rubber wheels, slush lead, c.1935, XX	60	90	120

BV52

BV53   BV71   BV49   BV87   BV74

BV46   BV4   BV6   BV68

BV57   BV21, cannon off   BV39

BV54   BV30   BV81

BV57A. Photo
by Ed Poole.

BV16   BV18   BV17
Photo by Ed Poole

Barclay, L to R: BV63, BV24. Courtesy Bob and Alice Wagner.

BV60   BV63   BV25   BV28   BV71

BV37   BV61   BV55   BV24

BV63   BV64   BV65

	C6	C8	C10
(BV 60) Sedan, 2-piece, No. 401, 2-door, 1930s "Barclay Toy," die-cast, 2-7/8" long	40	50	85
(BV 61) Sedan and "Tourist Trailer," "Made in U.S.A.," 1930s, 6-1/2" long	62	93	125
(BV 62) Silver Arrow Race Car, 5-1/2" long	22	33	45
(BV 63) Station Wagon, No. 404, die-cast, 1930s, 2-piece "Barclay Toy," 2-15/16" long	37	55	75
(BV 64) Steam-Roller, 3-1/4" long, traction type, slush lead with tin roof, No. 44	30	45	60
(BV 65) No. 363 Large Streamline Racer, in 1935 catalog, 6-7/8" long	45	68	90
(BV 66) Tank "4562" one man in turret, 3-7/8" long	17	26	35
(BV 67) Tank "4562" two men in turret, 3-7/8" long	21	31	42
(BV 68) Tank T41, 4-1/4" long	17	26	35
(BV 69) Tank, 2-5/8" long, man in turret, die-cast, black rubber tires	12	18	25
(BV 70) Tank 2-1/2" long (based on US M2 light tank)	12	18	25
(BV 71) Taxi, 3-1/4" long, c.1940s, slush	14	21	28
(BV 71A) Taxi, No. 318, die-cast, 3-1/4" long	25	38	50
(BV 72) Tractor, approx. 2-5/8" long, caterpillar type, slush lead, XX	17	26	35
(BV 73) (Unused)			
(BV 74) Trailer Truck variously "Railway Express," or with Moving Company name, c.1950s	5	8	10
(BV 75) Transport Set No. 330, 2 cars, 1960s, 4-1/2" long	25	40	75
(BV 76) No. 204 U.S. Army Truck, 2-1/2" long, no hitch, red wood hubs	11	16	22
(BV 77) "U.S. Army" Truck, white rubber wheels, 2-1/2" long, wire or peg hitch	12	18	25
(BV 78) Truck "U.S. Motor Unit," c.1940, white rubber tires, came 3 ways; no hitch, wire hitch, peg hitch, 3-1/4" long	17	26	35
(BV 79) Wheel-A-Rific speedway track, two lead racers, black rubber wheels, 10" of plastic track, sold for $1.00 c.1970	17	26	35
(BV 80) No. 46 wrecker, 3-1/2", c.1931	45	68	90
(BV 81) Wrecker, 3-15/16" long, c.1934, XXX	30	45	60

BV64   BV72   BV40

BV66   BV67   BV68
Photo by Craig A. Clark

BV67   BV66   BV70

BV68   BV5   BV69   cannon, 4" long post WWII

Photo by Ed Poole

BV69   BV70   BV71   BV71A
Photo by Craig A. Clark

Barclay, Top, L to R: Howitzer, 4 Wheels, loop hitch horizontal, Howitzer, 4 wheels, loop hitch vertical, BV78 with wire hitch, BV78 with peg hitch; Bottom, L to R: BV7, BV77 peg hitch, BV77 wire hitch, BV76, no hitch. Photo by Ed Poole.

	C6	C8	C10
(BV 82) Wrecker, 2-piece, No. 403, die-cast 1930s, "Barclay Toy," 2-7/8" long	40	50	85
(BV 83) Cannon Truck, moveable cannon, 4" long	37	56	75
(BV 84) Milk Truck in shape of bottle, No. 567	145	217	290
(BV 85) "Milk" Van Truck, 2-7/8" long, bottle on side	20	30	41
(BV 86) Officer's car, 2-1/2" long with megaphone on top	22	33	44
(BV 87) Side dump, approx. 1-1/2" long	7	11	15
(BV 88) Convertible with vacationers	50	75	100
(BV 89) 100/4 Build & Paint Auto Set, 6 vehicles, parts, paints, 1930s	No Price Found		
(BV 89A) No. 5004 Build and Paint Auto Set, c.1934	No Price Found		
(BV 90) 2004 Build & Paint Set, Truck, Coupe, Sedan, parts, paints, early	180	270	360
(BV 90A) 2004 Build & Paint Set, same number, only 2 vehicles	No Price Found		
(BV 91) "U.S. Mail" Truck, 1960s, approx. 2"	10	17	24
(BV 92) Moving Truck, c.1960s, approx. 2"	8	12	16
(BV 93) Log Truck, c.1960s, approx. 2"	7	11	15
(BV 94) Dump Truck, c.1960s, approx. 2"	7	11	15
(BV 95) Racing Car, c.1968, approx. 2"	5	8	10

BV79. Courtesy Toy Soldier Review.

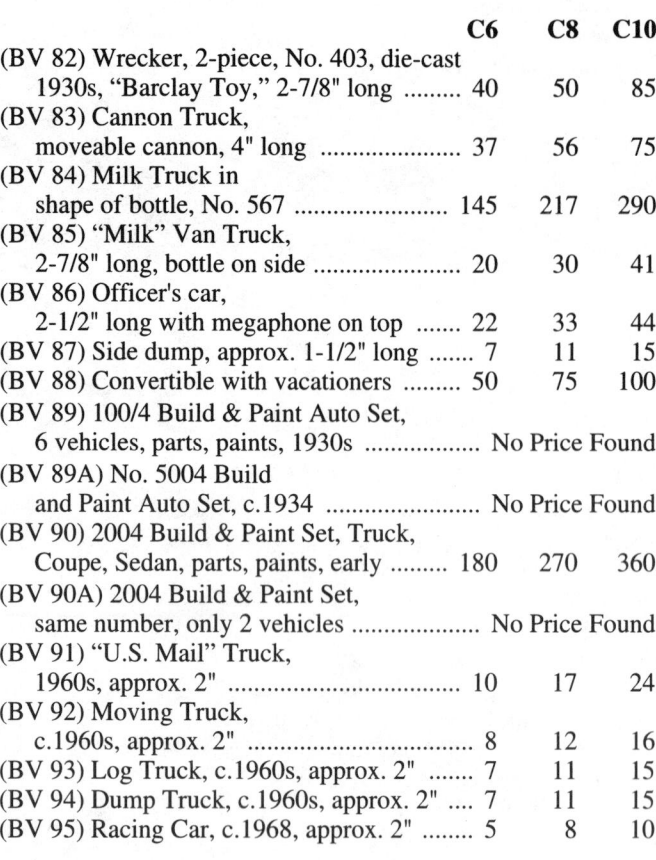

Barclay BV80

Barclay, L to R: BV80-BV10, BV26, BV59

BV82

Barclay BV83. Photo by Ed Poole.

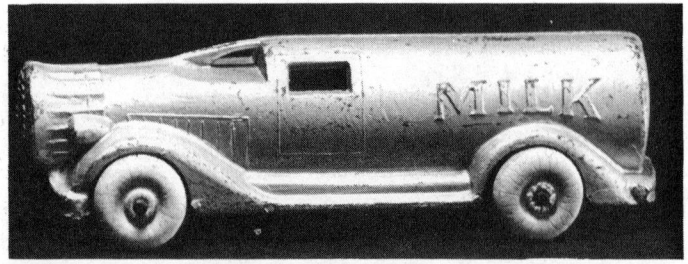

Barclay BV84. Courtesy Larry Burke.

Barclay
BV85

BV88

BV90, showing from Top to Bottom: BV140, BV145, BV144A. Photo by Roger Sanders.

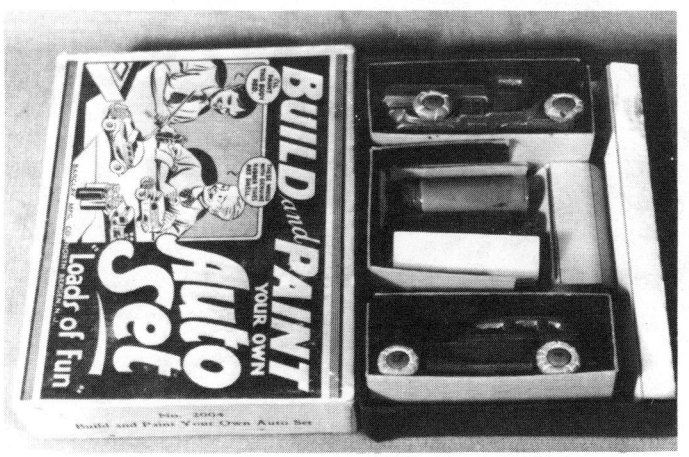

Barclay BV90A. Photo by Perry R. Eichor.

Another variation of BV91. Photo by Stan Alekna.

BV91. Photo from the Barclay files. Courtesy Toy Soldier Review.

Paint and decal variations of Barclay BV91; add five to ten dollars for the Woolworth truck. Photo by Stan Alekna.

Barclay, L to R: BV92, BV93, BV94, BV87. Courtesy Toy Soldier Review.

	C6	C8	C10
(BV 96) "Police" Car (like BV86 and BV97), approx. 2" long	5	8	10
(BV 97) "Chief" Police Car (like BV86 and BV96), approx. 2" long	5	8	10
(BV 98) Vintage Car, approx. 2" long	15	22	30
(BV 99) Oil Truck, c.1960s, approx. 2" long	8	13	18
(BV 100) Pepsi-Cola Truck, 1960s, approx. 2" long	8	13	18
(BV 101) Racing Car, c.1968, no fenders, approx. 2" long	5	8	10

	C6	C8	C10
(BV 102) Volkswagen, 1960s, approx. 2" long	10	17	24
(BV 103) U.S. Army Truck, c.1968, approx. 2" long	7	11	15
(BV 104) Hospital Truck, c.1968, approx. 2" long	8	13	18
(BV 105) Army truck, open bed, c.1968, approx. 2" long	7	11	15
(BV 106) Army Oil Truck, c.1968, approx. 2" long	8	13	18

Barclay: Decal variants of BV92. Photo by Stan Alekna.

Barclay, L to R: BV95, BV96, BV97, BV98. Courtesy Toy Soldier Review.

Barclay, L to R: BV99, BV100, BV101, BV102. From the Barclay files. Courtesy Toy Soldier Review.

Barclay: Decal variants of BV99. Photo by Stan Alekna.

Barclay: Variants of BV100, L to R: plain version, "Yoo Hoo," "Pepsi Cola," and "Coca Cola"; the latter two are particularly sought after. Photo by Stan Alekna.

Barclay, L to R: BV103, BV104, BV105, BV106. From the Barclay files. Courtesy Toy Soldier Review.

BV107. From the Barclay files. Courtesy Toy Soldier Review.

BV108. From the Barclay files. Courtesy Toy Soldier Review.

BV109

BV111

BV110

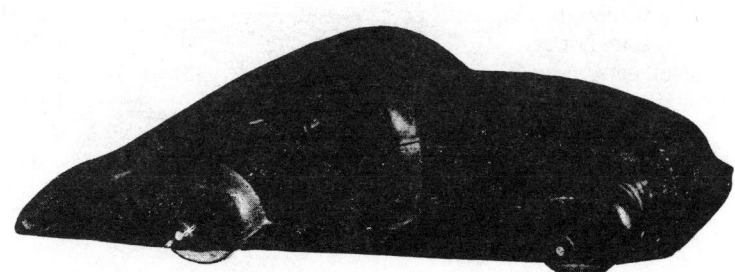

BV112

BV113

BV114

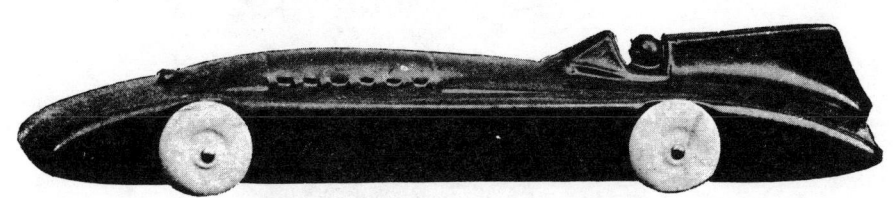

BV115

BV116

	C6	C8	C10
(BV 107) Double Transport Set No. 440, 4-1/2" long, 4 cars on upper and lower racks, 1963 on, hinged for unloading	72	108	145
(BV 108) 2-door Sedan, 1960s, 1-5/8" long	2	3	5
(BV 109) No. 203 Tractor, 2-1/8" long, peg hitch	11	16	22
(BV 110) Open coupe with driver in cap, early 30s	60	90	120
(BV 111) "Esso Gas" Truck, 1930s, 5" long	20	30	40
(BV 112) No. 361 Streamline Large Coupe	17	26	35
(BV 113) 1935 DeSoto AirFlow, 5-3/16" long	17	26	35
(BV 114) Car Carrier, 2 small cars, early 1930s	25	38	50
(BV 115) No. 371 Racing Car, large, 1930s, 4-1/4" long	16	24	32
(BV 116) No. 7 Tractor, c. late 20s early 30s	15	22	30
(BV 117) No. 1105 (or 1705) "Towing Service" Truck, large	82	124	175
(BV 118) 1929 Buick Sedan?, 3-1/4" long	27	41	55
(BV 119) No. 312 "Towing" Truck, in 1936 catalog, 3-3/8" long	50	75	100
(BV 120) No. 306 Racer, in 1936 catalog, 4-3/8"	55	83	110
(BV 121) No. 303 Streamline Racer, 4-3/8" long	55	83	110
(BV 122) No. 208 Hook and Ladder, in 1935 catalog, 3" long	16	24	32
(BV 123) No. 301 Coupe Streamline, 3-1/4" long	50	75	100
(BV 124) No. 207 Stake Truck, in 1935 catalog, 3-1/8" long	50	75	100
(BV 125) No. 362 Streamline Sedan, large, in 1935 catalog	41	61	82
(BV 126) No. 368 Fire Truck, 1930s, "Fire Dept. No. 99," 5-3/4" long	20	30	40
(BV 127) No. 1703 1935 Chrysler Airflow Sedan, large	17	26	35

BV117

BV118

BV119

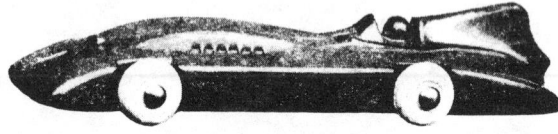

BV120

BV121

BV122

BV123

BV124

BV125

BV126

BV127

BV128

BV129

BV130

BV131 Delivery Truck

BV132

BV133

BV134

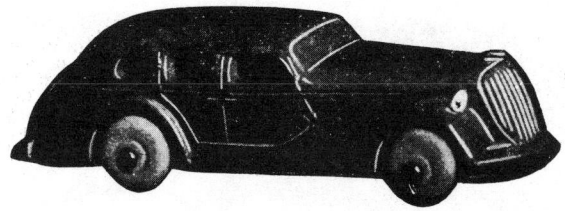

BV135

BV136

BV137

	C6	C8	C10
(BV 128) No. 42 Small Tractor, in 1931 magazine, 2-3/16" long	12	18	25
(BV 129) No. 39 Imperial Chrysler Coupe, c.1931	15	22	30
(BV 130) No. 5 Racer, in 1931 magazine, Golden Arrow	15	22	30
(BV 131) No. 206 Delivery Truck "Bakery Fine Cake Pies," c.1934, 3-1/8" long	70	105	140
(BV 132) No. 51 Coupe, c.1931, 2-3/16" long	18	27	35
(BV 133) No. 210 Fire Truck, c.1934, 3-1/8" long	25	38	50
(BV 134) No. 209 Fire Engine, c.1934, 3-1/8" long	25	38	50
(BV 135) No. 311 Sedan, c.1936	21	32	43
(BV 136) No. 309 "Delivery" Truck, c.1936, 3-1/2" long	12	18	25
(BV 137) No. 50 Fire Truck, c.1931, 2-3/8" long	22	33	45

	C6	C8	C10
(BV 137A) Like BV 137, but with gold hydraulics on both sides, wood hubs, rubber tires, 2-7/16" long	25	38	50
(BV 138) No. 56 Double-Decker Bus, c.1931, 3-1/4" long	22	33	45
(BV 139) No. 58 Auburn Speedster, c.1931	17	26	35
(BV 140) Sedan, c.1934	34	51	68
(BV 141) No. 205 Tow Car, in 1935 catalog, 3-1/16" long	34	51	68
(BV 142) No. 338 Contractor Set, approx. 6-1/4" long (has hole hitch for wire, unlike BV109's peg hitch), 1930s	No Price Found		
(BV 143) Large Streamline Coupe, 1930s	15	22	30
(BV 144) "Gasoline" Truck, small, c.1931, 2-5/16" long, 3 tank top	30	45	60
(BV 144A) Gas Truck, c.1935, 200 series?, 4 tank top, 3" long	25	38	50

BV137A. Photo by Craig A. Clark.

BV138

BV139

BV142

BV141

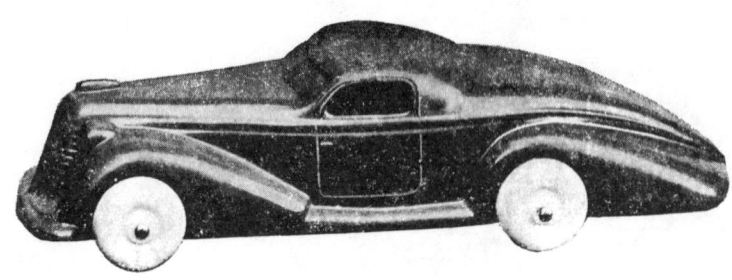

BV143

Barclay, L to R: BV144, BV144A, BV145. Photo by Craig A. Clark.

BV144A

	C6	C8	C10
(BV 145) Coupe, cast rear tire, c.1935, 200 series? 3-1/8" long	21	31	42
(BV 146) Coupe, removable spare tire, in 1935 catalog, 4-1/2" long	30	45	60
(BV 147) Dump Truck, spring action, ratchet, in 1935 catalog, 4" long	20	30	40
(BV 148) Sport Coupe, 2-7/8" long, removable spare tire, in 1935 catalog	32	48	65
(BV 149) Racing Car, large, raised exhaust pipe, driver, in 1935 catalog	17	26	35
(BV 149A) Racing Car, like above, 4" long, battery-powered headlight	No Price Found		
(BV 150) Race Car, open, driver, 4" long	70	105	140

	C6	C8	C10
(BV 151) Stake Truck, 4-3/8" long, in 1935 catalog	36	54	72
(BV 152) 2-Car transport set, approx. 4-3/4" long	42	63	85
(BV 153) 4-Car transport set, 10-1/4" long, open-cab Mack Truck (4) 2-1/2" cars, in 1935 catalog	No Price Found		
(BV 154) Roadster, 4-1/2" long, open, driver, dummy spare tire on each side, in 1935 catalog	80	120	160
(BV 155) Streamline Coupe, 5" long, in 1937 catalog	No Price Found		

Barclay, L to R: BV147, BV148, BV149. Photo by Craig A. Clark.

Barclay, L to R: BV148, BV147. Photo by Fred Maxwell.

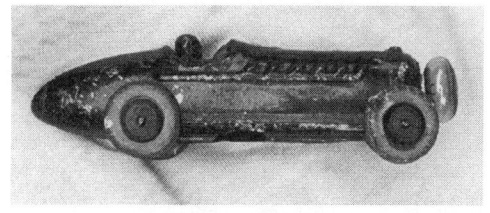

Barclay BV149A (bulb not original). Photo by Fred Maxwell.

Barclay BV150. Photo by Craig A. Clark.

Barclay BV151. Photo by Craig A. Clark.

Barclay BV152. Photo by Craig A. Clark.

Barclay BV153. Photo by David Leopard.

L to R: What appears to be Barclay BV154, somehow missing the driver, and BV146. Each seems to have been painted by a child, rather than at Barclay. Photo by Roy Bonjour.

Barclay, L to R: BV155, BV156. Photo by Craig A. Clark.

	C6	C8	C10
(BV 156) "White Horse" van, approx. 3" long (some have sticker reading "Welcome I.C.M.A. compliments THE WHITE MOTOR CO.")	55	83	110
(BV 157) No. 440 Double Decker Auto Transport, earlier version of BV107, truck has one side window, 1939-1963	25	40	75
(BV 158) Hospital Truck, Cab over, approx. 2" long	8	13	18
(BV 159) Convertible Sports Car, c.1960, driver & passenger	9	13	18
(BV 160) Volkswagen, c.1960s, slightly larger than BV102	12	18	24
(BV 161) Moving Truck, approx. 2" long, c. 1960	8	13	18
(BV 162) "U.S. Army" Sedan, approx. 2" long	6	9	12
(BV 163) "Taxi," approx. 2" long	5	8	10
(BV 164) VW Hot Rod version of BV102, approx. 2" long	12	18	24
(BV 165) Vintage Car, no windshield, lower seat than BV 98	5	8	10
(BV 166) Pickup Truck, No. 319	No Price Found		
(BV 167) Tow Truck, No. 316	No Price Found		
(BV 168) Stake Truck, "Trucking," in 1936 catalog, 3-1/2" long	No Price Found		

Barclay, L to R: BV158, BV104. Photo by Stan Alekna.

Barclay, L to R: BV157, BV75. Courtesy Bob and Alice Wagner.

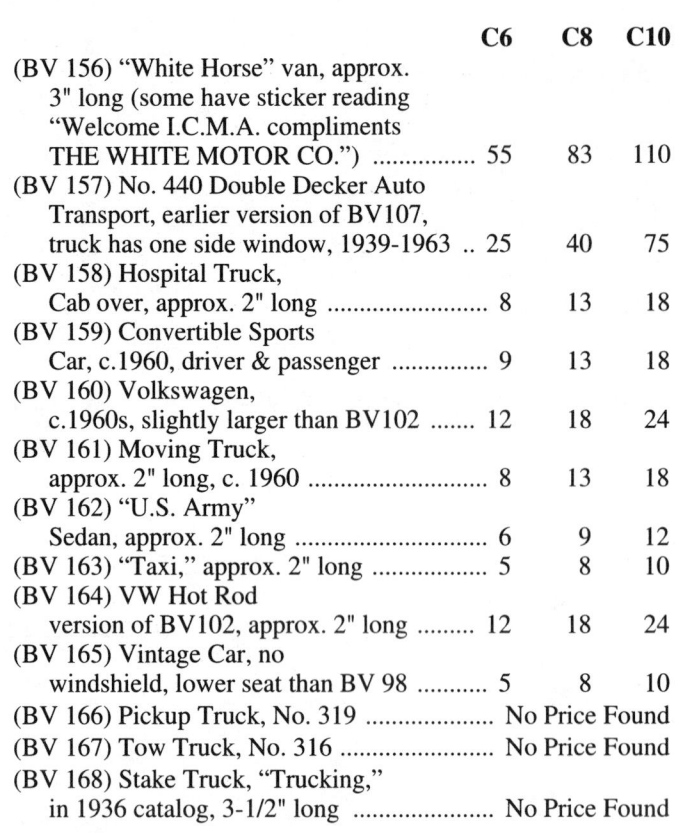

Barclay vehicles with the original factory tags, L to R: BV166, BV167. MacNary Collection Photo: RLM.

Barclay BV168. Photo by Craig Clark.

This 3" long "Gasoline" truck appears to be Barclay; no value found. Photo by Craig Clark.

At left, what seems to be a Barclay from the 1940s, though not yet verified; values in C6, C8, C10: $15, 25, 35; At right, No. 377 as a Delivery Truck; values $20, 30, 45. Courtesy Bob and Alice Wagner.

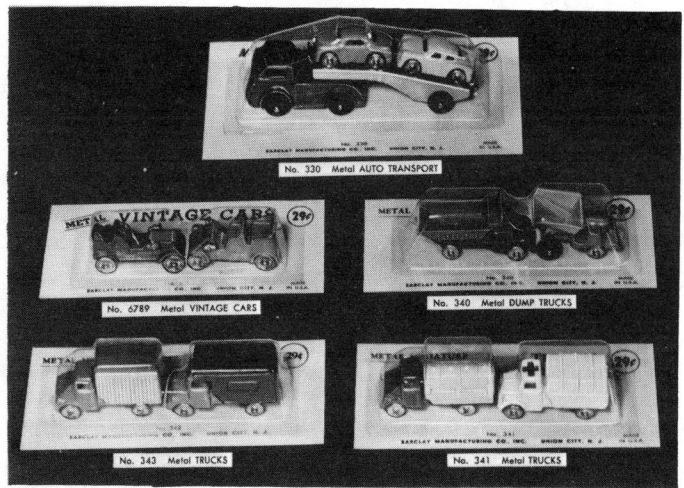

Barclay, L to R: What appears to be a Barclay coupe and sedan, though neither has been verified as such. Sold in the 1930s and 1940s; values in C6, C8, C10: $10, 20, 25. Courtesy Bob and Alice Wagner.

Barclay blister pack sets, c.1968. The no. 330 Auto Transport (BV75) is worth about $75 in mint. The others are worth about $35 in mint.. Photo from the Barclay files. Courtesy Toy Soldier Review.

325 TRAILER TRUCK

339 MINIATURE AUTOS

349 MINIATURE FOREIGN CARS

347 SPORTS CARS

Barclay Blister pack vehicles, c.1968. Value is about $35 in mint, except for the No. 339 pack of seven autos, which would go for about $55 in mint.. Photo from the Barclay files. Courtesy Toy Soldier Review.

Barclays in "bottle" bubble packs; value in mint about $25. Courtesy Toy Soldier Review.

BARR RUBBER

Barr Rubber was located in Sandusky, Ohio. The following list, with its codings, was compiled by Dave Leopard. Vehicles are broken down by type.

	C6	C8	C10
BA01 '35 Ford Coupe, 4" long	25	35	45
BA02 '35 Ford 2- door Slantback Sedan, 4" long	25	35	45
BT01 '35 Ford Stake Body Truck, 4-3/4" long	25	35	45
BT02 '35 Ford Panel Truck/Ambulance, 4-1/4" long	25	35	45
BT03 '35 Ford Army Truck, 4-3/4" long	30	40	50

Barr, L to R: BA02, BA01. Courtesy Dave Leopard, from his book Rubber Toy Vehicles.

Barr BT02, both versions. Courtesy Dave Leopard, from his book Rubber Toy Vehicles.

Barr, L to R: BT03, BT01. Courtesy Dave Leopard, from his book Rubber Toy Vehicles.

BEAUT MFG. CO.

Beaut Mfg. Co., North Bergen, New Jersey, was founded in 1946 by Eugene Buhler and Irving Reader, former machinist and salesman, respectively, for Barclay Mfg. Co. The company put out six toys: a Taxi, Police Car, Fire Engine, Sedan, Sedan Delivery, and a Child's Wagon. The company was successful at first, employing 10 people and selling to Woolworth's and many overseas buyers. It ceased its toy-making activities (it continued until 1982 as a general machine shop) around 1950, because of competition from plastic toys.

BEAUT "Fire" Car, No. 4, approx. 3-3/4" ...	10	15	20
BEAUT "Police" Car, approx. 3-3/4"	10	15	20
BEAUT Sedan, approx. 3-3/4"	10	15	20
BEAUT "Taxi," approx. 3-3/4", No. 1	10	15	20
BEAUT Sedan Delivery, 3-3/4"	20	30	40
BENBROS Military Land Rover, 1950s, 1/64 scale	20	30	40

BEAUT "Police" car (left) and "Taxi" (right). Photo by Bill Kaufman. Courtesy George Buhler.

BEST TOY & NOVELTY FACTORY

by Fred Maxwell, Slushmold *contributing editor, with the assistance of Perry Eichor and Ferd Zegel.*

John M. Best Sr., who founded Best Toy in Manhattan, Kansas, was an entrepreneur who stuck his neck out. Only senior citizens can understand how low our economy was in the 1930s, so starting a new business after watching other toy companies fail successively tells us something about Best and about the perennial appeal of good toys. To Best, the molding of potmetal toys must have seemed a good risk for a second income, as he was a printer who worked with metal alloys. Furthermore, he probably had been following the ups and downs of "those TOYS with the NUMBERS," for he had lived in Clifton, the home of Kansas Toy Company.

It started as a family hobby for his children, relatives, friends, and neighbors, according to Minnie Nelson, his daughter. Other employees we know of were John Best Jr., and his family, and Conrad Morsch, a molder. This hobby grew into a respectable business, supplying toy distributors and dime stores. The toys are readily found in today's toy markets. After several years of operation, it was sold to Ralstoy, a Ralston, Nebraska, company, in 1939.

At this point, we are not certain when Best started or what "number" in the series was his first molding. Although contradictory, evidence from family members suggests purchase of the assets of a Clifton toy company occurred about 1933. Nor do we know if he introduced any new patterns. Regardless, it was an important chapter in the story of those wandering molds. (See history of "Kansas Toy" in this book).

Of great assistance was a donation from Dee Buchanan, Mrs. Nelson's granddaughter, of a faded copy of a Best Toy brochure. It appears to be a pre-publication printer's mockup (undated); but its 42 illustrations (some shown here) were adequate to identify most of the Best and many of the Kansas toys in collections. With no paper trail to guide us previously, this was indeed a find; much of the hearsay errors and confusion of this family of toys was eliminated. Many thanks to all who helped and continue to help.

(Richard O'Brien adds this note: Dee Buchanan, great granddaughter of John Best Sr., also contributed a history in 1988 that may be of interest to readers: "About 55 years ago, John Milner Best Sr. and his wife Roseana, purchased a company from Kansas Toy & Novelty Company located in Vining, Kansas—actually a suburb of Clifton. The Bests owned a newspaper, printing plant, and book-bindery in Manhattan, Kansas. They moved the toy company to a building in back of their home at 530 Fremont Street, Manhattan. The family, in-laws and friends all worked making the lead cars produced by the toy company and were shipping them all over the world. There were also farm implements, tractors, airplanes, buses, and trains, as well as all types of cars. One of the Bests' grandchildren, Rosemary, remembers the Toy Factory well, as when she was about 3 years old and was playing about the factory, she fell into one of the lead-melting pots head first. Very fortunately the lead was not hot—so she just had a bad bruise on her head; whereas if the lead had been hot and melted it would indeed have been a tragedy.")

Best Toy reproductions can usually be distinguished from those of earlier makes in the "numbers" dynasty, if they have white rubber wheels and are embossed "Made in USA." However, some of the toys used the metal wheels (MW) of the Kansas Toy originals, or the later wood hubs with rubber tires (WHRT). It is also possible that Best modified or rebuilt his molds to create variations.

Best molded a great number of designs. To reduce redundancy in this book, we list them here, but will not describe them in detail, if they are adequately covered in Kansas Toy or Ralstoy lists. The following numbered toys and some unnumbered duplicates were found: 6, 10, 14, 17, 20, 25, 26, 27, 31, 32, 34, 35, 36, 37, 39, 40, 41, 42, 43, 45, 46, 47, 49, 51, 54, 55, 57, 58, 59, 60, 67, 70, 71, 72, 74, 76, 77, 78, 79, 80, 81, 85, 86, 87, 90, 91, 92, 93, 94, 95, 97, 99, 100, 101, 102.

	C6	C8	C10
BEV1 Racer, "85," 4". Record car w/large square fin, driver, HO, VG, 12 exhaust ports, WHRT	20	30	40
BEV2 Sedan, "86," 4". Lincoln? 2-door fastback, slant grille w/grid pattern, HL, divided w/s, rear wheel skirts	No Price Found		
BEV3 Sedan, "87." Brewster?	No Price Found		
BEV4 Sedan, "90," 3-1/2", 2-door airflow, hood reaches front bumper w/no grille, 4 OW, hard rubber wheels	No Price Found		
BEV5 Sedan, "91," 3-1/2". Cadillac? 2-door airflow, high style vee grille, faired front fenders	No Price Found		
BEV6 Coupe, "92," 3-3/4". Dodge? chopped top, Brewster-like heart shaped grille, HO, long streamlined front fenders	No Price Found		

	C6	C8	C10
BEV7 Coupe, "93," 3-5/8" Cadillac?, streamlined, hood similar to #91, grid pattern grille, 2 OW (see illustration of #96)	16	24	32

Best Toy Racers, L to R: No. 76, BEV1. Photo courtesy Perry Eichor.

BEV1, No. 85 - 4" long

BEV2, No. 86 - 4" long

BEV4, No. 90 - 3-1/2" long

BEV5, No. 91 - 3-1/2" long

BEV6, No. 92 - 3-3/4" long

Top row: BEV7, BEV8. Bottom row: BEV9A, BEV9B (repro). Courtesy Fred Maxwell.

Top row: BEV7, BEV14. Middle row: BEV6, (repro), BEV2 (repro). Bottom row: BEV5 (repro). Courtesy Perry Eichor.

BEV9a, No. 95 - 3-1/2" long

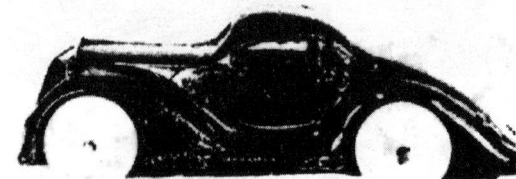

BEV10, No. 96 - 3-1/2" long

BEV11, No. 97 - 4-1/2" long

74   Best Toy & Novelty Factory

BEV13, No. 99 - 4" long

BEV14, No. 100 - 4" long

BEST TOY Tanker: BEV15, BEV16. Photo courtesy Perry Eichor.

No. 10 - Medium Racer

No. 76 - 4-1/4" long

No. 81 - 4-1/2" long

	C6	C8	C10
BEV8 Large Sedan, "94," 4-1/2", 2-door airflow, similar to #90, 4 OW, taxi lamp on roof		No Price Found	
BEV9a Sedan, "95," 3-1/2", 2-door airflow similar to #94, with 3 headlamps, 4 OW, trunk, hard rubber wheels. Chrysler-Briggs show car?		No Price Found	
BEV9b Sedan, "95," 3-1/2". Same as above with "Police Dept." shield on doors. Centered headlamp may be a siren. A version has "Police" painted on roof	45	68	90
BEV10 Coupe, "96," 3-1/2". Apparently same car as #93. Were both produced?		No Price Found	
BEV11 Large racer, "97," 4-1/2". Bluebird record car, driver, large fin, 12 exhaust ports, hard rubber wheels, faired	15	23	30
BEV12 Coupe, "98"		No Price Found	
BEV13 Coupe, "99," 4". Pontiac?, streamlined, HO, rearmount		No Price Found	
BEV14 Sedan, "100" 4". Pontiac, streamlined, 2-door, HO, HG, 4 OW, trunk		No Price Found	
BEV15 Cab Unit, "101," 3-1/4", International? sleeper cab, slanted grille, HO, 2 OW. Rare		No Price Found	
BEV16 Oil Transport, "No. 102," 4," streamlined "Gasoline" semi-trailer to #101, 4 tanks, 4 storage compartments. Total length of cab-trailer: 6-3/4"	47	70	95

No. 26 - 4" long

Box from a BEST TOYS Farm Set. All the Toys illustrated are from molds believed to have originated with Kansas Toys. Photo by Perry Eichor. Courtesy Fred Maxwell.

Bico

	C6	C8	C10
"Bico Bus to Joyville," open double-decker, passengers, driver	2000	3500	5000

Big Bang

	C6	C8	C10		C6	C8	C10
Big Bang Army Tank No. 5T, 8-1/8" long	35	50	100	Big Bang Motor Tank, No. 5T, 9-1/2" long, c.1933	100	200	350

Big Boy: See "Kelmet"

Bing Toy Works

Nuremberg, Germany 1866-1933

by Bob Smith

Bing Toy Works started producing tin toys in the 1880s. By 1914, it employed more than 5,000 people. Business flourished through the 1920s until the Great Depression. In 1932, after falling on hard times, a receiver was assigned to the company. About two years later, it ceased production of tin toys entirely. Karl Bub, another German toy manufacturer, took over the company soon thereafter. Bing automobiles are somewhat hard to find and are held in high regard by most collectors. The Model T series came not only in solid black, but in red, yellow, green, and blue litho. The color litho versions are hard to find.

	C6	C8	C10
BING Double-Decker Bus, 10" long	650	1100	1600
BING Dog Cart, Live Steam, leather seats, 10" long	3000	6000	9000
BING Fire Ladder Truck, c/w motor, composition figures, 13" long	2000	3500	5100
BING Fire Pumper, c/w motor, composition figures, 11" long	1800	3200	4500
BING Garage, Raceabout and Limousine. Autos 5-1/2" long, Garage 8" W x 6-1/2" D. Tin litho, c/w motor, c.1912	432	648	865
BING Garage with 2 open cars. Garage 8"W, 6-1/2"D. Car length 5-1/2". Tin litho, c/w motor. c.1925	400	600	800

BING Limousine c.1908, maroon & yellow striping, driver, c/w motor, 14" long, auctioned in 1995 for $4700.

Bing Garage, Raceabout, and Limousine; c.1912, autos 5-1/2" long. Photo by Bob Smith.

Bing Garage with two open cars, c.1925. Photo by Bob Smith.

Bing Limousine, c.1908, maroon with yellow striping. Courtesy Bill Bertoia Auctions. Photo by Jeanne Bertoia.

Bing Limousine, c.1915, 9-1/2" long. Photo by Bob Smith.

Bing "Model T" Ford Coupe, c.1924, 6-1/2" long. Photo by Bob Smith.

Bing "Model T" Ford Roadster, c.1924, 6-1/2" long. Photo by Bob Smith.

Bing Model T Fords, 6-1/2" long, c.1924. Bob Smith Collection. Photo by Len Rosenberg.

Bing "Model T" Ford Sedan, c.1924, 6-1/2" long. Photo by Bob Smith.

	C6	C8	C10
BING Limousine, c.1915, 9-1/2" long. Blue/black litho, c/w motor	900	1250	1800
BING Limousine, driver, windup, c.1920s, 15-1/4"	700	1100	1700
BING Model T Doctor's Coupe, black, c/w motor, 6-1/2"	225	338	450
BING "Model T" Ford Coupe Red/black/cream tin litho. 6-1/2" long, c/w motor. c.1924	330	485	660
BING "Model T" Ford Roadster. Red/black/yellow tin litho. 6-1/2" long, c/w motor. c.1924	600	900	1300
BING "Model T" Ford Sedan. Blue/black/cream tin litho. 6-1/2" long, c/w motor. c.1924	275	415	550
BING "Model T" Ford Touring Car. Color tin litho, 6-1/2" long, c/w motor. c.1924 (not pictured)	332	496	665
BING "Model T Fords". Sedan, Roadster, Touring, and Coupe, black paint. 6-1/2" long, c.1923 each	350	500	800
BING Open Two Seater, 9-1/2" long	1000	1700	2500
BING Stake Truck, driver, early, hand painted	1900	3000	5200
BING Touring Car. Type I spoked wheels, c/w motor, red/black, male driver, 6" long. c.1920	250	375	500
BING Touring Car. Type II - solid wheels, c/w motor, red/black, female driver, 6" long. c.1923	250	375	500

Bing "Model T" Fords, Sedan, Roadster, Touring, and Coupe, c.1923, 6 1/2" long. Photo by Bob Smith.

	C6	C8	C10
BING Touring Car, 13" long, windup	500	1000	1500
BING Vis a Vis, steam, c.1902, driver, 10" long, auctioned in 1995 for $10,600.			
BING "Yellow Taxi." Orange/black litho, c/w motor. 9" long, c.1924	800	1300	1850

Bing Touring Car, Type I, male driver, c.1920, 6" long. Photo by Bob Smith.

Bing Touring Car, Type II, female driver, c.1923, 6" long. Photo by Bob Smith.

Bing Vis-a-Vis, steam, c.1902. Courtesy Bill Bertoia Auctions. Photo by Jeanne Bertoia.

Bing "Yellow Taxi," c.1924, 9" long. Photo by Bob Smith.

	C6	C8	C10
BMC Pedal Car, C.1950s	200	300	400

BMC Pedal Cars, as seen in the 1952-53 Toy Yearbook.

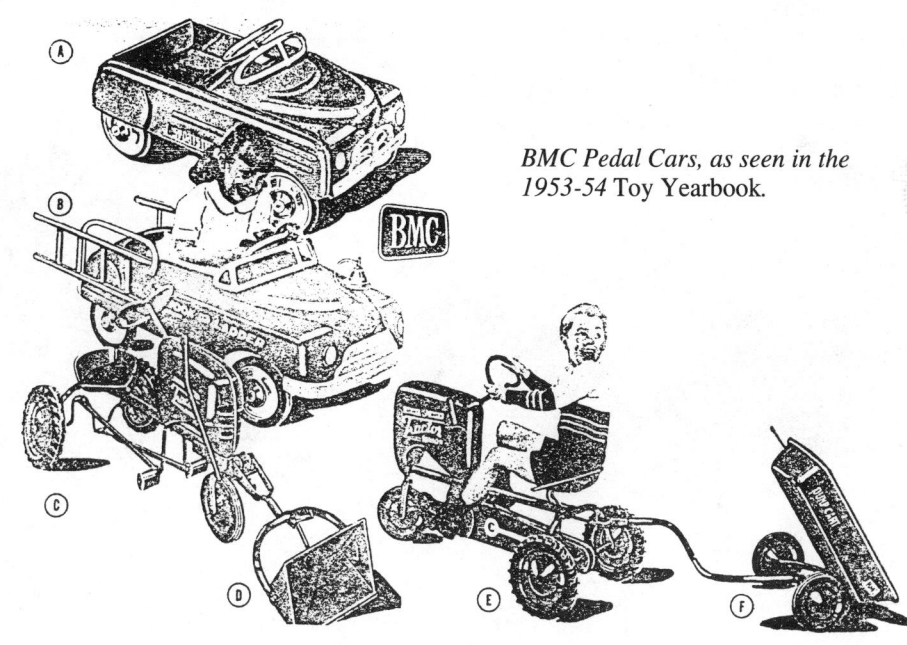

BMC Pedal Cars, as seen in the 1953-54 Toy Yearbook.

BONNIE BILT,
   Armored Car, U.S. Army 11   16   22

	C6	C8	C10
BONNIE BILT, Tank, plastic	6	9	12

BOYCRAFT

Boycraft was the brand name used by Steelcraft for the toys it supplied to Sears-Roebuck in the late 1920s and early 1930s.

	C6	C8	C10
BOYCRAFT Mack Dump Truck, 22" long, c.1920s	375	563	750
BOYCRAFT Steam Roller, 16" long	No Price Found		

Boycraft Mack Dump Truck, 22" long. Courtesy Bill Bertoia Auctions. Photo by Jeanne Bertoia.

Boycraft Steam Roller, 16" long. Courtesy Joe and Sharon Freed.

BRESLIN

Breslin Industries of Toronto made a number of lead-alloy toys, most or all of them copies, particularly of Barclay and Manoil. They can be easily distinguished from the originals as they usually read "Canada" or "Made in Canada."

	C6	C8	C10
BRESLIN Tank	30	40	50
BRESLIN Motorized Machine Gunner	30	40	50
BRESLIN Truck pulling Cannon	30	40	50

Breslin Truck Pulling Cannon. Barry S. Josephs Collection. Courtesy Hank Anton.

Breslin, L to R: Tank, Motorized Machine Gunner. Barry S. Josephs Collection. Courtesy Hank Anton.

BRIMTOY

BRIMTOY(England)	C6	C8	C10
Limousine, 1919, 11" long	300	450	600

Brimtoy Limousine, 1919, 11" long. Courtesy Bill Bertoia Auctions. Photo by Jeanne Bertoia.

BRINKS

	C6	C8	C10
BRINKS Armored Car, 9" long	250	375	575
BRINKS Truck Bank, aluminum, 8" long ...	40	60	80

Brinks Truck Bank, 8" long.
Courtesy James S. Maxwell Jr./
Virginia Caputo.

BRITAINS

Britains, of London, England, was originally owned by William Britain. In 1893, he introduced hollow-casting of toy soldiers. Britains is still in business and its soldiers are the most-collected military figures. It made, and continues to make, a number of vehicles. Understandably, many, perhaps the majority, are military. (Except where noted, photos by K. Warren Mitchell.)

Some Pre World War II Britains Ltd. Motor Vehicles (54mm Britains Armoured Corps Marching added for scale).
L to R, Back Row: 27d Armoured Car, 199 Motorcycle Machine Gun, 200 Dispatch Rider, 1321 Armoured Car, 1203 Tank (Carden Lloyd Type); Front Row: 1335 Lorry, Army, six wheeled type, 1448 Car, Staff, 1462 Covered Lorry, Caterpillar Type (cover missing), 1512 Army Ambulance, Motor Type.
Photo by Ed Poole.

	C6	C8	C10
BR27d Armored Car	No Price Found		
BR199 Motorcycle Machine Gun	40	75	110
BR200 Dispatch Rider	20	30	50
BR876 Bren Gun Carrier	35	65	85
BR1203 Tank (Carden Loyd Type)	110	155	230
BR1321 Armoured Car	150	325	400
BR1333 Lorry, Army, Caterpillar Type	125	200	300
BR1334 Lorry, Army, 4-Wheeled Type	105	130	210
BR1335 Lorry, Army, with Driver	115	165	230
BR1400 Speed Record Car, "The Blubird"	135	270	370
BR1413 Police Car with Two Officers	350	600	900
BR1432 Army Tender, covered, 10-wheel	125	200	325

Some of the Britains Ltd. Motor vehicles of the 1940s & 50s (Britains 54mm Tommy added for scale).
L to R, Back Row: 876 Bren Gun Carrier, 1334 Four Wheeled Army Lorry (towing 1717 Mobile unit, 2-pounder), 1335 six-wheeled Army Lorry, 1448 Staff Car, 1433 Covered Army Tender, caterpillar type (towing 1718 searchlight).
Front Row: 1512 Army Ambulance, 1877 Beetle Lorry (towing 1725 4.5" Howitzer and 1726 Regulation Limber), 1791 Dispatch Rider, 2102 Austin Champ (towing 2173 B.A.T. Gun).
Photo by Ed Poole.

	C6	C8	C10
BR1433 Army Tender, covered, caterpillar type	95	150	200
BR1448 Army Staff Car, officer and driver, first version smooth white tires, black fenders	175	310	385
2nd version - white tires, all khaki body	165	300	375

BR1334

BR1335

BR1400

BR1413

BR1432

BR1433

BR1433
Post-War

BR1448, L to R: first and second versions

BR1448,
3rd version

BR1448,
4th
version

	C6	C8	C10
3rd version, 1948-50, rectangular windshield, rubber tires	145	265	325
4th version, 1951-57, lead tires, painted gray, split windshield	150	285	350
5th version, 1958-59, black plastic tires	125	225	300
BR1462 Covered Lorry, R.A. Gun, drivers	150	350	450
BR1512 Army Ambulance, wounded man and stretcher, all doors open, 6" long	150	210	275
Postwar	95	150	210
BR1514 Corporation Motor Ambulance, driver, wounded and stretcher	350	600	850
BR1641 Underslung Heavy-Duty Lorry	200	350	550
BR1642 Heavy-Duty Lorry, driver, searchlight, battery and lamp	300	500	700
BR1643 Heavy Duty Lorry, underslung, with driver	600	900	1200
BR1656 John Cobb's Railton Wonder Car	200	350	500

	C6	C8	C10
BR1658 John Cobb's Railton Wonder Car, chromium-plated body, 10" long	125	200	325
BR1717 Mobile Unit, 2-pounder	30	50	70
BR1718 Mobile Searchlight	30	50	70
BR1725 4-1/2" Howitzer	13	20	30
BR1726 Regulation Limber	15	22	27
BR1727 Complete Mobile Howitzer Unit, 4 pieces, with limber and caterpillar trailer	300	550	750
BR1757 Balloon Barrage Unit (lorry, winch, balloon)	700	1000	1600
BR1791 Dispatch Rider	30	50	65
BR1832 10 Wheel Lorry with 2-pdr. AA Gun on Chassis	350	700	1000
BR1833 10-Wheel Lorry with Searchlight on Chassis	200	450	675
BR1855 Miniature Balloon Barrage Unit with Lorry, Winch and Balloon	125	250	350

BR1462

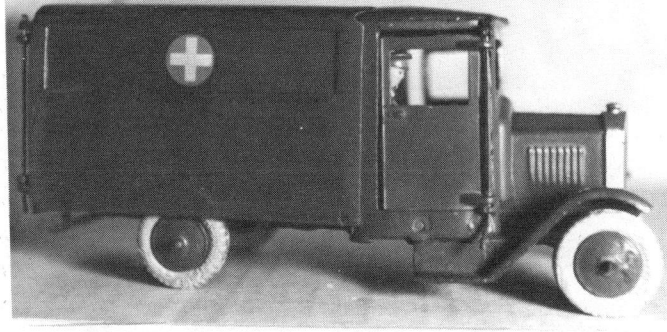

BR1512

BR1512 Post-War

BR1514

BR1642

BR1643

BR1727

BR1757

BR1832

BR1833

Britains BR1877 Pre-War with box. Photo by Ed Poole.

BR1877 Post-War

BR1897

BR2102

	C6	C8	C10
BR1876 Bren Gun Carrier			
with Full Crew, Pre-War	35	65	85
Post-War	30	55	75
BR1877 Beetle Lorry and Driver, Pre-War	60	95	135
Post-War	50	85	125
BR1879 Lorry and Trailer			
with hydrogen cylinders	115	165	210
BR1897 Motor Ambulance with doctor,			
wounded, nurses, orderlies, 18 pieces	175	325	450

	C6	C8	C10
BR2024 Light Goods Van with Driver	250	450	600
BR2102 Austin Champ	30	50	65
BR2150 (also 9770) Centurion Tank	150	275	375
BR2154 Centurion Tank,			
painted for Desert Warfare	250	450	600
BR2173 (also 9720)			
Batallion Anti-Tank Gun	10	14	18
BR2175 (also 9748) 155mm Gun,			
Mounted on Centurion Tank Body	200	350	500

BR2150

BR2175

BRITAINS FARM

	C6	C8	C10
BR641 Motorcycle with Sidecar	500	700	1250
BR748 Shell Gas Pump	11	19	25
BR749 Shellmax Gas Pump	10	17	22
BR750 BP Gas Pump	10	17	22
BR751 "Power" Pump	10	17	22
BR59F Lorry with Driver, 4-wheel	10	17	22
BR127F Fordson			
Tractor, metal wheels, driver	75	125	200
BR128F Fordson Major			
Tractor, driver, rubber tires	60	80	150
BR129F Timber Trailer with real log	25	50	75
BR134F Tractors & Implements	200	350	500
BR172F Fordson Power			
Major Tractor, no driver	50	75	100
BR173F Three Furrow Plough	7	11	16

BR641

L to R: BR748, 750, 751

BR59F

	C6	C8	C10
BR174F Muledozer		No Price Found	
BR175F Cultivator		No Price Found	
BR176F Acrobat Rake		No Price Found	

BR128F

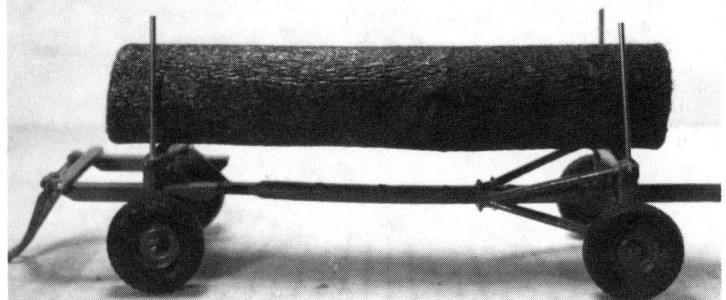

BR129F

BR172F with attached 174F

BR134F

BRITAINS LILLIPUT

	C6	C8	C10
LV/601 Open Sports Car	20	30	40
LV/602 Saloon Car	20	30	40
LV/603 Articulated Lorry	20	30	40
LV/604 Fordson Tractor with Driver	20	30	40
LV/607 Army Covered 3-Ton Truck, removable plastic top	25	38	50
LV/608 3-Ton Farm Lorry		No Price Found	
LV/609 Austin Champ, removable hood		No Price Found	
LV/610 Centurion Tank	25	38	50
LV/611 Sexton Self-Propelled Gun	27	41	55
LV/612 1-1/2 Ton Army Truck with spare wheel		No Price Found	
LV/613 1-1/2 Ton Covered Army Truck with spare wheel		No Price Found	
LV/614 Articulated Truck with spare wheel		No Price Found	
LV/615 Saracen Armoured Personnel Carrier		No Price Found	
LV/616 1-1/2 Ton Farm or Civilian Truck with spare wheel, measures 2-13/16" long		No Price Found	
LV/617 Local Authority Ambulance, cream, measures 3" long	8	15	20
LV/618 Army Ambulance, measures 3" long		No Price Found	
LV/619 Post Office Royal Mail Van, measures 3" long		No Price Found	
LV/620 3-ton Open Army Truck with spare wheel, measures 3-1/4" long		No Price Found	

L to R: LV611, LV610

	C6	C8	C10		C6	C8	C10
LV/SA Boxed Set containing: 1 LV/601, 1 LV/602, 1 LV/603, 1 LV/604 with driver, 1 LV/605 with Milkman, 1 LV/606, with accessories and Carter as listed in the 1951 Catalog Supplement	65	125	200	L11 Lilliput Railway Personnel & Vehicles: Saloon Car, lorry, sports car, articulated lorries, Austin "Champ," motorcyclists, station trolleys, packing cases, barrels, hampers, porters w/trolleys, guards, stationmaster, porters with luggage, news vendor, general public asst., 43 pieces		No Price Found	
L7 Lilliput Display Box containing Saloon Car, tractor, tumbrel cart and milk float, farmer, farmer's wife, stable lad, farm girl and dog, horses, cows and calf, sheep and lamb, pig, geese, hurdles and tree, 28-pieces	75	150	250				

Britains Lilliput LV/SA

Britains Lilliput L-7

BROOKLIN MODELS

by Vincent Rosa, with some excerpts from his work The Brooklin Collection Book *(1989).*

Love of cars, both prototype and model, is the reason John and Jenny Hall created Brooklin Models Ltd., a firm that makes the finest 1:43 scale replicas of white-metal model cars on the market today. Many collectors say that Brooklin models are the standard of the industry—very similar to the "standard of the world" description for Lionel toy trains or Britains toy soldiers. Brooklins today are known worldwide. The new Brooklin Collection includes some of the greatest and most controversial American motor cars made by U.S. manufacturers in the past five decades.

John began humbly in the basement of his Canadian home in the early 1970s, making models by hand with resin and no windows, using popsicle sticks, wood-burnt with the familiar early Brooklin Models logo to keep the resin casting from warping. Brooklin Models is named after a suburb of Ontario, Canada, called Brooklin.

When the Brooklin company was in its infancy, it experienced the greatest changes in technology and process. Therefore, the early Canadian models reflect many different changes as John, in an attempt to perfect his models, experimented with many forms of casting materials and color variations. 1974 was a pivotal year for John. It was early that year that he decided to leave his teaching position at Durham College and devote full-time to model-making and designing equipment to create finished scale-model cars. Most of the companies at this time were doing kits, not built-up models.

Meanwhile, back in the basement, John was dabbling in model-making and scratch-building models for himself and other collectors. He helped form the Canadian Toy Collector's Society (CTCS) with Ron Faithful and Tony Topley. Through the CTCS, John met many collectors from Canada and Buffalo, where John went to his first toy show called "Motoring in Miniatures." At the show, collectors persuaded him to make a Pierce Arrow. Thinking this was a good idea, John made two master models out of resin. He then cast 86 models at the laborious rate of 10 models per week. Thus, Brooklin Models began in 1974. The hand-painted Pierce Arrow with resin base became car #1. The Pierce Arrow was retired in 1993.

In 1975, John felt he could raise money at the Canadian Plowing Match held in Toronto by selling a model of a plow commemorating the event. Two thousand were produced, but only 200 were sold. The remainder were melted down. To say the least, it was not a financial success. Today, it is a rare and sought-after piece, as many Brooklin collectors have never seen one. There is one pictured in the hardcover *Brooklin Collection Book* by Vincent Rosa (1989).

Initially, John did everything to create a Brooklin Model. He carved the master, made the mold, cast the piece, and assembled the models. Two employees helped assemble and paint. As business improved, more people were hired. Today, the business supports 25 or more employees, including Jenny Hall, who runs the business office, and John, who oversees the entire operation.

In October 1979, John and Jenny decided to move back to the United Kingdom. This ceased all future production of Brooklin Models stamped "Made in Canada." They settled in Bath, England, a beautiful city filled with culture. The first factory was located in the Huggett Electrical building in Bath. John has used the Huggett's logo on many of his #16 Dodge models.

In England, new markets opened up and orders began to pour in. American cars are quite popular in Europe, so are Brooklin models. They have always been popular in America.

Today, John continues his original idea—to manufacture only models of American cars. He has chosen some of the most controversial cars of the past five decades. Each is a legend or classic in its own right. When asked why he models only American cars, John replies, "I think being influenced by living and working in North America is the obvious reason. And, of course, the sheer outrageous design and ostentation of the American car calls out to be modeled."

At the new Brooklin factory in Bath, Brooklin manufactures more than 50,000 models a year. Since 1988, the models have been marketed in a new box, which includes the Statue of Liberty, the New York City skyline, and an Edsel with an American flag banner. Gone are the old tan and brown logo boxes. These have been resurrected as of late for promotional issues, lending a nostalgic touch for the collector.

John and Jenny and Brooklin Models Ltd. have dedicated their craft to quality. Is John happy about his success—making his hobby his vocation? I would say yes. "I just wanted to make my cars," says John. "I've done what I set out to do. My greatest pleasure these days is watching the staff take over the skills and enthusiasm of the early days. Brooklin Models Ltd., is now a true company." Brooklin Models is still dedicated to three things: quality, quality, and quality. This is the standard by which all 1:43 scale models are judged. That is why Brooklin Models will continue to be the collector's choice for years to come.

BIOGRAPHY: Vincent Rosa grew up in Brooklyn, New York, and moved to Long Island, where he attended Adelphi-Suffolk-Dowling College. He holds a master's degree in history from Stony Brook University and looks forward to working on his doctorate. His hobbies include collecting Lionel Trains and toy soldiers of the British Victorian period. Vincent and his wife Bonnie operate a business called "Model Cars and Trains Unlimited," of Blue Point, New York, a firm that specializes in the sale of collectible trains, die-cast model cars, and toy soldiers of all types and varieties. Vincent's hobby-related works include: *Greenberg's Guide to Lionel H.O.* (Greenberg Publications, 1987, 1993). He has published his own copyrighted work, *The Brooklin Collection* (1989) and *The Official Brooklin Models Collector Guide* (1989). For information, call Vincent or Bonnie at (516) 363-2134. All materials and excerpts and listing format are copyright M.C.S. Productions, 1989, Vincent Rosa.

(NOTE: Prices are for Mint in the Box)

Bonnie & Vincent Rosa

BROOKLIN CODES

Code I: All pieces built, assembled, and decaled from the Brooklin factory in England. Also, those pieces produced in the factory, but partially assembled/partially or totally decaled outside, with total knowledge and approval of John Hall. These are considered 100-percent authentic Brooklin. For example, some CTCS, CPCTS, and promotionals such as Mobil and City of Toronto, Bay State Lobster, Model Auto Review, Coca-Cola, et. al.

Code II: Altered or modified Brooklin models outside the factory, done with full approval of the company. At present, there are only a few such models that fall into this category. The first is the series of convertibles produced by the Model Car Shop. Its first car was the Burgundy 1953 Skylark with wire wheels, and the second was the 1949 Red Mercury with wire wheels. The only other Code II piece presently is the plated (silver color) Edsel done by Danhausen.

Code III: Altered or modified Brooklin models outside the factory done without the approval of the company. There are many beautiful models in this category that can enhance your collection, but cannot be considered true Brooklin pieces. The excellent convertibles done by Jerry Rettig, the Orange County Fire Dept. Dodge Pickup done by TFC, and the Yellow Corvette with wire wheels done by the Model Car Shop are some examples.

Prototypes: These are pieces that may have been cast differently or paint-tested in color variation and were never intended for sale. These do not fall into any category above. There are many such models and the collector need not feel that his/her collection is incomplete without them. If, however, these pieces were put up for sale by the company or by an individual with permission of the company, then they would be Code I, such as the turquoise Mercury and the 11 Tucker samples given to the Tucker Club (so it could choose three promotional colors).

Discontinued Color/Style

Only 1,253 Shelby American G.T. 500 Fastbacks were built in 1968, making it one of the rarest cars in its class. It was the undisputed King of the 1960s muscle cars.

NOTE: Numbers 1, 16a, 17, 26a, and 31 were discontinued from the Brooklin Collection during 1992.

KEY

R	Regular Issue	5	One of a kind
D	Discontinued body style	6	First casting
C	Discontinued color	7	No gas cap
M	Made	8	With gas cap
W/C	With certificate	9	Numbered on baseplate
App.	Approximately	10	Smooth side
Int.	Interior	11	Small decals
Dk.	Dark	12	Rim linted sides
L	Means #14 in Tucker Canadian Issue		
Lt.	Light	13	No windows-van style
Med.	Medium	14	Large scale
M	Metallic	15	Last 250 made came with certificate
P	Promotional - Limited run	16	Gold trim
1	Resin baseplate	CPCTS	Canadian Pacific Coast Toy Show
2	No plastic windows	CTCS	Canadian Toy Collectors Society
3	Rare (not plentiful, hard to find, in demand)	CTCI	Classic Thunderbird Collectors International
4	Detailed chassis	PROTO	Prototype

MINT IN BOX: The only designation of trade as far as grading is concerned is MINT IN BOX.
NRS - No Reported Sales

CANADIAN ISSUES

Model No.	Year and Description	Key	Misc. Info.	Notes	Value ($)
1	**1933 PIERCE ARROW**				
	Blue/Grey	D-5-3	All resin	First issue	No Price Found
	Brown/Cream	D-5-3	All resin	First issue	No Price Found
	Blue/Grey	D-1-2-3	App. 30 m.	Second issue	No Price Found
	Maroon/Grey	D-1-2-3	App. 3 m.	Second issue	No Price Found
	Green/Grey	D-1-2-3	App. 30 m.	Second issue	No Price Found
	Brown/Cream	D-1-2-3	App. 30 m.	Second issue	No Price Found
	Champagne	R	Maroon Int.	Third issue	350
	Champagne	—	Red Int.	Third issue	350
	White	D-1-2-5-3			
	Silver Grey	D-M-1-2-3		Third issue	350
	Medium Blue	M		Third issue	350
	Silver Grey	M		Third issue	350

Model No.	Year and Description	Key	Misc. Info.	Notes	Value ($)
2	**1949 TUCKER**				
	Medium Blue	D-2-6-2-L	Grey Int.		200
	Dark Blue	D-2-6-2-L	Grey Int.		200
	Very Dark Blue	D-2-6-2-L	Grey Int.		200
	Black	D-2-3-6-L	Beige Int.		200
	Black	D-2-3-6-L	Lt. Grey Int.		200
	Maroon	D-3		14m.	No Price Found
	Medium Blue	D-M			200
	Dark Blue	D-R-M	Grey Int.		200
3	**1930 FORD VICTORIA 2 DR.**				
	White top Beige body	D-M-2	Tan Int.	Cream wheels	275
	White/Olive	D-2	Grey Int.	White wheels	250
	White/Olive	D-4	Tan Int.	White wheels	250
	White/Med. Brown	D-4	Grey Int.	White/wheels	105
	Beige/Olive	D-4	Tan Int.	White wheels	90
4	**1937 CHEVY COUPE**				
	Buff Green	D-R			325
	Medium Green	D			325
	Dark Green	D			325
	Dark Green	D-4			325
	Black	D-4-3		App. 18m.	Nrs.
5	**1930 MODEL A 2 DR COUPE**				
	Black top/Brown body	D	Tudor body	Orange wheels	525
	Black top/Brown body	D-4	Tudor body	White wheels	500
	Black/Black	D-3	Tudor body	White wheels	500
6	**1932 PACKARD**				
	Dk. Beige Top Maroon Body		Grey Int.		
	Lt. Beige/Maroon		Grey Int.		
	White/Maroon		Grey Int.		
	Dark Grey/Maroon				325
	Lt. Grey/M. Grey		Maroon fenders	Grey Int.	325
	Lt. Grey/Lt. Grey		Blue grey fenders		
	Med. Grey/Med. Grey		Med. blue fenders		
7	**1934 CHRYSLER AIRFLOW**				
	Cream (Off White)	R			190
8	**1940 CHRYSLER NEWPORT 4DR**				
	Lt. Green	M-R	Lt. Brown Int.		175
	Med. Green	M-R	Lt. Brown Int.		200
8A	**1941 CHRYSLER NEWPORT PACE CAR**				
	White - Dearborn Nat.				
	Car Convention	3	Red Int.	200 M.	475
9	**1940 FORD VAN**				
	Tan	P-3	Toledo Toy Show	213 m.	500
	Dark Blue	P-12-3	CTCS '79	60 m.	800
	Dark Blue	P-12-3	Marque	50 m.	600

ENGLISH ISSUES

Model No.	Year and Description	Key	Misc. Info.	Notes	Value ($)
1	**1933 PIERCE ARROW**				
	Light Blue	R-M	Grey Int.		65
	Med. Blue	M	Grey Int.		
	Dark Blue	M	Grey Int.		

Brooklin Models

Model No.	Year and Description	Key	Misc. Info.	Notes	Value ($)
	Champagne	M		100 m.	350
	Lt. Silver	M	Grey Int.		350
	Dk. Silver	M	Grey Int.		350
	Silver	M-P	Harrah's	Blue Int.	200
2	**1948 TUCKER**				
	Lt. Maroon	D-R-M-7			195
	Lt. Maroon	D-R-M-8			195
	Maroon	D-2-M			195
	Dk. Maroon	D-R-M-8			
2A	**1948 TUCKER**				
	Gold	R-M	Tan Int.		65
	Dark Gold	R-M	Tan Int.		65
	Maroon	P-M-3	Tan Int.	500 m. Tucker Club	200
	Silver	P-M	Tan Int.	Harrah's	175
	Lt. Brown	P-M	Grey Int.	Harrah's	175
	Gold	P-M	Beige Int.	Harrah's	175
	Lazer Red	P-M	Paramount Pictures	Semi-limited 1000 m.	200
	Stratus Silver	P-M	Paramount Pictures	Semi-limited 1000 m.	200
	Turquoise	P-M	Paramount Pictures	Semi-limited 1000 m.	200
	Green	5 Proto		No Price Found	
	Sierra Beige	5 Proto		No Price Found	
	Black	5 Proto		No Price Found	
	Signa Amber	5 Proto		No Price Found	
	Champagne	5 Proto		No Price Found	
	Zircon Blue	5 Proto		No Price Found	
	Jaguar Coral	5 Proto		No Price Found	
	White	5 Proto		No Price Found	
Bk 2 Bx	Lt Blue T.A.C.A. 2nd issue	P	Tucker Club		150
3	**1930 FORD VICTORIA 2DR**				
	Beige top/Med. Gr. Body	D-R-4-15	Beige wheels	Lt. Br. Int.	150
	Beige/light green	D-C-4	Beige wheels	Lt. Br. Int.	150
	Beige/Tan	D-4	White wheels	Lt. Br. Int.	175
	Beige/Lt. Olive	D-4	Beige wheels	Lt. Br. Int.	150
4	**1937 CHEVY COUPE**				
	Dark Green	D-R-4-15	Beige wheels		160
	Dark Green	D-C-4	Beige wheels		160
	Blue	D-P-3-9	Ill. Toy Show '86	100 m.	400
	Beige	D-P-3	Webers '87	70 m.	No Price Found
	Red	D-P	James Leake '87	150 m. 15th Auc.	
	Bright Green	D-P	Toledo Toy Show '87	100 m.	
	Blue	P	Ill. Toy Show	100 m.	
	White	P	Brooklin Club England	275 m.	
	"Police"	P	Bay Brooklin Club		150
4	**MODEL A FORD 2 DR COUPE**				
	Black top/Dk. Br. Body	D-3	Tudor body		250
	Black/Green	D-R-15			100
	Black/Lt. Green	D-C			100
	Black/Red	D-P	New Orleans Fire	100 m.	325
	Black/Red	D-P	Philly Fire	300 m.	300
	Black	D-P-3	Webers '86	69 M.	Nrs.
6	**1932 PACKARD STANDARD 8**				
	Lt. Brown top/Cream Body	R	Brown fenders	Lt. Br. Int.	125
	Blue-grey top silver	3	M. Lt. Blue fenders	Red Int.	200
	Grey Lt. Grey	3	Dk. grey fenders	Red Int.	200
	Tan/Lt. Grey	3	Brown fenders	Red Int.	200

Model No.	Year and Description	Key	Misc. Info.	Notes	Value ($)
7	**1934 CHRYSLER AIRFLOW**				
	Light Blue	R	Black wall tires		65
	Medium Blue	R	White wall tires		All Variants
	Medium Blue	R	Black wall tires		90 or more
	Dark Blue	R	White wall tires		
	Dk. Blue	R	Black wall tires		
8	**1940 CHRYSLER NEWPORT**				
	Yellow	R-D-15			125
8A	**1941 CHRYSLER PACE CAR**				
	White	R	Chrysler logo		65
	White	P	Motor Sport	140 m.	225
	White	P-3	Mtr. Sp. 60th Anv.	60 m.	350
9	**1940 FORD VAN**				
	Black	D-R-12	Ford		75
	Black	R	Ford		550
	Red	P-12-3	CTCS '80	Beige Int. 125 m.	550
	Red	P-3-10	CTCS '80	Lt. Br. Int. 125 m.	550
	Blue	P	CPCTS '84	100 m.	350
	Lt. Blue	P	CPCTS '87	150 m.	250
	Yellow	P-12-11	Coke	"Drink"	325
	Yellow	P-11	Coke	"Drink"	325
	Yellow	P	Coke	"Enjoy"	325
	Yellow	P	Coke	"Drink"	325
	Black	P	James Leake '85	250 m. 13th Auc.	200
	Orange	P	James Leake '88	150 m. 16th Auc.	225
	Yellow	P	Danhausen	150 m. 1st Issue	225
	Grey	P	Danhausen, red wh.	150 m. 1st issue	225
	Tan	P	Danhausen	2nd issue	225
	Grey	P	Danhausen, grey wh.	2nd issue	200
	Red	P-3	Indian River Fire	50 m.	500
	White	P	Nutmeg Ambulance	300 m.	200
	Red	P	Springfield Fire	100 m.	350
	Off White	P	Philly Ambulance	300 m.	350
	Maroon	P	Buchi Optik	60 m.	400
	Red	P	Old Toyland	100 m.	275
	Blue	P	Deaf Child Soc.	200 m.	220
	Dark Blue	P-3	BF Goodrich	50 m.	400-800
	White	P	Harrah's '85	400 m.	225
	Dark Brown	P	Hershey		375
	Maroon	P-3-9	J.U.N.K.	50 m.w.c.	800
	Beige	P-12-3	Lamberts	100 m.w.c.	650
	White	P-3	Mobil Bk. Tires	26 m.	No Price Found
	Beige	P-3	Model Auto	50 m.	450
	White	P-3	Maidenhead	150 m.	500
	Brown	P-3	Marque	50 m.	350
	Green	P-3	Randalls	50 m.	390.00
	Yellow	P	Shell-Model Garage	140 m.	175
	Cream	P	Spanish Armada	150 m.	200*
	Green	P-10	Toronto Works	50 m.	295-350
	Green	P-12	Toronto Works	50 m.	295-350
	Beige	P-3	Webers '84	67 m., Rare	No Price Found
	Maroon	P-3	Wessex Model	75 m., Rare	No Price Found
	Red	P	Yateley	150 m.	225
	Green	P	Huggett		110
	Red	P	Weeties		150.
10	**1949 BUICK ROADMASTER**				
	Lt. Silver Grey	R-C	Beige Int.	w/o hood orn.	65

Brooklin Models

Model No.	Year and Description	Key	Misc. Info.	Notes	Value ($)
	Med. Grey	R	Beige Int.	w/o hood orn.	75
	Dark Grey	R	Beige Int.	w, w/o hood orn.	75
	Black	3	Autosatisfaction	100 m. w/o hood orn.	
	Black	3	Beige Int.	w/hood orn.	200
	Maroon	P	Beige Int.	Mini cars	70

* Sleeper

Model No.	Year and Description	Key	Misc. Info.	Notes	Value ($)
11	**1956 LINCOLN CONTINENTAL MARK II**				
	Lt. Blue	R-M	Grey Int.		65
	Med. Blue	R-M	Grey Int.		70
	Dark Blue	R-M-C	Red Int.		75
	Black	P	Maroon Int.	500 m.	125
	Black	P-9	Accent, First Issue	White Int.	195
	Black	P-9	Accent, Grey Int.	400 m.	150
	White	5-Proto			No Price Found
	Gold	P-3	Autosatisfaction	50 m., Rare	No Price Found
12	**1931 HUDSON BOATTAIL**				
	Orange/cream fenders	R			70
	Beige top black body	P	CTCS '81 Red Fenders	250 m.	550
13	**1956 FORD T-BIRD**				
	Red	R			
	Dark Red	R			
	Beige	R	CTCI '82	300 m.	350
	Tan	P	CTCI '82	? m.	350
	Green	P	CTCI '88	200 m.	200
	White	P-9	Ill. Toy Show '87	100 m. w/c Red Int.	350
	White	P	Mini Cars	Black Int.	80
14	**1940 CADILLAC V-16 CONVERTIBLE**				
	Gold-Bronze	R-M			65
	Dark Bronze-Brown	R-M			75
	White top/red body	P	CTCS '83	400 m.	375
15	**1949 MERCURY**				
	Cream	C-R	Red or Grey Int.		200
	Med. Green	R-M			65
	Dark Green	R-M			75
	Dark Blue	P-M-9	Ill. Toy Show '88	100 m. w/c	200
	Turquoise Blue	Proto		6 m.	NRS
	Maroon	P	CTCS		175
19	**1935 DODGE VAN**				
	Grey body/red fenders	R-C	Burma Shave	Black run bds.	90
	Grey body/red fenders	R-C	Burma Shave	Red run bds.	90
	Grey body/black fenders	3	Burma Shave	Apr. 50 m.	250
	White	P	Bay St. Lobster	J. Leake Redo 50 m.?	300
	(16A) Lt. blue/dk. blue	R	City Ice		65
	Orange/Brown	P-3	Avon Club	75 m.	395
	Blue	P	Argus De LaMiniature	100 m.	295
	Cream/Orange	P	Bayview Model	50 m.	500
	White/Red	P	Dr. Bernardo's	100 m.	300
	Brown/black	P	Bimbo	100 m.	300
	Blue/Black	P	Buchi Optik	100 m.	300
	Pea Green/Green	P-M	Calandre	100 m.	300.
	Cream/Brown	P	Camel	75 m.	450
	Red/Black	P	Classic & Sport	200 m.	200
	Yellow/Black	P	Coca Cola		450
	Gold/Red	P-M-16	Collectors Gazette '86	24K. Gold, 200 m.	425
	Maroon/Black	P	CPCTS '83	50 m.	400
	Silver/Black	P-M	CPCTS '85	w/logo 100 m.	200

Model No.	Year and Description	Key	Misc. Info.	Notes	Value ($)
	Grey/Black	P	CPCTS '85	w/o logo ? m.	200
	Beige/Brown	P	CTCS '82	250 m.	225
	Beige/Brown	P	Gems & Cobwebs	100 m.	275
	Brown/Black	P	Hershey		300
	Green/Grey	P	Huggett Elec. '83	w/c 100 m.	325
	Red/Red	P-3	Indian River	50 m.	495
	White/Red	P	ITT Kruse '87	150 m.	175
	White/Red	P	J. Leake '84	12th Auction	275
	Red	P	Litchfield Fire	200 m.	275
	Dark Red	P	Litchfield Fire	200 m.	275
	White/Blue	P	London Mtr. Fair '85	100 m.	300
	Dark Blue	P-3	Maidenhead	100 m.	300
	Dark Blue/Red	P	Merley Museum	100 m.	300
	Lt. Blue/Dark Blue	P	Mini Wheels of Midland	50 m.	395
	Dark Green/Lt. Green		Model Auto Review	100 m.	295
	Yellow/Red	P	Old Toyland '87	100 m.	295
	Goldish Green/Black	P-M	Passport Transport	150 m.	275
	Maroon/Black	P-R	Dr. Pepper	Semi ltd.	70
	Red/Red	P	Philly Fire	App. 300 m.	295
	Black/Black	P-R	Sears	Semi ltd.	70
	Cream/Green	P	St. Martins	App. 150 m.	295
	Gold/Black	P-M-16	Spielgoed Otten	100 m.	250
	Yellow/Black	P-3	Weber's '85	68 m.	No Price Found
	Maroon/Gold	P	Wessex	75 m.	
	Maroon	P	Wessex Silver Key		120
16X	**1935 DODGE PICKUP**				
	Orange Body/Brown fenders	P	Avon	75 m.	400
	Green/Green	P	A.T.T. w pole	400 m.	350
	Green/Beige	P	CTCS '84	400 m.	300
	Yellow/Blue	P	CTCS '86	450 m.	290
	Burgundy/Cream	P	CPCTS '86	150 m.	300
	Blue/Cream	P-3	B.F. Goodrich	50 m.	200
	Green/Green	P-3	Huggetts	100 m.	300
	Orange/Brown	P	J. Leake '86	150 m. w/c 14th Auc.	300
	Blue/Black	P	Markham (250 made)	500 m.	200
	Red/Red	P	Orange Cty. FIre	400 m.	350
	Red/Brown, barrel seats	P	McDonald's	?Benefit #2	295
	Olive Green	P	New Eng. Telephone & Pole Truck	400 m.	250
	Red	P	Yately	150 m.	285
	Yellow	P	Brasilia Press	700 m.	75
	Red/Black	P	Yateley's	150 m.	185
17	**1952 STUDEBAKER STARLIGHT**				
	Black	C-R	Grey Int.		110
	Grey	R	Grey Int.		65
	Grey	R	Red Int.		70
18	**1941 PACKARD CLIPPER**				
	Maroon	R			65
	Gold/Bronze	P-M	CTCS '85	400 m.	350
	Khaki/White Stars	P	Military Staff Car	160 m.	400
	Yellow	P	American Taxi	500 m.	140
19	**1955 CHRYSLER C-300***	P	Brooklin Club Model, NRS (White)		65
	Red	R		500 m.	70
	Black/Tan	P	Mini Cars	500 m.	70
20	**1953 BUICK SKYLARK**				
	Aqua	R-M			

Model No.	Year and Description	Key	Misc. Info.	Notes	Value ($)
	White Convertible	P	Ketchner Oct. Fest.	100 m.	350
	Maroon Conv.	Code 2	Produced for Model Car Shop - Now Model Cars and Trains unlimited blue, PT, NY, Very Rare	50 pcs.	450
21	**1963 CORVETTE**				
	Blue	C-R-M			
	Red/Grey Int.	P	Mini Cars		70
	Red	P	Ill. Toy Show	100 m.	No Price Found
	White	R	Red Int.		65
	Silver	P-M-3		350 m.	300
	Red	P	Ill. Toy Show '87 Bk. Int.	100 m.	375
	Red	P			400
22	**1958 EDSEL CITATION**				
	Pink	R	Gold Name Decal		150
	Pink	R	Black Name Decal		75
	Lavender-Pink	R-C	Gold Name		
22A	Green, Metallic	R	W/Cont. Kit		65
23	**1956 FORD FAIRLANE VICTORIA**				
	White top/Green body	R	Marked #22 in error		90
	White top/Green body	R			65
24	**1968 SHELBY MUSTANG**				
	Blue	D-R-M			149
	Green	D-P-3	Model Expo	250 m? - How many are in the hands of collectors is not known - NRS	No Price Found

No. 24, Ford Shelby Mustang

Model No.	Year and Description	Key	Misc. Info.	Notes	Value ($)
24A	**1968 FORD MUSTANG**				
	Red	R			
25	**1958 PONTIAC BONNEVILLE CONV.**				
	Black	R-3	Burgundy Int.	40 m.	150
	Black	R	Grey Int.		65
26	**1956 CHEVY NOMAD**				
	White top/Lt. Blue body	R			65
	White/Coral	P	CTCS '87	375 m.	275
26X	**1956 CHEVY NOMAD VAN**				
	Red	P	Fire Chief		75
	Black	P	CPCTS '88	150 m.	195
	Black	P	Webers '88	71 m.	No Price Found
	Black	P	Das Automobile	200 m.	250
	Dk. Blue	P	Cars Only	150 m.	275
	Maroon	P	Wessex		150

Model No.	Year and Description	Key	Misc. Info.	Notes	Value ($)
27	**1957 CADDY ELDORADO BROUGHAM**				
	Silver	R-M			
28	**1957 MERCURY TURNPIKE CRUISER**				
	Bronze/Tan	R-M			65
	Blue (Monarch)	R-M	CTCS '88	450 m.	300
1989					
29	**1953 KAISER MANHATTAN**		**Standard Issue**	**1989**	**65.00**
	Blue	R	500 Produced for Rotterdam Shoppe		275
29X	Black	P			275
30	**1954 Dodge 500 Convt.**		**Standard Issue**	**1990**	**65**

New releases since 1990 follow. The most variations and collectible items since 1989 have appeared on the #31 Pontiac Van. Since Brooklin models changed its policy on the number of promotionals produced, a pattern for value has yet to be determined. Values tend to be regional and varied. The average production for promotional tends to be 750 models. The day when Brooklin models would make 50 models for a toy shop are clearly over. The higher the production runs, the lower the after-market prices tend to be.

Lower prices attract more collectors since they have a chance to own at least one or more promotional items.

NEW RELEASES

Model No.	Year and Description	Key	Misc. Inf.	Notes
31A	1953 Pontiac Sedan Delivery	R	Orange Gulf regular issue	1990
31X	1953 Pontiac Sedan Delivery	P	Part of boxed set Brooklin Video #1	Silver w/tonneau cover (blue)
31A	Mobil Gas	R	1952	1992
31A	Sunoco	R	1953	
32	1953 Studebaker Commander	R	Light Green, Reg. Issue	1990
33	1938 Phantom Corsair	R	Black Body	
33A	Tan	D	Original Brochure color, mini grid	
34	Maroon	R	Regular Issue, Dark Maroon	1991
35	1957 Ford Skyliner	R	Tan/gold chrome enhanced	
36	1953 Hudson Hornet	R	Green, Tan Interior	1992
37	1960 Ford Sunliner	R	Purple metal flake, Maroon top, convt.	1992
38	1938 Graham Sharknose	R	Khaki Tan	1992
39	1953 Olds Fiesta	R	Blue and white 2-tone - a first for Brooklin models	1992
40	1948 Cadillac	R	Dk. Navy Blue, Red Int.	1992

Brooklin 40. Courtesy Vincent Rosa.

Brooklin 41. Courtesy Vincent Rosa.

41	1959 Chrysler Convt.	R	Gold - Regular Issue	
41A	Light Milky Gold	R	Mistake a Brooklin Factory Released	
B	Pale Gold	R	Variation - of Reg. Issue (Color only)	175
42	1952 Ford F1 Ambulance	R	Jasper County Hospital Services	white w/decals 69
42	1952 Ford F1 Panel Special Delivery	CTCS "1992"	One of 500	185
42	1952 Ford F1		Alka Seltzer	185
43A	1948 Packard Station Wagon	R	w/wo. rack	69
44	1961 Chevy Impala	R	Red/White stripe	69
45A	1948 Buick Roadmaster	R	White/Beige Int.	69
46	1959 Chevy El Camino	R	Black/Red Int.	69
47	1965 Ford T-Bird	R	Red Conv.	69
48	1958 Chevy Impala	R	Baley Blue H/T	69
49	1954 Hudson Italia	R	Silver	69
50	1948 Chevy Aero Sedan	R	"Country Club Woody"	69
51	1951 Ford Victoria	R	2 tone green	69
52	1941 Hupmobile Skylark	R	Maroon	69
53	1955 Cameo Pick-up Truck	R	Red/White	69
*54	1953 Air Stream-Wanderer	R	Silver	*69
55	1951 Packard Mayfair	R	Maroon/Beige Top	69

* Perfect when coupled with BRK #50 or #51 (As set)
* Not released yet.
R = Regular Issue

BROOKLIN COLLECTION

New Editions for Release during 1996

Model No.	Year and Description	Key	Misc. Info.	Notes	Value ($)
BRK 50A	1948 Chevy Police Car	R	Black/Wht. Doors		69
BRK 60	1963 Olds Starfire	R	New for '96	N/R/A/Y*	
58	1963-1/2 Ford Falcon Sprint	R	Lt. Green Metallic		69
59	1957 Rambler Rebel	R		N/R/A/Y*	
57	1960 Lincoln Continental	R		N/R/A/Y*	
61	1960 Chevy Impala	R		N/R/A/Y*	
BRK 53X & 62	Chevy Cameo and Horse Trailer Set (Special)				159.95

Deletions and items discontinued from the Brooklin Collection as of January 1996 are:
BRK #18, 21, 23, 34A, 35.
BRK 18A will be re-issued as 1947 Packard Super Clipper - June 1996.
BRK #21A as 1964 "Vette" convertible, May 1996.
BRK 35A Top Down Conv., Oct. 1996.

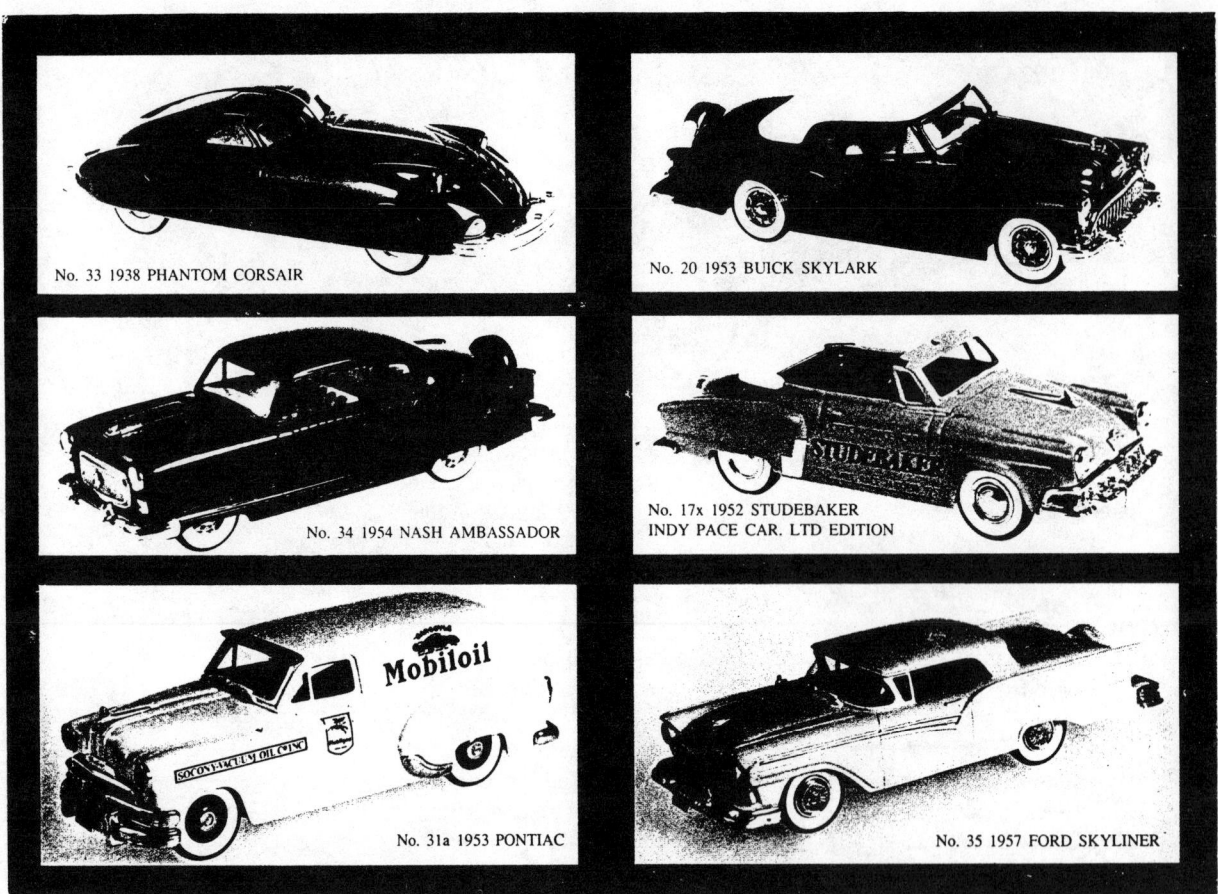

No. 33 1938 PHANTOM CORSAIR

No. 20 1953 BUICK SKYLARK

No. 34 1954 NASH AMBASSADOR

No. 17x 1952 STUDEBAKER INDY PACE CAR. LTD EDITION

No. 31a 1953 PONTIAC

No. 35 1957 FORD SKYLINER

Brooklins. Courtesy Vincent Rosa.

SPECIAL DEALER PROGRAMME

Model No.	Year and Description	Key	Misc. Info.	Notes
BRK 45 D.S.	1948 Buick Roadmaster	D.S.	Red	NRS
	1946 Lincoln Continental			
	Special Label	"Dealer Special"	Black/Dk. Beige Int.	N/R/A/Y

OTHER RANGES PRODUCED BY BROOKLIN MODELS:

A) Lansdowne - Models "Foreign"
B) Robeddie Models, "Foreign"

PROMOTIONAL GROUPS

Accent	11-11	CTCI	13-13
Autosatisfaction	10-11	Ill. Toy Show	4-13-21-15
Avon	16-16X	Indian River	9-16
Buchi Optic	9-16	J. Leake	16-9-16X-4-9
Coke	9-(9)-(9)-(9)-16	Maidenhead	16-9
CPCTS	16-9-16-(16)-16X-9-26X	Marque	9-9
CTCS	9-9-(9)-(12)-16-14-16X-18-16X-26	Old Toyland	9-16
Danhausen	9-9-9-9	Philly Fire	5-9-16
Goodrich	9-16X	Toledo Toy	9-4
Harrah	1-2-2-2-9	Weber	9-16-5-4-26X
Hershey	9-16	Wessex	9-16
Huggett	16-16X	Yately	9-16X

RECOMMENDED READING

Rosa, Vincent. 1974-1989 The Brooklin Collection. 1989, 80 pgs. This source listing for Brooklin Models is hardcover with color photos. $49.95 postpaid, comes with free Collector's Guide. Send to: Model Cars & Trains Ultd., 28 Arthur Ave., Blue Point, New York, 11715, (516) 363-2134.

QUICK GENERAL TIPS FOR THE COLLECTOR:

Type	Expect To Pay ($)
1st Production (Canada)	100 +
Farley (UK)	75 +
Current Production	70 +
Current Production Specials	90 +
Rare, Limited Edition	
Less Than 50 pieces	350-550
Less Than 10 units	1,000 +

Changes for 1992:

No. 17A - 1952 Studebaker convt. replaced No. 17 Studebaker Champion Coupe.

No. 20 - 1953 Buick Skylark available in red (only) as of October 1991.

No. 22A - Reworked Edsel, Improved casting replaced No. 22A Edsel Citation.

No. 31B - 1953 Pontiac Sedan Delivery, "Gulf Oil" re-placed by another Gas Co. livery, Mobilgas, and then Sunoco, making for an attractive Oil Co. Series. Set ongoing, yearly promotionals for the collector and service station enthusiast.

BUCKEYE

	C6	C8	C10
Buckeye Dump Truck	100	150	200
Buckeye Livestock Truck	115	172	230
Buckeye Pickup Truck	125	188	250
Buckeye Red Star Express Truck	160	240	320
Buckeye Semi Tractor	400	600	800

Buckeye Semi-Tractor.
Photo by Calvin L. Chaussee.

BUDDY "L"

Buddy "L" toys were first manufactured by the Moline Pressed Steel Company, Moline, Illinois, in 1921, and were named after the son of the owner, Fred Lundahl. Lundahl started the company about 8 years earlier, manufacturing auto and truck parts (fenders, etc.). The toys were originally made as special items for his son, but as Buddy Lundahl's playmates began to clamor for similar toys of their own, and their fathers began asking Lundahl senior to make duplicate toys for their sons, Lundahl went into the toy business.

Buddy "L" toys were large, typically 21 to 24 or more inches long for trucks and fire engines. Construction was of very heavy steel, strong enough to support a man's weight. These were made until the early 1930s when the line was modified and lighter weight materials were employed. Before this time, Fred Lundahl had died, having already lost control of the company. The company has changed names several times, being known as the Buddy "L" Corp., Buddy "L" Toy Co., etc., and in recent years dropping the quotes around the L.

Continuing to make toys till the present day, the company even put out a few wooden toys during WWII, when its main plant made nothing but war-related items. The early Buddy "L" trains are also popular and tend to be worth even more than the vehicles. Buddy "L" material from the pre-1932 period is almost indestructible; as a consequence, half of the pieces found are either very rusty or have been repainted at some point. The basic metal seems to hold up forever, but repainting and rust drops the price well below "good."

Following is a list of pre-1932 Buddy "L" toys compiled by Thomas W. Sefton.

Large Trucks

	C6	C8	C10
Buddy L 200 Express Truck 1921-31	900	1600	2300
Buddy L 201 Dump Truck (Ratchet) 1921-30	500	750	1000
Buddy L 201 A Hydraulic Dump Truck 1926-31	720	1080	1440
Buddy L 202 Coal Truck 1926-31	2500	4000	6200
Buddy L 202A Sand & Gravel Truck 1926-31	1500	2500	3500
Buddy L 203 Stake Truck 1921-24, 1926-28	800	1350	1900
Buddy L 203A Lumber Truck 1925-30	1500	2500	3500
Buddy L 203B Baggage Truck 1929-31	1400	2300	3270
Buddy L 204 Moving Van 1924-30	800	1200	1700

	C6	C8	C10
Buddy L 204A Railway Express 1926-31	1000	1700	2400
Buddy L 206, 206B Street Sprinkler Truck 1924-31	1100	1700	2400
Buddy L 206A Oil Truck 1925-30	900	1500	2200
Buddy L 207 Ice Truck 1926-31	500	750	1000
Buddy L 208 Coach 1928-31 (lt. Green Motorbus)	2000	3300	4800
Buddy L 209 Auto Wrecker 1928-31 (Tow Truck)	1800	2900	4000

Fire Trucks

	C6	C8	C10
Buddy L 205 Hook & Ladder 1924-31	800	1350	1850
Buddy L 205A Pumper 1925-30	1100	1800	2500

Buddy L 201 (restored). Photo by Calvin L. Chaussee.

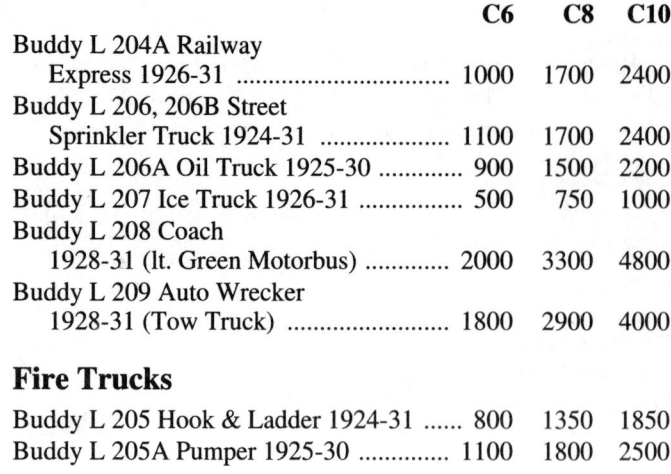

Buddy L 201A

Buddy L, top to bottom: 201A, 201. Photo by Tim Oei.

Buddy L pre-1932 203 Stake Truck (restored in photo). Courtesy Bill Bertoia Auctions. Photo by Jeanne Bertoia.

Buddy L, pre-1932, top to bottom: 202 Coal Truck, 202A Sand & Gravel Truck. Courtesy Bill Bertoia Auctions. Photo by Jeanne Bertoia.

Buddy L 203B

Buddy L Baggage Truck No. 203-B. Courtesy Joe and Sharon Freed.

Buddy L 204A

Buddy L 207

Buddy L 206A (restored). Photo by Calvin L. Chaussee.

Buddy L 209

Buddy L pre-1932 209 Auto Wrecker. Courtesy Bill Bertoia Auctions. Photo by Jeanne Bertoia.

Buddy L pre-1932 205 Hook & Ladder. Courtesy Bill Bertoia Auctions. Photo by Jeanne Bertoia.

Buddy L 205

Buddy L 205AB

Buddy L 205B

	C6	C8	C10
Buddy L 205AB (Working) Pumper 1930-31	1100	1800	2540
Buddy L 205B Aerial Ladder 1926-30	950	1600	2300
Buddy L 205C Insurance Patrol 1926-30	1400	2300	3300
Buddy L 205D Water Tower Truck (Working) 1930-31	2500	4200	7000

Model T Series

	C6	C8	C10
Buddy L 210 Flivver Truck 1925-30	900	1400	1900
Buddy L 210A Flivver Roadster 1925-27	550	850	1250
Buddy L 210B Flivver Coupe 1925-30	500	800	1200
Buddy L 211 Ford Dump Cart 1926-30	800	1550	2300

	C6	C8	C10
Buddy L 211A Ford Dump Truck 1926-30	1100	1700	2650
Buddy L 212 Ford Express Truck 1929-30	1400	2300	3225
Buddy L 212A One-Ton Ford Delivery Truck 1929-30	2000	3500	5000

Construction Equipment

	C6	C8	C10
Buddy L 220 Steam Shovel 1921-31	265	400	530
Buddy L 220A Heavy Steam Shovel 1929-30	400	600	800
Buddy L 220AB Heavy Shovel (on Treads) 1929-30	2500	4000	7000
Buddy L 230 Sand Loader 1925-31	165	250	330

Buddy L 210A. Courtesy Wilkinson Collection, Detroit Antique Toy Museum.

Buddy L 220 Steam Shovel. Courtesy Joe and Sharon Freed.

Buddy L 230

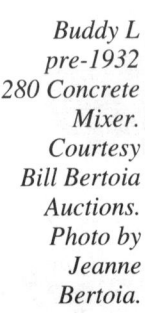

Buddy L pre-1932 280 Concrete Mixer. Courtesy Bill Bertoia Auctions. Photo by Jeanne Bertoia.

Buddy L 280 Concrete Mixer. Courtesy Thomas G. Nefos, Federal Shipping Network.

Buddy "L"

	C6	C8	C10
Buddy L 240 Small Derrick 1922-31	312	470	625
Buddy L 241 Large Derrick 1922-31	275	363	550
Buddy L 250 Overhead Crane 1924-27	700	1100	1600
Buddy L 250A Traveling Crane 1928-30 .	1200	1800	2500
Buddy L 260 Pile Driver 1926-28	750	1125	1500
Buddy L 270 Dredge (Clamshell) 1926-30	800	1200	1600
Buddy L 270A Tractor Dredge (on Treads) 1929-30	3000	5000	7500
Buddy L 280 Concrete Mixer 1926-30	500	750	1000
Buddy L 280A Mixer (on Treads) 1929-31	1100	1700	2600
Buddy L 290 Road Roller 1929-31	2100	3700	5280
Buddy L 300 Sand Screener 1929-30	700	1100	1700
Buddy L 350 Hoisting Tower 1929-31	500	900	1250
Buddy L 360 Aerial Tramway 1929-30 ...	1500	2400	3300
Buddy L 400 Trencher 1928-31	1800	2700	4200

End listing by Thomas W. Sefton

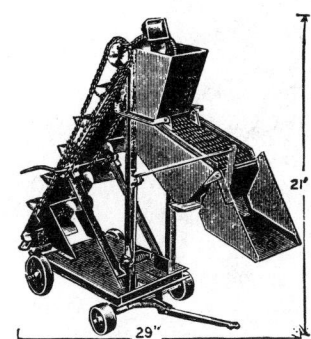

Buddy L 300

BUDDY L: 1932 and after

	C6	C8	C10
Buddy L Aerial Ladder Truck, 1933-34, 40" long	550	950	1300
Buddy L Aerial Ladder Truck No. 947, 1940	250	375	500
Buddy L Aerial Ladder Truck, 25" long	275	363	550
Buddy L Aerial Ladder Truck, wooden, 32" long	800	1300	1800
Buddy L Air Force Truck, No. 5577	100	150	200
Buddy L Airway Express Van No. 563	138	205	275

	C6	C8	C10
Buddy L "Allied Van Lines" moving van No. 366, 31" long	338	500	675
Buddy L "Allied Van Lines," wooden, 27" long	250	375	500
Buddy L Ambulance Truck	130	195	260
Buddy L Anti-Aircraft Air Force Blue Truck, GMC	42	63	85
Buddy L "Army Combat Car," wooden, w/cannon	140	210	280

Buddy L Aerial Ladder Truck, 25" long. Photo by Calvin L. Chaussee.

Buddy L Army Electric Searchlight Truck. Courtesy Continental Hobby House.

Buddy L "Army Supply Corps," 12" long. Photo by Calvin L. Chaussee.

Buddy L Army Tank No. 362, wood, 1943. Photo by Jack Matthews.

	C6	C8	C10
Buddy L Army Combination Set, No. 5560	200	300	400
Buddy L Army Electric Searchlight Truck No. 5545, 1957	138	208	275
Buddy L Army Half Track w/Cannon	138	208	275
Buddy L "Army Signal Corps" Truck, 1941-42, 12" long	140	210	280
Buddy L Army Supply Corps Truck, 12" long	45	68	90
Buddy L Army Tank, No. 362, wood, 1943, 13" long	45	68	90
Buddy L Army Transport, 27" with towed cannon, 6-spoke wheels	138	205	275
Buddy L Army Transport w/canvas-top trailer	238	357	475
Buddy L Army Truck 21," c.1940, cloth top	120	180	240
Buddy L Army Truck No. 506, 20-1/2" long	125	195	250
Buddy L "Army" Truck, 13" long, wooden, canvas top	115	162	230
Buddy L "Army" Truck, 16" long, wooden, canvas top	100	150	200
Buddy L "Army Supply Corps," cloth top	130	195	260
Buddy L "Army Transport" Truck, 19-1/2" long	175	263	350
Buddy L Atlas Van Lines	250	375	500

	C6	C8	C10
Buddy L Automatic Tail-Gate Loader with steering handle, 25" long	230	345	460
Buddy L Baggage Truck No. 11, 26-1/2" long, 1933	225	385	500
Buddy L Baggage Truck No. 41	72	108	145
Buddy L Baggage Truck No. 203-B, 1930-32, 26" long, auctioned in 1992 in very good-excellent condition for $8800.			
Buddy L Bell Telephone Truck, GMC, 3 linemen	138	205	275
Buddy L "Big Show Circus" Truck, wood, 1947, No. 484, 25-1/2" long	605	908	1210
Buddy L Brinks Armored Truck	230	345	460
Buddy L Buick Convertible, wooden, 18" long	275	413	550
Buddy L Bus, early 1930s, 23-1/2" long	375	525	750
Buddy L Camper, 1961	87	130	175
Buddy L Car Carrier, 1961	150	225	300
Buddy L Car Lift, 1960s	45	68	90
Buddy L Cattle Truck	70	105	140
Buddy L Chain Dump, 1920s	450	675	900
Buddy L Chemical Fire Truck, 1950s, 22" long	235	350	470
Buddy L Circus Tractor Trailer, 1960s	225	338	450
Buddy L City Baggage Dray No. 439, 1934, 19" long	250	375	500
Buddy L City Baggage Dray No. 839, 1939, 20-3/4" long	125	188	250

Buddy L "Army Transport" truck, (missing canvas) 19-1/2" long. Photo by Calvin L. Chaussee.

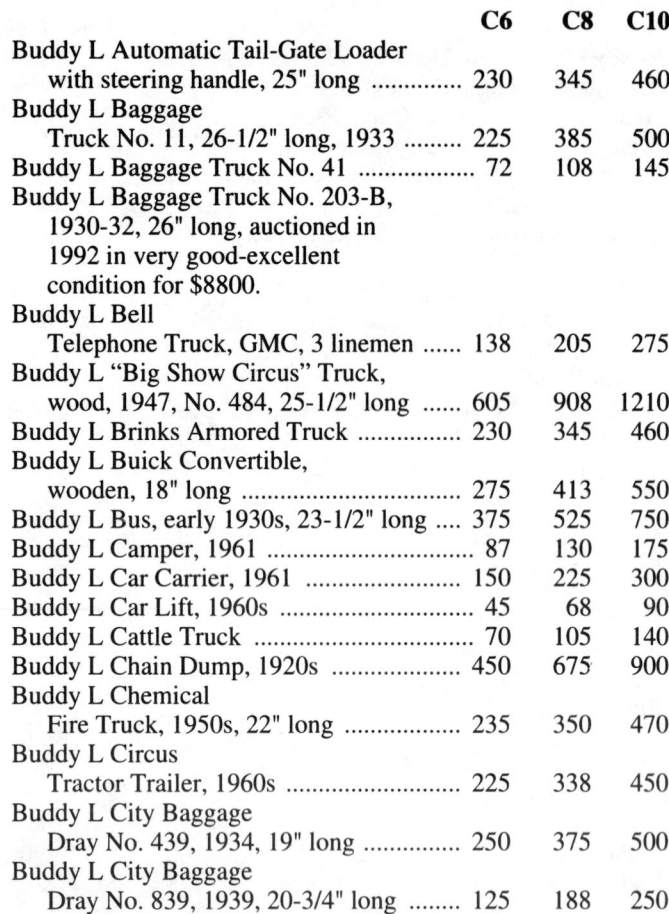

Buddy L Automatic Tail-Gate Loader with steering handle, 25" long. Photo by Calvin L. Chaussee.

Buddy L "Big Show Circus" truck, wood, 1947. No. 484. Photo by William G. Floyd.

Buddy L Bus, early 1930s, 23-1/2" long. Photo by Calvin L. Chaussee.

	C6	C8	C10
Buddy L "City Dray," 24" long	1500	2500	4000
Buddy L Coca-Cola Truck, 1950s, 14" long	155	233	310
Buddy L Coca-Cola Truck, wooden, 19" long, circa WWII, only 3 known, worth $4200 in mint 1984			
Buddy L Concrete Mixer, 1930s	200	300	400
Buddy L Concrete Mixer with Truck No. 54, 34-1/2" long, 1937	100	150	200
Buddy L Concrete Mixer No. 832, 1950- 51 with Motor Sound, 10-3/4" long	275	415	550
Buddy L Concrete Mixer, 1941, No. 932	100	150	200
Buddy L Concrete Mixer No. 5465, 1965	80	120	160
Buddy L Construction Truck, c.1960s	50	75	105
Buddy L Convertible, wooden, 18" long ...	400	600	800
Buddy L Country Squire Station Wagon, 15" long	108	162	215
Buddy L Curtiss Candy Truck	212	318	425

	C6	C8	C10
Buddy L Dairy Truck No. 2002 (Junior Line), 1930-32, 24" long	350	525	700
Buddy L Dairy Truck, late	105	158	210
Buddy L Dandy Digger No. 33	75	112	150
Buddy L Delivery Truck Deluxe Rider No. 803, 1945-48, 22-3/4" long	260	390	520
Buddy L Desert Rats Colt Jeep	75	112	150
Buddy L Double Hydraulic Self-Loader-N-Dump Truck No. 5892	100	150	200
Buddy L Dump Truck No. 434, 1936	212	318	425
Buddy L Dump Truck No. 634, 20-1/2" long	140	210	280
Buddy L Dump Truck (Junior Line), early, 24" long	1500	2500	4000
Buddy L Emergency Unit Tow Truck, 1950s	100	150	200
Buddy L Emergency Auto Wrecker No. 3317	100	150	200
Buddy L Engine No. 29, 1933-34, 25-1/2" long	225	338	450
Buddy L Excavator Truck and Shovel Set No. 948, 27-1/2" long, 1940	288	432	575

Buddy L Coca Cola truck, wooden, 19" long. Photo by Dick MacNary.

Buddy L Coca-Cola truck, 1950s, 14" long (missing bottles in photo). Photo by Calvin L. Chaussee.

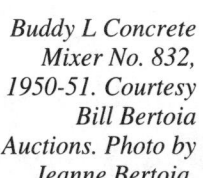

Buddy L Concrete Mixer No. 832, 1950-51. Courtesy Bill Bertoia Auctions. Photo by Jeanne Bertoia.

Buddy L Concrete Mixer, 1930s. Photo by Calvin L. Chaussee.

Buddy L Delivery Truck, Deluxe Rider No. 803. Courtesy Joe and Sharon Freed.

	C6	C8	C10
Buddy L Express			
Trailer Truck No. 35, 1934	475	715	950
Buddy L Express Truck,			
screenside, 1932	1200	2000	3000
Buddy L Farm Machinery Hauler	65	98	130
Buddy L "Farm Supplies" Hi-Lift			
Dump Truck, 20" long, 1954	125	188	250
Buddy L Farm Supply			
Truck No. 634, 1949	170	255	340
Buddy L Fast Delivery Truck No. 3313	75	112	150
Buddy L "Fast Freight," 20" long	100	150	200
Buddy L Fire Chief's Car with Siren			
No. 483, wood, 1947, 19-1/2" long	475	715	950
Buddy L Fire Engine, wood, 13" long	90	135	180

	C6	C8	C10
Buddy L Fire Hose Truck, 12" long	42	63	85
Buddy L Fire Ladder Truck, semi,			
rounded trailer fenders, 1960	100	150	200
Buddy L Fire Ladder			
Truck No. 859, 15" long	85	128	170
Buddy L Fire Ladder			
Truck, wooden, 20" long	87	130	175
Buddy L Fire Pumper, c.1960s	45	68	90
Buddy L "Fire Station," wooden, 17x15",			
with wooden chief car and ladder truck.			
Auctioned in 1992 in near-mint			
condition for $4070			
Buddy L "Firestone Service" Wrecker	500	800	1100
Buddy L Freight Hauler, GMC, 1957	200	300	400

Buddy L Double Hydraulic Self-Loader-N-Dump Truck No. 5892. Courtesy Thomas G. Nefos, Federal Shipping Network.

Buddy L "Emergency Auto Wrecker." Photo by Calvin L. Chaussee.

Buddy L "Farm Supplies" Hi-Lift Dump Truck, 1954, 20" long. Courtesy Islyn Thomas.

Buddy L Fire Chief's Car with Siren No. 483, 1947, wood. Photo by William G. Floyd.

Buddy L Fire Ladder Truck, Semi, rounded trailer fenders, 1960. Photo by Calvin L. Chaussee.

Buddy L "Hi-Lift Scoop-A-Dump." Photo by Thomas G. Nefos, Federal Shipping Network.

	C6	C8	C10
Buddy L Giraffe Truck	75	112	150
Buddy L Greyhound Bus, 7-1/2", 1950s	40	60	80
Buddy L Greyhound Bus, winds up, 16" long	225	338	450
Buddy L Greyhound Bus with Bell No. 481, wooden, 18-1/2" long	450	675	900
Buddy L Grocery Truck	150	225	300

	C6	C8	C10
Buddy L Half Track	72	108	145
Buddy L Heavy Machinery Truck	120	180	240
Buddy L High Lift Dumper, 1954	200	300	400
Buddy L "Hi-Lift Scoop-A-Dump"	75	112	150
Buddy L Highway Maintenance Dump	50	75	100
Buddy L Hook and Ladder Truck No. 859, wooden, 21-1/2" long	290	445	590

Buddy L Hose Truck No. 38. Courtesy Joe and Sharon Freed.

Buddy L "Hy-Way Maintenance" Mechanical Truck & Concrete Mixer No. 822. Photo by Tim Oei.

Buddy L "Hydraulic Highway Maintenance" truck, 17" long. Photo by Calvin L. Chaussee.

Buddy L "Ladder Truck," 1930. Courtesy Continental Hobby House.

Buddy L Merry-Go-Round Truck No. 5429. Courtesy Thomas G. Nefos, Federal Shipping Network.

Buddy L Mister Buddy Ice Cream Van. Courtesy Thomas G. Nefos, Federal Shipping Network.

	C6	C8	C10
Buddy L Hook & Ladder, 1961	100	150	200
Buddy L Horse Van, 18" long	100	150	200
Buddy L Hose Truck No. 38, 1933, 21-3/4" long	150	240	325
Buddy L Hot Rod	50	75	100
Buddy L Hot Rod Station Wagon	60	90	120
Buddy L Husky Dumper, late 1950s	112	168	225
Buddy L "Hy-way Maintenance" Mechanical Truck & Concrete Mixer No. 822, 1949, 36" long	350	525	700
Buddy L Hydraulic Aerial Truck No. 27, 1933-34, 40" long with ladders down	550	850	1200

	C6	C8	C10
Buddy L Hydraulic Dump Truck, 25" long, 1932	1100	1700	2500
Buddy L Hydraulic Dump Truck No. 10, 23-3/4" long, 1933-34	200	300	400
Buddy L Hydraulic Dump, 1938, 26" long	900	1400	2000
Buddy L Hydraulic Dump, No. 5859, 1949	325	488	650
Buddy L Hydraulic Dump, c.1960s	190	285	380
Buddy L "Hydraulic Highway Maintenance" Truck, 17" long	125	188	250
Buddy L Hydraulic Plow Truck	80	120	160
Buddy L Ice Cream Truck	65	98	130

Buddy L "Railway Express Truck" No. 480, wooden, 1947; the pressed steel hand truck came with it. Photo by William G. Floyd.

Buddy L "Riding Academy" No. 5455 truck. Courtesy Thomas G. Nefos, Federal Shipping Network.

Buddy L "Repair-It," 1953. Courtesy Mapes Auctioneers.

Brand New! First Time Offered!
Remote Controlled Electric Dump Truck

Buddy L Robotoy Dump Truck, as shown in the October, 1932 Butler Bros. catalog.

Buddy L "Sand and Stone" truck. Courtesy Continental Hobby House.

Buddy L Scarab No. 711 (bumpers missing in photo). Courtesy Heinz Mueller, Continental Hobby House.

	C6	C8	C10
Buddy L Ice Truck No. 12, 1933-34, 26-1/2" long	650	1050	1500
Buddy L International Delivery Truck No. 51, 1935, 24-1/2" long	200	300	400
Buddy L International Ice Truck, 28" long, 1939	550	825	1100
Buddy L International Wrecker	700	1100	1700
Buddy L Jr. Airmail Truck, 22" long	1500	2500	3500
Buddy L Jr. Baggage Truck, 22" long	1800	3000	4500
Buddy L Jr. Cement Mixer	300	450	600
Buddy L Jr. Dairy Truck, 22" long	1000	1800	2500
Buddy L Jr. Dump Truck, 22" long	800	1300	1800
Buddy L Jr. Milk Delivery Truck No. 2002	2000	3500	5000
Buddy L Jr. Oil Truck, 22" long	1200	2000	2800
Buddy L Jr. Steam Shovel, treads, 24" long	900	1400	2000
Buddy L Kennel Truck, 12 dogs	82	123	165
Buddy L "Ladder Truck," 1935	375	563	750
Buddy L Lift Gate Truck	75	112	150
Buddy L Long Distance Moving Van, wooden	250	375	500
Buddy L Lumber Truck, wooden, 30" long	425	638	850
Buddy L Machinery Hauler	138	205	275
Buddy L Mack Quarry Dump	37	56	75
Buddy L Mack Tandem, 1969	45	68	90
Buddy L Mack 30-Ton Dump	95	142	190
Buddy L "Marshall Field Company" 1966 Step Van	150	225	300
Buddy L Merry-Go-Round Truck No. 5429	88	132	175
Buddy L "Milk Delivery" Truck, early, 24" long	1700	2700	4000
Buddy L Milk Farms Truck, wooden	207	310	415
Buddy L Missile Launcher, GMC	90	135	180
Buddy L Mister Buddy Ice Cream Van	160	240	320
Buddy L "Motor Market," 22" long, 1937	200	300	400
Buddy L Pepsi-Cola Truck, wooden, auctioned in 1992 for $1595			
Buddy L Pickup Truck, early 1960s	62	93	125
Buddy L "Popsicle" Truck, wooden, 17" long	400	600	800
Buddy L "Pure Ice" Truck, wooden, 16" long	112	178	225
Buddy L Railway Express Truck, "Baby Ruth," "Butterfinger" tandem, 1935	1000	1700	2400
Buddy L "Railway Express" Truck, 1953, milk ad	130	195	260
Buddy L "Railway Express" Truck No. 480, wooden, 1947, 16-1/4" long	335	500	670
Buddy L Ranchero Stake Truck	112	168	225
Buddy L Red Baby Pickup, 26" long, doors open	1500	2500	3500
Buddy L Red Baby Pickup, 24" long	500	800	1200
Buddy L Repair-It, 24" long	142	213	285
Buddy L Repair-It, 15" long	160	240	320
Buddy L Ride-Em Dump No. 702, 20" long	230	345	460
Buddy L Ride-Em Fire Truck, c.1920s, elec. lights	900	1500	2200
Buddy L "Riding Academy" No. 5455 Truck, with 3 horses	60	90	120
Buddy L Robotoy Dump Truck with driver, operates on remote control	500	800	1100
Buddy L Sand & Gravel Truck No. 3312	107	160	215
Buddy L "Sand & Stone" Truck, 1950s, 15" long	75	112	150
Buddy L Sanitation Truck, late	75	112	150
Buddy L Scarab No. 211, no windup mechanism	250	375	500
Buddy L Scarab No. 711, winds up	175	263	350
Buddy L Scissors Dump	40	60	80
Buddy L Scoop Conveyor	75	112	150
Buddy L Scoop Dump	138	205	275
Buddy L Searchlight Truck, GMC, 1950s	75	112	150
Buddy L Service Truck, 1953	120	180	240
Buddy L "Shell" Truck, 13-1/2" long	190	285	380
Buddy L "Shell" Truck, 17-1/2" long, 1941	500	750	1050
Buddy L Signal Corps Unit, 1957, 24"	175	263	350
Buddy L Siren Pull-n-Ride	120	180	240
Buddy L Stake Truck, GMC, 1960s?	105	158	210
Buddy L Standard Oil Truck, 1933-34, 26" long	850	1300	2000
Buddy L Station Wagon, Ford, 1964, 14-1/2"	87	130	175
Buddy L Station Wagon, wooden, No. 371, 19" long	162	243	325

Buddy L Station Wagon, wooden. Courtesy Joe and Sharon Freed.

Buddy L "Sunshine Biscuits" van. Courtesy Joe and Sharon Freed.

	C6	C8	C10
Buddy L Steam Shovel and International Truck No. 16, 1937, 29-1/2" long, 13 1/2" high	110	165	225
Buddy L Steam Shovel, Mechanical, No. 30, 1935, 17-1/2" long, 13-1/2" high	200	325	450
Buddy L Steam Shovel No. 944	212	318	425
Buddy L Steam Shovel, 1938	112	168	225
Buddy L Steam Shovel on Treads (Junior Line) No. 2005, 1930-32, 24" long	150	275	400
Buddy L Stepside Pickup Truck, 1950s	75	112	150
Buddy L Store Delivery Truck	90	135	180
Buddy L "Sunshine Biscuits" Van	No Price Found		
Buddy L "Super Market Delivery" Truck	100	150	200
Buddy L Super Motor Market Truck	315	472	635
Buddy L Supply Truck w/load	125	188	250
Buddy L Surf Truck, 12" long, 1953	112	168	225
Buddy L Tank Truck, 27" long, 1930s	500	775	1100
Buddy L Tank Truck No. 438, 19-1/4" long, 1935	450	675	900
Buddy L Tank Truck No. 938, 21-1/2" long, 1941	225	338	450
Buddy L "Taxi," wooden	500	750	1000
Buddy L Telephone Truck, GMC	122	185	225
Buddy L Telephone Truck w/trailer	75	112	150
Buddy L "Texaco" Tanker, 27" long	150	225	300
Buddy L "Texaco" Tanker, 25" long, promo sold at gas stations	100	150	200

	C6	C8	C10
Buddy L Towing Service Truck, 25" long	212	318	425
Buddy L Timber Truck, wood, 25" long	165	248	330
Buddy L Town & Country Convertible, 1945, wood	350	525	700
Buddy L Traveling Zoo, post WWII	80	120	160
Buddy L Truck, open bed, wooden, 16" long	No Price Found		
Buddy L U.S. Mail Truck No. 5354, 1964	118	167	235
Buddy L U.S. Mail Truck, 21-3/4" long, "2592," c.1941	375	562	750
Buddy L "U.S. Mail" Truck, early 30s, 22" long	1200	2200	3100
Buddy L Utility Truck, GMC	82	124	165
Buddy L Utility Delivery Truck No. 946, 25" long, 1941-42	90	135	180
Buddy L "Van Freight Carrier," 20" long, 1940s	162	243	325
Buddy L Victory Jeep and Cannon, wood	100	150	200
Buddy L Volkswagen Bus, 1960s	112	168	225
Buddy L Water Tower, 1933-34, 48" long	1500	2500	3500
Buddy L Water Tower No. 28, 1936	1500	2500	3500
Buddy L Wild Animal Circus Truck	140	210	280
Buddy L Wrecker No. 13, 31" long, 1933	1000	1700	3000

Buddy L "Super Market Delivery" truck. Courtesy Continental Auctions.

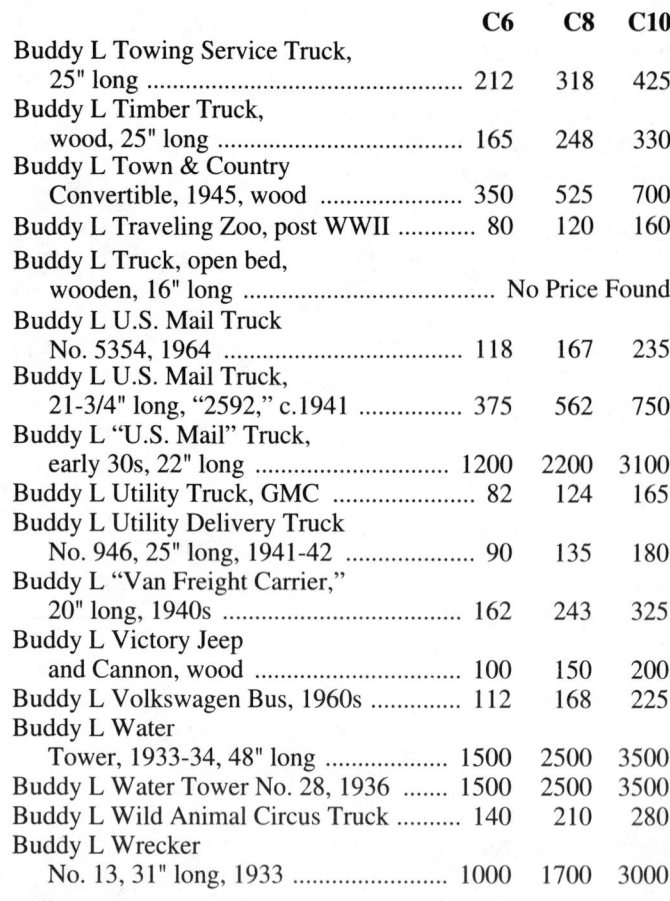

Buddy L Tank Truck, 1930s, 27" long (restored). Photo by Calvin L. Chaussee.

Buddy L "Texaco" tanker, 27" long. Courtesy Calvin L. Chaussee.

Buddy L Truck, open bed, wooden, 16" long. Courtesy Charles D. Richards.

	C6	C8	C10
Buddy L Wrecker			
No. 37, 1933, 24" long	150	250	400
Buddy L Wrecker, 1936-37, 27" long	600	950	1300
Buddy L Wrecker, 1938, 26" long	1000	1700	2400
Buddy L Wrecker			
No. 813, 1938, 32" long	80	140	200
Buddy L Wrecker			
No. W37, 25-1/4" long, 1939	90	145	200
Buddy L Wrecker			
No. 437, 1934, 24" long	375	525	750
Buddy L Wrecker No. 503,			
1940, 19-1/4" long, 1941-42	112	168	225
Buddy L No. 647, 1949, 26-1/4" long	175	263	350
Buddy L Wrecker, 16" long, c.1950s	112	168	225
Buddy L Wrecker, wooden, 18" long	115	172	230
Buddy L Wrecker, Emergency Towing			
Rider No. 903, 1949, 33" long	75	112	150
Buddy L Wrecker No. 903,			
33" long, 1950,			
"Buddy L Emergency Towing"	100	150	200

	C6	C8	C10
Buddy L Wrecker No. 937,			
1939, 25-1/4" long	130	180	285
Buddy L Wrecker No. 937,			
1941-42 version, 25" long	130	180	285
Buddy L Wrecker,			
1963, w/tools, No. 5427	100	150	200
Buddy L "Wrigley's Spearmint"			
Railway Express Truck			
No. 835, 25" long, 1938	700	1100	1500
Buddy L "Wrigley's Spearmint"			
Railway Express Truck, 1935,			
headlights light up, 23-1/8" long	750	1150	1600
Buddy L "Wrigley's Spearmint"			
Railway Express Agency Truck			
No. 953, 1940	800	1350	1850
Buddy L "Wrigley's Spearmint," 1957.......	175	263	350

Buddy L "U.S. Mail" truck, 21-3/4" long. Photo by Calvin L. Chaussee.

Buddy L Wild Animal Circus. Courtesy Thomas G. Nefos, Federal Shipping Network.

Buddy L Wrecker, wooden, 18" long. Photo by Perry Eichor.

Buddy L "Wrigley's Spearmint" Railway Express truck, 1935. Courtesy Rodney A. Heesacker.

BUFFALO TOYS

Buffalo Toys, of Buffalo, New York, began in 1924. It produced a number of lightweight steel toys up until WW II. The firm, apparently no longer making toys, folded in 1968.

	C6	C8	C10
Buffalo Toys Blue Bird Racer	150	225	300
Buffalo Toys Bumper Car, 10" windup	55	83	110
Buffalo Toys Mack Stake Truck, electric lights, c.1928, 25" long	300	450	700
Buffalo Toys Red Streak Racer, 24" long	312	468	625

	C6	C8	C10
Buffalo Toys Silver Bullet Racer, 26" long	350	525	700
Buffalo Toys Silver Dash	175	263	350
Buffalo Toys Silver Streak	300	450	600
Buick, 1947, plastic, 5-1/2" long, probably Irwin	5	8	10

Buffalo Toys Mack Stake Truck, electric lights, c.1928, 25" long. Photo by Bob Smith.

Buick, 1947, plastic, 5-3/8" long (probably Irwin). Courtesy James S. Maxwell/Virginia Caputo. Photo by Virginia Caputo.

BUILT-RITE

Built-Rite, of Lafayette, Indiana, began in 1922 as a cardboard-box manufacturer. About 1934, it began to produce cardboard construction toys, with its apparent heyday in the late 1930s and WWII. It is still in business, making card games, games, and puzzles under the name of "Warren."

Built-Rite No. 7 Private Garage, brick	30	40	50
Built-Rite No. 15 Commercial Garage	65	70	80
Built-Rite No. 17 Service Station	65	70	80
Built-Rite No. 20 Army Battery Set	80	100	125
Built-Rite No. 28 Garage and Super Service Station	65	75	85
Built-Rite No. 50 Army Raiders' Victory Unit, 28 pieces, Truck, Tank, AA gun, Jeep, Semitrack Truck, 20 soldiers, WWII	65	75	85

Built-Rite No. 56, 5 Miniature buildings, church, school, RR station, firehouse, drugstore	30	55	60
Built-Rite No. 83 Weapons Carrier	10	15	18
Built-Rite No. 84 Armored Car	10	15	18
Built-Rite No. 415 House, c.1943, 13"x20" boxed set with 19" house and garage, 27 pieces of furniture, sedan, baby buggy, shrubbery, etc.	75	90	100

Built-Rite No. 20. Photo by Ed Poole.

BURDETTE MURRAY

	C6	C8	C10
Burdette Murray Express Truck	1600	2700	3800

	C6	C8	C10
Burdette Murray White Standard Bed Truck	2000	3200	4600

BURNETT LIMITED

Birmingham/London, England, 1900-1930s

by Bob Smith

Burnett started producing toy cars around the turn of the century. Its cars were said to have excellent quality. Burnett moved the business to London in 1914 and continued to make toys into the 1930s. The company was then purchased by Chad-Valley. Burnett toy cars are quite rare.

	C6	C8	C10
Burnett Cargo Truck, maroon & black, c/w motor, driver, c.1926, 8-1/2" long .	600	800	1150

	C6	C8	C10
Burnett limousine, c.1925, blue/black, c/w motor, driver, 8" long	550	750	1100
Burnett Roadster, c.1925, green/black, c/w motor driver, folding windshield, 7-1/2" long	600	800	1150
Burnett Toyland Bus, 14-1/2" long	500	750	1050
Bus, "Twin Coach, Buffalo, Niagara Lines," 15-1/2" long, aluminum	2500	3500	6000

Burnett Cargo Truck, c.1926, 8-1/2" long. Photo by Bob Smith.

Burnett Limousine, c.1925, 8" long. Photo by Bob Smith.

Burnett Roadster, c.1925, 7-1/2" long. Photo by Bob Smith.

Bus, "Twin Coach, Buffalo, Niagara Lines," aluminum, 15-1/2" long. Courtesy James S. Maxwell/Virginia Caputo.

BW MOLDED PLASTICS

What is known about BW Molded Plastics is that in 1954 it was located at 1346 East Walnut St. in Pasadena, California, and that it made a variety of plastic toys, musical instruments, tea sets, ships, vehicles, etc.

	C6	C8	C10
BW873B, 5-piece Auto Parade Set; Pickup Truck, Convertible, Coupe, Ladder Truck, Racer		No Price Found	
BW879 "Roly" The Steam Roller, "fully mechanized"		No Price Found	

	C6	C8	C10
BW886 Jeep, 9-1/4" long		No Price Found	
BW887 Tank, 10" long		No Price Found	
BW888 Jaguar, 12-1/2" long		No Price Found	
BW??? Race Car, 3-1/2"	13	20	27
BW??? Fire Truck, 3-1/2"	13	20	27

Top Row: BW873B; Middle Row: BW879, BW886; Bottom Row: BW887, BW888. BW Molded Plastics from its catalog.

C.A.W. NOVELTY COMPANY

By Fred Maxwell, Slushmold Contributing Editor and Ferd Zegel, with the assistance of the Clay Center Historical Society, Gary Franson, Arlan and Gerry Conrad.

It is remarkable, indeed, that collectors had not found this fine company until 1990. Charles A. Wood not only ran a substantial operation, but he also made some of the finest replica toys in the slushmold industry. Ironically, Wood had one of the longest histories of the slushmold industry. Founded about 1925, his company was active until about 1940, when lead casting came to a halt with WWII.

Wood's output showed artistry, ingenuity, and meticulous craftsmanship. All his toys are smooth, crisp, detailed moldings, with extra touches such as open windshields and two or three colors per toy. The early production had metal disk wheels with painted black "tires," or metal-spoked. When you find open, V-shaped, divided windshield, drivers inside cabs and tri-motored aircraft with the outboard engines mounted on the landing gear struts, you wonder how he did it for the 5-cent price. Perhaps Wood explained it, for he once told a reporter that it sometimes took 3 or 4 years to make a mold. The molds are also works of art—machinist's art. This tells us something about his pride in his work and also that toy-making was not his primary occupation at the time.

Wood was born about 1891. He had lived and worked in Topeka and in nearby Clifton before coming to Clay Center. He was perhaps better known for his civic boosterism and good works. After he helped establish the local airport, he built and operated his own aircraft maintenance hangar. A master machinist, he made all his toy molds, production tools, and toy parts—even plastic wheels.

Although researching this slush industry for 20 years, I had only heard rumors of a "small molder in Clay Center." Then, a few years ago, I found a small monoplane with initials "CAW" under a tailplane. I put the pressure on Kansas friends, with the happy result that eventually I saw a mint collection owned by a relative of Wood's, as well as a few pieces and some paper memorabilia in the Historical Society Museum. What a pleasant surprise! Although we do not yet have a complete list, we have identified some of those "orphans" and some never heard of. Wood made airplanes, autos, novelties and trucks. Some of these have been well known to collectors, although unidentified. Clearly, this company and its toys deserve to be more fully known.

Note: The C&H Mfg. Co. was formed in 1940 by Rod Hemphill, the last C.A.W. employee, and Howard Clevenger. According to Mrs. Hemphill, they only used original C.A.W. molds. Apparently, this brave effort at revival managed to reproduce some toys before folding. These are heavier than C.A.W.'s and have black rubber wheels. Their claim to fame is in the publication of the accompanying partial flyer that allowed us to solve the paternity of these handsome orphans. However, judging from the catalog numbers and our incomplete list below, there must be several orphans out there. Can any of you collectors help? A C.A.W. trademark, seldom found (too costly?), was unique, lead, blind hubs fitted over a wire axle. They are sometimes found with ordinary nail axles piercing the hubs.

	C6	C8	C10
CWV1 Sport Roadster, no #, 3-1/2" Open Packard, driver w/cap (gilt or silver), no windshield (w/s), horizontal grille (hg), vertical louvers (vl), no headlamps, rear-mount (rm), metal disk wheels (mdw)	42	63	85
CWV2 Sport Roadster, no #, 3-1/2". Similar to above, Buick?, no w/s, plain grille, vl, rm, right side-mount (sm), mdw, (also spoked version (msw))	22	33	44

	C6	C8	C10
CWV3 Overland Bus, no #, 3-3/4". Fageol? Yellow Line? tour bus, hg, no headlamps, 12 windows, shallow "observer deck," mdw, left sm	12	18	24
CWV4 Fuel Tanker, no #, 3-3/4" Ford? truck, cab w/driver inside, no w/s, hg, 3 tanks, hose compart., msw	20	30	40
CWV5 Air Drive Coach, #25, 3-7/8". Blimp-like bus w/fin and rear propeller drive. (b. Also a version molded w/o prop.) 12 open windows (ow), white rubber wheels (wrw) with unique fitted hubs which cap hidden axles	22	33	45

L to R: C.A.W. CWV1, CWV2. Photo by Fred Maxwell.

C.A.W. CWV3. Courtesy Gary Franson.

C.A.W. CWV5. Photo by Fred Maxwell.

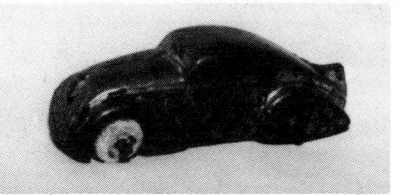

C.A.W. CWV6. Photo by Craig Clark.

TOYS THAT SELL THEMSELVES

Modern Metal Toys that Sell the Year Around, Realistic in Every
Detail. Finished in Bright Colors with the Best of Lacquers

No. 25 AIR DRIVE COACH
Length 3⅞ in. Height 1¾ in. Weight per
gro. 33 lbs. Retails for 10c.

Price per doz. ....

No. 32. DE SOTO SEDAN
Length 3⅞ in. Height 1⅞ in. Weight per
gro. 32 lbs. Retails for 10c.

Price per doz. ....

No. 30 STREAMLINE COUPE
Length 3 in. Height 1 in. Weight per gro.
19 lbs. Retails at 5c.

Price per doz. ....

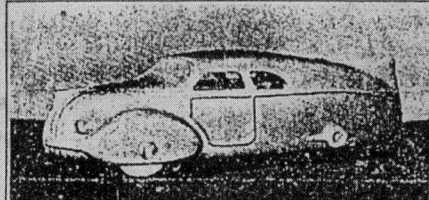

No. 33 WONDER SPECIAL
Length 3⅜ in. Height 1 in. Weight per gro
19 lbs. Retails for 5c.

Price per doz. ....

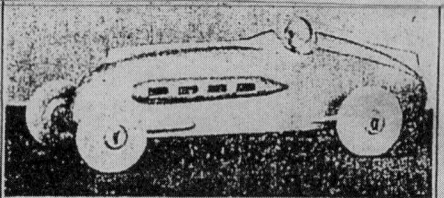

No. 31. MARVEL RACER
Length 3⅝ in. Height 1 3-16 in. Weight
per gro. 20 lbs. Retails at 5c.

Price per doz. ....

No. 38 NEW DESIGN RACER
Length 3⅜ in. Height 1¼ in. Weight per
gro. 20 lbs. Retails for 5c.

No. 39
TRANSPARENT WINDSHIELD RACER
Length 3 in. Height 1 in. Weight per gro.
15 lbs. Retails for 5c.

Each number packed one dozen
to box.

Colors: On all Airplanes 6 silver,
4 red, 2 green, to dozen. On all
Autos 6 red, 2 blue, 2 green, 2
silver to dozen.

Rubber Wheels on All Autos
Plastic Wheels on Airplanes Except No. 29

TERMS: 2% Ten Days, Net 30
Days. Prices are f. o. b. St. Louis,
Mo.

C & H Mfg. Co.

1610 So. Florissant Rd.
ST. LOUIS, MO.

No. 40 THREE PIECE AUTO SET
Three toys on card. Length 6⅜ in. Height 1 in. Weight per gro. 40 lbs. Retails for 10c
per card.

Price per doz. ....

C.A.W. vehicles, part of a catalog sheet issued by St. Louis' C&H Mfg. Co. about 1940 after the firm obtained C.A.W.'s molds.

C.A.W. Novelty Company

	C6	C8	C10

CWV6 Streamline Coupe, #30, 3".
Airflow, V-pattern grille, hood
ornament (ho), 4 ow, small rear fin,
small winged design on rear-wheel
skirts, mdw also wrw. Bottom pan
goes over rear axle, not under 16   24   32

CWV7 Wonder Special, #33, 3-3/8".
Airflow coupe, 3-wheeled
companion to #30 above, vg,
4 ow, wrw, front wheel skirts.
Pan goes over front axle 16   24   32

CWV8 Marvel Racer, #31, 3-5/8".
Streamlined FWD Indy type, driver,
torpedo tail with very small fin,
V-grille pattern, 8 exhaust ports,
alum. wheels. Also found in a
modern bubble-pack, w/lucent hard
plastic wheels, "Woodchuck Industries
Metal Toys, Clay Center, Ks." This
name may have been a new idea,
part of a recent market test .... No Price Found

CWV9 DeSoto Sedan, #32, 3-7/8".
Airflow, divided windshield,
bow, hl, vg, ho, wrw .... No Price Found

CWV10 New Design Racer #38, 3-3/8".
Streamlined coupe, rounded tail,
2 oval open windows show driver,
hood ornament loop (stringpull?),
wrw w/hubs .... No Price Found

CWV11 Transparent Windshield Racer,
#39, 3". Indy FWD 2 man racer
v-shaped vg, dual exhausts, boattail,
unique hubtires as in #25 (also wrw).
(Not complete if divided plastic
windshield is missing (fragile) .... No Price Found

CWV12 Three Piece Auto Set, #40,
as follows:
a. Midget coupe racer, no #, 2-1/16".
Hg, hl, divided open w/s, 2 ow,
2 colored body, mdw, headlamps
and cowl ventilators! .... No Price Found
b. Midget racer, no #, 2-1/8".
Gilt driver, vl, hg, mdw. (easily
confused w/Barclay #53) .... No Price Found
c. Austin Bantam, no #, 2". 2-door
Sedanette, 5 ow, hl, plain grille,
rm, mdw. (Easily confused with other
makers' Bantams) .... No Price Found

C.A.W. CWV7. Courtesy of Gary Franson.

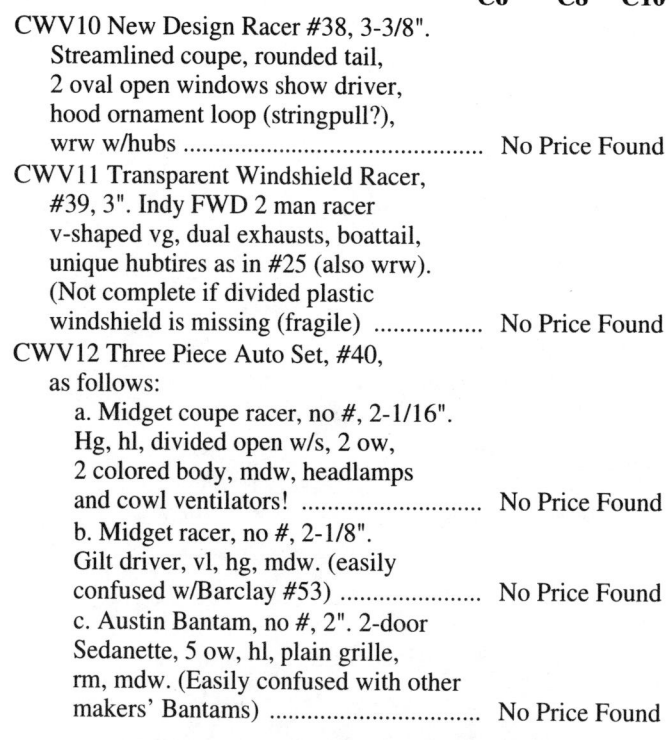

C.A.W. CWV8. Courtesy of Gary Franson.

C.A.W CWV9. Courtesy of Gary Franson.

C.A.W. CWV10. Courtesy of Gary Franson.

C.A.W. CWV11B. Courtesy of Gary Franson.

C.A.W., L to R: CWV12A, CWV4. Photo by Craig Clark.

C.A.W. CWV12B. Courtesy of Gary Franson.

CWV13 Dump Truck, no #, 3-1/8".
Ford?, hinged dump body, divided
open w/s, 2 ow, hg, mdw .... No Price Found
CWV14 Tank Truck, no #, 3-3/16". Ford?
3 fuel tanks, otherwise matching
above. Unusual 2-piece body
connected by rear axle. .... No Price Found

CWV15 Tank truck, no #. "Gasoline"
semi-trailer, 2 tanks. Cab w/divided
w/s and open windows shows it is
part of a set with CWV13 & CWV14 .... No Price Found

C.A.W. CWV13. Courtesy Ferd Zegel.

C.A.W.
CWV12C.
Photo by
Craig Clark.

C.A.W. CWV14. Courtesy of Gary Franson.

C.A.W. CWV15. Courtesy Ferd Zegel.

C.R.

(Charles Rossignol, Paris, 1868-1962)

By Bob Smith

Rossignol began making toy automobiles in 1895. The company became best known for the toy trains it produced in the nearly 100 years it was in business. In 1920, C.R. came out with a line of toy buses that lasted until the company closed its doors in 1962.

C.R. Dump Truck, c.1935, 16" long. Photo by Bob Smith.

C.R. Dump Truck, c.1935, 16" long.
Green/yellow c/w motor, head lamps,
dual side mount wheels 800   1200   1800

C.R. Rolls-Royce, tin litho, c/w motor, working lights. Courtesy Bill Bertoia Auctions. Photo by Jeanne Bertoia.

	C6	C8	C10
C.R. Large Bus	1200	2000	2800
C.R. Rolls Royce, tin litho, c/w motor, lights work, 14-1/2" long	1100	1900	2700
C.R. Streamline Sedan, windup, c.1930s, 14" long	315	462	630

*C.R. Streamline Sedan, windup, c.1930s, 14" long.
Courtesy Bill Bertoia Auctions. Photo by Jeanne
Bertoia.*

CARETTE, GEORGES

(Nuremberg, Germany 1886-1917)

By Bob Smith

Born in France, Carette went to Nuremberg to start his toy factory in 1886. He has become a legend in the hobby since. Next to Marklin, Carette is the most desirable of German toy-car makers. It is known for its fine detail and quality of materials. Carette stayed in business until 1917. At the onset of WWI, he fled to France, and his company was taken over by Karl Bub. The Carette limousines were made in three general lengths, 9-inch (22cm), 12.5-inch (32cm), and 15.5-inch (40cm). The larger size is the most desirable and usually sells for five figures.

	C6	C8	C10
Carette Landaulet Limo	2500	4000	6500
Carette Limousine, c.1910, chauffeur, 12-1/2" long	1200	2100	2900

Carette Limousine, driver, passenger, clockwork motor, 12-1/2" long. Courtesy Bill Bertoia Auctions. Photo by Jeanne Bertoia.

*Carette Limousine, c.1910, chauffer, 12-1/2" long.
Courtesy Bill Bertoia Auctions. Photo by Jeanne
Bertoia.*

*Carette Limousine, driver, luggage rack, high
headlamps, 15" long. Courtesy Bill Bertoia
Auctions. Photo by Jeanne Bertoia.*

Carette Limousine, c.1911, 9" long. Photo by Bob Smith.

	C6	C8	C10
Carette Limousine, doors open, roof rack, c.1911, 12-1/4"	1600	2700	4100
Carette Limousine, c/w motor, 16" long	2000	3500	5000
Carette Limousine, driver, passenger, c/w motor, 12-1/2" long	2000	3500	5000
Carette Limousine driver, luggage rack, high headlamps, 15" long	2500	4000	6000
Carette Limousine, white & green, 9"long, c/w motor, hand brake, head lamp, rubber tires, glass windows, c.1911	1200	2000	2800
Carette Open Car, 9", driver	500	750	1050
Carette Open Tourer, 4-seat, 2 bisque figures, 12-1/2" long, windup	6000	12,000	17,000

Carette/Bub Open Car, c.1911, 6-7/10" long. Photo by Bob Smith.

Carette Open Tourer, 4-seat, 2 bisque figures, 12-1/2" long windup. Courtesy Bill Bertoia Auctions. Photo by Jeanne Bertoia.

	C6	C8	C10
Carette Phaeton, 4-seat, 2 figures, 9" long	1200	2200	3400
Carette Open Phaeton, c.1906, 12" long, driver	2000	3500	5300
Carette/Bub Open Car, red/black, 6.7" long, c/w motor, tin plate or cloth dressed driver, hand brake, forward & reverse gear, c.1911	900	1300	1800
Carette Rear Entrance Tonneau, c/w motor, 8-1/2" long, four figures ...	1500	2500	4000

CASS TOYS

(Athol, Mass., 1890s to present)

Cass Delivery Truck Ridem, wooden, 30" long	25	38	50
Cass Dump Truck wooden ridem, 36" long	32	48	65
Cass Station Wagon, wooden, 19" long	60	90	120

Cass Tank, "General Lee," "224," wooden, 12" long	55	83	110
Cass Streamlined Truck ridem, 30" long	110	165	220
Cass Truck, wooden, 40" long ridem	150	225	300

Cass Tank, "General Lee," "224." Photo by Ron Fink.

CHAD VALLEY

(England)

	C6	C8	C10
Chad Valley Aerial Repair Truck, clockwork, 4"	175	262	350
Chad Valley "The Chad Valley Co. Ltd." Delivery Truck, 10" long	650	1100	1500
Chad Valley Double Decker Bus, "Chad Valley Toys," tin, 6"	65	98	130
Chad Valley Fordson Major Tractor, 6-1/2" long	100	150	200
Chad Valley Sedan, tin windup, rear luggage rack, 9-1/4" long	125	188	250

Chad Valley "The Chad Valley Co. Ltd." delivery truck. Courtesy Bill Bertoia Auctions. Photo by Jeanne Bertoia.

CHAMPION

The Champion Hardware Co., though in business from 1883 to 1954, produced toys only from 1930 to 1936, as a Depression stopgap. As might be expected from a hardware firm, its toys were cast iron. During its toy years the Geneva, Ohio, outfit was headed by C.I. Chamberlin.

Champion Airflow, 4-3/4" long		No Price Found	
Champion Coupe, Plymouth type, rumble seat opens, 7-1/2" long		No Price Found	
Champion Coupe, Reo type, 7-1/2" long ...	400	600	800
Champion Delivery Truck No. 536, 1930s, 8" long		No Price Found	
Champion Gas and Motor Oil Truck, 8" long, cast-iron, c.1930s	285	430	565

	C6	C8	C10
Champion 4-casting nickeled radiator car, approx. 4" long	175	262	350
Champion Mack Dump, 7" long, c.1930s	150	225	300
Champion Mack Express Truck, 7-1/2" long	100	150	200
Champion Mack Stake Truck, 4-1/2" long, c.1930	90	135	180
Champion Mack Stake Truck, 7-1/2" long	350	525	700
Champion Mack Wrecker, 9" long	375	562	750

Champion Delivery Truck No. 536. Photo by Rod Carnahan.

Champion Mack Dump, 7" long. Courtesy Wilkinson Collection, Detroit Antique Toy Museum.

Champion Motorcycles, L to R: CM2, CM1. Photo by Kent M. Comstock.

	C6	C8	C10

CHAMPION MOTORCYCLES (list by Kent M. Comstock)

	C6	C8	C10
(CM 1) Motorcycle, solo policeman, rubber tires, 5"	50	75	125
(CM 2) Motorcycle, solo policeman, nickel wheels, 5"	130	220	370
(CM 3) Motorcycle, solo policeman, rubber tires, 7-1/4"	150	250	400
(CM 4) Motorcycle, solo policeman, nickel wheels, 7-1/4"	175	275	450
(CM 5) Motorcycle with sidecar, policeman, rubber tires, 3"	60	90	120

Champion, L to R: CM2, CM3. Photo by Kent M. Comstock.

Champion Wrecker, 7-1/2" long. Photo by Bill Kaufman.

	C6	C8	C10
(CM 6) Motorcycle with sidecar, policeman and passenger, rubber tires, 5"	150	225	350
(CM 7) Motorcycle with sidecar, policeman and passenger, rubber tires, 6"	200	300	450
Champion Panel Delivery, 7-3/4" long	750	1300	1800
Champion Race Car, 2 riders, 5-1/2"	188	282	375
Champion Race Car, 6" long, cast-iron, detachable driver	170	255	340
Champion Race Car, 1935, 7-1/2" long	325	488	650
Champion Race Car, 9" long, c.1930s	150	225	300
Champion Sedan, 5-1/4" long	112	168	225
Champion Stake Truck, 8" long	300	450	600
Champion Wrecker, 9" long	250	375	500
Champion Wrecker, C-Cab, 8-1/4" long	850	1400	2090
Champion Wrecker, 7-1/2" long, cast-iron	250	385	550
Champion Wrecker, 4" long	112	172	225

Champion Panel Delivery, 7-3/4" long. Courtesy Bill Bertoia Auctions. Photo by Jeanne Bertoia.

CHEIN

Chein (pronounced "chain") was founded in 1903 by Julius Chein. The New Jersey company specialized in lithographed metal toys, the majority of them mechanical. In 1918, it was located at 310 Passaic Ave. in Harrison, New Jersey, with 250 employees. In 1934, it had 55 male and 92 female workers. In a 1946-47 directory, it listed 148 male and 132 female employees. Chein made toys until 1979, and is still in business today in Burlington, New Jersey.

	C6	C8	C10
Chein Airflow, windup, and garage	300	450	600
Chein Army Truck, cannon on back, 8-1/2" long, tin, early	75	125	225
Chein Army Truck, Mack, canvas top, 8" long	105	158	210
Chein Army Truck, open bed, 8-1/2" long, tin, early	90	135	235
Chein "Dan-Dee Dump Truck" windup	200	300	500
Chein "Greyhound" Bus, 9" long windup	120	200	400
Chein "Greyhound Lines" Push Toy, 9" long	175	300	425

Chein Army Truck, open bed, 8-1/2" long. Photo by Ed Poole.

Chein Macks, L to R: Army Truck, 8-1/2" long, Moving & Storage van, "Ice" truck, 8-1/2" long. Photo by Bob Smith.

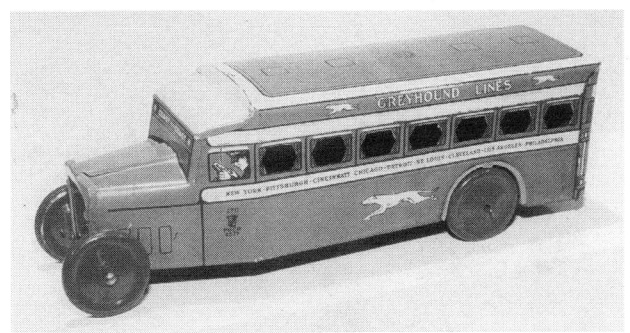

Chein "Greyhound Lines" push toy, 9" long. Photo by Bob Smith.

CHEIN HERCULES "C" CAB MACK TRUCKS

By Bob Smith

Chein introduced the Hercules series vehicles in 1925, the first model being the Dump Truck. It was made entirely of light-weight stamped-steel (heavy-gauge tin). Chein made at least 14 different Hercules models; the smallest being 17 inches long and stretching to 30 inches with the C-Cab Bull Dog Mack mobile clam truck (including boom). These toys generally retailed between $1 and $1.25. They were manufactured until the mid-1930s.

BIOGRAPHY: Bob Smith began collecting toys in 1978, after being influenced by some old friends who were members of the Genesee Valley Antique Toy Association (GVATA). Starting out by collecting Dinky Toys, he soon expanded his interests to Tootsie Toys, early Hill-Climber vehicles, pre-war tin cars, and early windup toys. He joined the GVATA and became its president for 10 years. Smith retired from the automobile business in 1991 after 27 years in auto sales. He now devotes full-time to the toy hobby. He promotes his well-known toy show in Rochester, New York. The RATS (Rochester Antique Toy Show) has grown to be one of the largest in the U.S. and is held twice a year (in June and November). Smith's articles about old toys and his antique toy ads are seen in numerous collectors magazines, which bring him in contact with collectors through out the world. Bob lives in Fairport, New York, with his wife Roberta and their two sons, Aaron and Evan.

Bob Smith

	C6	C8	C10
Chein Hercules Crane, 23" long, c.1925	125	200	300
Chein Hercules Dump Truck No. 250, open cab, 18" long, c.1925	400	550	750
Chein Hercules Fire Pumper No. 650, 18" long, c.1926	650	1050	1600

Chein Hercules Crane. Photo by Bob Smith.

Chein Hercules Fire Pumper No. 650. Photo by Bob Smith.

Chein Hercules Dump Truck No. 250 with original box. Photo by Bob Smith.

Chein Hercules Mack Coal Truck. Courtesy Bob Smith.

Chein Hercules Mack Army Truck. Courtesy Bob Smith.

Chein Hercules Mack Dump Truck. Courtesy Bob Smith.

Chein Hercules Mack Crane Truck No. 1100. Photo by Bob Smith.

Chein Hercules Mack Ice Truck. Courtesy Bob Smith.

	C6	C8	C10
Chein Hercules Mack Army Truck, 19-3/4 " long. Brown with canvas cover	350	600	1200
Chein Hercules Mack Coal Truck, 20" long, black cab, chassis, green bed. Tin coal chute, chute door opens	550	800	1300
Chein Hercules Mack Crane Truck No. 1100, 18" long	750	1250	1800
Chein Hercules Mack Dump Truck, 20" long. Black cab, chassis, red dump body. Tailgate opens	350	550	875
Chein Hercules Mack Ice Truck, 19-1/2" long. Black cab, green cargo box, step plate at rear of bed	550	800	1300
Chein Hercules Mack Log Truck, 18-1/2" long, all black	750	1100	1600

	C6	C8	C10
Chein Hercules Mack Mobile Clam Truck, 30" long (including boom). Green, red, black	No Price Found		
Chein Hercules Mack Motor Express Truck, 19-1/2" long. Black cab, orange stake bed	550	900	1350

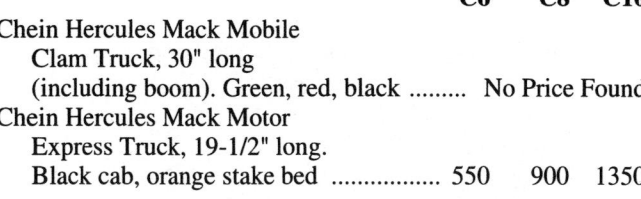

Chein Hercules Mack Mobile Clam Truck. Courtesy Bob Smith.

Chein Hercules Mack Log Truck. Courtesy Bob Smith.

Chein Hercules Mack Motor Express Truck with original box. Photo by Bob Smith.

Chein Hercules Mack Motor Express Truck. Courtesy Bob Smith.

Chein Hercules Mack Oil Tank Truck. Courtesy Bob Smith.

Chein Hercules Mack Ready-Mixed Concrete Truck. Courtesy Bob Smith.

	C6	C8	C10
Chein Hercules Mack Oil Tank Truck, 19" long. Black and orange	600	850	1350
Chein Hercules Mack Ready-Mixed Concrete Truck, 17" long. Deluxe model. Orange/black litho, rotating drum	750	1150	1800
Chein Hercules Mack Wrecking Truck, 23-1/2" long (including tow boom). Black cab, chassis, tow boom, red bed	550	800	1300
Chein Hercules Motor Express Semi-Truck No. 112, driver printed on glass, 15-1/2" long, c.1934	450	700	900

	C6	C8	C10
Chein Hercules Packard Dump Truck	250	375	500
Chein Hercules No. 8 Racer, 20" long. Driver, spare tire (mounted on rear). Red with yellow trim	700	1200	1800
Chein Hercules Roadster, 18" long. Red & black. Rumble seat, luggage rack	475	715	950
Chein Hercules Roadster, color variation of above, in green or yellow w/black fenders	550	800	1200
Chein Hercules "The Royal Blue Line" Pullman Bus, 18" long. Gray, red, black	750	1200	1750

Chein Hercules Mack Wrecking Truck. Courtesy Bob Smith.

Chein Hercules Motor Express semi-truck No. 112. Photo by Bob Smith.

Chein Hercules No. 8 Racer. Courtesy Bob Smith.

Chein Hercules Roadster. Courtesy Bob Smith.

Chein, L to R: Hercules Roadster; color variation in yellow. Photo by Bob Smith.

Chein Hercules "The Royal Blue Line" Pullman Bus. Courtesy Bob Smith.

	C6	C8	C10
Chein Hercules Wrecking Truck, open cab, 18" long	500	750	1250
Chein "Junior Truck," 1920s	90	150	250
Chein "Junior Oil Tank" Truck, 8-1/2" long, 1920s	90	150	250
Chein Limo, tin windup, 1930s, 7" long	225	338	450
Chein Mack Army Truck, 8-1/2" long	200	300	425
Chein Mack "Ice" Truck, 8-1/2" long	225	325	475
Chein Mack Moving & Storage Van	400	500	675
Chein "Peanuts" Bus, "Happiness Is An Annual Outing"	No Price Found		

Chein Hercules Wrecking Truck. Photo by Bob Smith.

Chein Army Truck, open bed, 8-1/2" long. Photo by Ed Poole.

Chein "Peanuts" Bus. Courtesy Continental Hobby House.

Chein Racer "52." Photo by Bob Smith.

Chein "Rapid Delivery" Truck No. 10. Photo by Bob Smith.

Chein Sedan, 6-window, 8-1/2" long. Photo by Bob Smith.

Chein Woodie Sedan, tin windup, with Chein Garage (no price found on latter). Photo by Dave Leopard.

	C6	C8	C10
Chein "Playland Whip" No. 340, 4 bumpem cars, windup	400	600	800
Chein "Racer No. 3," 1920s, 6-1/2" long windup	150	250	350
Chein Racer "52," tin windup, 6-1/2"	90	150	275
Chein "Rapid Delivery" Truck No. 10, tin windup	275	425	600

	C6	C8	C10
Chein Sedan, 6-window, 8-1/2" long, tin windup, c.1920s	250	475	675
Chein Roadster, tin litho, c.1925, 8-1/2" long	315	472	630
Chein Taxi, 7" long windup, 1920s	185	325	450
Chein Touring Car, tin litho, 7" long	250	375	500
Chein Woodie Sedan, tin windup, 5-1/4"	48	72	95
Chein Woodie Station Wagon, windup	100	150	200

CIJ
(France)

	C6	C8	C10
CIJ (France) P2 Alfa Romeo, c/w motor, hand- painted, hinged filler caps, moveable steering wheel, 20-1/2" long	1200	2000	2700

CITROEN
(France)

	C6	C8	C10
CITROEN (France) Fire Truck, c/w, removable hose reel	650	1100	1600
Citroen Truck, open bed, windup, door opens, 16-1/2" long	550	850	1300

CLARK, DAVID P. & CO.
(Dayton, Ohio, c.1898-1909)
By Bob Smith

D.P. Clark was the first manufacturer to use the heavy cast-iron flywheel on friction-drive Hill Climber toys, patented by Israel and Edith Boyer. The cars and trucks were made of heavy sheet metal, wood, and cast iron. Clark also made trains, animals, and other novelty toys with the friction mechanism. William Schieble, who was a partner in the company, bought Clark's half of the business in 1909. Schieble then changed the firm's name to the Schieble Toy and Novelty Co. Schieble filed for bankruptcy in 1931.

Back on his own, Clark went on to begin a new business. Naming his company the "Dayton Friction Toy Works," Clark felt free to use the patents from the now Schieble Toy Co. Lawsuits followed; Schieble was the winner. Clark sold the Dayton Toy Works to Nelson Talbot in 1924. He passed away soon thereafter. The company survived for 11 more years.

	C6	C8	C10
Clark No. 2 Automobile, 10-1/4" long	307	460	615
Clark No. 10 "Automobile" with driver, c.1908, 8-1/4" long	325	488	650
Clark Electric Runabout. Flywheel drive, 2 c.i. lady riders, wd., sheet mtl. & c.i. construction. Red/black/gold, 7-1/2" long, c.1902	550	800	1175
Clark Fire Hook & Ladder, c.1908, driver, 19" long	600	1000	1400

	C6	C8	C10
Clark Horseless Carriage. First toy with flywheel drive. Wood, tin & c.i. const. Blue/red, came lady passenger & driver, 11-1/2" long, c.1898	650	900	1200
Clark Horseless Carriage Push Toy, Spring suspension no flywheel mechanism. Wood, tin & c.i. const., green/red/yellow, 11" long. Possibly the first Clark toy. Patented November 2, 1897	450	675	900

	C6	C8	C10
Clark Open Touring Car. Flywheel drive, tin head lamps, red, 8" c.1903	238	360	475
Clark Police Patrol, Flywheel drive, five riders, red/gold, 9-1/2" long, c.1900	500	750	1050
Clark Runabout, Flywheel drive, wood head lamps, red, 7-3/4" long. c.1902	300	450	600
Clark Runabout, Flywheel drive, wd., sheet mtl. & c.i. const., red, 7-1/4" long, c.1903	250	375	500
Clark Steam Pumper. Flywheel drive, gold/red, 11" long, c.1908	300	450	600
Clark Steam Pumper. Flywheel drive. Wood, sheet metal & cast iron construction. Red, silver & gold, 10-1/4" long, c.1903	650	1050	1500

Clark No. 2 Automobile. Courtesy Joe and Sharon Freed.

What appears to be a variation (note the canopy) of D.P. Clark's No. 2 Automobile. No price found. Courtesy B.R. Blaydes.

Clark Electric Runabout, c.1902, 7-3/4" long. Photo by Bob Smith.

Clark Horseless Carriage: First toy with flywheel drive; 11-1/2" long. Photo by Bob Smith.

Clark Horseless Carriage Push Toy: Possibly the first Clark toy; 11" long.

Clark Police Patrol, c.1900, 9-1/2" long. Photo by Bob Smith.

Clark Open Touring Car, c.1903, 8" long. Photo by Bob Smith.

Clark Runabout, c.1903, 7-1/4" long. Photo by Bob Smith.

Clark Runabout, c.1902, 7-3/4" long. Photo by Bob Smith.

Clark Steam Pumper, c.1908, 11" long. Photo by Bob Smith.

Clark Steam Pumper, c.1903, 10-1/4" long. Photo by Bob Smith.

Hill-Climbing Friction Toys

No. 250. Chemical Engine.

10¾ inches long.
4   "   wide.
7½   "   high.

Equipped with ladder and chemical reservoir.

Packed 2 dozen in case.

Price, Doz., List..**$11.50**

No. 96. Automobile.

12¾ inches long.
4¾   "   wide.
7½   "   high.

Miniature representation of latest style Automobile. Runs forward, backward or in a circle.

Packed 2 dozen in case.

Price, Doz., List..**$16.50**

No. 100. Battleship.

19   inches long.
4   "   wide.
8¾   "   high.

Made of Sheet Steel, and painted gray. Boat rocks while in motion to reproduce actual sailing.

Has 4 Guns and 2 Turrets.
Packed 2 dozen in case.

Price, Doz., List..**$16.50**

No. 4. Hook and Ladder.

19½ inches long.
3¼   "   wide.
6¾   "   high.

Equipped with 3 ladders, and may be used for scaling purposes. Automatic gong that rings while machine is in operation.

Packed 2 dozen in case.

Price, Doz., List..**$16.50**

No. 1. Locomotive.

21   inches long.
5½   "   wide.
7⅛   "   high.

Representation of large American Locomotive. Capable of pulling ten cars.
Automatic Bell.

Packed 2 dozen in case.

Price, Doz., List..**$16.50**

No. 2. Automobile.

10¼ inches long.
3¾   "   wide.
7   "   high.

Contains four Passengers. Up-to-date equipment.

Packed 2 dozen in case.

Price, Doz., List..**$16.50**

No. 3. Fire Engine.

11½ inches long.
4   "   wide.
8   "   high.

Made of Sheet Steel. Automatic Gong that rings while engine is in motion.

Packed 2 dozen in case.

Price, Doz., List..**$16.50**

No. 310. Automobile.

17   inches long.
7   "   wide.
11   "   high.

Miniature reproduction of finest automobiles on the market. Carries six passengers.

Packed one-half dozen in case.

Price, Doz., List..**$72.00**

A page from a 1908 toy catalog showing D.P. Clark's Hill-Climbing friction toys. The numbers and descriptions appear to be the manufacturer's own.

Clark, David P. & Co.  131

Hill-Climbing Friction Toys

No. 10. "Automobile."
8½ inches long.
3½ " wide.
7½ " high.
Imitation of our modern Runabouts.
Packed 2 dozen in case.
Price, Doz., List... **$8.30**

No. 15. "Pullman Car."
13 inches long.
3½ " wide.
6 " high.
Substantially made and nicely painted.
Carries 6 passengers.
Packed 2 dozen in case.
Price, Doz., List... **$8.30**

No. 25. "Automobile."
9 inches long.
4½ " wide.
6 " high.
A strong, durable toy.
Carries 3 passengers.
Attractively painted.
Packed 2 dozen in case.
Price, Doz., List... **$8.30**

No. 35. "Cruiser."
13 inches long.
3 " wide.
7 " high.
Constructed of sheet steel.
Equipped with 4 lifeboats.
Packed 2 dozen in case.
Price, Doz., List... **$8.30**

No. 40. "Scorcher."
11 inches long.
4 " wide.
5½ " high.
A perfect model of up-to-date racers.
Speedy machine.
Packed 2 dozen in case.
Price, Doz., List... **$8.30**

No. 20. Police Patrol.
10½ inches long.
7½ " wide.
6 " high.
Made of steel. Equipped with 2 hand-cuffed prisoners, officer and chauffeur.
Packed 2 dozen in crate.
Price, Doz., List... **$8.30**

No. 220. "Patrol."
10½ inches long.
4 " wide.
7½ " high.
Very good design.
Two prisoners, 1 driver and 1 officer.
Packed 2 dozen in case.
Price, Doz., List... **$11.50**

No. 210. Combination.
13 inches long.
4 " wide.
7 " high.
May be used as Ambulance, Moving Van or Delivery.
Nicely painted.
Packed 2 dozen in case.
Price, Doz., List... **$11.50**

A second page from a 1908 toys catalog showing D.P. Clark toys.

CLEVELAND TOY

	C6	C8	C10
Cle-Play Transport	No Price Found		
Racer, aluminum, steel wheels, c. 1935, 13" long	175	262	350

Cleveland Toy "Cle-Play Transport." Photo by Dave Leopard.

Cleveland Toy Racer. Courtesy David W. Mapes Auctions.

COHN

	C6	C8	C10
Cohn Fire Chief pull car No. 34, 1940s, metal, 9" long	80	120	160
Cohn "Superior Sales Service" Garage, tin	150	225	300

Cohn Fire Chief pull car No. 34. Courtesy Don Hultzman.

COMET-AUTHENTICAST

Comet-Authenticast, owned by the Slonim family, began toy-making (as Comet) in about 1940 in Queens, New York. Though it began with only toy soldiers, it switched to making ID models for the government, virtually as soon as WWII began. After the war, it sold them as toys. It seems to have gone out of business in the early 1960s. Its vehicles appear to sell in the $8-$10 range, and probably more for something rare, like the Lee tank. In recent times, Quality Castings of Alexandria, Virginia, has been reissuing these toys, using the original molds, in a generally $4-$6 range.

1/108 Scale Metal Identification Models by Comet/Authenticast NY, NY. Russian Vehicles and Soldiers of World War II. L to R - Back Row: 5200 KV-1 Heavy Tank, 5201 KV-2 Heavy Tank, 5202 Josef Stalin, 5203 T34 Medium Tank.
Middle: Russian soldiers by Holger Erikson sold by Comet in sets R1 through 8, the latter two containing tanks also. Standing figure offers scale for tanks at 20mm tall.
Front: 5204 T70 light tank, 5205 ST2 Armored Carrier, 5206 T34/85 medium tank, 5207 Josef Stalin III. Photo by Ed Poole.

1/108 Scale identification models of WWII Japanese tanks by Comet/Authenticast. Authenticast GI in photo is 23mm tall. L to R - Back Row: 5051 Amphibian Tankette, 5052 Tankette, 5053 Medium Tank. Front Row: 5054 Medium Tank, 5055 Tankette, 5056 light tank, 5057 heavy medium tank. Photo by Ed Poole.

1/108 Scale identification models of WWII Germany vehicles by Comet/Authenticast. Also show are Authenticast German soldiers up to 21mm tall. L to R - Back Row: 5100 PzKwIII, 5101 PzKwl, 5102 Panzerjager, 5103 PzKw IV G, 5104 PzKw IV F. Middle: 5105 PzKw II, 5106 PzKw III, 5107 Tiger, 5108 8-Wheeled Armored Car.
Front: 5109 Pz35T, 5110 Panther, 5111 Sturmgeschutz, 5112 Half-Track. Photo by Ed Poole.

1/108 U.S. ID Models by Comet/Authenticast. Soldiers were sculpted by Holger Eriksson; tallest 20mm, L to R - Back Row: 5156 General Pershing, 5166 General Chaffee, 5167 Slugger II, 5168 Slugger, 5169 76mm Sherman.
Front Row: 5170 Airborne Tank, 5171 Armored Car (Staghound), 5172 Armored Car (Twin 50), 5173 DUKW, 5174 M32 Tank Recovery. Photo by Ed Poole.

Cold War U.S. 1/108 ID Models (cont'd); standing figures 15mm tall. Quality castings models substituted for nos. 5193, 5195 and 5196. By now Comet was producing for collectors and so belatedly brought out 5192 M3 Medium Tank. L to R - Back Row: 5190 T98 S.P. 105mm Gun, 5191 S.P. 155mm Howizer, 5192 M3 Tank, 5193 Hawk Missile - Transporter, Launcher and Mobile Radar with crew.
Front: 5194 Honest John Launcher and crew, 5195 Nike-Ajax Launcher and crew, 5196 M42 Duster Twin 40mm AA, 5197 Ontos S.P. Rocket Launcher. Photo by Ed Poole.

1/108 Scale identification models of WWII U.S. Vehicles Comet/Authenticast. Authenticast GI with Mine Detector is 20mm tall. L to R - Back Row: 5150 75mm Gun on Half Track, 5151 Heavy Tank M6, 5152 Sherman Tank, 5153 Greyhound Armored Car, 5154 Half-Track.
Middle: 5155 Hellcat, 5156 Priest, 5157 General Scott, 5158 General Stuart, 5159 Wolverine.
Front: 5160 Jeep, 5161 Weasel, 5162 Scout Car, 5163 Quack, 5164 King Kong. Photo by Ed Poole.

1/108 U.S. ID Models by Comet/Authenticast. Marching GIs are 20mm tall. Quality castings are shown in place of Authenticast 5177 and 5178. L to R - Back Row: 5175 LVTAA Amphibian Tank, 5176 LVT Amphibian, 5177 Utility Tank, 5178 Medium Tank 105mm.
Front: 5180 Walker Bulldog, 5179 General Patton, 5181 6x6 Truck, 5182 Command Car, 5183 Troop Carrier. Photo by Ed Poole.

1/108 Scale U.S. ID Models of the Cold War Era. Quality castings model is substituted for Authenticast 5189. Figures are 15mm tall. L to R - Back Row: 5184 Trailer, 5185 Weapons Carrier, 5186 M-67 Tank, 5187 M48 Tank, 5188 M103 Heavy Tank. Front Row: 5189 Atomic Cannon. Photo by Ed Poole.

The 1/108 Series Continues: Quality Castings of Alexandria VA not only reproduces but upgrades the Authenticast line. Here are some of the original German pieces. L to R - Back Row: 4017 Wespe, 4018 7.5 PAK, 4023 Opel Blitz, 4026 88 Flak on bogie wheels and off.
Middle: 4027 2 CM FLAF on & off trailer, 4031 3.7 PAK, 4035 7.5 INF gun, 4036 Kubelwagen, 4037 BMW cycle with 4037A MB variant, 4041 Pz38t.
Front: 4042 Wirblewing FLAK, 4044 Hetzer, 4045 Marder III, 4046 250/I Halftrack, 4049 Hummell, RFE Lost Silver DAK (added for scale 22mm tall). Photo by Ed Poole.

Quality Casting 1/108 German (continued). L to R - Back Row: 4051 5cm PAK, 4052 222 Armored Car, 4054 Brumbar, 4055 234/I Armored Car, 4058 Tiger II (Porsche Turret).
Front: 4061 7/2 Halftrack w/3.7 FLAK, 4062 2 cm QUAD FLAF and trailer, 4063 3.7 FLAK on trailer, 4064 88 PAK, 4065 105 Howitzer, 4066 Ferdinand, 4067 Elefant, 4068 250/7 Mortar Halftrack, oversize Authenticast (Erikson) GI 20mm tall for comparison. Quality makes many troops nearer to correct scale but squat and thick bodied. Photo by Ed Poole.

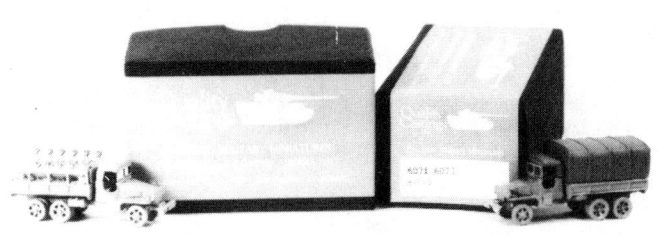

Quality Castings 1/108 Numbers 6033 (L) and 6031 (R) with boxes typically packed several kits each. These models replace old 6031 and 6033 which were Authenticast types 5181 and 5183 in the Quality line. Quality Castings' address is P.O. Box 11714, Alexandria, V, 22312. Photo by Ed Poole.

Two Comet/Authenticast 1/108 Models and boxes: Comet address given as NY, NY and Authenticast as Richmond Hill, NY; both indicate "Design Copyrighted 1943." 5009 Cromwell on left and 5010 Churchill on right. Photo by Ed Poole.

CONVERSE

Beginning in 1878, Converse helped make Winchendon, Massachusetts, "Toy Town U.S.A." It made wooden, tin, and steel toys and was felled in 1934 by the Depression. It was originally owned by Morton E. Converse.

	C6	C8	C10
Converse Auto with fringe on top, 3-seat, 1905, painted, pressed steel clockwork, rubber tires	600	900	1200
Converse Fire Engine Ladder Truck, bell, wooden headlight, 10", 1915	1250	1875	2500
Converse Fire Engine Ladder Truck, c.1915, wood headlamps, 18" long	1800	3000	4250
Converse Parcel Post, 1920s, 15" long	1500	2500	3700
Converse Pickup Truck, very early, open cab	500	750	1000
Converse Pierce-Arrow open touring car, steers	1200	2200	3000

	C6	C8	C10
Converse Roadster, 15-1/2" long, 1908 windup, open cab	1200	2200	3000
Converse Touring Auto, open, 4-seater	1200	2200	3000
Converse Touring Auto, 1910, pressed steel, canvas roof	1300	2200	3000
Converse Transitional Taxi, clockwork, 10-1/2" long	525	770	1050
Conway Packard Convertible, 1948, 12" long, clockwork, electric lights	175	263	350

Converse Transitional Taxi, 10-1/2" long. Courtesy Sotheby's NY.

COR-COR

According to Margaret E. Holland (as reported by Ross Hermann in the July 27, 1992 *Antique News*), the granddaughter of Cor-Cor founder Louis A. Corcoran, this Washington, Indiana firm began on 21st Street in 1926, then expanded to East 3rd and Vantress, and after a fire, built its final plant on Front Street. At this latter location the company changed its name to Corcoran Metal Products. At its height, the firm employed up to 590 people (in 1939 Corcoran, for obvious reasons, was named his county's "most valuable citizen"). Corcoran retired in 1941 because of failing health and died in 1945. His toys are marked "Cor-Cor" on the wheels.

	C6	C8	C10
Cor-Cor Airflow windup, electric lights, 18" long	1000	1600	2200
Cor-Cor Army Truck	No Price Found		
Cor-Cor Bus, 23" long	325	488	650
Cor-Cor Bus, electric lights	500	750	1000
Cor-Cor Chrysler Airflow	600	800	1200
Cor-Cor DeSoto Airflow	650	850	1250
Cor-Cor Dump Truck, dumps back or side to side, 23" long	225	338	450

	C6	C8	C10
Cor-Cor Fire Truck, 24" long	200	300	400
Cor-Cor Graham Paige sedan, 20" long, electric	600	1000	1600
Cor-Cor Ice Truck	No Price Found		
Cor-Cor Semi Truck	No Price Found		
Cor-Cor "Supplee Ice Cream" Truck	No Price Found		
Cor-Cor Van, painted metal, c.1928, 23" long	250	380	525

Cor-Cor "Supplee Ice Cream" truck. Photo by Tim Oei.

CORGI

(Britain)

Corgi is the registered trademark of Playcraft Toys. Its vehicles first appeared in 1956. Since Corgis are generally sold mint in the box, those are the prices shown here.

	MIB
Corgi 10 Tank and Transporter	150
Corgi 26 Beach Buggy & Sailboat	80
Corgi 34 David Brown 1412 Tractor & Trailer	80
Corgi 50 Massey-Ferguson tractor	38
Corgi 58 Beast Carrier	60
Corgi 61 Four Furrow Plow	35
Corgi 62 Farm Tipper Trailer	20
Corgi 64 Jeep FC150 Conveyor	100
Corgi 69 Massey Ferguson Tractor	120
Corgi 73 Massey Ferguson Tractor w/saw	110
Corgi 74 Ford Tractor with haybine scoop	100
Corgi 109 Pennyburn workman's trailer	35
Corgi 150 Vanwall	55
Corgi 151 Lotus Eleven	100
Corgi 152 BRM Formula 1	80
Corgi 152 Ferrari 312 B2 Formula 1	40
Corgi 153 Surtees T.S. 9b racer	45
Corgi 153 Bluebird	120
Corgi 154 Ferrari F-1	40
Corgi 154 Lotus	45
Corgi 155 Shado racer	45
Corgi 156 Cooper Maserati	40
Corgi 156 Embassy Shadow racer	50
Corgi 158 Lotus Climax F-1	50
Corgi 158 Elf Tyrrell Ford F-1	45
Corgi 159 Patrick Eagle Indy Car	45
Corgi 160 Hesketh 308 Formula 1 Car	30
Corgi 161 Santa Pod Commuter Dragster	45
Corgi 162 Quartermaster Dragster	38
Corgi 163 Capri, Glow Worm dragster	75
Corgi 164 Wild Honey Dragster	55
Corgi 166 Ford Mustang Organ Grinder Drag Funny	38
Corgi 167 U.S. racing buggy	42
Corgi 169 Arnold Sundquist's Jet Car	55
Corgi 200 Mini 1000	45
Corgi 201 Austin Cambridge	165
Corgi 202 Morris Cowley	132
Corgi 204 Morris Mini-Minor	75
Corgi 206 Hillman Husky	120
Corgi 208 Jaguar Saloon	132
Corgi 210 Citroen D.S. 19	100
Corgi 211 Studebaker Golden Hawk	110
Corgi 214 Ford Thunderbird	110
Corgi 215 Ford Thunderbird Open Sports	120
Corgi 217 Fiat 1800	75
Corgi 218 Aston Martin DB4	60
Corgi 219 Plymouth Wagon	120
Corgi 220 Chevrolet Impala	67
Corgi 221 Chevy Yellow Cab	100
Corgi 222 Renault FloRide	82
Corgi 223 Chevrolet Police Car	125
Corgi 224 Bentley Continental	125
Corgi 225 Austin Seven mini	100
Corgi 226 Morris Mini-minor	75

	MIB
Corgi 228 Volvo P1800	90
Corgi 229 Chevy Corvair	85
Corgi 230 Mercedes 220	95
Corgi 232 Fiat 2100	110
Corgi 233 Heinkel Car	85
Corgi 234 Ford Consul Classic	80
Corgi 235 Olds Super 88	100
Corgi 236 Motor School Car	100
Corgi 237 Oldsmobile Sheriff Car	100
Corgi 238 Jaguar Mark X	90
Corgi 239 VW Kharmann Ghia	90
Corgi 241 Ghia L6.4	68
Corgi 245 Buick Riviera	68
Corgi 246 Chrysler Imperial	98
Corgi 247 Mercedes 600 Pullman	75
Corgi 248 Chevrolet Impala	85
Corgi 249 Mini Cooper Deluxe Wicker Work	120
Corgi 252 Rover 2000	80
Corgi 253 Mercedes 220 Coupe	85
Corgi 256 VW Safari	225
Corgi 258 The Saint's Volvo	135
Corgi 259 Penguinmobile	65
Corgi 259 LeDande Coupe	105
Corgi 260 007 Aston Martin	275
Corgi 260 Metropolis Buick	60
Corgi 260 Renault 16	50
Corgi 261 Spider-Man Jeep	195
Corgi 261 James Bond Aston Martin	280
Corgi 262 Lincoln Continental	110
Corgi 263 Rambler Marlin	65
Corgi 263 Captain America Jetmobile	95
Corgi 264 Olds Toronado	85
Corgi 265 Supermobile	95
Corgi 266 Chitty Chitty Bang Bang	380
Corgi 267 Batmobile	325
Corgi 268 Green Hornet Black Beauty	450
Corgi 269 James Bond Lotus Esprit	110
Corgi 270 James Bond Silver Aston Martin	180
Corgi 271 Aston Martin (first)	150
Corgi 272 James Bond Citroen 2CV	90
Corgi 273 Rolls Royce Silver Shadow	90
Corgi 274 Bentley Series T	90
Corgi 275 Rover 2000 TC	68
Corgi 276 Olds Toronado	75
Corgi 277 Monkeemobile	410
Corgi 280 Rolls Royce Silver Shadow	40
Corgi 281 Rover 2000TC	60
Corgi 281 Austin Metro Royal Wedding	25
Corgi 282 Mini Cooper	50
Corgi 283 DAF City Car	50
Corgi 284 Citroen sm	50
Corgi 285 Mercedes Benz 240D	30
Corgi 285 Jaguar XJ12C	50
Corgi 287 Citroen Dyane	35

	MIB
Corgi 290 Kojak's Buick	70
Corgi 291 AMC Pacer X	25
Corgi 292 Starsky & Hutch Ford Torino	115
Corgi 293 Renault 5TS	15
Corgi 300 Chevrolet Stingray	100
Corgi 301 Iso Grifo 7 litre	52
Corgi 302 VW Polo	15
Corgi 302 Hillman Hunter	105
Corgi 303 Porsche 924 Rallye	30
Corgi 304 Mercedes Benz 300SL Hardtop Roadster	100
Corgi 306 Morris Marina	60
Corgi 310 Corvette Sting Ray	80
Corgi 311 Ford Capri 3 litre	50
Corgi 312 Jaguar E. Competition	105
Corgi 312 Marcos Mantis	55
Corgi 313 Ford Cortina w/Graham Hill figure	70
Corgi 314 Ferrari Berlinetta 250LM	55
Corgi 315 Simca 1000 Competition	80
Corgi 316 N.S.U. Sport Prinz	72
Corgi 318 Lotus Elan	105
Corgi 319 GT Miura-Lamborghini	60
Corgi 320 The Saint's Jaguar	95
Corgi 321 Porsche 924	30
Corgi 322 Rover 2000 Monte Carlo	150
Corgi 323 Citroen DS19 Monte Carlo	140
Corgi 324 Ferrari Daytona	35
Corgi 325 Ford Mustang Fastback	85
Corgi 327 MGB	125
Corgi 329 Mustang Mach	40
Corgi 330 Porsche	55
Corgi 331 Ford Capri GT	52
Corgi 332 Lancia Fulvia Sport Zagato	65
Corgi 334 Mini-Cooper Magnifique	48
Corgi 335 Jaguar E2x2	140
Corgi 336 007 Toyota 2000	465
Corgi 337 Corvette Sting Ray	85
Corgi 338 Chevy SS 350 Camaro	90
Corgi 339 Monte Carlo Mini	200
Corgi 341 Mini Marcos GT	60
Corgi 342 The Professionals Ford Capri	100
Corgi 342 Lamborghini	125
Corgi 343 Firebird	62
Corgi 344 Ferrari 206 DinoSport	62
Corgi 345 MGB-GT Competition	90
Corgi 347 Chevy Astro	65
Corgi 348 Vegas Thunderbird	72
Corgi 352 RAF Staff Car	105
Corgi 358 Olds H.Q. Staff Car, Military	150
Corgi 359 Army Field Kitchen	175
Corgi 370 Ford Mustang	16
Corgi 372 Lancia Fulvia Sport	35
Corgi 373 VW 1200 Police Car	60
Corgi 373 Peugeot 505	16
Corgi 377 Marco 3 litre	58
Corgi 378 Ferrari 308 GTS	15
Corgi 380 Alfa Romeo Pinin Farina	38
Corgi 381 GP Beach Buggy	36
Corgi 382 Porsche 911S	54
Corgi 383 VW1200	47
Corgi 384 Renault II GTL	16
Corgi 385 Mercedes 190E	10
Corgi 385 Porsche 917	27

	MIB
Corgi 386 Bertone Runabout	40
Corgi 389 Reliant Bond Bug	48
Corgi 392 Bertone "Shake" Buddy	30
Corgi 393 Mercedes Benz 350SL	48
Corgi 396 Datsun 240Z	50
Corgi 397 Can-Am Porsche 917	30
Corgi 400 VW 1300 Motor School	70
Corgi 402 Ford Cortina Police Car	50
Corgi 403 Ski Dumper	40
Corgi 405 Ford Transit Milk	20
Corgi 405 Chevrolet Ambulance	45
Corgi 406 Land Rover	80
Corgi 411 Lucozade Van	150
Corgi 412 Mercedes-Benz 240D Police	36
Corgi 413 Mazda Maintenance Truck	40
Corgi 414 Coast Guard Jaguar XJ	45
Corgi 416 R.A.C. Rescue Land Rover	72
Corgi 418 Austin Taxi	42
Corgi 419 Ford Zephyr Patrol Car	90
Corgi 420 Ford Airborn Caravan	90
Corgi 421 Bedford "Evening Standard"	200
Corgi 422 Riot Police Armored Car	40
Corgi 422 Corgi Toy Van	350
Corgi 424 Security Van	40
Corgi 425 Booking Office	420
Corgi 426 Citroen Safari	90
Corgi 428 Mr. Softee Truck	120
Corgi 430 T-Bird 1958 Bermuda Taxi	115
Corgi 433 VW Delivery Van	80
Corgi 434 Charlie's Angels Van	65
Corgi 435 Superman Van	60
Corgi 436 Spider-Man Van	45
Corgi 437 Cadillac Ambulance	128
Corgi 438 Land Rover	78
Corgi 443 Plymouth Station Wagon, U.S. Mail	110
Corgi 445 Plymouth Sports Station Wagon	100
Corgi 447 Walls Ice Cream Van	185
Corgi 448 Police Set	175
Corgi 450 Mini Van	80
Corgi 455 Karier Bantam	165
Corgi 457 ERF Platform Lorry	75
Corgi 458 ERF Earth Dumper	75
Corgi 459 Raygo Rascal	30
Corgi 460 Neville Cement Tipper	115
Corgi 463 Commer Ambulance	88
Corgi 464 Commer Police Van	128
Corgi 468 Routemaster Bus, Outspan	50
Corgi 470 Forward Control Jeep	45
Corgi 471 Smith's Mobile Canteen "Joe's Diner"	165
Corgi 471 London Transport Silver Jubilee bus	38
Corgi 472 "Vote for Corgi" Land Rover	130
Corgi 474 Walls Ice Cream (w/chimes)	225
Corgi 475 Safari	125
Corgi 477 Breakdown Truck	80
Corgi 478 Hydraulic Tower Wagon	90
Corgi 479 Commer Mobile Camera Van	145
Corgi 482 Range Rover Ambulance	45
Corgi 487 Chipperfield Circus Range Rover	140
Corgi 490 VW Breakdown Van	100
Corgi 491 Ford Estate Car	85
Corgi 494 Bedford Tipper Truck	75
Corgi 497 Man From U.N.C.L.E	380

	MIB
Corgi 497 Ford Escort "Radio Rentals"	16
Corgi 500 Police Car	35
Corgi 501 Range Rover	9
Corgi 503 Giraffe Truck	195
Corgi 506 Police "Panda" IMP	65
Corgi 509 Porsche Targa Police Car	60
Corgi 511 Performing Poodles Truck	525
Corgi 524 Route Master Bus-Stevenson's	20
Corgi 529 Route Master Bus-Graham Ward Calendar	20
Corgi 530 Route Master Bus-Yorkshire Post	20
Corgi 702 Breakdown Truck	20
Corgi 802 Popeye Paddle Wagon	485
Corgi 805 Hardy Boys Rolls Royce	250
Corgi 809 Dick Dastardly Car	100
Corgi 811 J.B. Moon Buggy	495
Corgi 908 AMX Recovery Tank	75
Corgi 909 Tractor Gun & Trailer	110
Corgi 1100 Low Loader	180
Corgi 1100 Mack Transcontinental	95
Corgi 1101 Warner & Swasey Hydraulic Crane	70
Corgi 1102 Crane Fruehauf Bottom Dumper	75
Corgi 1103 Chubb Pathfinder Crash Truck	80
Corgi 1104 Bedford Horse Transporter	75
Corgi 1105 Car Transporter	250
Corgi 1106 Decca Radar Van	125
Corgi 1106 Mack Container Truck "ACL"	95
Corgi 1107 Euclid Bulldozer	275
Corgi 1109 Ford Semi-Trailer	90
Corgi 1110 Mobile Gas Tanker	225
Corge 1110 JCB Crawler Loader	65
Corgi 1111 MF Combine Harvester	190

	MIB
Corgi 1116 Shelvoke Trash Truck	45
Corgi 1123 Circus Cage Wagon	165
Corgi 1126 Ecurie Ecosse Transporter	225
Corgi 1127 Simon Snorkel Fire Engine	100
Corgi 1128 Priestman Cub Shovel	60
Corgi 1130 Chipperfield Horse Transporter	325
Corgi 1137 Ford Semi-Trailer Truck	240
Corgi 1138 Ford Car Transporter	145
Corgi 1139 Chipperfield Circus Menagerie Truck	595
Corgi 1142 Ford Holmes Wrecker	130
Corgi 1143 American LaFrance Fire Engine	125
Corgi 1144 Berliet Wrecker Truck	80
Corgi 1145 Mercedes Unimog-Goose Dumper	50
Corgi 1146 Tri-Deck Car Transporter	185
Corgi 1147 Scammell Tractor & Trailer, "Ferrymasters"	120
Corgi 1150 Unimog Snow Plow	50
Corgi 1151 Mack Exxon Tank Truck	63
Corgi 1152 Mack Tanker, "Esso"	75
Corgi 1154 Mack Crane Truck	150
Corgi 1156 Volvo Concrete Mixer	60
Corgi 1159 Ford Car Transporter	75
Corgi 1160 Gulf Petrol Truck	90
Corgi 1163 Human Cannonball Truck	85
Corgi 1170 Ford Car Transporter	50
Corgi 1192 Ford Van "Lucas"	15
Corgi 6547 Ford Tractor-Conveyor on Trailer	150
Corgi 9001 1927 Bentley	65
Corgi 9011 1915 Model T Ford	40
Corgi 9013 1915 Ford	70
Corgi 9031 1910 Renault	65
Corgi 9041 1912 Rolls Royce	63

COURTLAND TOYS (WALT REACH)

by Joe and Sharon Freed, copyright 1996

Walter Rudolph Reach, founder of Courtland toys, was born in Jersey City, New Jersey, in 1905. Educated in local schools, Reach eventually worked his way to Camden, New Jersey, where, in 1937, he opened a successful sign-painting business. Beyond the usual commercial trade, he performed extensive contract work for the Campbell Soup Company. In fact, he painted some of the early Campbell advertising signs now eagerly sought by advertising collectors. Within a few years, Reach, sensing a rising wave of patriotism within the country, began a second business—The Camden Flag and Banner Company, again taking advantage of his artistic skills. The early war years saw a decline in his work for Campbell, but the flag and banner business flourished.

In the summer of 1943, Reach's friend, Harold Salter, a salesman working for a well-known Philadelphia toy distributor, A. Ponnock & Sons, approached Reach for suggestions on how he might dispose of a railroad boxcar full of "prepared" cardboard. Reach acquired the cardboard at a bargain price, with the thought he'd find some way to capitalize on this potential windfall. He decided on cardboard toys. He quickly fashioned

two toys: a two-wheel rabbit cart and a horse cart. Sales success soon followed as a war-weary public, hungry for low-cost toys, snapped up the entire stock. Both toys sold well, although the horse cart was the more popular toy (it out-sold the rabbit toy).

With the capital from the cardboard toys, Reach founded the Courtland Manufacturing Company, incorporating on May 29, 1944. His friends and business associates formed the company's management team. 1944 was also the year of his first true Courtland toy. A 12-inch tractor and trailer truck, made entirely of wood and marked "Courtland" on the sides of the trailer, was introduced to the trade, and achieved widespread sales success. His wooden Courtland success was short-lived, as his connections with Campbell soon provided him with a ready supply of "rejected" tin from its canning process. (Additionally, over the next several years, Reach purchased "reject" tin-plate from J&L Steel of Bethlehem, Pennsylvania.) A Courtland line of tin toys quickly followed; by the late fall of 1945, several toy trucks and playsets fashioned from tin were introduced.

With Reach designing the toys, and his father Erwin as the plant's manager, Courtland was off and running. During 1945, toy production at the Haddon Avenue factory focused on 42 dedicated employees. Courtland would eventually employ more than 350 persons, most with family ties to each other, where father and son, mother and daughter teams were quite common. By late 1945, Courtland began installing mechanical motors in a select number of toys, boosting sales even higher. Courtland prospered with gross sales in 1946 exceeding $600,000. In 1946, Courtland toys could be found in 43 states and 13 foreign countries. As evidence of the swift and dynamic growth of the company, the top three domestic orders for tin toys in 1946 came from Sears, Roebuck & Co. of Chicago, for $21,827.26; Loft Candy Company, Long Island, New York, for $14,704.50; and Butler Brothers of Chicago, for $11,711.74.

Reach and his management staff instituted a "child toy testing" program at the plant, whereby a small room in the building was set aside for local children to evaluate the play value of new toy designs by playing with the toys. He observed the children at play to see which toys kept their interest and which toys were played with the least, or not selected for play at all. Reach, over the years, pointed with pride to his "child testing" program, believing that this type of testing was greatly responsible for his overall success.

1947 toy sales were five times greater than the same period the preceding year, and factory production was taxed to its production capacity of 20,000 toys a day. During that same year, Courtland's Export Division came into being under the direction of John H. Jackson. The Export Division, located in Basking Ridge, New Jersey, was tasked with the responsibility of coordinating all sales to foreign countries and to administer a newly negotiated contract with General Metal Toys LTD of Canada. Courtland had, in fact, just completed and shipped the first such order of Walt Reach Courtland Toys with the General Metal Toys LTD markings.

Over the next few years, Courtland introduced several toy innovations, including the streamline design of its trucks and cars and, most notably, the famous "Guaranteed For Life" mechanical motor. This motor, completely enclosed and designed for easy removal from the toy, was offered in both key-wind and friction action, and came with a colorful printed warranty with each toy sold. Hailed by the trade as a decisive marketing tool, the "Motor Guaranteed For Life" warranty provided buyers with the unique opportunity to exchange defective motors for new motors.

Gross sales of more than one million dollars was reported for the first time in 1948 as toy sales reached a total of $1,292,374.48. In 1949, sales rose to a staggering $1,906,378.22. Also, during 1949, Courtland Man-ufacturing moved to a newly renovated plant at 6th & Jefferson Street in Camden. During the planning phase for the renovated plant, Reach hired a manufacturing consultant to design the production assembly line so that an entire toy—from start to finish, including piece assembly (hand work), packaging, boxing, sealing, and labeling— could be completed with no toy ever leaving the flow of the production line.

Reach, having borrowed heavily to secure and outfit his new production facility, was hit a severe financial blow, when on, June 24, 1950, the United States, under a United Nations mandate, entered the Korean Conflict. Essential war materials, which included tin, were diverted to the war effort, effectively denying him the backbone of his toy production. The availability of tin for toy-making was reduced to a trickle, with the only source once again being "reject" tinplate. Recalling the early years of the company, this scenario was nothing new to him. What was new this time was that he found himself competing with other toy and novelty manufacturers across America for the meager supply of available tin.

A second, and more devastating blow to Courtland was the discovery, in the fall of 1950, of the introduction of counterfeit toys. These cheap, look-alike knock-offs, with inferior mechanical motors, were flooding the toy market under the Courtland name. The perpetrator(s), in addition to producing counterfeit Courtland toys, was also printing bogus "Motor Guaranteed For Life" warranty certificates. This caused a two-fold problem. Not only was Courtland faced with the loss of the sale of the toy, but it was also forced to exchange Courtland motors for defective motors, and there were many. To refuse this exchange, at least initially, would have, in all probability, destroyed the highly regarded guarantee. His initial thoughts were that the toys came from an Asian country, such as China or Japan. Subsequent investigating revealed the possibility the toys were coming from Canada, or at least entering the United States from Canada. (The mystery of where the toys originated and by whom, has never seen solved.)

With the combination of the effects of the war, the decline in sales due to counterfeit toys, and the need to pay the mortgage on the new plant, Reach suddenly found himself with a cash-flow problem. Searching desperately for funds, he turned to the Geo. Borgfeldt Company, a large, national toy distributor, to secure the necessary financial assistance. Besides the debt-service, one of the concessions he made to Borgfeldt was that the sole distribution of all Courtland toys went to Borgfeldt. Sales continued to sag, and Reach, desperate to hold the company together, approached persons, now known to be less than honorable, for help. Help they did…they helped themselves to his company by taking over the directorship and management positions, firing the original directors, and draining the company of its money by paying themselves high salaries and huge bonuses. Employee rosters were quickly reduced to a minimum.

Within two years, and without Reach, the fledgling toy empire with so much potential evaporated. Reach, however, was a fighter. Moving to Philadelphia with his family and dreams in 1953, he opened the Courtland Toy Company, attempting to remanufacture several of the original toys and a few new designs under that name; thus, the toys with the Courtland Toy Company, Philadelphia markings. By 1953, though, time had passed for tin-plate as a material for mass toy production. Plastics were in. Even though Reach had used some plastics in his original streamline Courtland designs produced in the 1949 to 1951 period, he could not retool for plastic-injection molding without considerable expense. Finally, Courtland Toys were truly committed to history and the drive to rival Louis Marx as America's toy king was no more.

Special thanks to Marie Reach, Walt's widow, for the above information. Marie, a most gracious lady, opened her home and her memories of Walt and his Courtland toys to us. Marie, herself employed at the Courtland plant in Camden, provided numerous documents, photographs, artifacts, and anecdotes for our future book on the history of Courtland toys. We want to express our sincere thanks to Marie.

Walt Reach, as shown in the July, 1946 Toys & Novelties. Courtesy Dick MacNary.

COURTLAND NON-POWERED VEHICLES

(List by Joe and Sharon Freed)

	C6	C8	C10
Courtland all-wood open high-side trailer, 13" long	500	750	1000
600 Courtland Open Van tractor-trailer L 13", W 3", H 3-1/4" 1946 retail price 49¢	125	200	300
610 Courtland Side Dump Tractor-trailer L 13", W 3", H 3-1/4" 1946 retail price 49¢	100	175	275
620 Courtland Log Truck Tractor-trailer. L 13", W 3", H 3-1/4" 1946 retail price 59¢	150	225	350
700 Courtland Side dump Tractor-trailer. L 13", W 3", H 3-1/4" 1946 retail price 49¢	125	200	325
800 Courtland Easter Greetings Rabbit Truck, 9" long	325	525	750

Courtland all-wood open high-side trailer. Courtesy Joe and Sharon Freed.

Courtland No. 610 Side Dump. Courtesy Joe and Sharon Freed.

620 Courtland (non-power). Courtesy Joe and Sharon Freed.

Courtland No. 800 Easter Greetings Rabbit Truck (non-power). Courtesy Joe and Sharon Freed.

The Courtland No. 900 Truck Assortment, non-powered, as found in July 1946 Toys & Novelties. Courtesy Dick MacNary.

Courtland, L to R: 900 Fire Patrol Truck; 900 Moving and Storage Truck. Courtesy Joe and Sharon Freed.

Courtland Tractor-Trailer, Same tractor as No. 2000 except marked "Loft-Fresh Candy." Courtesy Joe and Sharon Freed.

	C6	C8	C10
900 Courtland Truck Assortment, 4 trucks with box	No Price Found		
900 Courtland Ice Cream Truck, L 9", W 3", H 2-3/4", 1946 retail price 39¢	125	200	300
900 Courtland Moving and Storage Truck, 1946, retail price 39¢, L 9", W 3", H 2-3/4"	150	225	350
900 Courtland Fire Patrol No. 2 Truck, 1946, retail price 39¢, L 9", W 3", H 2-3/4"	100	175	275
900 Courtland Express and Hauling Truck, retail price 39¢, 1946, L 9", W 3", H 2-3/4"	100	175	275
1050 Courtland Logging Camp Train Set, 1946 retail price $1.79, L 26-3/4", W 3", H 3-1/4"	No Price Found		
1060 Courtland Trailer Truck Parade, 1946, retail price $1.79, L 13" W 3", H 3-1/4" ...	No Price Found		

	C6	C8	C10
1070 Courtland Big 4 Truck Parade, 1946 retail price $1.79, The four 900, L 9-1/2", W 3-1/4", H 3"	No Price Found		
1200 Courtland Side Dump Tractor-Trailer, L 13", W 3", H 3-1/4"	175	250	375
Courtland Tractor-Trailer. Same tractor as No. 2000 except marked, "Loft-Fresh Candies"	350	550	850

Courtland Non-Powered tractor-trailer marked "Loft-Fresh Candy" (extremely rare). Courtesy Dutkins of Cherry Hill, NJ.

COURTLAND FRICTION-POWERED VEHICLES

(List by Joe and Sharon Feed)

	C6	C8	C10
3875 Courtland Mechanical "Gulf" Gasoline Tractor-Trailer L 13", W 3", H 3-1/4"	225	350	475
4000 Courtland Woody Sedan, red & tan, L 7-1/4", W 3-1/4", H 2-3/4"	65	75	100
4000 Courtland Woody Sedan, blue & tan, Note: This is one of only four Courtland styled toys stamped "A Walt Reach Toy by Courtland Toy Co. Phila., PA. Made in U.S.A." The only known Courtland-			

styled toys marked with the Courtland Toy Company, Philadelphia stamping is this No. 4000 sedan, a non-powered "Fire Chief" car, a private garage similar to No. 9075 and a mechanical parking meter bank, L 7-1/4", W 3-1/4", H 2-3/4" ....

	C6	C8	C10
(No. 4000 sedan ...) L 7-1/4", W 3-1/4", H 2-3/4"	65	75	100
4060 Courtland Space Rocket Patrol Car, 1952 retail price 98¢, L 7-1/4", W 3-1/4", H 2-3/4"	150	200	250
5450 Courtland "Pop-Up" Ladder Fire Truck, L 13", W 3", H 3-1/4"	250	350	450
7500 Courtland Mechanical State Police Car with siren, L 7-1/4", W 3-1/4", H 2-3/4"	150	200	250
7500 Courtland Mechanical Fire Chief Car with siren, L 7-1/4", W 3-1/4", H 3-1/4"	150	200	250

Courtland. Upper left No. 3875 Gulf Gas Truck; Bottom left No. 2800 Wholesale Case (unopened); Center, No. 7800 Traffic Signal; Lower right No. 500 Mechanical Truck set; Right rear No. 7500 Parking Meter. Courtesy Joe and Sharon Freed.

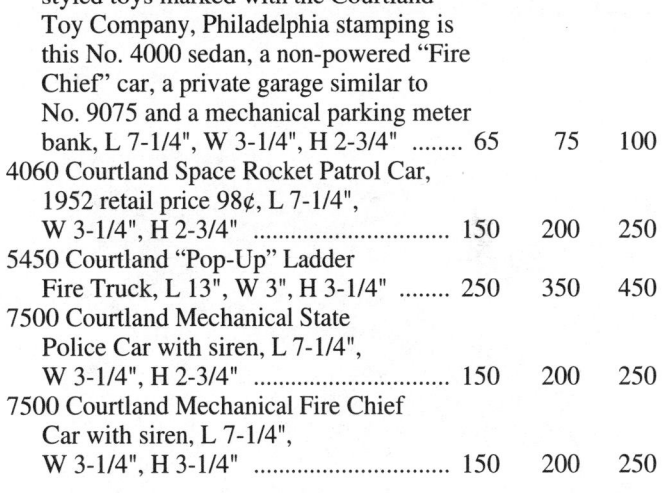

Courtland 3875 (friction). Courtesy Mapes Auctioneers.

Courtland No. 4000 Woody Sedan. Courtesy Joe and Sharon Freed.

Courtland No. 4060 Space Rocket Patrol Car. Courtesy Joe and Sharon Freed.

	C6	C8	C10
XXXX Courtland Dump Truck w/dual rear wheels, L 10-1/2", W 3", H 3-3/8"	250	350	475
7600 Courtland FBI Riot Squad Car L 7-1/4", W 3-1/4", H 2-3/4"	175	200	250
XXXX Courtland Mechanical Military Gun Car, painted gun shield, L 7-1/2", W 3-1/4", H 2-1/2"	250	350	475
XXXX Variation of above, lithographed gunshield	275	375	500
Courtland Mechanical Gasoline Tractor-Trailer, similar to No. 2000 Gasoline Truck with Trailer. Marked "Gasoline-Motor Oils," Philadelphia, PA. L 13", W 3", H 3-1/4"	100	150	200

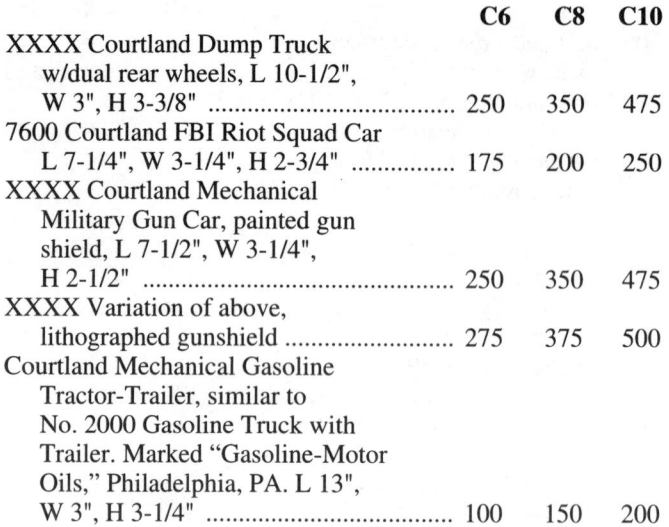

Courtland "Pop-Up" Ladder Fire Truck. Courtesy Joe and Sharon Freed.

Courtland Mechanical Military Gun Car, variation with litho gun shield. Courtesy Joe and Sharon Freed.

Courtland Dump Truck with dual rear wheels, friction. Courtesy Joe and Sharon Freed.

COURTLAND TIN WIND-UP VEHICLES

(List by Joe and Sharon Freed)

	C6	C8	C10
No. 500 Mechanical Truck Set, w/box, 4 trucks - No. 2000, 2100, 2200, 2300	600	900	1400
No. 600 Trucking Terminal Set, 2 trucks, w/box	450	750	1100
No. 1070 Mechanical Big 4 Truck Parade, 1947 retail $3.39, 9" long, 3" wide, 2-3/4" high	No Price Found		
No. 1200 Mechanical Trailer-Truck, 1947 retail $1.00, 13" long, 3" wide, 3 1/4" high	200	250	375
No. 1300 Mechanical Ice Cream Truck, retail 79¢, 9" L, 3" W, 2-3/4" H	150	200	250
No. 1300 Mechanical Moving & Storage Truck, 1947 retail 79¢, 9" long, 3" wide, 2-3/4" high	175	250	375

Truck from Courtland No. 600 Mechanical Truck Terminal Set. Courtesy Joe and Sharon Freed.

Courtland No. 500 Mechanical Truck Set. Courtesy Joe and Sharon Freed.

Courtland No. 1300 Mechanical Ice Cream Truck. Photo by Bob Smith.

Courtland 1600. Courtesy Joe and Sharon Freed.

Courtland Motor Guaranteed for Life No. 2000 Mechanical Gasoline Tractor-Trailer (packed in individual boxes all with motor guarantee certificate). Courtesy Joe and Sharon Freed.

Courtland Motor Guaranteed for Life No. 2050 Mechanical Milk tractor-trailer. Courtesy Joe and Sharon Freed.

Courtland Motor Guaranteed for Life No. 2100 Mechanical Hook & Ladder tractor-trailer. Courtesy Joe and Sharon Freed.

	C6	C8	C10
Same as above, w/No. 130 litho on the sides of the truck bed	175	250	375
No. 1300 Mechanical Fire Patrol No. 2 Truck, 1947 retail 79c, 9" long, 3" wide, 2-3/4" high	125	200	275
No. 1300 Mechanical Express and Hauling Truck, 1947 retail 79¢, 9" long, 3" wide, 2-3/4" high	125	200	275
No. 1400 Mechanical "Automatic Ladder" Fire Truck, 1947 retail $1.00, 9" long, 3" wide, 2-3/4" high	175	250	350
No. 1500 Mechanical Road Roller Truck, 9" long, 3" wide, 3-1/4" high	250	350	450
No. 1600 Mechanical Dump Truck, 7" long, 3" wide, 2-3/4" high	100	150	200
No. 2000 Mechanical "ESSO" Gasoline Tractor-Trailer, 13" L 3" W, 3-1/4"H	250	350	450
No. 2000 Mechanical Gasoline Tractor-Trailer, 13" L, 3" W, 3-1/4" H	250	350	450
No. 2050 Mechanical Milk Tractor-Trailer, "American Dairies," 13" long, 3" wide, 3-1/4" high	350	575	800

	C6	C8	C10
NOTE: 1951 catalog shows Milk Trailer markings that read the same as above except "Approved" is used in the place of the words "Vitamin D". This variation is not known to have been produced.			
No. 2100 Mechanical Hook and Ladder Tractor-Trailer, 13" L, 3" W, 3-1/4" H	100	150	200
No. 2150 Mechanical Emergency Rescue Squad Tractor-Trailer, 13" long, 3" wide, 3-1/4" high	150	200	250
No. 2200 Mechanical Logging Tractor-Trailer, 13" L, 3" W, 3-1/4" H	150	200	250
No. 2300 Mechanical Open Van Tractor-Trailer, 13" L, 3" W, 3-1/4" H	125	175	225
No. 2350 Mechanical Open Van Tractor-Trailer, 13" L, 3" W, 3-1/4" H	150	200	250
No. 2375 Mechanical Heavy Duty Sand and Gravel Tractor-Trailer, 13" long, 3" wide, 3-1/4" high	175	225	275
No. 2400 Mechanical Trailer Tow Truck, 13" long, 3" wide, 3-1/4" high	225	325	400
No. 2600 Mechanical Freight Haulers Tractor- Trailer, 13" L, 3" H, 3-1/4" W	200	300	375

Courtland Motor Guaranteed for Life No. 2150 Mechanical Emergency Rescue Squad. Courtesy Joe and Sharon Freed.

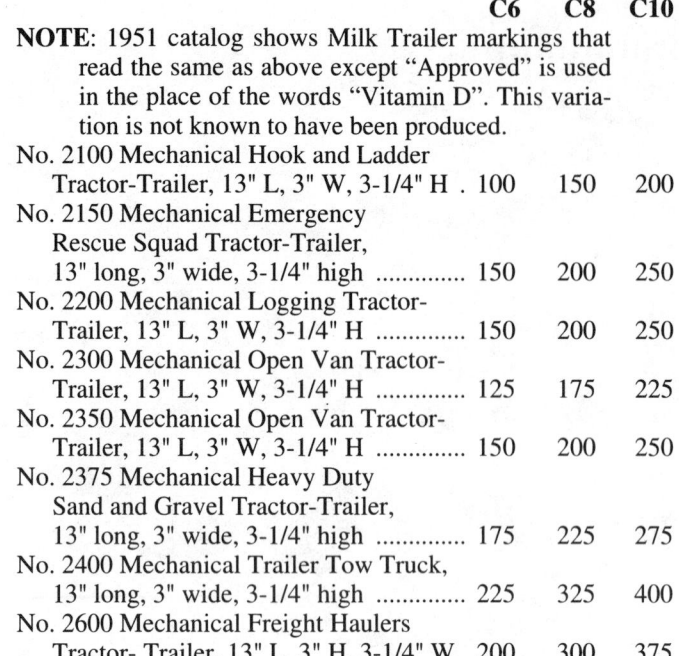

Courtland Motor Guaranteed for Life No. 2200 Mechanical Logging tractor-trailer. Courtesy Joe and Sharon Freed.

Courtland 2300 Mechanical Open Van tractor-trailer. Courtesy Joe and Sharon Freed.

Courtland 2375. Courtesy Joe and Sharon Freed.

Courtland No. 3000 Mechanical Road Roller Truck. Courtesy Joe and Sharon Freed.

Courtland, Top to Bottom: 3100 Mechanical Dump Truck, 1600 Dump Truck. Courtesy Joe and Sharon Freed.

Courtland 3900. Courtesy Joe and Sharon Freed.

Courtland No. 4000 City Meat Market Delivery Sedan. Courtesy Joe and Sharon Freed.

Courtland 4000 "Modern Bakery." Courtesy Continental Hobby House.

Courtland 4000 Fire Chief Car, red and white, with red plastic bubble on hood. Courtesy Joe and Sharon Freed.

	C6	C8	C10
No. 2700 Mechanical Side Tipper Tractor-Trailer, 13" L, 3" H, 3-1/4" W	200	300	375
No. 2800 Assortment consists of 2 No. 2000 Gasoline Trucks, 2 No. 2050 Milk Trucks, 2 No. 2200 Log Trucks, 2 No. 2350 Open Van Trucks, 2 No. 2600 Freight Hauler Trucks and 2 No. 2700 Side Tipper Trucks - Wholesale Assortment Only, in Mint $3000			
No. 3000 Mechanical Road Roller Truck, 9" long, 3" wide, 3-1/4" high	250	350	450
No. 3100 Mechanical Dump Truck, 7" long, 3" wide, 3-1/4" high	100	125	150
No. 3200 Mechanical Stake Bed Truck, 7" L, 3" W, 3-1/4" H	125	150	175
No. 3800 Assortment consists of 6 No. 3200 Stake Bed Trucks and 6 No. 3100 Dump Trucks. Wholesale Assortment Only .... No Price Found			
No. 3900 Courtland Mechanical Side Tipper Tractor-Trailer, "Black Diamond Coal Company-340," 13" L, 3" H, 3-1/4" W	250	350	450

	C6	C8	C10
No. 4000 City Meat Market Delivery Sedan, 7-1/4" L, 3-1/4" W, 2-3/4" H	75	125	150
No. 4000 Modern Bakery Delivery Sedan, 7-1/4" L, 3-1/4" W, 2-3/4" H	100	150	175
No. 4000 Fire Chief Car, red & white, 7-1/4" L, 3-1/4" W, 2-3/4" H	75	100	125
Same as above, all red	100	125	150
No. 4000 Checker Cab Car, green & yellow, 7-1/4" L, 3-1/4" W, 2-3/4" H	175	200	325
Same as above, green and white	200	225	350
No. 4500 Express Service Pickup, 7-1/4" L, 3-1/4" W, 2-3/4" H	75	100	125
No. 4500 Country Produce Pickup, 7-1/4" L, 3-1/4" W, 2-3/4" H	75	100	125
No. 4500 Modern Decorators Pickup, 7-1/4" L, 3-1/4" W, 2-3/4" H	100	125	150
No. 5000 Mechanical Operation No. 51 Crane Truck, 13" long, 3-5/8" wide, 5" high	225	325	400
No. 5100 Mechanical "Black Diamond" Coal Truck, 10-1/2" long, 3" wide, 3-3/8" high	150	225	300
No. 5200 Mechanical No. 51 Steam Shovel, 15-1/2" long, 3-3/4" wide, 9-1/2" high	135	185	235

Courtland No. 7000 "Fire Chief" car, first version. Courtesy Joe and Sharon Freed.

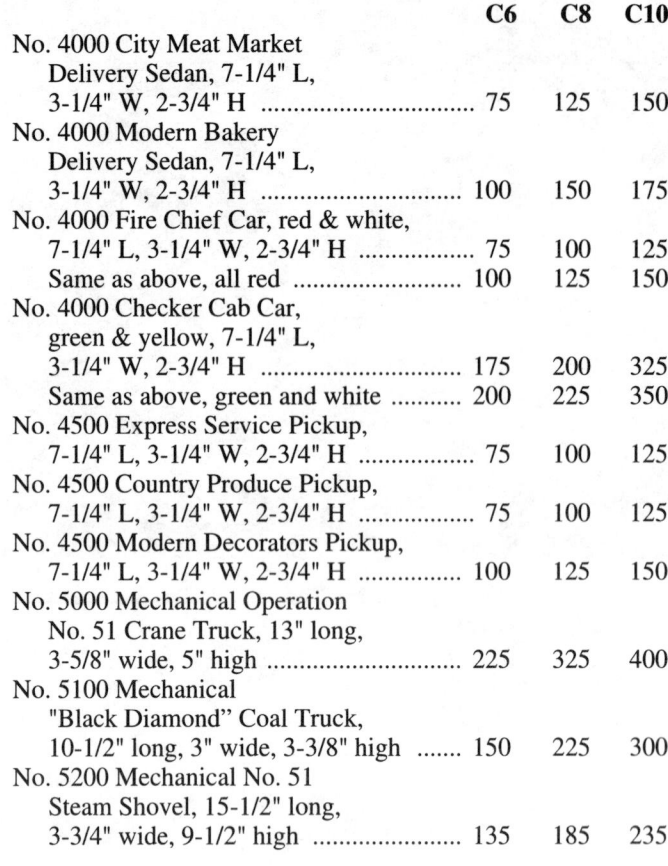

Courtland No. 4000 Checker Cab Car. Courtesy Joe and Sharon Freed.

Courtland No. 5000 Mechanical Operating No. 51 Crane Truck. Photo by Bob Smith.

Courtland "Motor Guaranteed for Life" No. 5100 "Black Diamond" Coal Truck. Courtesy Joe and Sharon Freed.

	C6	C8	C10
No. 5300 Mechanical Combination Steam Shovel carried by low-boy tractor-trailer, 15-1/2" L, 3-7/8" W, 10-1/2" H	350	550	775
No. 5800 Assortment consists of 3 No. 2300 Aluminum Open Van Trucks, 3 No. 2150 Emergency Rescue Squad Trucks, 3 No. 2375 Sand & Gravel Trucks & 3 No. 2400 Towing Service Trucks. Wholesale Assortment Only	No Price Found		
No. 6000 Mechanical Farm Tractor w/scraper, rear tires are large rubber and front are small rubber tires, 8-3/4" long, 4-3/4" wide, 4-1/2" high	100	150	200
No. 6050 Mechanical Farm Tractor w/o scraper, rear tires are large rubber and front are small rubber tires, 7-1/2" long, 4-3/4" wide, 4-1/2" high	75	100	150
No. 6075 Mechanical Farm Tractor w/o scraper, rear tires are large tin litho while the front are small rubber tires, 7-1/2" long, 4-3/4" wide, 4-1/2" high	250	350	450

	C6	C8	C10
No. 6100 Mechanical Caterpillar Tractor w/rubber treads, 6" long 3" wide, 4-1/2" high	250	350	450
No. 6500 Mechanical Ice Cream Scooter, 6-1/2" long 3" wide, 4-1/2" high	200	300	400
No. 7000 Mechanical Fire Chief Car w/siren, 7-1/4" long, 3-1/4" wide, 2-3/4" high	125	175	225
No. 7500 Mechanical State Police Car w/siren, 7-1/4" long, 3-1/4" wide, 2-3/4" high	150	200	250
No. 7500 Mechanical Parking Meter and Bank, base 6" x 6", 24-1/2" high.	150	225	300

NOTE: This is one of only four Courtland toys stamped "A Walt Reach Toy by Courtland Toy Co., Phila. PA. Made in U.S.A." The only known Courtland styled toys marked with the Courtland Toy Company, Philadelphia stamping is this mechanical parking meter bank, a No. 4000 sedan, a non-power "Fire Chief" car, and a private garage similar to No. 9075

	C6	C8	C10
No. 7800 Traffic Signal, battery-powered	275	400	550

Courtland 5300. Courtesy Joe and Sharon Freed.

Courtland 6050. Courtesy Continental Hobby House.

Courtland No. 6075 Mechanical Tractor w/Tin wheels. Courtesy Joe and Sharon Freed.

Courtland No. 6100 Mechanical Caterpillar Tractor with rubber treads. Courtesy Joe and Sharon Freed.

	C6	C8	C10

No. 8500 Mechanical Chrome Trimmed Tow Truck, tow boom shows detail, 8" long, 3-1/4" wide, 3-1/2" high 125   200   275

No. 8500 Mechanical Chrome Trimmed Tow Truck, tow boom is solid color, 8" long, 3-1/4" wide, 3-1/2" high 225   350   450

Courtland 9050 Fire Department with automatic garage door. 7-3/4" x 10-1/8" x 6-3/4", found to have a non-powered fire chief car with the Courtland Toy Co., Phila. PA, markings, it is quite possible that some of the 9050 garages were also manufactured in Philadelphia 45   55   75

9075 Private Garage with automatic door, 7-3/4" x 10-1/8" x 6-3/4". Since the non-powered car which accompanies this garage is found with Courtland Toy Co., Phila. PA, markings, it is quite possible that some of the 9075 garages were also manufactured in Philadelphia 50   75   100

Courtland No. 8500. Courtesy Joe and Sharon Freed.

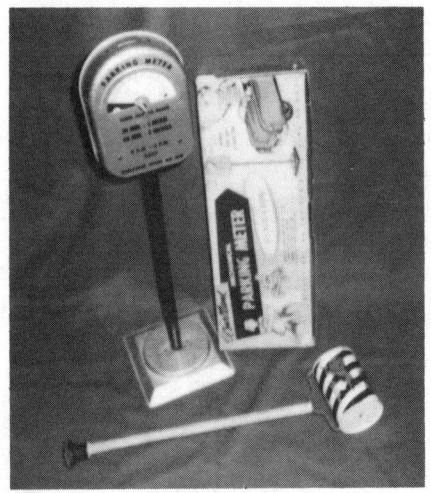

Courtland No. 7500. Courtesy Joe and Sharon Freed.

Courtland 9050. Courtesy Joe and Sharon Freed.

Courtland 9075 Private Garage. Courtesy Joe and Sharon Freed.

COX

(See also Thimbledrome)

	C6	C8	C10		C6	C8	C10
Cox Adam 12, gas powered	90	135	180	Cox Gas Dune Buggy	30	45	60
Cox Army Jeep, gas powered	72	112	150	Cox Matador, gas powered	90	135	180
Cox Corvette, 1966, 8," gas powered	90	135	180	Cox Vega Funny Car, gas powered	37	56	75
Cox Ford GT-40, gas powered	112	168	225	Cox Volkswagen, powered	37	56	75
Cox Funny Car, 12" long, plastic	7	11	15				

CRAFTOYS

By Fred Maxwell and Ron Eccles

Craftoys, a small Omaha firm, had a brief career casting slushmold vehicles before the war's need for lead brought the potmetal era to a long halt. We have discovered little more about the company than the accompanying sales sheet. It acquired some of the molds when Ralstoy was reorganizing about 1940. For those readers accustomed to identifying by "those numbers," note: #92 sedan has the same number as a Best Toy coupe, but they are not the same car, #100 racer is obviously not the same as Best #100 sedan. Second-hand Kansas Toy molds were used for #78 mixer, #81 racer,

#102 gasoline semi-tanker, #101 fire truck, #103 speed car, #104 oil truck, and #105 station wagon, possibly came from Ralstoy. The ancestry of Kansas toy is evident in #17 tractor and the freight-train set. The designs of the RR coal car, stockcar, and tank car were changed. Thus, we come to end of the line as "those toys with the numbers" roll into history. These catalog numbers may or may not be found on the toys. Black rubber wheels are seen to be characteristic of this line, but they are not exclusive with Craftoy.

Craftoy Tractor, "17," "Fordson," "Made in USA," farm tractor, driver, rear wheels larger, visible engine, 2-1/2"	8	12	16
Craftoy Cement Mixer, "78," 2 open windows, "Made in USA," 3-3/4"	8	12	16
Craftoy Racer, "81," Miller FWD Indy racer, "Made in USA," 4-1/2"	10	15	20
Craftoy Sedan, #92, streamlined 2-door sedan, 4 open windows, screen pattern grille, 4" long	No Price Found		
Craftoy Racer #100, Indy type, driver, removable tin hood, rounded nose available in repros, 4-1/4" long	No Price Found		

Craftoy? Racer, no #, Indy type, driver, removable tin hood, slanted nose, available in repros, 3-3/4" long .... No Price Found

Craftoy Fire Truck, #101, Hose Truck or Insurance Patrol, 4 open windows, 4-1/2" long .... No Price Found

Craftoy Tanker, "102" 1938, International K-Line?, "Gasoline," semi-trailer, 2 open windows, See Ralstoy, 6-3/4" long .... No Price Found

Craftoy Speed Car, #103, streamlined closed racer, body trimmed in fantasy streamlines, 4-1/4" long, available in repros .... No Price Found

Craftoy Oil Truck, #104, 1938 International?, COE, "Gas," "Oil" tanker, 2 open windows, 3-3/4" .... No Price Found

Craftoy Station Wagon, #105 streamlined, 4 open windows, 3-3/4" .... No Price Found

Top: Craftoy #100, Bottom: Craftoy ? Racer, Indy type, driver, removable tin hood. Photo by Fred Maxwell.

Craftoy Tanker "102." Courtesy Ferd Zegel.

No. 102--Gasoline Transport
S. P. 25¢
Size 6¾ inches
Packed ½ Doz. to Ctn.
Doz. Wgt. 4 lbs.
Color--Cab, Blue; Truck, Red

No. 105--Station Wagon
S. P. 10¢
Size 3¾ inches
Packed 1 Doz. to Ctn.
Doz. Wgt. 2¼ lbs.
Color--Red

No. 100--Racer with
removable Hood
S. P. 10¢
Size 4¼ inches
Packed 1 Doz. to Ctn.
Doz. Wgt. 2 lbs.
Color--Hood, Red;
Body, Aluminum

No. 104--Oil Truck
S. P. 10¢
Size 3¾ inches
Packed 1 Doz. to Ctn.
Doz. Wgt. 2¼ lbs.
Color--Red

**Craftoys
Inc.**

Factory
2230 South 16th Street
Omaha 9, Nebraska

Executive Office
417 Omaha Loan Building
Omaha 2, Nebraska

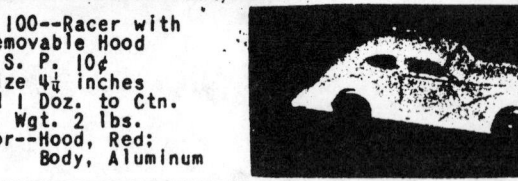

No. 92--Sedan
S. P. 10¢
Size 4 inches
Packed 1 Doz. to Ctn.
Doz. Wgt. 2 lbs.
Color--Red

No. 101--Fire Truck
S. P. 10¢
Size 4½ inches
Packed 1 Doz. to Ctn.
Doz. Wgt. 2¼ lbs.
Color--Red

No. 103--Speed Car
S. P. 10¢
Size 4¼ inches
Packed 1 Doz. to Ctn.
Doz. Wgt. 2¼ lbs.
Color--Red

No. 17--Tractor
S. P. 10¢
Size 2½ inches
Packed 1 Doz. to Ctn.
Doz. Wgt. 2¼ lbs.
Color--Red

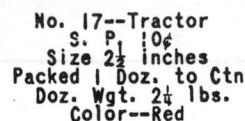

No. 78--Cement Mixer
S. P. 10¢
Size 3¾ inches
Packed 1 Doz. to Ctn.
Doz. Wgt. 2 1/3 lbs.
Color--Blue

No. 81--Racer
S. P. 10¢
Size 4½ inches
Packed 1 Doz. to Ctn.
Doz. Wgt. 2 lbs.
Color--Aluminum

No. 3600--Freight Train (5 Pcs.)   Colors--Locomotive, Aluminum
S. P. 49¢   Coal Car, Black
Size 16½ inches   Stock Car, Blue
Packed 1 Doz. to Ctn.   Tank Car, Green
Doz. Wgt. 8 lbs.   Caboose, Red
TERMS: 2% ten days, net 30 days, F.O.B. Omaha, Nebraska

A Craftoys flyer.

Craftoy Speed Car No. 103. Drawing by Deb Eccles.

Craftoy Speed Car No. 103. Photo by Perry R. Eichor.

Craftoy Oil Truck #104. Photo by Fred Maxwell.

CRAGSTAN

(Japan)

	C6	C8	C10
Cragstan Ambulance, friction	70	105	140
Cragstan Fire Chief Car, friction	82	123	165
Cragstan "G Men Car," tin friction, 6-1/2" long	60	90	120
Cragstan Greyhound Bus, friction, 9" long	35	52	70

Cragstan "G MEN CAR," tin friction, 6-1/2" long. Photo by Ron Fink.

D&L PLASTICS

(Pittsburgh)

	C6	C8	C10
Future Car, 1940s	20	30	40

DAISY

	C6	C8	C10
Daisy "Tank-Daisymatic No. 64," Rapid Fire Tank, 1960s, battery-operated, 8" long, four actions	110	165	220
Daisy "Tank-Daisymatic No. 80," 1965, battery-operated, 8-1/2" long, five actions, with darts	100	150	200

	C6	C8	C10		C6	C8	C10
Tractor Trailer	200	300	400	Semi-Stake Truck, 18" long, cast aluminum, c.1940s	300	425	600

Day Time Lines Semi-Stake Truck, cast aluminum, c.1940s, 18" long. Photo by Bob Smith.

DAYTON FRICTION TOY WORKS

Dayton, Ohio (1909-1935)

See David P. Clark history

	C6	C8	C10
Dayton Armored Car, Flywheel drive, sheet metal const., red/gold, 11" L, c.1909	250	450	600
Dayton Bus, c.1920s	350	525	700
Dayton Coal and Ice Truck, tin friction c.1920	250	450	600
Dayton Coupe, 12", 1928, pressed steel	175	250	450
Dayton Coupe, 12-1/2" long, c.1920..........	400	550	800
Dayton Coupe, friction, 17" long, tin	500	650	900
Dayton "Dayton Friction," pressed steel, rubber tires, 1920s, 14-1/2" long	250	400	550
Dayton Delivery Van, friction	250	400	550
Dayton Dump Truck	375	550	750
Dayton Fire Ladder Truck, 18" long	200	350	550
Dayton Fire Ladder Truck, 22" long, friction	250	350	550
Dayton Fire Pumper Truck, flywheel drive, sheet metal const., white/gold, 14-3/4" long, c.1909	450	600	800
Dayton Roadster, 14" long, c.1930s	200	300	400
Dayton Seven-Passenger Touring Car. Flywheel drive, sheet metal const., red/gold, 13-1/4" L, patent date April 2, 1909...	150	225	300
Dayton Stake Truck	300	450	600
Dayton Touring Car, 13-1/2" long, unpowered	300	450	600

Dayton Armored Car, 11" long, c.1909. Photo by Bob Smith..

Dayton Fire Pumper Truck, 14-3/4" long, c.1909. Photo by Bob Smith.

Dayton Coupe, tin, friction, 17" long. Photo by Terry Sells.

Dayton Seven-Passenger Touring Car, c.1909, 13-1/4" long. Photo by Bob Smith.

DELUXE

(Richmond Hill, Queens, New York)

	C6	C8	C10
DeLuxe "DeLuxe Service Station," 1940s ..	40	75	100

DeLuxe "DeLuxe Service Station" with box. Photo by Ron Fink.

DENT HARDWARE COMPANY

Dent, of Fullerton, Pennsylvania, was in business from 1895 to 1973. Henry H. Dent, with four partners, was the owner. Cast-iron toys seem to have first emerged in 1898. Dent is known for particularly fine castings in its vehicles. It was also one of the first man-ufacturers to try (with little success) aluminum toys (in the 1920s). Toys seem to have been phased out during the hard times of the Depression. Dent marked few, if any, of its toys.

	C6	C8	C10
Dent "American Oil Co.," cast-iron Truck, approx. 10-1/2" long	800	1200	1600
Dent "American Oil" Truck, 15" long	1200	2000	2800
Dent "Breyer's Ice Cream," removable doors, 1932, 8-1/2" long	700	1150	1700
Dent Bus, cast-iron, 6-1/4" long	375	563	750
Dent "Bus Line," 9" long	400	600	800

	C6	C8	C10
Dent Bus, 10-1/2" long	500	850	1200
Dent Coast to Coast Bus, 7-1/2" long	125	187	250
Dent "Coast to Coast" Bus, 10" long	300	450	600
Dent "Coast to Coast" Bus, c.1925, 15" long	750	1000	1500
Dent "Contractors" Mack Dump, open cab, 10-1/2" long	1200	2200	3000

Dent "American Oil Co." truck, 15" long. Courtesy Bill Bertoia Auctions. Photo by Jeanne Bertoia.

Dent "American Oil Co.," 10-1/2" long. Courtesy Phillips NY.

Dent "Breyer's Ice Cream." Courtesy Bill Bertoia Auctions. Photo by Jeanne Bertoia.

Dent, L to R: pattern for "Coast to Coast" bus, c.1925, 15" long, "Public Service" bus 13-1/2" long and its brass pattern. Courtesy Bill Bertoia Auctions. Photo by Jeanne Bertoia.

Dent "Freeman's Dairy" truck, 6" long. Courtesy Bill Bertoia Auctions. Photo by Jeanne Bertoia.

Dent "Junior Supply Co. New York Philadelphia." Courtesy Sotheby's NY.

 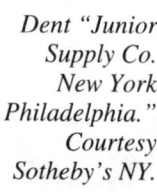

	C6	C8	C10
Dent Convertible	400	700	1000
Dent Coupe, 5" long	125	188	250
Dent Dump Truck, 15-1/4", C-cab	800	1350	1900
Dent "Express J&B" Stakebed Truck, 14-1/2", 1915, driver	500	800	1100
Dent Fire Pumper, 11" long, early, tiny driver	700	1200	1600
Dent Fire Pumper, 11" long, normal-sized driver, hose	500	850	1200
Dent Fire Truck, cast-iron, 7" long	150	225	300
Dent Fire Ladder Truck, 8-1/2" long, with driver	450	675	900
Dent Fire Truck with ladder and men, cast-iron, 18" long	900	1350	1800
Dent Fordson Tractor	250	375	500
Dent "Freemen's Dairy" Truck, 6", sliding doors, milkman	650	1100	1550

	C6	C8	C10
Dent hose reeler with men, cast-iron, large	500	750	1000
Dent Ice Truck, 6" long	155	233	310
Dent Ice Truck, 10" long, c.1920s	450	675	900
Dent "Interurban" Bus, cast-iron, 9" long	250	375	500
Dent "Interurban" Bus, cast-iron, 10-1/2" long	500	750	1000
Dent "Junior Supply Co. New York Philadelphia," c.1923, 16" long	2000	3500	5000
Dent La Salle, 4-1/4" long	475	710	950
Dent La Salle Panel Truck	450	700	950
Dent Ladder Truck, 10" long, two drivers	250	375	500
Dent Ladder Truck, 12" long	300	450	600
Dent Mack Cement Truck, 11-1/4" long, extremely rare, auctioned in 1992 in Good-Very Good condition for $47,300			
Dent Mack Dump Truck, 4-1/2" c.1925, iron wheels	55	82	110

Dent "New York-Chicago" Bus, 10-1/4" long. Courtesy Bill Bertoia Auctions. Photo by Jeanne Bertoia.

Dent "Police Patrol," approx. 8-3/4" long. Courtesy Phillips NY.

Dent "Pioneer" Fire Ladder Truck, driver, 13-1/4" long. (The toy shown here has been recently painted.) Courtesy Bill Bertoia Auctions. Photo by Jeanne Bertoia.

Dent "Public Service" Bus, 13-1/2." Courtesy Sotheby's NY.

Dent Road Roller, 4-1/2" long. Courtesy Bill Bertoia Auctions. Photo by Jeanne Bertoia.

Dent Road Sweeper, 7-3/4" long. Courtesy Bill Bertoia Auctions. Photo by Jeanne Bertoia.

Dent, L to R: Touring Car, passengers, driver, 9-1/4" long, Touring Car, passenger, driver, 12" long. Courtesy Bill Bertoia Auctions. Photo by Jeanne Bertoia.

	C6	C8	C10
Dent Mack Express State Truck, auctioned in 1992 for $4,400			
Dent Mack Express Van, auctioned in 1992 for $9,900			
Dent Mack Tank Truck, auctioned in 1992 for $3,960			
Dent Model T 2- door Sedan, iron wheels, c.1925	125	187	250
Dent "New York-Chicago" Bus, 10-1/4" long	375	562	750
Dent "Patrol," 6-1/2" long, c.1920s	125	187	250
Dent Phaeton, driver	170	255	340

Dent "Valley View Dairy," 8" long. Courtesy Bill Bertoia Auctions. Photo by Jeanne Bertoia.

	C6	C8	C10
Dent "Pioneer" Fire Ladder Truck, driver, 13-1/4" long	1200	2000	3000
Dent "Police Patrol," 8-3/4" long	750	1125	1500
Dent "Public Service" Bus, c.1926, 13-1/2" long	1800	3000	4500
Dent Road Roller, 4-1/2"	80	120	160
Dent Road Sweeper, auctioned in 1994 in excellent condition for $3,700			
Dent Runabout, 6" long, driver, tiller	212	368	425
Dent Sedan, 4-1/2" long, 1920s	100	150	200
Dent Sedan, 7-1/2" long, spare tire, has stop and go light, full bumpers on front	900	1350	1800
Dent Sedan, 7-1/2" long, 1920s	425	638	850
Dent Stake Truck, 15-1/2" long, driver, 4 tin milk cans	1800	3500	5000
Dent Steam Roller, cast-iron, 6" long	45	68	90
Dent Touring Car, passengers, driver, 9-1/4" long	500	800	1200
Dent Touring Car, driver & passenger, 12" long	500	750	1000
Dent "Valley View Dairy," 8" long	550	900	1400
Dent Yellow Cab, approx. 7-3/4" long	850	1275	1700

DINKY

Dinky toys were first made in England in 1932 under the name "Modeled Miniatures." They were later called "Meccano Miniatures." In 1934, they were dubbed "Dinky" (which means "fetching" in England).

CIVILIAN DINKY

Prices are for Mint in the Box, since that is how most Dinky civilian vehicles are sold.

	MIB
14C Coventry Fork Lift	100
22A Maserati Sport 2000	150
23G Cooper Bristol Racing Car	150
23H Ferrari Racer	100
23J H.W.M. Racer	150
24A New Yorker Convertible	175
24B Peugeot	150
24C Citroen DS19	180
24D Plymouth Belvedere	160
24H Mercedes 190SL	130
24L 2CV Vespa	200
24V Simca 9 Arnode	150
24X Ford Vedette	165
24Y Studebaker	125
25 Ford Zodiac Police Car	85
25M Bedford Tipper	100
25V Bedford Refuse Truck	110
27 Motorcart	150
27F 1948 Plymouth Station Wagon	200
30A Chrysler Airflow	250
30E Breakdown Lorry	No Price Found
33 Simca Glass Truck	185
33 AN Simca Bailly	150
34B Royal Mail	90
36A Log Lorry	205
36F British Salmson	120

	MIB
36F Taxi	120
39A Unic Auto Transporter	310
39E Chrysler Royal	675
42A Police Box	90
44AA Motorcycle Patrol & Sidecar	80
60Y Fuel Tender	400
61 Ford Prefect	80
62 Singer Roadster	80
64 Austin Lorry	90
66 Bedford Flat Truck	110
71 Dublo Volks Van	120
73 Dublo Range Rover & Horse Trailer	125
101 Sunbeam Alpine Sports Car	225
103 Austin-Healey 100 Sports Car	250
103 Spectrum Patrol	220
104 Spectrum Pursuit Vehicle	300
105 Triumph TR2	225
106 Austin Atlantic Convertible	100
106 Thunderbird 2	125
106 "The Prisoner" mini moke	105
107 Sunbeam Alpine	125
108 Sam's Car	165
110 Aston Martin	160
111 Triumph TR2 Competition	225
112 Purdy's TR7	85
113 MGB	110

	MIB
120 Jaguar XKE	135
122 Volvo 265	25
123 Princess 2200 HL Saloon	40
124 Rolls Royce Phantom V	82
127 Rolls Royce Phantom V	45
128 Mercedes Benz 600	55
129 VW Bug	95
130 Ford Consul Corsair	90
131 Cadillac Tourer	100
131 Jaguar Type E 2 + 2	100
131 Jaguar Type G	100
132 Ford 40-RV	70
132 Packard Convertible	190
134 Triumph Vitesse	65
138 Hillman Imp	65
139A 1949 Ford Sedan	60
140 Morris 1100	75
141 Vauxhall Victor	100
142 Jaguar Mark X	85
143 Ford Capri	120
144 VW1500	90
146 Daimler 2-1/2 litre V8	95
148 Ford Fairlane	110
149 Citroen Dyane	45
150 Rolls Royce Silver Wraith	95
151 Triumph 1800 Saloon	90
152 Rolls Royce Phantom V Limousine	70
155 Ford	80
156 Rover 75	150
156 Saab 96	135
157 Jaguar XK120	165

Dinky, L to R: 157 Jaguar KX120 Coupe, 344 Estate Car. Courtesy Phillips NY.

	MIB
157 BMW 2000 Tilux	50
158 Rolls Royce Silver Shadow	80
160 Mercedes Benz 250 SE	70
161 Mustang Fastback	60
162 Ford Zephyr Saloon	150
162 Triumph 1130	90
163 Bristol 450 Sports Coupe	125
163 Volkswagen 1600 TL Fastback	75
164 Ford Zodiac	70
164 Vauxhall Crest Saloon	150
165 Ford Capri	95
166 Sunbeam Rapier	155
167 Aceca	130
168 Singer Gazelle	145
168 Ford Escort	50
169 Ford Corsair 200E	65
169 Studebaker Golden Hawk	145
170 Lincoln Continental	95

	MIB
171 Hudson Sedan	150
172 Studebaker	175
173 Nash Rambler	120
173 Pontiac Parisienne	65
174 Ford Mercury Cougar	70
174 Hudson Hornet	155

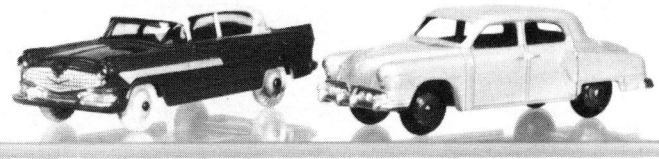

Dinky, L to R: 174 Hudson Hornet Sedan, 172 Studebaker Land Cruiser. Courtesy Phillips NY.

	MIB
175 Hillman Minx	190
176 Austin A105 Saloon, first Dinky with windows	170
176 N SU R 80	75
177 Opel Kapitan	125
178 Mini Clubman	40
178 Plymouth Plaza	130
179 Studebaker President	150
180 Packard Clipper Sedan	130
180 Rover 3H	40
181 Volkswagen	135
182 Porsche 356A Coupe, deep pink	150
184 Volvo	125
185 Alfa Romeo Coupe	125
186 Mercedes Benz	80
187 DeTomaso Mangusta	50
187 VW Karmann Ghia	125
188 Jensen FF	75
189 Lamborghini Marzal	55
189 Triumph Herald	105
190 Monteverdi 375L	75
190 Caravan	105
191 Dodge Royal Sedan	145
192 DeSoto Fireflite Sedan	140
192 Range Rover	45
193 Rambler Wagon	125
195 Fire Chief's Car	35
196 Holden Special	85
197 Morris Mini Traveler	145
198 Rolls Royce Phantom V	105
199 Austin Countryman	110
200 Matra 630	40
201 Plymouth Rally '76	40
202 Fiat Abarth 2000	35
208 VW Porsche 914	60
210 Alfa Romeo 33 LeMans	70
212 Ford Cortina Rally	85
213 Ford Capri Rally	50
217 Alfa Scarabo	40
220 Ferrari P5	60
221 Corvette Stingray	60
222 Hesketh 308E	45
223 McLaren M8A CanAm	33
225 Lotus FI Racing Car	50

	MIB			MIB
226 Ferrari 312	45	271 Bedford Royal Van		40
227 Beach Buggy	32	271 Ford Fire Appliance		40
230 Talbot-Lago race car	135	272 Police Accident Unit		45
231 Mercedes-Benz	125	275 Brinks Truck		60
232 Alfa Romeo race car	125	276 Ford Ambulance		40
233 Cooper Bristol race car	135	277 Superior Ambulance		95
236 Connaught Racer	135	278 Plymouth Yellow Cab		50
237 Mercedes Racer	155	279 Diesel Road Roller		65
238 Jaguar Racer	160	279 Plymouth Taxi		28
239 Vanwall Racer	125	280 Observation Coach		150
240 Cooper Racer	60	281 Pathe News Camera Car		180
242 Ferrari Racer	50	282 Land Rover Fire Appliance		110
242 Simca Versalles	90	283 B.O.A.C. Coach		40
243 BRM racer	55	284 London Taxi		45
245 Sports Car Gift Set	295	285 Merryweather Fire Engine		95
250 Police Mini Cooper S	75	286 Ford Transit Fire Truck		70
250 Streamlined Fire Engine	115	287 Police Accident Unit		60
251 Pontiac Police Car	75	289 London Bus		40
252 Pontiac RCMP Police Car	100	290 Double Decker Bus		155
254 Police Rangerover	45	291 Atlantean Bus		40
254 Austin Taxi	110	292 Ribble Regent Bus		70
255 Zodiac Police Car	95	295 Atlas Bus		100
257 Canadian Fire Chief's Car	150	297 Cadillac Ambulance		100
258 DeSoto Police Car	165	300 Massey Harris Tractor		125
259 Fire Engine	120	301 Field-Marshall Tractor		85
260 Royal Mail Van	170	308 Leyland Tractor		60
261 Telephone Service Truck	165	319 Tipping Trailer		35
263 Airport Fire Rescue Tender	80	320 Harvest Trailer		40
264 Ford Fairlane Police Car	125	321 Manure Spreader		70
265 Plymouth Taxi	150	322 Disc Harrow		45
266 ERF Fire Tender	80	340 Land Rover and Trailer		175
267 Bedford Dump	75	341 Land Rover		35
268 Renault Dauphine mini car	150	342 Motocart		75
268 Range Rover Ambulance	30	343 Dodge Farm Truck		195
269 Jaguar Police Car	175	344 Estate Car		60
270 Ford Panda Police Car	55	352 Ed Straker's Car		90

DINKY (MECCANO), MILITARY TOYS: 1937-1980

by William W. Kilborn

When Dinky Toys were first issued in 1933, they were intended to add a touch of realism to the "Hornby" train models. The first offering to the public was a set of six small accessories referred to as "Model Miniatures" and were commonly known as the "22 Series." In the original 22 Series group of six die-cast vehicles, one product is of particular interest to us who are military model collectors, this being No. 22F, which resembled an army tank of the era. It had two cast components, one large casting for the main body and side skirts and a smaller one for the turret, which actually rotated. A fair amount of attention was paid to the louvers and rivets on both castings. The tank was propelled by two large wheels on the outside and three smaller ones on the inside, fitted to each side of the larger casting which, in turn, carried the rubber treads. The treads were originally manufactured in red rubber and later in green. The metal

casting was originally green with an orange turret, which makes the tank nonbelievable in military terms, but later versions were painted drab gray with green treads, which were sold as individual items. The original tank was available in the boxed set only and marked "Hornby Series Model Miniatures No. 22." In the later 1930s, the base was altered and stamped to read "Dinky Toy."

The reason I have taken the time to describe this piece under the company's history is that I personally feel that the tank was intended as part of a market-feeler, to see where interest lay in future production of military toys. From records I have read, the tank led in production quantities and demand over the other five items produced in this original set.

Nineteen thirty-seven saw the introduction of what developed into the finest range of mass-market die-cast military toys ever produced until the birth of Solido.

Nineteen thirty-eight saw further consolidation of the vehicle range, which by then contained almost three varieties. During WWII, the Dinky operations were interrupted by the war effort. One of the few new or adapted models during this period was a replica of a petrol tanker painted gray with the word "pool" in white on its sides. The unfortunate part of this period was that many of the toy dies were lost during the equipment shuffling to make room for the wartime production. Christmas 1945 saw production get underway again, and some 50 different toy models went out to the retailers for sale to the public. The hopes for a quick return to the pre-war status quo were, however, not to be fulfilled, as metal alloys were put to priority use for much-needed domestic products, and to feed the giant export projects on which the British economy now depended for its survival.

However, by 1952 the post-war boom was gathering momentum as railway accessories and model planes were re-introduced. New products flowed from the design studios to the production lines until finally, in 1954, the production of the first new group of army vehicles arrived on the scene. Also, one of the most significant events of that year for future collectors was the renumbering of all models. The suffix system was no longer manageable, and a block number system was allocated to types of vehicles. The larger-scale "Super Dinky Toys" in blue striped boxes with a white background were also introduced in the mid-1950s. It was 1958 before Dinky replied to the challenge of domestic competition from "Corgi," which entered the market in 1956, by fitting special features to their models. Pausing for a breath from the introduction of gimmicks to keep abreast of their competition, in 1961 the company produced 20 or so new models and changed over from plain to tread tires on all their vehicles (although military models had them since the mid-1950s).

In June 1969, the company again made a significant change in its vehicle products to attempt to stay with the competition by the introduction of speed wheels, which were eventually to become standard on everything. Six years earlier, after the takeover by Lines Bros., the name of the firm was changed to "Meccano-Triang Ltd." —a bad omen, for, in 1971, after a general recession in the toy trade, the company's bank loans were recalled and the whole of the Lines Group went into liquidation. The Meccano assets were transferred to a new company, "Maoford Ltd.," which was subsequently named "Meccano (1971) Ltd." New toys were desperately needed. In 1972, the company went into the kit business for the first time.

But by now, the hand of doom was resting on production and even the introduction of space toys would not delay the inevitable, as the Binns Road factory was effectively closed on Nov. 30, 1979. The closure did not save the parent company, which was also having difficulty in the American market. Although Dinky Toy continued to be produced elsewhere for several years, the eventual low labor cost and success of mass-plastic extrusion manufacturing from the Asian export market was the real culprit behind the demise of one of the English-speaking world's finest toy manufacturers, which, in its heyday, produced about 3,000 varieties of transportation toys during a marvelous history of almost 50 years in England, France, and India.

BIOGRAPHY: William Kilborn is a professor of interior design at Ryerson Poltechnical Institute in Toronto. His collecting pursuits include Marx Trains (for more than 20 years, Train Collectors Association member for more than 10 years); Toy Soldier Bands since 1975; and Military Dinky Toys since 1973. He is a contributing editor to *Toy Soldier Review*.

Establishing A Value

Dollar values in today's world are always changing; therefore, I have always found it more beneficial to deal in formulas when trying to establish fees or prices. Thanks to Jack Wilson of *Collectors Press* in Bradford, England, I can now put forth our combined efforts into my own hypothesis, as follows:

Step #1 Mint Prices: Mint Boxed Condition

A. Over 45 years old: original price x 75 = m/b
B. Over 25 years old: original price x 40 = m/b
C. Over 15 years old: original price x 20 = m/b
D. Under 14 years old: original price x 5% per annum (not compounded)

The exceptions to the above formulas depend on amount of production and the number of years in production; for example if an article was only made for one year,

but had a production run of 90,000 units, the price applied to the above might only double. Therefore, the rarer the piece, the higher the price applied to the above formulas. Now we have established Mint Boxed value but only if you know the last original price while in production. Otherwise, you will have to accept the selling price of dealers and collectors.

Step #2: Establishing Condition Price

Taking a mint boxed model with an estimated value of $20, the different values, according to condition in military collecting, are:

1. Excellent (boxed): Shows some sign of play and moisture rust, 20% off mint boxed price—$16.
2. Near Mint (no box) or Excellent (boxed): Some rust, no scratches, all decals in place, 30% off mint boxed price—$14.

3. Very Good (boxed): Some rust, scratched, all decals, no paint missing, 45% of mint boxed prices—$11.

4. Very Good (no box): Some rust, scratches, no missing parts or paint, 55% off mint boxed prices—$9.

5. Good (no box): Rust, paint chipped, decals partially missing, no missing parts, 60% off mint boxed—$8.

6. Fair (no box): Rusted wheels axle and base, scratches, chipped, missing paint, decals gone, missing tires or chains, but not broken, paint still good for the purpose of reconditioning (50% there). Negotiated price only below 60% of the original value.

Note that all deductions are taken from the original mint-box price and that my formula does not deal with broken or missing components or with pieces having less than 40 percent of the original paint-finish gone; such pieces have no real value to the collector, unless reconditioned, and then they should only bring 50 percent of excellent, not mint boxed! In addition, it should also be noted that boxes can bring $3 to $50, depending on age and condition, for which I have not worked out a formula. Prices shown above are mainly based on my purchased price between 1979 and 1989, when I stopped collecting Dinky and went into other military lines; plus updates from the English monthly newspaper *Toy Collectors Gazette*, 1992.

Note: Early military Dinky, except for boxed sets, were sold in yellow boxes with black lettering, 6 or 12 pieces to the box, thus eliminated Mint/Boxed as a value or condition

William W. Kilborn

of the item. It should also be noted that pre-war items differed from re-issue as follows: pre-war, smooth hub caps; post-war, rimmed hub caps.

DINKY MILITARY PRODUCTION, PERIODS AND TYPES

British Vehicles: Pre-War (1937-41) and re-issued (1945-50)

SERIES	ARTICLE	YEARS OF MFG	N/M	VALUE EX	VG
22F	Tank Grey or (orange)	1933	$200	$150	$75
22S	Search Light Lorry 6 to a box (small)	1935/41	$350	$250	$150
37C	Dispatch Rider RCS.	1938/41	$70	$40	$25
150A	Royal Tank Corp Officer	1937/41	$20	$15	$10
150B	Royal Tank Corp Private (seated)	1937/41	$25	$20	$15
150C	Royal Tank Corp NCO	1937/41	$30	$20	$10
150D	Royal Tank Corp Driver (seated)	1937/41	$20	$15	$15
151A	Medium Tank	1937/41	$300	$200	$100
151B	Transport Wagon (reissued)	1937/41	$200	$150	$100
		1953-54	$100	$80	$50
151C	Cooker Trailer	1937/41	$125	$100	$80
151D	Water Tank Trailer	1937/41	$120	$90	$70
152A	Light Tank (reissued)	1937/41	$100	$80	$60
		1954-55	$50	$40	$30
152B	Reconnaissance Car (")	1937/41	$100	$80	$60
		1954-55	$75	$50	$40
152C	Austin Staff Car	1937/41	$125	$100	$75
153A	U.S. Jeep white star	1954/55	$100	$80	$50
156 Set	Mechanized army set 12pc.	1937/41	$200m/b		
	151 a,b,c,d-152, a,b,c			$1500	$1000
	161 a,b-162, a,b,c-			n/m boxed	boxed
160	Ranco Seated Gunners (3)	1939/41	$60	$40	$30
160A	Royal Artillery NCO	1939/41	$20	$15	$10
160B	Royal Artillery Gunner (seated)	1939/41	$20	$15	$10

22S Searchlight Lorry. W. Kilborn Collection.

151A Medium Tank (without markings) 1932-41. W. Kilborn Collection.

151A Medium Tank with Markings. W. Kilborn Collection.

151B Transport Wagon, 1937-41. W. Kilborn Collection.

Meccano "Dinky" military vehicles issued pre WWII (standing Dinky figures at far left are 30mm tall. Figures shown are from sets 150 and post war descendants of sets 150 & 160).
L to R - Back Row: 22f Tank, 37c Royal Corps of Signals Dispatch Rider, 151a Medium Tank, 151d Water Tank Trailer, 151c Cooker trailer, 151b Transport Wagon.
Middle Row: 151b Transport Wagon, 152a Light Tank, 152b Reconnaissance Car, 152c Austin 7 Car.
Front Row: 161b AA Gun on trailer, 161a Searchlight on Lorry, 161c Gun, 162b Trailer, 162ad Light Dragon. Photo by Ed Poole.

152A Light Tank reissue. W. Kilborn Collection.

152B Reconnaissance Car Reissue. W. Kilborn Collection.

152C Austin Staff Car, 1937 issue. W. Kilborn Collection.

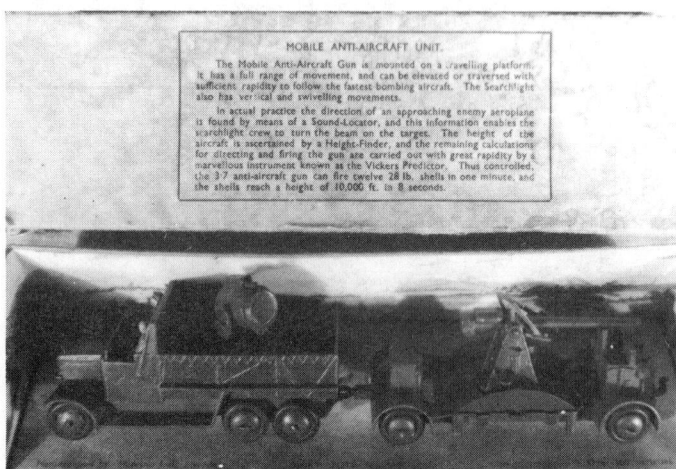

153A U.S. Jeep, postwar. W. Kilborn Collection.

Set No. 161 Mobile Anti-Aircraft Unit. W. Kilborn Collection.

L to R: 161A Transport Lorry with Searchlight, 1937, 151C Cooker, 151D Water Tanker, 1937. W. Kilborn Collection.

161B Anti-Aircraft Gun reissued. W. Kilborn Collection.

162A, B, C. Lt. Dragon Set with 18 pounder, reissued. W. Kilborn Collection.

SERIES	ARTICLE	YEARS OF MFG	VALUE		
			N/M	EX	VG
160C	Royal Artillery Gunlayer	1939/41	$25	$20	$15
160D	Royal Artillery Gunlayer (standing)	1939/41	$20	$15	$10
161 set	Mobile Anti-Aircraft	1939/41	$1000m/b		
	Unit 161 a.b.c. (with box prices)		$800	$600	
161A	TransportLorry with Search Light	1939/41	$500	$300	$250
161B	AA Gun on Trailer (reissued)	1939/41	$140	$110	$80
		1954/55	$70	$50	$40
1162A	Lt. Dragon Motorized	1939/41	$100	$80	$65
	Tractor (reissued)	1954/55	$75	$50	$35
162B	Ammunition Trailer (")	1939/41	$50	$35	$25
		1954/55	$20	$15	$10
162C	18 PD. Gun (reissued)	1939/41	$50	$35	$25
		1954/55	$20	$15	$10

SETS (Complete with boxes)

SERIES	ARTICLE	YEARS OF MFG	VALUE		
			N/M	EX	VG
150	Royal Tank Corp. Personnel 150 A,B,C,D, 6 pcs.	1937/41	$120	$90	$60
151	Royal Tank Corp. Medium Set 151A,B,C,D 4 pcs.	1937/41	$300	$200	$100
152	Royal Tank Corp, Light Set 152A,B,C 3 pcs.	1937/41	$250	$200	$150
160	Royal Artillery Personnel 160A,B,C,D 6 pcs.	1939/40	$120	$90	$60

Note: Early military Dinky except for boxed sets were sold in yellow boxes with black lettering, 6 or 12 pieces to the box, thus eliminating MINT/BOXED as a value or condition of the item. It should also be noted that pre-war items dirrered from re-issue as follows: 1) pre-war, smooth hub caps 2) post-war, rimmed hub caps British Vehicles post-war (1954-1977):

British Vehicles: (1954-1977)

NUMBER	DESCRIPTION	YEAR	CONDITION	VALUE
341	Land Rover Trailer Army (sold with #669 Super Dinky set)	1954	M/B	$40
601	Austin Paramoke	1966/77	M/B	$95
603	Army Personnel Privates	1955/71	M/B	$50
621	3 Ton Army Wagon	1954/63	M/B	$85
622	10 Ton Army Truck	1954/64	M/B	$85

L to R: 601 Austin Paramoke, 673 Scout Car. W. Kilborn Collection.

Top to Bottom: 622 Foden 10-ton Truck, 689 Artillery Tractor. W. Kilborn Collection.

NUMBER	DESCRIPTION	YEAR	CONDITION	VALUE
623	Army Covered Wagon	1954/63	M/B	$90
624	Daimler Ambulance #30H	1944/54	M/Box (4)	$85 each
625	Austin Covered Lorry/30s	1948/54	M/Box (4)	$75 each
626	Military Ambulance	1956/65	M/B	$85
640	Bedford Army Truck #25w	1944/54	M/Box (4)	$75 each
641	1 Ton Cargo Truck	1954/62	M/B	$85
642	R.A.F. Pressure Fueller	1957/60	M/B	$185
643	Army Water Tanker	1958/64	M/B	$95
651	Centurion Tank	1954/70	M/B	$95
660	Tank Transporter	1956/64	M/B	$180
661	Recovery Tractor	1957/65	M/B	$135
665	'Honest John' Launcher	1964/76	M/B	$175
666	Missile Erector/Platform	1959/64	M/B	$285
667	Missile Service Platform	1960/64	M/B	$275
669	U.S. Army Jeep #405 sd/tr	1944/54	M/B	$50
670	Armoured Car	1954/70	M/B	$60
673	Scout Car	1953/62	M/B	$60
674	Austin Champ Jeep	1954/70	M/B	$60
674	Austin Champ "UN white"	1954/70	M/B	$300
675	Ford Fordor U.S. Army #139	1944/54	M/Box (4)	$100each
676	Armoured Personnel Car	1955/62	M/B	$55

624 Daimler Ambulance, 625 Austin Lorry, 675 U.S. Ford. W. Kilborn Collection.

640 Bedford Army Truck (two versions - black grille or chrome). W. Kilborn Collection.

Top to Bottom: 641 1-ton truck, 677 Command Vehicle. W. Kilborn Collection.

Top to Bottom: 642 RAF Tanker, 661 Recovery Tractor. W. Kilborn Collection.

660 Tank Transporter with 651 Centurion Tank. W. Kilborn Collection.

665 Honest John Missile Launcher. W. Kilborn Collection.

666 Missile Erector Platform. W. Kilborn Collection.

667 Missile Servicing Platform Vehicle. W. Kilborn Collection.

669 Jeep Sold with 341 Trailer as a set. W. Kilborn Collection.

Top - L to R: 674 UN white Austin Champ, 674 Khaki; Bottom - L to R: 643 Water Tanker, 626 Ambulance. W. Kilborn Collection.

 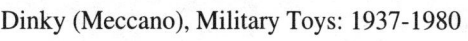

NUMBER	DESCRIPTION	YEAR	CONDITION	VALUE
677	Armoured Command Vehicle	1952/61	M/B	$100
686	Field Artillery Tractor	1957/70	M/B	$100
687	Trailer and 25 Pdr.	1957/70	M/B	$30
688	Gun Set	1957/70	M/B	$90
689	Medium Artillery Tractor	1957/65	M/B	$105
692	5.5 Medium Gun	1955/62	M/B	$75
693	7.2 Howitzer	1958/67	M/B	$40

Top to Bottom: 676 Personnel Carrier, 670 Armoured Car, 688 Tractor, 687 Gun Trailer, 686 Field Gun. W. Kilborn Collection.

British Vehicles Military: Late Models (1977-1980)

NUMBER	DESCRIPTION	YEAR	CONDITION	VALUE
602	Armoured Command Car	1980	M/B	$75
604	Landrover Bomb Disposal	1977	M/B	$35
609	U.S. 105mm Howitzer	1977	M/B	$22
612	Commando Jeep	1980	M/B	$38
616	AEC. Arctic Transporter	1977	M/B	$100
617	Volkswagen Anti-tank gun	1977	M/B	$75
618	AEC. Arctic Trans./Helicopter	1980	M/B	$150
619	Bren Gun Set	1980	M/B	$80
620	Berliet Missile Launch	1973	M/B	$90
622	Bren Gun Carrier	1977	M/B	$60
625	6 Pdr. Anti-tank Gun	1977	M/B	$45
654	155mm. Mobile Gun	1980	M/B	$75
654	155mm. Mobile Gun	1980	M/B	$75
656	Static 88mm. Gun	1980	M/B	$90
667	Armoured Patrol Car	1977	M/B	$35
668	Foden Army Truck	1980	M/B	$55
680	Ferret Armoured Car	1977	M/B677	$40

Top to Bottom: 623 Bedford Truck & 692 Medium Gun, 621 Bedford Truck & 693 Howitzer. W. Kilborn Collection.

617 Volkswagen & Anti-Tank Gun Set. W. Kilborn Collection.

Dinky 616 and 618, from U.S. catalog No. 12.

620 Berliet Missile Launcher Vehicle. W. Kilborn Collection.

*Top to Bottom: 668 Foden Truck, large scale,
604 Landrover Bomb Disposal Unit, 687
Convoy Army Truck. W. Kilborn Collection.*

NUMBER	DESCRIPTION	YEAR	CONDITION	VALUE
681	D.U.K.W.	1977	M/B677	$25
682	Stalwart Load Carrier	1977	M/B677	$35
683	Chieftain Tank	1980	M/B616	$70
687	Convoy Truck	1980	M/B	$27
690	Scorpion Tank	1979	M/B	$80
691	Striker Anti-tank Vech.	1979	M/B	$65
692	Leopard Tank	1980	M/B	$55
694	Hanomog Tank Destroyer	1980	M/B	$100
696	Leopard Anti-Aircraft T.	1979	M/B	$120
699	Leopard Recovery Tank	1977	M/B	$75

French Military Vehicles: (1946-1977)

NUMBER	DESCRIPTION	YEAR	CONDITION	VALUE
24M	Willy's Jeep	1946/49	M/B	$300
80A	Panhard EBR Tank	1957/63	M/B	$95
80B	Willy's Hotchkiss Jeep	1957/60	M/B	$95
80BP	Willy's Hotchkiss Jeep	1958/63	M/B	$100
80C	AMX13 Char Tank	1958/67	M/B	$100
80D	Berliet 6x6 Truck	1958/67	M/B	$125
80E	155mm. Field gun	1958/67	M/B	$105
80F	Renault Ambulance	1959/67	M/B	$80
800	Renault SINAPAR Radio Tk	1974	M/B	$45
802(819)	155mm. Fieldgun	1973/77	M/B	$40

French Dinky, Top to Bottom: 80C AMX Tank RT No. 813 AMX Self-Propelled Gun, 80A Panhard EBR in box. W. Kilborn Collection.

French Dinky - Top to Bottom: 80D/818 Berliet Army Truck, 80E/819 Howitzer. W. Kilborn Collection.

French Dinky, Top to Bottom: 80E 155m Fieldgun, 824 Berliet Gazelle. W. Kilborn Collection.

French Dinky 800 Renault Sinpar Radio Truck. W. Kilborn Collection.

French Dinky, Top to Bottom: 808/2 GMC Wrecker Sahara, 808/3 Wrecker Khaki. W. Kilborn Collection.

NUMBER	DESCRIPTION	YEAR	CONDITION	VALUE
808/2	GMC Wrecker Sahara	1972/73	M/B	$170
808/3	GMC Wrecker Khaki	1974	M/B	$150
807	Renault Ambulance Tous	1973	M/B	$70
809	GMC Truck 6x6	1970	M/B	$250
810	Dodge Command Car	1973	M/B	$195
813	AMX Self Propelled Gun	1965	M/B	$195
814	Panhard AML Amoured Car	1962/67	M/B	$110
815	Panhard EBR Tank	1962/67	M/B	$85
816	Berliet Gazelle Rkt. Launch	1969	M/B	$140
821	UNIMOG Covered Truck	1960	M/B	$95
822	M3 Half Track	1960	M/B	$115
823	Field Kitchen	1962/67	M/B	$85
823	GMC Tanker	1969	M/B	$320
824	Berliet Gazelle Truck	1963	M/B	$150
825	D.U.K.W. Amphibian	1964	M/B	$165
826	Berliet Wrecker	1963	M/B	$225
827	Panhard FL10 Tank	1963	M/B	$110
828	Jeep/Anti-Tank Missiles	1964	M/B	$125
829	Jeep with recoil rifle	1964	M/B	$100
883	AMX Bridge Layer	1964	M/B	$180
884	Brockway Bridging Truck	1962	M/B	$295
890	Berliet Tank Transporter	1960	M/B	$265
1406	Sinpar 4x4 Military Pol.	1977	M/B	$75.00
816/2	Hotchkiss Willy's Jeep	1958/59	M/B	$250

with tow hook

French Dinky, Top - L to R: 80H/807 Ambulance, 820 Ambulance; Bottom: 825 D.U.K.W. Amphibian. W. Kilborn Collection.

French Dinky, Top to Bottom: 809 GMC Truck 6x6, 823 GMC Tanker reissue. W. Kilborn Collection.

French Dinky, top L to R: 810 Dodge Car, 828 Jeep with missiles; bottom L to R: 829 Jeep with cannon, 815 Renault Sin Par. W. Kilborn Collection.

French Dinky, Top to Bottom: 814 Panhard Aml; L: 80B Hotchkiss Jeep, R: 80BP Hotchkiss Jeep. W. Kilborn Collection.

French Dinky, Top to Bottom: 815 Panhard EBR boxed; 890 Berliet Transporter. W. Kilborn Collection.

French Dinky, 821 Mercedes Benz Unimog, 823 Field Kitchen Trailer. W. Kilborn Collection.

French Dinky 822 M3 Half Track. W. Kilborn Collection.

French Dinky 826 Berliet Crane. W. Kilborn Collection.

French Dinky 827 Panhard EBR. W. Kilborn Collection.

French Dinky 883 AMX Bridge-Layer Tank. W. Kilborn Collection.

French Dinky 884 Brockway Bridgelayer Truck. W. Kilborn Collection.

French Dinky 1406 Renault Sinpar set, Air Force colors with figures. W. Kilborn Collection.

Some Dinky Military Vehicles made in France (French Dinky); Dinky standing soldier is 30mm tall.
L to R, back row: 810 Dodge Command Car, 813 155mm Self Propelled Gun, 80A (renumbered 815A) Panhard Armored Car - gun barrel not original, 822 Half track M3 towing 823 Army Field Kitchen; Front Row: 825 DUKW, 829 Gun-Carrier Jeep, 883 AMX Bridge-laying Tank, 884 Brockway Bridge Truck (Bridge Rails & Pontoons Missing). Photo by Ed Poole.

DISTLER

(Germany)

	C6	C8	C10
Distler BMW Wanderer, windup	250	375	500
Distler Coupe, driver, c/w motor	600	1000	1400
Distler Eccentric Saloon Car, windup, 8" long, driver's head springs through roof	500	800	1100
Distler Electro Magic 7500 Porsche Cabriolet, battery-driven	450	675	900
Distler Jaguar	340	510	680
Distler Limousine, tin litho, battery headlights, chauffeur, c/w motor, c. 1920s, 12" long	900	1500	2200
Distler Packard Convertible, c.1950s	225	338	450
Distler Uncle Wiggly Car	1500	2500	4000

Distler BMW Wanderer windup. Photo by Tim Oei.

Distler Electro Magic 7500 Porsche Cabriolet, battery driven, with original box. Photo by Tin Oei.

DOEPKE "MODEL TOYS"

by Ray Funk

Doepke Model Toys advertised its toys as outlasting all others—three-to-one. The company's full title was the "Charles Wm. Doepke Mfg. Co., Inc." of Rossmoyne, Ohio. Each toy was an authorized replica of the actual thing, and the decals and coloring exact. At the end of World War II, Doepke hit the market with five models, first in a line of heavy-duty metal operating replicas, employing metal tread or authentic miniature tires, either Goodyear or Firestone. This, to the best of my knowledge, has never been done so perfectly, even in the model kits of today.

These toys had rubber smoke stacks and received the approval of *Parents Magazine* and other advocates of good toys at that period. The first five numbers were 2000, 2001, 2002, 2006, 2007. Why not 3, 4, and 5? Perhaps Doepke had toys planned for these numbers that fell through. Following is a description of the Doepke vehicles:

Ray Funk is a leading collector and authority on trains and other toys, as well as a collector and authority on comic books and western literature.

No. 2000, Wooldridge H.D. Earth hauler, bright yellow, four huge tires, 25 inches long, 10 pounds. The actual manufacturer's address is listed as Sunnyvale, Calif. I'm sure most of you have seen the John Wayne movie "The Fighting Seabees," which used several of these, along with Caterpillar bulldozers and road graders. These Wooldridges caught my eye with their maneuvering ability, and could traverse the roughest terrain easily. Two long doors, the length of the bottom of the dirt-hauling area, could be released to deposit a load. Original price: $14.75 in 1945.

Doepke No. 2000 Wooldridge. Photo by Ray Funk.

No. 2001, Barber-Greene high-capacity bucket loader, 13 inches high, 10 pounds, dark green, all steel and rolling on steel tread. It was designed as a toy to load earth haulers. Handcrank operated. Original price: $14.75.

No. 2006, Adams diesel road-grader, dark orange, 26 inches long, 14 pounds, all six wheels, three axles and blade adjustable to all angles, steerable via steering wheel. Original price: $14.75.

Doepke 2006. Photo by Calvin L. Chaussee.

No. 2007, Unit Mobile Crane, dark orange, 11-1/2 inches long, 19-1/2" boom, 8-1/2 pounds, adjustable side jacks, steered via a drawbar, block and tackle and removable operating clam shell as standard accessory. Original price: $14.75.

Doepke 2001. Photo by Calvin L. Chaussee.

No. 2002, Jaeger concrete mixer, bright yellow, 15 inches long, 8 pounds on four wheels, steerable via draw bar (all model toys steered exactly like the real thing). Though perhaps the best-detailed, it was the poorest selling toy. While you could mix concrete in them, it wasn't feasible, due to a small amount received versus cleaning time. Original price: $10.75 to $13.75.

Doepke No. 2007 Unit Mobile Crane. Photo by Ray Funk.

Doepke 2002. Photo by Calvin L. Chaussee.

Doepke 2008 as shown in Doepke catalog.

No. 2009 was released and No. 2000 dropped. No. 2009 was a Euclid earth-hauler truck, with uncoupling four-wheel tractor to use to tow other toys, 27 inches long, 11 pounds, Euclid green, or light road-grader orange, trailer dumped in the same way as the Wooldridge. Original price: $14.75.

Doepke 2009 in Doepke catalog. Courtesy Ray Funk.

No. 2010, American-LaFrance pumper fire truck, 18 inches long, 7 pounds, bright red with chrome trim, ladder, bell, fire extinguisher, hoses and nozzle, a reservoir that held water for hand-operated pressure pump. Original price: $16.75.

Doepke catalog illustration of Model No. 2010. Courtesy Ray Funk. Photo by Bill Kaufman.

No. 2011, Heiliner earth scraper, 29 inches long, 13 pounds, bright dark red, loaded and dumped and operated on four wheels as the Wooldridge did. Original price: $16.75.

Doepke 2011 as shown in a Doepke catalog. Courtesy Ray Funk.

No. 2012, Caterpillar D6 tractor and bulldozer, caterpillar yellow, 15 inches long, 7 pounds, with real bulldozer treads for sharp realistic turning (removable only by using punch and hammer to remove connecting pin from between two of the pads) and adjustable bulldozer blade, plus heavy draw bar. Diesel motor was cast metal. Original price: $13.75.

Doepke 2012. Photo by Calvin L. Chaussee.

No. 2013 eliminated and replaced No. 2001. No. 2013, Barber-Green mobile high-capacity bucket loader, 22 inches long, 12 inches high, 10 pounds, buckets on chains and rubber conveyor belt, adjustable and steered by steering wheel. Original price: $19.75.

Doepke No. 2013 Barber-Greene. Courtesy Thomas G. Nefos, Federal Shipping Network.

No. 2014, American La-France aerial ladder truck, 23 inches long, 42-inch extended ladder height, 11 pounds, bright red and chrome, bell, red light, adjustable side jacks, single unit truck steered by steering wheel. Original price: $20.75.

Doepke Model Toys were doomed to extinction by lower-priced, lighter-constructed imitators of lesser quality, but none ever had, before or after, the heavy-duty constructed realism and operating qualities as had the one and only "Model Toys." Of the Doepke Model Toys that were mass-produced, several had variations in their basic construction from time to time. Usually these changes were an elimination of the more intricate operating procedures and had little or no effect on the toy's overall outward appearance.

In *Antique Toy World*, Philip Sayer wrote a two-part article on Doepke and featured pictures of nearly all toys manufactured by the firm. The ones that were produced in such limited numbers (only one to a few), are mentioned and often times described. Also listed are nearly all of the slight changes in mass-produced toys, though I could not (perhaps overlooked it) find mention of the change in the D-6 Caterpillar. The first models to hit the market have the front axles held tightly forward by springs, so when being pushed forward and they strike a solid object to climb over, there is some give to absorb the shock and protect the tract pads. Later models eliminated this and opted for simple axle wells. Had I not had both types, this slight change would have easily gone unnoticed.

It would seem that Doepke would accept orders to make model toys of the real thing for the actual producers, and the toys with the most allure, playability, and feasible mass-production design and entertainment value, would be mass produced. The others had only one to a few produced, as mentioned. This is no doubt the explanation for the number gaps between the marketed items. Among the scarcer articles produced, were even a few automobiles, avidly sought after by collectors that have delved into this company's past history to any depth.

	C6	C8	C10
Doepke No ?? Farm			
Tractor-N-Wagon, wooden	68	102	135
Doepke No. 2000 Wooldridge			
H.D. Earth Hauler, 25" long	125	188	250
Doepke No. 2001 Barber-Greene high			
capacity bucket loader, 13" high	242	365	485
Doepke No. 2002 Jaeger			
Concrete Mixer, 15" long	210	315	420
Doepke No. 2006 Adams			
Diesel Road Grader, 26" long	112	168	225
Doepke No. 2007 Unit			
Mobile Crane, 11-1/2" long	150	225	300
Doepke No. 2008 American			
La France Aerial Ladder Truck	190	285	380
Doepke No. 2009 Euclid			
Earth Hauler Truck, 27" long	142	215	285
Doepke No. 2010 American-La			
France pumper fire truck, 18" long	160	240	320

	C6	C8	C10
Doepke No. 2011 Heiliner			
Earth Scraper, 29" long	155	233	310
Doepke No. 2012 Caterpillar			
D6 tractor and bulldozer, 15" long	288	432	575
Doepke No. 2013 Barber-Greene			
mobile high-capacity bucket			
loader, 22" long, treads	190	285	380
As above, wheels	225	338	450
Doepke No. 2014 American-La France			
aerial ladder fire truck 23" long	275	413	550
Doepke No. 2015 Clark Airport			
Tractor and Baggage Trailers	225	338	450
Doepke No. 2017 MG, 1954, 15" long	200	300	400
Doepke No. 2018 Jaguar, 1955	343	515	685
Doepke No. 2023 Searchlight			
Truck, 1955	750	1300	1700

Doepke 2013 on wheels.

Doepke 2014 (bell at middle). Photo by Calvin L. Chaussee.

Clark AIRPORT TRACTOR and Trailers

Here's an exciting, new Model Toy that's loaded with customer appeal—a rugged scale miniature of the Clark Airport Tractor that hauls air freight and baggage!

Like all Model Toys, the AIRPORT TRACTOR and TRAILERS are wonderfully realistic in appearance and performance. Trailers bear the emblems of leading airlines—an authentic touch that will thrill and impress all youngsters.

Doepke 2015. Part of an ad in the May, 1954 Hobby Merchandiser. Courtesy Bob Bard.

Doepke 2017, as seen in the May, 1954 Hobby Merchandiser. Courtesy Bob Bard.

Doepke No. 2018 Jaguar. Photo by Calvin L. Chaussee.

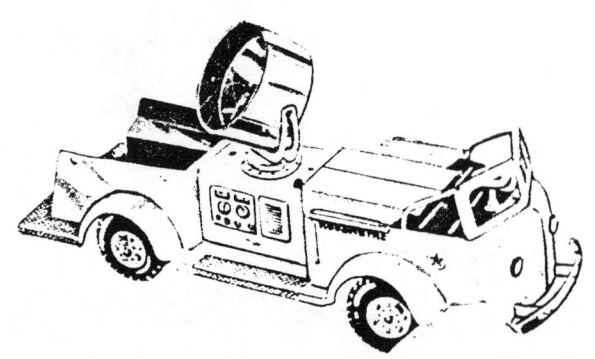

Doepke 2023 as seen in the 1955-56 Toy Yearbook.

DOLL & CO.

	C6	C8	C10
Doll & Co. Touring Car, Open, live steam motor, hand painted tin, 3 doors open, 19" long	1500	2700	4000

	C6	C8	C10
Doll & Co. Truck, open bed, live steam, chain driven, 19" long	2000	3700	6600

DOOLING BROTHERS

(Los Angeles)

The three brothers began their firm in 1939. There were seven different cars and one variation

	C6	C8	C10
Dooling Arrow (1948 to late 1950s)		No Price Found	
Dooling F Car, Hornet powered	700	1100	1600
Dooling Mercury Deluxe, rear drive		No Price Found	
Dooling Mercury Midget		No Price Found	
Dooling Mercury Second Series, front drive		No Price Found	
Dooling Pee Wee, 12" long		No Price Found	
Dooling Streamliner, 16" long		No Price Found	

Dooling Brothers Mercury "18" gasoline-powered racer. This was auctioned in Jan., 1993 for $1550. It was made in California in limited quantities between 1939 and 1945. Courtesy Jeff Bub Auctions.

DRUGE

Druge Bros. Mfg. Co. was located at 888-92nd Avenue, Oakland, California. In 1948 its "Hyster" sold for the very high price of $9.75.

	C6	C8	C10
Druge Cari-Car Lumber Carrier	100	150	200
Druge "Hyster" Lumber Carrier	120	180	240

Druge "Hyster" Lumber Carrier. Photo by Tim Oei.

DUNWELL

Dunwell was the trade name given to its toys by Metal Products Co. of Clifton, New Jersey. Its trucks seem to have been sold from 1953 to 1958. Its line resembles Tonka's and is rare.

	C6	C8	C10		C6	C8	C10
Dunwell "Auto Transport"	200	300	400	Dunwell Log Truck	175	265	350
Dunwell Dump Truck	100	150	250	Dunwell "Red Star			
Dunwell "Grain Hauler"	100	150	250	Express Lines" Truck	300	450	650
Dunwell "Land-o-Lakes"				Dunwell "Snowcrop" Refrigerator Semi	300	450	650
Semi, 1956 mail offer	250	375	500	Dunwell "Steel Carrier Co." Semi	100	150	250
Dunwell "Livestock Transport"	175	265	350	Dunwell Wrecker	150	225	300

Dunwell "Auto Transport." Photo by Roy Bonjour.

Dunwell Grain Hauler. Photo by Tim Oei.

Dunwell "Livestock Transport." Photo by Tim Oei.

Dunwell Log Truck. Photo by Tim Oei.

Dunwell "Red Star Express Lines" c. 1953. Photo by Bob Smith.

Dunwell "Steel Carrier." Photo by Tim Oei.

DYNA-MODEL PRODUCTS COMPANY

(Dyna-Mo)

by Fred Maxwell

Dyna-Model Products Co., 93 S. St., Oyster Bay, Long Island, New York, may have pioneered the scale-models industry dominating today's markets with its "Dyna-Mo" brand of HO toys to be used in train layouts. They are rather high quality pot-metal toys, identified by their method of assembling body parts, clamping axles between small posts, and the standardized appearance of the undersides of the whole line.

Probably produced in the 1930s, and perhaps in the post-war era, the toys were made by a coarse die-casting process. The earlier vintage cars were made into two to five parts, exclusive of wheels and axles, to be pinned, clamped, or glued together; body, frame, steering wheel, top, and windshield. Some were packaged as kits, with instructions printed on the box: "Pinch ends of axel [sic] after installing wheels" (R-26). The toys were factory painted in as many as four colors per toy.

	C6	C8	C10
D1 Dyna "R-26 HO Surrey, 35c": 1-3/4". Horseless carriage, tiller steering, 3 colors, 3-piece body, kit	4	6	8
D2 Dyna Touring Car: 2". Antique Stanley Steamer, open tonneau, rt. hand steering, 4 colors, 4-piece	4	6	8
D3 Dyna Speedster: 2". Antique Mercer, rt. hand steering, 4 colors, 3-piece.	4	6	8
D4 Dyna Roadster: 1-7/8". Antique Buick? Open rt. hand steering, 4-piece, 3 colors	4	6	8
D5 Dyna Touring Car: 1-7/8". Antique. Realistic folded top attachable with hinge pins, left hand steering, 5-piece, 2 colors	4	6	8
D6 Dyna "R-61 HO Model T Ford 1914 touring with top 60c": 1-5/8". 1-piece body, top up, 3 colors. "Cut plastic windshield to fit, darken edges with ink or paint and glue top and windshield in place, in slots provided"	4	6	8
D7 Dyna Touring car: 1-3/4". 1914 Ford, top down cast in 1-piece body, glued windshield, 3 colors	4	6	8
D8 Dyna Roadster: 2". 1920s Packard convertible, top down, rumble seat, one piece body, glued windshield, spoked wheels, 3 colors	6	9	12
D9 Dyna Roadster: 2". Packard, same as above, top up, 3 colors	6	9	12
D10 Dyna Touring: 2". Packard, same as above, top down, 3 colors	6	9	12
D11 Dyna Roadster: 2". Model A Ford? Top down, open rumble seat, disc wheels, 1-piece body, unpainted	2	3	4
D12 Dyna Sedan: 2". Buick Sedan, 1930s. Open windshield and windows, 2 colors	4	6	8
D13 Dyna "R-68 HO Buick convertible 55c". 2-3/8". Late 1930s. Open, 2-door Sedan, top down, 1-piece body, solid cast windshield, disk wheels	6	9	12
D14 Dyna Sedan: 2-3/8", Buick 2-door. airflow, open windshield and windows	6	9	12

	C6	C8	C10
D15 Dyna Taxi: 2-3/8". Buick Sedan, late 1930s. Open windshield and windows, 2 colors	6	9	12
D16 Dyna Convertible, 2-3/8". Cadillac 2-door Sedan, late 1930s	6	9	12
D17 Dyna Sedan: 2-3/8". Cadillac 2-door Sedan, open windshield and windows, incl. rear, late 1930s	6	9	12
D18 Dyna Taxi: 2-3/8". Cadillac sedan, late 1930's, open windshield and windows including rear, 2 colors	6	9	12
D19 Dyna Sedan: 2-3/8". Pontiac 4-door airflow, open windshield and windows incl. rear	6	9	12
D20 Dyna Limousine: 2-1/2". Cadillac, late 1930s, open windows as above	6	9	12
D21 Dyna Delivery Van: 2-3/8", Pontiac, late 1930s, open windshield and door windows	4	6	8
D22 Dyna Pickup Truck: 2-1/2". GMC?, late 1930s, open windows, spoked wheels, 2-piece, 3 colors	4	6	8

Dyna-Model, top L to R: D1, Ford T Roadster, 1-7/8", D7, D3, Franklin steam touring 2-1/8" Middle, L to R: D5, D6, D9, D10, D8; Bottom, L to R: D11, Cadillac Sedan 2", D23, D16. Photo by Fred Maxwell.

	C6	C8	C10
D23 Dyna Wrecker: 2-3/4", GMC?, late 1930s, open windows, 3-piece, 4 colors	6	9	12
D24 Dyna Dump Truck: 2-3/4". Open windows, hinged body with realistic load of coal. 3-piece, 2 colors, dual rear wheels	8	12	16
D25 Dyna Pickup Truck: 2". GMC?, 1930s, one piece, open windows, one color	4	6	8
D26 Dyna Pickup Truck: 2". Mack? "US Army," Air Corps star decals, late 1930s, 2-piece body, 2 colors	4	6	8
D27 Dyna Truck: 2". Mack? Same chassis as above, but tarpaulin covered, 2-piece body	4	6	8

Dyna-Model, top L to R: D14, D20?, D12, Cadillac 2-door Sedan, 2-3/8"; Middle, L to R: D15, D18, D21; Bottom, L to R: D22, D23, D24. Photo by Fred Maxwell.

EBO

(Germany)

	C6	C8	C10
Delivery Truck, early, tin litho, c/w motor, driver, 8" long	400	600	800

ELASTOLIN (HAUSSER)

by Jack Matthews

O&M Hausser (brothers Otto and Max) was founded in 1904 in Ludwigsberg near the German city of Stuttgart in Southern Germany. Hausser, Lineol's larger and fiercest competitor, made a somewhat larger variety of military toys and in the same popular 7.5cm scale but its pieces are generally considered to be a bit less sturdy and well-made (with a few exceptions). Thus, they do not command quite the same prices as do Lineol. Elastolin was Hausser's trade name.

Elastolin postwar No. 730 Prime Mover, U.S. Crew; value as shown $1,200. Photo by Jack Matthews.

Elastolin No. 730/10 6-wheel Prime Mover; value as shown $3,000. Photo by Jack Matthews.

Elastolin No. 730N Prime Mover, camouflaged; value as shown $2,200. Photo by Jack Matthews.

Elastolin No. 731, large Prime Mover; value as shown $16,000. Photo by Jack Matthews.

Elastolin postwar No. 731 Prime Mover. "Chrysler" front, U.S. crew; value as shown $2,200. Photo by Jack Matthews.

Elastolin No. 733/2 Kubelwagen (Staff Car)—War Production; value as shown $750. Photo by Jack Matthews.

Elastolin No. 733/10 Communications Car (very rare); value as shown $4,000. Photo by Jack Matthews.

Elastolin No. 733/12 Command Car with luggage (very rare); value as shown $4,000. Photo by Jack Matthews.

Elastolin No. 734 Zugsmachine (rare); value as shown $4,000. Photo by Jack Matthews.

Elastolin No. 738 camouflaged Ambulance with rubber tires; value as shown $3,000. Photo by Jack Matthews.

Elastolin No. 739N; value as shown $2,200. Photo by Jack Matthews.

Elastolin No. 739N Flakwagen, camouflaged, with British crew; value as shown $2,750. Photo by Jack Matthews.

Elastolin post-war No. 743 with British crew; value as shown $1,200. Photo by Jack Matthews.

Elastolin No. 743N; value as shown $2,000. Photo by Jack Matthews.

Elastolin No. 743N with Luftwaffe crew; value as shown $2,000. Photo by Jack Matthews.

Elastolin No. 744 Panzer Spahwagen (very rare); value as shown $12,000. Photo by Jack Matthews.

Elastolin postwar No. 744, "Chrysler front" version, U.S. crew; value as shown $1,200. Photo by Jack Matthews.

Elastolin No. 745 Communications Truck, camouflaged (rare); value as shown $3,750. Photo by Jack Matthews.

Elastolin No. 745 Communications Truck, light gray (rare); value as shown $3,500. Photo by Jack Matthews.

Elastolin No. 794 Heavy Truck towing Kitchen Wagon with crew (very rare); value as shown $4,250. Photo by Jack Matthews.

Elastolin No. 0/730 (very early tank and exceptionally rare); value as shown $2,400. Photo by Jack Matthews.

Elastolin No. 0/740 (early and rare); value as shown $2,400. Photo by Jack Matthews.

Elastolin 1/733 Kubelauto; value as shown $650. Photo by Jack Matthews.

Elastolin No. 1/733 Kubelauto with metal wheels (rare)—Kreigsproduction; value as shown $700. Photo by Jack Matthews.

Elastolin No. 1/734 Zugwagen (early and rare); value as shown $3,000. Photo by Jack Matthews.

Elastolin No. 1/740 AA Truck (early and rare); value as shown $2,750. Photo by Jack Matthews.

Elastolin 1/742 Searchlight Truck with Luftwaffe crew (early and rare); value as shown $3,000. Photo by Jack Matthews.

Elastolin No. 1744 Panzer Spahwagen (early and rare); value as shown $3,000. Photo by Jack Matthews.

Elastolin early tank (very rare); value as shown $350.

Elastolin, early and very rare; value as shown $3,000. Photo by Jack Matthews.

ELDON

(Los Angeles
1010 E. 62nd St.,)

	C6	C8	C10
Eldon Aerial Ladder Truck, 21" long	40	60	80
Eldon Concrete Truck, 17" long	44	66	85
Eldon Corvette, 14" long	44	66	85
Eldon Delivery Truck	40	60	80
Eldon Dump Truck, 18" long	30	45	60
Eldon Ford Lift Gate Truck, 18" long	30	45	60
Eldon Hot Rod, 18" long	80	120	160
Eldon Hot Rod Kit, bat-op, snap-together ...	32	48	65
Eldon Mighty Tow Truck	45	68	90
Eldon Road Race slot car set, 1965.............	35	55	70
Eldon Stake Truck	40	60	80
Eldon Steam Shovel	20	30	40
Eldon Tank Transport, military	48	72	95
Eldon Wrecker, 18" long, plastic	40	60	80

Eldon Aerial Ladder Truck, 21" long. Photo by Terry Sells.

ELMAR PRODUCTS COMPANY

(15 W. 24th St., New York City, c.1950s)

Elmar Rocket Shooting Tank. Courtesy Islyn Thomas.

	C6	C8	C10
Elmar Rocket			
Shooting Tank, 3-1/2" long .... No Price Found			

EMPIRE FORCES

(Gardel Industries, 106 E. 19th St., New York City, c.1943-44)

	C6	C8	C10
Empire Forces E5 Tank,			
composition (also in plaster) .... No Price Found			
Empire Forces E6 Tank,			
composition (also in plaster) .... No Price Found			

Empire Forces tanks. L to R: E5, E6

ERIE

(Parker White Metal)

Listing by Dave Leopard

According to James Apthorpe, Erie toys were made by Parker White Metal Company, which apparently began in Erie, Pennsylvania, but moved to Fairview (west of Erie) in the early 1960s. However, according to company officials he contacted, the firm made toys only prior to WWII. It printed no catalogs.

	C6	C8	C10		C6	C8	C10
EV01 Lincoln Zephyr				EV05 Packard Roadster,			
Sedan, 1936, 5-1/2" long, painted	40	50	60	1936, 6" long, painted	45	68	90
EV02 Lincoln Zephyr				EV06 Packard Roadster,			
Sedan, 1936, 5-1/2" long, plated	45	55	65	1936, 6" long, plated	47	70	95
EV03 Lincoln Zephyr				EV07 Packard Roadster,			
Sedan, 1936, 3-1/2" long, painted	25	30	35	1936, 3-1/2" long, painted	25	30	35
EV04 Lincoln Zephyr				EV08 Packard Roadster,			
Sedan, 1936, 3-1/2" long, plated	35	52	70	1936, 3-1/2" long, plated	30	35	40

	C6	C8	C10
EV09 (Unused)			
EV10 Ford Pickup Truck, 1935, low sides, 5" long, plated	45	55	65
EV11 Ford Pickup Truck, 1935, high sides, 5" long, large rear window	40	50	60
EV12 Ford Pickup Truck, 1935, high sides, 5" long, small rear window	40	50	60
EV13 Ford Ice Truck, 1935, "Pure Ice Co.," 5" long	50	60	70
EV14 Ford Tow Truck, 1935, "Servel Body," 5" long	50	60	70

	C6	C8	C10
EV15 Cabover Truck, c.1937, no tailgate, 3-1/4" long	20	25	30
EV16 Cabover Truck, c.1937, tailgate, updated, 3-1/4" long	20	25	30
EV17 Tow Truck, c.1939, no chassis, 4-1/4" long	30	35	40
EV18 Sedan, c.1939, futuristic, fin on trunk, no chassis, 4-1/4" long	30	35	40
EV19 Coupe, c.1939, futuristic, no chassis, 4-1/4" long	30	35	40
EV20 Sedan, c.1939, sharknose, no chassis, 4-1/4" long	30	35	40

Erie EV20. Photo by James Apthorpe.

ERTL

Ertl was begun by Fred Ertl Sr., in 1945, working out of his Dubuque, Iowa, home. As business expanded, the firm moved to Dyersville, Iowa. Ertl had learned about using sand molds in his native Germany; very early in the company's history, he began working directly from the original blueprints to make his toy tractors, trucks, and other wheeled toys. Ertl's specialty is farm toys, with rights obtained from such manufacturers as International Harvester and John Deere. Today, Ertl is the largest manufacturer of toy farm equipment in the world; in addition, it makes a number of other toys, such as cars, trucks, and airplanes.

	C6	C8	C10
Ertl Allis-Chalmers B-112 Tractor	70	110	165
Ertl Conoco Tanker	75	120	175
Ertl Fleetstar Hi-Side Dump Truck, red/wht	125	185	250
Ertl Fleetstar Tilt Bed, green	125	185	250
Ertl Fleetstar 10-Wheel Dump Truck, red	125	185	250
Ertl Ford 8000 Tractor, early	25	40	60
Ertl GE Truck, white	15	22	30
Ertl Gleaner C-280 w/corn picker	25	45	60
Ertl Grain Hopper, early	22	34	48
Ertl IHC Farmal 806, square fender	100	175	230
Ertl International Fleetstar Gravity Feed Truck	150	250	350
Ertl International Scout, maroon, or blue	85	135	195
Ertl John Deere 500 Bulldozer w/blade	40	70	100
Ertl John Deere 6600 Combine	60	100	140
Ertl Loadstar Box Van, lavender/white	200	375	575
Ertl Loadstar Concrete Truck, red/white	200	350	500
Ertl Loadstar Dump Truck	140	250	325
Ertl Loadstar Grain/Cattle Stake Truck	140	250	325

	C6	C8	C10
Ertl Loadstar Tilt Bed, green/gray	125	175	300
Ertl Loadstar Tow Truck, white/red	150	275	425
Ertl Mary Kay Cosmetics Trailer Truck	65	115	150
Ertl Mobile Tanker	40	65	88

Ertl Fleetstar Dump Truck, 10 wheel. Photo by Bob Smith.

Ertl Fleetstar Hi-Side Dump Truck. Photo by Bob Smith.

Ertl Grain Hopper, 14-1/2" long. Courtesy Harvey K. Rainess.

Ertl International Fleetstar Gravity Feed Truck.

Ertl International Scout (both). Photo by Bob Smith.

Ertl Loadstar Box Van. Photo by Bob Smith.

Ertl

	C6	C8	C10
Ertl Picker	25	40	60
Ertl Texaco Tanker No. 2.	150	250	350

	C6	C8	C10
Ertl "Van Lines"			
Pup Trailer only, white	100	150	225
Ertl White Cab-Over Dump Truck,			
white/red	165	265	400

Ertl Loadstar Concrete Truck. Photo by Bob Smith.

Ertl Fleetstar Tilt Bed. Photo by Bob Smith.

Ertl Loadstar Tilt Bed. Photo by Bob Smith.

Ertl Loadstar Tow Truck. Photo by Bob Smith.

Ertl, L to R: "Ertl Van Lines" pup trailer, Loadstar straight cab and chassis. Photo by Bob Smith.

Ertl White Cab-Over Dump Truck. Photo by Bob Smith.

	C6	C8	C10
Erwin, Ford w/windshield wipers	40	60	80
Erwin Race Car	55	82	110

F&F CEREAL PREMIUMS

by Dave Leopard

The toy vehicles that were included in Post cereals during the 1950s and 1960s were made by the F&F Mold and Die Works of Dayton, Ohio, a company that specialized in manufacturing plastic premiums for the food industry. The Fiedler and Fiedler company was in business from 1945 until 1987, and its entire product-line consisted of plastic premiums.

The small plastic vehicles, about 3 inches long, were included in Post Grape-Nut Flakes, Corn Flakes, Rice Krispies, etc. over a period of about 15 years, beginning in 1954. Most of the cereal premiums were cars, but they also made speedboats, which were marked "Century," several versions of a tractor-trailer truck, which were marked "Ford" on the cab and "Fruehauf" on the trailer, and two versions of a Greyhound bus.

All of the F&F vehicles from 1954 to 1967 are clearly marked with its trademark. Two earlier Fords, a 1950 and a 1951 sedan, have magnets glued underneath the roof, are the same scale and are very similar to other F&F vehicles. Collectors disagree as to whether these early Fords are in fact F&Fs. Likewise, a series of 1969 Mercurys, identical to earlier F&F vehicles in scale, style, and materials, are marked "JVZ Co." Whether these Fords and Mercurys are properly identified as F&F or not, they are very similar and fit nicely with known F&F vehicles.

1950 Ford 4-Door Sedan	6	9	12
1951 Ford 4-Door Sedan	6	9	12
1954 Mercury XM-800 Show Car	5	8	10
1954 Mercury Monterey Convertible	8	12	15
1954 Mercury Monterey 4-Door Sedan	5	8	10
1954 Mercury Monterey 2-Door Sedan	5	8	10
1954 Ford Crestline Sunliner	5	8	10
1954 Ford Crestline Hardtop	5	8	10
1954 Ford Crestline 4-Door Sedan	5	8	10
1954 Ford Customline 2-Door Sedan	5	8	10
1954 Ford Customline Ranchwagon	5	8	10
1955 Ford Country Sedan (wagon)	8	10	15
1955 Ford Customline 2-Door Sedan	6	9	12
1955 Ford Fairlane Crown Victoria	5	8	10
1955 Ford Fairlane Sunliner	5	8	10
1955 Ford Thunderbird Convertible	7	11	15

	C6	C8	C10
1957 Ford Convertible	8	12	15
1957 Ford 4-Door Hardtop Sedan	8	12	15
1957 Ford Highway Patrol	8	12	15
1957 Ford Ambulance	3	4.50	6
1957 Ford Firechief Car	8	12	15
1959 Ford Thunderbird Hardtop	6	9	12
1959 Ford Thunderbird Convertible	6	9	12
1960 Plymouth Convertible	3	4.50	6
1960 Plymouth Hardtop Coupe	3	4.50	6
1960 Plymouth Station Wagon	3	4.50	6
1961 Ford Thunderbird Convertible	8	10	15
1961 Ford Thunderbird Hardtop	8	10	15
1961 Ford Thunderbird Roadster (single seat)	10	15	20
1966 Ford Mustang Convertible	6	10	12
1966 Ford Mustang Hardtop	6	9	12
1966 Ford Mustang Fastback	6	9	12
1967 Mercury Cougar Hardtop	3	5	7
1969 Mercury Cougar Hardtop	3	5	7
1969 Mercury Cyclone Fastback	6	10	12
1969 Mercury 2-Door Hardtop	6	10	12

F&F: Front, 1955 Ford Fairlane Sunliner; Rear, 1954 Mercury XM-800 Show Car, 1954 Ford Customline Ranchwagon. Courtesy Dave Leopard. Photo by Rick Lacaire.

F&F, L to R: Ford Highway Patrol, Ford Ambulance. Photo by Gary Linden.

	C6	C8	C10
1969 Mercury 4-Door Sedan	6	10	12
Ford Tractor/Trailer (flatbed)	8	10	15
Ford Tractor/Trailer (lowboy)	8	10	15
Ford Tractor/Trailer (moving van)	8	10	15

	C6	C8	C10
Ford Tractor/Trailer (enclosed trailer)	8	10	15
Ford Tractor/Trailer (oil tanker)	8	10	15
Greyhound Bus	8	12	16
Greyhound Scenicruiser Double-Decker Bus	8	10	15

FALLOWS TOYS

Fallows Toys, Frederick &
   Henry, Horseless Carriage with driver,
   8" long, cast iron and tin, c.1905 900   1350   1800

Fallows Toys, Frederick & Henry,
Horseless Carriage with driver, 8" long.
Courtesy Wilkinson Collection,
Detroit Antique Toy Museum.

FIRESTONE

The following list, with its codings, was compiled by David Leopard.

FA01 1939 Mercury fastback
   4-door Sedan, 4-3/4" long 60   75   90
FA02 1935 Ford 2-door
   Humpback Sedan, 4-7/8" long 50   60   75
FA03 1936 Ford 2-door
   Humpback Sedan, 4-7/8" long 70   105   140

Firestone FA-03 (both) with original box.
Photo by Ron Smith.

FISCHER, HEINRICH & CO.

(Nuremberg, Germany, 1908-1931)

by Bob Smith

Fischer's easily recognized mark, a fish swimming through the letter A, is a unique trademark usually found on the rear of the car. The George Borgfeldt store of New York City purchased many of the toys produced by Fischer for the U.S. market. Not all of the Fischer toys carried his mark, however. "Nifty" toys, for example, was one of the trademarks used by the company. The great comic character tin toy, "Toonerville Trolley," is one of the best known Fischer toys made under the Nifty trademark.

	C6	C8	C10
Fischer Automatic Dump Truck, c/w motor, 10-1/2" long	550	825	1200
Fischer Double-Decker Bus, tin c/w, c.1910, 7-1/2" long	680	1000	1500

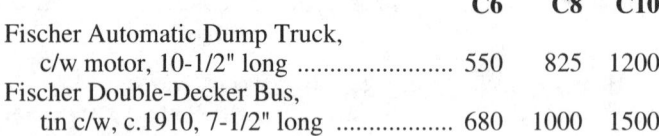

Fischer Limousine, c.1910, maroon, black stripes. Courtesy Bill Bertoia Auctions. Photo by Jeanne Bertoia.

Fischer Double-Deck Bus, tin clockwork, c.1910, 7-1/2" long. Courtesy Harvey K. Rainess.

Fischer Limousine, c.1918, 7-1/2" long. Photo by Bob Smith.

Fischer Limousine, c.1915, 9" long. Photo by Bob Smith.

Fischer Torpedo, c.1912, 8" long. Photo by Bob Smith.

	C6	C8	C10
Fischer Limousine, chauffeur, c/w motor, 10" long	465	700	930
Fischer Limousine, c.1910, maroon, blk. stripes, driver, overhead rack, 13" long	1700	2800	4500
Fischer Limousine, green/black, c.1915, 9" long, c/w motor, back doors open	650	975	1275
Fischer Limousine, c.1918, 7-1/2" long, green/black, c/w motor, head lamps, windshield	550	825	1175

	C6	C8	C10
Fischer Limousine, luggage rack, driver, 9" long	650	1000	1300
Fischer Torpedo, c.1912, 8", red/yellow tin litho, c/w motor,	700	1000	1375
Fischer Tourer, chauffeur, 2 women, 8-1/2" long	500	750	1000
Fischer Town Coupe, tin, c/w motor, approx. 7" long	800	1300	2200

FISHER-PRICE

Fisher-Price was founded by Herman Fisher and Irving Price on Oct. 1, 1930, in East Aurora, New York. It made (and makes) colorfully lithographed quality wood toys for small children.

	C6	C8	C10
Fisher-Price 7 Looky Fire Truck	85	125	170
Fisher-Price 145 Husky Dump Truck	50	75	100
Fisher-Price 234 Nifty Station Wagon	225	325	450
Fisher-Price 472 Peter Bunny Cart	225	275	375
Fisher-Price 615 Tow Truck	30	45	60
Fisher-Price 629 Tractor	25	38	50
Fisher-Price 674 Black Sports Car	62	93	125

Fisher-Price 7 Looky Fire Truck. Courtesy John Murray.

Fisher-Price 234 Nifty Station Wagon. Courtesy John Murray.

Fisher-Price 472 Peter Bunny Cart. Courtesy John Murray.

Fisher-Price 733. Photo by Kent M. Comstock.

	C6	C8	C10
Fisher-Price 718 Tow Truck	25	38	50
Fisher-Price 724 Jalopy	11	16	22
Fisher-Price 733 Mickey			
Mouse Safety Patrol	262	393	525
Fisher-Price 745 Elsie's Dairy Truck	400	575	700

Fisher-Price 745 Elsie's Dairy Truck.

FREIDAG

According to a well-illustrated article by Fred Mac-Adam in the March 1993 *Antique Toy World*, William Freidag formed Freidag Mfg. Co. and Foundry in Freeport, Illinois, in 1920. He pronounced his last name "Friday." Freidag's cast-iron toys are obscure but significant and can easily be confused with those by another maker. Thus, collectors might find it helpful to obtain a copy of the MacAdam article when they're uncertain about any cast-iron toy from 1920 to 1932, when Freidag went out of business.

	C6	C8	C10
Freidag Auto with chauffeur, 1920s	375	562	750
Freidag Bus, 6-3/4" long	225	338	450
Freidag Coupe, 5-3/4" long, 1924	290	435	580
Freidag Double-Decker Bus, 9-1/4" long ..	850	1400	2100
Freidag Panel Delivery Truck,			
7-1/2" long	1200	2200	3200
Freidag Pickup Truck, 7-1/2" long	500	750	1000
Freidag Racer, c.1930s,			
6-1/2" long, driver, passenger	400	600	800
Freidag Roadster, 1922, 9-1/4" long	500	750	1000
Freidag Taxi with black driver	600	1000	1400
Freidag Taxi, 7" long, 1920s	450	675	900
Freidag Truck, flatbed, 10" long	500	750	1000
Freidag Yellow Cab, 5" long	550	850	1250

Freidag Double-Decker Bus, 9-1/4" long. Courtesy Bill Bertoia Auctions. Photo by Jeanne Bertoia.

Freidag, L to R: Pickup Truck, 7-1/2" long, Panel Delivery Truck, 7-1/2" long. Courtesy Bill Bertoia Auctions. Photo by Jeanne Bertoia.

Freidag Roadster, 1922, 9-1/4" long. Courtesy Bill Bertoia Auctions. Photo by Jeanne Bertoia.

"FUTURISTIC"

Discovered by collector Dave Leopard, these slush-cast lead-alloy vehicles obviously belong together. FU1 appears to be pre-WWII and the others postwar. The manufacturer is unknown

	C6	C8	C10
FU1 Car Pulling House Trailer, 6", white tires		No Price Found	
FU2 Coupe with fin, 4-1/4" long, black tires		No Price Found	
FU3 Oil Truck, 3-3/4" long black tires, "Super Oil"		No Price Found	

"Futuristic" FU1. Photo by Dave Leopard.

"Futuristic" FU2. Photo by Dave Leopard.

"Futuristic" FU3. Photo by Dave Leopard.

G&K

	C6	C8	C10
G&K Delivery Truck, tin windup, driver, early, 5-1/2" long	475	715	950
G&K Motorcycle w/seat-like sidecar, tin windup, early, 6-1/2" long	800	1300	1800

GAMA

	C6	C8	C10
Gama Aerial Ladder w/pump	138	210	275
Gama Cadillac	350	550	850
Gama Crane w/Clam Bucket	125	188	250
Gama Tractor & Trailer, 17" long	95	140	190

GT1 Gama pre-war, large, with chain treads; value as shown $500. Photo by Jack Matthews.

GT2 Gama pre-war, large; value as shown $500. Photo by Jack Matthews.

GT3 Gama pre-war, large; value as shown $500. Photo by Jack Matthews.

GT4 Gama post-war, large; value as shown $350. Photo by Jack Matthews.

GT5 Gama postwar, large; value as shown $350. Photo by Jack Matthews.

GT6 Gama postwar, large; value as shown $350. Photo by Jack Matthews.

GT7 Gama postwar, large; value as shown $350. Photo by Jack Matthews.

GT8 Gama postwar, large; value as shown $300. Photo by Jack Matthews.

GT9 Gama prewar, medium size; value as shown $200. Photo by Jack Matthews.

GT10 Gama prewar, medium size; value as shown $150. Photo by Jack Matthews.

GT12   *GT13*
Gama prewar, small, L to R, value as shown: $100, $125. Photo by Jack Matthews.

GT11 Gama prewar, small; value as shown $200. Photo by Jack Matthews.

GT16   *GT17*
Gama prewar, small (5-6"); value as shown $125 each. Photo by Jack Matthews.

GT14   *GT15*
Gama prewar, small; value as shown $125 each. Photo by Jack Matthews.

GT18 Gama prewar, small, with box; value as shown $175. Photo by Jack Matthews.

GT19 Gama Montage tank, small, with original box; value tank alone in mint $200. Courtesy Joe and Sharon Freed.

GT20 Gama Montage Tank, small (6-1/4"); value tank alone in mint $200. Courtesy Harvey K. Rainess.

GT21 Gama Tank, WWII type, 3-1/4", No. 634, windup, with box. Courtesy Harvey K. Rainess.

Gama, early; value as shown $250. Photo by Jack Matthews

Gama; value as shown $150. Photo by Jack Matthews.

GARLAND

	C6	C8	C10
Garland Red Flyer			
Hydraulic Dump (Made in Detroit)	125	188	250

*Garland Red Flyer Hydraulic Dump,
25" long. Photo by Jerry Combs.*

GARRETT

Garrett Flexible Products of Garrett, Indiana, began in 1978. Its owner was F.H. Thurman, who designed Auburn Rubber's trucks, cars, etc., in the 1950s. He also designed the Garrett line, which was sometimes known as Rubber Toys Unique, with some toys marked "Unique."

	C6	C8	C10
Garrett Corvette Sting Ray, 7" long	15	22	30

GARTON

	C6	C8	C10		C6	C8	C10
Garton "Fire Department"				Garton Hod Rod Pedal Car	400	650	900
Ladder Pedal Car, 1949	700	1100	1600	Garton Woody Pedal Car, 1937	1300	2500	3900
Garton Ford Pedal Car, c.1950s	700	1100	1700				

GAY PLASTICS

	C6	C8	C10		C6	C8	C10
"Gay Police," 3-wheeler, 8" long	35	52	70	Gay Plastics Truck	5	8	10

GENDRON

	C6	C8	C10
Gendron Buick Pedal Car, 1920	5000	9500	18,000
Gendron Federal Knight Dump Truck,			
offered in "museum quality" in 1992 for $11,000			
Gendron "Racer" Pedal Car, 38" long	1300	2000	3000
Gendron/Sampson			
Army Truck, 27" long	800	1300	2000
Gendron/Sampson			
Chemical Fire Truck, 28" long	1200	2000	2800
Gendron/Sampson			
Coal Truck, 26" long, steel	1000	1600	2500
Gendron/Sampson Dump			
Truck, 27" long, pressed steel	850	1350	1900

*Gendron Stearns pedal car, c.1920, 41" long.
Courtesy Bill Bertoia Auctions.
Photo by Jeanne Bertoia.*

A Garrett flyer.

	C6	C8	C10
Gendron/Sampson Screen			
Side Express Truck, 27" long	650	1100	1500
Gendron/Sampson			
Stake Truck, 26" long	1500	2300	3500
Gendron/Sampson			
Tank Truck, 29" long	800	1400	2000

	C6	C8	C10
Gendron Sportster			
Pedal Car, 41" long	2000	3500	5300
Gendron Stearns			
Pedal Car, c.1920, 41" long	1000	1700	2640

GENERAL TOY OF CANADA

	C6	C8	C10
General Toy of Canada			
Racer No. 3, tin windup, 4-3/4" long	75	112	150

GIBBS

	C6	C8	C10		C6	C8	C10
Gibbs "Gibbs No. 701" Truck	150	250	350	Gibbs Service Station	350	525	700

GIFTCRAFT

	C6	C8	C10
Giftcraft (possibly only the distributor)			
TA01 Fastback Sedan c.1946 Nash,			
solid rubber, 4" long	15	22	30

Giftcraft, TA01.
Photo by Dave Leopard.

GILBERT: See "A.C. Gilbert"

GILMARK

	C6	C8	C10		C6	C8	C10
Gilmark Esso Gasoline Truck	12	18	25	Gilmark Sedan w/opening hood	8	12	16
Gilmark Rocket				Gilmark Tractor/Trailer			
Car, driver, 4" long, 1950s	20	30	40	Hi-Way Transporter	8	12	16

GIRARD

Girard Model Works was founded by C.G. Wood in 1906, in Girard, Pennsylvania. His son Frank was soon made a partner. In 1918, it began making mechanical toys for an unidentified New York firm. In 1920, it sold them under the name "Wood's Mechanical Toys." The business eventually passed into other hands and had 1,000 employees in 1931. In the Depression, Girard laid off its salesman, Louis Marx, who stalled Girard customers as he tried to get a plant of his own in business. Since Marx was better-known to buyers than the people at Girard, he emerged triumphant. In 1934, Marx took over the firm. Girard remained in business until 1980, though its last toys seem to have been made in 1975.

	C6	C8	C10		C6	C8	C10
Girard Army Truck, cloth top, c.1940	150	225	300	Girard Bus with			
Girard Auto Transport,				driver, 12-1/2" long windup	188	282	375
c. early 1930s, carries two trucks	275	413	550				

	C6	C8	C10
Girard Coupe, 6" long	30	45	60
Girard Coupe, 14" long, battery operated headlights	350	525	700
Girard Fire Chief Car, 15" long	200	300	400
Girard "Fire Chief Siren Coupe," 14" long windup	275	450	600
Girard Fire Truck, 12" long, 1920s	50	75	100
Girard "Gasoline" Tanker, c.1939	85	135	225
Girard Ladder Truck, 7" long, 1930s	175	263	350
Girard Pierce-Arrow Coupe, 14" long, c.1932, green, orange & cream, windup	250	350	500
Girard Pump Truck, battery operated headlights, 10" long	100	150	200
Girard Race Car No. 2, 8" long windup	300	450	600

	C6	C8	C10
Girard Race Car, 1920s, pull rod	138	205	275
Girard Roadster, 14-1/2" long, electrified	212	318	425
Girard Side Dump, 11-1/2" long	150	225	300
Girard Stake Truck, 10" long, electric headlights	150	225	300
Girard Tank Truck, 11-1/2" long, wood wheels	92	138	185
Girard Touring Bus, painted tin, c.1920, 12" long	150	225	300
Girard "Toyland Dairy" Truck & Trailer	375	565	700
Girard Truck w/3 Trailers, 1928	130	195	260
Girard Truck with Trailer, 1930s, 17" long	100	150	200

Girard "Fire Chief Siren Coupe." Photo by Bill Kaufman.

Girard Pierce-Arrow Coupe, c.1932, 14" long. Photo by Bob Smith.

Girard Stake Truck, 10" long, electric headlights. Courtesy Charles L. Jackson.

Girard Touring Bus. Courtesy Mapes Auctioneers & Appraisers.

GLASS

	C6	C8	C10		C6	C8	C10
Glass Gas Pump, 1930s	200	325	450	Glass Motorcycle & Cop, 1930s	250	400	600

GLOBE CO.

	C6	C8	C10
Globe Co. Motorcycle w/Cop, 1930s, 8" long	650	1150	1675
Globe Co. Roadster, separate driver, kids in rumble seat, cast-iron, 11-1/2" long	500	750	1000

Globe Co. Roadster, separate driver, kids in rumble seat, 11-1/2" long. Courtesy Bill Bertoia Auctions. Photo by Jeanne Bertoia.

GONG BELL

	C6	C8	C10
Gong Bell "Mickey Mouse Bus Lines - Walt Disney Stars"	250	375	500
Gong Bell Milk Truck 13" long, wooden bottles	225	338	450
Gong Bell Racer, 20" long, c.1930s	150	225	300

Gong Bell "Mickey Mouse Bus Lines - Walt Disney Stars." Courtesy Wilkinson Collection, Detroit Antique Toy Museum.

GOODEE

By Dave Leopard

Goodee die-cast vehicles were made by the Excel Products Company of East Brunswick, New Jersey. All of the prototypes for Goodee vehicles appear to be in the 1953 to 1955 range. It would seem that Goodee vehicles were produced in two sizes: about 3 inches and 6 inches, although I have listed only the ones I have actually seen. Some of the larger models had windup motors, which would increase their value.

Large Size

1953 GMC Pickup Truck	15	20	25
1953 Ford Police Cruiser	15	20	25
1954 DeSoto Station Wagon	15	20	25
1955 Ford Fuel Truck	15	20	25
American LaFrance Pumper	15	20	25
Military Jeep	15	20	25

Small Size

1953 GMC Pickup Truck	10	12	15
1953 Studebaker Coupe	12	15	20
1953 Lincoln Capri Hardtop	10	12	15
1953 Cadillac Convertible	10	12	15
1953 Ford Police Cruiser	10	12	15
1954 DeSoto Station Wagon	10	12	15
1955 Ford Fuel Truck	10	12	15

Goodee 1953 GMC Pick up, large and small versions. Photo by Dave Leopard.

	C6	C8	C10			C6	C8	C10
American LaFrance Pumper	10	12	15		Step Van	10	12	15
Military Jeep	10	12	15		Land Speed Racer	10	12	15
Moving Van	10	12	15		Land Speed Racer (bubble fenders)	10	12	15

GREY IRON

Grey Iron began in 1840 as the Brady Machine Shop in Mount Joy, Pennsylvania. Toy-making began as early as 1903, almost entirely in iron (occasionally in lead and aluminum). Its best-known products are toy soldiers. It is still in business today as Donsco-John Wright, located in Wrightsville, though still casting in Mount Joy.

	C6	C8	C10
Grey Iron Ford Coupe w/driver 8-3/8" long	475	515	950
Grey Iron Ford Coupe w/driver, 5-5/8" long	No Price Found		
Grey Iron, Convertible Midget, 1-1/2" long	20	30	40
Grey Iron, Coupe Midget, 1-1/2" long	20	30	40
Grey Iron, Delivery Truck, Midget, 1-1/2" long	20	30	40
Grey Iron, Racer, Midget, 1-1/2" long	20	30	40
Grey Iron, Sedan, Airflow Type, Midget, 1-1/2" long	20	30	40
Grey Iron, Sedan, older, Midget, 1-1/2" long	20	30	40
Grey Iron, Sedan, 1927, 9" long	1000	1500	2000

Grey Iron "Midget" Vehicles, approx. 1" long. Photo by Stan Alekna.

GREY-IRON-CASTING-CO. **MOUNT JOY, PA., U.S.A.**
THE GUARANTEED LINE

TOY AUTOMOBILES.

Ford Coupes.

Perfect replicas of latest models. Substantially built and practically unbreakable.

Attractively finished in Black Enamel, with Nickel Trimmings, Yellow Wheels and Balloon Tires.

Complete with driver and detachable spare tire.

No. 100. 8⅜ inches long. 4⅜ inches high. 3½ inches wide.
1 in a box. 3 dozen in a case. 140 lbs. per case.

No. 50. 5⅝ inches long. 3¼ inches high. 2½ inches wide.
4 in a box. 6 dozen in a case. 230 lbs. per case.

No. 50X. Same as No. 50, but without driver and spare tire.
4 in a box. 6 dozen in a case. 210 lbs. per case.

The Grey Iron Ford Coupe, as seen in Grey Iron's catalog No. 24 (1924?).

Grey Iron Ford Coupe, missing driver, 8-3/8" long. Courtesy Bill Bertoia Auctions. Photo by Jeanne Bertoia.

GRIMLAND

(Marietta, Georgia)

	C6	C8	C10
Grimland Allied Vans, 7-1/2" long	58	87	115

GUNTHERMANN, S.G.

(Nuremberg, Germany. 1887 to present)

By Bob Smith

Gunthermann's toy business flourished well into the 1900s. S.G. Gunthermann passed away in 1890. His widow married the company manager, Adolf Weigel. Weigel's initials were added to the "SG" logo until his death in 1919. The initials were removed and the logo was changed back to the original SG. The company was sold to Seimens in 1965 and is still in business today.

	C6	C8	C10
Gunthermann Auto Candy Container, driver in open, closed cab	550	900	1400
Gunthermann "Blue Bird" Racer, tin litho, c/w motor, 20" long	1000	1700	2350
Gunthermann Clown Car, c/w motor, 6" long	900	1700	2300
Gunthermann Double-Decker Bus, electric headlights, early 1930s, 12" long	475	638	950
Gunthermann Fire Ladder Truck, 4 firemen, overhead ladder, 16" long	1800	3000	4400
Gunthermann Fire Pumper, c.1898, hand-painted tin, c/w motor, 2 firemen, 8-1/4" long	1500	2700	3900
Gunthermann Fire Pumper, 3 firemen (composition), 8-1/4" long	1600	2800	4000
Gunthermann Fire Pumper, windup, early, 7-3/4" long	800	1300	2000
Gunthermann "Georgian Window" Limousine c.1908, driver, c/w motor	1100	1700	2500
Gunthermann "Gordon Bennett" Coupe, 5-3/4" long	1200	2200	3000

	C6	C8	C10
Gunthermann Hansom-type Auto	750	1300	1750
Gunthermann Horseless Carriage, c/w motor, driver, 7" long	1100	1700	2500
Gunthermann Kaye Don's Sunbeam Silver Bullet Racer, 22" long	800	1400	2000
Gunthermann Limousine, c.1920, 12" long. Green/black, c/w motor, 4 opening doors, painted driver	1150	1650	2400
Gunthermann Motorcycle & Rider, 7" long	1500	2800	3700
Gunthermann Motorcycle & Rider, 8-1/4" long	1000	1700	2400
Gunthermann Open Phaeton, driver, windup, 7" long	650	1100	1600
Gunthermann Paris-Berlin Race Car	1100	1700	2500
Gunthermann Taxi, convertible back, driver, c/w motor, c.1912, 10-1/2" long	1100	2100	2900
Gunthermann Two-Seat Open Car, c.1899, driver in top hat, 7" long	850	1450	2100
Gunthermann two-way Limousine/Touring Car, 10-1/4" long. Brown/yellow, c/w motor, adjustable steering and headlamps. A removable top converts car to touring model, c.1920s	850	1250	2000

Guntherman "Blue Bird" Racer with original box. Courtesy Bill Bertoia Auctions. Photo by Jeanne Bertoia.

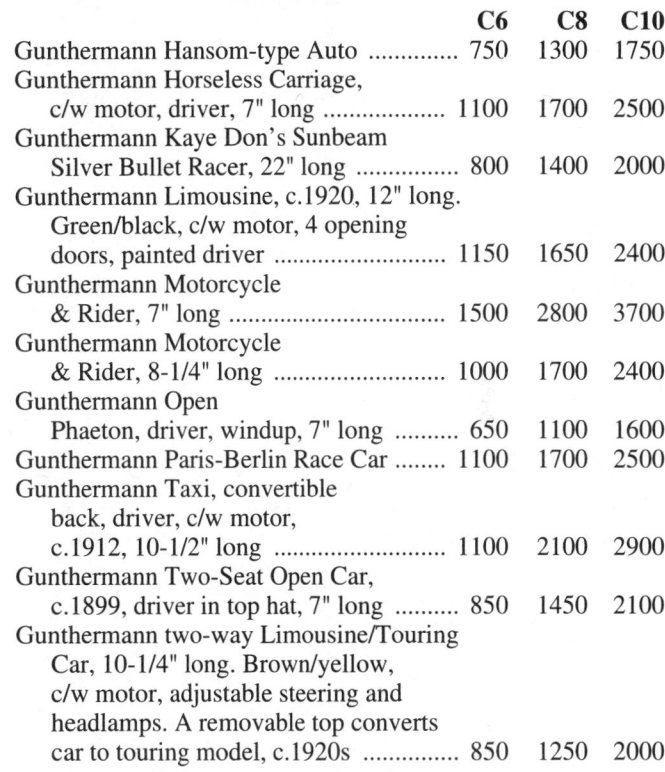

Guntherman Kaye Don's Sunbeam Silver Bullet with original box. Courtesy Bill Bertoia Auctions. Photo by Jeanne Bertoia.

Gunthermann Limousine, c.1920, 12" long. Photo by Bob Smith.

Guntherman Two-Seat Open Car, c.1899. Courtesy Bill Bertoia Auctions. Photo by Jeanne Bertoia.

*Gunthermann two-way Limousine/touring Car, c.1920s, 10-1/4"
long. Photo by Bob Smith.*

	C6	C8	C10
Gunthermann Vis-à-Vis, driver, windup, 5" long	800	1400	2000
Gunthermann Vis-à-Vis, driver, windup, 10-1/4" long	1250	2500	3100

*Guntherman Vis-a-Vis, driver, windup, 10-1/4" long
(repainted figure). Courtesy Bill Bertoia Auctions.
Photo by Jeanne Bertoia.*

GYRO

In 1926 Richard B. Munday became head of Dayton Friction Works, where he patented a horizontal flywheel and called his toys "Gyro" after the gyroscope.
Gyro shut its doors in 1935.

Gyro Coal & Ice Dump Truck	250	375	500

*Gyro toys, as seen
in the 1929 Butler Bros.
Christmas catalog.*

HAFNER

Chicago's Hafner began in 1900 as the Toy Auto Company, though it may not have produced its first model until the following year. By 1904, the firm's name became W.F. Hafner. Hafner set off on his own in 1914 (the first company eventually evolving into American Flyer) with the Hafner Manufacturing Company, his son joining him in 1918. This latter outfit manufactured windup trains until it was purchased in 1950 by Wyandotte.

	C6	C8	C10
Hafner "Auto Express Co." Truck, 8-1/2" long, steel clockwork	450	675	900
Hafner Runabout with upholstered driver's seat, steel clockwork, 7" long	450	675	900
Hafner Touring Car, 10" long, pressed steel, clockwork	750	1125	1500
Hafner Transitional Phaeton, 9-1/2" long, 2 figures	1500	2500	3500

Hafner, L to R: "Auto Express Co.," Runabaout with upholstered driver's seat. Courtesy Sotheby's NY.

Mechanical Runabout.

Modeled a f t e r the popular American style Runabout seen on our streets. Made of sheet steel formed and clinched, finely painted and varnished and decorated with gold ornamentation. A plush cushioned seat is fitted to it, and will carry a doll as large as 12 inches. Fitted with steering gear which permits accurate adjustment to run in any circle or a straight line. Large rubber tires of ¼ inch in diameter make the running almost noiseless.
Price...95¢

Hafner's Runabout, as shown in the 1903 Siegel Cooper Co. toy catalog.

Hafner Touring Car, 10" long. Courtesy Sotheby's NY.

Hafner Transitional Phaeton. Courtesy Bill Bertoia Auctions. Photo by Jeanne Bertoia.

HALSAM

Halsam is best known for its American Logs (similar to Lincoln Logs, but preferred by some collectors), which went into production in 1934. It was also well-known for its blocks, and, as can be seen by the accompanying illustrations, its trucks came with loads of them. No sales were found for any of Halsam's vehicles.

TRAILER PULL TOYS WITH BLOCKS

This line of pull toys packed with blocks of vivid colors gives real, double play value. All blocks contained in the trucks have rounded corners and are finished in harmless, brilliant enamels. Each truck individually packed.

No. 449—TRUCK WITH BLOCKS. Extreme length 11 inches, width 3 inches. Contains 10 only 1-5/16 inch blocks. Packed ¼ dozen sets in a package..................Per doz. $4.00

No. 450—TRUCK WITH BLOCKS. Extreme length 15½ width 3 inches. Contains 10 only 1-5/16 inch blocks. Packed ¼ dozen sets in a package.............Per doz. $4.00

No. 451—TRUCK WITH BLOCKS. Extreme length 17 inches, width 4 inches. Contains 24 only 1¾ inch blocks.

Per doz. $16.00

A Halsam trailer truck as shown in the September 1934 Butler Bros. catalog.

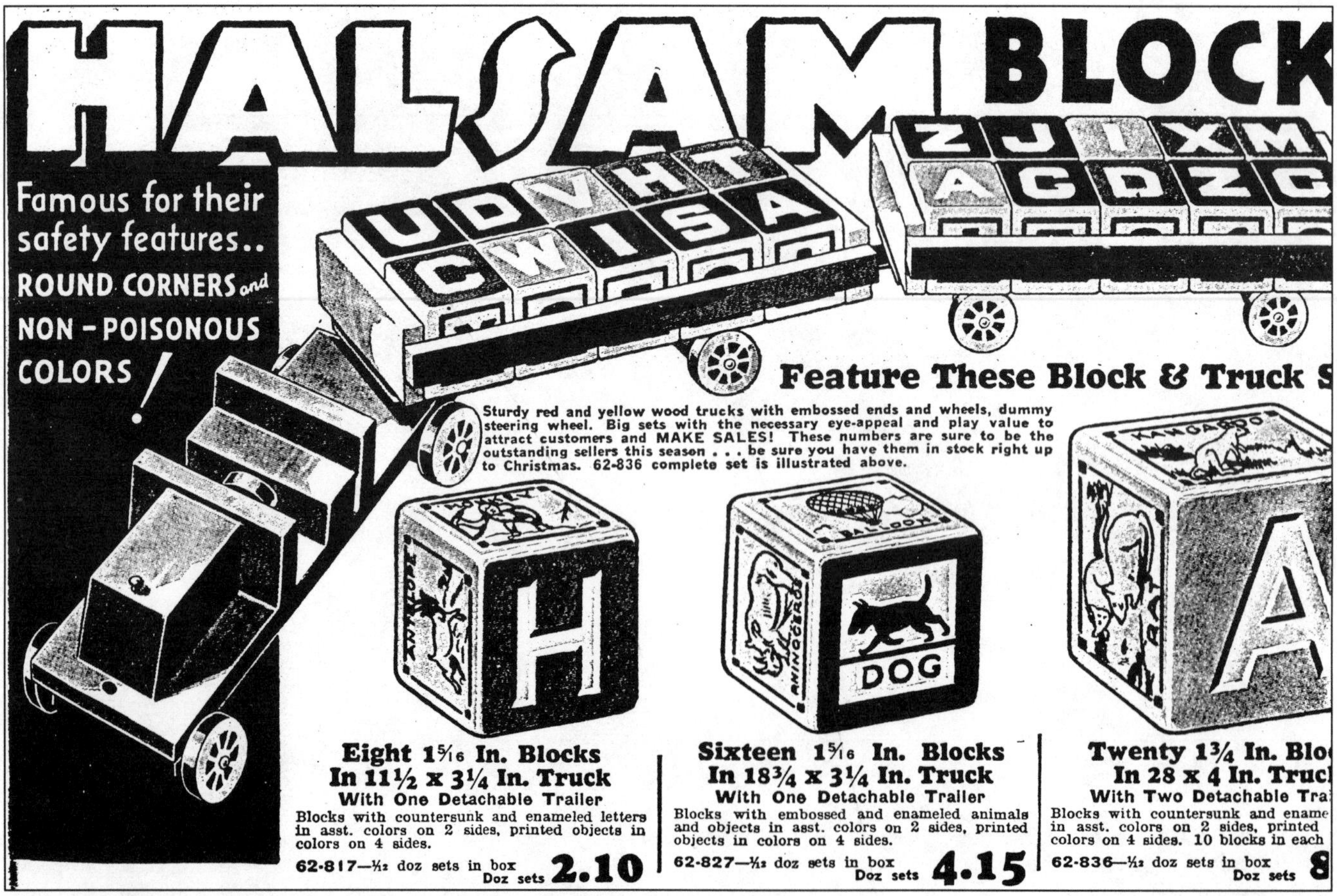

A Halsam trailer truck as shown in the September 1934 Butler Bros. catalog.

HANDI-CRAFT CO.

	C6	C8	C10
Handi-Craft Co. Auto Casting Set No. 891, 1940s, price with box	72	105	145

HAPPY SAM

	C6	C8	C10
Happy Sam driving wood truck, c.1920s, 8" long	80	120	160

HARRIS

Harris Toy Company of Toledo, Ohio, seems to have begun production of cast iron toys during the late 1880s. The firm, which also jobbed for Dent, Hubley and Wilkins, stopped making toys in 1913.

	C6	C8	C10
Harris Tiller Auto, driver	450	675	900

HAUSER: See "Elastolin"

Elastolin, Top to Bottom:
Troop Carrier;
Truck with Cannon, 11" long.
Courtesy Sotheby's NY.

HENRY, M.A.

(New York)

Henry, M.A., Tank, 8" long, composition ...... No Price Found

Henry, M.A., Tank,
8" long, composition.
Photo by Harold Haseley.

HESS PROMOTIONAL TOYS

A Holiday Tradition

by Thomas G. Nefos

One can trace the roots of the Amerada Hess Corp. (formally Hess Oil & Chemical) back many years before a promotional toy was even considered. Hess entered retail gasoline marketing around 1958 with a minority purchase of the Meadville Corp. Meadville operated clean, oversized service stations under the brands of Save Way and Safeway in some large Northeast cities. The Hess branch was introduced in 1959; by 1962 the company operated about 28 stations under its own brand name. By 1965, several other fuel companies were bought, and some of their stations were renamed as "Hess."

It wasn't until 1964 that the first toy tanker truck was sold at Hess stations. Almost every year since then (around Thanksgiving Day) a high quality plastic toy vehicle bearing its name has been offered. These highly detailed toys are said to be exact replicas of actual vehicles in the Hess fleet (from 1987 to present, the toy's design was changed to reflect non-fleet vehicles). The toys are produced in limited quantities, and over the past few years, customers have been restricted to two toys, because of great demand. Each vehicle is packaged in a colorful box and batteries are included in the purchase price. A great deal of respect has been given to these toys by collectors, in view of their limited production and quality construction. It's important to note that to maintain the value, keep all the packaging that comes with the toy (box, inserts, battery card, etc.).

The 1964 toy truck commonly referred to as the "B Mack" was manufactured by Marx in Hong Kong and sold at the stations for $1.39. The cab of the truck was green with yellow fenders and red chassis. The tank trailer featured a green and white body with the Hess name applied to both sides of the tank and cab. The truck had operating head and tail lights, powered by a battery located under the tank. It came with a small red funnel that enabled the tank to be filled with liquid and a drain hose to empty it. This unique toy truck can be hard to find in original condition today.

Not commonly known by collectors, this same truck design was offered under the private labeling of several other fuel companies: Billups Pretroleum, Aetna (which was the North Carolina-based Taylor Oil Co., operating under the Travelers Brand), Wilco (also on the Delhi-Taylor supply system), Service of North Carolina, and Gant. Each of these marketers sold the B Mack toy truck in 1964. By 1965, the Billups brand name had been eliminated in the East and their stations sold to Hess. Hess continued the toy promotion the following year (1965) with the reissue of the B Mack.

Nineteen sixty-six brought the only non-land vehicle to date in the Hess toy collection: the Hess Voyager. This replica of an oil tanker ship, made by Marx in the United States, was outfitted with battery-operated lights on the bow and stern, as well as port and starboard. The Hess name appeared on the ship's stack and both sides of the bow. The toy came with a battery installation card inside the box and sold for $1.89.

In 1967, Hess offered a newly-designed semi-tanker truck often referred to as the "red velvet bottom." This term describes the box, not the truck. The "split window" (two-piece windshield) cab was done in the company colors of green, yellow, and red, with the tank trailer being green and white. The box, which was only available that year, had a red velvet base on which the truck could be displayed and a card in the box explained the battery was already installed. This truck sold for $2.89 and was made by Marx in the United States.

The 1968 and 1969 trucks sold for $1.49 and were basically a reissue of the 1967. This truck was manufactured by Marx, but in Hong Kong. Here are some guidelines to help you distinguish between the three years. In 1967, the velvet based box used clearly stated "Made in the U.S.A." and the Marx logo was not present. In 1968 to 1969 the velvet box was not used, the box lid was marked "Made in Hong Kong" and "Hess Oil & Chemical Corp. Home Office Perth Amboy, New Jersey," and the Marx logo can be found on the battery cover of the truck.

The merger of Hess Oil and Chemical with Amerada Petroleum Corp. took place in 1969, producing the present day name of Amerada Hess. To commemorate this occasion, the 1968-69 toy truck, re-labeled with the new name, was given to Hess employees. This extremely rare truck occasionally appears on the collector market, even though it wasn't sold publicly.

As the 1970 holiday season approached, everyone wondered what Hess would offer next (this type of anticipation is still evident today). 1970 brought the first pumper-style fire truck ($1.69) with detachable hoses and ladder. The truck, made in Hong Kong by Marx, featured a revolving (motor driven) red emergency light, instead of head and tail lights. The box featured a full-length picture of the truck, which came with a battery instruction card.

The same fire truck was reissued in 1971 ($1.69) with the box being the only difference. The '71 is referred to as the "Seasons Greetings" truck. The usual full-color picture of the toy was not in this plain white cardboard box. Instead, a simple label stating, "Hess--

Seasons Greetings" was used. The reason is unclear. However, in this case, the box makes a significant difference in the toy's value today.

Nineteen seventy-three was the first year that Amerada Hess opted not to offer a toy promotion at its stations. However, another variation of the 1968 semi-tanker appeared from 1972 to 1974. These two trucks do have slight modifications you should be aware of. The landing gear or "feet" on the trailer in 1968 were square, while the 1972 to 1974 are round. Additionally the 1972 to 1974 box now reads "Amerada Hess Corporation." Selling prices: 1972 ($1.79) and 1974 ($1.89).

A new addition brings a new design in 1975. The first semi-box truck with opening side and rear doors made its appearance. This truck carries the company colors of green, red, and yellow on the cab. The box trailer is done in green, white, yellow and housed three miniature oil drums, along with battery powered head and tail lights. The truck sold for $1.99 and is stamped on the bottom "Made in Hong Kong" and "Amerada Hess Corporation." Although very rare, a "Marx--Made in the U.S.A." version of this same truck was manufactured. This version is identifiable by the stamp on the bottom of the trailer, and has a slightly larger box, which reads "Made in the United States of America." Both trucks were packaged with different battery-installation cards.

The 1975 truck was slightly modified and became the 1976 holiday promotion. In 1975, the cab was fabricated in one piece, as opposed to the 1976 version, which was made in two separate pieces (the fenders can be removed from the upper cab). The three miniature oil drums were still provided, but Hess labels were added to them. This year's cost to the customer was $2.29.

In keeping with the times, a newly designed tractor was featured on the 1977 semi-tanker truck. Once again, the company colors were prominent, along with the traditional lighting system. The underside of the tanker was dated in Roman numerals (1977) along with "Made in Hong Kong" and "Amerada Hess Corporation." The packaging included a battery-installation card and the price tag was $2.39.

In 1978 ($2.49), with a minor change, the reissue of the 1977 truck appeared at the gas stations in time for the holiday season. The only difference is the size of the Hess label located on the rear of the tank trailer. In 1977, the label size was 1-1/2 inches by 1 inch, which makes the Hess name appear flatter. In 1978, the Hess label appeared a bit taller, measuring 1-1/2 inches by 7/8 inch.

There was no promotional toy in 1979. Amerada Hess, in maintaining high standards of service, provided training to its service-station personnel on location by means of a modified GMC motor home. In 1980, a toy replica of the Hess Training Van was chosen as the holiday promotion. This van sold for $3.29 and featured an opening door, a pop-up TV antenna, and operating lights. Its detail was so complete, it sported miniature New Jersey license plates, windshield, and sideview mirrors. The underside states "Made in Hong Kong" and "Amerada Hess Corporation." The copyright date of 1978 can be confusing, since the van was sold in 1980. A battery-installation card was included in the packaging.

Nineteen eighty-one was the third and final year to date that Hess decided not to offer a holiday promotional toy. This decision didn't affect the toy's popularity when the 1982 truck ($4.69) made is debut. This replica of a 1933 Chevy home-delivery oil tanker is said to be fashioned after the original truck that Leon Hess drove as a young man in the oil business. In fact, the box reads "The First Hess Truck." This '33 Chevy had operating lights, opening doors, and a hose reel with a rubber hose located on the passenger side of the vehicle. Roman numerals dated the truck (1980), even though it wasn't offered until 1982. The underside was stamped "Made in Hong Kong" and "Amerada Hess Corporation" with the operating instructions printed on the box.

A reissue of the '33 Chevy appeared in 1983, with a new feature: a savings bank. Hess advertised this popular toy as a "built-in bank in the tank" truck because of this unique addition. Your coin could be inserted into the top of the tank body and removed by turning one of the simulated filler caps. The selling price increased to $5.29.

Continuing with the addition of the savings bank, 1984 brought a newly-designed semi-tanker similar to 1977-78 trucks, except for the addition of the bank. The underside of the truck was marked "Made in Hong Kong" and "Amerada Hess Corporation." Roman numerals dated (1984) the toy. Instructions were printed on the box, as well as a separate card in the packaging. Price: $4.99.

Two previously offered trucks were used in 1985. Depending on your geographic location, you could buy the 1933 Chevy in the Northeast or the 1984 tanker bank in the Southeast. To the best of my knowledge, this was the only time two different toys were offered in the same year.

The second fire truck in the Hess series was offered as a savings bank in 1986. This red aerial ladder truck included flashing emergency lights and head/tail lights. The white ladder could be fully rotated and extended, with the coin slot located under the ladder to the rear of the truck. Coins could be removed through a small trap door, conveniently located in the back of the fire truck. Stamped on the underside "Made in Hong Kong" and "Amerada Hess Corporation" and dated with Roman numerals (1986), the toy sold for $5.49.

Nineteen eighty-seven brought an entirely new color scheme to the Hess toys; white and green. In previous years, the actual company colors were used. The "18 Wheeler" box truck offered in 1987 had sliding cargo doors, which concealed three miniature Hess-labeled oil drums. Clearance lights were added to the traditional head and tail lights, along with a savings bank. This truck was manufactured in two places and carries the name of origin on the truck and box: "Made in Hong Kong" or "Made in China" and "Amerada Hess Corporation." Roman numberals (1987) were used to date the truck, which sold for $5.99.

The 1988 Hess toy truck and friction-powered racer sold for $6.95. The new white and green colors gave this toy a clean, crisp appearance and the customer two toys in one package for the first time. Once again, the toy was produced in both Hong Kong and China, with operating instructions printed on the box.

A third fire truck ($8.99) was used for the 1989 promotion. The body of the truck was the same as 1986, but with a color change (white body and red aerial ladder). This year's toy featured a savings bank, lights, and the addition of sound (dual sirens). It was dated by Roman numerals (1989) and was manufactured in China.

Nineteen ninety brought back the familiar semi-tanker truck (white and green). This truck boasted 36 working lights and dual sounds (air horns/ back-up alarm.). The tanker, which was made in China, sold for $9.99.

As certain toys became more popular, they were reissued. This was the case of the 1991 toy truck and friction-powered racer sold in that year. Looking much like its predecessor, it had a newly-designed race car and slightly larger truck cab. This edition was made in China and sold for $10.99.

Thanksgiving day 1992 will long be remembered for yet another advancement in an already outstanding promotional toy. The "18 Wheeler with Race Car" went on sale at Hess gas stations. The white and green semi-box truck was outfitted with clear side windows on the trailer to showcase a friction-powered car. The rear door opened to expose a movable ramp, and the lighting system was enhanced to include the race car, which had battery-powered front and rear lights. Manufactured in China, the toy truck sold out quickly at $11.99.

Thomas G. Nefos is publisher/editor of The National Toy Connection. *This publication was developed to enhance collecting transportation and promotional toys. He has written several articles on Hess toys, was a contributing writer to the book* The Hess Toy Collector, *and publishes a price guide annually on the subject.*

PRICE GUIDE TO "HESS PROMOTIONAL TOYS"

(Original Selling Prices in Parentheses)

1964 ($1.39) $1,900.00
    B Model Mack Tanker Truck -
    made in Hong Kong

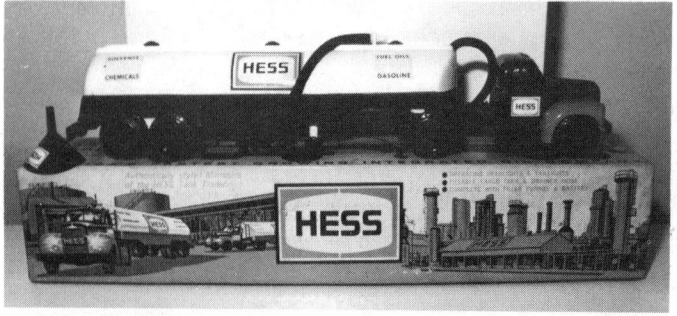

1964 "B Mack" Tanker. Courtesy Thomas G. Nefos National Toy Connection.

1965 same as 1964

1966 ($1.89) $2,300.00
    "Hess Voyager" Tanker Ship - made in U.S.A.

1967 ($2.89) $2,400.00
    Split window Tank Truck with "Red Velvet"
    base on box - made in U.S.A.

1968 ($1.49) $675.00
    Same as 1967 except no red velvet box -
    made in Hong Kong

1969 Same as 1968

1969 Never sold publicly $2,500.00
    Split Window Tank Truck Amerada Hess -
    Hong Kong

1970 ($1.69) $695.00
    Red Pumper Fire Truck Hong Kong by Marx

1967 "Red Velvet" Truck. Courtesy Thomas G. Nefos National Toy Connection.

1971 ($1.69) $3,000.00
    Same as 1970 except for box -
    "Season's Greetings"

1972 ($1.79) $395.00
    Split Window Tanker Truck same as 1968
    with some minor changes

1973 No promotion offered

1974 ($1.89) $350.00
    Split Window Tanker Truck same as 1968
    with some minor changes

1975 Box Truck. Courtesy Thomas G. Nefos National Toy Connection.

1977/78 Tanker Truck. Courtesy Thomas G. Nefos National Toy Connection.

1st Truck in Series: 1970 Pumper F/T.

1975 ($1.99) $395.00
    Box-type Tractor/trailer with 3 oil drums -
    no labels on drums - 1-piece cab -
    made in both Hong Kong and the U.S.A.

1976 ($2.29) $395.00
    Same as 1975 except oil drums have "Hess"
    labels - 2-piece cab - made in Hong Kong

1977 ($2.39) $175.00
    Tanker Tractor/trailer - made in Hong Kong -
    rear label is 1-1/2" x 1"

1978 ($2.49) $185.00
    Same as 1977 except the rear label is 1" x 7/8"

1979 No promotion offered

1980 ($3.29) $395.00
    GMC Training Van - made in Hong Kong

1976 Box Truck. Courtesy Thomas G. Nefos National Toy Connection.

1981 No promotion offered

1982 ($4.69) $95.00
    33 Chevy Tanker Delivery Truck
    "first Hess truck" - Hong Kong

1983 ($5.29) $95.00
    Same as the 1982 - made in Hong Kong

1984 ($4.99) $95.00
    Similar to 1977 except it was issued as a bank

1980 Hess Training Van. Courtesy Thomas G. Nefos National Toy Connection.

1987 "18 Wheeler" Box Truck. Courtesy Thomas G. Nefos National Toy Connection.

1982 '33 Chevy. Courtesy Thomas G. Nefos National Toy Connection.

1985 Reissue 1933 Chevy $125.00
    Same as the 1982 except it was issued as a bank.

1986 ($5.49) $100.00
    Red Aerial Ladder Fire Truck made in
    Hong Kong - bank

1987 ($5.99) $75.00
    Box-type Tractor/trailer with 3 Hess labeled
    drums - made in both Hong Kong and China

1988 ($6.95) $70.00
    Race Car Transporter with friction powered
    car - made in both Hong Kong and China

1989 ($8.99) $65.00
    White Aerial Ladder Fire Truck dual
    siren sounds - bank made in China

1990 ($9.99) $45.00
    White Semi-tanker Truck with back-up/air
    horn sounds - made in China

1991 ($10.99) $35.00
    Reissue of 1988 with some slight changes -
    made in China

1992 ($11.99) $40.00
    18-wheeler box truck with race car -
    made in China

1988, 1991, 1992 Hess Promos. Courtesy Thomas G. Nefos National Toy Connection.

Hess 1989 Ladder Fire Truck. Courtesy Thomas G. Nefos Federal Shipping Network.

  Price Guide to "Hess Promotional Toys"

1993...$28.00
    Patrol Car, white and green w/sirens and lights,
    larger scale than previously-issued toys.

1994...$1,000.00
    Hess Premium Diesel Truck, same as 1990
    tanker except not sold to general public;
    given as gift to bulk diesel fuel dealers.

1994...$25.00
    Rescue Truck, white and green w/red ladder
    (larger scale than previously-issued toys).

1995...$35.00
    Toy Truck and Helicopter, white and green
    flatbed semi w/helicopter cargo -
    both have working lights.

WILCO PROMOS

1966...$2,500.00
    B Mack Tanker Truck - Same color as the
    Hess 1964/65- silver "W" tooled into grille

1967...$550.00
    Split Window Tanker-blue body
    with white trim

1968...$1,200.00
    Oil Tanker Ship - green body

NO PROMOTIONAL TOYS IN THE 70s

1985...$95.00
    Semi Tanker Truck Bank - blue body,
    white trim and red letters

1986...$85.00
    '33 Chevy Tanker Bank - blue body,
    white trim and red letters

1988...$25.00
    Semi Box Truck - no barrels white body,
    blue trim with red/blue letters

1989...$35.00
    Race Car Transporter - white body, blue trim,
    red/blue letters

1990...$30.00
    Aerial Ladder Fire Truck - white body,
    blue trim with red letters

1991...$25.00
    Semi-tanker Truck - white body,
    blue trim, red letters

1992...$25.00
    Race Car Transporter

HESS TOY COMPANY

(Nuremberg, Germany 1825-1934)

By Bob Smith

    Founded in 1825 by Matthieu Hess, this is one of the oldest toy makers in Germany. Matthieu passed away in 1886 and left the business to his son, Johann Leonard; thus began the "J.L.H." trademark. Most Hessmobile cars used a unique friction mechanism which had a power-lock on top of the cowl and a hand crank in the front. When cranking the handle, a momentum would build up. You would then lift the power-lock, releasing the driveshaft to turn the rear wheels.

	C6	C8	C10
Hess Limousine, blue/black, 9" long, friction drive, c.1920	700	950	1300
Hess Limousine, green/red, clockwork, 9" long	500	750	1000
Hess Limousine, green/black 7-1/2" long, friction drive, c.1920	575	675	900
Hess Open Two-Seat Auto tin litho, approx. 8" long	750	1250	1800
Hess Open Two-Seat Car, 10-1/2" long	750	1400	1870
Hess Racer, driver, 5" long	500	800	1100
Hess Speedster, driver, crank friction drive, 8" long	275	415	550
Hess Two-Seat Open Racer, tin litho, c/w motor, 8-3/4" long	750	1250	1800
Hessmobile Open Phaeton, c.1918, driver, 8-1/2" long	800	1300	1900
"Hessmobile" Racer, driver, hand crank, 8" long	412	618	825

Hess, from Top: Limousine, 9" long, c.1920; Limousine, 7-1/2"long, c. 1920.

	C6	C8	C10
"Highway Patrol" (TV series) car	50	75	100

HILL CLIMBER VEHICLES

By Bob Smith

Hill Climber Vehicles were first produced in the late 1800s. A patent was issued to Israel D. Boyer on Nov. 2, 1897. This patent date is found on some Clark friction toys, though they were most likely produced after the turn of the century. The "Hill Climber" name was adopted by most of the friction-toy manufacturers in the early 1900s. Four companies in Dayton, Ohio—D.P. Clark Co., Dayton Friction Toy Works, Schieble Toy & Novelty Co., and Republic Tool Co.—had a rivalry in the industry that lasted for 40 years. Research has found that the designers and engineers of Hill Climber toys were known to jump from one firm to another, bringing their trade secrets with them. This caused some similarities in color and style, making it difficult for the collector to recognize who made the toy. In the beginning, all Hill Climber Vehicles had a primitive, husky look to them. They had wooden bodies, with cast-iron wheels, buggy tops, and pressed-steel dashboards, and always had a huge cast-iron fly-wheel to propel them up a hill. They were painted by hand in a dark green or blue color, with accent striping of gold or yellow. The Hill Climber, with its unique style, is very easily recognized as an American-made toy.

(Hill Climbers under the various above-named companies.)

HILLER

	C6	C8	C10
Hiller Comet Race Car, "3," fuel-powered, c.1940-42	800	1300	1800
Hiller Comet Race Car, "4," non-powered, 18" long	550	825	1200

Hiller Comet Race Car "3." Photo by William G. Floyd.

HOGE

Hoge Fire Chief Car, 15" long	250	450	650

Hoge Fire Chief Car, 15" long. Photo by Bob Smith.

HOLGATE

Holgate was founded by Cornelius Holgate in Philadelphia. About 1930 it began turning out educational wooden toys. It merged with Playskool in 1958; now owned by Hasbro.

	C6	C8	C10
Holgate Army Tank, 10 wheels, wooden, 12" long	65	82	130

HOLMES COAL CO.

	C6	C8	C10
"Holmes Coal Co". Pressed Steel Delivery Truck, 17-1/2" long	400	600	800

*"Holmes Coal Co."
(Possibly Marx).
Courtesy Sotheby's NY.*

HOT WHEELS: See "Mattel"

HUBLEY

The Hubley Manufacturing Company was founded at least as early as 1892 by John Hubley. It made iron toys from the start at its plant in Lancaster, Pennsylvania. All toys at the beginning were cast iron, and some early toys included coal ranges, circus wagons, and mechanical banks. Hubley's cast-iron toys were popular almost from the start and have long been collector's items, because they were well-made and attractive. By 1940, however, the cast-iron toy, due to the increased cost of freight and foreign competition, was slowly becoming a thing of the past. At this time, when Hubley was the largest producer of cast-iron toys and cap pistols in the world, it began to introduce die-cast zinc alloy toys. During WWII, Hubley was 98 percent engaged in war production.

Since the war, Hubley has manufactured die-cast toys and plastic toys exclusively. In 1952, Hubley manufactured 9,763,610 toys and 11,184,878 cap pistols, about 10 times the amount of toys and pistols it produced in 1930, but with a line of toys 80 percent smaller than in 1930. It is the combination of the relative scarcity (and multiplicity) of the older toys, plus the preference by collectors for cast-iron over die-cast zinc alloy and plastic toys, that makes the pre-WWII toys the most attractive to collectors. Hubley was acquired by Gabriel Industries in late 1965, and puts out holster sets, cap pistols, vehicles, hobby kits, and a number of other toys.

	C6	C8	C10
Hubley Air Compress Truck, 7" long, c.1950s	37	56	75
Hubley Ahrens Fox Hose Reel, 11-1/4" long	2000	4500	8000
Hubley Allis Chalmers Model WC Tractor, driver, 7" long	108	162	215
Hubley American LaFrance Ladder & Hose Truck, 15" long	112	168	225
Hubley Army Ambulance No. 476, late	60	90	120
Hubley Army Motor Truck No. 807 with driver, 15" long	1100	1800	2400
Hubley Auto, 6-1/2" long	80	120	160
Hubley Auto, 7-1/2" long, No. 358, c.1928	150	225	300
Hubley Auto, 9", 1922, Chevy?	400	600	800

Hubley Auto Transport, all-metal truck with four different-color plastic Cadillacs, 18" long without ramp. Courtesy Harvey K. Rainess.

"HUBLEY"
9 STYLES
Rubber Tires!

Average 3¾ In.

9 Styles—Roadster, coupe, sedan, phaeton, wrecker, etc., streamline models, beautiful 2-color enamel finishes, nickeled radiator and lamps, some styles with black enameled trunks.

61-1920—1 doz in box..........Doz **.80**

Order numbers below for individual items
61-1925—Sedan..................... } 1 doz in box
61-1926—Phaeton...................
61-1927—Coupe..................... Doz
61-1928—Truck.....................
61-1929—Roadster................. **.80**

Hubley autos, as shown in a September 1934 Butler Bros. catalog.

	C6	C8	C10
Hubley Auto Carrier, 10" long with three cars and one Pickup Truck, c.1939	338	505	675
Hubley Auto Carrier, 1950s, 2 Packards	80	120	160
Hubley "Auto Express," 9" long, cast-iron	900	1450	2000
Hubley Auto Transport, all-metal truck w/4 different-color plastic Cadillacs, 18" long without ramp	175	263	350
Hubley Avery Tractor, 4-3/4" long, very early, "No. 2"	120	180	240
Hubley Auto c.1950s, black plastic wheels, die-cast	12	18	25
Hubley "Beetle Bug," VW, 1969, metal w/sunroof	50	75	100
Hubley Bell Telephone Truck, 3" long	200	300	400
Hubley Bell Telephone Truck 3-3/4" long	150	235	310

	C6	C8	C10
Hubley Bell Telephone, 5-1/4" long	200	320	450
Hubley Bell Telephone, 7" long, 2 ladders, tools	600	1000	1400
Hubley Bell Telephone, 8-1/4" long, w/tools	400	600	800
Hubley Bell Telephone Truck; 9-1/4" long, 1931, with derrick and windlass, auger, trailer with 10" pole, three digging tools, and two loose ladders	550	950	1300
Hubley "Bell Telephone," 12" long, with tools	175	263	350
Hubley Bell Telephone Truck, 14" long, 1950s, accessories	85	128	170
Hubley Bell Telephone, post-WWII, 24" long	60	90	120

Hubley Bell Telephone, Post-War, 24" long,. Courtesy Thomas G. Nefos, Federal Shipping Network.

	C6	C8	C10
Hubley Black & White Cab, 1920s	1200	2000	3000
Hubley "Borden's Milk Cream," deluxe version, 7-1/2" long, rubber tires, clicker	1250	1875	2500
Hubley "Borden's Milk Cream," standard version, 6" long	1000	1500	2000

Hubley Bell Telephone Trucks, in ascending order: 3", 3-3/4", 5-1/4", 7", 8-1/4", 9-1/4" long. Courtesy Bill Bertoia Auctions. Photo by Jeanne Bertoia.

Hubley, L to R: "Borden's Milk Cream," 6" long, Borden's Milk Truck, 3-5/8" long. Courtesy Bill Bertoia Auctions. Photo by Jeanne Bertoia.

	C6	C8	C10
Hubley Bus, 5-1/2" long, c.1938, rubber wheels	50	75	100
Hubley Bus, 8" long, 1930s	60	90	120
Hubley Bus, 9" long, die-cast, c.1950s	20	30	40
Hubley Cadillac, 7" die-cast, 1941	40	60	80
Hubley 2278 Car and 2279 House Trailer, c.1939	150	225	300
Hubley Caterpillar Tractor, 3-1/4" long, driver in cab	100	150	200

Hubley "Borden's Milk Cream," 7-1/2" long. Courtesy Phillips NY.

	C6	C8	C10
Hubley Borden's Milk Truck, 3-5/8" long	250	375	500
Hubley Bulldozer, 9" long	62	93	125
Hubley Bulldozer, die-cast, front scoop, c.1950, 10-1/4" long, rubber treads	78	118	155
Hubley Bulldozer, 12" long	150	225	300

Hubley Bulldozer, 12" long. Photo by Calvin L. Chaussee.

Hubley Caterpillar Tractor, 3-1/4" long. Courtesy Mapes Auctioneers & Appraisers.

	C6	C8	C10
Hubley Caterpillar Tractor, 9" long	62	93	125
Hubley Cattle Truck, plastic, 12" long	30	45	60
Hubley Cement Mixer, 3-1/2" long, Wonder, 1930s	125	188	250
Hubley Cement Mixer, 18" long	400	600	800

	C6	C8	C10
Hubley Bus, (futuristic type), 3-1/2" long, c.1935	60	90	120
Hubley Bus (futuristic) No. 617, 7-3/4" long	150	225	300

Hubley Cattle Truck, plastic, 12" long. Photo by Terry Sells.

Hubley Bus (futuristic) No. 617. Courtesy Mapes Auctioneers.

Hubley Cement Mixer Truck, 8" long. Courtesy Bill Bertoia Auctions. Photo by Jeanne Bertoia.

	C6	C8	C10
Hubley Cement Mixer Truck, 8" long	2000	3800	6500
Hubley Champion Stake Truck, 8-1/2" long, 1930s, white rubber tires ..	140	210	280
Hubley Chemical Truck with ladders, 13" long	200	300	400
Hubley Chevrolet 1932 Coupe, kit, w/box	12	18	25
Hubley Chevrolet 1932 Phaeton kit, 1960s, w/box	27	41	55
Hubley Chevrolet 1932 Roadster kit, 1960s, w/box	20	30	40
Hubley Chrysler Airflow, 4-1/2" long, take-apart body	125	188	250
Hubley Chrysler Airflow, 6-3/4" long, take-apart body	312	468	625
Hubley Chrysler Airflow, 8" long, electrified, white rubber tires on wood hubs	600	900	1200
Hubley Chrysler Airflow Racing Car, c.1938	100	150	200
Hubley "Coal" Truck, c.1922, 9-1/2" long	438	657	875

Hubley Compressor Truck, Ingersoll Rand, 8-1/4" long. Courtesy Bill Bertoia Auctions. Photo by Jeanne Bertoia.

	C6	C8	C10
Hubley Corvette, 13-1/2" long, No. 509	162	243	325
Hubley Coupe, 6-1/2" long, c.1939	110	165	220
Hubley Coupe, 4-1/2" long, 1920s	100	150	200
Hubley Coupe, 3-1/2" long, 1930s	40	60	80
Hubley Coupe, 1933 Ford	90	135	180
Hubley Coupe Roadster, rumble seat, 11" long, rubber tires	125	187	250
Hubley Crane, 1940s, wooden wheels	67	100	135

Hubley "Coal" Truck, c.1922, 9-1/2" long. Courtesy Christie's East.

	C6	C8	C10
Hubley Coal Truck, cast-iron, with driver, 16-3/4" long	1200	1800	2500
Hubley "Coast to Coast" Bus, cast-iron, 1927, 13" long	450	675	900

Hubley Crane, 1940s, wooden wheels. Courtesy Harvey K. Rainess.

	C6	C8	C10
Hubley De Soto Airflow, 4" long	100	150	200
Hubley Delivery Van, 4-1/2" long, 1932	700	1300	1800

Hubley "Coast to Coast" bus, cast iron, 1927, 13" long. Courtesy Bill Bertoia Auctions. Photo by Jeanne Bertoia.

Hubley Delivery Van, 1932, 4-1/2" long. Courtesy Bill Bertoia Auctions. Photo by Jeanne Bertoia.

	C6	C8	C10
Hubley Compressor Truck, Ingersoll Rand, 8-1/4" long	2500	4500	7000
Hubley Convertible, 7" long, die-cast & iron	100	150	200
Hubley Convertible, hardtop, 1950s	50	75	100

	C6	C8	C10
Hubley Diesel Low Boy w/grader	115	172	230
Hubley Diesel "Road Roller," 10" long	50	75	100
Hubley Duesenberg Town Car, 9" long build-it model, w/box	26	39	52
Hubley Dump Truck, 1930s, 3-1/2" long	40	60	80
Hubley Dump Truck, 5-1/2" long	50	75	100
Hubley Dump Truck, c.1938, 7-1/2" long	1000	1600	2400
Hubley Dump Truck, 1952	112	168	225

Hubley Dump Truck, Mack, 1930s, 6 tires, 10-3/4" long; driver missing in photo. Courtesy James S. Maxwell/Virginia Caputo. Photo by Virginia Caputo.

	C6	C8	C10
Hubley Dump Truck, Mack, 1930s, 6 tires, 10-3/4" long	1000	1800	2800
Hubley Dump Truck, No. 902, late	55	83	110
Hubley Dump Truck, plastic & metal, 8" long	25	38	50
Hubley "Elgin, The" Street Sweeper, 8" long, cast-iron, 1931	3500	5000	7500

Hubley Elgin. Courtesy Chic Gast.

Hubley Fire Engine Pumper, Ahrens-Fox, 7" long	400	600	800
Hubley Fire Engine Pumper, Ahrens-Fox, 10" long	250	375	500
Hubley Fire Engine Pumper, 1930s, 5" long	65	98	130
Hubley Fire Engine Pumper, post war? 7" long	55	82	110
Hubley Fire Engine Pumper, c.1930s, 2 firemen, 8-1/2" long	275	362	550
Hubley Fire Engine Pumper, c.1920, 12-1/2" long, cast-iron, black rubber tires, driver, boiler-trailer	350	525	700
Hubley Fire Engine Pumper, 14" long, two firemen, early, No. 554, auctioned in 1992 for $6820.			
Hubley Fire Engine Pumper, early, No. 504	350	525	700

	C6	C8	C10
Hubley Fire Engine Pumper, 1930s, No. 2254	170	255	340
Hubley Fire Engine Pumper, terraplane front, 1930s, 6-1/4" long	185	275	370
Hubley Fire Engine Pumper w/searchlight, 7" long, c.1950s	55	83	110
Hubley Fire engine No. 526, 10-1/2" long, c.1936	175	263	350
Hubley Fire engine, die-cast, white rubber tires with wooden rims, c.1941	40	60	80
Hubley Fire Ladder Truck, early, 7-1/2" long	130	195	260

Hubley Fire Ladder Truck, early, 7-1/2" long. Photo by Rod Carnahan.

Hubley Fire Ladder Truck, 8-1/2" long, early	250	375	500
Hubley Fire Ladder Truck, 14" long, driver, c. early 1930s	500	800	1200
Hubley Fire Ladder Truck, 19-1/2" long	850	1400	1900
Hubley Fire Truck with searchlight, white rubber tires with wooden rims	55	82	110
Hubley Fire Truck, 5" long	100	150	200
Hubley Fish Hatchery Truck, 1950s, w/net, fish	65	98	130
Hubley "5-Ton Truck," 17" long, 8 wooden barrels, c.1920	750	1200	1700

Hubley "5 Ton Truck." Courtesy Sotheby's NY.

Hubley Flatbed Truck No. 506, all metal	118	177	235
Hubley Ford Coupe, 1936	40	50	80
Hubley Ford Model A Coupe kit, 1960s, w/box	25	38	50
Hubley Ford Model A Phaeton kit, 1960s, w/box	25	38	50
Hubley Ford Model A Pickup kit, 1960s, w/box	25	38	50

Hubley Flatbed Truck No. 506. Courtesy Harvey K. Rainess.

	C6	C8	C10
Hubley Ford Model			
A Roadster kit, 1960s, w/box	32	48	65
Hubley Ford Model A			
Station Wagon kit, 1960s, w/box	25	38	50
Hubley Ford Model			
A Town Car kit, 1960s, w/box	25	38	50
Hubley Ford Model			
A Victoria kit, 1960s, w/box	25	38	50
Hubley Ford Tractor & Disc	85	128	170
Hubley Fordson Front-End Loader,			
cast iron, c. early 1930s, 9" long	1000	1800	2700
Hubley Fuel Truck, cast-iron, 5-1/2" long .	100	150	200
Hubley Grader	56	84	112
Hubley "General" Steam Shovel, 6" long ..	175	263	350
Hubley "General" Steam Shovel, 7" long ..	375	562	750
Hubley "General"			
Steam Shovel, 8-1/4" long	300	450	600
Hubley "General" Steam Shovel, 9" long ..	400	625	850

Hubley "General," 9" long.

Hubley "General" Steam Shovel,			
10-1/2" long	440	660	880
Hubley "General" Steam Shovel, 15" long	450	700	1000
Hubley Graham, 4" long	85	125	170
Hubley Gulf Tank Truck	100	150	200
Hubley Hook & Ladder No. 463..................	28	42	56
Hubley Hook & Ladder No. 468..................	130	195	260
Hubley Hook & Ladder No. 473..................	82	123	165
Hubley Hook & Ladder Truck,			
19-1/2" long, cast-iron	200	300	400
Hubley Huber Road Roller, 3-1/2" long	75	112	150
Hubley Huber Road Roller, 5-3/8" long	125	188	250
Hubley Huber Road Roller,			
windup, 1932, 7-1/2" long	3500	6500	9500
Hubley Huber Road Roller, 4-1/2" long	110	165	220

Hubley Huber Road Rollers, lengths 5-3/8", 4-1/2", 3-1/2". Courtesy Bill Bertoia Auctions. Photo by Jeanne Bertoia.

Hubley Huber Road Roller, 8" long. Courtesy Bill Bertoia Auctions. Photo by Jeanne Bertoia.

Hubley, Huber Road Roller, 8" long. Courtesy Mapes Auctioneers & Appraisers.

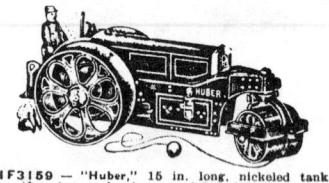

1F3159 — "Huber," 15 in. long, nickeled tank, scarifier lowers by lever, painted driver, steering wheel steers, can be used as a pull toy. ½ doz. in box................Doz **$24.00**

Hubley "Huber" Road Roller, 15" long, as shown in December, 1929 Butler Bros. catalog.

	C6	C8	C10
Hubley Huber Road Roller, 8" long	455	682	910
Hubley Huber Road Roller, 13" long	2500	3850	5000
Hubley Huber Road Roller, 14" long	1600	2500	3800
Hubley Huber Road Roller, 15" long	3000	4500	6000
Hubley "Hubley Tanker,"			
plastic, 12-1/2" long		No Price Found	
Hubley "Hubley Transport,"			
plastic, 13" long auto carrier	125	188	250
Hubley Indianapolis			
500 Racer, 9" metal kit	150	225	300
Hubley "Jaeger" Cement Mixer	475	712	950
Hubley Jaguar, die-cast, 7-1/2" long	62	93	125
Hubley Jeep, metal, 6-3/4" long	15	22	30
Hubley Jeep & Speedboat, late	25	38	50

Hubley "Hubley Tanker," plastic, 12-1/2" long. Photo by Terry Sells.

Hubley "Hubley Transport," plastic, 13" long. Photo by Terry Sells.

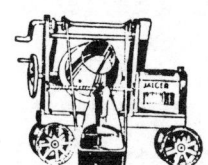

Hubley "Jaeger" Cement Mixer, 1929.

1F3111—"Jaeger" Concrete Mixer, 6¾ x6⅛, yellow enameled chassis with motor front, blue enameled uprights, bright aluminum hopper, nickeled wheels, operated by turning crank & wheel.
⅙ doz. in box.
Doz $11.50

Hubley Jaguar, die-cast, 7-1/2" long. Photo by Bob Smith.

	C6	C8	C10
Hubley Kiddietoy			
Auto Transport, Cadillacs	80	120	160
Hubley Kiddietoy Convertible, c.1930s	100	150	200
Hubley Kiddietoy Fire			
Truck, plastic, w/rubber wheels	17	26	35
Hubley Kiddietoy Ladder			
Truck, 1950s, 6" long	67	100	135
Hubley Kiddietoy Motor Express,			
6-1/2" long, tailgate opens, plastic	30	45	60

	C6	C8	C10
Hubley Kiddietoy No. 452 Tow Truck,			
6-3/8" long, 1950s, "No. 2" on roof	37	56	75
Hubley Kiddietoy No. 454			
Hook & Ladder, 7" long	65	98	130
Hubley Kiddietoy No. 457 Racer,			
6-1/2" long, die-cast, rubber tires	46	69	92
Hubley Kiddietoy No. 461			
Stake Truck, Ford, 1946	45	90	170
Hubley Kiddietoy No. 465			
Buick Convertible, 7" long	65	98	130
Hubley Kiddietoy No. 472 Tractor	42	63	85

Hubley Kiddietoy Motor Express, tailgate opens, all plastic, 6-1/2" long. Courtesy Harvey K. Rainess.

Hubley Kiddietoy No. 5 "Taxi"	7	12	25
Hubley Kiddietoy No. 315			
Road Roller, 6" long, plastic	50	75	100
Hubley Kiddietoy No. 356			
Log Truck, 12" long	72	105	145
Hubley Kiddietoy No. 432			
MGTD Roadster, 6" long	110	165	220

Hubley Kiddietoy No. 5 "Taxi." Courtesy Bob and Alice Wagner.

Hubley Kiddietoy No. 461 Stake Truck. Courtesy Bob and Alice Wagner.

	C6	C8	C10
Hubley Kiddietoy No. 476 Dump Truck	70	105	140
Hubley Kiddietoy No. 510 Dump Truck	125	188	250
Hubley Kiddietoy No. 520 Fire Ladder Truck, 19" long	250	375	500
Hubley Kiddietoy "Patrol" Stake Truck, c.1937	27	41	55
Hubley Kiddietoy Pickup Truck, c.1930s	100	150	200
Hubley Kiddietoy Pumper, c.1950s, 6" long	67	100	135
Hubley Kiddietoy Sedan, 2-door, c.1930s	100	150	200
Hubley Kiddietoy Sedan, 4-door, c.1930s	115	172	230
Hubley Kiddietoy Tractor, c.1960s, die-cast, 5-1/2" long	12	18	25
Hubley Kiddietoy Wrecker, 8" long	67	105	135
Hubley Ladder Truck c. late 1930s, 5" long	45	67	90
Hubley Ladder Truck, terraplane front, c. 1930s, 6" long	70	105	140
Hubley Ladder Truck, 7" long, c.1920s	175	263	350
Hubley Ladder Truck, 7-1/4" long, c.1930s, 3 ladders, 2 axes	225	338	450
Hubley Ladder Truck, 10" long, c.1930s	110	165	225
Hubley Ladder Truck, c.1929, 13" long	500	750	1000
Hubley Ladder Truck, 13-1/2" long, c.1940	375	562	750

Hubley, L to R: Ladder Truck, 1929, 13" long, Ahrens Fox Fire Hose Reel, 11-1/4" long. Courtesy Bill Bertoia Auctions. Photo by Jeanne Bertoia

	C6	C8	C10
Hubley Ladder Truck, 16" long, with eagles, early	700	1150	1600
Hubley LaSalle, c.1940, die-cast	90	135	180
Hubley Life Saver Truck, c.1930, hole in rear is large enough to hold pack of Life Savers, 4-1/4" long	700	1150	1600

Hubley Life Saver Truck holds pack of Life Savers. Courtesy Bill Bertoia Auctions. Photo by Jeanne Bertoia.

	C6	C8	C10
Hubley Life Saver Truck, small hole in rear, can't hold Life Savers		No Price found	
Hubley Limousine, 7" long, 6-door, c.1920s	165	250	330
Hubley Lincoln Zephyr, die-cast, 5-1/4" long	25	38	50
Hubley Lincoln Zephyr, 6" long	120	180	240

Hubley Lincoln Zephyrs, L to R: 6" long; die-cast, 5-1/2" long. Courtesy Bill Bertoia Auctions. Photo by Jeanne Bertoia.

	C6	C8	C10
Hubley Lincoln Zephyr, 7-1/4" long	233	350	465
Hubley Lincoln Zephyr and House Trailer, cast-iron, 14" long overall	400	600	800
Hubley Log Truck, 13" long	100	150	200
Hubley Log Truck, 16" long	70	105	140
Hubley Log Truck No. 469	45	100	200
Hubley Log Truck with five chained logs, black rubber tires, die-cast, approx. 19" long	138	205	275
Hubley Log Truck, plastic, No. 356, 12" long	75	112	150
Hubley Low Boy Hauler w/Road Grader, 21" long	115	172	230
Hubley Low Boy Truck, Trailer, Tractor	200	300	400
Hubley Mack Dump Truck, 8-1/2" long	600	950	1400
Hubley Mack Dump Truck, 11-1/2" long, with driver	900	1400	2200
Hubley Mack Gasoline Truck, 8-3/4" long	700	1100	1500

Hubley Mack Gasoline Truck, 8-3/4" long. Courtesy Bill Bertoia Auctions. Photo by Jeanne Bertoia.

Hubley Mack Gasoline Truck, 10-3/4" long. Courtesy Bill Bertoia Auctions. Photo by Jeanne Bertoia.

	C6	C8	C10
Hubley Mack Gasoline Truck, 10-3/4" long	800	1350	1800
Hubley Mack Gasoline Truck, 13-1/4" long, c.1925	550	900	1300
Hubley Mack Stake Truck	200	300	400
Hubley Mack Truck Steam Shovel-Digger, c.1920, nickel wheels and scoop, 7" long	450	675	920
Hubley "Merchants Delivery" c.1920s, 6" long	400	600	800

	C6	C8	C10
Hubley MG, 9" long	60	90	120
Hubley MG, 5-3/4" long	48	72	95
Hubley Mighty Metal Power Shovel	100	150	200
Hubley "Milk Cream" Truck, c.1930s, cast iron, 3-1/2" long, white rubber tires	262	393	525
Hubley "Mr. Magoo Car," c.1961, 9" long, five actions, includes cloth roof top, battery op	145	215	290
Hubley Model T Coupe, 4" long	100	150	200
Hubley Monarch Tractor, 5-1/2" long	600	900	1200
Hubley Motor Express Tractor and Trailer, black rubber tires, 500 series, approx. 19" long	130	195	260
Hubley "Motor Express," 12"long, plastic	70	105	140
Hubley 2287 "Motor Express" Truck and Trailer, 8" long	175	263	350
Hubley "Motor Express" No. 352, plastic, 12" long	75	112	150

Hubley "Merchants Delivery," 1920s, 6" long. Courtesy Bill Bertoia Auctions. Photo by Jeanne Bertoia.

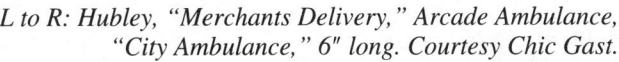

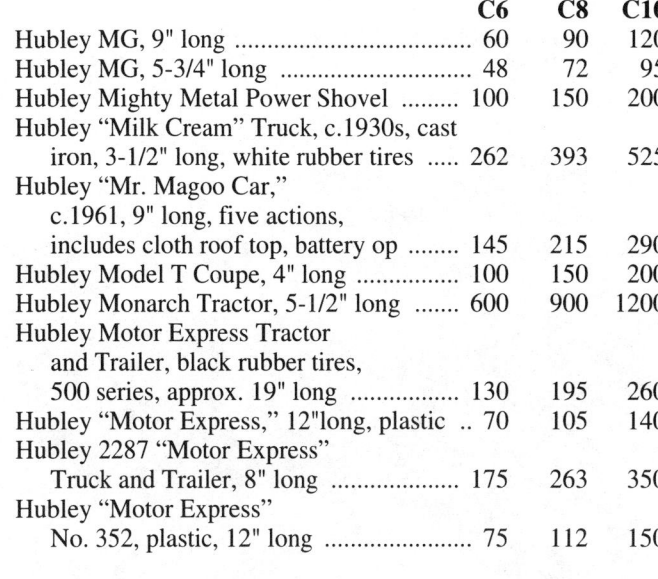

L to R: Hubley, "Merchants Delivery," Arcade Ambulance, "City Ambulance," 6" long. Courtesy Chic Gast.

Hubley MG, die-cast, 9" long. Photo by Bob Smith.

Hubley "Milk Cream" truck. Courtesy James S. Maxwell/ Virginia Caputo. Photo by Virginia Caputo.

Hubley Nite Coach, metal wheels, went on "Nu-Car" carrier, 1930s, 3-1/2" long. Courtesy Chic Gast.

	C6	C8	C10
"HUBLEY MOTORCYCLES"-see end of Hubley section			
Hubley Motorized Steam Pumper, 4" long, c.1930s	50	75	100
Hubley Nite Coach, 3-1/2" long, metal wheels, went on "Nu-Car" carrier, c.1930s	30	45	60
Hubley "Nucar Transport" with trailer, 17" long, 4 cars	500	900	1250

Hubley "Nucar Transport." Courtesy Christie's East.

	C6	C8	C10
Hubley Oliver Orchard Tractor, 5-1/2" long	88	132	175
Hubley Packard Sedan, 5-1/2" long, c.1939-1940s	25	40	75
Hubley Packard, 15 parts, c.1929, straight eight, 11" long, auctioned 1994, excellent, minor repairs, for $16,000			
Hubley Packard Dietrick Convertible model kit, w/box	25	38	50
Hubley Packard, 1930 "Phaeton" kit, w/box	25	38	50

Hubley Packard Sedan, 1939-40s, 5-1/2" long. Courtesy Bob and Alice Wagner.

1F3109—"Packard," 11 in. long, green & black enameled body, stripped, hood and front doors open, imit. engine, disc wheels, imit. balloon gray tires, nickeled driver. ⅓ doz. in box. **Doz** **$14.00**

Hubley Packard, 1929.

	C6	C8	C10
Hubley Packard Roadster kit, w/box	25	38	50
Hubley "Panama" Digger, approx. 3-1/2" long (hard to find)	300	450	600
Hubley "Panama" Digger, 9-1/2" long	800	1200	1650
Hubley "Panama" Digger, Mack, 13" long	1100	1650	2200

Hubley "Panama," 9-1/2" long.

Hubley "Panama" digger, Mack, 13" long.

	C6	C8	C10
Hubley "Patrol," 8-1/4" long, driver, 3 firemen	312	468	625
Hubley "Patrol," 15-1/2" long, driver, policeman	700	1200	1600
Hubley Pickup, 3-1/2" long, cast-iron	22	33	45
Hubley PickUp Dump No. 470, 1958 Ford, 9-1/2" long, die-cast	20	30	40
Hubley Piledriver, late, 12" long	90	135	180
Hubley Pipe Truck No. 803, 9-1/2" long, c.1950s	35	52	70
Hubley Power Shovel, 14" long	60	90	120
Hubley Racer, die-cast, black rubber tires, 4" long	25	38	50
Hubley Racer, 5-1/2" long, c.1930s, 2 passengers	125	188	250
Hubley Racer, 6" long, driver, tail fin, c.1930s	210	325	450
Hubley Racer, 6-1/2" long, driver, c.1930s	200	300	400

	C6	C8	C10
Hubley Racer, 6-1/2" long, plastic	44	66	88
Hubley Racer, driver, 7" long, c.1930s	215	322	430
Hubley Racer, driver, 7" long, electric headlights	No Price Found		
Hubley Racer, animated exhaust stacks, 8" long, driver	550	875	1250
Hubley Racer, animated exhaust stacks, 11" long, driver	1200	2000	3000
Hubley Racer, Closed Cabin, c.1930s, 8" long	250	375	500
Hubley Racer, driver, rubber tires, 8" long	125	188	250
Hubley Racer, 8-1/2" long, c.1930s, tail fin, exhaust stacks, driver	650	1000	1500
Hubley Racer, die-cast, 12" long	65	93	130
Hubley Racer "No. 1," 8" long	250	375	500
Hubley Racer No. 5, early wheels, 9-3/8" long	1100	1800	2600
Hubley Racer No. 5, painted and nickeled iron and aluminum, 9-1/2" long, raise hood-see motor	1300	2000	3000
Hubley Racer No. 5, die-cast, large wheels	75	112	150
Hubley Racer No. 7, 5-1/4" long, early '30s	188	282	375

	C6	C8	C10
Hubley Racer No. 8, streamlined, 7-1/4" long	225	338	450
Hubley Racer No. 22, 7-3/8" long, aluminum & cast-iron, c.1940	105	158	210
Hubley Racer 629, c.1936, 6-3/4" long	300	475	650
Hubley Racer No. 677, 8-1/2" long	700	1200	1600
Hubley Racer, "1790," 5" long approx	160	240	320
Hubley Racer, 2241, 7-1/2" long, c.1930s	45	68	90
Hubley Racer No. 2330, aluminum	500	800	1200
Hubley "Railway Express" Truck, 5" long, rubber tires	200	300	400

Hubley "Railway Express" truck, 5" long. Courtesy Mapes Auctioneers & Appraisers.

	C6	C8	C10
Hubley Renault Dauphine, plastic	45	68	90
Hubley Road Grader, 10" long, die-cast	27	41	55
Hubley Road Grader 12" long	70	105	140
Hubley Road Grader, 15" long, c.1950s	40	60	80
Hubley Road Roller, Hercules, 4-5/8" long	80	120	160

Hubley Racer No. 5, painted and nickeled iron and aluminum, 9-1/2" long (hood panels in photo recast). Courtesy Christie's East.

Hubley Racer No. 22, aluminum and cast iron, 1940, 7-3/8" long. Photo by Rod Carnahan.

Hubley Road Roller, Hercules, 4-5/8" long. Courtesy Bill Bertoia Auctions. Photo by Jeanne Bertoia.

	C6	C8	C10
Hubley Road Roller, c.late 1920s, 8" long, driver	300	450	600
Hubley Road Roller, plastic, wood wheels	25	38	50
Hubley Road Scraper No. 481	37	52	75
Hubley Roadster, c.early 1920s, 7-1/4" long, driver	900	1600	2200
Hubley School Bus, c.1960s, die-cast, 9" long	35	52	70
Hubley Sedan, c.1920, cast-iron, 7" long	100	150	200

Hubley Racer "1790." Photo by Bill Kaufman.

	C6	C8	C10
Hubley Sedan, c.1928, cast-iron, 7" long ...	150	225	300
Hubley Sedan, die-cast, 7" long	62	93	125
Hubley Sedan, c.1930s, cast-iron, 4-door, 6" long	110	165	220
Hubley Sedan, 5" long, sidemount tire, c.1930s	165	198	230
Hubley Sedan, early, 4-1/8" long	67	100	135
Hubley Sedan, c.1938, 2-door, 3-1/2" long, looks like Ford, rubber wheels	60	90	120
Hubley Service Car, 4-1/4" long	60	90	120
Hubley Service Car, 5" cast iron, including wheels, c.1930s	200	300	400
Hubley 726 Shovel Truck, 10" long, c.1930	No Price Found		
Hubley Shovel Truck, 8-1/2" long, c.1938	550	900	1250
Hubley Speedster No. 6, early, 7" long	225	350	435
Hubley Sport Car No. 485	70	105	140
Hubley Stake Dump, die-cast	30	45	60
Hubley Stake Truck, c. late 1930s	160	240	325
Hubley No. 460 Stake Truck	44	66	88
Hubley No. 614 Stake Truck, c.1930s	75	112	150
Hubley Stake Bed Truck, cast-iron, 3-1/2" long	50	75	100
Hubley Stake Bed Truck, 5" long	95	142	190
Hubley Stake Bed Truck, 7" long	225	338	450

Hubley, Stake bed truck, 7" long. Courtesy Mapes Auctioneers & Appraisers.

	C6	C8	C10
Hubley Stake Truck with trailer, No. 927. Two pieces, 21" long	40	60	80
Hubley No. 452 Stake-type Truck, black rubber tires, c. post-WWII	40	60	80
Hubley Station Wagon, c.1940s, 1950s, 8-1/2" long, No. 476	35	52	70
Hubley Steam Roller, 5" long	150	225	300
Hubley Steam Shovel, 4-1/2" long, No. 325	115	173	230
Hubley Stock Truck, plastic, 12" long	112	168	225
Hubley Studebaker Car Carrier, 10" long, c.1930s	200	300	400
Hubley Studebaker Roadster, frame and body separate	300	450	600
Hubley Studebaker Stake Truck	20	30	40
Hubley Studebaker Touring Car, cast-iron	325	518	650

	C6	C8	C10
Hubley Studebaker Town Car, cast-iron, 5" long	250	375	500
Hubley Take-Apart Coupe, 6" long	225	338	450
Hubley Take-Apart Roadster, c.1930s	120	180	240
Hubley Take-Apart Sedan, 6" long, c.early 1930s	150	230	325
Hubley Take-Apart Stake Truck, 4-3/4" long	200	300	400
Hubley Take-Apart Stake Truck, 6-1/2" long	500	750	1000
Hubley Take-Apart Station Wagon, c.1920s	250	400	550

Hubley Woody Station Wagon, take-apart, 5" long. Courtesy Bill Bertoia Auctions. Photo by Jeanne Bertoia.

	C6	C8	C10
Hubley Take-Apart Tow Truck, early	238	355	475
Hubley Taxi, die-cast, black rubber tires	20	30	40
Hubley Telephone Truck, plastic	25	38	50
Hubley "10 Ton" Stake Truck, cast-iron, 7" long	300	425	600
Hubley "10 Ton" Stake Truck, 8-1/4" long	350	525	700

Hubley "10 ton" stake truck, cast iron, 7" long. Photo by Bob Smith.

Hubley "10 Ton" Stake Truck, 8-1/4" long. Courtesy Bill Bertoia Auctions. Photo by Jeanne Bertoia.

	C6	C8	C10
Hubley Thunderbird	120	180	240
Hubley Touring Auto, c.1921, 11-1/2" long	No Price Found		
Hubley Touring Auto, c.1915, 9-1/2" long, cast-iron, chauffeur and rider	750	1125	1500
Hubley Touring Auto, 7" long, c.1920s	165	248	330
Hubley Tow Truck, 8-3/4" long, cast-iron, c.1930s	140	210	280

steer... roll like real!

MAN, DO THEY GO! IT'S ALMOST LIKE GETTING THE REAL THING FOR CHRISTMAS!

Woolworth's AMERICA'S CHRISTMAS TOY STORE

4-PC. FIRE SET EVEN HAS OWN SPOTTER PLANE! By land, air, everyone's there! Motorcycle, plane, Fire Chief, 2-section hook and ladder engine! 4 ladders reach 18¾". Plastic. **1.98**

STEERING WHEEL TURNS. Tractor's big wheels roll down highway or over sod. Metal, 7" long. **98c**

LUMBER TRUCK IN 2 SECTIONS. Plastic lumber truck, hood lifts. Trailer stands alone. 1 foot long. Hauls load of 9 boards. **1.49**

Trailer stands on dolly wheels!

RACY MODEL CAR. Carries a spare on back, as foreign sportsters do! 9", metal. **1.49**

GET PHONE POLES UP! Bell truck has trailer, pole, 3 tools. Winch. Metal. Assembles to 13". **1.49**

By THE HUBLEY MANUFACTURING CO.

Not shown: 5½" metal tractor, 59c
Metal hook-and-ladder, 7½", 59c
7¼" metal logging truck, 59c

Some prices slightly higher in West

Hubleys, as shown in Woolworth's 1954 Christmas catalog-comic book.

	C6	C8	C10
Hubley Tow Truck, Ford, 9" long, die-cast	62	93	125
Hubley Tractor No. 472	40	60	80
Hubley Tractor No. 490	50	75	100
Hubley Tractor, Ford 961, with plow, 15" long	100	150	200
Hubley Tractor, Ford 4000, 10-1/2" long	40	60	80
Hubley Tractor, Ford 6000	80	120	160
Hubley Tractor, 960 H	68	102	135
Hubley Tractor, scale model, 7" long	88	132	175
Hubley Tractor, steam boiler in front, 4-3/4" long, c. early 1920s	125	187	250
Hubley Tractor, 5", c.1930s	250	450	600
Hubley Tractor, die-cast, with scoop, 13" long	58	87	115
Hubley Tractor Loader No. 501, 11" long, c.1950s	78	118	155
Hubley Tractor Shovel, driver, 9-1/2" long	750	1300	1750
Hubley Tractor Trailer c.1950s	75	112	150
Hubley Tractor Trailer and Road Scraper No. 506, die-cast, 19" long	150	225	300
Hubley Trailer Truck, c.1936-38.	100	150	200
Hubley Transitional Fire Patrol, 12" cast-iron, driver, firemen, c.1920	1000	1500	2000

	C6	C8	C10
"Hubley U.S.A." Airflow type, c.1937, approx. 3-1/2" long	20	30	40
Hubley Volkswagen	35	52	70
Hubley Water Tower, early, 14" long, 2 drivers	850	1400	2000
Hubley Wrecker, chrome wheels, Service Car	45	68	90
Hubley Wrecker, 3-1/2" long	42	63	85
Hubley Wrecker, 4-1/2" long, rubber wheels, c.1930	110	165	220
Hubley Wrecker, 4-3/4" long	75	112	150
Hubley Wrecker, 6" long, c.1940, white wheels on large hubs	100	150	200
Hubley Wrecking Truck, 1930, cast-iron, rubber tires, 7-1/2" long	150	225	300
Hubley Wrecker, No. 452	30	45	60
Hubley Wrecker, 10" long, Ford, No. 474	82	123	165
Hubley Yellow Cab, 8" long, rear luggage racks folds down	300	450	600
Hubley Yellow Cab, c.1920s, 7-3/4" long	550	850	1200
Hubley Yellow Cab, c.1920s, 8-1/4" long, spare tire	600	950	1400

Hubley Yellow Cab; rear luggage rack folds down. Photo by Chic Gast.

Hubley Yellow Cab, 1920s, 7-3/4" long. Courtesy Sotheby's New York.

HUBLEY MOTORCYCLES

List by Kent M. Comstock

Kent M. Comstock, who has contributed photos, and much information, regarding motorcycles to various sections of this book, is a lifelong motorcycle enthusiast. It was his interest in antique motorcycles that got him interested in toys. He was at an Antique Motorcycle Club (AMC) meet in Wauseon, Ohio, in 1985 when he saw small cast iron motorcycles trading for hundreds of dollars. He was hooked. He believes toy replicas are great collector pieces for motorcycle enthusiasts. "The Harleys, Indians and Hendersons made out of iron are very realistic and representative of their period. They were all authorized and very well detailed." He strongly advises new collectors to buy what they like, as they'll be able to continue to enjoy the toy even if it dips in price.

	C6	C8	C10
HM 1 Motorcycle solo, "Cop," rubber or nickel wheels, 4" long	50	75	100
HM 2 Motorcycle with sidecar "Cop" rider and passenger, 4" long	110	165	220
HM 3 Motorcycle racer "Speed," 4-1/4" long	165	248	330
HM 4 Motorcycle tandem, "PDH" rubber or nickel wheels, 4-1/8" long	100	150	250
HM 5 Motorcycle trike "Crash Car," rubber or nickel wheels, 4-3/4" long	50	75	125

Hubley HM1

Hubley HM2, passenger missing. Photo by Max Heiss.

Hubley, L to R: HM8, HM7. Photo by Kent M. Comstock.

	C6	C8	C10
HM 8 Motorcycle trike "Flowers," rubber or nickel wheels, blue, 4-1/2" long	500	800	1200
HM8A Motorcycle trike "Flowers," 5-1/4" long, auctioned 1994, very good, for $3100			
HM 9 Motorcycle policeman "Harley-Davidson," nickel wheels, 5-1/2" long .	275	363	550

	C6	C8	C10
HM 10 Motorcycle policeman "Harley-Davidson" swivel head, rubber or nickel wheels, 7-1/4" long	700	1200	1600
HM 11 Motorcycle Hillclimber "HD-45" rubber or nickel wheels, 6-1/2" long	400	600	800
HM 12 Motorcycle Racer nickel wheels, 5-3/4" long	375	550	800
HM 13 Motorcycle civilian driver, rubber or nickel wheels, 6-1/4" long	250	400	600
HM 14 Motorcycle with sidecar, civilian driver and passenger, 6-1/2" long	300	500	750
HM 15 Motorcycle policeman "PD" 1950's die-cast with plastic driver, 8-1/2" long	450	675	900
HM 16 Motorcycle trike "Traffic Car" Indian, rubber tires, 9" long	800	1400	2200
HM 16A "Traffic Car," 11-1/2" long	1500	2500	3500

Hubley Motorcycles, L to R: HM8A, HM8, HM7. Courtesy Bill Bertoia Auctions. Photo by Jeanne Bertoia.

Hubley HM9. Photo by Kent M. Comstock.

Hubley HM10. Courtesy David Mapes Auctions.

Hubley HM12. Photo by Kent M. Comstock.

Hubley HM11. Photo by Kent M. Comstock.

Hubley HM15. Photo by Kent M. Comstock.

Hubley HM13. Photo by Kent M. Comstock.

Hubley HM16. Courtesy Sotheby's NY.

Hubley HM17. Photo by Max Heiss.

	C6	C8	C10
HM 17 Motorcycle policeman, battery operated headlight, 6" long	300	450	600
HM 18 Motorcycle with demountable cop, battery operated headlight, 8-1/2", red	600	750	1000
HM 19 Motorcycle with sidecar, 2 demountable cops, battery operated headlight, 8-1/2" long, red ...	1150	1900	2650
HM 20 Motorcycle with sidecar, "Harley-Davidson," 2 demountable cops, 9" long, olive green	700	1000	1400
HM 21 Motorcycle with sidecar, "Indian," 2 demountable cops, 9" long, red	600	900	1200
HM 22 Motorcycle with detachable civilian rider, "Harley-Davidson," 9" long, olive green, blue, or orange ...	1000	1750	2500
HM 23 Motorcycle with detachable cop, "Harley-Davidson," 9" long, olive green, blue, or orange	850	1500	1880

	C6	C8	C10
HM 24 Motorcycle with detachable cop, "Indian" nickel 4-cylinder motor, 9-1/4" long, red, green, or yellow	800	1300	1800
HM 25 Motorcycle Package Truck, "Harley-Davidson Parcel Post," with detachable blue rider, 9-1/2" long	1300	2000	2900
HM 26 Motorcycle Package Truck, "Indian Air Mail," with detachable blue rider, 9-1/2" long	1100	2000	2700
HM 27 Motorcycle Trike "Indian Crash Car," demountable rider, axes and hose reel, 11-1/2" long	1500	2000	3000

Hubley HM19. Courtesy Sotheby's NY.

Hubley HM20. Photo by Kent M. Comstock.

Hubley HM21. Photo by Kent M. Comstock.

Hubley HM22. Photo by Kent M. Comstock.

	C6	C8	C10
HM 28 Motorcycle trike "Indian Traffic Car," demountable rider, 12" long, red and blue	1500	2000	3000
HM 29 Motorcycle with sidecar, "Indian Armored Car," 2 demountable cops, 8-1/2" long, red	1200	2000	2750
HM 30 Motorcycle, plastic Kiddietoy, 5" long	15	22	30
HM 31 Motorcycle, trike "Say It With Flowers," cast-iron, 10-1/2" long, auctioned 1994, excellent, for $18,000			
HM 32 Motorcycle, Harley-Davidson, with policeman, swivel head, 6-1/2" long, early, "Harley" on both sides	500	750	1000

	C6	C8	C10
HM 33 Motorcycle, Harley-Davidson, sidecar, civilian driver, woman passenger, 9" long	800	1400	2200
HM 34 Motorcycle, removable rider, 4-1/4" long	50	75	125
HM 35 Motorcycle, Harley-Davidson with sidecar, 2 policemen, rubber or nickel wheels, 5-1/4" long	250	350	500

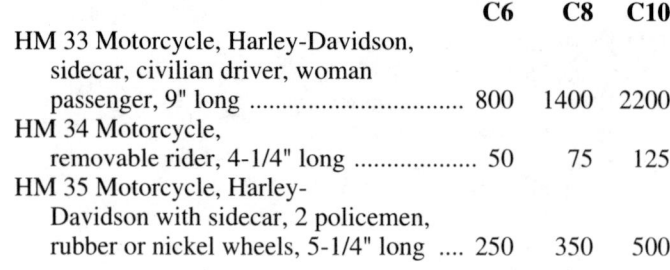

Hubley Motorcycle HM23. Courtesy Bill Bertoia Auctions. Photo by Jeanne Bertoia.

Hubley HM24. Photo by Kent M. Comstock.

Hubley HM25. Courtesy Sotheby's NY.

Hubley HM26. Courtesy Sotheby's NY.

Hubley Motorcycle HM26. Courtesy Bill Bertoia Auctions. Photo by Jeanne Bertoia.

Hubley HM27. Photo by Kent M. Comstock.

Hubley Motorcycles

Hubley Motorcycle HM28. Courtesy Bill Bertoia
Auctions. Photo by Jeanne Bertoia.

Hubley Motorcycle
HM29. Courtesy Bill
Bertoia Auctions. Photo
by Jeanne Bertoia.

Hubley HM30. Photo by Terry Sells.

Hubley HM31. Courtesy Sotheby's NY.

Hubley HM34. Photo by Kent M. Comstock.

Hubley HM32. Courtesy Wilkinson Collection, Detroit Antique
Toy Museum.

Hubley Motorcycle, HM35. Photo by Kent M. Comstock.

Hubley Motorcycles  237

	C6	C8	C10
HM 36 Motorcycle trike "Indian Crash Car," 9-3/8" long, auctioned 1994, excellent, for $4500			
HM 37 Motorcycle trike Popeye Spinach Cycle, separate rider, 5-3/8" long	650	1100	1750
HM 38 Motorcycle, Popeye Patrol, 8-3/8" long	2000	3500	5500
HM 39 Motorcycle Trike "Crash Car," 6-1/2" long	225	338	450
HM 40 Motorcycle, Kiddietoy, plastic, 5" long	15	22	30

Hubley Motorcycle HM36, with hose reel and cans. Courtesy Bill Bertoia Auctions. Photo by Jeanne Bertoia.

Hubley Motorcycles, L to R: HM37, HM38. Courtesy Bill Bertoia Auctions. Photo by Jeanne Bertoia.

Hubley Motorcycle HM39. Courtesy Bill Bertoia Auctions. Photo by Jeanne Bertoia.

IDEAL

	C6	C8	C10
Ideal American LaFrance Aerial Ladder Truck	95	143	190
Ideal American LaFrance Fix-It Tow Truck w/1952 Pontiac car & tools	150	225	300
Ideal Army Ambulance, 5" long	20	30	40
Ideal Army Jeep, "Mighty Mo," siren, plastic, 1953, 13" long	25	38	50

	C6	C8	C10
Ideal Army Van, 4" long	20	30	40
Ideal Atomic Rocket Launching Truck, 12" long	32	48	65
Ideal Auto Laundry	55	83	110
Ideal Barracuda Coupe, 1964, plastic, 4" long	15	23	30
Ideal Bulldozer, plastic	50	75	100
Ideal Cadillac, 4-door, 1948, plastic, 4" long	25	38	50
Ideal Car Trailer, c.1945, plastic, 3" long	20	30	40

Ideal, L to R: Army Ambulance, Van, 6" long. Courtesy Bob and Alice Wagner.

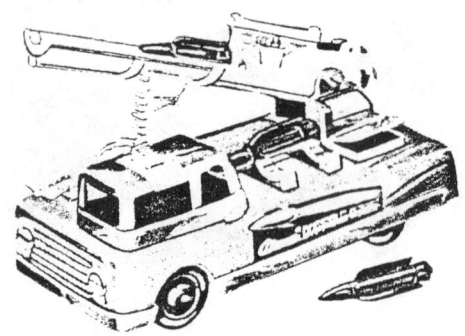

Ideal Atomic Launching Truck, as shown in a 1955-56 Toy Yearbook.

	C6	C8	C10
Ideal Car Trailer, plastic, 4 cars, 27" long	40	60	80
Ideal Carousel Truck	50	75	100
Ideal Cattle Truck, 13" long	25	38	50
Ideal Coal Truck, 1949, 5-1/2" long	21	31	42
Ideal Corvette	75	112	150
Ideal "Dairy Farm" Van	27	41	54
Ideal Danger Patrol Truck, 1950s	90	135	180
Ideal Dragnet Talking Police Car	60	90	120
Ideal Dump Truck, 5-3/4"	21	32	42
Ideal Emergency Van, 6" long	10	35	45
Ideal FBI Car No. 3072, Talks	No Price Found		

Ideal Cattle Truck. Photo by Terry Sells.

Ideal Dump Truck, plastic. Photo by Dave Leopard.

Ideal FBI Car No. 3072, talks. Photo by Tim Oei.

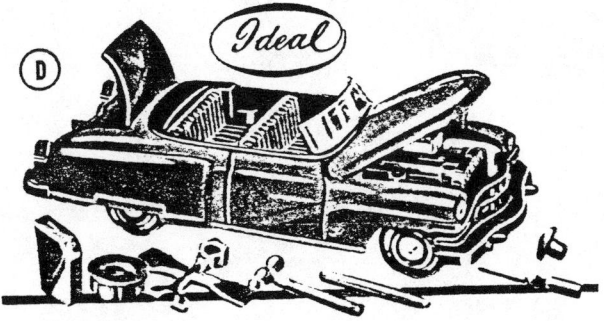

Ideal Fix-It Convertible, as shown in the 1953-54 Toy Yearbook.

D, Ideal Fix-It Tow Truck and Car with dented fender. 20-1/2" plastic and metal truck holds tools for chaining tires and fender. Also has battery-operated searchlight, crank-operated tow crane, "fire extinguisher." $9.95.

E, Ideal Danger Patrol truck, 12-3/4" long, of plastic and metal, with friction motor. Includes tool chest, "oxygen" tank, ladders, road block, control box with "microphone," etc. Red light flashes as truck moves. $3.98.

F, Ideal Dragnet Talking Police Car. Official 14-1/2" "Dragnet" plastic and metal car. Crank produces "radio voice." Has built-in swivel chair, table, battery-operated searchlight, camera, binoculars, rifles, etc. $3.98.

Illustration from the 1955-56 Toy Yearbook.

	C6	C8	C10
Ideal Fire Pumper	34	51	68
Ideal Fix-It Cadillac, 12" long	75	112	150
Ideal Fix-It Fire Chief Fire Truck	72	108	145
Ideal Fix-It Sport Convertible, 13" long	65	98	130
Ideal Fix-It Tow Truck	90	135	180
Ideal Fix-It Tow Truck and Car with Dented Fender, 20-1/2" long, metal and plastic			No Price Found

	C6	C8	C10
Ideal Fix-It Truck 8-1/2" long, with tools, plastic	62	93	125
Ideal Ford Truck	40	60	80
Ideal Ford Wagon	40	60	80
Ideal "Gambles" Semi Truck, 12" long, plastic	36	54	72
Ideal Hy-Speed Car Wash w/car, 1950s	32	48	65
Ideal Ice Cream Truck, 5-1/2" long, 1948-54	30	60	100
Ideal Jeep, c.1945	20	30	40
Ideal Jet Racer	50	75	100
Ideal Ladder Truck	65	98	130
Ideal Mercedes Sedan, 9" long.	35	52	70
Ideal Motorific 1951 GMC Wrecker	20	30	40
Ideal Nellybelle Jeep	14	21	28
Ideal Oldsmobile, 1954, 19" long	150	225	300
Ideal Panel Truck No. 3085, 1951-52..........	27	41	54
Ideal Panel Truck No. 1-1729	20	30	40
Ideal Patton Tank, 6" long	12	18	25
Ideal Pickup Truck, American, 1948, 4" plastic	20	30	40
Ideal Pickup Truck, Ford, 1940, 4" plastic ..	14	21	27
Ideal Pickup Truck, streamlined, 4-1/2" long, 1950s, No. 1-788	7	11	14
Ideal Pickup Truck, streamlined, with canopy and gas tank filler, 4-1/2" long, 1950s	4	10	20
Ideal Police Car	6	9	12
Ideal Race Car, 8" windup	60	90	120
Ideal Race Car, 10" windup	50	75	100

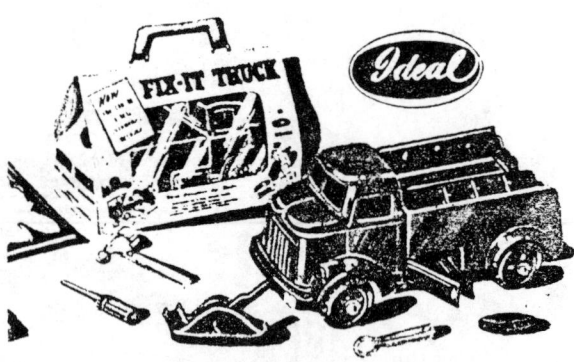

Ideal Fix-It Truck, as shown in a 1952-53 Toy Yearbook.

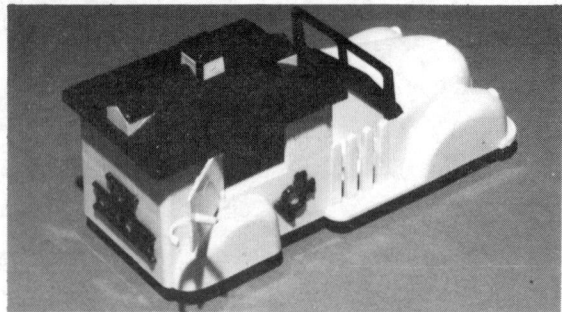

Ideal Ice Cream Truck. Courtesy Bob and Alice Wagner.

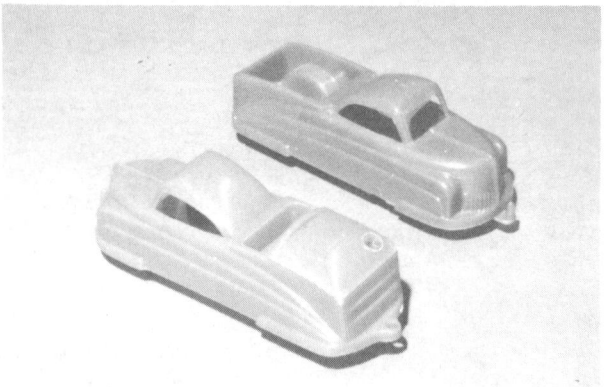

Ideal, L to R: Pick-up truck, streamlined, with canopy and gas tank filler, 4-1/2," Pick-up truck, streamlined, 4-1/2." Courtesy Bob and Alice Wagner.

Ideal Jeep, c.1945, on original box. Photo by Terry Sells.

Ideal Robert the Robot. Photo by Don Hultzman.

Ideal Rolls Royce, plastic, 8" long. Photo by Ron Fink.

Ideal Scooter. Photo by Terry Sells.

Ideal Rocket Cycle. Photo by Terry Sells.

Ideal Sanitation Truck, 5-1/2" long. Photo by Terry Sells.

Ideal Sedan, 9-1/4" long. Photo by Terry Sells.

Ideal Shell truck. Photo by Terry Sells.

	C6	C8	C10
Ideal Robert the Robot, battery-operated ...	150	225	300
Ideal Rocket Car, 11" long, w/windup launcher	No Price Found		
Ideal Rocket Cycle, 6-1/2" long	100	150	200
Ideal Rocket Launcher Truck, 12" long	55	83	110
Ideal Rolls-Royce, 12" long	11	16	22
Ideal Rolls-Royce, 8" long, plastic	12	18	25
Ideal Sanitation Truck, 5-1/2" long, plastic	20	35	50
Ideal Scooter, 4" long, plastic	No Price Found		
Ideal Sedan, 5" long	14	21	28
Ideal Sedan w/Teardrop Trailer, 8-1/8"	26	39	52

	C6	C8	C10
Ideal Sedan, 9-1/4" long, plastic	20	35	50
Ideal Semi, 12" long	26	39	52
Ideal Service Truck, 8" long	22	33	45
Ideal Service Van, 5" long	20	30	40
Ideal Shell Truck, 12-1/2" long	25	38	50
Ideal Signal Corps Truck, 5" long	20	30	40
Ideal Speed King Dream Racer, plastic, 13" long	50	75	100
Ideal Speedy Pete pulltoy racer, early 1950s	60	90	120
Ideal Steam Shovel, 7-1/2" long	22	33	45
Ideal Steering Farm Tractor	7	11	15
Ideal Steve Canyon Glider Bomb Truck, 17"	60	90	120
Ideal "Television Repair" truck	40	60	80
Ideal Tow Truck, 17" long, plastic and metal	100	150	200
Ideal Tractor, 1948, plastic, 4" long	20	30	40
Ideal Trailer No. 1-409	7	11	15
Ideal Turbo-Jet Car No. 4867	60	90	120
Ideal Two-Car Garage	No Price Found		
Ideal Van, 6" long	10	35	45
Ideal Van, sliding front door, 4-1/2" long	10	25	60
Ideal Work truck	35	52	70
Ideal XP-600 Fix-It car of tomorrow, 16"	85	128	170

Ideal Steam Shovel, plastic. Photo by Dave Leopard.

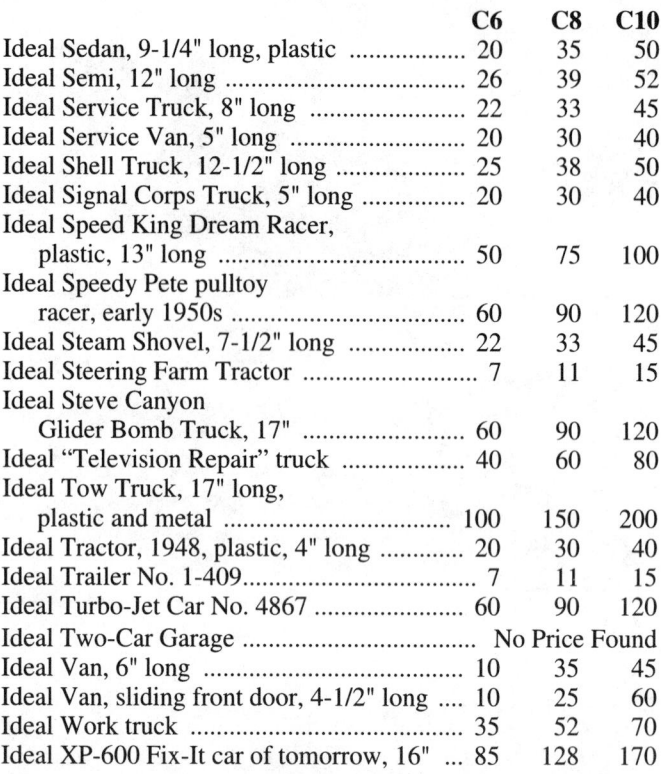

Ideal Turbo-Jet Car, No. 4867. Photo by Tim Oei.

Ideal Two-Car Garage, plastic. Photo by Dave Leopard.

Ideal, back row: Van, sliding front door, "Dairy Farm" van; Front: Van, 6" long. Courtesy Bob and Alice Wagner.

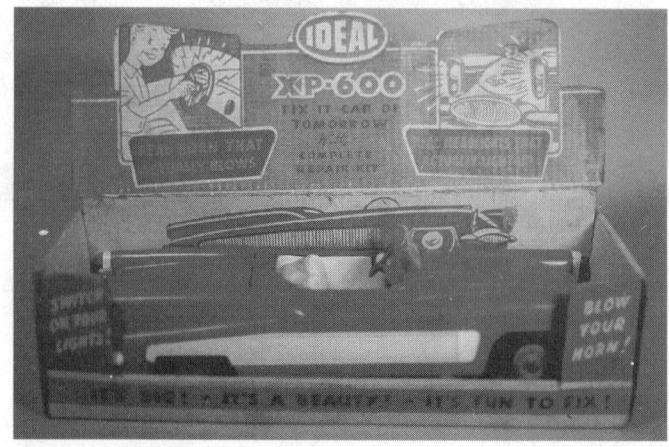

Ideal XP-600 Fix-It Car of Tomorrow in original box. Photo by Terry Sells.

	C6	C8	C10
Ingap Mouse Car, windup; Italian, 6" long, eccentric wheels, arms extend	1650	2475	3300

Ingap Mouse Car. Courtesy Christie's East.

IRWIN TOY CORPORATION

Irwin was founded in 1922 by Irwin Cohn. Located at first in New York City, it began as a maker of celluloid baby rattles and pinwheels, soon becoming the largest manufacturer of pinwheels in the United States. In the late 1940s, it produced the first polyethylene toy, a 7-inch car. Irwin, which eventually moved to Leominster and Fitchburg in Massachusetts (with an additional plant in Nashua, New Hampshire), sold out to Miner Industries in 1973.

	C6	C8	C10
Irwin Army Bus	27	41	55
Irwin Army Cadillac			
Staff Car, plastic windshield	15	22	30
Irwin Army Dump Truck, plastic	12	18	25
Irwin Barney Rubble Car	12	18	25
Irwin Big Mike Tow			
Truck, battery operated	55	82	110
Irwin Buick Convertible, 1948, 5" long	10	15	20
Irwin Chevrolet Panel Delivery, 6" long	10	15	20
Irwin Chevrolet Pickup Truck,			
5.3" long, 1952........................	10	15	20
Irwin Dream Car			
Convertible, 16" long, metal	200	300	400
Irwin Dump Truck, 8-1/2" long, 1950s	15	22	30

	C6	C8	C10
Irwin Ford Sunliner,			
9" long, plastic friction	50	75	100
Irwin GI Joe Motorcycle & Sidecar	100	150	200
Irwin Horse Van, 16" long	25	38	50
Irwin Human Cannonball Truck,			
19" long, 1960s, has net, 2 figures	41	62	83
Irwin Ice Cream Truck, plastic	55	82	110
Irwin Jaguar Roadster, 6" long	35	52	70
Irwin Log Truck	20	30	40
Irwin Packard Sedan			
friction, 9" long, 1952..............................	25	30	35
Irwin Pickup Truck, metal, 6" long	24	36	48

Irwin Chevrolet Pick-Up Truck, 5.3" long. Photo by Dave Leopard.

Irwin Pickup Truck, metal, 6" long. Photo by Ron Fink.

	C6	C8	C10
Irwin Plumbing & Heating			
Truck w/tools, etc., 1960s	62	93	125
Irwin Police Car, plastic, 12" long	25	38	50
Irwin Pontiac Hardtop			
Coupe, friction, 6" long, 1952	15	20	25
Irwin Racer	17	26	35
Irwin "Skipper" Convertible, 1962	150	225	300
Irwin State Police Car,			
plastic friction, 6-1/2" long	15	22	30
Irwin Steeraway Wonder Car	95	143	190
Irwin Taxi Cab, 12" long, trunk opens	125	188	250
Irwin Telephone Repair Truck	100	150	200
Irwin Tow Truck, 8"	27	41	55

Irwin Police Car, plastic friction, 12" long. Photo by Ron Fink.

Irwin Pontiac Hard-top Coupe, friction. Photo by Dave Leopard.

Irwin State Police Car, plastic friction, 6-1/2" long. Photo by Ron Fink.

IVES

	C6	C8	C10
Ives Horseless Carriage			
Runabout, 6-1/2" long, 6" high to			
the top of jockey cap on driver	2500	3750	5000
Ives Steamer, cast-iron,			
19-1/2" long, two drivers	500	750	1000

J&S

	C6	C8	C10
J&S Hudson w/suspension, die-cast	68	102	135

JANE FRANCIS TOYS

by Jane Francis

In 1942, the scarcity of toys during the war started me making stuffed toys for a Pittsburgh hospital gift shop, Allegheny General, where I was a Medical Librarian. It wasn't long before I was making the "Gingham Dog," the "Calico Cat," and "Jumbo, The Elephant" for several hospital gift shops in the Pittsburgh area. The toy buyer at Gimbel's called one day and asked me to make 12 dozen stuffed toys. This was the real beginning of Jane Francis Toys.

I located a woman who had had a great deal of experience in an Eastern sewing factory. She agreed to sew in her own home. Twelve dozen were made and delivered one day ahead of schedule.

It wasn't long before other major department stores in Philadelphia, Baltimore, and Washington were ordering and more sewers were found. A giraffe and a turtle were added to the line.

Pearce Woolen Mills in nearby Latrobe was manufacturing army blankets and we purchased the combings from the blankets to stuff the toys. The Association for the Blind took the contract to stuff the toys. Now we were off and running.

Home sewers were unable to meet production, so we found a sewing factory in Canton, Ohio to cut and sew the bodies. They were shipped back to Pittsburgh where they were stuffed and packed for shipment. After the first few weeks a string tab, saying "Jane Francis Toys" was attached to each animal. By this time we had a commissioned agent to handle sales. Its sales office was at 200 Fifth Ave., New York.

The war was winding down and my husband decided to join the operation and bring out a line of die-cast cars and trucks, spinning toys, and a Gulf Service Station.

The die-cast line went well until the advent of plastic toys. At approximately the same time, a man by the name of Frank Snedden invented and patented the first automatic shut-off hose nozzle. He was about to retire from Westinghouse and decided to sell his patents and dies. A purchase was negotiated.

A fire at our location in Wilkinsburg (Pittsburgh) prompted us to move to Somerset. At that location, a partner was brought into the business. The partnership did not work out, and in 1951, we started the A.W. Francis Co. to manufacture lawn and garden accessories.

(A shorter history by Jane Francis states her firm operated in Wilkinsburg from 1942 through 1946 and in Somerset from 1947 through 1949. The line of die-cast cars was introduced in 1945. The last Jane Francis toys were manufactured in 1949. Jane Francis Vanyo, the Francis' daughter, in 1993 stated that the successor company, A.W. Francis, was still in business in Somerset under the name Green Garden, Inc., producing lawn and garden accessories.)

	C6	C8	C10
JF01 Pickup Truck, 6-1/2" long	30	40	50
JF02 Pickup Truck, 5" long, No. 347............	20	25	30
JF03 Pickup Truck, 5" long, No. 447............	20	25	30
JF04 Tow Truck, 5" long, No. 447	30	35	40
JF05 Gulf Truck, tin cover, 5" long, No. 447...............................	30	40	50

	C6	C8	C10
JF06 Sedan, fastback, futuristic, 6-1/2" long	25	30	40
JF07 Sedan, fastback, futuristic, 6-1/2" long, with windup motor	30	40	50

Jane Francis JF02. Photo by Dave Leopard.

Jane Francis JF04. Photo by Dave Leopard.

Jane Francis JF05. Photo by Dave Leopard.

Jane Francis produced this Gulf Service Station in the late 1940s. Robert H. Mauler of Jessup, Maryland, secured a gross of these stations many years ago, in mint condition; value complete in mint $750. Courtesy Barbara Francis Vanyo.

JAPANESE BATTERY-OPERATED TOYS

by Don Hultzman

"Made in Japan" are the words toy collectors look for in their pursuit of high-quality mechanical tin toys. Before WWII, these words were synonymous with cheap, poor-quality, drab-looking toys made from recycled materials and ideas. Most of the toys were people-animal oriented, with less emphasis on vehicle, nautical, or aircraft-type toys. They were powered either by a spring or a flywheel and didn't last too long or do too much, as far as play-value goes. These inexpensive, poor quality toys kept Japan a third-rate toy-manufacturing nation until after WWII, when Japan's surrender resulted in economic chaos for this industrial nation.

In its quest for economic recovery and to compete in a toy market already dominated by Germany and America, the Japanese knew they had to come up with a new, different and exciting type of toy that would make them more desirable than their competitors. Japanese toy designers concentrated their technology on a different type of toy operation. Not satisfied with the limited action and short duration of spring-driven or flywheel-propelled toys, the toy engineers developed a small electric motor, powered by flashlight batteries. This mini-motor took up less room than other mechanisms, had a longer-running duration, and enabled the toy to perform more functions. This development opened up an entirely new dimension in toy design and introduced the concept of the battery-operated toy!

The toy designers integrated this new concept into hundreds of automaton-like toys, capable of as many as eight different types of actions, all in one cycle. These unique toys were an instant hit with the foreign market, especially in the United States. These clever, unusual, and high-quality toys made Japan the dominant toy producer and exporter for the next 20 to 30 years.

Again, Japan flooded the market with these ingenious, well-made toys while quality control remained a high priority. These merits were not only apparent in their figural toys, but also in their vehicle line. Here, Japanese toy makers concentrated on very fine detail and quality, especially in their scale-model passenger cars, with the ultimate goal of making them look like the real thing, and they succeeded. Their workmanship carried over into their other vehicle lines, such as motorcycles, emergency, and construction vehicles, as well as their novelty (silly) and comic character cars, trucks, and space toys.

No other nation was able to equal or surpass the impetus and determination of the Japanese toy makers, until Japan relinquished its domination by re-aligning its economy in the electronic-automotive field.

Now that they are approaching middle age, it is no wonder that these fine toys remain in great demand today and are often very pricey!

Don Hultzman confesses he has always been a collector of toys, but didn't really get serious about the hobby until about 10 years ago. He not only collects toys, but also repairs them. Born and raised in Cleveland, he received a Master's degree in Guidance and Administration at Kent State and is currently employed by the Panama City School System as a school counselor. He does free-lance writing as a science consultant to the encyclopedia department of World Publishing Co., and lives in Brunswick Hills, Ohio. Many of his tin windup toys can be seen in the 1983 MGM movie "A Christmas Story" and the 1994 movie "My Summer Story."

Condition of a Toy and its Relation to Price

The value of a battery-operated toy depends not only on its desirability, rarity, and complexity, but very much on its condition. A toy in "mint" condition is generally worth twice as much as a toy in "good" condition. A toy in "very good" condition will be equally priced between "good" and "mint."

C-10- "mint," means just that—the condition in which the toy was originally issued-perfect-regardless of age. It will also be in perfect mechanical condition, complete with all accessory parts, when applicable, and will look "brand new." The cloth or fur (plush) covering on some battery toys may reveal some discoloration (yellowing) due to age, but this should not affect its value as a "mint" toy, as long as it is clean. All toys in this category must be in perfect working condition. The original box in mint condition will significantly enhance the value of any "mint" toy.

C-8- "Very Good," indicates the condition of a battery toy that has seen some use and is starting to show its age. It will still be in perfect working order and have all its accessory parts, where applicable. It will have some age-soiling, but will have no rust or corrosion. Overall, it will have an appearance of freshness and still be highly desirable to the fussy collector.

C-6- "Good," applies to a battery toy that has seen considerable use, wear and tear, some age soiling, but still in perfect working condition with no missing parts or accessories. The "wet" toys may show some slight surface rust that can be easily removed. A toy in "good" condition is still a welcome addition to any toy collection, but will be targeted for upgrading by a piece in better condition.

Any battery toy below the condition of "good" will reflect a drastic reduction in value. Toys in good shape, but missing accessory parts, will not lose as much value as those that are severely rusted, corroded, painted over, have parts broken off and are totally inoperable. These "poor" toys are usually collected for their "scrap value" by the toy repairer, and seldom are they worth more than $10.

The key to grading is to use common sense and avoid wishful thinking. Since grading the condition of a toy may be difficult at times, consulting with an expert in the field, if possible, could clear up any lingering doubts. (See back section of this guide for references of toy collectors.)

Guidelines for the Care and Repair of Your Battery-Operated Toy
by Don Hultzman

Your prized battery toy needs T.L.C. and when it stops working, you now have a frustrating disaster on your hands. To avoid this, the following suggestions should be of some help:

Battery toys, like other mechanical toys, should be operated periodically to keep them loosened up. Using a lightweight spray lubrication now and then will help considerably, if the mechanism is accessible. Do not over-lubricate, as the excess may stain any cloth-or-fur-covering on some battery toys.

A good quality car wax or polish will keep the lithographed and bare metal parts looking like new-especially on the "wet" toys. Always test an obscure lithographed area to make sure the polish doesn't soften or dissolve the paint. Care should be exercised when polishing metal parts adjoining any cloth or plush covering, as the substance may stain the coverings. Light surface rust usually disappears with a careful polishing. Nothing can be done for deep rust or corrosion without ruining the value of the toy. Repainting will only further reduce the value and is not recommended.

Should your battery toy fail to operate, the following steps might be helpful:

1. Make sure it is not gunked-up, and that no moving parts are binding.
2. Make sure the battery contacts are not dirty or corroded-if so clean them with crocus cloth. ALWAYS USE FRESH BATTERIES!
3. Lightly tap the toy with your finger or **lightly** nudge one of the moving parts while the switch is on.

If none of these steps work, your toy needs major surgery. This means the toy must be completely torn down, repaired, and reassembled. Most battery toys are repairable as long as they have not been destructively tampered with and no parts are missing or corroded beyond repair. This job is best left to an expert in toy repair and should never be attempted by those who don't know what they are doing. Expert repairs will not affect the value of a battery toy, so long as the repair is **undetectable** and the toy looks and functions **exactly** as it did before the repair. Such repairs are acceptable in toy collecting circles. Expert repairs are also expensive, but are well worth the investment if it means the difference between a "mint" and one below the grade of "good" toy, since an inoperable toy is practically worthless, regardless of condition.

	C6	C8	C10
"American Circus Television Truck" 1950s, Exelo Co., 9-1/4" long, six actions, RARE, (includes detachable metal antenna)	600	900	1200
"Anti-Aircraft Jeep," 1950s, "K" Co., 9-1/2" long, five actions	100	150	200
"Anti-Aircraft Jeep," 1950s, T-N Co. 11" long, six actions, (includes detachable tin radar antenna)	150	225	300
"Antique Gooney Car," 1960s, Alps Co., 9" long, four actions	70	105	140
"Armored Attack Set," 1960s, Marx Co., jeep 6-1/4" long and tank 5-1/4" long, plus 15 2" plastic figures	200	300	400
"Army Radio Jeep--J1490" 1950s Linemar Co., 7-1/4" long, four actions	90	135	180

	C6	C8	C10
"Auto-top Ferrari Convertible," 1960s, Bandai Co., three actions, 11" long	450	675	900
"Automatic Toll Gate," 1955, Sears, 16"x17" base, six actions, (includes 8" tin Valiant)	150	225	300
"Batmobile," 1972 National Periodical Publications, ASC Co., 12" long, three actions	200	300	400
"Big Ring Circus Truck," 1950s, M-T Co., 13" long, three actions	150	225	300
"Big Shot Cadillac," 1950s, T-N Co., 10" long, four actions, Rare	200	300	400
"Big Wheel Coca-Cola Truck," 1970s, Taiyo Co., three actions	80	120	160
"Big Wheel Family Camper" 1970s, 10" long, three actions	80	120	160

	C6	C8	C10
"Big Wheel Ice Cream Truck," 1970s 10" long, three actions	70	105	140
"Bulldozer," 1950s, T-N Co., 7-1/2" long, five actions	80	120	160
"Bulldozer," 1950s, M-T Co., 11" long, six actions	90	135	180

	C6	C8	C10
"B-Z Porter" Baggage Truck 1950s, M-T Co., 7-1/2" long, 6-1/2" high, minor toy, includes three pcs. of luggage (tin)	150	205	300
"Cadillac" Car, 1949, Ashai Toy Co., 10" long, three actions	150	225	300

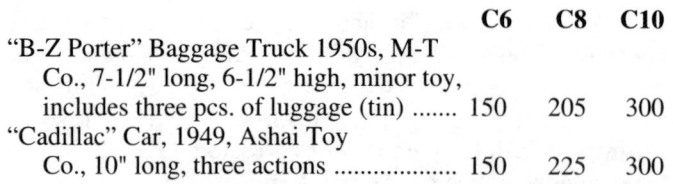

Anti-Aircraft Jeep. Photo by Don Hultzman.

Antique Gooney Car. Photo by Don Hultzman.

Batmobile. Photo by Don Hultzman.

Big Wheel Coca-Cola Truck. Photo by Don Hultzman.

Bulldozer, Shaking Old-Timer Car, Tractor. Photo by Don Hultzman.

Caterpillar Tank M-1. Photo by Don Hultzman.

	C6	C8	C10
"Caterpillar Tank M-1," 1950s, M-T Co., five actions, 8-1/2" long, 11" long with barrel extended	150	220	300
"Chaparral 2F," Car, 1960s, Alps Co., 11" long, five actions	90	135	180
"Chemical Fire Engine," 1950s, HTC Co., 10" long, four actions	110	165	220
"Circus Fire Engine," 1960s, M-T Co., 11" long, four actions	140	210	280
"Climbing Donald Duck On His Friction Fire Engine," 1950s Linemar Co., four actions, 12" long	400	600	800
"Clown Circus Car," 1960s, M-T Co., 8-1/2" long, 9" high, five actions	130	195	260
"Coin Taxi," 1960s, Daiya Co., 6-1/2" long, Minor toy	50	75	100
"Comic Hungry Bug," VW auto, 1970s, Tora (S-T) Co., 7-3/4" long, five actions	40	60	80
"Comic Musical Car," 1960s, T-N Co., four actions, 6" long, 8-1/2" tall	70	105	140
"Comic Road Roller," 1960s, Bandai Co., four actions, 9" long	70	105	140
"Corvair Bertone," 1970s, Bandai Co., four actions, 12" long	50	75	100

	C6	C8	C10
Corvette Sting Ray Sport Coupe, 1968, Eldon Co., 13-1/2" long, Minor toy	100	150	200
"Cragstan Beep Beep Greyhound Bus," 1950s, Cragstan Co., 20" long, three actions	120	180	240
Cragstan Firebird III, 1956, Alps Co., 11-3/4" long-3 actions	300	450	600
"Crane Tractor," 1950s, SKK Co., 7-1/2" long, 11-1/2" high extended	70	105	140
"Crazy Car," 1950s, Marusan Co., five actions, 9" long	70	105	140
"Desert Patrol Jeep," 1960s, M-T Co. 11" long, four actions, includes turret gunner	100	150	200
Dick Tracy Police Car, 1949, TN Co., 9" long--4 actions	100	150	200
"Disney Fire Engine," 1950s, Linemar Co., 11" long, four actions	440	660	880
"Disneyland Fire Engine," 1950s, Linemar Co., 18" long, five actions	300	450	600
Dreamboat Hot-Rod--See Hot Rod			
"Dump Truck No. 7343," 1960s, T-N Co., 10-1/4" long, seven actions	150	225	300

Crazy Car. Photo by Don Hultzman.

Expert Motor Cyclist. Photo by Tim Oei.

Farm Truck, Alps. Photo by Don Hultzman.

Farm Truck, T-N. Photo by Don Hultzman.

	C6	C8	C10
"Electric School Bus," 1950s, M-T Co., 9-1/2" long, minor toy	80	120	160
"Electro Special Racer," 1950s, Yonezawa Co., 10" long, three actions	100	150	200
"Electro Toy Racer," 1950s, Yonezawa Co., three actions, 10" long	1000	1500	2000
"Electronic Fire House," 1940s, Banner Co., 7" square, minor toy (includes plastic fire engine)	80	120	160
"Expert Motor Cyclist," 1950s, MT Co., 12" long, five actions	450	675	900
"Farm Truck," 1960s, Alps Co., 11" long, three actions	120	180	240
"Farm Truck," 1950s, T-N Co., five actions, 9" long	100	150	200
"F.D. Fire Engine," 1960s, Y-M Co., 10" long, 12" high when ladder is extended, four actions	100	150	200
Ferris Wheel Truck, 1950s, T-N Co. 11" long, four actions	400	600	900
"Fire Chief No. 8 Car," 1960s Y Co., 11-1/4" long, three actions	90	135	180
"Fire Chief Mystery Action Car,"1960s, T-N Co., 9-3/4" long, four actions	120	180	240

	C6	C8	C10
"Fire Command Car," 1950s, T-N Co., five actions	170	255	340
"Fire Engine," 1950s, Marusan Co., four actions, 9" long	150	225	300
"Fire Engine," 1950s T-N Co., (Electro Toy), three actions, 9" long-ladder extends 13"	150	225	300
"Fire Engine," 1950s, Y Co., 12" long, ladder extends 16", six actions	100	150	200
"Fire Engine," c.1950s, S-H Co., 3 actions, 8" long	100	150	200
"Firebird Racer," 1950s, Tomiyama Co., four actions, 14-1/4" long	300	450	600
"Ford Model T," 1950s, Nihonkogei Co., 10-1/4" long, four actions (includes detachable tin roof)	60	90	120
"Ford Mustang 2" x 2," 1960s, Wenmac-AMF Co., four actions, 16" long	70	105	140
"Fork Lift Truck," 1960s, M-T Co., 10-1/4" high, Minor Toy	100	150	200
"Go Kart," 1960s, M-T Co., 6-1/2" long, minor toy (includes control wire with steering key)	100	150	200

F.D. Fire Engine, Fire Engine, Fire Chief Mystery Action Car, Police Motorcycle Cop. Courtesy Don Hultzman.

Fire Command Car. Photo by Don Hultzman.

Fork Lift Truck. Photo by Don Hultzman.

Go-Kart, M-T Co. Photo by Don Hultzman.

	C6	C8	C10
"Go Kart," 1950s, Rosko Co., 10" long, three actions, includes detachable head	100	150	200
"Go-Stop Benz Racer," 1950s, Marusan Co., three actions, 11" long	150	220	300
"Grand-Pa Car," 1950s, Y Co., 9" long, four actions	60	90	120
"Greyhound Bus," 1950s, KKK. Co., Minor Toy, 7-1/4" long	100	150	200
"Greyhound Bus-Scenicruiser," 1950s, I.Y. Metal Toy Co., 16" long, three actions	100	150	200
"Greyhound bus with Headlights," 1950s, Linemar Co., 10-1/4" long, three actions	120	180	240
"Handy-Hank Mystery Tractor," 1950s, T-N Co., 9" long, four actions	90	135	180

Greyhound Bus. Photo by Don Hultzman.

King Size Fire Engine. Photo by Don Hultzman.

	C6	C8	C10
"Happy Clown Car," 1960s, Y Co., 6-1/2" long, three actions.	80	120	160
"Happy Tractor," 1960s, Daiya Co., 8" long, four actions	40	60	80
"Highway Drive," 1950s, T-N Co., 15-1/2" long, three actions (includes tin magnetic car)	60	90	120
"Highway Patrol Police Special," 1960s, Y Co., five actions, 11-1/2" long	100	150	200
"Highway Patrol Jeep," 1950s, Daiya Co., 10" long, four actions	70	105	140
"Highway Skill Driving," 1960s, K Co., 13" long, three actions	70	105	140
"Hot Rod" Car, 1950s, T-N Co., 10" long, Minor Toy	200	300	400
"Hot Rod Custom 'T' Ford," 1960s, Alps Co., four actions, 10-1/2" long	100	150	200
"Hot Rod Limousine," 1960s, Alps Co., four actions, 10-1/2" long	200	300	400
"Ice Cream Truck," 1960s, Bandai Co., 10-1/2" long, five actions	150	225	300
"James Bond's Aston-Martin"--See "007 Aston Martin"			
"James Bond-007 Car-M101," 1960s, Daiya Co., 11" long, seven actions, includes ejectable driver--See "M101 Aston Martin"			

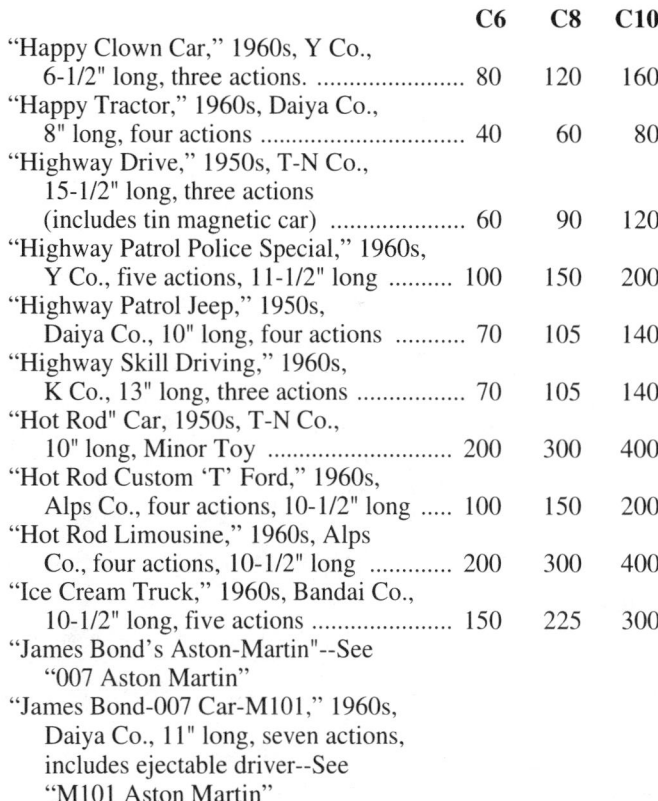

John's Farm Truck. Photo by Don Hultzman.

Kissing Couple. Photo by Don Hultzman.

	C6	C8	C10
"Jeep-USA," 1950s, TKK Co., 12-1/2" long, a minor toy	60	90	120
"Jeep No. 10560," 1950s, Cragstan, 5-1/2" long, a minor action toy	70	105	140
"John's Farm Truck," 1950s, T-N Co., 9" long, seven actions	140	210	280
"K-55 Electric Tractor," c.1950s, M-T Co., 3 actions, 7" long	70	105	140
"King Size Fire Engine" 1960s, Bandai Co., three actions, 12-1/2" long	150	225	300
"Kissing Couple," 1950s, Ichida Co., 10-3/4" long, five actions	150	225	300
"Ladder Fire Engine," 1950s, Linemar Co., five actions, 13" long	170	255	340
"Love-Beetle-Volks," 1960s, K.O. Co., 10" long, three actions	60	90	120
"M-101 Aston Martin Secret Ejector Car," 1960s, Daiya Co., 11" long, six actions, (includes ejectable passenger)	200	300	400
"Magic Action Bulldozer," 1950s, T-N Co., 9-1/2" long, three actions	100	150	200
"Marvelous Car," T-Bird, 1956, T-N Co., three actions, 11" long	250	375	500
"Marvelous Fire Engine," 1960s, "Y" Co., 11" long, four actions	100	150	200

	C6	C8	C10
Melody Camping Car, 1970s, "Y" Co., 10" long, three actions	100	150	200
Merry-Go-Round Truck, 1950s, M.T. Co., 11" long, four actions	400	600	800
"Mickey Mouse and Donald Duck Fire Engine," 1960s, M-T Co., 16" long, three actions	200	300	400
"Mickey Mouse Sand Buggy," 1960s M-T Co., 11" long, four actions	150	225	300
"Military Air Defense Truck," 1950s, Linemar Co., four actions, 15-1/4" long	100	150	200
"Military Command Car," 1950s T-N Co., five actions, 11" long	150	225	300
"Million Bus," 1950s, KKK Co., three actions, 12" long, RARE	1250	1875	2500

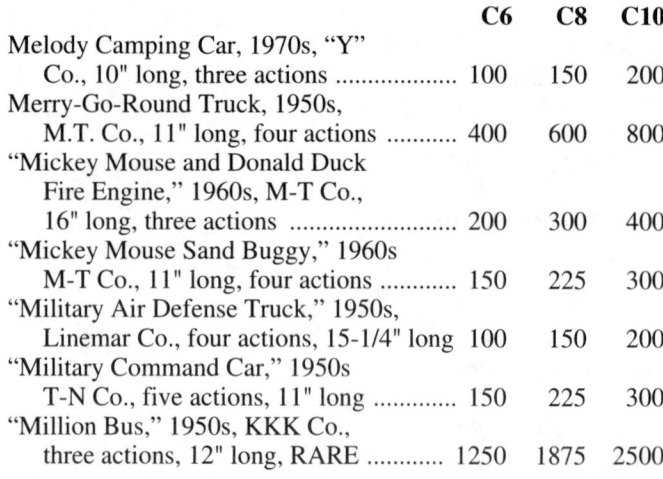

Marvelous Fire Engine. Photo by Don Hultzman.

M-101 Aston-Martin Secret Ejector Car.

Military Command Car. Photo by Don Hultzman.

Mobile Satellite Tracking System. Photo by Don Hultzman.

	C6	C8	C10
"Mobile Satellite Tracking Station," 1960s, Y Co., six actions, 9" long, (includes detachable antenna) RARE	400	600	800
"Monkee-Mobile," 1967, ASC Co., (Aoshin Co.) Minor Toy, 12" long	250	375	500
"Motorcycle Cop," 1950s, Daiya Co. 10-1/2" long, 8-1/4" high, five actions	200	300	400
"Musical Cadillac Car," 1950s, Irco Co., 9" long, Minor Toy	300	450	600
"Musical Comic Jumping Jeep," 1970s, M-T Co., 12" long, six actions	90	135	180
"Musical Ice Cream Truck," 1960s Bandai Co., 10-1/2" long, five actions	100	150	200
"Mystery Fire Chief Car No. 81," 1950s, Sanshin Co., 9-1/4" long, three actions	120	180	240
"Mystery Police Car," 1960s, T-N Co., 9-3/4" long, 6" wide, 4" high, three actions	100	150	200
"Newbuggy Crazy Car, 1970s, M-T Co., 10" long, Minor Toy	50	75	100
"News Service Car," 1960s, TPS Co., 10" long, four actions	150	225	300
"Nutty Mads Car" (Drincar), 1960s, Marx Co., 9-1/4" long, three actions	200	300	400
"007 Aston Martin," 1966, Gilbert Co., 11-1/2" long, eight actions, (includes ejectable passenger)	250	375	500
"007 Secret Agent's Car," (Impala), 1960s, Spesco Co., (Joy Toy), 15" long, five actions	200	300	400
"Ol' MacDonald's Farm Truck," 1960s, Frankonia, four actions (includes plastic pig, cow and chicken)	110	165	220
"Old Fashioned Fire Engine," 1950s, M-T Co., four actions, 12-1/2" high	110	165	220
"Old Fashioned Car," 1950s, S-H Co., 10" long, four actions	50	75	100
"Old Ford Touring Car," 1950s, Z Co., 10" long, four actions	50	75	100

Monkee-Mobile. Photo by Don Hultzman.

Mystery Police Car. Photo by Don Hultzman.

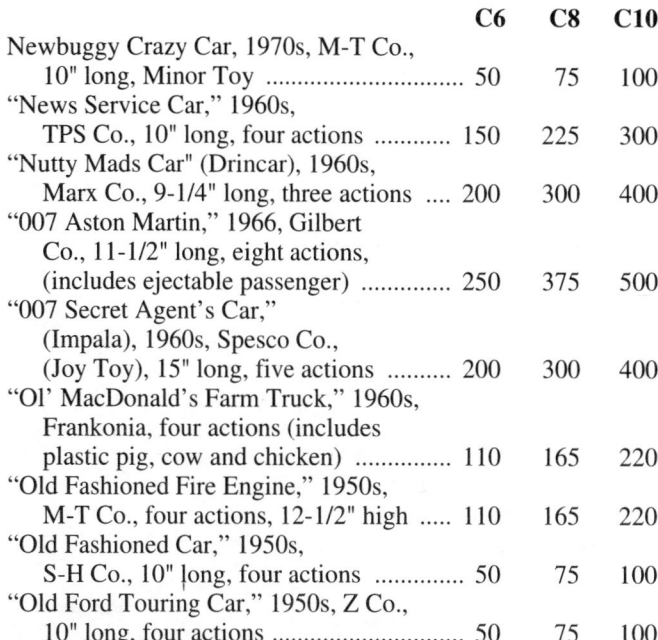

Musical Ice Cream Truck. Photo by Don Hultzman.

"Ol' MacDonald's Farm Truck." Courtesy Mapes Auctioneers & Appraisers.

	C6	C8	C10
"Old Time Automobile," 1950s, "Y" Co., 8-3/4" long, three actions (includes detachable tin litho driver and steering wheel)	100	150	200
"Old Timer," Car, 1950s, Cragstan Co., 9" long, three actions	100	150	200
"Oldtimer Automoball," 1950s, M-T Co., 10" long, three actions, includes celluloid ball	90	135	180
"Oldtimer Sunday Driver," 1960s, Daiya Co., 9" long, four actions	70	105	140
"Passenger Bus," 1950s "Y" Co., 16" long, four actions	300	450	600
"Patrol Auto-Tricycle," 1960s, T-N Co., 19" long, 7-1/2" high, four actions	160	240	320
"P.D. No. 5--Police Patrol Car," (Buick), 1960s, Askakusa Toy Co., 11-1/2" long, three actions	90	135	180

	C6	C8	C10
"Pickup Truck," T-N Co., 10" long, four actions	90	135	180
"Piston Action Bulldozer," 1960s, Linemar Co., 7-1/2" long, two cycles	100	150	200
"Police Auto Cycle," 1960s, (motorcycle and plastic driver), Bandai Co., five actions, Remote Control	150	225	300
"Police Motorcycle," 1950s, M-T Co., 11-3/4" long, seven actions	160	240	320
"Police No. 5," Police Car, 1950s, T-N Co., four actions, 9-1/2" long	100	150	200
"Police Patrol Jeep," 1960s, T-N Co., four actions, lights, bump & go, noise, smoke, 9-1/4" long	100	150	200
"Pom Pom Tank," 1950s, S&E Co., 12" long, five actions	100	150	200
"Popcorn Vendor Truck," 1960s, T-N Co., 9" long, three actions	130	195	260
"Porsche With Visible Engine," 1964, Bandai Co., 10" long, three actions	90	135	180
"Power Shovel," 1950s, Alps Co., 15" long, extended, six actions	150	225	300
"RCA-NBC Mobile Color TV Truck," 1950s, Yonezawa Co., 9" long, four actions	350	525	700

Old Fashioned Fire Engine. Photo by Don Hultzman.

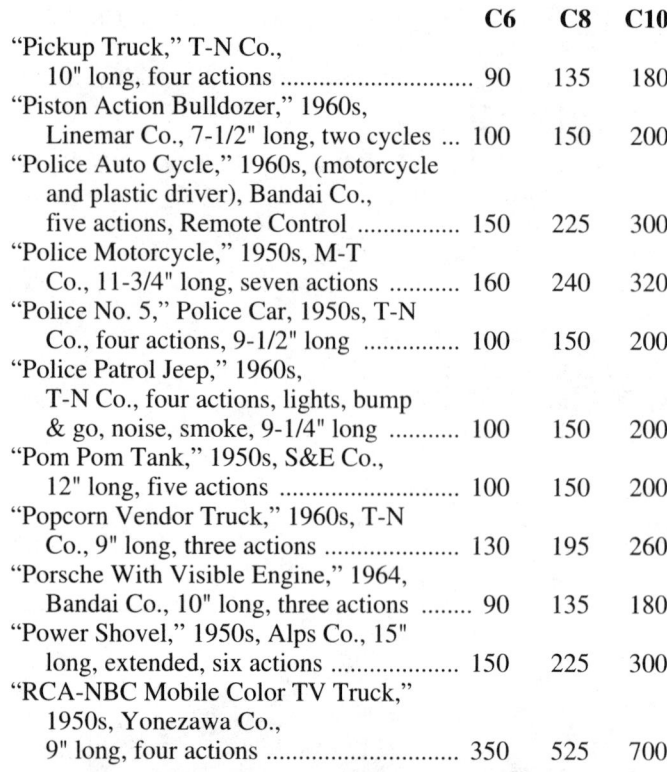

"Old Timer" car, Cragstan. Courtesy Mapes Auctioneers & Appraisers.

Police Auto Cycle. Photo by Don Hultzman.

Police Motorcycle. Photo by Don Hultzman.

Japanese Battery-Operated Toys

	C6	C8	C10
"Racecar #25," 1950s, Alps Co., three actions, 9" long, RARE	800	1200	1600
"Radar Jeep," 1950s, T-N Co., 11" long, four actions	100	150	200
"Reversible Diesel Electric Tractor," 1950s, Marx Co., Minor Toy	90	135	180
"Road Construction Roller," 1950s, Daiya Co., 8-1/2" long, four actions	90	135	180
"Road Grader," 1960s, T-N Co., 12" long, three actions	80	120	160
"Road Roller," 1950s, M-T Co., 9" long, four actions	110	165	220
"Robotank TR-2," 1960s, T-N Co., four actions, 5" high	200	300	400
"Romance Car M-841," 1950s, "M" Co., 8" long, three actions	110	165	220
Santa Claus on Hand Car	100	150	200
"Santa Claus on Scooter," 1960s, M-T Co., 10" high, four actions	100	150	200
"School Bus," 1950s, Cragstan, 20-1/2" long, a Minor Toy	60	90	120
Searchlight Jeep, 1950s, T-N Co., 16" long overall, (7-1/2" Jeep & 8-1/2" artillery) four actions	100	150	200
"Secret Service Action Car," (Green Hornet motif), 1960s, ASC Co., 11" long, four actions, RARE	300	450	600

	C6	C8	C10
"Shaking Classic Car," 1960s, T-N Co., 7" long, four actions	60	90	120
"Shaking Old-Timer Car No. 2511-1," 1960s, T-N Co., 9" long, four actions, includes plastic driver	60	90	120
"Sheriff Car," 1950s, T-N Co. four actions, 10" long	90	135	180
"Sight Seeing Bus," 1960s, Bandai Co., 14-1/2" long, four actions	150	225	300
"Sight Seeing Bus," 1950s, Yonezawza Co., Minor Toy, 9" long	150	225	300
"Siren Fire Car," 1950s, M-T Co., 9" long, four actions	130	195	260
"Siren Patrol Car," 1960s, M-T Co., four actions, 12-1/2" long	80	120	160
"Siren Patrol Motorcycle," 1960s, M-T Co., three actions, 12" long	200	300	400
"Smoky Bill on Old Fashioned Car," 1960s, T-N Co., 9" long, four actions	110	165	220
"Smokey the Bear Jeep," 1950s, M-T Co., 10" long, four actions	300	450	600

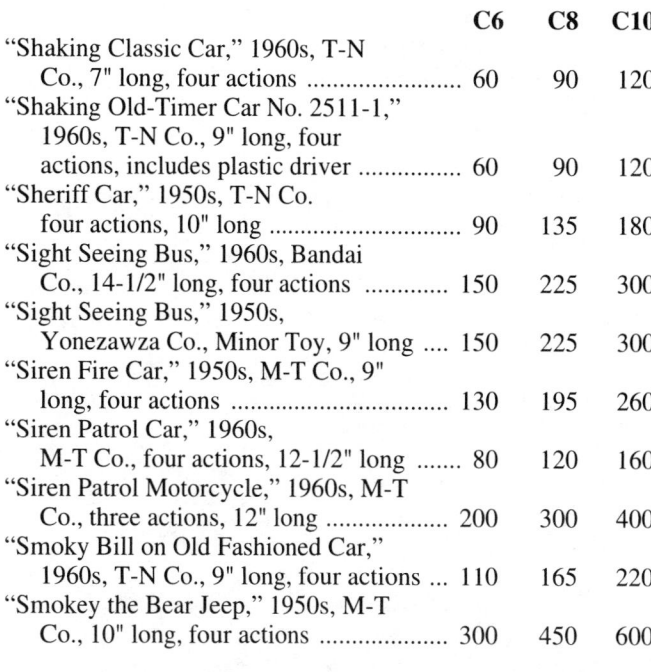

Power Shovel. Courtesy Don Hultzman.

Police No. 5. Photo by Don Hultzman.

Steam Roller (Road Roller). Photo by Don Hultzman.

Santa Claus on Scooter. Courtesy Don Hultzman.

	C6	C8	C10
"Smoking Bulldozer," 1960s, WKC Co., 9" long, four actions	100	150	200
"Smoking Volkswagen," 1960s, Aoshin Co., 10-1/2" long, four actions	60	90	120
"Smoky Joe-Fancy Mobile," 1960s, T-N Co., four actions, smokes, lights, bump & go, noise, 9" long	90	135	180
"Sports Car Race Set," 1960s, TPS Co., Minor Toy, 8"x14" base, includes four plastic racecars	100	150	200
"Steam Roller (Road Roller)," 1950s, T-N Co., (Rosko), 12" long with trailer, four actions	150	225	300

	C6	C8	C10
"Steam Roller," 1950s, "Y" Co., 8" long, four actions (includes tin trailer)	110	165	220
"Steerable Tank," 1950s, Linemar Co., 9" long, five actions	60	90	120
"Strange Explorer," 1960s, DSK Co., 7-1/2" long, four actions	70	105	140
"Sunbeam Jeep No. 1," 1940s, 10" long, unmarked, three actions	100	150	200
Sunbeam Side Car (Motorcycle) 1950s, Marusan Co., 9-1/2" long, three actions	800	1200	1600
"Sunday Driver," 1950s, M-T Co., 10" long, four actions (includes detachable driver)	70	105	140
"Superman Truck," 1950s, Linemar Co., 10-1/4" long, three actions, RARE	800	1200	1600
"Surrey Jeep," 1960s, T-N Co., 11" long, three actions	90	135	180
"Talking Police Car-Mystery Action," 1960s, Y Co., 14" long, three actions	70	105	140
"Tank M-4 Combat Tank," 1960s, Taiyo Co., 11-1/2" long, 13" with gun barrel extended, five actions	80	120	160
"Tank M-35," 1950s, HTC Co. 8" long, three actions	110	165	220

"Strange Explorer" with box. Courtesy James S. Maxwell/ Virginia Caputo. Photo by Virginia Caputo.

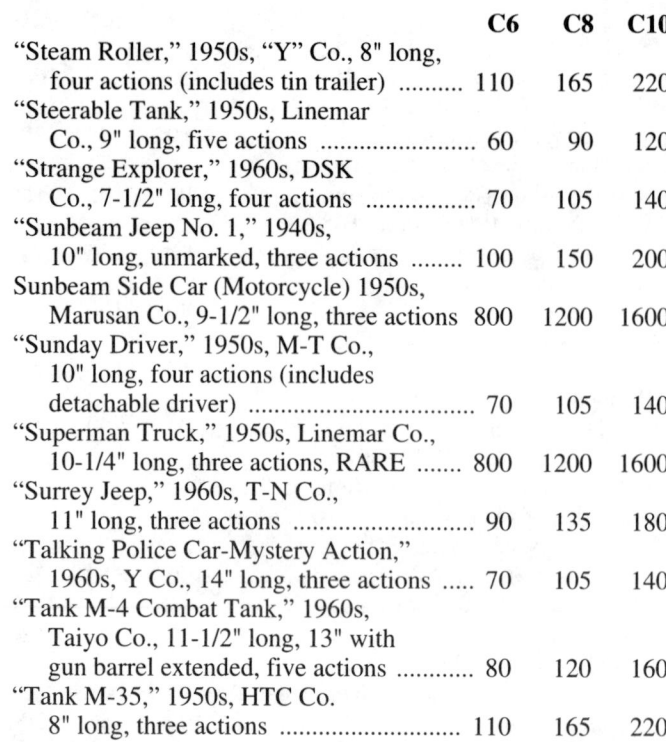

Sunbeam Jeep No. 1. Photo by Don Hultzman.

Sunday Driver. Photo by Don Hultzman.

L to R: "Tank M-4 Combat Tank," "Tank X-3," "Tank M-103." Courtesy Don Hultzman. Photo by Ron Chojnacki.

	C6	C8	C10
"Tank M-41," 1970s, J Co., 8-1/4" long, four actions	110	165	220
"Tank M-48-T," 1960s, T-N Co., 8-1/4" long, four actions	100	150	200
"Tank M-56," 1940s, M-T Co., 7-1/2" long, wheel drive	100	150	200
"Tank M-71," 1950s, M-T Co., 5-3/4" long, five actions	100	150	200
"Tank M-81," 1960s, M-T Co. 8-1/2" long, seven actions	100	150	200
"Tank M-103," 1950s, M-T Co., 7" long, three actions	90	135	180
"Tank M-107-US Army," 1950s, Y Co., 6" long, four actions, includes four missiles	110	165	220
"Tank M-X," 1950s, T-N Co., 8-1/2" long, five actions	70	105	140
"Tank T-5," 1950s, T-N Co., 8-1/2" long, three actions, includes detachable radar antenna	120	180	240
"Tank X-3, (Explorer Defense), 1950s, Cragstan Co. 7-3/4" long, five actions, includes six cartridge shells	130	195	260
"Tank X-75," 1950s, M-T Co., 9" long, three actions, includes tin gun and darts	110	165	220
Tank-Daisymatic #64	100	150	200
Tank-Daisymatic #80	100	150	200
"Tank Robot," 1960s, S-H Co., five actions, 10" tall	250	375	500
"Taxi," (yellow cab), 1950s, Linemar Co., 7-1/2" long, five actions	70	105	140
"Taxi Cab," 1950s, "Y" Co., 8-1/2" long, five actions	70	105	140
"Taxi Cab," 1960s, "Y" Co., four actions, 9" long	80	120	160
"Teddy-Go-Kart," 1960s, Alps Co., 10-1/2" long, four actions	90	135	180
The Swinger (Mustang Mach I), c.1960s, T.P.S. Co.--10-1/2" long, three actions	50	75	100
"Tiny Jeep," 1950s, WACO Co., 4-1/4" long, minor action	30	45	60

	C6	C8	C10
"Tiny Tank," 1950s WACO Co., 4-1/4" long, minor action	30	45	60
"Tom and Jerry Highway Patrol," 1960s, M-T Co., 8" long, three actions	120	180	240
"Tom and Jerry Jumping Jeep," 1960s, M-T Co., 9" long, three actions	150	225	300
"Tractor," 1950s, Showa Co. 7-1/2" long, four actions, includes litho tin figure (driver)	110	165	220
"Tractor," 1960s, Y Co., 6" long, three actions	100	150	200
"Tractor On Platform," 1950s, T-N Co., tractor 9" long, trailer 7" long, minor toy	100	150	200
"Turn-O-Matic Gun Jeep," 1960s, T-N Co., 10" long, five actions	100	150	200
"Twin Racing Cars," 1950s, Alps Co., three actions, 7" long--10" long with coupling rod)	200	300	400
"Visible Ford Mustang," 1960s, Bandai Co., 10" long, four actions	90	135	180
"Volkswagen Convertible," 1950s, T-N Co., three actions, 9-3/4" long	250	375	500

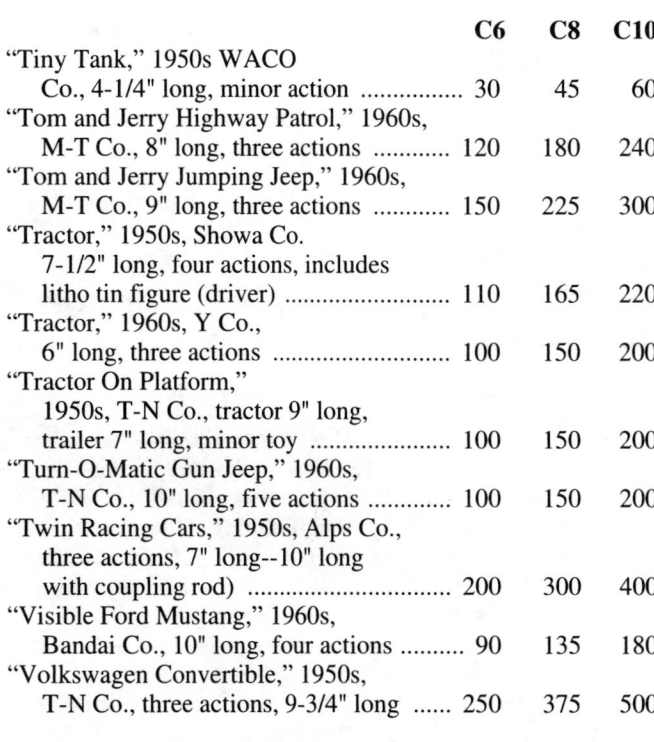

Tank (M-81), Tank (M-35), Tank (M-56), Tank (M-107).

Turn-O-Matic Gun Jeep. Photo by Don Hultzman.

Twin Racing Cars. Photo by Don Hultzman.

	C6	C8	C10
"Volkswagen-Eletrik," 1950s, Mignon Co., 8-1/2" long, three actions	100	150	200
"Volkswagen No. 7653," 1960s, Bandai Co., 10" long, three actions	80	120	160

	C6	C8	C10
"Volkswagen With Visible Engine," 1960s, K.O. Co., 7" long, three actions	110	165	220
"Volkswagen With Visible Engine No. 4049," 1960s, Bandai Co., 8" long, three actions	110	165	220

JAPENESE (ETC.) TIN CARS

by Ron Smith

Tin toy cars have been manufactured since the first horseless carriages roamed the streets of the United States and Europe. They ranged in size and price from the tiny 1-inch penny toy to the 28-inch Eldorado, which sold for $10. Although there are German, Spanish, and French toy cars listed here, our concentration will be the 1950s Golden Era of Japanese tin toy cars.

These examples enjoy much popularity today, and prices have been raised by the limitlessness of some people's insanity. Keep one thing foremost in your mind when trying to sell a toy at the mint price; the person who paid that price already has one.

(All photos by Ron Smith except where noted.)

Ron Smith has always loved toy cars and planes. He can still show you his first Dinky Toy his aunt bought for him in 1940 in Fred Harvey's Toy Store inside Cleveland's Terminal Tower Building. Born and raised in Shaker Heights, Ohio, Smith served in the U.S. Navy, attended John Carroll University, and, for the last 14 years, has been employed by Arrow Distributing of Solon, Ohio. He has collected die-cast cars, trucks and planes, cast-iron toys, and plastic promotional cars. For the last 10 years, he has specialized in tin-plate cars and planes. Ron lives in Solon with his wife Joan and their two cats, Trouble and Bogart.

Ron Smith.

No.	Year	Model	Manufacturer	Power	Size	C6	C8	C10
J1	1960s	Aston-Martin DB5 (James Bond)	Gilbert	Friction	11-1/2"	75	100	300
J2	1960s	Aston-Martin DB6	Asahi Toy Co.	Friction	11"	100	200	400
J2A	1959	Austin Healey 100 Six Coupe	Bandai	Friction	8"	60	80	200
J2B	1959	Austin Healey 100 Six Convertible	Bandai	Friction	8"	60	80	200
J2C	1960s	BMW1500	Ichiko	Friction	8"	90	150	275
J3	1953	Buick	Marusan	Friction	7"	75	125	250
J4	1954	Buick Station Wagon	Unknown	Battery	8"	75	150	200
J5	1955	Buick Roadmaster	Yoshiya	Friction	11"	200	300	400
J6	1958	Buick Century	Yonezawa	Friction	12"	400	600	1300
J7	1958	Buick Century	Bandai	Friction	8"	60	80	100

J1

J2

J2C

J5

J6

J7

J8

J13

J16. Photo by Tim Oei.

J17B

No.	Year	Model	Manufacturer	Power	Size	C6	C8	C10
J8	1959	Buick	T.N.	Friction	11"	80	125	250
J9	1959	Buick	Ichiko	B/O-Friction	12"	100	250	300
J10	1960	Buick	Ichiko	Friction	17-1/2"	150	250	600
J11	1961	Buick	T.N.	Friction	11"	50	100	200
J12	1961	Buick Emergency Car	T.N.	Friction	14"	50	95	125
J13	1963	Buick Wildcat	Ichiko	Friction	15"	125	250	400
J14	1966	Buick Le Sabre	Ashai Toy Co.	Friction	19"	100	200	400
J15	1968	Buick Sportswagon	Asakusa	Friction	15"	100	150	200
J16	1950	BMW 600 Isetta	Bandai	Friction	9"	150	200	250
J17	1950	BMW Isetta (three wheels)	Bandai	Friction	6-1/2"	75	125	200
J17B	1960s	Coke Truck	Japan	Battery	12"	125	225	400
J18	1950	Cadillac	Marusan	Friction	11"	400	600	1100
J19	1950	Cadillac	Marusan	Battery	11"	500	800	1500
J20	1952	Cadillac	Alps	Friction	11-1/2"	300	500	1000
J21	1952	Cadillac	T.N.	Battery	13"	75	150	350
J22	1954	Cadillac	Gama	Friction	12"	200	300	500
J23	1954	Cadillac	Joustra	Battery	12"	200	300	500
J24	1959	Cadillac Sedan	Bandai	Friction	12"	75	100	175

J18

J20

J21

J23

J24

J24

J25

J25

J29

J31

J31

J34

J37

J38

No.	Year	Model	Manufacturer	Power	Size	C6	C8	C10
J25	1959	Cadillac Convertible	Bandai	Friction	12"	75	100	175
J26	1960s	Cadillac	Bandai	Friction	17"	125	175	375
J27	1960	Cadillac	Yonezawa	Friction	18"	150	200	350
J28	1961	Cadillac 60	Unknown	Friction	9"	95	125	150
J29	1961	Cadillac Fleetwood	SSS	Friction	17-1/2"	150	300	600
J30	1962	Cadillac	Yonezawa	Friction	22"	100	250	400
J31	1963	Cadillac	Bandai	Friction	17"	125	200	350
J32	1965	Cadillac	Ashahi Toy Co.	Friction	17"	100	200	300
J33	1965	Cadillac	Ichiko	Friction	22"	300	400	600
J34	1967	Cadillac	K.O.	Friction	10-1/2"	100	150	300
J35	1967	Cadillac	Unknown	Friction	10-3/4"	75	100	125
J36	1967	Cadillac El Dorado	Ichiko	Friction	28"	200	300	600
J37	1953	Chevrolet Corvette	Bandai	Friction	7"	75	100	150
J38	1958	Chevrolet Corvette	Yonezawa	Friction	9-1/2"	200	300	500
J39	1962	Chevrolet Corvette	Bandai	Friction	8"	30	50	75
J40	1965	Chevrolet Corvette	Bandai	Friction	8"	40	60	80
J41	1964	Chevrolet Corvette	Ichida	Battery	12"	150	225	350
J42	1968	Chevrolet Corvette	Taiyo	Battery	9-1/2"	35	50	75
J43	1960s	Chevrolet Corvair	Bandai	Friction	8"	30	50	75
J44	1963	Chevrolet Corvair	Ichiko	Friction	9"	50	65	95
J45	1967	Chevrolet Camaro	Taiyo	Friction	9-1/2"	10	20	30
J46	1967	Chevrolet Camaro	T.N.	Friction	14"	150	250	400
J47	1967	Chevrolet Camaro	Modern Toys	Friction	11"	25	50	75
J48	1971	Chevrolet Camaro Rusher	Taiyo	Battery	9-1/2"	10	20	35
J49	1954	Chevrolet	Marusan	Friction	11"	500	800	1000
J50	1955	Chevrolet	Marusan	Battery	10-3/4"	500	900	1500
J51	1956	Chevrolet Station Wagon	Bandai	Friction	9-1/2"	75	125	175
J52	1956	Chevrolet Pick Up	Bandai	Friction	9-1/2"	75	125	175
J53	1956	Chevrolet Convertible	Bandai	Friction	9-1/2"	100	150	225
J54	1958	Chevrolet Red Cross Ambulance	Bandai	Friction	8"	20	30	50
J55	1958	Chevrolet Pick Up Truck	Bandai	Friction	8"	50	65	90
J56	1958	Chevrolet Convertible	Bandai	Friction	8"	60	90	125

J42

J41

J48

J46

J49

J50

J57

J59

J60

J60A

J62

J63

No.	Year	Model	Manufacturer	Power	Size	C6	C8	C10
J57	1958	Chevrolet Station Wagon	Bandai	Friction	8"	50	60	85
J58	1958	Chevrolet Sedan	Bandai	Friction	8"	75	100	125
J59	1959	Chevrolet Sedan/Convertible/Wagon	SY	Friction	11-1/2"	200	300	500
J60	1960	Chevrolet	Marusan	Friction	11-1/2"	200	300	500
J60A	1960	Chevrolet H.T.	Japan	Friction	9"	100	150	200
J61	Unused							
J62	1961	Chevrolet Impala Sedan	Bandai	Friction	11"	100	150	300
J63	1961	Chevrolet Impala Convertible	Bandai	Friction	11"	100	150	300
J64	1962	Chevrolet Secret Agent	Unknown	Battery	14"	75	110	150
J65	1962	Chevrolet	Unknown	Friction	11"	125	250	350
J66	1963	Chevrolet Impala	Unknown	Friction	18"	150	225	400
J67	1960	Citroen DS 19 Convertible	Bandai	Friction	12"	100	150	300
J68	1960	Citroen DS 19 Sedan	Bandai	Friction	12"	100	150	300
J69	1960	Citroen ID 19 Station Wagon	Bandai	Friction	12"	100	150	300
J70	1950	Chrysler	Guntherman	Friction	11"	100	200	500
J71	1955	Chrysler	Yonezawa	Friction	8"	100	200	300
J72	1957	Chrysler New Yorker	Alps	Friction	14"	500	700	1000+
J73	1958	Chrysler	Unknown	Battery	13"	200	300	600

J64

J65

J66

J71

J72

J73

J74

J77

J81A

J82

J84

J85A

J86

J86

No.	Year	Model	Manufacturer	Power	Size	C6	C8	C10
J74	1959	Chrysler Imperial Convertible	Bandai	Friction	8"	75	90	125
J75	1959	Chrysler Imperial Sedan	Bandai	Friction	8"	75	90	125
J76	1960	Chrysler Valiant	Bandai	Friction	8"	20	40	50
J77	1962	Chrysler Imperial	Asahi Toy Co.	Friction	16"	500	700	1000+
J78	1960	DKW 1000 Convertible	Bandai	Friction	8"	90	125	200
J79	1960s	Datsun Bluebird 1200	Bandai	Friction	8"	60	75	125
J80	1950s	Divco Dugans Bakery Truck	Unknown, Japan	Friction	7-1/2"	300	400	600
J81	1930s	DeSoto	Masudaya	Friction	8"	300	400	800
J81A	1950s	DeSoto H.T.	Japan	Friction	7"	50	75	150
J82	1958	Dodge Sedan	T.N.	Friction	11"	300	400	600
J83	1959	Dodge Truck	Unknown	Friction	24"	350	500	900
J84	1959	Dodge Pick Up	Unknown	Friction	18-1/2"	350	500	900
J85	1968	Dodge Yellow Cab	T.N.	Friction	12"	90	125	200
J85A	1969	Dodge H.T.	Buddy L	X	13"	50	70	90
J86	1958	Edsel Convertible/Sedan	Haji	Friction	10-1/2"	300	400	800
J87	1958	Edsel Wagon	Haji	Friction	10-1/2"	200	300	400
J88	1958	Edsel Ambulance	Haji	Friction	11"	200	250	300
J89	1958	Edsel Station Wagon	T.N.	Friction	11"	150	200	300
J90	1958	Edsel H.T.	Asahi	Friction	10-3/4"	300	400	600
J91	1958	Edsel H.T.	Toy Nomura	Friction	8-1/2"	100	150	250
J92	1958	Edsel	Yonezawa	Friction	10-1/2"	300	400	600
J92A	1960s	Ferrari Berlinetta	Bandai	Friction	9-1/2"	75	125	200
J92B	1946	Ford	Italy	Wind Up	10"	100	200	400
J93	1949	Ford Sedan	Guntherman	Wind Up	11"	150	300	400
J94	1951	Ford Sedan	Guntherman	Wind Up	11"	150	300	400
J95	1950	Ford Good Humor Ice Cream Truck	KTS, Japan	Friction	10-3/4"	150	250	350
J95A	1954	Ford H.T.	Marusan	Friction	11"	125	175	350
J96	1955	Ford Pick Up	Bandai	Friction	12"	150	250	300
J97	1955	Ford Station Wagon	Bandai	Friction	12"	150	250	300
J98	1955	Ford Ambulance	Bandai	Friction	12"	150	250	300
J99	1955	Ford Panel Truck "Flowers"	Bandai	Friction	12"	200	400	600

J87

J89

J91

J92A

J92B

J93

J95A

J96

J97

J98

J99

J100

No.	Year	Model	Manufacturer	Power	Size	C6	C8	C10
J100	1955	Ford Convertible	Bandai	Friction	12"	300	500	700
J101	1956	Ford H.T.	Yonezawa	Friction	12"	300	500	800
J102	1956	Ford Convertible	Haji	Friction	11-1/2"	400	600	1000+
J103	1956	Ford Sedan	Marusan	Friction	13"	500	800	1000+
J104	1956	Ford Wagon	Nomura	Friction	10-1/2"	75	100	200
J105	Ford	Fairlane Sedan	Ichiko	Friction	10"	100	200	300
J106	1957	Ford H.T.	T.N.	Friction	12"	100	200	300
J107	1957	Ford Sedan/Con./Wagon/Pick Up	Joustra	Friction	12"	200	250	300
J108	1957	Ford Sedan/Conv./Wagon/Pick Up	Bandai	Friction	12"	200	250	300
J109	1957	Ford Station Wagon	Nomura	Friction	7-1/2"	60	80	100
J110	1958	Ford Retractable Top	K. Japan	Friction	10"	70	90	150
J111	1958	Ford Retractable Top	T.N.	Battery	11"	100	125	175
J112	1958	Ford Country Squire Station Wagon	Bandai	Friction	8"	40	60	80
J113	1958	Ford Fairlane H.T./Conv.	Bandai	Friction	8"	40	60	80
J114	1958	Ford Fairlane H.T./Conv.	Sankei Gangu	Friction	9"	90	115	125
J114A	1958	Ford H.T.	Japan	Battery	12"	150	250	475
J115	1959	Ford Fairlane Skyliner	Sankei Gangu	Friction	9"	90	115	125
J116	1959	Ford Station Wagon	T.N.	Friction	12"	100	150	200
J117	1959	Ford Retractable	T.N.	Friction	11"	100	150	200

J102

J103

J104

J105

J106

J107

J114A

J116

J117

J119

J120

J121

J122

J125

No.	Year	Model	Manufacturer	Power	Size	C6	C8	C10
J118	1960s	Ford Falcon	Bandai	Friction	8"	20	30	50
J119	1960	Ford	Haji	Friction	11"	100	200	300
J120	1961	Ford Country Sedan	Bandai	Friction	10-1/2"	125	150	250
J121	1962	Ford Country Sedan	Asahi	Friction	12"	200	300	600
J122	1964	Ford H.T.	Ichiko	Friction	13"	200	400	600
J123	1964	Ford H.T.	Rico	Friction	17"	300	500	800
J124	1964	Ford Convertible	Rico	Friction	17"	300	500	800
J125	1965	Ford Galaxie H.T.	MT	Friction	11"	125	150	250
J126	1968	Ford Torino	S.T.	Friction	16"	200	250	400
J127	1956	Ford Thunderbird	T.N.	Friction	11"	200	300	400
J128	1956	Ford Thunderbird H.T. Clear Top	T.N.	Friction	11"	200	300	400
J129	1956	Ford Thunderbird	T.N.	Battery	11"	200	300	400
J130	1959	Ford Thunderbird	Bandai	Friction	8"	50	60	80
J131	1959	Ford Thunderbird Convertible	Bandai	Friction	8"	50	60	80
J132	1961	Ford Thunderbird Retractable	Yonezawa	Battery	11"	90	120	175
J133	1962	Ford Thunderbird Retractable	Yonezawa	Battery	11"	90	120	175
J134	1963	Ford Thunderbird Retractable	Yonezawa	Battery	11"	90	120	175
J135	1964	Ford Thunderbird Convertible	Asahi	Friction	12-1/2"	150	200	400
J136	1964	Ford Thunderbird H.T.	Asahi	Friction	12"	150	200	400

J126

J127

J129

J134

J134

J136

J137

J138

J139

J140

J143

J147B

J155

J161B

No.	Year	Model	Manufacturer	Power	Size	C6	C8	C10
J137	1964	Ford Thunderbird	Ichiko	Friction	16"	100	200	400
J138	1965	Ford Thunderbird H.T.	Bandai	Friction	10-3/4"	60	85	125
J139	1965	Ford Mustang F.B.	Bandai	Friction	11"	45	65	90
J140	1965	Ford Mustang H.T./Conv.	Bandai	Fric/Bat.	11"	75	125	150
J141	1965	Ford Mustang (FBI)	Bandai	Friction	11"	75	100	125
J142	1965	Ford Mustang Convertible	Yonezawa	Battery	13-1/2"	90	125	200
J143	1966	Ford Mustang F.B.	T.N.	Friction	17"	100	175	250
J144	1967	Ford Mustang	Bandai	Battery	13"	45	65	100
J145	1960s	Ford Taurus 17M Convertible	Bandai	Friction	8"	30	40	60
J146	1960s	Ford GT	Bandai	Battery	10"	65	85	125
J147	1957	Ferrari 250 G. Convertible	A.T.C.	Friction	9-1/2"	200	300	500
J147B	1960s	#3 Ferrari	Bandai	Friction	8"	85	150	190
J148	1958	Ferrari	Bandai	Battery	11"	90	150	300
J149	1960	Ferrari Super America Coupe	Bandai	Friction	12"	100	200	300
J150	1960s	Ferrari Super America Convertible	Bandai	Friction	12"	100	200	300
J151	1960s	Fiat 600 Sedan	Bandai	Friction	8"	50	65	95
J152	1950s	International Cement Mixer	SSS	Friction	19"	275	300	600
J153	1950s	International Grain Hauler	SSS	Friction	23"	275	300	600
J154	1960	Jaguar XK150 H.T. Conv.	Bandai	Friction	9-1/2"	75	125	200
J155	1960s	Jaguar XKE Convertible	T.T.	Friction	10-1/2"	95	125	175
J156	1960s	Jaguar XKE Coupe	Lendolet Auto	Friction	10-1/2"	50	75	100
J157	1960s	Jaguar XK140	Bandai	Friction	9-1/2"	40	60	90
J158	1960s	Jaguar XKE	Bandai	Battery	10"	90	125	200
J159	1960s	Jaguar 3.4 Sedan	Bandai	Friction	8"	50	60	100
J160	1960s	Jaguar 3.4 Convertible	Bandai	Friction	8"	50	60	100
J161	1965	Jaguar XKE120	Alps	Friction	6-1/2"	90	150	350
J161B	1950s	Lancia	Bandai	Friction	8"	50	90	150
J162	1954	Lincoln	Unknown	Friction	12"	175	275	400
J163	1955	Lincoln Sedan	Yonezawa	Friction	12"	250	325	600
J164	1956	Lincoln Continental Mark II	Linemar	Friction	12"	400	600	1000+
J165	1956	Lincoln	Ichiko	Friction	16-1/2"	150	250	375

J163

J164

J165

J166

J167

J168

J169

J170A. *Photo by Strine.*

J176

J177

J193

J195

No.	Year	Model	Manufacturer	Power	Size	C6	C8	C10
J166	1959	Lincoln Continental Mark III Conv.	Bandai	Friction	12"	90	150	200
J167	1959	Lincoln Continental Mark III Sedan	Bandai	Friction	12"	90	150	200
J168	1960	Lincoln H.T./Convertible	Yonezawa	Friction	11"	100	150	300
J169	1964	Lincoln	Unknown	Friction	10-1/2"	90	175	275
J170	1950s	Lotus Elite	Bandai	Friction	8-1/2"	25	35	45
J170A	1960s	Lotus Ford Racer	Junior	Battery	16"	200	400	600
J171	1960s	Land Rover "88" Station Wagon	Bandai	Friction	8"	30	40	60
J172	1950s	Mercedes Limousine	Tipp & Co.	Friction	14"	500	800	1000+
J173	1950s	Mercedes Benz Racer	Line Mar	Friction	9-1/2"	95	150	185
J174	1950s	Mercedes Benz Racer W196	Marusan	Battery	10"	150	200	250
J175	1960s	Mercedes	Ichiko	Friction	12-1/2"	115	155	200
J176	1960s	Mercdes Benz 219 Sedan	Bandai	Friction	8"	50	80	100
J177	1960s	Mercedes Benz 219 Convertible	Bandai	Friction	8"	50	80	100
J178	1960s	Mercedes Benz 230 SL	Modern Toys	Battery	15"	175	210	250
J179	1960s	Mercedes Benz 230 SL	Alps	Battery	10"	65	75	95
J180	1960	Mercedes Benz 230 SL	Yanoman	Battery	14-1/2"	125	155	185
J181	1960s	Mercedes Benz 250 SE	Ichiko	Battery	13"	110	140	185
J182	1960	Mercedes Benz 250 S	Daiya	Friction	14"	110	155	175
J183	1950s	Mercedes Benz 300 SL	T.N.	Battery	11"	125	150	200
J184	1950s	Mercedes Benz 300 SL	KS	Battery	7"	45	65	85
J185	1950s	Mercedes Benz 300 SL	Dist. Cragstan	Battery	9"	65	95	125
J186	1950s	Mercedes Benz 300 SL	Bandai	Friction	8"	65	95	125
J187	1957	Mercedes Benz 300 SL	Marusan	Friction	8-1/2"	150	250	325
J188	1960s	Mercedes Benz 600	Unknown	Friction	10"	95	125	175
J189	1960s	Mercedes Benz Taxi	Bandai	Battery	10"	75	100	125
J190	1962	Mercedes Benz	SSS	Battery	12"	200	250	350
J191	1970	Mercedes Benz	Ichiko	Friction	24"	125	150	200
J192	1954	Mercury H.T.	Rock Valley Toys	Battery	9-1/2"	100	125	200
J193	1956	Mercury H.T.	Alps	Friction	9-1/2"	400	500	1000
J194	1958	Mercury Station Wagon	Bandai	Friction	8"	60	80	100
J195	1958	Mercury H.T.	Yonezawa	Friction	11-1/2"	250	325	600
J196	1967	Mercury Cougar H.T.	Taiyo	Battery	10"	25	45	65
J197	1967	Mercury Cougar H.T.	Asakusa Toys	Friction	15"	175	225	300
J198	1952	MG TF	Unknown	Friction	8-1/2"	50	75	95
J199	1954	MG TD	SSS	Friction	6-1/2"	35	65	85
J200	1955	MG TF	Bandai	Friction	8"	95	125	150
J200B	1955	MG	SSS	Friction	6"	50	70	100
J201	1957	MGA	A.T.C.	Friction	10"	175	250	400
J202	1960s	MG Magnette Mark III Sedan	Bandai	Friction	8"	95	125	150
J203	1960s	MG Magnette Mark III Convertible	Bandai	Friction	8"	95	125	150
J204	1960s	Messerschmitt 4 Wheels Convert.	Bandai	Friction	8"	200	250	350

J197

J200B

Japenese (etc.) Tin Cars

J205

J207A

J208

J209

J210

J213

J214

J215

No.	Year	Model	Manufacturer	Power	Size	C6	C8	C10
J205	1960s	Messerschmitt 4 Wheels Sedan	Bandai	Friction	8"	200	250	350
J206	1950s	Nash	MSK	Battery	8"	40	70	90
J207	1956	Nash Ambassador	Sankei Gangu	Friction	8"	100	125	150
J207A	1952	Oldsmobile	Y	Friction	11"	150	350	500
J208	1956	Oldsmobile Sedan	Ichiko/Kanto	Friction	10-1/2"	200	400	600
J209	1956	Oldsmobile Super 88 Sedan	Masudaya	Friction	16"	300	400	600
J210	1958	Oldsmobile Sedan	A.T.C.	Friction	12"	200	300	400
J211	1958	Oldsmobile Super 88 Sedan	A.T.C.	Friction	13"	250	325	425
J212	1958	Oldsmobile Sedan	Y	Friction	16"	300	400	700
J213	1959	Oldsmobile Sedan	Ichiko	Friction	12-1/2"	75	125	175
J214	1961	Oldsmobile Convertible/Wagon	Yonezawa	Friction	12"	75	125	180
J215	1966	Oldsmobile Toronado	Bandai	Battery	11"	65	110	150
J216	1968	Oldsmobile Toronado	Ichiko	Friction	17-1/2"	300	400	500
J217	1950s	Opel Sedan	Yonezawa	Fric/Bat	11-1/2"	70	90	125
J218	1954	Pontiac Star Chief	Asahi	Friction	11"	250	350	500
J218A	1954	Pontiac HT/Conv.	Minister-India	Friction	11"	Newer Issue		15

J216

J217

J218A

J218B

J218C

J218D

276   Japenese (etc.) Tin Cars

J219

J220

J222

J222

J223

J224

J225

J226

No.	Year	Model	Manufacturer	Power	Size	C6	C8	C10
J218B	1950s	Pontiac Conv.	KS	Friction	14"	150	300	450
J218C	1950s	Pontiac Coupe	KS	Friction	14"	150	300	450
J218D	1956	Pontiac H.T.	TN	Friction	8"	150	300	500
J219	1967	Pontiac Firebird	Akasura	Friction	15-1/2"	90	150	275
J220	1967	Pontiac Firebird	Bandai	Friction	10"	30	55	75
J221	1967	Pontiac Firebird (w/wipers)	Bandai	Battery	9-1/2"	40	55	75
J222	1953	Packard Convertible/Sedan	Alps	Friction	16"	500	800	1500
J223	1957	Packard Hawk Convertible	Schuco	Battery	10-3/4"	300	400	500
J224	1956	Plymouth H.T.	Unknown	Friction	8-1/2"	200	400	600
J225	1956	Plymouth H.T.	Alps	Battery	12"	300	400	600
J226	1957	Plymouth Fury H.T.	Y	Friction	11-1/2"	300	400	600
J227	1958	Plymouth Fury	Bandai	Friction	8"	75	90	150

J227

J228

J230

J231

J232

J233B

J233C

J233D

J234B

J235

J235B

J235C (Rare)

No.	Year	Model	Manufacturer	Power	Size	C6	C8	C10
J228	1959	Plymouth Hardtop	A.T.C.	Friction	10-1/2"	200	400	600
J229	1959	Plymouth Convertible	A.T.C.	Friction	10-1/2"	250	400	600
J230	1961	Plymouth Sedan	Ichiko	Friction	12"	125	250	400
J231	1961	Plymouth Station Wagon	Ichiko	Friction	12"	125	150	200
J232	1961	Plymouth T.V. Car	Ichiko	Battery	12"	125	175	300
J233	1964	Plymouth Fury H.T.	Kusama	Friction	10"	60	80	100
J233B	1960s	Porsche	T.T.	Friction	9-1/2"	75	125	200
J233C	1960s	Porsche	JNF (Ger.)	Wind Up	9"	200	400	600
J233D	1960s	Porsche	Geshia (Ger.)	W/W	9"	200	400	600
J234	1960	Porsche 911	Bandai	Battery	10"	65	95	125
J234B	1960s	Porsche 9115	T.T.	Friction	9-1/2"	75	125	200
J235	1950s	Porsche Speedster	Distler	Battery	10-1/2"	350	400	600
J235B	1960s	Rolls	HTC	Friction	6"	75	100	150
J235C	1960s	Rolls Royce Sedan	TN	Friction	10"	300	500	800
J236	1960	Rolls Royce "Silver Coupe" Conv.	Bandai	Friction	12"	100	150	200
J237	1960s	Rolls Royce "Silver Coupe" Sedan	Bandai	Friction	12"	100	150	200
J238	1960s	Rolls Royce (with Electric Lights)	Bandai	Battery	12"	100	200	300

J236

J237

J239

J240

J242

J243

J251. Photo by Tim Oei.

J252

J258

J260

J262A

J264

J265

J265A

No.	Year	Model	Manufacturer	Power	Size	C6	C8	C10
J239	1960	Rolls Royce	T.N.	Friction	10-1/2"	175	250	375
J240	1960s	Rambler Rebel Station Wagon	Bandai	Friction	12"	50	85	125
J241	1960	Renault	Bandai	Friction	7-1/2"	95	150	200
J242	1960s	Studebaker Avanti	Bandai	Friction	8"	125	175	300
J243	1954	Studebaker	Yoshiya	Friction	9"	150	200	300
J244	1960s	Saab 93 B	Bandai	Friction	7"	40	60	80
J245	1960s	Subaru 360	Bandai	Friction	7"	75	100	125
J246	1960s	Triumph TR-3 Convertible	Bandai	Friction	8"	50	75	150
J247	1960s	Triumph TR-3 Coupe	Bandai	Friction	8"	50	75	150
J248	1960s	Toyopet Crown	Bandai	Friciton	9"	40	50	75
J249	1960s	Toyota	Ichiko	Friction	16"	150	275	325
J250	1967	Toyota 2000 GT	A.T.C.	Friction	15"	150	275	325
J251	1960s	Vespa	Bandai	Friction	9"	50	75	125
J252	1960	VW Karmann-Ghia (Coupe/Conv.)	Bandai	Friction	7"	100	150	250
J253	1960s	Volkswagen Bus	A.T.C.	Friction	12"	125	175	350
J254	1960s	Volkswagen Pick Up Truck	Bandai	Friction	8"	50	60	75
J255	1960s	Volkswagen Bus	Bandai	Friction	8"	50	60	75
J256	1960s	Volkswagen Bus	Bandai	Bat/Fric	9-1/2"	75	125	175
J257	1950s	Volkswagen Bus	Tipp & Co.	Battery	9"	300	400	600
J258	1950s	Volkswagen Convertible	T.N.	Friction	9-1/2"	100	150	250
J259	1960s	Volkswagen Convertible	Bandai	Battery	7-1/2"	50	70	90
J260	1960s	Volkswagen Convertible	Bandai	Battery	11	110	145	185
J261	1960s	Volkswagen Convertible	Taiyo	Battery	10-1/2"	25	45	90
J262	1960s	Volkswagen	Bandai	Friction	8"	25	40	60
J262A	1950s	Volkswagen	German	Wind Up	6"	75	150	300
J263	1960s	Volkswagen	Bandai	Battery	10-1/2"	25	50	75
J264	1960s	Volkswagen	Bandai	Battery	11"	25	50	75
J265	1960s	Volkswagen with/without Sun Roof	Bandai	Friction	15"	60	90	125

J265B

J274

J276

J278A

 Japenese (etc.) Tin Cars

J284

J286

J287

J288

J289. *Photo courtesy Sonny Glassbrener.*

J290

J291

No.	Year	Model	Manufacturer	Power	Size	C6	C8	C10
J265A	1950s	Volvo	Sweden	Wind Up	11"	600	700	1800
J265B	1960s	Volvo	KS	Friction	7"	100	200	350
J266	1960s	Willys Jeep FC - 150 Pick Up	T.N. Toy Nomura	Friction	11"	50	75	95
J267	1950s	Zuendapp Janus	Bandai	Friction	8"	125	150	300
J268	1950s	Mazda Auto Tricycle K 360	Bandai	Friction	6"	75	100	200
J269	1950	Daihatsu Midget	Kokyu Shokai	Friction	5"	75	100	200
J270	1950s	Daihatsu Midget	Yonezawa	Friction	7"	75	100	200
J271	1950s	Mitsubishi Auto Tricycle Leo	Bandai	Friction	5"	75	100	200
J272	1950s	Mitsubishi Auto Tricycle	Bandai	Friction	11"	100	150	300
J273	1950s	Orient Auto Tricycle	Yonezawa	Friction	9"	75	100	200
J274	1950s	Mazda Auto Tricycle	Bandai	Friction	8"	75	100	200
J275	1950s	Daihatsu Auto Tricycle	Nomura	Friction	11"	100	150	300
J276	1950s	Buick Futuristic Le Sabre	Yonezawa	Friction	7-1/2"	100	200	400
J277	1963	Corvair Bertone	Bandai	Battery	12"	75	150	200
J278	1950s	Dream Car Buick Phantom	Tipp & Co.	Friction	12"	300	400	600
J278A	—	Dream Car	Y	Friction	17"	600	800	1500
J279	1960s	Dream Car Firebird III	Alps	Friction	11"	100	200	300
J280	1960	Ford Gyron	Ichida	Battery	11"	75	100	150
J281	1956	GM's Gas Turbine Powered Firebird II	Ashahi	Friction	8-1/2"	100	200	500
J282	1950s	Pontiac Dream Car	Mitsubishi	Friction	10"	100	200	500
J283		Atom Jet Car	Y	Friction	30"	500	1000	2000
J284		Atom Car	Yonezawa	Friction	17"	200	400	800
J285	1950s	Record Racer NSU	Bandai	Friction	18"	100	150	200
J286	1950s	Agajanian Racer No. 98	Y	Friction	18"	500	800	2000
J287	1950s	Champion's Racer No. 98	Y	Friction	18"	500	800	1500
J288	1950	Champion Racer No. 42	Gem	Friction	18"	500	750	1200
J289	1950	Champion Racer No. 15	German	Friction	18"	500	750	1200
J290	—	Electrospecial #21	Y	Battery	10"	300	500	800
J291	—	Midget Special #6	Y	Friction	7"	300	500	700

JEP

(J de P, Paris, 1899-1965)

by Bob Smith

J de P was founded in 1899 as the *Societe Industrielle de Ferblanterie (SIF)*. The name was changed to *Jouets de Paris* (J de P) in 1928, as the company introduced a new line of toy cars. Four years later, the name was again changed to *Jouets en Paris* (JEP). This name stayed until 1965, when the company went out of business.

	C6	C8	C10
JEP Bugatti Racer, tin litho, c/w motor, "2," 8-1/2" long	340	510	680
JEP Bus, 10-1/2" long, windup	438	657	875

	C6	C8	C10
JEP (J de P) Delage Limousine. Green/black c/w motor, horn, batt/op. spot light, full steering, 13-1/2" long c.1929	300	450	600
JEP Hispano Suiza, c/w motor, lights work, 20" long	2000	4000	6600

JEP Delage Limousine, c.1929, 13-1/2" long. Photo by Bob Smith.

JEP "Madeline-Bastile" Autobus, c.1928, 10-1/4" long. Photo by Bob Smith..

	C6	C8	C10
JEP (J de P) "Madeline-Bastille" 6 wheel Autobus. Green/cream, c/w motor, front/rear wheel steering, 10-1/4" long, c.1928	1200	1600	2100
JEP Peugeot Coupe, pre-WWII, clockwork	200	300	400
JEP Plymouth, door opens, windup, 13"	400	600	800
JEP Rolls Royce Open Phaeton, steel, electric headlights, c/w motor, 19-1/2" long	2000	3500	5000

JEP Rolls Royce Open Phaeton, steel, electric headlights, clockwork motor, 19-1/2" long. Courtesy Bill Bertoia Auctions. Photo by Jeanne Bertoia.

JO HAN: See "Promotionals"

JONES & BIXLER

	C6	C8	C10
Jones & Bixler, Auto, cast-iron, driver, rider	1200	2000	3200
Jones & Bixler, "Express J & B" Truck, 15-1/2" long	900	1350	1800
Jones & Bixler "Peerless" Racer, 5" long, cast-iron	500	800	1100
Jones & Bixler Red Devil Touring Car, driver, 8-1/2" long, cast-iron	550	850	1200

Jones & Bixler "Express J&B" truck. Courtesy Sotheby's NY.

THE JUDY COMPANY

History and listings by Dave Leopard

The Judy Company of Minneapolis made educational toys, including a farm set called "Happy's Farm Family" (patented in 1945) which included a solid rubber car, pickup truck, and tractor, along with human and animal figures.

	C6	C8	C10
JA01 Sedan, 2 dimensional, (part of set), solid rubber, 5-1/4" long	15	20	25
JT01 Pickup Truck, 2 dimensional (part of set), solid rubber, 5-1/4" long	15	20	25
JF01 Farm Tractor, 2 dimensional (part of set), solid rubber, 3-1/2" long	15	20	25

Judy vehicles at top of box, L to R: JF01, JT01, JA01. Courtesy Dave Leopard from his book Rubber Toy Vehicles.

KAHN

Kahn Cadillac & Trailer with furniture, bushes, c.1950, plastic .... No Price Found

KANSAS TOY & NOVELTY COMPANY

by Fred Maxwell, Slushmold Contributing Editor with assistance of Perry Eichor, Ferd Zegel and the Clifton Historical Society

Arthur Haynes, an auto mechanic, started molding toys in his Clifton, Kansas, shed for local stores in 1923. With clever hands and an artist's eye, he charmed his friends and local townspeople with his bright-colored toys. He made his patterns from advertising pictures, from local vehicles, and probably from other makes of toys, such as Tootsietoy. He made his own production tools. His range was diverse, for he made miniatures of aircraft, autos, trains, farm equipment, a zeppelin and a few animals, novelties, and charms.

Haynes believed that he invented hollow-casting of metal toys, so he must have started with solid toys. One day, he dropped his full mold, spilling its hot metal. To his delight he had a perfect, hollow auto toy, with promise of savings of metal and shipping costs.

This was a town enterprise from the beginning. Jess Foster, news editor, helped with alloy mixtures. Mr. Hadsell, the Union Pacific agent (see RR #38, an early promotional?), suggested they send samples to Woolworth's in New York. Clayton D. Young, a traveling salesman, saw the toys, joined the company, and built a profitable business with the chain stores, including Kress, Kresge and Sears-Roebuck; he became a partner. At its peak of international sales in the late 1920s, the firm employed as many as 65 in two shifts during the Christmas order season.

They were young people who had grown up together, a happy gang who joked and sang at their work. This informality was reflected in the local name, "the Hoopie Factory." Two or three of their early toys, #26 and #33, were stripdowns--hoopies, probably raced locally. Whether "Whoopee", tractor toy #48, was a local spelling of this or whether it celebrated a fat, cheering order, is not known. Certainly a lot of happy whoopee-e-e-s must have floated from hoopie-land.

Teamwork there must have been, for a molder, according to Ernest Istas, could produce 2,000 toys a day. Helen Istas was the secretary. Bill Haynes was another molder, showing the family nature of the work force, with its clippers (trimmers), painters, clampers (axles), and boxers. "Butch" Morgison, one of our sources, was each of these during his long career with the company. We found that Clayton Stevenson (see "Lincoln White Metal Works" and "Midwest Toy"), a basement toy-maker and then employee of a foundry, furnished some molds and patterns. He must have created those realistic designs from three-piece molds with their intricate front-ends (see "8", "58", "60", "80", "88," and "91"). These features must have slowed production and added to costs, but made for collector value and rarity.

During its good years, KT&N created more designs and produced more toys than any white-metal maker, save Barclay. Young withdrew his share and retired around 1930. With the loss of these assets and the onset of the Great Depression, the company went downhill. George Hoeffer (sp?) reorganized the company and moved the factory down the road, but this effort lasted only a few months. A happy era was coming to an end. This later history is scanty, but there is evidence that Haynes kept trying until toy #100 in 1935.

High-numbered toys are rare and changes of wheel types suggest that he was having problems. Perhaps he had always overreached, for looking back at the diversity of his toys and novelties, it is remarkable from a few mechanics in a small Plains town. Perhaps this was what caught my eyes many years ago. Pot-metal toys have been intriguing and fun.

NOTES: Because KT&N founded a molding dynasty, with its molds still in use today after passing through several companies, I have included extra details and comments with this history to eliminate collector and dealer confusion. We found that "those toys with the numbers" was more collector gossip than a good rule. Many KT&N toys were not numbered, some of them twins of the numbered versions, and not all numbered toys were KT&N. Numbered toys are shown in "quotes."

Some toys were made in two or three versions/variations.

Some toys were made in two or three sizes (5¢, 10¢, and 15¢. Can you believe?).

Most wheels were metal (disc or simulated spoked or wire. Tractor/farm wheels were large disc or open spoke with wide rims; a unique track-laying version with rubber tracks used metal or wood wheels.) Rubber tires on wood hubs (popularized by Tootsietoy Grahams in 1932) were tried on #75 and later, followed by soft rubber (balloon) wheels and hard-rubber white discs with painted black tires.

Many had string-pull loops or knobs on the lower grille.

All colors were used, including gold, silver, and pink (for little girls?).

A few were found with bi-colored bodies (sales samples?). Many early toys were finished in Egyptian lacquer, a japanning so thin the bright metal gleamed through. A mint example with this unique finish has a modern, glittery look.

"Made in USA" embossing is a clue to Best Toy and later, for this copyright addition came from laws of the mid-1930s. Black rubber tires were used later by Ralstoy and others.

For KT&N airplanes, cannon, and novelties, see "Aircraft" and "Miscellaneous" sections in *Collecting Toys*. For additional pictures and different views see "Best Toy & Novelty" in this book.

The "dynasty" mentioned above included Best Toy, Ralstoy, Craftoy, and Eccles Bros., in that order. The Ralstoy of today, with its line of die-cast trucks, is the same company on a different track.

The following sequential listing has been carefully researched, but additions are still trickling in. The first toy is controversial. One source said it was a solid casting; probably true, but did it ever reach the market? Some said it was the large Indy racer; others said it was the midget racer without a driver. I vote for this rare coupe, KTVO, because it is crude and uniquely engraved on its mold "Arthur L. Haynes."

For collectors who find variations useful, the following abbreviations are used:

HRDW:	white hard-rubber disk wheels
HG:	horizontal grille pattern
HL:	horizontal hood louvers
HO:	hood ornament, cap or motometer
LI:	landau irons, on convertibles
MDW:	metal disc wheels
MDSW:	metal solid-spoke wheels
MSW:	metal open-spoke wheels
MWW:	metal simul. "wire" wheels
OW:	open windows
RM:	rearmount spare
SM:	sidemount spare
SP:	string-pull knob or loop, in front
T:	trunk, external
UV:	unnumbered version
VG:	vertical grille
WS or W/S:	windshield
WV:	windshield visor
WHRT:	wood hubs, rubber tires

Fred Maxwell

Fred Maxwell, collector and occasional author, has been collecting antique aircraft and vehicle toys since 1965. This retirement hobby was started from scratch, for his lead soldiers were missing when he returned home from college. He founded Capital Miniature Auto Collectors Club in 1969 to promote interest in the Central Atlantic states. He felt challenged by the lack of public knowledge and the ambiguity of that orphan category: Pot Metal or Slushmold Toys.

	C6	C8	C10
KTV0 Large Coupe, no #. Crude, high-bodied "Ford," HO, HG, no headlamps, SP, VL, 5 windows, door handles, wheel type unknown because only a reproduction has been found, 3-1/4"			No Price Found
KTV1 Midget Racer, no #. No driver, torpedo tail, HO, SP, VL, HG. 5/8" MDW w/simulated lug nuts, lacquer finish, 3" long	20	30	40
KTV2 Midget Racer, no #, same as above, 3", w/driver, plain MDW, lacquer. Easily confused with another maker's copy. See #31 and #67	70	105	140
KTV3 Large Indy Racer, no #, driver, boattail, HO, MDW, lacquer, 6" long			No Price Found
KTV4 Coupe, no #, crude, slant roof, no head lamps, shallow rear body, no fenders, hood similar to first racer above, lacquer. First "hoopie" or stripdown made? 3-1/8" long	32	48	65
KTV5 Sedan, no #. Crude limousine or stretch taxi, 6 windows, louvered rear quarters, HO, VL, HG, T, SP, large MDW, lacquer, 3-3/8" long			No Price Found

	C6	C8	C10
KTV6 Coupe, "8," 3-1/4". Cadillac Convertible? A 3-piece mold casting different from the 3 #8 versions below; basic body suggests same pattern-maker, if not KT&N then Midwest Toy. Rectang. VG, HO, no headlamps, VL, MWWSM, WV, 2 OW, body trim, kickplates, door handles, LI, T, MEWBT. A carefully crafted, rare model			No Price Found

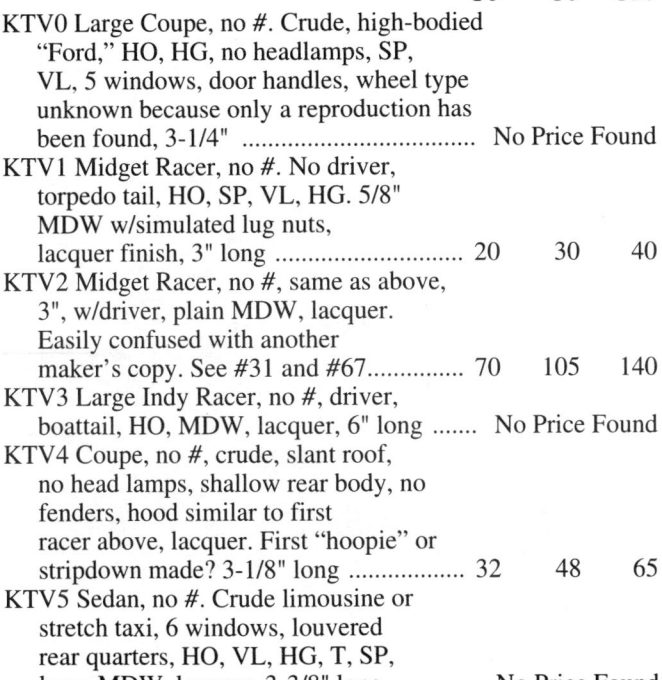

Kansas Toy Racers, Top row: KTV1, KTV2.
Bottom row: KTV14, KTV24, KTV52. Photo by Fred Maxwell.

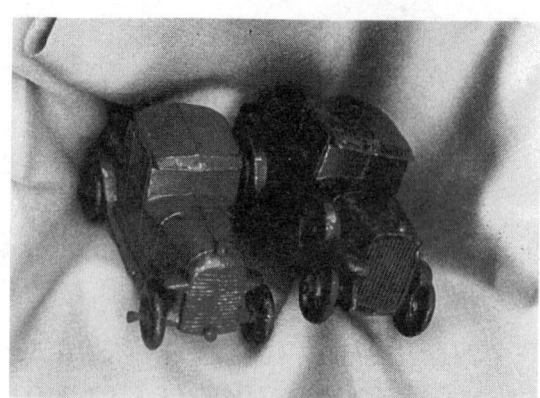

Kansas Toy, L to R: KTV7, KTV6. Photo by Fred Maxwell.

Kansas Toy Autos, Top row: KTV4, KTV5.
Middle row: KTV7, KTV7.
Bottom row: KTV26, KTV26, KTV43. Photo by Fred Maxwell.

Kansas Toy Coupes in two scales KTV9, KTV26. Photo by Ferd Zegel.

Kansas Toy, Top row: KTV7, KTV15.
Bottom row: KTV45, KTTV67. Photo by Perry Eichor.

Kansas Toy Bus KTV12. Photo by Fred Maxwell.

KTV13. Drawing courtesy of Deb Eccles.

Kansas Toy, L to R, Top: KTV14, KTV35, KTTV69.
Middle: Best "85," KTV52, KTTV71.
Bottom: Craftoy? KTV24, Best "97." Photo by Fred Maxwell.

  Kansas Toy & Novelty Company

	C6	C8	C10

KTV7 Coupe, "8," 3-1/8". Convertible,
LI, VL, HG, WV, SP, RM, MWW,
no HO, no headlamps, enamel
finish. Also UVs with "Chrysler,"
headlamps and HO; or with MDSW 20   30   40

KTV8 Coupe, "8," 3-1/8". Trunk
Convertible, T, HO, VG, SM, MDW .... No Price Found

NOTE: #8 is the lowest numbered vehicle found. Its realistic, high quality signals the ending of a novice toymaker's experimental phase. The coupes above have the same 1924 Chrysler hood and nice details like landau irons and kickplates, but not all had headlamps. The basic body expanded into this series of coupes, #14 roadsters, and sedans (all (?) unnumbered), lacquered or enameled, with 3 types of wheels: MDW, MDSW, and MWW. They were unnamed or named: Chrysler, Chevrolet. The large coupe, KTV9, is a scale-up of #8. Only 3 of these large pieces are known: the racer KTV3, John Deere tractor KTV19, and a Sedan #88.

KTV9 Large coupe, no #, 5"
Chrysler Convertible, MWW and
2 golf doors. Larger version of #8 .... No Price Found

KTV10 Sedan, no #, 2-7/8". "Chevrolet,"
6 windows, LI, WV, VL, SP, RM, MWW   16   24   32

KTV11 Sedan, no #, 3-1/4". "Chevrolet,"
as above, HG, HO, MSW .... No Price Found

KTV12 Overland Bus, "9," 3-1/2".
"Fageol," solid windows .... No Price Found

KTV13 Overland Bus, no #, 3-1/2".
"Fageol," 9 male passengers, driver
and "baggage" cast on windows, HG,
RM, MDW. Also an UV w/various
family passengers on windows 26   39   52

Kansas Toy ? KTV16. Courtesy Bob Straub.

Kansas Toy and Novelty, L to R: KTV17, KTV47, KTV46. Photo by Chic Gast.

	C6	C8	C10

KTV14 Indy Racer, "10," 3-1/8". Driver,
boattail, exhaust right, VL, HG, HO,
SP, MSW or MWW. Also UV 10   15   20

KTV15 Roadster, "14," 3-1/8". Open
"Chrysler," solid W/S, plain
grille, HO, VL, SP, RM, MDSW 18   27   36

KTV15A Roadster, no #, 3-1/8".
Same as above, HG, 2 golf club doors ..... No Price Found

KTV16 Roadster, no #. Similar to
above, with open rumble seat. KTN?

KTV17 Farm Tractor, "17," 2-7/8".
"Fordson," driver, HG, crank, no tow
hook, large 1-1/4" and 3/4" MDW with
4 holes in disks. Also found with same
size 6 spoke wheels. (See #57) 20   30   40

KTV18 Farm Tractor, no #, 2-5/8". Same
basic body as above; "Fordson" on
radiator and crankcase, VG and towhook,
with smaller, plain MDW, 3-piece
molded grille .... No Price Found

KTV19 Large Farm Tractor, no #,
4-7/8". Deere Model D. A finely crafted
replica in 2 colors, steering shaft, fly
wheel, belt drive wheel, rear fenders,
large 2" and 1" 12-spoke wheels .... No Price Found

Kansas Toy Deere Model D Tractor - KTV19. Photo by Ferd Zegel.

Kansas Toy KTV20. Photo by Fred Maxwell.

Kansas Toy Farm Vehicles KTV23, KTV21, KTV54. Photo by Fred Maxwell.

Kansas Toy: KTV22 (mid 1930s), KTV25 (1920s). Photo by Perry Eichor.

Kansas Toy KTV26. Courtesy Bob Ackerly.

Kansas Toy Vehicles, Top row: KTV24, KTV26, KTV37. Middle row: KTV38, KTV40, KTV43. Bottom row: KTV45, KTV52, KTV53. Photo by Fred Maxwell.

Kansas Toy, L to R: KTV33, KTV41. Courtesy Ferd Zegel.

	C6	C8	C10
KTV20 Truck, "20," 3-1/8". Ford? Solid w/s, 2 OW, 3 tanks, VL, HG, rear faucet, MWW. Versions w/and w/o driver. Also an UV	37	56	75
KTV21 Steam Tractor, "25," 3". "Case," crew of 2, tow loop, large front, small rear MSW and flywheel. (See #71.) Also an UV with no name	25	38	50
KTV22 Racer, "26," 4". "Bearcat" stripdown, long hood, motometer, 3 intakes, driver, open frame, left 4 cyl. exhaust. (See #33.)		No Price Found	
KTV23 Separator-Thresher, "27," 3". Tow hook, auto-type MSW (not tractor rims), lacquer or enamel. Also UV. (See #72.)	20	30	40
KTV24 Midget racer, "31," 2-1/8". Driver, torpedo tail, VL, HG, HO, MWW, lacquer. Also UV. (See #67.)	14	21	28
KTV25 Racer, "33," 3". "Bearcat" stripdown, smaller version of #26 above	85	128	170
KTV26 Coupe, "35," 2-1/4". Convertible, LI, VL, HG, HO, RM, MWW. Also an UV	20	30	40
KTV27 Locomotive-tender, "36," 4-3/8". "KT & N RR" 6 MSW, 4 MDW, 0-6-4		No Price Found	
KTV28 "Pullman" Car, "37," 3-1/2". "KT & N RR," 4 MDW		No Price Found	
KTV29 Box Car, "38," 3-1/4". "KT & N RR," Union Pacific shield (an early promotional?), 4 MDW		No Price Found	

	C6	C8	C10
KTV30 Tank Car, "39," 3-1/8". "KT & N RR," ladder, filler, MDW		No Price Found	
KTV31 Caboose, "40," 2-3/4". "KT & N RR," stack, brakeman's cab, MDW		No Price Found	
KTV32 Stock Car, "41," "KT & N RR," MDW		No Price Found	
KTV33 Dump Truck, "42," 3-1/2". Ford? Driver, no cab, diamond emblem on hinged dump body, VL, HG, SP, MWW	30	45	60
KTV34 Steam Road Roller, "43," 3-1/4". Driver, SP, boiler, wooden rollers	20	30	40
KTV35 Racer. "46," 2-7/8". 1929 Golden Arrow record car, driver, large tail fin, MWW	12	18	24

Kansas Toy, L to R, Top: KTV33A, Ralstoy?, KTV38. Middle: KTV23, KTV21, KTV34. Bottom: KTV46, KTV18, KTV47. Photo by Perry Eichor.

Three versions of the original Kansas Toy #42 truck:. Top row: Kansas Toy version, KTV33. Bottom row: Ralstoy, RAV1, Earlier version (Ralstoy?). Photo by Perry Eichor.

Kansas Toy and Novelty KTV34. Photo by R.F. Sapita.

Kansas Toy KTV35. Photo by Fred Maxwell.

KTV36 Warehouse Tractor, "48,"
3". "Caterpillar," "Whoopee," driver,
VL, HG, HO, SP, tow loop, MWW.
Also an UV 25   38   50

KTV36A Farm Tractor. Same as above
but with larger 3/4" track-laying wheels,
metal or wood, for rubber track .... No Price Found

KTV37 Tour Bus, "49," 2-3/8". 1928
Pickwick COE "Nite Coach," HG,
SP, MDW duals. Also an UV. See #59 ..... No Price Found

KTV38 Pickup Truck, "51," 2-3/4".
Ford w/cab, VL, HG, tow loop,
MDW, lacquer. Also an UV .... No Price Found

KTV39 Roadster, "54," 2-3/8".
Buick, driver w/cap, rumble seat,
T, plain hood and grille, no headlamps,
SM, MWW. Also an UV. (See #77.) 20   30   40

KTV40 Roadster, "54," 2-1/4".
Same as above, no trunk 52   78   105

KTV41 Truck-Semi, "55," 4".
Ford, stake trailer, VL, HG, MDW .... No Price Found

KTV42 Farm Tractor, "57," 1-3/4"
Fordson, driver, SP, MDW rear,
MSW front. Smaller version of
#17. Also an UV .... No Price Found

KTV43 Sedanette, "58," 2-1/4".
Austin Bantam, unique fighting cock
on door panels, 4 OW, HL, VG, RM,
MWW, 3-piece molded grille .... No Price Found

KTV44 Tour Bus, "59," 3-3/8". 1928
Pickwick COE double-deck
night-coach, screen grille. Larger
version of #49 above. Also an UV
with dual wheels 75   112   15

Kansas Toy Vehicles, L to R: KTV36, KTV58. Photo by Fred Maxwell.

Kansas Toy KTV36. Photo by Fred Maxwell.

Kansas Toy KTV39. Photo by Fred Maxwell.

Kansas Toy, Top: KTV41. Bottom, L to R: KTV53 (repro), trailer for KTV41. Photo by Fred Maxwell.

Kansas Toy KTV43. Courtesy Ferd Zegel.

Kansas Toy KTV44. Photo by Fred Maxwell.

*Kansas Toy Autos with Hard Rubber Wheels,
L to R: KTTV59, KTV45. Photo by Fred Maxwell.*

*Kansas Toy
KTV51.
Courtesy
Ferd Zegel.*

*Kansas Toy Vehicles with Wood Hubs, L to R: KTTV64,
KTTV65. Photo by Fred Maxwell.*

*Kansas Toy Towed Implements, Top row: KTV46, KTV49.
Bottom row: KTV47, KTV50. Photo by Fred Maxwell.*

Kansas Toy KTV56. Photo by Perry Eichor.

Kansas Toy KTTV64. Photo by Craig A. Clark.

*Kansas Toy, Top row: KTTV66, KTTV63.
Middle row: KTTV68, KTV45.
Bottom row: KTV43. Photo by Perry Eichor.*

	C6	C8	C10

KTV45 Sedan, "60," 3-1/2". 1930 Reo Royale? or Chrysler 2-door brougham, plain hood, vee-VG, square rear deck, MDW, MDWSM. Also an UV with MWW and MWWSM, 3-piece molded grille 30   45   60

NOTE: The following is a unique towed farm set with several hinged or moving parts, each a different color and large 1-1/4" spoked tractor wheels. "61" and "62" have been seen with tin snap-on seats (odd).

KTV46 Planter, "KTN No. 61," 4". V-blade plough with seed hopper, 4-piece incl. wheels and 3 colors 35   52   70

KTV47 Disc Harrow, "62," 4". 8 discs on same 1-5/8" wide frame as #61. 13 pieces, incl. discs and wheels, 4 colors ... 35   52   70

KTV48 Plough, "63," 4". Single blade on same shaft as #61 35   52   70

KTV49 Dirt Tumble, "64," 4". Adjustable dumping scoop, 1-1/2" wide on same frame as #62. 6 pieces, 4 colors 35   52   70

KTV50 Dirt scraper, "65," 3-5/8". Blade, 1-7/8," adjustable, on same frame as #62 .... No Price Found

	C6	C8	C10

KTV51 Coupe, "66," 3-1/2", Stream-lined 3-wheeler, 6 OW, MWW .... No Price Found

KTV52 Midget Racer, "67," 1-1/2". Driver, torpedo-tail, VL, HG, HO, MDW. Smaller version of #31. Also an UV .... No Price Found

KTV53 Fire Engine, "70," 2-1/4". Seagrave ? pumper, driver, VL, HG, MDW .... No Price Found

KTV54 Steam Tractor, "71," 2-1/2". Crew of 2, tow-loop. Small version of #25 20   30   40

KTV55 Separator-Thresher, "72," 2+". Tow hook for #71 .... No Price Found

KTV56 Army Tank, "74," 2-1/4". "US Army," WWI type, high turret, large front, small rear wheels. OD color .... No Price Found

KTV57 Racer, no #, 1". Miniature solid-cast version of #10, moving wheels, charm loop on nose .... No Price Found

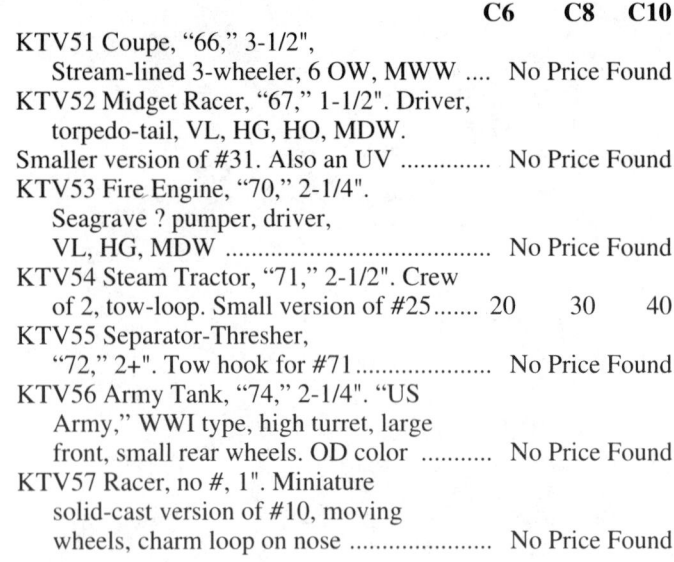

Kansas Toy KTV70 (both). Courtesy Ferd Zegel.

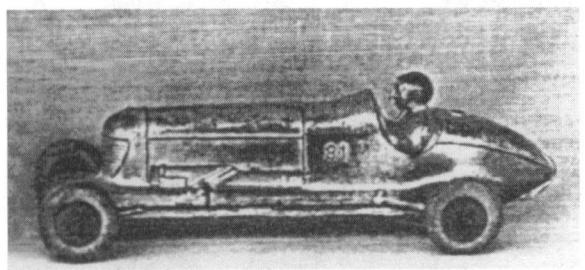

Kansas Toy Racer - KTV69. Courtesy Bob Ackerly.

Kansas Toy KTV72. Courtesy Bob Ackerly.

This is probably an ad for Kansas Toy vehicles. It ran in the April, 1933 Butler Bros. catalog. Fred Maxwell typed the numbers in.

	C6	C8	C10
KTV58-KTV60 Unused.			
KTV61 Army Tank, "74," 2-1/4". "US Army," 2 gun turret, OD color. A different tank than #74 above	No Price Found		
KTV62 Coupe, "75," 4-1/4". Graham like (Tootsietoy) VG, SM, T, WHRT, 1933 issue	No Price Found		
KTV63 Racer, "76," 4-1/4". Auburn speedster, low driver, headrest fairing, SP, HG, slanted louvers, large oval fin, kickplates, HWRW or WHRT	25	38	50
KTV64 Roadster, "77," 4". Open sport Duesenberg, W/S down, driver, VG, slanted louvers, SM, T, WHRT	25	38	50
KTV65 Concrete Mixer, "78," 3-3/4". Truck with water tank & mixing barrel, VG, HL, WHRT. Found both with and w/o a bottom pan. Sometimes called a fuel tanker	No Price Found		
KTV66 Sedan, "79," 4-1/4". 2-door, Graham like, 4 OW, VG, HL, RM, WHRT w/5 removable tires. Found both with and w/o bottom pan	20	30	40

	C6	C8	C10
KTV67 Coupe, "80," 3-1/2". Convertible, top up, LI, 2 OW, VG, T, MWW w/MWW SM, 3-piece molded grille	30	45	60
KTV68 Coupe, "80," 3-1/2". Same as above except HRDW w/MDW SM (a different casting re sidemounts).	No Price Found		
KTV69 Racer, "81," 4-3/8". Miller FWD, driver, 8 cyl. right exhaust, HG, WHRT, 1933 issue	No Price Found		
KTV70 Sedan, "82," 4". Pierce-Arrow Silver Arrow fastback, 6 OW, HRDW, 3-piece molded grille	No Price Found		
KTV71 Indy Racer, "83," 4-5/8". FWD, driver, VG, HL, right exhaust, WHRT	No Price Found		
KTV72 Sedan, "84," 3-5/8". DeSoto? Airflow, 4 OW, HO, HG, HL, HRDW, 1934 issue	No Price Found		

NOTE: There are so few original KT&N higher-numbered toys in today's market, compared to later reproductions, that it is not known which went into production. They are shown earlier in this book as Best Toys to save duplication.

KARL BUB

("KBN," Nuremberg, Germany, 1851-1966)

by Bob Smith

Bub had one of the longest reigns in the toy business. He took over the Carette Toy Co. in 1917, after Georges Carette fled to France at the onset of WWI. He also took over the Bing Toy Works in 1932. Bub used much of the technology practiced by Carette. His toys were of the better-quality toys to come out of Germany in the early 1900s. Bub produced many of the fine toys sold by FAO Schwarz Co. of New York.

	C6	C8	C10
Karl Bub Coupe, rumble seat, c/w motor	No Price Found		
Karl Bub Limousine, windup, 8" long	250	375	500
Karl Bub Limousine, windup, driver, 11" long	700	1200	1800
Karl Bub Limousine Green/black, 9-3/4" long. Doors open, front crank c/w motor	700	1150	1600
Karl Bub Limousine, clockwork, c.1920s, 14" long	2000	4000	7500
Karl Bub Limousine. Red/black, c/w motor, 14" long. Opening doors, hand brake, c.1915	1200	1800	2500
Karl Bub Mercedes Limousine. Green/black, 13-1/2" long. Doors open, windshield folds, head lamps, tool box's c/w motor, head lamps, steering, c.1928	950	1500	2100
Karl Bub Roadster, driver, c.1908, 9" long	800	1400	2200

	C6	C8	C10
Karl Bub Sedan, 1919, high headlamps, windup, 14" long	750	1300	2120
Karl Bub Tourer, two seat, 9-1/2" long, windup	900	1700	2400

Karl Bub Limousine, 9-3/4" long. Photo by Bob Smith.

Karl Bub Limousine, clockwork, c.1920s, 14" long. Courtesy Sotheby's NY.

Karl Bub Limousine, c.1915, 14" long. Photo by Bob Smith.

Karl Bub Mercedes Limousine, c.1928, 13-1/2" long. Photo by Bob Smith.

Karl Bub Roadster, driver, c.1908, 9" long. Courtesy Bill Bertoia Auctions. Photo by Jeanne Bertoia.

Karl Bub Sedan, 1919, high headlamps, windup, 14" long. Courtesy Bill Bertoia Auctions. Photo by Jeanne Bertoia.

KELMET

(Also known as Trumodel and Big Boy)

Kelmet was founded in Chicago in 1925 by several wholesale toy representatives. It was their wish to compete with the large steel-toy vehicles of the period. Work was done to at least some extent through A.C. Gilbert. White trucks were a Kelmet staple. The toys were big (about 2 feet) and heavy (about 10 pounds).

	C6	C8	C10
Kelmet Aerial Ladder Truck, 30" long	800	1250	1700
Kelmet "Army Truck," 1929, 25" long	800	1350	2000
Kelmet Chemical Truck	900	1400	2000
Kelmet Coal Pocket Loader	1200	2000	3000
Kelmet Crane Truck	2500	4000	6000
Kelmet Sand Loader	1000	1700	2400
Kelmet Scissor Dump Truck, 25" long	600	950	1400
Kelmet Steam Shovel, Big Boy	325	488	650
Kelmet Tank Truck, 27" long	1500	2700	4700
Kelmet Trumodel Derrick with power hoist and tip bucket	1000	1700	2400
Kelmet White Dump Truck, 25" long, No. 501	1200	2000	2700
Kelmet White Fire Truck (ladder)	1200	2000	3000

Kelmet Aerial Ladder Truck, 30" long (restored in photo). Courtesy Bill Bertoia Auctions. Photo by Jeanne Bertoia.

Kelmet "Army Truck," 1929, 25" long. Courtesy Joe and Sharon Freed.

Kelmet White Dump Truck, No. 501. Courtesy Joe and Sharon Freed.

KENTON

Kenton Lock Manufacturing Co. was incorporated in May 1890, in Kenton, Ohio. In November 1894, it became the Kenton Hardware Manufacturing Co. Around this period, it began producing toys. In 1903, it brought out its first toy auto line, calling them the "Red Devils," since most cars in those days were painted red. The firm was a guild. In 1930, L.S. Bixler, of Jones & Bixler, was its president. The firm used cast iron.

	C6	C8	C10
Kenton Ambulance, cast-iron, 7" long	750	1300	1700
Kenton "Army Motor Truck 807," 14" long, cast-iron	600	950	1300
Kenton Auto, very early, clockwork, tiller, driver in top hat, approx. 4" long	250	400	550
Kenton Auto, 6" long, cast iron	1000	1700	2400
Kenton Auto Dray Truck, black driver, passenger, 9" long	1000	1800	2500
Kenton "Auto Express 548" w/driver, 9-1/4" long	1500	2700	3800
Kenton Auto Hansom, 7-3/4" long	400	600	800
Kenton Boat-tail cut-down speedster, 1910, 7" long	120	180	240
Kenton Buckeye Ditcher, 9" long	500	800	1100

	C6	C8	C10
Kenton Buckeye Ditcher, 11-3/4" long	1500	2700	3975
Kenton Bus, double-decker, 1920s, 6" long..	400	600	800
Kenton Bus, double decker, 1920, 7-1/4" long	1100	1650	2200
Kenton Bus, double decker, c.1920s, 8-1/8" long	1000	1800	2500
Kenton Bus, double-decker, 9-1/2" long	500	750	1000
Kenton Bus, double-decker, 12" long	500	800	1200
Kenton Bus, double-decker, 13-1/2" long	1500	2800	4500
Kenton Bus, 8" long, cast-iron	340	510	680
Kenton Bus, 1920s, 10-3/4" long	375	525	750
Kenton Bus, 12-3/4" long	600	1000	1400
Kenton Bus, Twin Coach, 8-1/2" long	1000	1600	2350
Kenton Cattle Truck, 8" long, cast-iron, c.1938	150	225	300
Kenton Cement Mixer Truck, 1932, 8-1/2"	1500	2700	4000

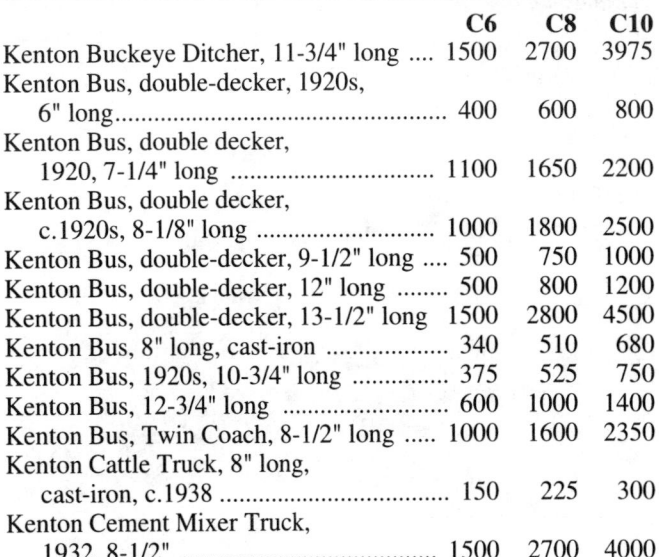

Kenton Ambulance, cast iron, incorrect driver, 7" long. Courtesy Sotheby's NY.

Kenton "Army Motor Truck 807," incorrect driver in photo. Courtesy Sotheby's NY.

Kenton Auto Hansom, 7-3/4" long. Courtesy Bill Bertoia Auctions. Photo by Jeanne Bertoia.

Kenton Buckeye Ditcher, 12-1/2" long. Courtesy Sotheby's NY.

Kenton Bus, double-decker, 1920s, 6" long. Courtesy Bill Bertoia Auctions. Photo by Jeanne Bertoia.

Kenton Bus, double decker, 8-1/8" long. Courtesy Sotheby's NY.

Kenton Bus, double-decker, 9-1/2" long. Courtesy Phillips NY.

Kenton Bus, double-decker, 12" long. Courtesy Bill Bertoia Auctions. Photo by Jeanne Bertoia.

Kenton Bus, double-decker, 13-1/2" long. Courtesy Sotheby's New York.

Kenton Bus, 12-3/4" long. Courtesy Bill Bertoia Auctions. Photo by Jeanne Bertoia.

	C6	C8	C10
Kenton Circus Truck, 10" long	1300	2000	2700
Kenton "City Service" Truck, C-cab, 10-1/4" long	1500	2800	3700
Kenton "Coal" Dump Truck, 8-1/2" long ..	140	210	280
Kenton "Coal" Dump Truck w/driver, 10-1/2" long, c. 1932	800	1350	2000
Kenton "Coast-to-Coast" bus	350	525	700
Kenton "Contractors" Dump Wagon, cast-iron, 8-1/2" long	500	750	1000
Kenton "Contractors" Dump Truck, 3-bucket, 9-3/4" long	500	800	1150
Kenton Coupe, 5" long	230	345	460
Kenton Coupe, 6-1/2" long	425	638	850
Kenton Coupe, 8" long	700	1100	1600

Kenton Coupe, 1926, separate driver, 10" long, auctioned in 1994, near mint, for $9,000

	C6	C8	C10
Kenton Dump Truck, 6" long	337	505	675
Kenton Dump Truck, hinged self-locking gate, 8-1/2"	500	800	1100
Kenton Emergency Truck, c.1930s, black rubber tires, takes batteries for headlights and spotlight	180	270	360
Kenton Fire Apparatus Truck	400	600	800
Kenton Fire Pumper, 5-3/4" long, early	120	180	240

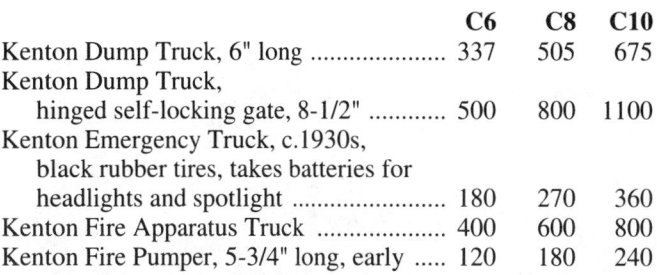

Kenton "Contractors" Dump Wagon. Courtesy Sotheby's NY.

Kenton "Coal" Dump Truck with driver, 10-1/2" long. Courtesy Bill Bertoia Auctions. Photo by Jeanne Bertoia.

Kenton Dump Truck, hinged self-locking gate, 8-1/2" long. Courtesy Bill Bertoia Auctions. Photo by Jeanne Bertoia.

Kenton "Contractors" Dump Truck, 3-bucket, 9-3/4" long. Courtesy Bill Bertoia Auctions. Photo by Jeanne Bertoia.

Kenton Fire Pumper, early with driver, 10-1/2" long. Photo by Rod Carnahan.

Kenton Fire Pumper, 18" long, has gong. Courtesy Mapes Auctioneers & Appraisers.

Kenton Ice Truck, driver, 7-7/8" long. Courtesy Bill Bertoia Auctions. Photo by Jeanne Bertoia.

Kenton Ice Truck, tractor trailer, 1930s, 10-1/2" long. Courtesy Bill Bertoia Auctions. Photo by Jeanne Bertoia.

Kenton "Jaeger" cement mixer. Courtesy Sotheby's NY.

Kenton "Jaeger" Cement Mixer Truck, 8" long. Courtesy HAKE'S American & Collectibles.

Kenton "Jaeger" Cement Mixer, rubber wheels, 9"?. Courtesy Sotheby's NY.

Kenton Ladder Truck, approx. 7-1/2" long; from a 1927 Kenton catalog.

Kenton Limousine, driver, c.1915, 7-3/4" long. Courtesy Christie's East.

Kenton Overland Circus with hippo, 7-1/4" long. Courtesy Bill Bertoia Auctions. Photo by Jeanne Bertoia.

Kenton "Patrol" Wagon, driver, 3 firemen, c.1920s-30s, 9" long. Courtesy Bill Bertoia Auctions. Photo by Jeanne Bertoia.

	C6	C8	C10
Kenton Fire Pump Truck, early with driver, approx. 10" long	185	278	350
Kenton Fire Pumper, 11-1/2" long, 1911	No Price Found		
Kenton Fire Pumper, 14-1/2" long, 1920s	800	1200	1600
Kenton Fire Pumper, 18" long, c.1920, has gong	350	525	700
Kenton Fire Truck, 15" long with pumper	1200	2000	2800
Kenton Franklin, air-cooled, 8-1/2" long	1300	1950	2600
Kenton Hose Reel Fire Truck, 8-3/4" long	325	488	650
Kenton "Hose" Truck, approx. 6-3/4" long, open cab, c.1920s, green, driver, rider, hose, ladders	350	525	700
Kenton Hudson, postwar, electric lights	50	75	100
Kenton Ice Truck, tongs and glass ice, 7-1/2"	1000	2000	3000
Kenton Ice Truck, driver, 7-7/8"	425	638	850
Kenton Ice Truck, tractor trailer, 1930's, 10-1/2" long	1000	1700	2400
Kenton Jaeger Cement Mixer, 6-1/2" long, iron wheels	262	393	525
Kenton Jaeger Cement Mixer, 7" long	550	825	1250
Kenton Jaeger Cement Mixer, 7-3/8" long	650	950	1500
Kenton Jaeger Cement Mixer, 8" long	1000	1500	2000
Kenton "Jaeger Mixer," cast-iron Cement Truck, 9" long	1000	2000	3000
Kenton Ladder Truck, approx. 7-1/2" long, cast-iron	300	450	600
Kenton Ladder Truck, 9" long, driver, early 1930s	90	135	180
Kenton Ladder Truck, 11-1/2" long	280	420	560
Kenton Ladder Truck, pressed steel ladders, 16" long	500	850	1100
Kenton Ladder Truck, 17-1/4" long	750	1200	1700
Kenton Ladder Truck, 20" long	1100	1800	2500
Kenton Ladder Truck, 22" long	1500	2400	3500
Kenton Limousine, driver, c.1915, 7-3/4" long	500	750	1000
Kenton "Merchant Delivery"	450	675	900
Kenton "Oil Gas" Truck, 10-1/2" long	800	1400	2100
Kenton Overland Circus cage truck with driver, 7-1/2" long	900	1500	2000
Kenton Overland Circus with hippo, 7-1/4" long	700	1150	1600

Kenton "Pickwick Nite Coach," 11" long. Courtesy Phillips NY.

Kenton "Pickwick Nite Coach" L to R: 7-1/2" long, 9-1/2" long. Courtesy Bill Bertoia Auctions. Photo by Jeanne Bertoia.

Kenton Road Roller "Galion Master," 7" long. Courtesy Bill Bertoia Auctions. Photo by Jeanne Bertoia.

Kenton, L to R: Sedan, 1923, separate driver, 10" long, Coupe, 1926, separate driver, 10" long, Sedan, 1926, separate driver, 10-1/4" long. Courtesy Bill Bertoia Auctions. Photo by Jeanne Bertoia.

Kenton Runabout Auto, cast iron, driver, c.1908, 6-1/2" long. Courtesy Christie's East.

Kenton "Seeing New York 899." Courtesy Bill Bertoia Auctions. Photo by Jeanne Bertoia.

	C6	C8	C10
Kenton Overland Circus			
with lion, 9" long	800	1300	1800
Kenton Overland Circus			
Calliope Truck, 10" long (Rare)	No Price Found		
Kenton "Patrol" Wagon, driver,			
3 firemen, 9" long, c.1920s-1930s	650	1100	1600
Kenton Phaeton Touring Car, 12"	350	562	700
Kenton "Pickwick Nite Coach,"			
14" long, cast-iron	1900	2750	3800
Kenton "Pickwick Nite Coach," 11" long	No Price Found		
Kenton "Pickwick Nite Coach,"			
9-1/2" long	1400	2500	3700
Kenton "Pickwick Nite Coach,"			
7-1/2" long	600	1100	1500
Kenton "Pickwick Nite Coach," 6" long	500	850	1200
Kenton Pontiac, 4-1/2" long	262	393	525
Kenton Pontiac & Trailer, 10" long	350	525	725
Kenton Racer, 7-1/2" long	142	213	285
Kenton Racer, 9" long, early, cast-iron	600	1000	1400
Kenton Red Devil Auto,			
1906, with driver, 6" long	225	338	450
Kenton Reo Sedan, 1929, 8" long	No Price Found		
Kenton Road Grader, 5-1/2" long	125	188	250
Kenton Road Grader, 7-1/4" long, 1950	135	205	275
Kenton Road Grader, cast-iron,			
7-1/2" long, rubber tires,			
nickel-plated moveable blade	155	230	310

	C6	C8	C10
Kenton Road Roller,			
"Galion Master," 5-1/2" long	115	172	230
Kenton Road Roller,			
"Galion Master," 7" long	150	225	300
Kenton Roadster, 6" long, driver, c.1908	300	450	600
Kenton Runabout Auto, 5" long, 1900	170	225	340
Kenton Runabout Auto, cast-iron,			
driver, c.1908, 6-1/2" long	700	1050	1400
Kenton Sand & Gravel Truck, 1940s	165	248	330
Kenton Sedan, 4" long	110	165	225
Kenton Sedan, 7" long, late 1930s,			
rubber tires, take apart body	1400	2100	2800
Kenton Sedan, 8-1/2" long	2000	3000	5000
Kenton Sedan, 1923, separate driver,			
10" long, auctioned 1994, mint, for $6,000			
Kenton Sedan, 1926, separate driver,			
10-1/4" long, auctioned 1994,			
excellent, for $23,000			
Kenton "Seeing New York 899" Bus with			
Mama Katzenjammer,Uncle Heine,			
Alphonse, Gloomy Gus,			
Happy Hooligan, 10-1/2"	2000	3900	6350
Kenton "Speed" Stake Truck, 9-1/8" long	450	850	1250
Kenton "Speed" Stake			
Truck, c.1927, 5-1/2" long	50	75	100
Kenton Sprinkler Truck, early, 8"	300	450	600
Kenton Stake Truck, 6" long	337	405	675
Kenton Steam Roller,			
"Galion Master," 6-1/2" long	225	338	450
Kenton Steam Shovel			
Marion, 7-1/4" long	600	900	1200

Kenton "Speed" stake truck, 9-1/8" long. Courtesy Bill Bertoia Auctions. Photo by Jeanne Bertoia.

Kenton "Speed" stake truck, c.1927, 5-1/2" long. Courtesy Bill Bertoia Auctions. Photo by Jeanne Bertoia.

Kenton Touring Car, open, driver and passenger, 8-1/2" long (air-cooled Franklin). Courtesy Sotheby's NY.

Kenton Touring Car, open, driver, passenger, 1923, 9" long. Courtesy Bill Bertoia Auctions. Photo by Jeanne Bertoia.

	C6	C8	C10
Kenton Tank, cast-iron, 2-1/2" long	80	120	160
Kenton Touring Car, 6", driver	225	338	450
Kenton Touring Car, open, driver & passenger, 7-3/4" long, detachable steering wheel, 1924			No Price Found

	C6	C8	C10
Kenton Touring Car, open, driver and passenger, 1923, 9" long	650	975	1300
Kenton Tow Auto, 1920s, 9-1/2" long	1600	2400	3200
Kenton Yellow Cab, 1950s, 6-3/8" long	300	450	600

KEYSTONE

Keystone, of Boston, had an odd assortment of products: movie projectors, steel trucks, wooden boats and pressed-wood forts and garages. Founded in June, 1922 or 1923 by Chester Rimmer and Arthur Jackson, it was first located in a small shop in Malden, Massachusetts under the name Jacrim, using parts of partners' last names. Rimmer retired in 1958 and sold out to various companies. Its address in Boston was 288 A Street. All numbers and descriptions in bold type are Keystone's own.

Keystone "Bus Station Waiting Room"; value in Good $100. Photo by Ron Fink.

Keystone "Bus Terminal"; value in Good $100. Photo by Ron Fink.

Keystone Garage "Storage"; value in Good $150. Photo by Ron Fink.

Keystone Garage "Washing Lubrication"; value in Good $150. Photo by Ron Fink.

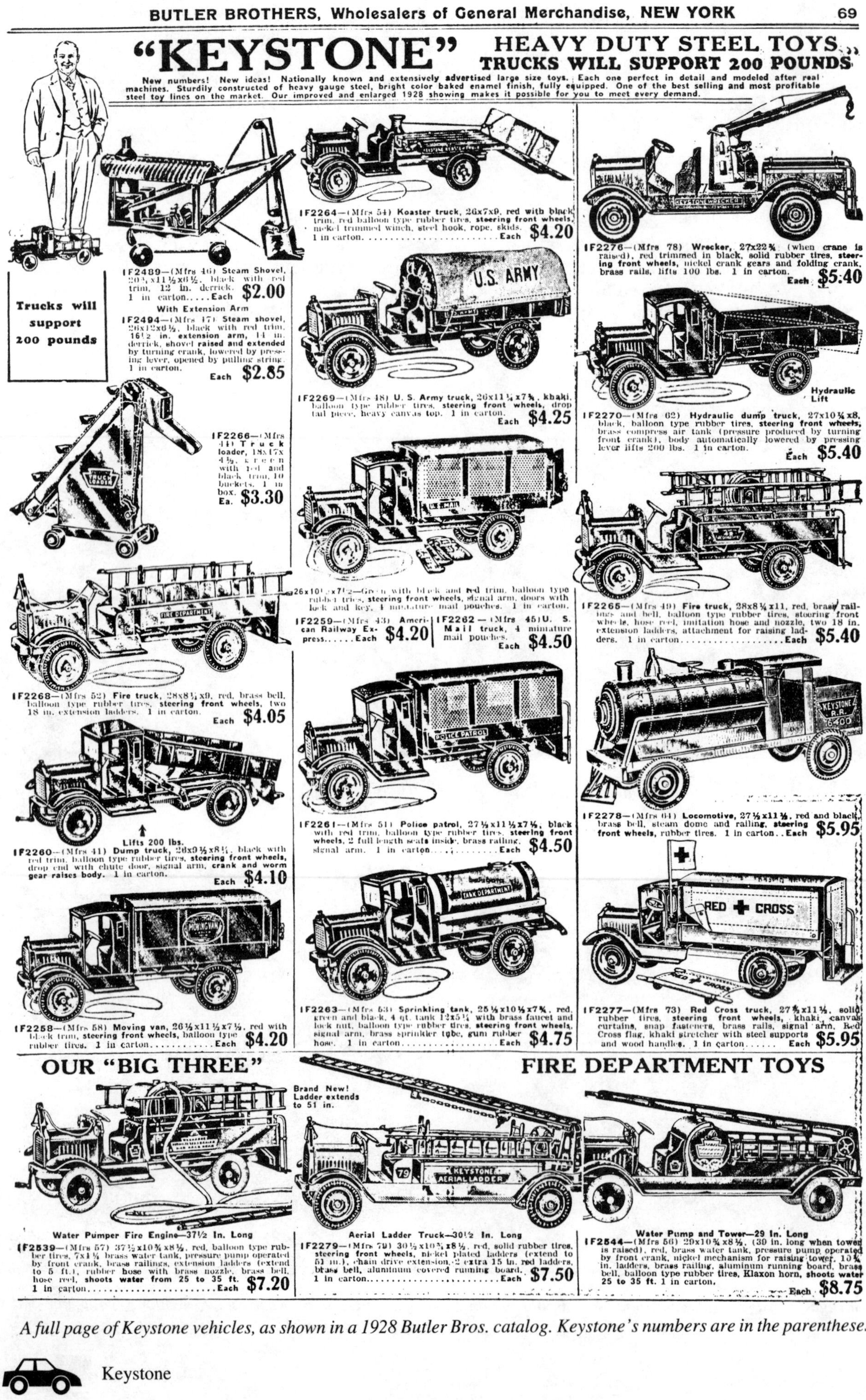

BUTLER BROTHERS, Wholesalers of General Merchandise, NEW YORK 69

"KEYSTONE" HEAVY DUTY STEEL TOYS
TRUCKS WILL SUPPORT 200 POUNDS

New numbers! New ideas! Nationally known and extensively advertised large size toys. Each one perfect in detail and modeled after real machines. Sturdily constructed of heavy gauge steel, bright color baked enamel finish, fully equipped. One of the best selling and most profitable steel toy lines on the market. Our improved and enlarged 1928 showing makes it possible for you to meet every demand.

Trucks will support 200 pounds

1F2489—(Mfrs 46) Steam Shovel, 20¾x11½x6½, black with red trim, 12 in. derrick. 1 in carton.....Each $2.00

With Extension Arm

1F2494—(Mfrs 47) Steam shovel, 26x12x6½, black with red trim, 16½ in. extension arm, 14 in. derrick, shovel raised and extended by turning crank, lowered by pressing lever, opened by pulling string. 1 in carton. Each $2.85

1F2264—(Mfrs 54) Koaster truck, 26x7x9, red with black trim, red balloon type rubber tires, steering front wheels, nickel trimmed winch, steel hook, rope, skids. 1 in carton..........................Each $4.20

1F2276—(Mfrs 78) Wrecker, 27x22¾ (when crane is raised), red trimmed in black, solid rubber tires, steering front wheels, nickel crank gears and folding crank, brass rails, lifts 100 lbs. 1 in carton. Each $5.40

1F2269—(Mfrs 48) U. S. Army truck, 26x11¼x7¾, khaki, balloon type rubber tires, steering front wheels, drop tail piece, heavy canvas top. 1 in carton. Each $4.25

Hydraulic Lift

1F2270—(Mfrs 62) Hydraulic dump truck, 27x10¾x8, black, balloon type rubber tires, steering front wheels, brass compress air tank (pressure produced by turning front crank), body automatically lowered by pressing lever lifts 200 lbs. 1 in carton. Each $5.40

1F2266—(Mfrs 44) Truck loader, 18x17x4½, green with red and black trim, 10 buckets. 1 in box. Ea. $3.30

26x10½x7½—Green with black and red trim, balloon type rubber tries, steering front wheels, signal arm, doors with lock and key, 4 miniature mail pouches. 1 in carton.

1F2259—(Mfrs 43) American Railway Express......Each $4.20

1F2262—(Mfrs 45) U. S. Mail truck, 4 miniature mail pouches. Each $4.50

1F2265—(Mfrs 49) Fire truck, 28x8¼x11, red, brass railings and bell, balloon type rubber tires, steering front wheels, hose reel, imitation hose and nozzle, two 18 in. extension ladders, attachment for raising ladders. 1 in carton..................Each $5.40

1F2268—(Mfrs 52) Fire truck, 28x8¼x9, red, brass bell, balloon type rubber tires, steering front wheels, two 18 in. extension ladders. 1 in carton. Each $4.05

Lifts 200 lbs.

1F2260—(Mfrs 41) Dump truck, 26x9½x8¼, black with red trim, balloon type rubber tires, steering front wheels, drop end with chute door, signal arm, crank and worm gear raises body. 1 in carton. Each $4.10

1F2261—(Mfrs 51) Police patrol, 27½x11½x7⅛, black with red trim, balloon type rubber tires, steering front wheels, 2 full length seats inside, brass railing, signal arm. 1 in carton..........Each $4.50

1F2278—(Mfrs 64) Locomotive, 27½x11⅛, red and black, brass bell, steam dome and railing, steering front wheels, rubber tires. 1 in carton..Each $5.95

1F2258—(Mfrs 58) Moving van, 26½x11½x7½, red with black trim, steering front wheels, balloon type rubber tires. 1 in carton...........Each $4.20

1F2263—(Mfrs 53) Sprinkling tank, 25¼x10½x7¾, red, green and black, 4 qt. tank 12x5¼ with brass faucet and lock nut, balloon type rubber tires, steering front wheels, signal arm, brass sprinkler tube, gum rubber hose. 1 in carton..................Each $4.75

1F2277—(Mfrs 73) Red Cross truck, 27⅝x11½, solid rubber tires, steering front wheels, khaki canvas curtains, snap fasteners, brass rails, signal arm, Red Cross flag, khaki stretcher with steel supports and wood handles. 1 in carton...... Each $5.95

OUR "BIG THREE" FIRE DEPARTMENT TOYS

Brand New! Ladder extends to 51 in.

Water Pumper Fire Engine—37½ In. Long

1F2539—(Mfrs 57) 37½x10¾x8½, red, balloon type rubber tires, 7x4¼ brass water tank, pressure pump operated by front crank, brass railings, extension ladders (extend to 5 ft.), rubber hose with brass nozzle, brass bell, hose reel, shoots water from 25 to 35 ft. 1 in carton......................Each $7.20

Aerial Ladder Truck—30½ In. Long

1F2279—(Mfrs 79) 30½x10¾x8½, red, solid rubber tires, steering front wheels, nickel plated ladders (extend to 51 in.), chain drive extension, 2 extra 15 in. red ladders, brass bell, aluminum covered running board. 1 in carton.......................Each $7.50

Water Pump and Tower—29 In. Long

1F2544—(Mfrs 56) 29x10¾x8½, (39 in. long when tower is raised), red, brass water tank, pressure pump operated by front crank, nickel mechanism for raising tower, 10¾ in. ladders, brass railing, aluminum running board, brass bell, balloon type rubber tires, Klaxon horn, shoots water 25 to 35 ft. 1 in carton. Each $8.75

A full page of Keystone vehicles, as shown in a 1928 Butler Bros. catalog. Keystone's numbers are in the parentheses.

All American C-5 "Cattle Liner." Photo by Bob Smith.

All American D-3 Dyna-Dump. Photo by Roy Bonjour.

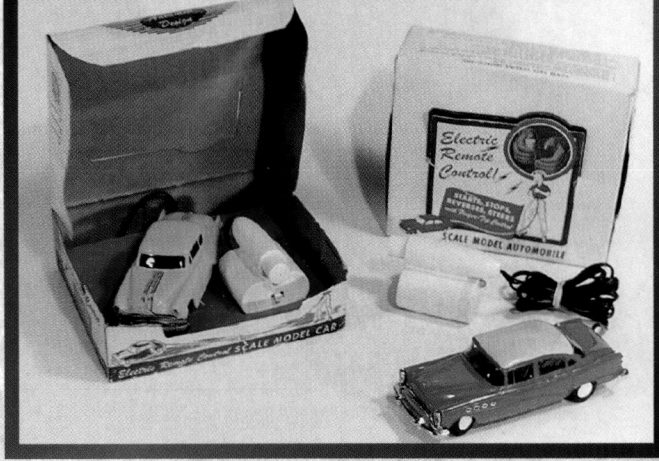

AMT Promo scale 1950s battery-powered and air-driven steering "Electric Remote Controlled" cars. L to R: Pontiac, Buick. These pieces, when sold mint in the box, are worth about $175. Photo by Tim Oei.

Arcade AR23. Courtesy Bill Bertoia Auctions. Photo by Jeanne Bertoia.

Arcade, L to R: AR21, AR22. Courtesy Bill Bertoia Auctions. Photo by Jeanne Bertoia.

Arcade, L to R: AR1, AR261. Courtesy Bill Bertoia Auctions. Photo by Jeanne Bertoia.

Arcade AR41 (both).
Courtesy Bill Bertoia
Auctions. Photo by
Jeanne Bertoia.

Arcade AR93.
Courtesy Bill Bertoia Auctions.
Photo by Jeanne Bertoia.

L to R: Arcade AR83, Hubley Ahrens Fox Fire Hose Reel, 11-1/4" long.
Courtesy Bill Bertoia Auctions. Photo by Jeanne Bertoia.

The fifth bus from the left is Realistic RV3. The rest are Arcade, L to R: AR112A, AR112, AR116, AR170, AR116.
Courtesy Bill Bertoia Auctions. Photo by Jeanne Bertoia.

Arcade buses, L to R: AR113, AR113B, AR113 color variation, AR113A. Courtesy Bill Bertoia Auctions. Photo by Jeanne Bertoia.

Arcade, L to R:
AR208A, AR120
(the latter, with
"Louisville Ky"
on it, worth half
again the standard
AR120). Courtesy
Bill Bertoia Auctions.
Photo by
Jeanne Bertoia.

Arcade AR118. Courtesy Bill Bertoia Auctions. Photo by Jeanne Bertoia.

Arcade AR162. Courtesy Bill Bertoia Auctions. Photo by Jeanne Bertoia.

Arcade AR237 variants: The "USCO" at left was auctioned in the condition shown in 1994 for $16,000, and the one at right, as shown, at the same auction, for $11,000. Courtesy Bill Bertoia Auctions. Photo by Jeanne Bertoia.

Arcade AR259. Courtesy Bill Bertoia Auctions. Photo by Jeanne Bertoia.

Arcade AR260. Courtesy Bill Bertoia Auctions. Photo by Jeanne Bertoia.

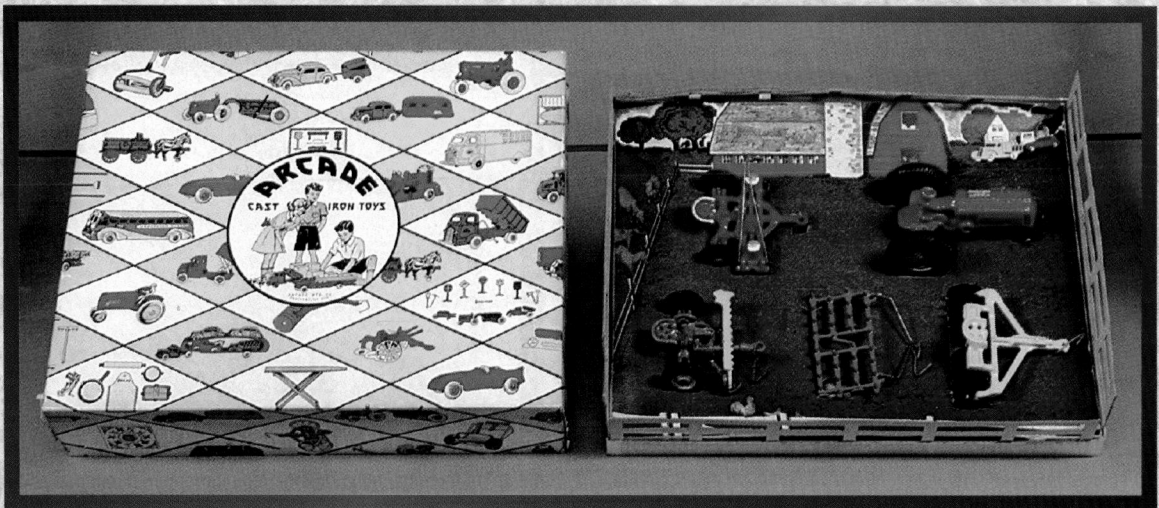

This Arcade Farm Set, 12x15" box, all mint, sold at auction in 1994 for $975. Courtesy Bill Bertoia Auctions. Photo by Jeanne Bertoia.

Archer A29. Photo by Terry Sells.

Banner, L to R: Side Dump, Dump, 5-1/4" long. Courtesy Alice and Bob Wagner.

The vehicles page from the 1936 Auburn Rubber catalog.

Barclay, L to R: BV157, BV75. Courtesy Alice and Bob Wagner.

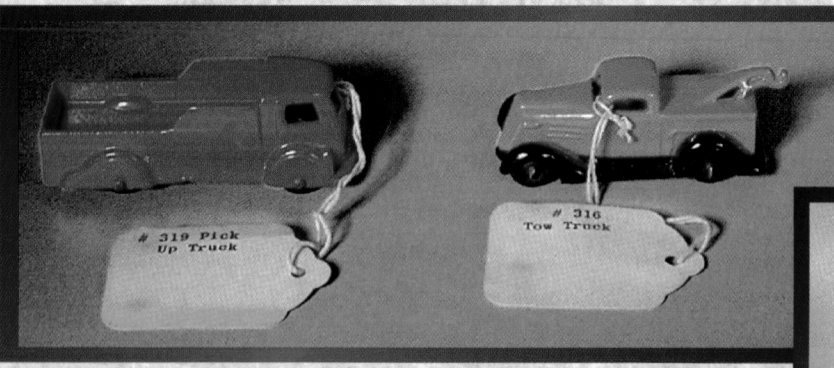

Barclay, L to R: BV166, BV167; both with Barclay factory tags. Photo by Dick MacNary.

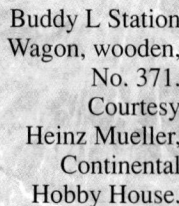

Buddy L Station Wagon, wooden, No. 371. Courtesy Heinz Mueller, Continental Hobby House.

Top to Bottom: Best BEV1, Kansas Toy KTV25, Lincoln White Metal LWV2. Photo by Chic Gast.

Buddy L "Hy-Way Maintenance" Mechanical Truck & Concrete Mixer No. 822. Photo by Tim Oei.

Buddy L 207 Ice Truck Photo by Tim Oei.

L to R: C.A.W. CWV11, CWV12C, Kansas Toy KTV43. Photo by Chic Gast.

Buddy L Army Truck, wood. MacNary Collection. Photo: RLM.

Racers, L to R: Champion, 1935, 7-1/2" long, Arcade AR191, Williams, 8-1/2" long, Arcade ARA, Williams 7-1/8" long. Courtesy Bill Bertoia Auctions. Photo by Jeanne Bertoia.

Courtland 800 Easter Greetings Rabbit Truck, non-powered. Photo by Bob Smith.

Dent "American Oil" truck, 15" long. Courtesy Bill Bertoia Auctions. Photo by Jeanne Bertoia.

Distler BMW Wanderer windup. Photo by Tim Oei.

Distler BMW Wanderer windup, rare yellow US version. Photo by Tim Oei.

Distler Electro Magic 7500 Porsche Cabriolet, battery driven, with original box, battery, and literature. Photo by Tim Oei.

Elastolin No. 731 large Prime Mover. Photo by Jack Matthews.

Elastolin No. 739N with British Crew (camouflage); value as shown $2,400. Photo by Jack Matthews.

A.C. Gilbert Gilmotor windup truck. Courtesy Sharon and Joe Freed.

Gunthermann Vis-a-Vis, driver, windup, 10-1/4" long. Courtesy Bill Bertoia Auctions. Photo by Jeanne Bertoia.

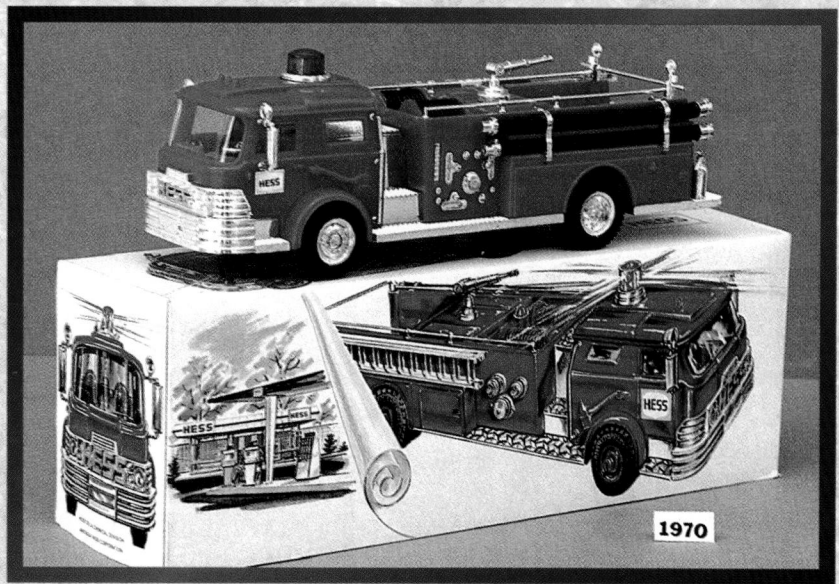

Hess 1970 red pumper fire truck. Courtesy Thomas G. Nefos, National Toy Connection.

Hubley Motorcycles HM8, HM7. Photo by Kent M. Comstock.

Hubley Motorcycle HM13. Photo by Kent M. Comstock.

Hubley Motorcycle HM16. Courtesy Bill Bertoia Auctions. Photo by Jeanne Bertoia.

Hubley Racers, L to R: No. 5, painted and nickeled iron & aluminum, 9-1/2" long, Animated exhaust stacks, 11" long, driver, No. 5, early wheels, 9-3/8" long, No. 8, streamlined. Courtesy Bill Bertoia Auctions. Photo by Jeanne Bertoia.

Hubley Motorcycle HM24. Photo by Kent M. Comstock.

Hubley Motorcycle HM27, with accessories. Courtesy Bill Bertoia Auctions. Photo by Jeanne Bertoia.

L to R: Hubley "General" steam shovel, 9" long, Arcade AR144, Hubley "General" steam shovel, 8-1/4" long. Courtesy Bill Bertoia Auctions. Photo by Jeanne Bertoia.

Hubley Packard, 15 parts, 1929. Clint Seeley Collection.

Hubley "Panama" digger, Mack, 13" long. Courtesy Bill Bertoia Auctions. Photo by Jeanne Bertoia.

Hubley, "Panama" digger, Mack, 13" long. Courtesy Sharon and Joe Freed.

Hubley Yellow Cab, 1920s, 7-3/4" long. Photo by Chic Gast.

Japanese (Etc.) Tin Cars: J286. Photo by Tim Oei.

Japanese Battery-Operated: Atom Motorcycle. Rider jumps on and off; five actions total. Photo by Tim Oei.

Kenton, L to R: Coupe, 1926, separate driver, 10" long, Sedan, 1923, separate driver, 10" long, Sedan, 1926, separate driver, 10-1/4" long. Courtesy Bill Bertoia Auctions. Photo by Jeanne Bertoia.

Top, L to R: Kenton "Jaeger Mixer," 9" long, Hubley Compressor Truck, 8-1/4" long, Hubley Cement Mixer Truck, 8" long, Kenton Jaeger Cement Mixer, 7-3/8" long.
Bottom, L to R: Kenton "Jaeger" cement mixer, 7" long, Dent Road Sweeper, 7-3/4" long, Hubley Elgin Street Sweeper, Kenton Cement Mixer Truck, 1932, 8-1/2" long. Courtesy Bill Bertoia Auctions. Photo by Jeanne Bertoia.

Kenton Bus, double-decker, 12" long. Courtesy Bill Bertoia Auctions. Photo by Jeanne Bertoia.

Keystone No. 56 Water Pump Tower. Courtesy Sharon and Joe Freed.

Kilgore cast iron, L to R: Low Boy Machinery Hauler, 1931, 12-1/4" long, Ford Wrecker, 1931, 10-3/4" long, Aviation Semi Tanker, Ford, 12-1/4" long. Courtesy Bill Bertoia Auctions. Photo by Jeanne Bertoia.

Kingsbury Greyhound Bus, windup, c.1937, 18" long. MacNary Collection. Photo: RLM.

Lehmann tin windups, L to R: "Lehmann's Autobus 590," "Uhu," "Tut Tut." Courtesy Bill Bertoia Auctions. Photo by Jeanne Bertoia.

Lincoln White Metal, L to R: LWV5, LWV6. Photo by Perry Eichor.

Top, clockwise to bottom: Tootsietoy 1947 Mack Pure Oil Tanker Truck, 6", 1954 to 1959, missing Pure Oil Decals, ($80), Tootsietoy Service Station Rack for 4" vehicles ($15-$35), Manoil 707, Tootsietoy Gas Pump Island included in sets 4550, 4200, 5710, 1693, 1815, 1743 and in assorted blister packs ($25-$45). Photo by Impact Photographic Group, Winston-Salem, NC. Caption by John Gibson.

Marx, L to R: Racer No. 3, Racer No. 4, "Midget Special" race car - driver in old headgear & goggles, 5" long, No. 2 Racer. MacNary Collection. Photo: RLM.

Marx, L to R: "Drive-UR-Self" Car, "Blondie's Jalopy," Reversible Coupe, "Charlie McCarthy & Mortimer Snerd Private Car," Lonesome Pine trailer and car. Courtesy Bill Bertoia Auctions. Photo by Jeanne Bertoia.

Marx cars with original boxes, top, L to R: Charlie McCarthy in his Benzine Buggy, "Beat It!" "The Komical Kop"; bottom, L to R: "Whoopee Car" (Yale-Princeton), "Funny Flivver." Courtesy Bill Bertoia Auctions. Photo by Jeanne Bertoia.

Marx, L to R: "Midget" Racer No.7, Racer No. 5, Racer No. 7. MacNary Collection. Photo: RLM.

Marx "Fire Chief" car, right-hand drive (made in England). MacNary Collection. Photo: RLM.

Late 1930s French Meccano constructional car with original box, alternative parts, and instruction sheet. Courtesy Gates Willard. Photo by E.W. Willard.

Meccano 2-Seater Sports Car (non-constructional) Courtesy Gates Willard. Photo by E.W. Willard.

Metalcraft, L to R: Coca Cola Truck, 11" long, "Heinz" truck, with original box. Courtesy Bill Bertoia Auctions. Photo by Jeanne Bertoia.

Minic Rolls-Royce Sedanca with electric headlamps as sold by Bloomingdale's department store in New York City for $1.98. Price tag is on underside of box. Also shown are key and catalogue in color (as included with every Minic in its box), plus separate instruction/information sheets. Courtesy Gates Willard. Photo by E.W. Willard.

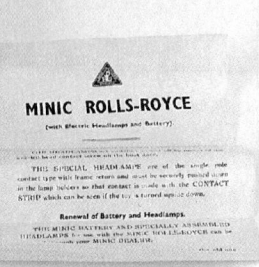

Minic No. 2 Service Station with pumps and oil bin and equipped with electric lamps, advertising Shell and Pratt's. Courtesy Gates Willard. Photo by E.W. Willard.

Minic Bentley Tourers, L to R: 37M, 55ME. Courtesy Gates Willard. Photo by E.W. Willard.

Nosco Vizy Vee Stockar Racer. Photo by Terry Sells.

Nosco Cop-Cycle. Photo by Kent M. Comstock.

Oh Boy No. 100. Photo by Bob Smith.

An original Peter-Mar flyer. Courtesy Mary Gaeta.

Plasticville Gas Station and Plasticville Sedan.
Courtesy Thomas G. Nefos, National Toy Connection.

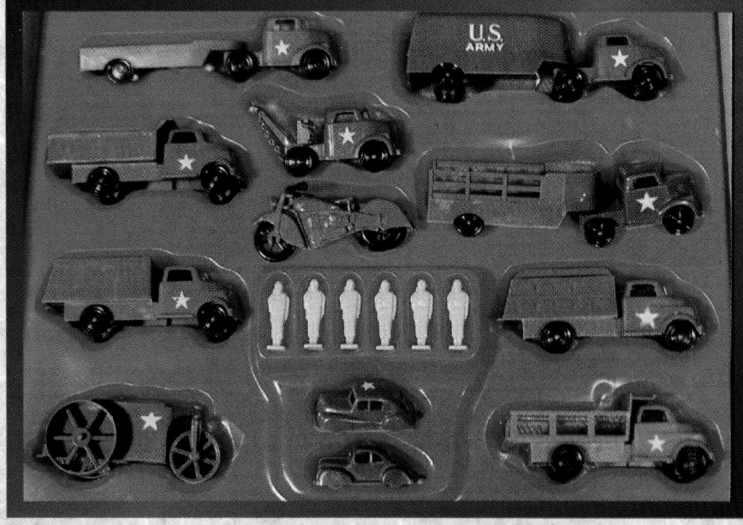

Pyro 21-piece U.S. Army Set contents. Photo by Terry Sells.

Renwal No. 56. Photo by Terry Sells.

Renwal No. 91. Courtesy Alice and Bob Wagner.

Renwal No. 46. Courtesy Alice and Bob Wagner.

Smitty No. 409-G GMC Mobilgas Tanker. Photo by Tim Oei.

Steer O Toys Convertible. Photo by Tim Oei.

Strauss, top: "Green Racer"; bottom, L to R: "Red Flash Racer," Racer No. 21. Photo by Bob Smith.

Thomas Toys
No. 237 Motorcycle
& Sidecar.
Photo by Kent M.
Comstock.

"Sturditoy Oil Company" tanker.
Photo by Tim Oei.

Tonka 1961, No. 140 Sanitary Truck. According to research by Patrick O'Neil, this truck is extremely rare because, according to a retired Tonka executive, it was discontinued in early March of 1961 because of an "unfortunate accident." Photo by Patrick O'Neil.

Tootsietoy, top, clockwise to bottom: vehicles pictured are from the #7600 Bild-A-Truck set issued 1954-58: it includes 2 1947 Mack Trailer Trucks, 1 stakeside trailer w/5 removable stakes, 1 van trailer, 1 tanker trailer, 6 wooden logs, 2 sets tandem wheels, 2 sets undercarriage connectors, 2 Pure Oil stickers, box/liner/accessories box value - $300-350-450. Missing from picture are logs, 1 set tandem wheels, 2 undercarriage connectors, oil stickers for tanker and accessories box. Photo by Impact Photographic Group, Winston-Salem, NC.
Caption by John Gibson.

Tonka, 1954, No. 750. Photo by Mark McManus.

Vindex, L to R: VM1, VM2 (riding cop missing). Courtesy Bill Bertoia Auctions. Photo by Jeanne Bertoia.

Vindex, L to R: Packard Club Sedan, 1929, Oldsmobile Sedan, 1929.
Courtesy Bill Bertoia Auctions. Photo by Jeanne Bertoia.

Vindex "P&H" power shovel.
Courtesy Bill Bertoia Auctions.
Photo by Jeanne Bertoia.

Williams "Coast to Coast Cartage Co." stake trailer truck, 10-1/8" long.
Courtesy Bill Bertoia Auctions. Photo by Jeanne Bertoia.

Woodhaven Animate Climbing Tractor, tin
windup with plow.
Courtesy John Monteleone.

Wyandotte L to R: WY046, WY045. Photo by Brian Seligman.

Wyandotte Coupe with
Trailer WY27.
Courtesy Harvey K.
Rainess.

Wyandotte Circus
Truck, WY63.
Courtesy Brian Seligman.

Wyandotte L to R: WY294, WY126.
Photo by Brian Seligman.

Wyandotte L to R: WY299, WY208. Photo by Brian Seligman.

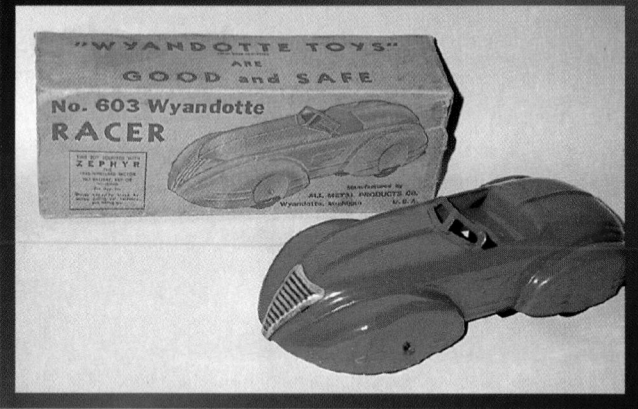

Wyandotte No. 603 Racer (unlisted), windup, 1930s, 9" long;
value in mint $300. Courtesy Don Hultzman.

Wyandotte WY126, two views. Photo by Brian Seligman.

Wyandotte Cord, WY162, 1936/37, black rubber tires, wood
hubs, rev. windup motor, 13-3/8" long. Photo by Tim Oei.

NO. 741—WOOD FIRE DEPARTMENT

This set contains one knock-down fire station; ladder truck with removable ladder and a sound alarm operated by turning wheel on sound box. Packed in an individual display box.

NO. 752—WOOD TRAFFIC SET

This set contains one knock-down garage, one ice truck and one dumping coal truck. Dumping motion on coal truck operated by lever on side of chassis. Packed in an individual display box.

NO. 734—LUMBER SET

A construction set containing one lumber truck equipped with load of construction lumber suitable for the building of many objects. Also contains two packages of building lumber, wheels, axles, block, hammer and nails. Building lumber drilled for easy nailing and may be used many times. Packed in an individual display box.

Keystone wood toys, from a Keystone catalog. The Fire Station, in C6, C8, C10 is worth $85, 128, 170. The Garage in C6, C8, C10 is worth $125, 188, 250. No price found for the Lumber Set, or its "Construction Lumber Co." truck. Courtesy Ron Fink.

	C6	C8	C10
Keystone No.? "Dugan Brothers" "Ridem" Truck, 27" long	1200	2200	3200
Keystone No. 41 Dump Truck, 26-1/2" long	450	750	1100
Keystone No. 43 American Railway Express, 26" long	1000	1700	2500
Keystone No. 44 Truck Loader, 17-3/4" high	500	800	1100
Keystone No. 45 U.S. Mail Truck, 26" long	750	1300	1850

	C6	C8	C10
Keystone No. 46 Steam Shovel, 26" long when arm is extended	425	638	850
Keystone No. 47 Steam Shovel, 34-1/2" long when arm is extended	250	375	500
Keystone No. 48 U.S. Army Truck, 26" long	432	648	865
Keystone No. 49 Fire Truck, 27-1/2" long	275	412	550
Keystone No. 51 Police Patrol, 27-1/2" long	700	1200	1700
Keystone No. 52 Fire Truck, 27-1/2" long	600	1100	1500
Keystone No. 53 Sprinkler Truck, tank 12" long	800	1300	2000

Keystone Garage "Washing-Lubrication-Parking"; value in Good $100. Photo by Ron Fink.

A Keystone tank, wooden, metal firing mechanism, c.WWII, 6" long ; no price found. Photo by Ed Poole.

Keystone No. 41. Courtesy Sotheby's NY.

Keystone, top to bottom: 41 Dump Truck, 43 American Railway Express. Courtesy Bill Bertoia Auctions. Photo by Jeanne Bertoia.

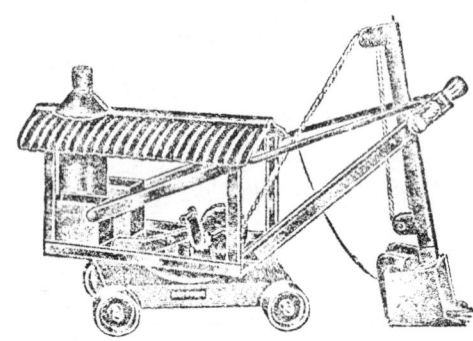

Keystone No. 47. From the September, 1931 Butler Bros. catalog.

Keystone No. 48. Photo by Calvin L. Chaussee.

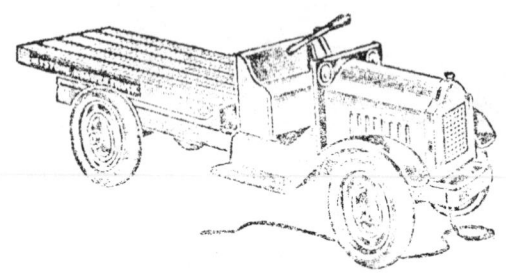

Keystone 55. From the September, 1931 Butler Bros. catalog.

Keystone 56. From the October, 1932 Butler Bros. catalog.

Keystone No. 58. Courtesy Mapes Auctioneers, Vestal, NY.

Keystone 60. From the October, 1932 Butler Bros. catalog.

	C6	C8	C10
Keystone No. 54 Koaster Truck, with skids, hoist cable, windlass, 26" long when skids retracted	800	1350	1825
Keystone No. 55 Koaster Truck, without skids and windlass	450	675	900
Keystone No. 56 Water Pump Tower, 29" long	700	1250	1650
Keystone No. 57 Chemical Pump Engine, 27-1/2" long	700	1200	1600
Keystone No. 58 Moving Van, 26" long	750	1300	1850
Keystone No. 59 Water Tower	1300	2100	3000
Keystone No. 60 Riding Steam roller, 26" long	232	348	465

	C6	C8	C10
Keystone No. 62 Hydraulic Dump Truck, 26" long	325	488	650
Keystone No. 73 Ambulance, military, 27" long	775	1400	1950
Keystone No. 78 Wrecking Car, 27" long	775	1400	1950
Keystone No. 79 Aerial Ladder, 30-1/2" long	600	1000	1400
Keystone No. 84 "Coast to Coast" Bus, windup, 31" long	1100	1900	2700
Keystone No. ?? Express Truck windup, 20" long	105	158	210
Keystone No. ?? Ladder Truck, 24" long	250	385	525
Keystone No. ?? Milk Truck, 27" long	1400	2300	3300

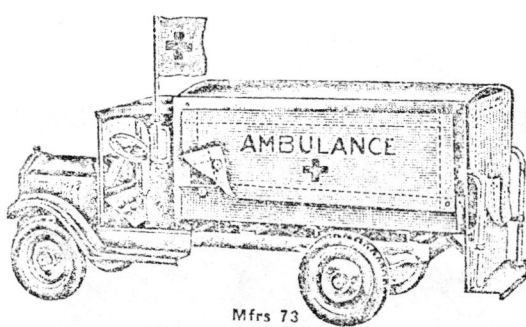

Keystone No. 73. From the September, 1931 Butler Bros. catalog.

Keystone 84. From the October, 1932 Butler Bros. catalog.

Keystone No. ?? Plastic Bus, 7-1/4" long. Photo by Terry Sells.

Keystone No. ?? Plastic Sedans, 4-1/2" long. Photo by Terry Sells.

	C6	C8	C10
Keystone Pure Milk Divco, No. D-402, motor drive	150	225	300
Keystone No. ?? Steam Shovel Ridem	200	300	400
Keystone No. ?? Dump, Cab Over, 25" long	230	345	460
Keystone No. ?? Mack Fire Truck, Ridem, Cab Over engine	235	355	470
Keystone No. ?? Plastic Bus, 7-1/4" long	No Price Found		
Keystone No. ?? Plastic Sedan, 4-1/2" long, c.1950, hood lifts, gas tank fills & drains	27	41	55
Keystone No. ?? Ridem Dump Truck, c.1945, 29" long	200	300	400
Keystone No. ?? Ridem "Water Tower with Real Pump," 1945, 29" long	200	300	400
Keystone No. ?? Steam Roller, red and black, air pressure whistle, brass bell, 20" long	400	600	800
Keystone No. ?? "World's Greatest Circus" Truck, 26" long, c.1930s	1500	2700	4000
Keystone Service Center w/vehicles	70	105	140

Keystone "Ridem Dump Truck," c.1945. Courtesy Joe and Sharon Freed.

Keystone No. ?? Ridem "Water Tower with Real Pump," 1945. Courtesy Joe and Sharon Freed.

Keystone No. ?? "World's Greatest Circus" truck; one of two variations. Photo by Calvin L. Chaussee.

KILGORE

Kilgore, of Westerville, Ohio, appears to have begun toy-making in the 1920s. Its toys were cast iron and low priced. Cap pistols were its most popular line. But it also did well with a number of attractive trucks, fire engines, and cars, as well as scattered aircraft and ships. Some subsidiary manufacturing was done in Lancaster, Pennsylvania, and Canada. In 1937, Kilgore began making plastic cars, trucks, planes, and buses, and later added plastic cap pistols, placing it among the first (if not the first) companies to produce plastic toys. Kilgore remained in business until at least 1978. The first owner, a Mr. Kilgore, sold out in 1921.

	C6	C8	C10
Kilgore Arctic Ice Cream Truck, 6-3/8" long, w/3 interchangeable bodies	550	800	1200
Kilgore Arctic Ice Cream Truck, 8" long	600	1000	1400
Kilgore "Arctic Ice Cream" Truck, 9" long	500	750	1000
Kilgore Auto, "LF 1300A," with driver	180	270	360
Kilgore Aviation Semi Tanker Ford, 1931, 12-1/4" long	2000	4000	5200
Kilgore Bus, double decker, c.1930, 6" long	450	675	900

	C6	C8	C10
Kilgore Bus, plastic, advertised in 1937, 4"	20	25	30
Kilgore Convertible with Rumble Seat, 7" long, early 1930s, with driver	160	240	320
Kilgore Coupe, 4" long, cast-iron	60	90	120
Kilgore Coupe, streamlined, plastic, 4", advertised in 1939	22	33	45
Kilgore Coupe, cast-iron, 1930s, 5"	70	105	140
Kilgore Dump Truck, cast-iron, c.1934, 5-3/4" long	160	240	320

Kilgore toys, as seen in the November, 1932 Butler Bros. catalog.

Kilgore Arctic Ice Cream Truck, 6-3/8" long, with 3 interchangeable bodies (includes stake & dump, plus Arctic Ice Cream). Courtesy Bill Bertoia Auctions. Photo by Jeanne Bertoia.

Kilgore, Arctic Ice Cream Truck.

Kilgore Aviation Semi Tanker Ford, 1931, 12-1/4" long. Courtesy Bill Bertoia Auctions. Photo by Jeanne Bertoia.

Kilgore Bus, double decker, c.1930, 6" long. Courtesy Christie's East.

Kilgore Coupe, streamlined, plastic. Photo by Dave Leopard.

Kilgore Dump Truck, cast iron, c.1934, 8-1/2" long. Courtesy James S. Maxwell/Virginia Caputo. Photo by Virginia Caputo.

Kilgore "Express" Truck, plastic. Photo by Dave Leopard.

	C6	C8	C10
Kilgore Dump Truck, 7" long, 1930s	180	270	360
Kilgore Dump Truck, 8-1/2" long, cast-iron, c.1934	800	1500	2180
Kilgore "Express" Truck, plastic, 4", advertised in 1937..................	22	33	45
Kilgore "Fire Chief" Sedan, plastic, 4", advertised in 1937..................	22	33	45
Kilgore Fire Ladder Truck, 7-1/2", c.1920s	200	300	400
Kilgore Fire Pumper, 5" long, cast-iron	88	132	175
Kilgore Fire Pumper, 4" long, cast-iron	80	120	160
Kilgore Ford Deluxe Sedan, 1934, 7" long	No Price Found		
Kilgore Ford Wrecker, 1931, 10-3/4" long	1200	2100	3100
Kilgore Livestock Truck, 6-1/4" long	165	248	330
Kilgore Livestock Truck, 7" long, 1930s ...	700	1050	1400
Kilgore "Livestock" Truck, 8" long	600	900	1200
Kilgore Low Boy Machinery Hauler, 1931, 12-1/4" long, auctioned 1994, very good, for $2300			
Kilgore Model T Coupe, 5" long	200	300	400

	C6	C8	C10
Kilgore Motorcycles: see end of Kilgore section.			
Kilgore Open Town Car, plastic, 4" long	15	20	25
Kilgore Packard Luxury Sedan, 8-1/4", take-apart body	800	1200	1600
Kilgore Pierce-Arrow Roadster, 6-1/8", take-apart body	250	375	500
Kilgore Police Car, plastic, 4" long, 1937	22	33	45
Kilgore Pontiac, 10" long, cast-iron, 1930 (See Stutz)			
Kilgore Race Car, Rocket, 1930s, 6-1/2" ...	225	338	450
Kilgore Race Car, Rocket, 1930s, 4-1/4" ...	112	168	225
Kilgore Roadster, 4" long	68	102	135
Kilgore Roadster, 6" long, driver, rumble seat	230	345	460
Kilgore Roadster, 8" long, driver, rumble seat	375	563	750
Kilgore Sedan, 3-1/4" long	70	105	140
Kilgore Sedan, 5" long	175	263	350
Kilgore Stake Truck, take-apart, 5" long ...	112	168	225
Kilgore Stake Truck, 3-1/2" long	62	93	125

Kilgore "Fire Chief" Sedan, plastic. Photo by Dave Leopard.

Kilgore "Livestock" truck, 8" long. Photo by Rod Carnahan.

Kilgore Stake Truck, take-apart, 5" long. Courtesy Bill Bertoia Auctions. Photo by Jeanne Bertoia.

Kilgore Stutz Roadster. Courtesy Sotheby's NY.

Kilgore Tank, 2-1/2" long. Photo by Ed Poole.

Kilgore "Taxi." Photo by Dave Leopard.

Kilgore "Toy Town Delivery" Truck, 6-1/8" long. Courtesy Bill Bertoia Auctions. Photo by Jeanne Bertoia.

When Kilgore adopted Bakelite Plastics—

"JEWELS FOR PLAYTHINGS"
found nation-wide markets

THE adoption of Bakelite plastics proved a master stroke of merchandising for the Kilgore Mfg. Co. Serious disadvantages of toys formerly made from cast iron ... limitations in design and manufacture, and excessive weight that prevented distant shipment ... were eliminated. Now, since Kilgore "discovered" Bakelite plastics, they state:

"We have been able to expand into other items which can be marketed nation-wide and have created various specialties which never could have been developed if we had not changed our manufacturing facilities to make them out of Bakelite materials."

The new Bakelite plastics toys justify the title "Jewels for Playthings." Sharp edges are gone; details are precise; colors are rich and permanent. The toys are lighter, safer, more attractive and practically "child-proof."

Your playthings too may profit from the sales and production advantages of Bakelite plastics. They are available in all colors ... in transparent, translucent and opaque effects ... in phenolic, urea, cellulose-acetate and polystyrene types. Write for Portfolio 48 of illustrated booklets describing these materials.

Bakelite Corporation, 247 Park Avenue, New York
Chicago: 43 East Ohio Street
BAKELITE CORP. OF CANADA, LTD., 163 Dufferin Street, Toronto
West Coast: Electrical Specialty Co., Inc., San Francisco, Los Angeles, Seattle

BAKELITE

The registered trade marks shown above correspond respectively, or unlimited quantity, it symbolizes the entire manufactured by Bakelite Corporation. Under the capital "B" is the number of present and future uses of Bakelite Corporation's products.

PLASTICS HEADQUARTERS

VISIT THE BAKELITE EXHIBIT, HALL OF INDUSTRIAL SCIENCE, NEW YORK WORLD'S FAIR 1939

This June, 1939 Playthings ad shows Kilgore's new plastic toys in the foreground, with the cast iron versions at the rear. Courtesy Playthings Magazine.

	C6	C8	C10
Kilgore Stutz Roadster, 13 parts	1100	1500	2500
Kilgore Tank, 2-1/2" long, cast-iron	30	45	60
Kilgore "Taxi," plastic, 4", advertised in 1937	22	33	45

	C6	C8	C10
Kilgore "Toy Town Delivery" Truck, 6-1/8" long	200	300	400
Kilgore Tractor w/scoop	100	150	200

KILGORE MOTORCYCLES

(list by Kent M. Comstock)

	C6	C8	C10
(KM1) Motorcycle Solo, police, white rubber tires, 4"	75	100	150
(KM2) Motorcycle Trike "Special Delivery," white rubber tires, 4-1/4"	150	225	350
(KM3) Motorcycle with sidecar, nickel wheels, 4-1/4"	125	200	300
(KM4) Motorcycle with sidecar, nickel wheels, 5"	175	250	400
(KM5) Motorcycle Solo, rubber tires, 5-3/4"	150	225	350
(KM6) Motorcycle Solo, removable rider, rubber tires, 6-1/2"	400	600	1000

	C6	C8	C10
(KM7) Motorcycle with delivery box, nickel wheels, 5-7/8"	250	500	750

NOTE: All Kilgore MC have cast-in drivers except for #6 which has a removable driver. This is not a complete list, although it is close.

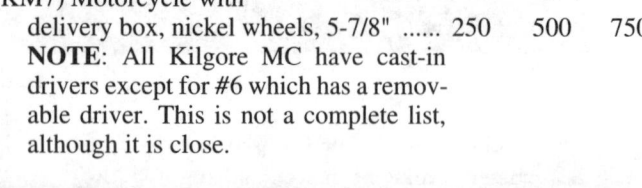

Kilgore, L to R: KM2, KM4. Photo by Kent M. Comstock.

Kilgore Motorcycle KM7. Photo by Kent M. Comstock.

KINGSBURY

Kingsbury had its origins in 1886 in Keene, New Hampshire. Its owner was Harry T. Kingsbury, who bought the Wilkins Toy Co., apparently not phasing out that firm's name until 1919. Steel and spring motors characterize Kingsbury's toys, with cars, fire engines, farm equipment, and racing cars as its primary output. Kingsbury is still in business, but apparently gave up toy production in 1942.

Kingsbury Aerial Ladder Truck, pressed steel windup c.1941, 24" long, ladder rises automatically to height of 38 inches when the truck runs into any obstruction, fireman on ladder climbs up and down by turning crank at base of ladder, early version new in 1905..	250	375	575
Kingsbury Aerial Ladder Truck, windup, c.1920s, 33" long	1200	2000	2850
Kingsbury Aerial Ladder Truck, c.1920s, 9" long windup	262	393	525

Kingsbury Airflow, c.1934, pressed steel, rubber tires, 14" long	275	375	600
Kingsbury Airflow, clockwork, 14" long ..	275	375	600
Kingsbury Army Truck, c.1941	112	168	225
Kingsbury Auto, very early, 9-3/4" long, steel windup	350	525	700
Kingsbury Auto Delivery Truck No. 749, c.1908	750	1300	1800
Kingsbury Bluebird Racer	800	1300	2000
Kingsbury Brougham Sedan, 13" long, pressed steel windup	600	1000	1400

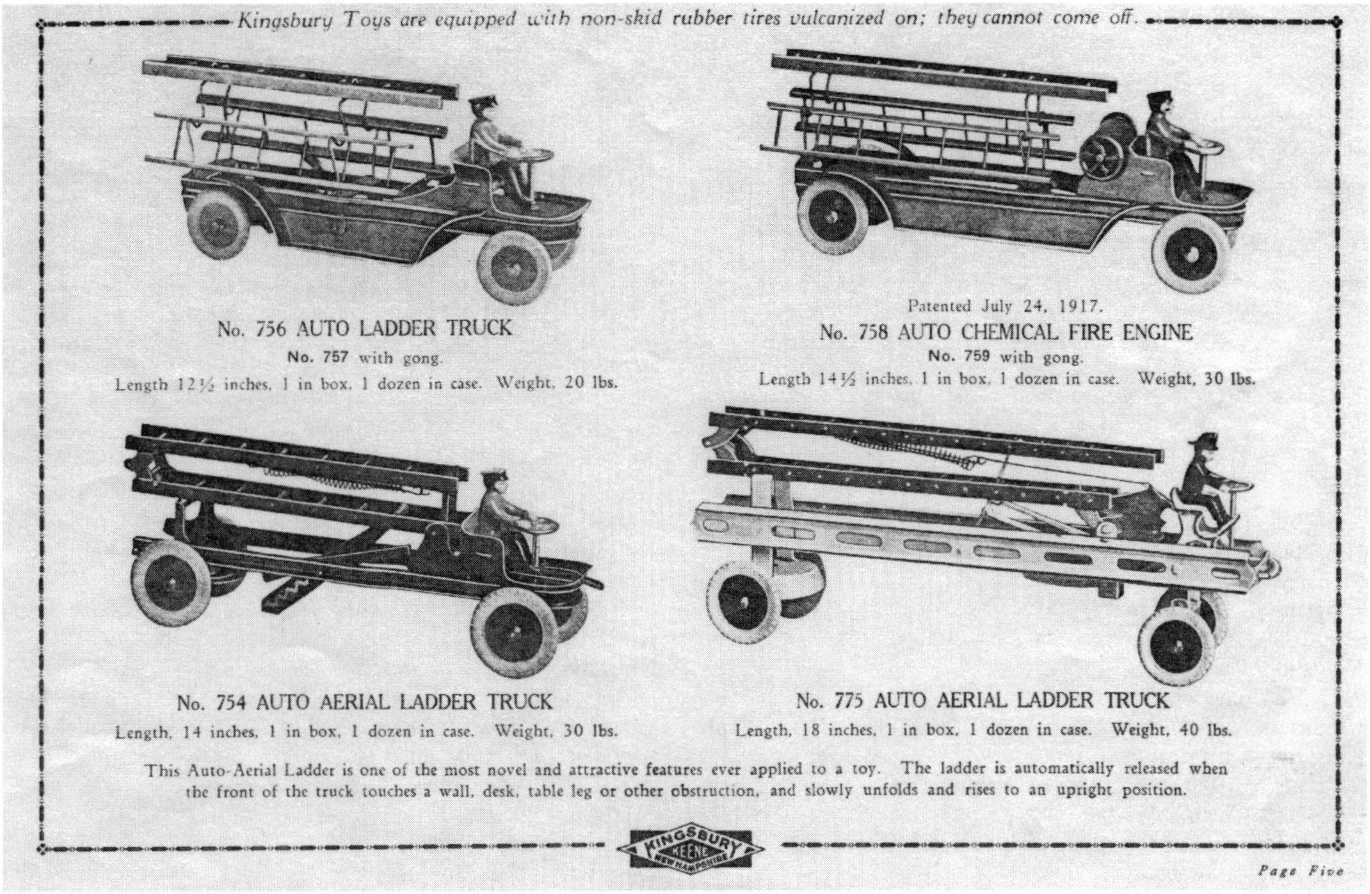

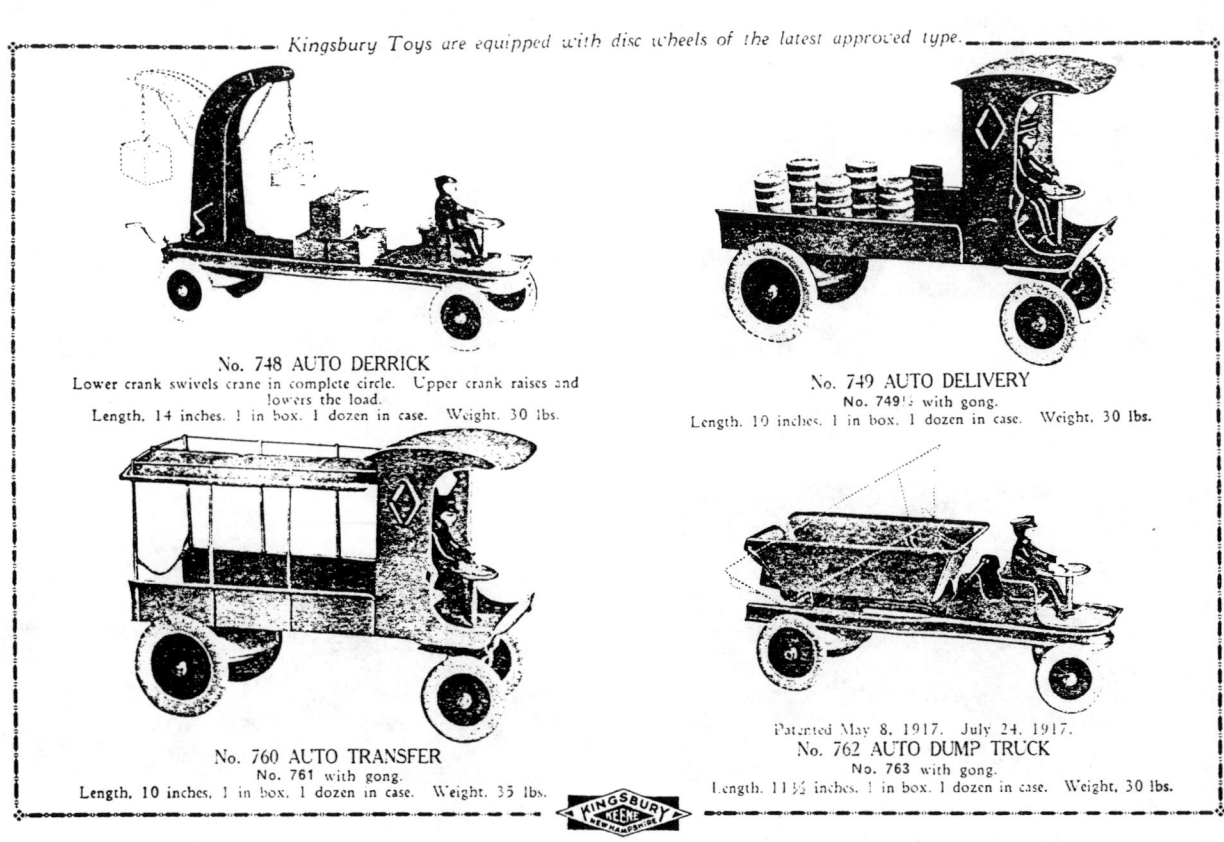

Kingsbury Toys are equipped with non-skid rubber tires vulcanized on; they cannot come off.
No. 756 AUTO LADDER TRUCK
No. 757 with gong.
Length 12½ inches, 1 in box, 1 dozen in case. Weight, 20 lbs.
Patented July 24, 1917.
No. 758 AUTO CHEMICAL FIRE ENGINE
No. 759 with gong.
Length 14½ inches, 1 in box, 1 dozen in case. Weight, 30 lbs.
No. 754 AUTO AERIAL LADDER TRUCK
Length, 14 inches, 1 in box, 1 dozen in case. Weight, 30 lbs.
No. 775 AUTO AERIAL LADDER TRUCK
Length, 18 inches, 1 in box, 1 dozen in case. Weight, 40 lbs.
This Auto-Aerial Ladder is one of the most novel and attractive features ever applied to a toy. The ladder is automatically released when the front of the truck touches a wall, desk, table leg or other obstruction, and slowly unfolds and rises to an upright position.
KINGSBURY KEENE NEW HAMPSHIRE
Page Five

An illustration from a c.1922 Kingsbury catalog.

Kingsbury Toys are equipped with disc wheels of the latest approved type.
No. 748 AUTO DERRICK
Lower crank swivels crane in complete circle. Upper crank raises and lowers the load.
Length, 14 inches, 1 in box, 1 dozen in case. Weight, 30 lbs.
No. 749 AUTO DELIVERY
No. 749½ with gong.
Length, 19 inches, 1 in box, 1 dozen in case. Weight, 30 lbs.
No. 760 AUTO TRANSFER
No. 761 with gong.
Length, 10 inches, 1 in box, 1 dozen in case. Weight, 35 lbs.
Patented May 8, 1917. July 24, 1917.
No. 762 AUTO DUMP TRUCK
No. 763 with gong.
Length, 11½ inches, 1 in box, 1 dozen in case. Weight, 30 lbs.
KINGSBURY KEENE NEW HAMPSHIRE

Some very early-looking Kingsbury trucks; from a 1924 or thereabouts catalog.

Kingsbury Airflow. Courtesy Mapes Auctioneers & Appraisers.

Kingsbury Auto Delivery Truck No. 749, c.1908. Courtesy Phillips NY.

	C6	C8	C10
Kingsbury Cab Over Semi-truck	155	250	325
Kingsbury Cannon Truck, very early, 11" long, clockwork	150	250	350
Kingsbury Cannon Truck c.1939, 15" windup	150	250	350
Kingsbury Caterpillar, 8-1/2" long, windup	150	250	350
Kingsbury Cattle Truck, 19" long, 1930s	100	185	275
Kingsbury Chemical Fire Truck, c.1929, c/w motor, 14" long	1000	1800	2500
Kingsbury Chemical Ladder Truck, 35" long	1300	2200	3000
Kingsbury Combination Chemical Truck, 26" long	1500	2500	3500
Kingsbury Contractors Tractor	150	225	300
Kingsbury Coupe, c.1930, rumble seat, electric light, 12-1/2" long	325	488	650

	C6	C8	C10
Kingsbury Coupe No. 244	800	1300	1900
Kingsbury Coupe No. 344, 13-1/2" long	550	950	1350
Kingsbury Coupe No. 444, 13-1/2" long, electric lights	500	800	1100
Kingsbury Coupe No. 74200	550	950	1300
Kingsbury Coupe, has music box, electric lights, windup, 14" long	500	825	1150
Kingsbury Coupe, 11" long, windup	800	1400	1900
Kingsbury Delivery Stake Truck, 1923, 9" long, driver	225	338	450
Kingsbury DeSoto, 14-1/2" long, pressed steel windup, c.1938	275	375	600
Kingsbury Divco Borden's Van	350	525	700
Kingsbury Divco Grocery Van	312	468	625
Kingsbury Divco U.S. Air Mail Truck	300	450	650
Kingsbury Dray Stake Truck, early 1930s	150	225	300
Kingsbury Dump Truck, tin, driver, 10" long	225	337	450
Kingsbury Dump Truck, 11-1/2" long	500	750	1000
Kingsbury Dump Truck, early 1930s, 16" long, clockwork	350	525	700
Kingsbury Express Truck, late	200	275	375
Kingsbury "Fire Chief" Coupe, 1930s, 14" long	350	575	800
Kingsbury "Fire Chief" Coupe, 12-1/4" windup	800	1300	1800
Kingsbury Fire Pumper, 9-1/2" long	200	300	400
Kingsbury Fire Pumper, 11" long, very early, clockwork, iron and steel	300	450	625
Kingsbury Fire Pumper, 1930s, 20" long	300	450	600

Kingsbury Cannon Truck c.1939, 15" long. Photo by Orville C.

Kingsbury Coupe, c.1930, rumble seat, electric lights, 12-1/2" long. Courtesy Christie's East.

Kingsbury "Fire Chief" Coupe. Photo by Bob Smith.

	C6	C8	C10
Kingsbury Fire Pumper, 1920s, 23" long .	1000	1700	2400
Kingsbury Fire Truck, mechanical ladder, cast-iron driver, 1915, 9-1/2" long	235	355	470
Kingsbury Fire Truck, 18" long	220	330	440
Kingsbury Ford Sedan & House Trailer, 1937, 23" long, pressed steel	350	535	700
Kingsbury Golden Arrow Racer, 20" long, pressed steel windup	465	700	930
Kingsbury Greyhound Bus, windup, 18" long	500	750	1000
Kingsbury Huckster Truck, 9-1/2" long	800	1200	2090
Kingsbury Ladder Truck, 10-1/2"	100	150	200
Kingsbury Ladder Truck, 19" long, early	1700	3000	4700
Kingsbury Ladder Truck, 22" long, steel, driver	150	250	350
Kingsbury Ladder Truck, 33" long	1000	2300	3600
Kingsbury Ladder Wagon Fire Truck, tin, rubber tires, 23-1/2" long	100	175	275
Kingsbury Lincoln Zephyr & Travel Trailer, 22-1/2" long, c.1936	325	500	700
Kingsbury "Little Jim" Delivery Truck, 13" long	300	450	550

	C6	C8	C10
Kingsbury "Little Jim" Tow Truck, 11" long	300	450	650
Kingsbury "Little Jim" Tractor	250	375	500
Kingsbury "Little Jim" Truck	700	1100	1600
Kingsbury Mail Truck, early, 7" long, driver	500	800	1100
Kingsbury "Panama" Dump Truck, 14" long, clockwork, 1923	750	1000	1400
Kingsbury Phaeton Auto, 1900, rubber slip tires, 9-1/2" long	750	1125	1500
Kingsbury "Pure Milk" Truck	132	198	265
Kingsbury Rack Truck, 16" long, pressed steel windup	350	525	700
Kingsbury Roadster, 11" long	350	525	700
Kingsbury Roadster, No. 242, 13" long, electric headlights, spring motor, luggage rack	400	600	800
Kingsbury Roadster, No. 433 - Same as No. 242			
Kingsbury Sand Loader, 12" long	125	188	250
Kingsbury Sedan No. 300	1300	2000	2900
Kingsbury Stake Truck, c.1926, clockwork, 25" long	300	450	600
Kingsbury Studebaker Cannon Truck	150	225	400
Kingsbury Sunbeam Racer, sheetmetal, red with rubber tires on steel wheels, clockwork motor, 19" long	500	750	1050
Kingsbury Tractor, mechanical, 8" with driver	160	240	320

Kingsbury Fire Pumper, 1930s, 20" long. Photo by Calvin L. Chaussee.

Kingsbury Golden Arrow Racer, 20" long. Courtesy Wilkinson Collection, Detroit Antique Toy Museum.

Kingsbury Greyhound Bus, windup, c.1937, 18" long. Photo by Bob Smith.

Kingsbury Lincoln Zephyr & Travel Trailer, c.1936, 22-1/2" long. Photo by Bob Smith.

Kingsbury "Little Jim" Delivery Truck, 13" long. Photo by Calvin L. Chaussee.

Kingsbury Sand Loader, 12" long. Photo by Calvin L. Chaussee.

	C6	C8	C10
Kingsbury Tractor and Cart, tin, with iron driver, white rubber wheels, c.1930s	150	250	450
Kingsbury Transit Truck, 1930s, 19" long	150	250	400
Kingsbury Truck with C Cap, 10" long, tin	175	262	350

	C6	C8	C10
Kingsbury Windup Car, curved dash, driver, 9" long	225	337	450
Kingsbury Wrecker, 13" long, pressed steel, windup	250	375	500
Kingsbury Yellow Cab, 1934.....................	350	525	700

KINGSTON PRODUCERS

(Kokomo, Ind.)

Kingston Duesenberg, 12", w/transformer & steel track	1500	2700	3700
Kingston Dump Truck	150	225	300
Kingston Electric Truck	150	225	300

Kingston Electricar, 15" long, the Red Arrow, 1930s	150	225	300
Kingston Electricar Set, racer & truck	500	750	1000
Kingston Ice Truck	150	225	300
Kingston Wrecker	150	225	300

KNAPP

Knapp "Electric Automobile," c.1903. Courtesy Sotheby's NY.

Knapp "Electric Automobile" c.1903, pressed steel, 11" long, battery-activated	1500	2400	4000

LAKETOY

	C6	C8	C10
Laketoy "John Wanamaker"			
Delivery Van, 10-1/2" long, wooden	180	270	360

LANSING SLIK-TOYS

(Listing and history by Dave Leopard)

Lansing Slik-Toys were made in Lansing, Iowa, and sometimes bear the name "Kipp," in addition to the "Lansing" and "Slik-Toy" trademarks. Most Slik-Toys are made of aluminum in a single casting, but some were made of hard plastic. All Slik-Toys I have seen have a four-digit number beginning with "9." If a toy bears such a number, even if it has no other markings, it is almost surely a Slik-Toy.

A Lansing Slik-Toys ad as seen in the July, 1946 Toys & Novelties. *Courtesy Dick MacNary.*

*Lansing Slik-Toys, L to R:
Pickup No. 9703, Tank Truck
No. 9705, Sedan No. 9702.
Photo by Dave Leopard.*

	C6	C8	C10
Bulldozer	65	98	130
Combine	150	225	300
Corn Picker (goes with Oliver 77 Tractor)	225	338	450
Grader, 9-1/2" long	50	75	100
Grader, 17" long	88	132	175
Oliver 77 Tractor, approx. 7-3/4" long	142	217	285
Sand & Gravel Dump, 12" long	70	105	140
Stakebody Truck, 11" long, No. 9500	40	50	60
Sedan, fastback, 7" long, No. 9600	25	30	40
Sedan, fastback, 7" long, No. 9600, taxi version	30	40	45
Pickup Truck, 7" long, No. 9601	25	30	40
Open Stake Truck, 7" long, No. 9602	25	30	40
Tank Truck, 7" long, No. 9603	25	30	40
Sedan, 4-door, 6" long, No. 9604	20	25	35
Pickup Truck, 6" long, No. 9605	20	25	35
Firetruck, 6" long, No. 9606	20	25	35
Tank Truck, 6" long, No. 9607	20	25	35

	C6	C8	C10
Tractor/trailer rig (milk tanker), 8" long, No. 9610	30	35	45
Tractor/trailer rig (grain trailer), 8" long, No. 9611	25	30	40
Tractor/trailer rig (log trailer) 18" long, No. 9612	25	30	40
Tractor/trailer rig (flatbed trailer), 8" long, No. 9613	25	30	40
Stake Truck, 6" long, No. 9616	20	25	35
Wrecker, 5" long, No. 9617	20	25	30
Metro Van, 5" long, No. 9618	25	30	40
Firetruck, 3-1/2" long, No. 9700	20	25	35
Roadster, 3-1/2" long, No. 9701	20	25	35
Sedan, c.1949 Buick, plastic, No. 9702	15	20	30
Pickup Truck, 4" long, plastic, No. 9703	20	25	35
Station Wagon, 4", plastic, number 9704	20	25	30
Tank Truck, 4", plastic, No. 9705	20	25	30
Fire Truck, 4" long, plastic, No. 9706	15	20	30

LAPIN

(Newark, N.J.)

Listing by Dave Leopard

1939 4-door Sedan, 4"	17	26	35	1949 Cadillac Convertible, 6"	20	30	40
1939 Coupe, 4"	17	26	35	1949 Cadillac Sedan, 9"	20	25	30
1939 City Bus, 4"	20	25	30	1949 Cadillac Convertible, 9"	20	25	30
1949 Cadillac Sedan, 6"	14	21	27	1949 Chevrolet Stake Truck, 5"	7	11	15

Lapin 1939 4-Door Sedan. Photo by Bob and Alice Wagner.

Lapin 1939 Coupe. Photo by Bob and Alice Wagner.

Lapin 6" Cadillacs. Courtesy Bob and Alice Wagner.

Lapin Chevrolet Stake Truck. Courtesy Bob and Alice Wagner.

LEE STOKES INDUSTRIES

Lee Stokes started his firm in 1945 in New Oxford, Pennsylvania. Except for the first three, he created his own models (31 different types were sold; six in 0-gauge, the rest in HO, to take advantage of the post-war interest in HO-gauge trains and accessories). The cars were made of a very tough compound of plaster and urea formaldehyde, so they stand up well. The firm, with 8 employees, sold internationally, as well as in the United States. It moved to Bel Air, Maryland, in 1950 and closed in 1955. Stokes died in 1991. Prices average $30, and up to $50 for the Rolls-Royce.

A 1948 Lee Stokes kit.

LEHIGH BITSI-TOYS

These are heavy die-cast toys with black rubber tires, produced around 1950. Text and listing by Dave Leopard.

	C6	C8	C10
LV1 Tractor/Trailer, "Modern" decal, c.1948 Reo, 5-1/2"	20	25	30

	C6	C8	C10
LV2 1949 Chevrolet Coupe, 2-1/2".	10	15	20

LEHMANN, ERNST PAUL

(Brandenburg, Germany, 1881-present)

By Bob Smith

Lehmann began manufacturing toys in 1881, using the EPL trademark. Its founder passed away in 1934, but the company continued in business under the management of his cousin, Johannes Richter. At the end of WWII, Richter moved to West Germany. He opened a new factory in Nuremberg in 1951. The Lehmann Company is still in business making toys.

Lehmann Toys have become a common word among early tin-toy collectors. These wonderful mechanical machines are more sought-after than any other windup toy and usually command a high price. The company used many different color variations from year to year on some of its toys, giving the collector a wide variety to choose from. While some Lehmanns are very rare, it is not too difficult to build a collection of them. Most Lehmanns carry a model number for easy reference. A box adds 20 to 40 percent in value

	C6	C8	C10
Lehmann "Aha" Delivery Van,			
5-1/2" long, 1920s tin windup	500	750	1050
Lehmann Auto Post tin windup, 5" long	650	1100	1500
Lehmann Autobus, tin windup	800	1400	2000

	C6	C8	C10
Lehmann "Autohutte"			
Garage No. 771, 6" long	200	300	400
Lehmann Baker & Chimney Sweep, tin			
windup, c.1900-1935, 5-1/4" long	2000	3800	6000
Lehmann Berolina Car, tin windup	1500	2500	3500
Lehmann "Deutsche Reichspost,"			
1927 postal truck w/driver, windup	800	1400	2200
Lehmann "Echo" Motorcycle No. 725,			
1907, 9" long tin windup	1000	1500	2500

Lehmann "Aha." Courtesy Bill Bertoia Auctions. Photo by Jeanne Bertoia.

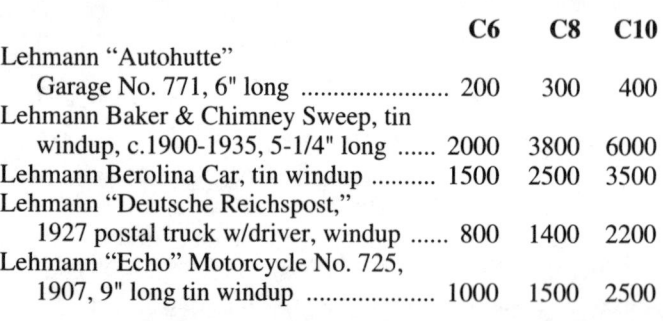

Lehmann "Lehmann's Autobus 590." Courtesy Sotheby's NY.

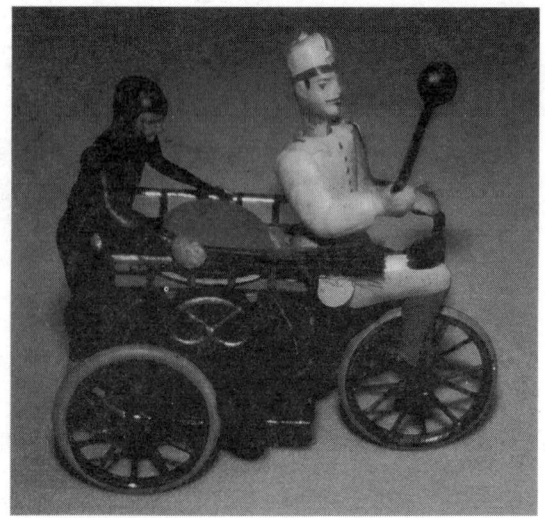

Lehmann Baker & Chimney Sweep. Photo by Kent M. Comstock.

Lehmann "Echo" motorcycle. Photo by Kent M. Comstock.

Lehmann Galop racer No. 1. Courtesy Bill Bertoia
Auctions. Photo by Jeanne Bertoia.

Lehmann, top L to R: Gnom Series No. 835, 813; Bottom, L to
R: Gnom Series No. 808, 807. Photo by Bob Smith.

Lehmann Gnom No. 808 "Autohutt," with two No. 807 sedans.
Photo by Bob Smith.

Lehmann Ito. Courtesy Christie's East.

Lehmann "Li La." Courtesy Sotheby's NY.

Lehmann
"Mensa."
Photo by
Bob Smith.

Lehmann Mixtum.
Courtesy Bill Bertoia
Auctions. Photo by
Jeanne Bertoia.

	C6	C8	C10
Lehmann "EHE & Co." open bed, tin windup	320	480	640
Lehmann Galop Racer No. 1, tin windup with garage	800	1200	1600
Lehmann Gnom series #835 "BV-Aral" Tanker, Blue/gray, 4-1/2" long, tin litho, C.1938	200	350	550
Lehmann Gnom series #813 Opel Dump Truck, Red/green, 4-1/2" long, tin litho. c.1935	200	300	500
Lehmann Gnom series #808 Racing Car, Diff. colors, 4-1/2" long, tin litho.	200	300	500
Lehmann Gnom series #807 Sedan. Diff. colors, 4-1/2" long, tin litho. c.1935	200	350	500
Lehmann Gnom #808 "Autohutt" Garage w/two #807 Sedans, Tin litho. c.1935	500	750	1200
Lehmann "Ito" Sedan, 1920s, 6-1/2" long tin windup	500	750	1000
Lehmann Lana Auto tin windup	1200	2000	2800
Lehmann "Lehmann's Autobus 590" tin windup	1000	1800	2400
Lehmann "Li La" Early Car, 5-1/2" long tin windup	1000	1700	2500

	C6	C8	C10
Lehmann "Lo Lo" Early Car, driver, tin windup	500	750	1100
Lehmann "Lu Lu" Delivery Truck, tin windup, 7-1/4" long	1500	2700	4000
Lehmann Mensa Delivery Van, No. 688, Red/blue, c/w motor, 3 wheel, steering, 5-1/4" long, c.1912	1000	1600	2200
Lehmann Mixtum Comic Car, 4" long	1200	2200	3200
Lehmann "Motor Car Kutsche," 1897, 5-1/2" long, tin windup	270	405	540
Lehmann "Motor Coach," 1920's, 5-1/2" long, tin windup	325	525	700
Lehmann "Naughty Boy" tin windup	650	1000	1300
Lehmann "New Century Cycle," 1907, 5" long tin windup	370	555	740
Lehmann "Oho," c.1903 tin windup	325	500	650
Lehmann "Onkel" tin windup	375	562	750
Lehmann Panne Touring Car, tin windup, 6-1/2" long	550	850	1200
Lehmann Peter Clown Car	1000	1600	2200
Lehmann "Sedan" tin windup, 5-1/2" long	275	412	550
Lehmann "Terra" tin windup	650	1000	1500

Lehmann "Motor Coach." Courtesy Sotheby's NY.

Lehmann "Naughty Boy."

Lehmann "Onkel"; from a Lehmann catalog.

Lehmann Tut Tut. Courtesy Christie's East.

	C6	C8	C10
Lehmann "Tut-Tut," man in car with horn, 6-3/4" long, tin windup	650	1000	1500

	C6	C8	C10
Lehmann "Uhu" Amphibious Car, tin windup	800	1400	2050

Lehmann "Uhu." Courtesy Sotheby's NY.

LIDO

Lido was founded in October 1947 by brothers Seymour and Effrem Arenstein, with the purchase of Elite Toy Co. from David Krotman. Krotman made plastic bubble pipes, scissors, and a horn. Since his firm was near the Lido Country Club, he also used that name. For $6,800, the Arensteins bought the molds and the name. They opened Lido at 321 Rider Avenue in the Bronx, and about 1960 or 1961 moved to 1340 Viele Avenue, also in the Bronx. Lido's toys were small, always plastic, and eventually, the Arensteins were known as the "Louis Marxes of low-end." At peak, the firm employed close to 1,000 people. In the years after the 1950s, it employed several thousand indirectly in Hong Kong, Japan, and Taiwan. The brothers sold out, due to disagreements, to Bala Corporation of Philadelphia, which liquidated a year later. What was left was eventually bought by Gabriel Industries. From 1973 to 1990, Seymour Arenstein owned Joy Toy.

	C6	C8	C10
Lido Auto, trailer hitch, 9-1/2" long	15	22	30
Lido Convertible, c.1950's	8	12	17
Lido Fire Truck, 3" long	4	6	8
Lido Jeep & Trailer	5	8	10
Lido Plymouth Sedan, 10" long	4	6	9
Lido Racer, 3"	4	6	8
Lido Service Truck, 3-1/2"	8	12	17

Lido Auto, trailer hitch, plastic, 9-1/2" long. Photo by Ron Fink.

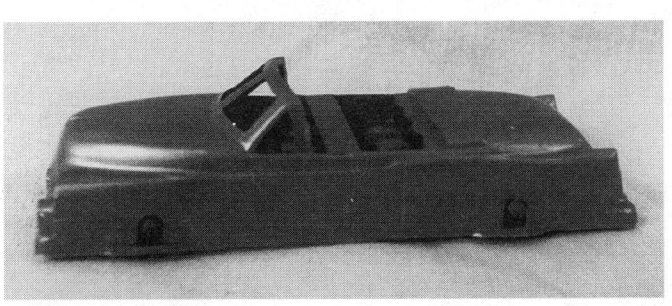

Lido Convertible, c.1950s. Photo by Dave Leopard.

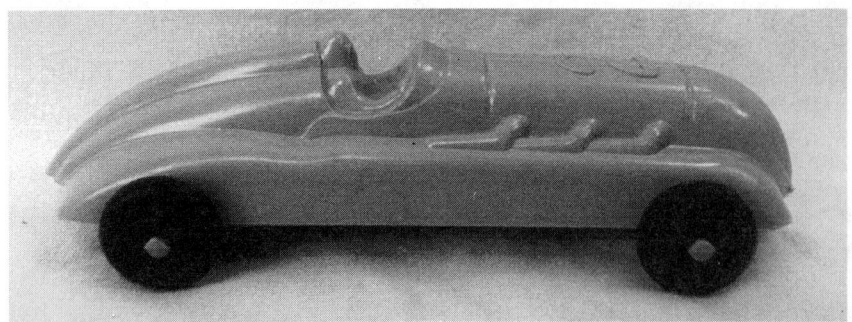

Lido Racer. Photo by Dave Leopard.

LIMOUSINE

	C6	C8	C10
Limousine, license plate "N.Y. 1918" litho, approx. 6" long, tin windup	140	210	280

Limousine, license plate "N.Y. 1918." Courtesy James S. Maxwell/Virginia Caputo. Photo by Virginia Caputo.

LINCOLN LOGS

Lincoln Trailer Truck No. 2977,
    sold as early as 1939 .... No Price Found

Turned stained wood, each set
builds many different models of
log cabins, houses, etc., each set
in box with instructions.

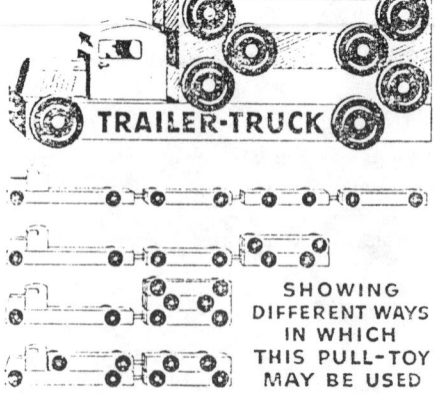

No. 2977 — LINCOLN TRAILER TRUCK. Extreme length 29 inches. Length folded 9¾ inches. All pieces made of hardwood in natural finish with red enamel wheels. A unique presentation of the ever popular truck idea combined with flat cars, which may be arranged in a number of interesting ways. Truck fitted with hook for attaching pull cord. Packed in a box.

Each $1.32

A Lincoln Logs Trailer Truck as shown in a 1940-41 L. Gould catalog.

Some collectors may be unaware that Lincoln Logs briefly advertised that its logs could be turned into vehicles; from a 1929 Butler Bros. Christmas catalog.

LINCOLN TOYS

(Windsor, Ontario, Canada)

	C6	C8	C10
Lincoln Toys "Allied Van Lines" Truck, 23" long	175	275	375
Lincoln Toys Auto Transport, 24" long	150	225	375
Lincoln Toys Cement Truck, 13" long	95	143	190
Lincoln Toys Coca-Cola Truck, 16" long	330	550	800
Lincoln Toys Crane Truck	175	263	350
Lincoln Toys Dump Truck, 7" long	100	150	200
Lincoln Toys Dunlop Wrecker, 13" long	100	175	250
Lincoln Toys "Express" Truck	90	135	180
Lincoln Toys "Heinz" Pickle Truck	300	450	600
Lincoln Toys Ice Truck, 1949	225	338	450
Lincoln Toys Ladder Truck, steel, 1950s	90	135	180
Lincoln Toys "Lincoln Transport," early 50s, 24" long	175	263	350
Lincoln Toys "Lincoln Van Lines"	230	345	460
Lincoln Toys "Phil Wood" Dump Truck, 7"	65	98	130
Lincoln Toys "SandTruck" Dump, 14" long	100	175	200
Lincoln Toys Shovel, 16" long	112	168	225
Lincoln Toys Telephone Service Truck	150	250	300

Lincoln Toys "Sand Truck" dump, 14" long. Photo by Bob Smith.

LINCOLN WHITE METAL WORKS

By Fred Maxwell, Slushmold Contributing Editor, Perry Eichor and Ferd Zegel

This Lincoln, Nebraska, firm is now recognized as the maker of many of those high-quality pre-war slush-mold "orphan toys." This long obscurity is all the more surprising because Clayton E. Stevenson, its founder, was a many-talented personage in the Dime Store Toy industry—an artist, skilled craftsman, and salesman with worldwide contacts. He had made toys at home since the early 1920s (see "Mid-West Metal Novelty Co."); as a salesman for Western Diecasting Co., he furnished some molds to Kansas Toy and may have furnished some to Tip Top Toy and others. He may also have invented three-piece molds, which were his specialty. The third piece was used to cast those uniquely realistic re-entrant front-ends (grille, head-lamps, fenders), but had to be pulled away in order to open the mold and dump the hot toy. These molds and the even more complex molds for those beautiful tri-motored aircraft (Lincoln's Fokker and C.A.W.'s Fords) were surprising in this competitive industry, because it slowed production and added to costs. For us collectors it created rarity.

He had a remarkably long toy-making career—about fifteen years—through the Great Depression. What we know came from a Christmas story in the Nov. 20, 1931, *Nebraska State Journal*, an article in the January 1984 *Antique Toy World*, and from bio-graphical information, photos, and toys saved by his daughter, Marian Horn. Stevenson, an auto mechanic, was born in 1896 and raised in Axtell, Kansas. He and his wife Esther moved to Lincoln in 1931 and started marketing toys in his name at 1250 Dakota Street. For a new business, he had a rapid rise. In his first season he made "800,000 toys in three months." He was man-ager, purchaser, worker, and salesman. As his business grew (30,000 toys a day and 27 to 30 laborers at one time), he moved to a larger facility at 2204 Y Street. In 1935, he was listed at 3433 J Street. The toys were sold to Woolworth, Kress, Kresge, and Schwartz Paper Co., stores, as well as all over the country, especially Cali-fornia and New York, and even abroad.

The factory was sold in 1940, after nine (?) years of production, due to shortages of lead and rubber and the rising costs of labor—all due to expansion of war pro-duction. (We were not told who bought what, although a few clues point to nearby Ralstoy. Although 1940 is the date given by a family member, I did not find the business listed in Lincoln directories after 1937.)

A variety of toys were made—"tiny airplanes, midg-et racers, larger speed cars, brilliant sedans, small coupes, tri-motor plane models, and miniature sawmills. They ranged in size from 3 inches to 7 (?) inches in length". Stevenson, who did the modeling, used pictures of planes and cars shown in magazines. In 1931 for his midget racer, he used a picture of a Miller special. His sedan was a replica of the front-drive Cord. His coupe was a Nash model. His tri-motor plane was taken from a photo of a Ford product, other patterns were issued later. Early toys used metal wheels and tin propellers and had neat patterned bottom-pans. Later toys had rubber wheels. This list below is incomplete; we were dependent on the few toys we have found. Can any of you collectors of rare Slush add to this history? Have you seen a Cord sedan? Could Stevenson have patterned or produced the Cord sold by Tommy Toy Co.? Have you seen a Nash coupe? Others from three-piece molds?

	C6	C8	C10
LWV1 Indy Racer, Miller FWD Special, driver, rounded grille, horizontal cooling fins alongside hood, torpedo tail, 5-1/8" long			No Price Found
LWV2 Speed Car, Bluebird record car, driver, V-8 engine with intake ports, triangular fin with wing design embossed, 6" long			No Price Found
LWV3 Speed Car, Bluebird, smaller version of above, 4" long	55	83	110
LWV4? Speed Car, A V-12 version of Bluebird with triangular fin, Lincoln?, 4-5/8" long			No Price Found

	C6	C8	C10
LWV5 Sedan, Pierce-Arrow Silver Arrow, vertical vee-grille, head-lamps and front fenders faired, 6 open window (OW), divided windshield (W/S), plain pan, 3-1/2" long			No Price Found
LWV6 Sedan, 2-door Chrysler Airflow, hood ornament (HO), divided open W/S, horizontal louvers (HL), plain pan, 3-3/4"			No Price Found
LWV7 Sedan, 2-door Pontiac, HO, grid pattern grille, HL, 4 OW, trunk, 3-7/8" long			No Price Found
LWV8 "Wrecker," high style with chopped top, Graham-like grille, 2 OW, fenders faired bumper to bumper, solid crane with grid pattern			

Lincoln White Metal, L to R: LWV1, mid 1930s, LWV28, mid 1930s.. Photo by Perry Eichor.

Lincoln White Metal, Top: LWV2; Bottom: LWV3. Photo by Perry Eichor.

Lincoln White Metal, L to R: LWV5, LWV15, LWV6. Photo by Perry Eichor.

	C6	C8	C10

and hook, patterned pan
"Made in USA," 3-1/2" long .... No Price Found

LWV9 Fire Engine Pumper with fireman
on rear step. Graham-like grille,
fenders faired bumper to bumper,
patterned pan "Made in USA,"
3-3/4" long, "Patrol No. 79" .... No Price Found

LWV10 Tanker Truck, COE, 2 OW,
6 tanks, 8 compartments, patterned
pan, "Made in USA," 3-3/4" .... No Price Found

LWV11 Railcar, Streamline "UNION
PACIFIC" and shield symbol, 2 OW
in cab, 18 OW in passenger section,
hidden rubber wheels, patterned pan,
"Made In USA," 4-1/2" long .... No Price Found

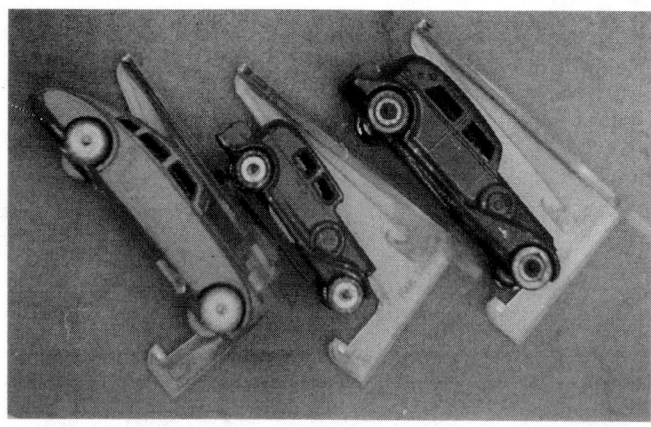

Lincoln White Metal, L to R: LWV5, LWV17, LWV16. Photo by Fred Maxwell.

Lincoln White Metal LWV8. Photo by Perry Eichor.

Lincoln White Metal LWV9. Photo by Perry R. Eichor.

Lincoln White Metal, Top: LWV10; Bottom: LWV11. Photo by Perry Eichor.

Lincoln White Metal LWV10. Photo by Fred Maxwell.

Lincoln White Metal LWV12. Photo by Fred Maxwell.

Lincoln White Metal, L to R: LWV12, LWV32, variation of LWV12 (unlisted). Photo by Fred Maxwell.

Lincoln White Metal LWV13. Courtesy Perry Eichor.

	C6	C8	C10
LWV12 Fire Engine, steam pumper, 2 man crew, hose reel compartment, HO, HG 3-1/4" long			No Price Found
LWV13 Speed Car, Bluebird, w/crossed flag on fin , V12, horizontal trim, patterned pan, 4-1/8" long			No Price Found
LWV14 Coupe, streamlined Pontiac, HO, VG, HL 2 OW, H trim on front fenders, embossed folded "trunk rack," patterned pan, 3-3/8"			No Price Found

	C6	C8	C10
LWV15 Coupe, Graham? slanted vee-grille, divided WS, 2 OW, SM, T, from 3-piece mold, 3-3/8" long			No Price Found
LWV16 Coupe, Oldsmobile, streamlined, slanted vee-grille, HO, HL, divided WS 2 OW, RM, patterned pan, 4" long			No Price Found
LWV17 Coupe, streamlined Lincoln?, slanted vee-grille, divided WS, 2 OW, patterned pan, 3-1/2" long			No Price Found
LWV18 Coupe, Graham?, VG, SM, 2 OW, LI, T from 3-piece mold, 3-1/2"			No Price Found
LWV19 Coupe, slanted hood, rear-mount hub for rubber tire, 4-1/2", slanted grille (see Tootsie Graham)			No Price Found
LWV20 Coupe, vertical hood, wrap-around?, rear window, T			No Price Found
LWV21 Brougham, Graham?, vertical vee-grille, SM, 4 OW, T, from 3-piece mold, 3-1/2" long			No Price Found
LWV22 Stake Truck, slanted HG, divided WS, 2 OW, open stakes, rounded pan, 3-1/2" long			No Price Found
LWV23 Limousine, Graham? VG, MDWSM, 4 OW, LI, T, from 3-piece mold, 3-1/4" long			No Price Found
LWV24 Limousine, Nash?, VG, VL, MWWSM, 4 OW, T, from 3-piece mold, 2-1/2" long			No Price Found
LWV25 Indy Racer, small, 2-man, FWD, rounded hood, 4 cyl., exhaust left side			No Price Found
LWV26 Tractor, small Fordson			No Price Found
LWV27 Bus, Overland, HO, HG, VL, 10 OW, 3-1/2" long			No Price Found

Lincoln White Metal, top to Bottom: LWV14, LWV18, LWV21. Photo by Fred Maxwell.

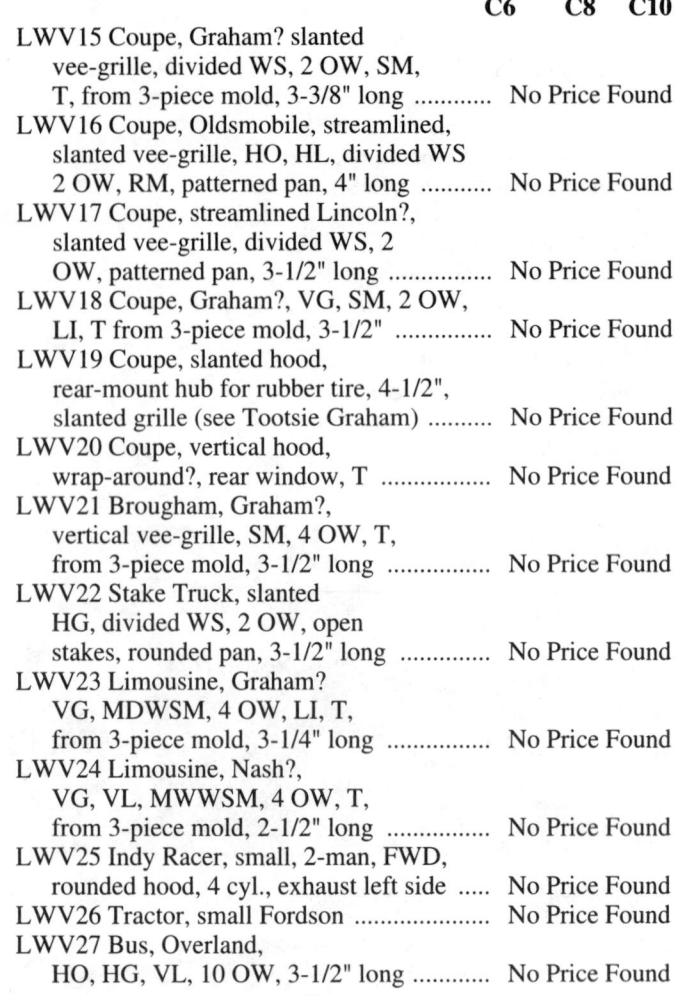

Lincoln White Metal LWV19. Courtesy Ferd Zegel.

Lincoln White Metal LWV22. Courtesy Bob Ackerly.

LWV28 Indy Racer,
    large, driver, slanted vee-grille,
    horizontal cooling fins, torpedo tail .... No Price Found
LWV29 Indy Racer, large,
    driver, unusual grille design .... No Price Found
LWV30 Indy Racer, large,
    different version of above .... No Price Found
LWV31 Sedan, Lincoln Auto Co.? .... No Price Found
LWV32 Sedan, Ford V-8 .... No Price Found
LWV33 Racer. Indy Miller type,
    smaller version of LWV1, 4" .... No Price Found
LWV34 Racer. Indy
    Miller type, similar to above, 4-1/4" .... No Price Found

LWV35 Sedan. 2-door DeSoto?, HO, HL,
    4 OW, very streamlined airflow rear .... No Price Found
NOTE: Some of the above are so rare that they may not have been put into production.

Lincoln used several types of wheels: metal disc and metal "wire" with black painted "tires"; white rubber "balloon tires" then standard in the industry. Abbreviations used above same as used for Kansas Toy Co. Many of the above list came from private collections or photographs. I have not seen realized prices for several years. Collectors of rare, quality slushmold toys should expect to pay above-average prices.

Lincoln White Metal, top to bottom: LWV24, LWV23, LWV15. Photo by Fred Maxwell.

Lincoln White Metal LWV31. Photo by Fred Maxwell.

Lincoln White Metal LWV34. Courtesy Ferd Zegel.

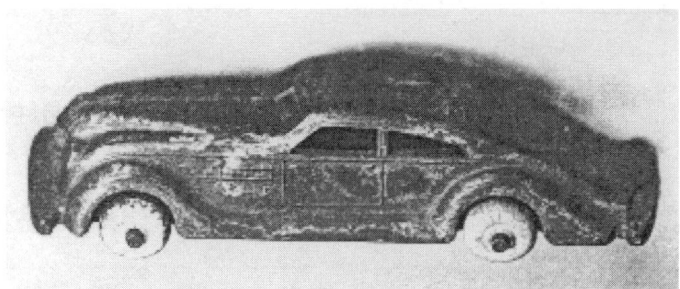

Lincoln White Metal LWV35. Courtesy Bob Ackerly.

LINDSTROM

The Lindstrom Tool & Toy Company made wind-ups of light-pressed steel, as well as tin. It was located in Bridgeport, Connecticut, and began making toy cars about 1913. It seems to have ceased production sometime in the 1940s.

	C6	C8	C10
Lindstrom Bumper Car, 6-1/2" long, tin windup	60	90	120
Lindstrom Ladder Truck, Mack type	138	247	275
Lindstrom "Long Distance Moving Van," trailer only	75	112	150
Lindstrom Lumber Truck no. 160, steerable front wheels, tin, with driver, 10" long	125	187	250
Lindstrom "Parcel Post No. 2" Truck, tin windup	200	300	400

	C6	C8	C10
Lindstrom Racing Car, 1930s, tin windup, 6" long	90	135	185
Lindstrom "Skeeter Bug," 1930s, (bumper car) 7" long, tin windup	120	180	240
Lindstrom Steam Roller No. 181, mechanical, 12" long	50	75	100
Lindstrom "U.S. Mail No. 1" Truck, early, 7" long	500	800	1200

"SPEED DEVIL" RACING CARS

8 STYLES—5¾ in. long, metal, strong spring motor propels racer at amazing speed, white rubber tires on wood wheels, detachable key, asst. litho color combinations.
Assortment—Each car in 4-color litho box.

62-5007—1 doz in box......Doz .92

Set of 10—5 with motors, 5 without motors, in litho box.
62-5109—½ doz sets in box....................Doz sets 8.00

Lindstrom "Speed Devil" racing cars, as shown in the Butler Bros. November/December 1936 catalog; no price found.

LINEMAR: See "Marx"

LINEOL

By Jack Matthews

Germany's Lineol was founded by Oscar Weiderholz in 1906, in the Berlin suburb of Brandenburg. Its military tinplate line was considered superior to all others (although in sales, Elastolin dominated the field). They were authentic; most were painted in camouflage colors. With but a few exceptions, all Lineol military tinplate toys were made in scale for its 7.5cm. (2-15/16 inch) composition toy soldiers.

All vehicles in this section have their prices listed as part of the photo caption.

Lineol No. 1009, early; value as shown $4,500. Photo by Jack Matthews.

Lineol No. 1010, early; value as shown $4,500. Photo by Jack Matthews.

Lineol No. 1041 Ambulance; value as shown $3,500. Photo by Jack Matthews.

Lineol No. 1011 Troop Lorry, early; value as shown $3,500. Photo by Jack Matthews.

Lineol 1206/5 Staff Car with luggage rack (very rare); value as shown $4,250. Photo by Jack Matthews.

Lineol No. 1205/5 Communications Car (very rare); value as shown $4,500. Photo by Jack Matthews

Lineol No. 1211 Command Staff Car; value as shown $1,500. Photo by Jack Matthews.

Lineol No. 1210; value as shown $1,500. Photo by Jack Matthews.

Lineol No. 1211 Staff Car/Command; value as shown $1,300. Photo by Jack Matthews.

Lineol No. 1215 Armored Car (rare); value as shown $3,500. Photo by Jack Matthews.

Lineol No. 1218 Bridge Truck (very rare); value as shown $6,500. Photo by Jack Matthews.

Lineol No. 1225/5 6-wheeled Prime Mover, gray, last vehicle made; value as shown $3,500. Photo by Jack Matthews.

Lineol No. 1225/5 6-wheel Prime Mover, camouflage top, last one made; value as shown $3,000. Photo by Jack Matthews.

Lineol No. 1280 Panzer Tank; value as shown $1,500. Photo by Jack Matthews.

Lineol early tank; value as shown $450. Photo by Jack Matthews.

	C6	C8	C10
Lionel (Trains) Electric Racing Automobile set	1600	2500	3750
Log Truck (Beck), steers via horn on top of cab, late 1940s, large	60	90	120

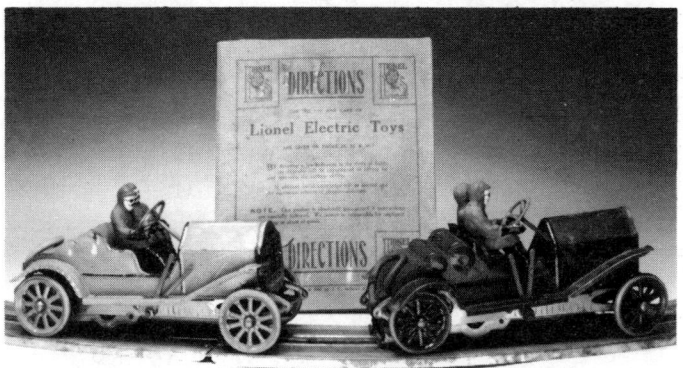

Lionel Electric Racing Automobile Set. Courtesy Sotheby's NY.

LLEDO MODELS

By Iain C. Baillie

Lledo was a company founded in 1982 by (*and named by reverse eponymity by*) Jack Odell (who had been one of the founders of Lesney Products & Co.).

The aim was to create a British manufacturer of die-cast models at more modest prices than some of the existing manufacturers. The company is now probably the only major die-cast producer who actually manufactures in the UK (at Enfield in Essex).

In 1996 the company was purchased by HCG Group Limited (the Hobbies Collectables and Gifts Group).

The first six models were launched in April 1983 as "Days Gone" and consisted of five horse-drawn vehicles and one early motor, a 1920 Model "T" Ford Van which has probably been its most popular with well over 1,000 liveries. The scale of the early models was erratic, especially for buses and trucks. Most models were motor vehicles from the 20s to the 40s with some later vehicles, but in 1996, it launched a new range, "Vanguard," for the 50s and 60s and they consist of 1:45 scale for cars and 1:64 scale for trucks.

From the beginning Lledo exploited the collectibles market and over the years many millions of models have been produced. Its product proved very popular in the promotional market and steps were taken to distinguish general release lines from promotional lines.

The company developed a systematic numbering system comprising a casting number preceded by DG for those models in general release and LP for promotional releases (with a different face-plate). The Vanguard series are identified by VA and then the casting number and there is a PM series of models only released in promotional lines. There are about 88 DG/LP castings and 26 PM castings. There are also a series of Marathons (M or MP) which is a series of 6 castings of

trucks or buses on a larger scale. Each casting number in each series is followed by a 3 digit livery number while the chief guide to this series of models, the RDP guides, applies a final letter to define variants (which can be extremely important in identifying the more expensive models). Specific lines were (1) a grey series of 144 sets of 17 of the DG castings issued in 1986 for promotional use in the USA; (2) a US dedicated series (the so-called 500 series) which did not have printing of logos and comprised about 8 of the DG castings; (3) about 8 castings released under the name Edocar in the Netherlands in 1986; (4) "Fantastic Set of Wheels" in 1985 developed for the USA and distributed by Hartoy Inc. in bubble packs.

The models on general release are generally produced by tampo printing whilst those for promotional distribution are produced either by label printing for small runs or occasionally by tampo printing for larger runs. There is a code 1 label producer Stevelyn & Co., of Hertfordshire, whose models are identified by the prefix SP and are generally runs of about 500.

The models are probably primarily popular in Great Britain but there has been considerable expansion of their distribution in the USA and a U.S. collectors club has been formed.

Because of the concentration on the collectable market from the beginning, there is virtually no demand for these models except in mint boxed form (MIB). This also means that many of the models can be secured for relatively low prices ($10 to $15) but it seems unlikely there will be any significant increase in price for the average model. This does have the advantage for the collector that a complete set of the castings (amounting to more than 150) can be secured for a relatively modest investment, although individual liveries may cost considerably more. Promotional releases tend to fetch higher prices because of the scarcity as compared to general release liveries. However, limited editions certificated editions are increasing quite rapidly in price. For example a two model Vanguard limited edition released in 1996 has already doubled in price.

Some typical prices would be as follows:

DG1-000C Horse-drawn tram Westminster $15 (however, variant DG1-000E is quoted at $160).

The famous DG6 1920 Ford Model T: most prices for general release models are from $10 to $40 but for the LP series tend to be from $20 to $100 and some are even quoted at $250. DGG-033C, a Barclay Bank livery, has been quoted at $1600.

With nearly 140 castings and possibly some 7000 in total different liveries, detailed pricing becomes more impossible but the above figures will give some guide to a collector.

A complete list of the castings/liveries can be found in the Annual Guides published by RDP Publications, PO Box 1946, Halesowen, West Midlands B63 3T6 which publishes the Lledo Guides, Days Gone Collector, and Lledo Information Service but does not give prices.

Iain C. Baillie is a Scots born naturalised American living with his wife Joan in London but, to confuse the issue, their only son lives in California. Iain is an intellectual property lawyer qualified in the USA and Europe and Senior European Partner of a US law firm. He was originally drawn to model vehicles because of the brand names in the models and tends to specialise in Lledo but has also collections of Matchbox and Corgi. He is not sure how these all fit with his collection of military figurines, ducks (model), and ship models to say nothing of neck ties. He is an avid science fiction fan but not a collector of SF memorabilia.

Lledos. Photo by Iain C. Baillie.

Iain C. Baillie.

LONDONTOY

By Dave Leopard

Londontoy die-cast vehicles were produced in London, Ontario, for about five years (1945 to 1950). They were also molded in the United States by the Leslie Henry Company, by special arrangement with Londontoy. The U.S. versions are characterized by the absence of the "Made in Canada" marking, and the larger American versions sometimes had a three-dimensional baseplate, which simulated the vehicle drivetrain. The larger versions were sometimes equipped with a heavy flywheel friction motor or a windup mechanism. Oil tankers and beverage trucks sometimes bore advertising for actual brand names. Either motors or advertising would add to the values below: (O'Brien: There is evidence Londontoy made toy soldiers in 1941, suggesting the 1941 vehicles were also produced in that year.)

	C6	C8	C10
4" Size			
1941 Ford Pickup Truck	15	20	25
Oil Tanker	15	20	25

	C6	C8	C10
1941 Chevrolet Master Deluxe Coupe	15	20	25
Beverage Truck	15	20	25
1941 Ford Open Cab Firetruck	15	20	25
City Bus	20	25	30

6" Size

	C6	C8	C10
Six-window Sedan	No Price Found		
Panel Delivery	No Price Found		
Candian Greyhound Bus	No Price Found		
Thunderbolt Racer	No Price Found		
Beverage Truck	20	25	30
Oil Tanker	20	25	30
1941 Ford Pickup Truck	20	25	30
1941 Chevrolet Master Deluxe Coupe	20	25	30
Firetruck	20	25	30
City Bus	No Price Found		

Larger Than 6"

	C6	C8	C10
Tractor and Van Trailer	60	80	100
Dump Truck	No Price Found		
Stake Body Truck	No Price Found		
Moving Van (tin body)	No Price Found		
Car Transporter	No Price Found		
Lumber Truck	No Price Found		

Londontoy 4" and 6" 1941 Pickup Trucks. Photo by Dave Leopard.

Londontoy, L to R: 4" 1941 Ford Open Cab Firetruck, 6" Firetruck. Photo by Dave Leopard.

Londontoy 4" and 6" Oil Tankers. Photo by Dave Leopard.

Londontoy 4" and 6" 1941 Chevrolet Master Deluxe Coupes. Photo by Dave Leopard.

LUMAR: See "Marx"

LUPOR METAL PRODUCTS

(New York)

	C6	C8	C10		C6	C8	C10
Lupor Ambulance, 7", friction	52	78	105	Lupor Police Car, 1949 Ford, friction, 7" long	44	66	88
Lupor Army Ambulance, friction, 7" long ...	50	75	100				
"Lupor Citrus Fruit" Trailer Truck	42	63	85	Lupor Race Master, 11" long tin windup	100	150	200
Lupor Fire Chief Car No.57	48	72	95				

	C6	C8	C10		C6	C8	C10
Lupor Racer No. 8, 1930s, tin windup	138	205	275	Lupor Seafood Transport Trailer Truck	42	63	85
Lupor Racer, 12" long, no windup	30	45	60	Lupor Sedan, friction, 7" long	38	57	75
				Lupor Trailer Truck	25	38	50

M&L TOY CO. INC.

M&L was incorporated Oct. 21, 1947. It was located on Paterson Plank Road, in Union City, New Jersey, and got its name from the two brothers (or father and son) who owned it, Morris and Louis (last name unknown). The company may have begun in 1946 and lasted till at least 1948. It made vehicles, trains, "jeweled swords," water guns, mechanical toys, and plastic horns. Most or all of its vehicles seem to have been sold unpainted and with plastic wheels. The alloy used in the vehicles was more than 99 percent zinc, with a smidgen of aluminum added. Most or all of its toys were copies. There were about 30 employees. By 1948, it was at 123-33rd Street in Union City. Many, and perhaps all of its vehicles, were copies of discontinued Barclays.

	C6	C8	C10
M&L (1) Racer, 2-3/4" long	17	25	34
M&L (2) Cabin Racer	12	18	25
M&L (3) Fire Pumper	12	18	25
M&L (4) Fire Ladder Truck	12	18	25
M&L (5) Coupe, 1930s, spare tire post	12	18	25
M&L (6) Sedan, streamlined	12	18	25

M&L (1) Racer. Photo by Craig A. Clark.

Top: M&L (2) Cabin racer, cast headlamps. Bottom: Barclay prototype, rhinestone headlamps missing. Photo by Perry Eichor.

M&L (3) M&L (4). Photo by Craig A. Clark.

M&L (5). Photo by Bill Conover.

M&L (6). Photo by Bill Conover.

MANOIL

Manoil was owned by two brothers, Jack and Maurice Manoil. Its sole sculptor was Walter Baetz, the man responsible for Manoil's striking seven early vehicles, which were Manoil's first toys, debuting in 1934. The firm, originally located in Manhattan, then Brooklyn, and finally in Waverly, New York, closed down about 1955.

	C6	C8	C10
Manoil 700 Sedan, futuristic	40	60	80
Manoil 701 Sedan, futuristic	45	68	90
Manoil 702 Coupe, futuristic	45	68	90
Manoil 703 Wrecker, futuristic	80	120	160
Manoil 704 Roadster, futuristic, Pat. No. 95791	45	68	90
Manoil 705 Sedan, futuristic, Pat. No. 95792	45	68	90

	C6	C8	C10
Manoil 706 Rocket, futuristic bus-like vehicle, Pat. No. 95793	60	90	120
Manoil 70 Soup Kitchen, large number	9	13	18
Manoil 70A Soup Kitchen, small number	9	13	18
Manoil 71 Shell Carrier with Soldier on Shell Box, has loop	11	16	23

No. 700 - SEDAN

Manoil 704. Courtesy K. Warren Mitchell.

No. 701 - SEDAN

Manoil 705. Photo courtesy Bob and Alice Wagner.

No. 702 - COUPE

Manoil 706. Courtesy K. Warren Mitchell.

No. 703 - WRECKER

Manoil, c.1935. Courtesy Marjorie and Peter Ruben.

Manoil 69 cannon, metal wheels, wood wheels, wood wheels variant. Manoil Vehicles, Top row, L to R: 70, 71; Middle row: 71 with variant on wheel support , 72, 73 with front tow loop, 74; Bottom row: 75, 75A with siren cast separately, 75A siren cast integrally. Photo by Ed Poole.

	C6	C8	C10
Manoil 71A Same as above, no loop	10	15	20
Manoil 72 Water Wagon, larger number	10	15	20
Manoil 72A Same as above, small number ..	10	15	20
Manoil 72B No. number	10	15	20
Manoil 73 Tractor, loop front	10	15	20
Manoil 73A Tractor, plain front	11	16	23
Manoil 74 Armored Car with Anti-Tank Gun	22	33	45
Manoil 75 Armored Car with Anti-Aircraft Gun	27	41	55
Manoil 75A Armored Car with Siren, siren cast separately	25	38	50

	C6	C8	C10
Manoil 75A Armored Car with Siren, siren cast with vehicle	32	48	65
Manoil 95 Tank	8	12	17
Manoil 96 Large Shell on Truck	9	13	18
Manoil 97 Pontoon on Wheels	22	33	45
Manoil 98 Torpedo on Wheels	10	15	20
Manoil 103 Gasoline Truck	10	15	20
Manoil 104 Chemical Truck	11	16	22
Manoil 105 Five Barrel Gun on Wheels	12	18	25
Manoil (MC5) Tank, composition	12	18	25

L to R: 95, 96, 97, 98

L to R: 103, 104, 105, 200. Photo by Ed Poole.

MC5

Manoil Post-War Vehicles

	C6	C8	C10
Manoil "4 Speedsters" boxed set - Roadster, Sedan, Fire Engine, Oil Truck, price w/box	250	375	500

	C6	C8	C10
Manoil 707 Sedan	22	33	44
Manoil 708 Roadster, horizontal radiator	27	41	55

Manoil, L to R: 708A, 708. Photo courtesy Bob and Alice Wagner.

Manoil 711 with original box. Courtesy Old Toy Soldier *magazine.*

Manoil 711, showing the climbing fireman and the fireman clinging to the side of the truck; no price found for the extremely rare 1" high figures. Courtesy Old Toy Soldier *magazine.*

Manoil 712 with original box. The 1" high firemen are extremely rare; no price found for them. Courtesy Old Toy Soldier magazine.

No. 713   BUS

No. 710 - OIL TANKER

No. 709 - FIRE ENGINE

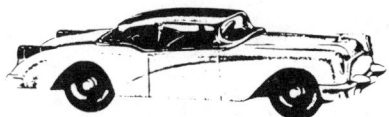

No. 716 - SEDAN

No. 707 - SEDAN

No. 717 - HARD TOP CONVERTIBLE

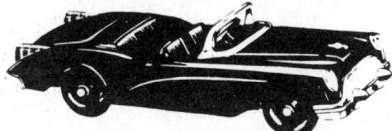

No. 718 - CONVERTIBLE

No. 719 - SPORT CAR

No. 715 - COMMERCIAL TRUCK has removable panels, as shown above

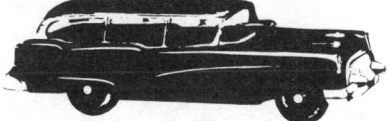

No. 720 - RANCH WAGON

Manoil Post-War Vehicles. Courtesy Marjorie & Peter Ruben.

No. 714 - TOWING TRUCK

Manoil Post-War Vehicles. Courtesy Majorie & Peter Ruben.

No. 708 - ROADSTER

 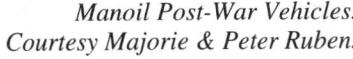

	C6	C8	C10
Manoil 708A Roadster, vertical radiator	50	75	100
Manoil 709 Fire Engine, 4" long	18	28	38
Manoil 710 Oil Tanker	13	19	26
Manoil 711 Aerial Ladder	200	300	400
Manoil 712 Pumper	200	300	400
Manoil 713 Bus	12	18	24

	C6	C8	C10
Manoil 714 Towing Truck	10	15	20
Manoil 715 Commercial Truck	10	15	20
Manoil 716 Sedan	10	15	20
Manoil 717 Hard Top Convertible	12	18	24
Manoil 718 Convertible	10	15	20
Manoil 719 Sport Car	10	15	20
Manoil 720 Ranch Wagon	10	15	20

Manoil Plastic Vehicles

	C6	C8	C10
Manoil P-7 Roadster	12	18	25
Manoil P-8 Sedan	12	18	25
Manoil P-9 Pick-Up	12	18	25
Manoil P-10 Towing Truck	12	18	25

	C6	C8	C10
Manoil P-11 Road Scraper	12	18	25
Manoil P-12 Tractor	12	18	25
Manoil P-13 Dump Cart	12	18	25

P-7 Roadster

P-8 Sedan

P-9 Pick-Up Truck

P-10 Towing Truck

P-11 Road Scraper

P-13 Dump Cart
P-12 Tractor

MARKLIN VEHICLE CONSTRUCTION SETS

by Gates Willard

Well-known today for currently manufactured toy trains, the German Marklin Company enjoyed a fine reputation for quality toys long before 1933 to 1934, when a series of constructional motor vehicles was introduced. Marklin had been making multi-purpose construction sets similar in concept to Erector in the United States and Meccano in England, but now it was building specialized sets that would appeal to the young automotive engineer.

A clever merchandising scheme was developed. You could buy a boxed set of parts to build a complete chassis, but a motor would have to be purchased separately. The body of your choice was still another kit to buy, and up to six types were available by the late 1930s. If you wished to have other types of vehicles, alternative body kits were available. Complete sets with body, motor and chassis were also sold, and some sets included more than one body, but Marklins were costly, and, in the 1930s, many could afford to buy only one piece at a time. The quality of finish is superb, and some pieces are decorated with hand striping.

The group of constructional vehicles could be referred to as "The 1100 series." However, there was no 1102. The 1100 Series was revived after the war, but 1104P, 1106T, 1108G, 1110B, 1133R, and 99R were not made again. Marklin phased out the remaining constructional vehicles in the mid-1950s. Why is no value guide possible for Marklin toys? Very few are changing hands in the 1990s, and not enough data exists to develop a reliable and useful listing of values.

The following lists use the factory prewar numberings.

* - Means not reissued postwar.

1101C Chassis
1103St Streamlined Coupe Body. Early is 2-tone blue, later is all green with brown roof.
*1104 Pullman Limousine Body. Early is beige and green. Later is ivory with gray roof.
1105L Lorry (Pickup) Body. Red/Green.
*1106T Tanker Body. Red/Blue.
1107R Racing (Sports Car) body, red/white.
*1108G Armored Car Body, camouflaged (more than one pattern).
1109M Clockwork motor.
*1110B Electric Lighting Set
*99R Driver (lightweight composition material)
*1133R Mercedes Racing Car, red, complete with chassis and motor. Smaller Scale
1133AL Mercedes Racing Car, aluminum. Complete with chassis and motor. Smaller Scale

Since 1990, Marklin has issued seven limited-edition constructional vehicles that look as though they could be members of the original 1100 series, but there are many detail differences. The Tanker, Racing Car, and Lorry are very similar to the originals, but the three vans and the Fire Engine are probably based upon 1930s prototypes that had never reached production. Perhaps one of these could have been the missing link, Number 1102! All of the "new" Marklins have electric headlights and were completely assembled at the factory. It remains to be seen whether there will be additions to the series.

VEHICLE	YEAR PRODUCED	FACTORY NUMBER
Reichspost (Postal Van) yellow/black	1990	1990
Fire Engine, red	1991	1991
Lorry, red/green	1992	1992
Standard Tanker, red/blue	1993	1993

Marklin: Assembled No. 1101C chassis with parts box, cast iron key, and tools; 1109M clockwork motor is installed. Courtesy Gates Willard. Photo by Ed Poole.

Marklin 1103 St. Streamlined Coupe. Courtesy Gates Willard. Photo by E.W. Willard.

Marklin 1104P Pullman Limousine. Courtesy Gates Willard. Photo by E.W. Willard.

Marklin 1105L Lorry. Courtesy Gates Willard. Photo by E.W. Willard.

Marklin 1106T Tanker, shown with original box; two tinplate cars were included. Photo by E.W. Willard. Courtesy Gates Willard.

Marklin 1107R racing car with original composition 99R driver; behind it is the unassembled car in its box. Courtesy Gates Willard. Photo by E.W. Willard.

Marklin 1108G Armored Car. Photo by E.W. Willard. Courtesy Gates Willard.

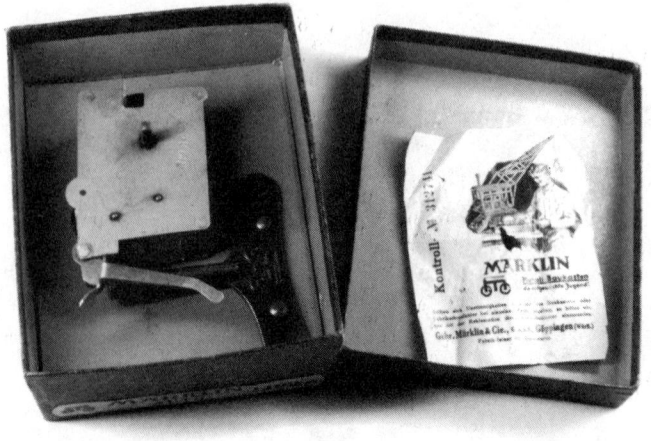

Marklin boxed 1109M Clockwork Motor with cast-iron key. Courtesy Gates Willard. Photo by E.W. Willard.

VEHICLE	YEAR PRODUCED	FACTORY NUMBER
Geld Transporter (Armored Truck), blue/black	1993	1101
Reichspost (Postal Van), dark red/black	1994	1989
Racing Car, red/white	1995	1103

End Marklin by Gates Willard

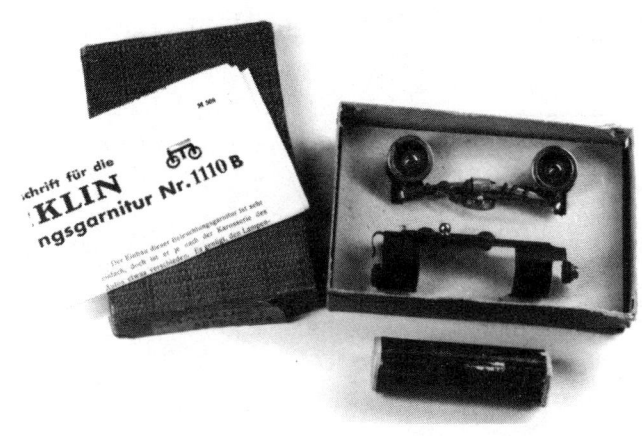

Marklin box 1110B Lighting Set with instructions and original battery. Courtesy Gates Willard. Photo by E.W. Willard.

Marklin 1133R Mercedes Racing Car (smaller scale) with composition driver and cast iron key. Courtesy Gates Willard. Photo by E.W. Willard.

Marklin limited edition trucks L to R: Postal Van (1990), Fire Engine (1991), and Lorry (1992); all have working electric headlights. Courtesy Gates Willard. Photo by E.W. Willard.

Marklin, L to R: Standard Tanker (1993), Geld Transporter (1993). Courtesy Gates Willard. Photo by E.W. Willard.

Marklin, L to R limited editions: Reichspost Van (1994), Racing Car (1995). Courtesy Gates Willard. Photo by E.W. Willard.

	C6	C8	C10
Marklin Mercedes Racing Car, 12" long, windup	425	638	850
Marklin Road Working Machine, 3-5/8" long	100	150	200
Marklin Armored Car, camouflaged, 14-1/2" long	1000	1700	2400
Marklin Kubelwagen, die-cast, 3-1/2" long	325	490	650

	C6	C8	C10
Marklin 308 ELR Racer, 12"	250	375	500
Marklin Troop Carrier, die-cast metal, 4-1/2" long	325	490	650
Marklin Troop Carrier, die-cast metal, 10 wheels, 5" long	450	675	900
Marklin Water Truck, early, faucet works, 15" long	1300	2500	3600

Marklin Road Working Machine, 3-5/8" long. Courtesy James S. Maxwell Jr./Virginia Caputo. Photo by Virginia Caputo.

Marklin Kubelwagen, die-cast, 3-1/2" long. Photo by Terry Sells.

Marklin Troop Carrier, die-cast metal, 4-1/2" long. Photo by Terry Sells.

Marklin Troop Carrier, die-cast metal, 5" long. Photo by Terry Sells.

Marklin Water Truck, early, working faucet, 15" long. Courtesy Bill Bertoia Auctions. Photo by Jeanne Bertoia.

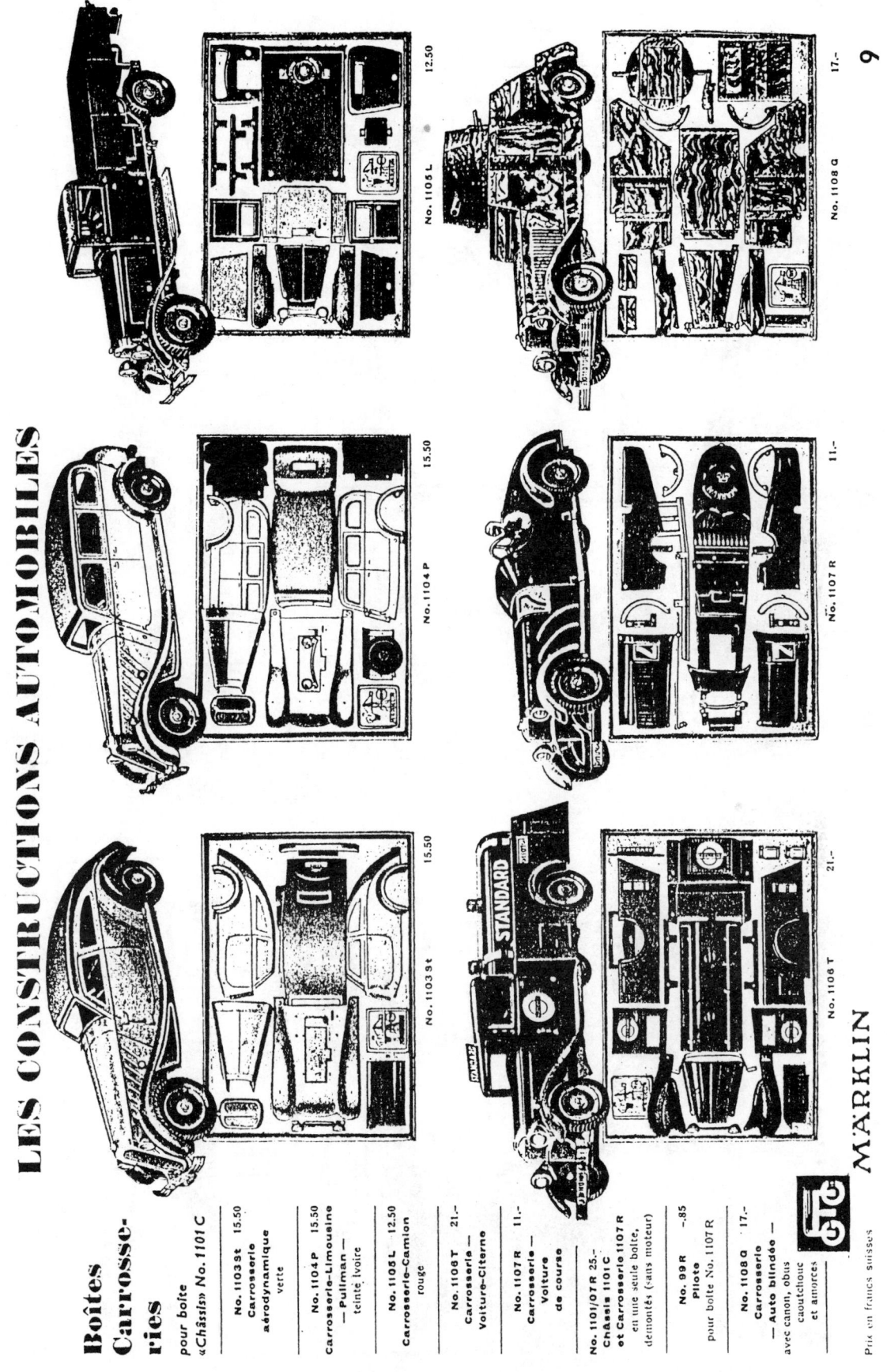

LES CONSTRUCTIONS AUTOMOBILES

MARKLIN

Boîtes Carrosseries

pour boîte
«Châssis» No. 1101 C

No. 1103 St   15.50
Carrosserie
aérodynamique
verte

No. 1104 P   15.50
Carrosserie-Limousine
—Pullman—
teinté ivoire

No. 1105 L   12.50
Carrosserie-Camion
rouge

No. 1106 T   21.—
Carrosserie —
Voiture-Citerne

No. 1107 R   11.—
Carrosserie —
Voiture
de course

No. 1101/07 R   25.—
Châssis 1101 C
et Carrosserie 1107 R
en une seule boîte,
démontés (sans moteur)

No. 99 R   —.85
Pilote
pour boîte No. 1107 R

No. 1108 Q   17.—
Carrosserie
— Auto blindée —
avec canon, obus
caoutchouc
et amorces

Prix en francs suisses

1939-40 Marklin catalog. Courtesy Gates Willard.

Les Constructions — Automobiles

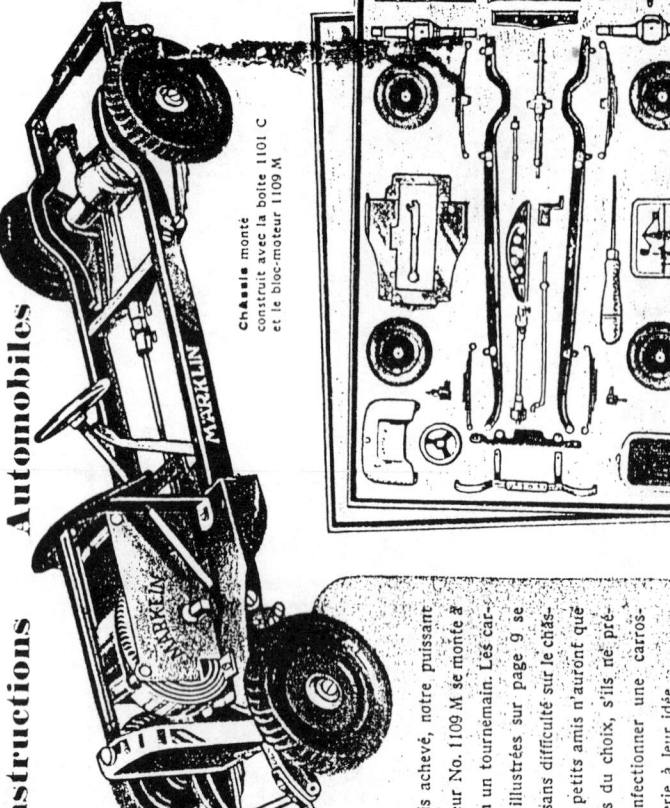

Châssis monté
construit avec la boîte 1101 C
et le bloc-moteur 1109 M

Le châssis achevé, notre puissant bloc-moteur No. 1109 M se monte à l'avant en un tournemain. Les carrosseries illustrées sur page 9 se montent sans difficulté sur le châssis et nos petits amis s'ils ne préfèrent confectionner une carrosserie à leur idée.

No. 1101 C   16.—
Boîte CHÂssis – boîte fondamentale–contenant toutes les pièces pour construire le châssis ci-dessus (sans moteur). Manuel illustré avec historique de l'auto

La boîte Châssis No. 1101 C constitue la boîte fondamentale, elle sert de point de départ à toutes les voitures. Cette boîte permet de réaliser un véritable châssis d'automobile de 36 cm de longueur. Toutes les parties sont conformes, le cadre, la suspension, le différentiel, le cardan, la direction etc. Le manuel qui est joint à la boîte, facilite le montage par des descriptions détaillées et de nombreuses illustrations

La fabrique ne livre pas directement aux particuliers

No. 1110 B   3.—
Phares électriques
avec ampoules 2½ volts
(sans pile-torche)

No. 1109 M   6.—
Bloc-Moteur
boîte avec moteur et clef, pour chassis 1101 C

MÄRKLIN

Voiture de course Mercédès

Nouvelle boîte de construction contenant toutes les pièces. y compris le moteur, pour monter la fameuse Mercédès qui a gagné tant de grandes épreuves. Châssis avec roues indépendantes, direction réglable, carrosserie aérodynamique, puissant moteur à grande vitesse. Livrée avec pilote. Montage facile, manuel illustré.

Longueur châssis 21 cm,
longueur totale 29 cm.

Voiture de course Mercédès, construite avec la boîte 1133 AL. Voiture livrée toute montée pour les amateurs qui ne s'intéressent pas au montage et démontage. Teinte aluminium

No. 1133 R teinte rouge 21.—   No. 1133 AL teinte aluminium 21.—
Boîte de construction Mercédès
ensemble complet de pièces détachées suivant dessin ci-contre, pour monter la voiture de course ci-dessus. Voir aussi texte en tête de la page.

W 99 Pilote pour voiture de course   —.50

8

1939-40 Marklin catalog. Courtesy Gates Willard.

LOUIS MARX

By the 1950s, Louis Marx was the largest manufacturer of toys in the world—six large factories in the United States and ownership of interest in factories in seven other countries. Marx, born in Brooklyn in 1896, was working for "Toy King" Ferdinand Strauss when he was in his teens. By 20, his energy and enterprise had made him a director of that company. A falling out with Strauss persuaded him to go into business for himself. In 1921, he and his brother began making their own toys, including some adaptations of items by the now-defunct Strauss. Marx's watchword seems to have been quality at the lowest possible price, and he was such a favorite with toy buyers that he had virtually no need for salesmen or advertising.

Marx made virtually every type of toy, with the exception of dolls. In April 1972, he sold his company to the Quaker Oats Company, who, in 1976, sold it to Europe's largest toy manufacturer, Dunbee-Combex-Marx. The company went into bankruptcy in 1980. Marx died in 1982, at the age of 85. In 1982, American Plastics bought much of the Marx assets; in 1990, it began producing toys from the original molds. In the first Marx break-up, certain rights and molds were retained in Mexico, and these continue to be used.

	C6	C8	C10
Marx A&P Truck, 28" long	135	202	270
Marx "Acme Markets" Trailer Truck, late	150	250	400
Marx Aerial Ladder Truck, late	135	202	270
Marx Aerial Water Tower Truck, 15" long windup	275	363	550
Marx "Aero Oil Company" Truck, 5-1/2" long, friction, c.1930	225	375	500
Marx Air Force Truck, "Air Defense Group" ridem toy, 32" long, No. 3290	125	188	250

	C6	C8	C10
Marx Air Force Truck, canvas top, 20" long	105	158	210
Marx Airflow, 4"	88	132	175
Marx Airport Transport Bus, 6-1/2" long	32	48	65
Marx "Allied Van Lines," tin friction, Linemar, c.1950s	100	150	200
Marx "Allstate Super Trailer"	325	490	650
Marx "Ambulance" with siren, 1930s tin windup, 14-1/2" long	250	375	550

Marx "Aero Oil Company" truck. Photo by Bob Smith.

Marx "Allstate Super Service" station; value in Good $75. Photo by Ron Fink.

Marx "Ambulance" with siren, 1930s tin windup. Courtesy David W. Mapes Auctions.

Marx Amos & Andy Fresh Air Taxi. Photo by Bob Smith.

	C6	C8	C10
Marx Ambulance, "M.D. War Dept.," 1930s tin windup	300	425	700
Marx Ambulance No. 8500, approx. 14" long, 1930s	150	275	475
Marx Ambulance No. 8600, approx. 14" long, 1930s	240	360	525
Marx American LaFrance Hose Truck, late, 21" long	175	263	350
Marx "American Railroad Express Agency, Inc.," early 1930s, open cab, 7"	150	250	400
Marx "American Railway Express Agency" Van, 9" long, closed driver's window, windup	300	450	600
Marx "American Railway Express Agency" Van, Bulldog Mack windup	250	375	500
Marx "American Tractor" with implements, 1920s, 10" long, tin windup	132	198	265
Marx American Truck Co. No. 65 Moving Truck, friction	65	98	130

	C6	C8	C10
Marx Amos & Andy Fresh-Air Taxi, tin windup, 8" long, 1930s	500	800	1250
Marx Anti-Aircraft Unit No. 1 Fire Control Truck, friction, plastic and tin	90	135	180
Marx "Anti-Aircraft Unit No. 12" Civilian Defense Truck, friction, plastic, 12" long	110	165	220
Marx "Armored Bank," 6" long, c.1940	75	112	150
Marx Armored Trucking Co. tin windup	150	275	400
Marx "Army Command Car," friction, tin and plastic, 19-1/2" long. Siren and flashing signal light	No Price Found		
Marx Army Corps of Engineers, 20" long, canvas top	125	188	250
Marx Army Jeep: See Marx Willys Steel Jeep			
Marx Army Scout Stake Truck, c.1940	60	90	120
Marx Army Staff Car, 1930s, tin windup	162	243	325

Marx "Anti-Aircraft Unit No. 12" Civilian Defense Truck, friction, plastic, 12" long. Photo by Terry Sells.

Marx "Armored Bank," 6" long. MacNary Collection. Photo: RLM.

Marx "Army Command Car," friction, tin and plastic, 19-1/2" long. Photo by Terry Sells.

Marx Automatic Fire House. Photo by Don Hultzman.

Marx Beat It! The Komical Kop. Courtesy Ed Hyers Antique Toys.

Marx Brake Kar with screeching noise. Courtesy Continental Hobby House.

Marx "Brightlite Filling Station" with original box. Photo by Bob Smith.

Marx Bulldozer Climbing Tractor. Courtesy Continental Hobby House.

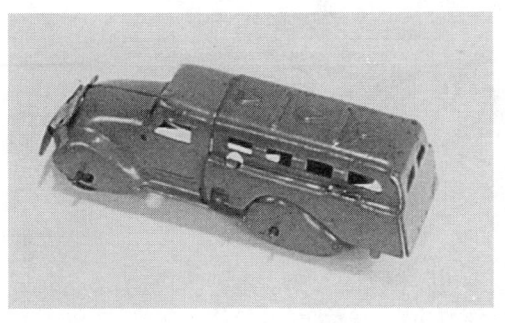

Marx Bus, c.1940, 4-1/2" long. MacNary Collection. Photo: RLM.

Marx Cadillac, Untouchables type. Photo by Gary Linden.

	C6	C8	C10
Marx "Army Staff Car," W-601158, with flasher and siren, 11" long, 1940s tin windup	225	338	450
Marx Army Staff Car, 9" long, plastic friction	9	14	18
Marx Army Tractor, 1930s windup	135	203	270
Marx Army Troop Carrier, plastic, w/searchlight	62	93	125
Marx Army Truck, 10" long, cloth cover, 1930s tin windup	350	525	700
Marx Army Truck, tin litho, c.early 1930s, 8" long	108	162	215
Marx Army Truck, cab plastic	85	128	170
Marx Army Truck, w/covered trailer & cannon trailer, c.1940	200	300	400
Marx Army Truck w/cannon, c.1950s	65	98	130
Marx Arrow Racer No. 2 tin windup, 1930s, 4" long	78	117	155
Marx Auto, 4" long, c.1937	27	41	55
Marx Auto Hauler, 1930s, with two Airflows	135	198	270
Marx Auto Hauler, windup, 2 cars, c.1950, 10" long	150	225	300
Marx Auto Hauler, 3 1965 Mustangs, friction, 18" long	175	263	350
Marx Auto Hauler, 4 plastic cars	135	202	270
Marx Auto-Laundry Car Wash	125	188	250
Marx Auto Transport, Mack C-Cab, 12" long windup, 3 cars, c.1920s	250	375	575
Marx Auto Transport, 21" long, 3 cars, c.1950s	225	338	450
Marx Auto Transport, 31" long, c.1958, includes 2 Corvettes, 2 T-Birds, everything tin	275	363	550
Marx Auto Transport, 1950s, with two tin litho cars, 34" long	150	225	300
Marx Auto Transport, 4 steel cars, c.1939	175	263	350
Marx "Auto Transwalk" No. T-50447B, 1930s truck with 3 cars	185	278	350

	C6	C8	C10
Marx "Automatic Fire House," 1950s, Fire Chief Car, 7-1/2" long, Volunteer Fire Dept. Garage, 19" long, tin windup	110	165	220
Marx Automatic Garage, comes with one friction car	35	52	70
Marx "Automatic Reversing Road Roller," 1925, 9" long tin windup	200	300	400
Marx Baby Wrecker Truck, battery-operated	50	75	100
Marx Bakery Truck "Rolls, Pies & Cakes," 11" long	125	188	250
Marx Beat It the Komikal Kop, 1930s tin windup	250	375	500
Marx Big Boss Car Carrier, 42" long	80	120	160
Marx Big Bruiser Tow Truck, 1960s	50	75	100
Marx Big Job Dump Truck, 28" long, plastic	50	75	100
Marx Big Lizzie Car, early 1930s, 7-1/4" long tin windup	150	225	300
Marx "Big Load Van Company," 13" long wind-up, Bulldog Mack, 1930s	235	352	470
Marx Big Parade, moving vehicles, soldiers, etc. 24" long tin windup	500	900	1200
Marx "Big Shot" Cannon Truck, plastic, 22" long, fires cap-loaded missiles	52	76	105
Marx "Big Silver" Mack Dump Truck tin windup	250	375	500
Marx "Blondie's Jalopy" tin windup, 16" long	1500	2300	3100
Marx Blue Bird Gas Station	150	225	300
Marx Bluestreak Racer, No. 3, tin windup c.1930s, 4" long	55	83	110
Marx Bottom Dump, late	40	60	80
Marx Bouncing Benny Pull Car, 7" long, 1939	150	225	300
Marx Brake Kar with screeching noise	105	157	210
Marx "Brightlite Filling Station"	250	375	600
Marx "Bud Bowman's Milk Express" Truck	185	278	370

Marx Carousel Truck, friction. Photo by Scott Smiles.

Marx "Caterpillar" climbing tractor. Courtesy Continental Hobby House.

Marx Charlie McCarthy in his Benzine Buggy. Photo by Bob Smith.

Marx "Coast to Coast" Delivery Truck, 1930s, 6" long. MacNary Collection Photo: RLM

Marx Coca Cola truck, 1950s, shelf sidecases. Photo by Don Hultzman.

Marx Coca-Cola truck, plastic, 10-1/2" long. Photo by Terry Sells.

Marx "City Sanitation Dept." Photo by Bill Kaufman.

Marx Coca-Cola Truck, Linemar, tin friction, 3" long. Courtesy James S. Maxwell/Virginia Caputo. Photo by Virginia Caputo.

Marx Coca-Cola truck, Sprite decal, 20" long. Photo by Richard MacNary.

	C6	C8	C10
Marx Bulldozer ClimbingTractor, caterpillar type, c.1950s, 10-1/2" long tin windup	200	300	400
Marx Bumper Auto, streamlined, c.1939, large bumpers, tin windup	120	180	240
Marx Bus, c.1940, 4-1/2" long	90	135	180
Marx "Busy Bridge" tin windup	325	488	650
Marx "Busy Parking Station," 1930s, 17" long, with 2" tin race car, wind-up	150	225	300
Marx Cadillac Coupe, 1931 windup, 12" long	432	648	865
Marx Cadillac Roadster, 13" long, trunk w/tools on luggage carrier, 1930s tin windup	250	400	550
Marx Cadillac, Untouchables type, 5-1/4" long	35	52	70
Marx Car Carrier windup, carries Airflow	58	85	115
Marx Cargo Truck, 16" long, post WWII	80	120	160
Marx Carousel Truck, 8" long, "1967"	50	75	100
Marx Carpenter Stakebed Truck with dolly, approx. 14" long	100	150	200
Marx Carwash & Garage, tin litho	125	188	250
Marx "Caterpillar" Climbing Tractor c.1950s, 10" long tin windup	90	135	180
Marx "Charlie McCarthy and Mortimer Snerd Private Car" tin windup	1100	1800	2600
Marx Charlie McCarthy in his Benzine Buggy tin windup	405	608	810
Marx "Chief-Fire Dept. No. 1" "Friction Drive," c.1948	90	135	180
Marx Circus Truck, plastic, 10"	110	165	220
Marx "Cities Service Towing Service," 20-1/2" long	175	250	375
Marx "City Hospital Ambulance," tin windup, 10" long	475	713	950
Marx "City Sanitation Dept. Help Keep Your City Clean," c.1940, 12-3/4" long	150	250	350
Marx Climbing, Fighting Tank, tin windup	175	263	350
Marx Climbing, Fighting Tank, 5-1/2" long, tin, plastic	22	33	45
Marx Climbing Tractor, sparkling, 1960s, 8-1/2" long tin windup	90	135	180

	C6	C8	C10
Marx "Cloverdale Farms" Milk Truck, 11-1/2" long	100	150	200
Marx Coal Truck, electric motor and lights, early	200	300	450
Marx Coal Truck, No. 964J	122	188	245
Marx Coal Dump Truck No. 964, 21" long	140	210	280
Marx "Coast to Coast" Delivery Truck, 1930s, 6" long	75	112	150
Marx "Coca-Cola" Truck, Linemar tin friction, 3" long	50	75	100
Marx "Coca-Cola" Truck, 17" long	210	315	420
Marx "Coca-Cola" Truck, 20" long, Sprite decal, stamped steel, late 1940s to early 1950s	160	275	400
Marx "Coca-Cola" Truck, 1950s, shelf sidecases	200	300	400
Marx "Coca-Cola" Truck, plastic, 10-1/2" long	175	263	350
Marx "Coke Coal City Coal Co." Truck, tin windup	255	383	510
Marx Comicar the Snappy Flivver	275	403	550
Marx "Construction" Tractor Hauler, 14" long, reverses, has driver	175	263	350
Marx Contractors & Builders Dump Truck, 1939, 11" long	100	150	200
Marx Convertible Roadster, 1930s, nickel-plated tin. 11" long	200	300	400
Marx "Coo Coo Car" 1920s, 7-1/2" long	175	415	550
Marx Cord Convertible, 11" long	250	375	500
Marx Corvette Coupe, plastic friction, 8" long	42	63	85
Marx Coupe, steel windup, electric headlights, 14" long	390	585	780
Marx Crane Truck, approx. 20" long	188	292	375
Marx Crazy Dora nodder-head tin windup	100	150	200
Marx "Crescent Ice" Truck 11" long, c.1950s	80	120	160
Marx Curtiss Candy Truck, plastic	10	20	30
Marx "Dagwood the Driver" Crazy Car, 1935, 8" long	500	750	1000
Marx Dairy Truck & Trailer, w/bottles, 1930s	175	263	350
Marx "Dan Dipsy Car," 1950s, 5-1/2" long, plastic nodder, windup	138	205	275
Marx "Daredevil Motor Drome," 1930s, 5-1/2" high, 9" diameter, 2" windup car	100	150	200

Marx Coo-Coo Car. Photo by Don Hultzman.

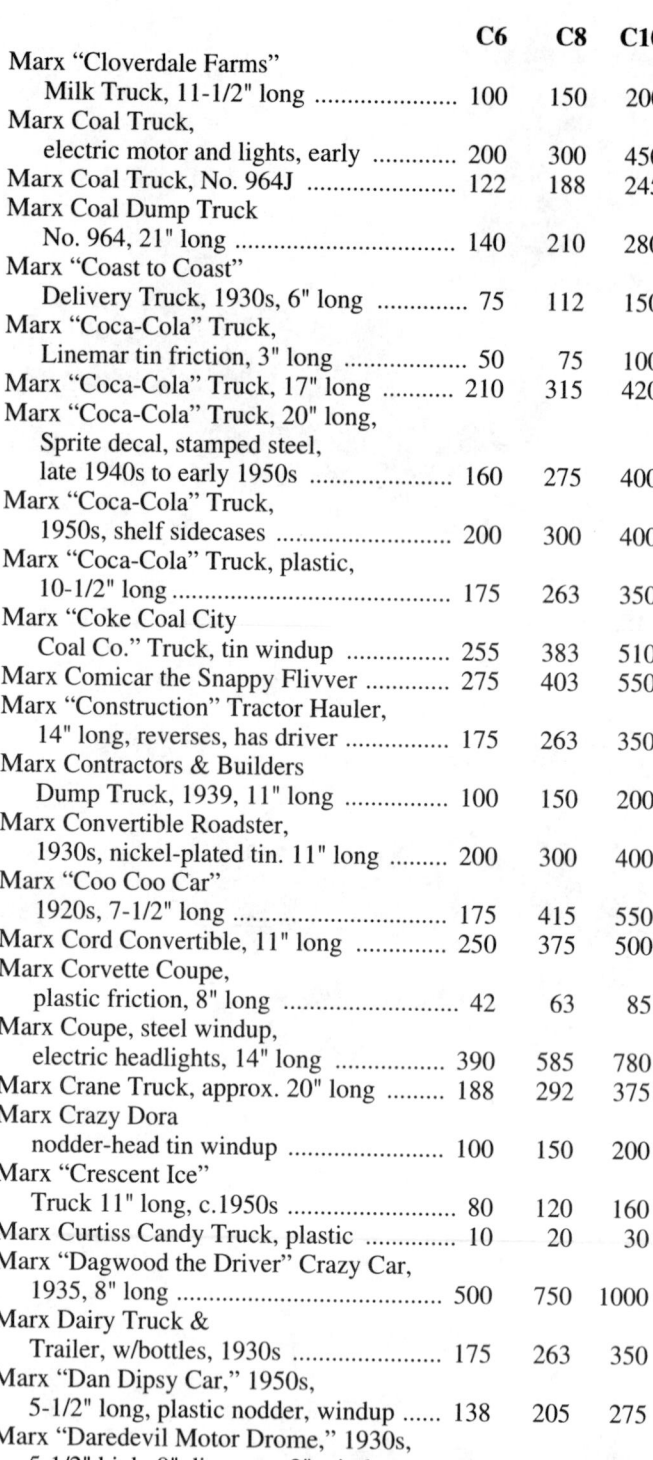

Marx "Curtiss Candy Company" truck. Photo by Gary Linden.

Marx Deluxe Coupe, windup, electric headlights, 15" long. Photo by Bob Smith.

Marx "Deluxe Delivery" truck. Courtesy Thomas G. Nefos, Federal Shipping Network.

Marx De Luxe Tractor, 6 wheels, 4 in treads, c. 1932. Photo by Orville C. Britton.

Marx Dick Tracy Squad Car No. 1, 6-3/4" long.

Donald Duck Dipsy Car. Photo by Don Hultzman.

Marx Doughboy Tank, two extending side turrets; from the October, 1932 Butler Bros. catalog.

Marx Doughboy Tank WWII pot helmet, c.1950. Courtesy Harvey K. Rainess.

Marx Doughboy Tank, no extending side turrets.

	C6	C8	C10
Marx "Day & Nite Service Service Center"	75	112	150
Marx DC Semi Tractor Trailer, late	100	150	200
Marx Delivery Van, plastic	60	90	120
Marx "Delivery" Van	75	112	150
Marx Deluxe Auto Transport, approx. 22" long, 2 plastic cars	75	112	150
Same as above, no cars	50	75	100
Marx Deluxe Coupe, windup, elec. lights, 15" long	450	650	950
Marx "Deluxe Delivery" Truck, 13"	125	188	250
Marx "Deluxe Delivery" Truck, 1950s 11" long tin windup	138	215	275
Marx Deluxe Mechanical Coupe, 8", 1930s	155	235	310
Marx De Luxe Tractor, 6 wheels, 4 in treads, tin windup, c.1932	250	375	500
Marx "Dept. of Police" Car, 1930s friction, 8"	225	328	450
Marx Dick Tracy "Police Station" with 7" long automatic siren car, 1950s	400	600	800
Marx Dick Tracy Riot Car, c.1946, 7-1/2" long, friction motor	140	210	280
Marx Dick Tracy Squad Car, convertible, 20" long, c.1948, friction, battery light, Tracy & Sam Catchum in plastic	175	263	350
Marx Dick Tracy Squad Car No. 1, 11" long, friction	225	338	450
Marx Dick Tracy Squad Car No. 1, 6-3/4" long, friction	155	233	310
Marx "Dipsy Doodle Bug" Dodgem car (Dan or Dora) 6" high tin windup	67	105	135
Marx Disney Parade Roadster 4 characters	240	360	480
Marx "Donald Duck Convertible," 1950s, Linemar, 5" long, tin friction	250	350	500

	C6	C8	C10
Marx Donald Duck Crazy Car, 1950s, Linemar, 5-1/2" long windup	275	363	550
Marx Donald Duck Dipsy Car, 1950s, 5-1/4" long tin windup (plastic Mickey or Donald)	260	390	520
Marx Donald Duck "Dipsy Car - Donald Duck," 1950s, Linemar windup, 6" long	350	525	700
Marx "Donald Duck Disney Flivver," 1950s, Linemar, 5-1/2" long	250	375	500
Marx "Donald Duck Dump Truck," 1950s, Linemar, 5" long	250	375	500
Marx Donald Duck Fire Chief Crazy Car, Linemar tin windup, rubber hat	750	1300	1700
Marx "Donald Duck In His Convertible," 1950s, Linemar friction, 6" long	225	338	450
Marx "Donald Duck on Tractor," 1950s, Marx friction, 3-1/2" long, plastic	120	180	240
Marx "Dora Dipsy Car," 1950s, 5-1/2" long plastic nodder, windup	188	282	375
Marx "Dottie the Driver," 1950s, 6-1/2" long windup	80	120	160
Marx Doughboy Tank, two extending side turrets, with top turret, 9-1/4" long, 1930 tin windup, soldier with gun pops out	160	240	320
Marx Doughboy Tank, no extending side turrets, tin windup	150	225	300
Marx Doughboy Tank, WWII pot helmet, c.1950	130	195	260
Marx "Driver Training Car," 1950s, 6" long tin windup	105	160	250
Marx "Drive-UR-Self Car," 1950s, 11" long tin windup	225	338	450
Marx Dump Truck, 4-1/2" long, c.1940	50	75	100
Marx Dump Truck, steel windup, c.1940, 4 1/2" long	60	90	120
Marx Dump Truck, 7-1/2" long, c.1941	60	90	120
Marx Dump Truck, 9-1/2" long, late	50	75	100
Marx Dump Truck, 13" long, tin windup	200	300	400
Marx Dump Truck, 14" long	37	56	75

Marx Dump Truck, 4-1/2" long. MacNary Collection. Photo: RLM.

Marx Dump Truck, steel wind-up, 4-1/2" long. Courtesy James S. Maxwell/Virginia Caputo. Photo by Virginia Caputo.

Marx E-12 Tank: Sponsons swing down for flint replacement. Very similar to the Sparkling Climbing Fighting Tank with Recoiling Cannon, but without that latter feature. Photo by Bill Holt.

Marx Easter Stake Truck, c.1940, 6" long. MacNary Collection Photo: RLM.

Marx Electric Combat Tank. Courtesy Heinz Mueller, Continental Hobby House.

Marx Electric Motor Driven Coupe, electric front and rear lights, 15" long. Photo by Bob Smith.

Marx "Fire Chief" car, right-hand drive (made in England). MacNary Collection. Photo: RLM.

Marx Fire Chief Car, windup. Photo by Bill Kaufman.

Marx Fix-All Motorcycle, plastic, 12" long. Photo by Terry Sells.

Marx Funny Flivver with original box. Courtesy Bill Bertoia Auctions. Photo by Jeanne Bertoia.

Marx G-Man Pursuit Car. Courtesy Gary Linden.

	C6	C8	C10
Marx Dump Truck, 17" long, No. 695B	75	112	150
Marx Dump Truck, No. 1018, 18" long, c.1950s	192	290	385
Marx Dump Truck, 20" long, late, No. 2083	50	75	100
Marx Dump Truck, two-color, No. T751, c.1930s	82	124	165
Marx Dump Truck, No. 1084	30	45	60
Marx Dump Truck, 1955 Chevy	62	93	125
Marx Dump Truck, hard plastic	42	63	85
Marx Dump Truck, w/treads, c.1920s	137	205	375
Marx E-12 Tank, sponsons swing down	88	132	175
Marx Earth Hauler, c.1964	110	165	220
Marx "East-West Fast Freight" Trailer Truck	80	120	160
Marx Easter Stake Truck, c.1940, 6" long	150	225	300
Marx Easter Stake Truck, 7" long	162	243	325
Marx Easter Stake Truck, 10-1/2" long, 1938	190	275	380
Marx Electric Combat Tank, battery-operated	80	120	160
Marx Electric Lighted Car, silver finish, Pontiac, 10" long	60	90	120
Marx Electric Motor Driven Coupe, elec. lights, c.1933, 15" long	350	550	850
Marx Electric Speedway, Cars, track, transformer	300	450	600
Marx "Electrically Lighted Truck and Trailer Set" No. T-5715 c.1930s, 15" long	150	220	300
Marx "Elmer's Racing Fuel" Trailer Truck, 1950s, tin	112	168	225
Marx Falcon with plastic bubble top, black rubber tires	125	188	250
Marx "Fanny Farmer" Candy Truck, plastic	125	188	250
Marx Farm Tractor, battery operated	40	60	80
Marx Fighting Tank No. 462, plastic top, 6" long windup	37	56	75
Marx Fire Chief Car, c.1920s	175	263	350
Marx Fire Chief Car, 1948 Hudson, 12" long	162	245	325
Marx Fire Chief Car, friction	68	102	135
Marx "Fire Chief" Car, right-hand drive (made in England), 7-1/2" long	100	150	200
Marx "Fire Dept. Chief" Car, c.1950s, 11" long tin windup	40	60	80
Marx Fire Dept. Car	100	150	200
Marx Fire Engine Pumper, friction, late 1920s	275	363	550
Marx Fire Ladder Truck, 6" long, c.1940	50	75	100

	C6	C8	C10
Marx Fire Ladder Truck, 14" long	60	90	120
Marx Fire Truck, friction, 25" long	225	338	450
Marx Fire Truck, plastic, with siren, 1950s	70	105	140
Marx "Firestone" Truck, 14-1/2"	312	468	625
Marx "1st Batt. F.D. Chief's Car," 16" long, siren, battery headlights, tin windup	215	322	430
Marx Fix-All Convertible and Wrecker set	125	188	250
Marx Fix-All Farm Tractor, 1953	112	168	225
Marx Fix-All Hardtop Convertible, w/tools, equipment	88	132	175
Marx Fix-All Jeep, with removable fabric top, hood, wheels including spare, and tires	125	175	400
Marx Fix-All Mercury Station Wagon	115	172	230
Marx Fix-All Motorcycle, 12" long, plastic	No Price Found		
Marx Fix-It Jaguar, 12" long, plastic	88	132	175
Marx Fix-It Tow Truck, w/accessories	100	150	200
Marx Ford Convertible, 1951, 11" long	55	83	110
Marx "Funny Flivver," c.1925 tin windup, 8" long	160	240	320
Marx G-Man Pursuit Car, 1930s, tin windup	300	450	600
Marx G-Man Pursuit Car No. 7000, 15" long, 1930s	375	562	750
Marx Gang Buster Car No. 7200, approx. 14" long, 1930s	550	825	1100
Marx Gas Island, 1930s	100	200	300
Marx "Gasoline" Trailer Truck, windup	188	282	375
Marx General Alarm Firehouse	350	525	700
Marx "Giant King Racer" c.1930s, "711," tin windup	110	165	220
Marx Giant Reversing Tractor Truck with tools, "Hauling," 14" long, c.1950s tin windup	100	150	200
Marx "Glendale Coal Company" Dump	125	188	250
Marx Glendale Wrecker	100	150	200
Marx "Gold Star Transfer Company" Trailer Truck	132	198	265
Marx "Gravel" Truck, 13" long	88	132	175
Marx "Gravel" Truck, 9" long	55	83	110
Marx Grocery Truck, 1950s, 14-1/2" long	62	93	125
Marx Guided Missile Truck No. 4488	220	330	440
Marx "Gulf" Service Station	300	450	600

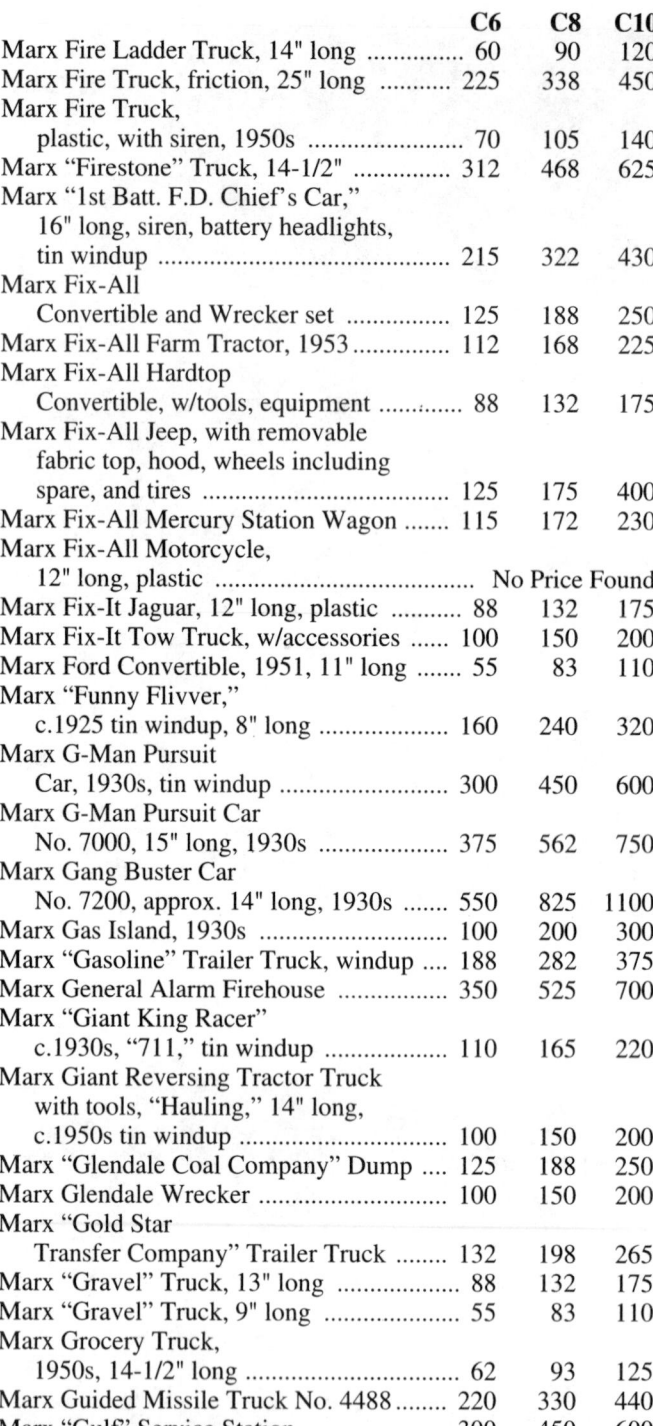

Marx "Gravel" truck. Photo by Calvin L. Chaussee.

Marx Giant King Racer, "711," as shown in the 1929 Butler Bros. Christmas catalog.

Marx "Heliport Service Center"; value in Good $100. Photo by Ron Fink.

Marx Highboy Climbing Tractor. Photo by Don Hultzman.

Marx "Hi-Way Express" truck. Photo by Calvin L. Chaussee.

Marx Hydraulic Dump. Courtesy Heinz Mueller, Continental Auctions.

Marx "Honeymoon Garage," with the two cars that were sold with it. Photo by James Apthorpe.

Marx "Joy-Rider." Courtesy Bill Bertoia Auctions. Photo by Jeanne Bertoia.

Marx "Lifesavers" truck, plastic, 9-1/2" long. Photo by Terry Sells.

	C6	C8	C10
Marx Gyro Rocket Car	85	128	170
Marx Happitime Service Station	238	357	475
Marx Hauler and Closed Van Trailer, plastic	62	93	125
Marx Hauler and Open Van Trailer, plastic	90	135	180
Marx "Hauling" Tractor, windup, 14" long, 6-wheel	150	220	300
Marx "Heavy Duty Express" Truck, cloth cover	95	142	190
Marx Heavy Duty Hydraulic Dump	72	108	145
Marx Heavy Duty Power Shovel	112	168	225
Marx "Highboy Climbing Tractor," c.1950s, 10-1/2" long tin windup	75	112	150
Marx Highboy Tractor, sparkles, c.1950s, 10" long tin windup	100	150	200
Marx High-Lift Loader c.1964	112	168	225
Marx Highway Patrol Car (TV series), plastic & metal, friction, 9" long	88	132	175
Marx Hi-Mac Dump Truck & Driver	125	188	250
Marx "Hi-Way Express" Truck	175	275	400
Marx "Hi-Way Express Van Lines" Truck	130	195	260
Marx "Home Dairy" Truck with bottles, 10" long	138	205	275
Marx Honeymoon Garage, tin litho, 1930s	90	135	180
Marx Hot Rod Coupe, plastic, 5"	42	63	85
Marx Hot Rod, open cab, driver, plastic, 7-1/2"	45	68	90
Marx Hot Rod "777 Super"	160	240	320
Marx Howard Johnson's Truck, 10" long, plastic	100	150	200
Marx Hydraulic Dump	100	150	200
Marx "Ice" Truck, c.1941	75	125	200
Marx Ice Truck w/tongs & ice	262	393	525
Marx Intercity Delivery, 18" long	100	150	200
Marx International Task Force Truck, with soldiers	55	82	110
Marx Invasion Force Truck	45	68	90
Marx Jalopy Pickup Truck, 7" long, tin windup	80	120	160
Marx Jeep: See Marx Willys Steel Jeep			
Marx "Joy-Rider," 1929, 8" long, College Boy driver, tin windup	250	375	500
Marx Jumpin' Jeep, c.WWII 6" tin windup	140	210	280
Marx Kellogg's Express Stake Truck	80	120	160

	C6	C8	C10
Marx "King Racer" 1930s, 8-1/2" long, tin windup	500	800	1100
Marx Landau, 6" long	38	58	75
Marx Lazy-Day Dairy Farm Pick-up Truck and trailer, 22" long	115	172	230
Marx Lazy-Day Farms Stake Truck 18" long, late	65	98	130
Marx "Liberty Bus Co.," 1930s	150	225	300
Marx "Lifesavers" Truck, plastic, 9-1/2" long	90	135	180
Marx Light Duty Climbing Tractor, 1930s tin windup	162	243	325
Marx "Limping Lizzie" Car, tin windup	200	300	400
Marx Linemar "Air Defense Pom-Pom Gun," battery operated, 14" long, five action	120	180	240
Marx Linemar Army Pickup Truck, tin friction, 6-1/2" long	35	52	70
Marx Linemar Army Searchlight Truck	100	150	200
Marx Linemar Army Stake Truck, tin, friction, 7" long	35	52	70
Marx Linemar? "Ferris Wheel Truck," battery operated, four actions, 11" long, c.1950s	140	210	280
Marx Linemar Friction Car, 8-1/2" long	30	45	60
Marx Linemar Futuristic Roadster, 1955, 12" long		No Price Found	
Marx Linemar Mercedes Racer, 9"	138	208	275
Marx Linemar "Military Police Car," 1950s, battery operated, 8-1/2" long, six actions	90	135	180
Marx Linemar "NBC Television Truck," 1950s, battery operated, five actions, 9" long	240	360	480
Marx Linemar, "NAR Television Truck," 1950s battery operated, 12" long, four actions, includes six film strip inserts	280	420	560
Marx Linemar "Old Jalopy," small, 1950s tin windup	48	72	95
Marx Linemar Police Car, 1954 Chevy, 7-1/2" friction	60	90	120
Marx Linemar Searchlight Truck, Studebaker	90	135	180
Marx Linemar Stake Truck, friction, 15-1/2"	108	162	215

Marx Linemar "Air Defense Pom-Pom Gun." Courtesy Don Hultzman.

Marx Linemar Army Pickup Truck, tin friction, 6-1/2" long. Photo by Ron Fink.

Marx Linemar Army Stake Truck, tin friction, 7" long. Photo by Ron Fink.

Marx Linemar Futuristic Roadster (with box), 1955, 12" long. Photo by Carl Thatcher.

Marx Linemar Taxi, "Yellow Cab." Photo by Don Hultzman.

Marx Lonesome Pine trailer and auto. Photo by Bob Smith.

Marx Lumar Rocker Dump. Photo courtesy Heinz Mueller, Continental Auctions.

Marx "Lumar 24 Hour Service Center" with Parking Tower; value in Good $125. Photo by Ron Fink.

	C6	C8	C10
Marx Linemar "Steerable Tank," 1950s, 9" long battery operated, 5 actions	50	75	100
Marx Linemar Taxi "Yellow Cab," battery-operated, 7-1/2" long, five actions	60	90	120
Marx Linemar "Television Truck," 1950s, battery operated, 11" long, 3 actions	200	300	400
Marx Livestock Truck	75	112	150
Marx Loader Dump, 17" long	100	150	200
Marx "Loblaws" Trailer Truck, late	132	198	265
Marx Lone Eagle Oil Company windup Tank Truck, 12" long, Bulldog Mack	700	1100	1600
Marx "Lonesome Pine" Trailer and Convertible Sedan, 1930s, 19" long	360	540	720
Marx Lotus Ford Racer, 9", plastic	37	56	75
Marx Lowboy, 1953, 34" long	112	168	225
Marx Lumar Aerial Ladder Truck	118	177	235
Marx Lumar Allied Van Lines	50	100	175
Marx Lumar Army Truck	80	120	160
Marx Lumar Army Truck & Electric Searchlight Trailer	100	150	200
Marx Lumar Auto Transport, 28" long	145	218	290
Marx Lumar Carry All Low Boy	32	48	65
Marx "Lumar Contractors" 962 Dump Truck, approx. 17" long	110	165	220
Marx "Lumar Contractors" Steam Shovel	70	105	140
Marx Lumar Contractors Crane	65	98	130

	C6	C8	C10
Marx Lumar Dairy Truck	75	100	175
Marx Lumar "Dump" Truck	100	150	200
Marx Lumar Dump, 22" long	85	128	170
Marx Lumar "Emergency Searchlight Unit," 19" long, tin litho	138	208	275
Marx Lumar Hi-Lift Loader	90	135	180
Marx Lumar Hook & Ladder, 33" long	212	318	425
Marx Lumar Hydraulic Dump	75	112	150
Marx Lumar Jeep & Trailer	112	168	225
Marx Lumar Police Car, 1954 Chevy, battery operated	68	102	135
Marx Lumar Power Grader	52	78	105
Marx Lumar Rocker Dump, 18" long	60	90	120
Marx Lumar Rocket Truck	77	108	155
Marx Lumar Scoop-A-Dump	140	210	280
Marx Lumar Searchlight Truck, 19" long	138	208	275
Marx Lumar Shop-Rite Trailer Truck, 1970s, 24"	27	41	55
Marx Lumar Stake Truck, 14" long	60	90	120
Marx Lumar Steam Shovel	75	112	150
Marx Lumar Telephone Service Truck	120	180	240
Marx Lumar "U.S. Army" Truck, 18-1/2" long, cloth top	75	112	150
Marx Lumar Utility Truck w/tools	200	300	400
Marx "Lumar Van Lines," straight body	175	275	400
Marx Lumar Van Lines Trailer Truck, 17" long	175	235	350

Marx Lumar Utility Truck. Courtesy Heinz Mueller. Continental Hobby House.

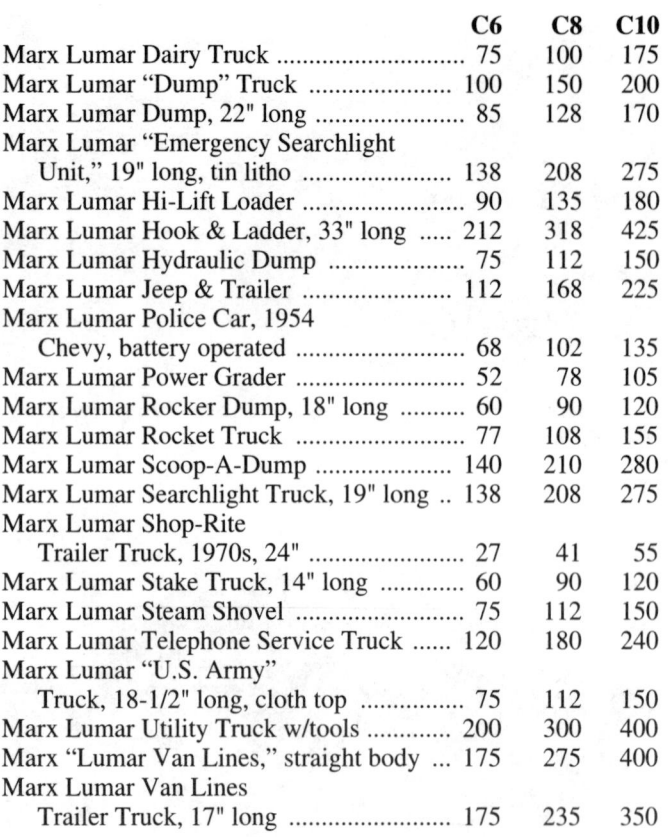

Marx "Lumar Van Lines," straight body. Photo by Bob Smith.

Marx "Magnetic Crane" Truck. Photo by Bob Smith.

Marx Mechanical Coupe, 8" long. Photo by Bob Smith.

Marx "Merchants Transfer" truck. Photo by Bob Smith.

Marx Mickey Mouse Dipsy Car. Courtesy Don Hultzman.

Marx "Midget Climbing, Fighting Tank." Courtesy K. Warren Mitchell.

Marx "Midget Climbing Fighting Tank," 3rd version, 1951. Courtesy Harvey K. Raines.

Marx "Midget" racer No. 7, pre-war. MacNary Collection. Photo: RLM.

Marx "Midget Special." Courtesy Scott Smiles.

Marx "Midget Special" race car; driver in old headgear and goggles, 5" long No. 2 racer. MacNary Collection. Photo: RLM.

Marx "Mid-Town Service Center." Photo by Ron Fink.

	C6	C8	C10
Marx Lumar Willys Jeep	75	112	150
Marx M.D. War Dept. Ambulance, 1930s	650	975	1300
Marx Machinery Moving Truck No. 1016	90	135	180
Marx "Mack Dump Truck," 1930s (City Coal Co.) 13" long, tin windup	350	525	700
Marx Mack Tank Truck	250	375	500
Marx Magic Barn with tractor	95	143	190
Marx "Magic Garage and Car," 1950s, garage 10" long, car 7" long, windup	85	128	170
Marx Magnetic Crane, 17"	138	205	275
Marx "Magnetic Crane" Truck, 8-1/2" long, 1940s	425	640	850
Marx "Main Street" tin windup, 1929	263	395	525
Marx Maintenance Truck, 6" long, c.1929, 2 ladders at each side of truck	30	45	60
Marx "Mammoth Truck Train" No. T-50-12345, c.1930s, truck with five trailers	175	262	350
Marx "Marbrook Farms" Sparkling Tractor & Trailer Set, c.1950s, 21" long tin windup	75	112	150
Marx Marco Oil Tanker, c.1940	150	225	300
Marx Marcrest Dairy Stake Truck	100	150	200
Marx Marcrest Livestock Semi, 20" long	115	173	230
Marx "Marshall's" Delivery Van, late	100	150	200
Marx Marx-A-Power Giant Bulldozer, battery operated	68	102	135
Marx Mayflower Van, 13" long	115	173	230
Marx "Meadow Brook Dairy" Stake Truck w/trailer	225	338	450
Marx "Meat" Delivery Truck, plastic 9-3/4"	90	135	180
Marx Mechanical Coupe, 8" long tin windup, c.1933	275	400	575
Marx Mechanical Gasoline Truck windup	325	488	650
Marx "Mechanical Roadster," 1950s, 11" long tin windup	100	150	200
Marx Mechanical Sparkling Tank, late	35	52	70
Marx "Mechanical Speedway Racer" tin windup	125	188	250
Marx Mechanical Station Wagon tin windup	125	188	250
Marx "Mechanical Taxi Cab," 1950s, 11" long tin windup	80	120	160
Marx "Mechanical Tractor" 6" long, c.1930s tin windup	110	165	220
Marx "Mechanical Tractor with Earth Grader," 21-1/2" long, c.1950s tin windup	105	158	210

	C6	C8	C10
Marx Mechanical Tractor, plastic & tin windup, 6"	62	93	125
Marx Mechanical Trailer Truck windup	300	450	600
Marx "Merchants Transfer" Truck, tin windup, 1929, 10" long	275	450	700
Marx Mickey Mouse Dipsy Car, 1950s, 5-1/4" long, tin car, plastic Mickey	200	300	400
Marx "Mickey Mouse Motorcycle," 1950s, Linemar, tin friction, 3-1/2" long	300	450	600
Marx "Midget Climbing Fighting Tank," approx. 5-1/2" long c.1935 tin windup	75	112	150
Marx "Midget Climbing Fighting Tank," 3rd version, 1951	60	90	120
Marx Midget Climbing Tractor, 5-1/2" long, c.1950 tin windup	60	90	120
Marx "Midget" Racer No. 7, premier windup	100	150	200
Marx "Midget Racer," 1950s, 6" long, plastic windup	50	75	100
Marx "Midget Special," race car - driver in old headgear and goggles, 5" long, No. 2 racer, 1930s, tin windup	100	150	200
Marx "Midget Special" race car driver in old headgear and goggles, 5" long No. 7 racer, 1930s, tin windup	100	150	200
Marx "Midtown Service Center"	200	300	400
Marx Mighty Marx Jeep	10	15	20
Marx Military Power-Mite Bulldozer	45	68	90
Marx Military Power-Mite Dump Truck	45	68	90
Marx Milk Truck, Studebaker type	450	675	910
Marx Milton Berle Car, 1950s tin windup	208	312	415
Marx Mobile Crane, c.1940	80	120	160
Marx "Mortimer Snerd's Tricky Auto," 1939 tin windup	438	658	875
Marx Model T Ford, plastic	40	60	80
Marx "Moto-Fix" Truck	80	120	160
Marx Motor Market, 14" long	123	185	245
Marx Motorcycle Policeman with sidecar, "Police," "3," license plate reads "102D," approx. 8" long, c.1940 tin windup	200	325	450
Marx "Motorcycle Trooper," 1935 tin windup	175	275	400
Marx Moving Van, c.1940, 4-1/2" long	100	150	200
Marx Mystery Car, press down to operate	145	218	290

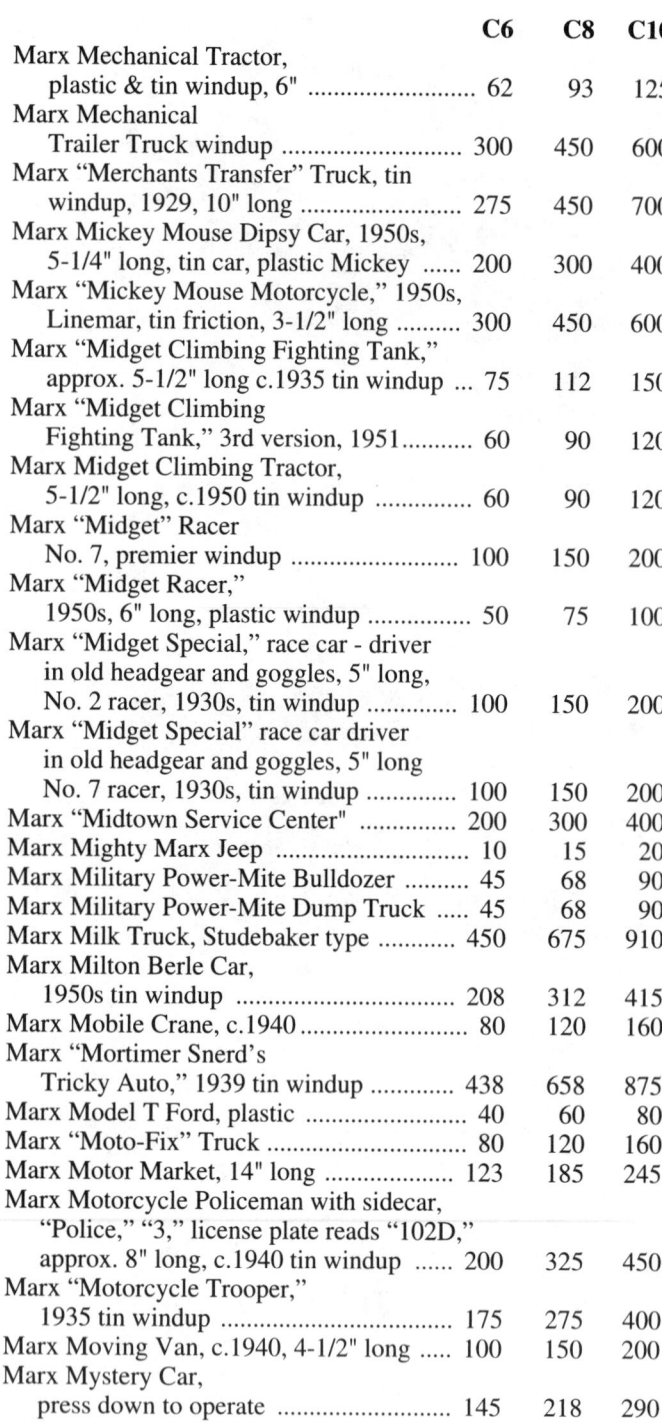

Marx Motorcycle Policeman with sidecar, "Police," "3." Courtesy Phillips NY.

Marx Moving Van, c.1940, 4-1/2" long. MacNary Collection. Photo: RLM.

  Louis Marx

Marx Mystic Motorcycle. Courtesy Scott Smiles. Photo by Mike Adams.

Marx "New Flivver" with original box. Photo by Bob Smith.

Marx "Nutty Mads Car." Courtesy Don Hultzman.

Marx Old-Fashioned Antique Automobile. Photo by Gary Linden.

Marx "Old Jalopy" large and small (the small is Marx Linemar). Courtesy Ed Hyers Antique Toys.

Marx "P.D." motorcycle cop, windup, siren, late 1930s, 8" long; value in C6, C8, C10: $200, 275, 375. Courtesy Kent M. Comstock.

	C6	C8	C10
Marx "Mystery Police Cycle," 1930s, 4-1/2" long tin windup	175	275	400
Marx Mystery Taxi, c.1930s, press down to operate	100	150	275
Marx "Mystic Motorcycle," c.1930s tin windup	75	112	150
Marx Navy Jeep: See Marx Willys Steel Jeep			
Marx Nellybelle Jeep, w/steel cage insert & 3 figures	150	250	500
Marx "New Flivver," 1920s, 7" long tin windup	250	350	500
Marx "New Rocket Racer," 1930s, 16" long	200	300	400
Marx "Newberry's" Semi Truck	120	180	240
Marx North American Van Lines windup, 14" long	150	225	300
Marx Nutty Mad Car, friction, 4" long, c.1965	70	105	140
Marx "Nutty Mads Car" (Drincar) 1960s, 9-1/4" long, battery operated, 3 action	140	210	280
Marx Old-Fashioned Antique Automobile, plastic	20	30	35
Marx "Old Jalopy" tin windup	128	192	255
Marx "Old Jalopy" tin windup, College Boys, post WWII	150	225	300
Marx "P.D." Motorcyclist, approx. 4" long tin windup	150	225	325

	C6	C8	C10
Marx "P.D." Motorcycle Cop, windup, siren, 8" long, late 1930s.	200	275	375
Marx "P.D" Police Motorcycle with sidecar, 3-1/2" long 1930s tin windup	200	325	450
Marx Paddy Wagon, 5" long, c.1920s	150	225	300
Marx Panel Truck, plastic, 8-1/4" long		No Price Found	
Marx Panel Wagon	40	60	80
Marx "Parcel Post U.S. Mail," 8-1/2" long, early, tin windup	225	338	450
Marx "Pathe News," camera atop car	1500	2700	4300
Marx Pepsi-Cola Truck, 1950s, plastic, 7" long	100	150	200
Marx Pepsi-Cola Truck, 8" long, 1945	75	150	250
Marx Pepsi-Cola Truck, 11" long, 1950s	50	125	200
Marx Pepsi-Cola Truck, plastic, 7" long	145	215	290
Marx Pepsi-Cola Truck, plastic, 10-1/2" long		No Price Found	
Marx "Pet Shop Delivery," 1950s, 10" long	55	82	110
Marx Peter Rabbit Eccentric Car, tin windup	125	188	250
Marx Pickup Truck, electric headlights, c.1941, 11" long	75	150	200
Above, with box & load	100	200	300
Marx Pickup Truck, 1968, 6" long	12	18	25
Marx "Pinched" tin windup, c.1927	450	700	1000
Marx "Polar Ice" Truck, steel, 14" long	175	300	425

Marx Panel Truck, plastic, 8-1/4" long. Photo by Terry Sells.

Marx "P.D." Police motorcycle w/sidecar. Courtesy Gary Linden.

Marx Pepsi-Cola Truck, plastic, 7" long. Photo by Terry Sells.

Marx Pepsi-Cola Truck, plastic, 10-1/2" long. Photo by Terry Sells.

Marx Pickup Truck, electric headlights, c.1941, 11" long, with original box. MacNary Collection. Photo: RLM.

Marx "Polar Ice" Truck, steel, 14" long. Photo by Terry Sells.

Marx Police Car, 1954 Chevy. Photo by Gary Linden.

Marx Power Grader. Courtesy Continental Hobby House.

Marx Racer No. 3. MacNary Collection. Photo: RLM.

Marx Racer No. 4. MacNary Collection. Photo: RLM.

Marx Racer No. 5. MacNary Collection. Photo: RLM.

Marx Racer No. 7. MacNary Collection Photo: RLM.

Marx Racer No. 8, nickel-plated. Photo by Perry R. Eichor.

	C6	C8	C10
Marx Police Car, 1954, Chevy		No Price Found	
Marx "Police Patrol" Motorcycle with sidecar, 1935 tin windup	150	225	300
Marx "Police Siren Motorcycle," 1930s, 8" long tin windup	175	275	400
Marx "Police Squad Sidecar," windup, 8" long, yellow	200	325	450
Marx Pontiac, friction, 1954, 10" long	30	45	60
Marx Popeye "Dippy Dumper" Truck	450	675	900
Marx "Popeye Transit Co." Trailer Truck	550	825	1200
Marx Power Caterpillar Climbing Tractor, tin windup	125	188	250
Marx "Power Grader" No. 1759, black or white wheels, 17-1/2" long	35	52	70
Marx Power House Dump Truck, late, 25" long	50	75	100
Marx Power Shovel, c.1964	90	135	180
Marx Powerhouse Dump Truck	250	375	500
Marx "Power Snap Caterpillar Climbing Tractor," 1950s, 8" long tin windup	80	120	160
Marx Precinct Police Patrol Armored Truck, 10-1/2" long tin windup, circa early 1930s	2000	3000	4000
Marx Pure Milk Dairy Truck with glass bottles, pressed steel, tin wheels, c.1940	125	225	350
Marx Racer No. 2, 1930s tin wind-up, 13" long	82	123	165
Marx Racer No. 2, 1930s, 5" long, tin windup	75	112	150
Marx Racer No. 3, 1930s, 5" long, tin windup	75	112	150
Marx Racer No. 3, plastic windup	162	243	325
Marx Racer No. 4, 1930s, 5" long, tin windup	75	112	150
Marx Racer No. 4, 1942 tin windup, sedan-like	88	132	175
Marx Racer No. 5, 1930s, 5" long, tin windup	75	112	150
Marx Racer No. 7, 1930s, 5" long, tin windup	75	112	150
Marx Racer No. 8, nickel-plated	100	150	200

	C6	C8	C10
Marx Racing Car, "12," c.1940, two-man team, tin wind-up	110	165	220
Marx Racing Car, "12," litho, plastic driver, c.1950s, windup	300	450	600
Marx Racing Car, "21," 7" long, early	175	263	350
Marx Racing Car, "27," litho, plastic driver, c.1950 windup	150	225	300
Marx Racing Car "61" windup, 1930s, 6" long	90	135	180
Marx Radar Jeep, with plastic seats, console interior, operationg machine gun (2-1/2" long), and 1-1/2" diameter radar screen; two figures	75	300	600
with 2-wheel trailer (jeep and trailer wheels match); add	30	45	100
with 4-wheel electric searchlight trailer (military), wheels match; add	40	60	150
with 4-wheel trailer, plastic rotating (turn with wheels) radar screen (8-3/4" long) and one or two figures (wheels match); add	50	100	400
Marx Rapid Express Truck	135	202	270
Marx RCA Panel Truck, 8" long, 1950s, with accessories	112	168	225
Marx REA Express Truck No. 1021	325	488	650
Marx "Reads" Drugstore Stake Truck, c.1940, 14"	162	243	325
Marx "Reads" Drugstore Truck, plastic cab, 14-1/2"	150	225	300
Marx "Reversible Coupe," "The Marvel Car," c.1938 tin windup	275	415	550
Marx Reversing Road Roller, tin windup	125	188	250
Marx Reversing Tank, 1930s tin windup	65	98	130
Marx "Rex" Race Car, 1920s tin windup	162	244	325
Marx "Rex Mars Planet Patrol," 1950s tin windup, 9-1/2" long	212	318	425
Marx Ridem Fire Truck, 30" long	162	243	325
Marx Road Grader, heavy-duty, 17" long	37	56	75
Marx Road Roller, 8-1/2" long, c.1930 has driver, tin windup	125	188	250

Marx Radar Jeep. Photo by Richard Jansen.

Marx Radar Jeep's four-wheel trailer, plastic rotating (turn with wheels) radar screen. Photo by Richard Jansen.

Marx "Rex" Race Car. Courtesy Thomas G. Nefos, Federal Shipping Network.

Marx "Rookie Cop," c.1950. Courtesy Kent M. Comstock.

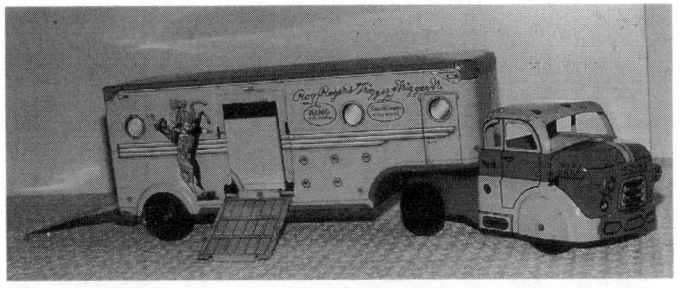

Marx Roy Rogers Horse Trailer. Courtesy Harvey K. Rainess.

Marx "Sand" Mechanical Dump Truck c.1939, 9" long.

Marx "Royal Van Co.." Courtesy Mapes Auctioneers & Appraisers.

Marx Sears "Happi-Time Service" station; value in Good $75. Photo by Ron Fink.

	C6	C8	C10
Marx Roadside Rest, 4 pumps, car, garage, 1930	450	700	1000
Marx Rocker Dump No. 1752, 17-1/2" long	110	165	220
Marx "Rocket Racer," 1930s, tin windup	215	322	430
Marx "Rookie Cop" with siren, 1930s, 8-1/2" long tin windup	232	348	465
Marx "Rookie Cop" windup, 8" long, yellow, around 1950	188	282	375
Marx Roy Rogers Horse Trailer	225	338	450
Same as above, plus Jeep	245	368	490
Marx Royal Bus Line, 10" long tin windup	100	150	200
Marx "Royal Coupe," 1920s, 9" long	375	563	750
Marx "Royal Oil Company" Mack Truck, 9"	400	600	800
Marx "Royal Van Co.," "We Haul Anywhere," 9" long tin windup	350	525	700
Marx Sabre Car	87	132	175
Marx "Safe Driving School" - see Driver Training Car.			
Marx "Sand" Mechanical Dump Truck c.1939, 9" long	45	68	90
Marx "Sand & Gravel" Dump Truck, 10" long, 1940s	100	150	200
Marx Sand & Gravel w/scoop, 16" long	70	105	140
Marx Sand & Gravel Dump Truck, 21" long	115	172	230
Marx "Sand and Gravel Truck - Builders Supply Co.," 1920 tin windup	100	150	200
Marx Sand Loader	60	90	120
Marx Scenic Bus, plastic, 10" long	40	60	80
Marx School Bus, 12" long	35	52	70

	C6	C8	C10
Marx Scoop Dump, 20" long, postwar	138	206	275
Marx Searchlight Truck, 9" long, c.1941	118	178	235
Marx Secret Agent Car	110	165	220
Marx Sedan, 4-1/2" long, c.1940	75	112	150
Marx "Service Station," 1929	262	393	525
Marx "Sheriff Sam & His Whoopee Car," 1950s, 6" long tin windup	180	270	360
Marx "Sheriff Sam & His Whoopee Car," 1960s, 6" long tin windup	88	132	175
Marx Shop-Rite Tractor/Trailer	100	150	200
Marx Side Dump Truck, four-color No. T-475 c.1940	60	90	120
Mack Side Dump Truck and Trailer, No. T-4045, c.1930s	100	150	200
Marx "Signal Corps" Truck, plastic	60	90	120
Marx Silver Streak Racer, plastic windup, 6"	70	105	140
Marx "Sinclair" Truck, steel	200	325	475
Marx "Single Track Speedway," 1938, 8 track sections, 4" long windup car	60	90	120
Marx "Siren Fire Chief" c.1930, "F.D. 1st Batt.," 15" long	375	550	750
Marx "Siren Police Car," 1930s	215	322	430
Marx "Siren Police Patrol," 1930s, 15" long	375	550	750
Marx Snappy Gus Car	500	750	1050
Marx "Sparkling Climbing Fighting Tank," cannon recoils, tin windup	138	206	275
Marx "Sparkling Climbing Tank," 1939	140	210	280
Marx Sparkling Climbing Tractor, 1940s tin windup	150	225	300
Marx Sparkling Climbing Tractor, 8-1/2" long, c.1950s tin windup	62	93	125
Marx "Sparkling Climbing Tractor and Trailer," 16" long, c.1950s tin windup	55	82	110
Marx Sparkling Doughboy Tank	175	263	350

Marx "Siren Fire Chief." Photo by Bob Smith.

Marx "Siren Police Patrol." Photo by Bob Smith.

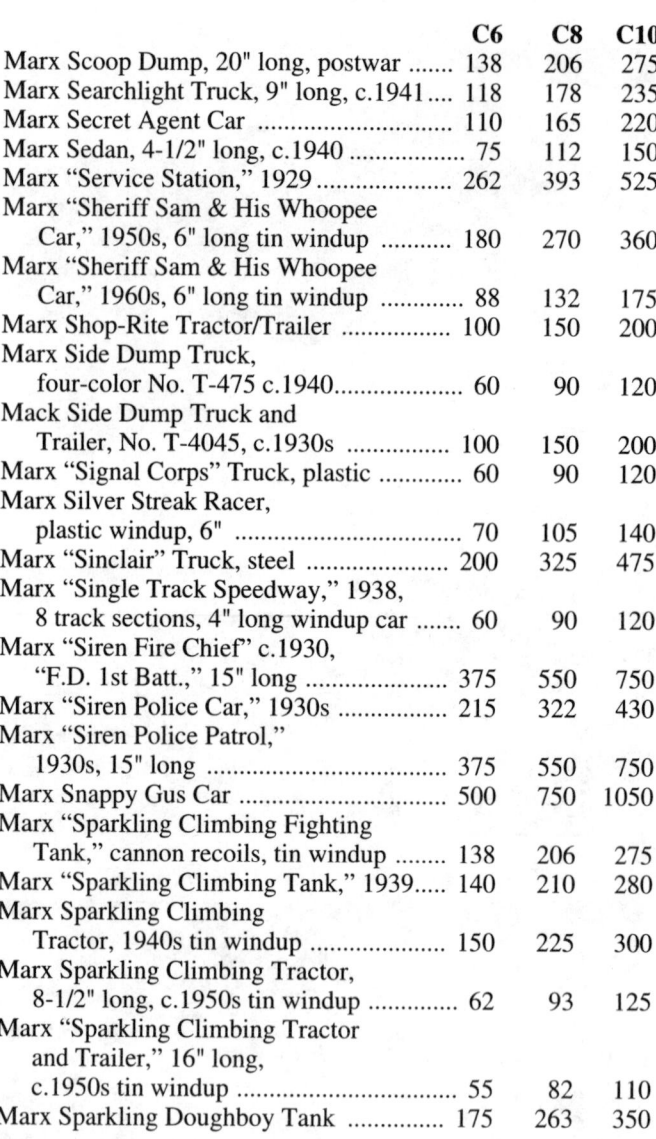

Marx "Sparkling Climbing Fighting Tank;" cannon recoils. Courtesy Charles D. Richards.

*Marx Sparkling Climbing Fighting Tank with Recoiling Cannon, 10"
long. Photo by Bill Holt.*

*Marx Sparkling Tank, 4" long. Courtesy
Continental Hobby House.*

*Marx Stake Truck, 4-1/2" long. Mac-
Nary Collection. Photo: RLM.*

Marx "Speed Boy Delivery." Courtesy Kent M. Comstock.

Marx Superman Tank, Linemar, battery-operated, 10-1/4" long. Courtesy Christie's East.

	C6	C8	C10
Marx Sparkling Heavy Duty Bulldog Tractor with Road Scraper, c.1950s, 11" long tin windup	125	188	250
Marx "Sparkling Hot Rod Racer," 1950s plastic windup, 8" long	37	56	75
Marx Sparkling Jet Futuristic Car, friction motor, 10" long	87	132	175
Marx Sparkling Soldier Motorcycle, c.1940 tin windup	250	375	500
Marx Sparkling Super Power Tank, c.1950s, 9-1/2" long tin windup	110	165	220
Marx Sparkling Tank, 4" long tin windup	55	82	110
Marx Sparkling Tank, prewar, tin windup, 9"	120	180	240
Marx "Sparkling Tractor," tractor with plow blade, 1939 tin windup	140	210	280
Marx Sparkling Turn Over Tank, tin windup	40	60	80
Marx "Speed Boy Delivery" (Motorcycle), 1930s, 9-3/4" long, battery lights, tin windup	250	400	575
Same as above, no lights	262	393	525
Marx "Speed Boy 4" windup, 9-1/2" long motorcycle	250	375	500
Marx "Speedway Bus" plastic windup, 4" long	25	38	50
Marx Speedway Coupe, battery lights, 8" long tin windup	250	375	500
Marx Speedway Jeep	25	38	50
Marx Sports Coupe, 1930s, 15" long	200	300	400
Marx Stake Truck, 4" long, c.1941	27	41	55
Marx Stake Truck, 4-1/2" long, c.1940	50	75	100
Marx Stake Truck, 6" long, c.1941	88	132	175

	C6	C8	C10
Marx Stake Truck, 12" long, 1930s, two-color	65	98	130
Marx Stake Truck, 20" long, c.1939	100	150	200
Marx Stake Truck, No. 1008	60	90	120
Marx Stake Truck No. E-271, three-color, c.1941	100	150	200
Marx Streamline Convertible, friction	138	207	275
Marx "Streamline Speedway," 1938, tin figure 8 track, 2 windup cars, 31" long	140	210	280
Marx Streamlined Coupe, hardtop, no windshield supports, c.1937, steel, 6" long	180	270	360
Marx Streamlined Coupe, tin windup	110	165	220
Marx Studebaker Dump, 1950s	110	165	220
Marx Studebaker Shovel Truck	125	188	250
Marx Studebaker Stake Truck, 1950s	100	150	200
Marx Stutz, 11" long	650	1050	1450
Marx Stutz Electric Car with driver, 1930, 36" long tin windup	225	338	450
Marx "Sunnyside Service Station," 1930s, complete	400	600	800
Marx Super Hi-Way Service Wrecker	42	63	85
Marx "Super Hot Rod 777"	150	225	300
Marx "Super Service" Center	175	263	350
Marx "Super Streamline Racer," 1950s, 17" long tin windup	120	180	240
Marx Superman Rollover Tank, 1940s, 4" long	400	600	800
Marx "Superman Tank," 1950s, Linemar Co., 10-1/4" long, battery operated, 3 actions	500	750	1000
Marx Superman Tank, Linemar, 4" long	500	800	1100
Marx Take-Apart Jaguar, 1950s	115	172	230
Marx Tank, friction, 1940, tin, sparkles, 3-1/2"	20	30	40
Marx Tank No. 4 "U.S. Army" windup	100	150	200
Marx Tank, late, machine gun on top of turret	55	82	110

Marx Tank No. 3; 2 guns on top of roof. Courtesy Harvey K. Rainess.

Marx Tank Truck, c.1940, 4-1/2" long . MacNary Collection. Photo: RLM.

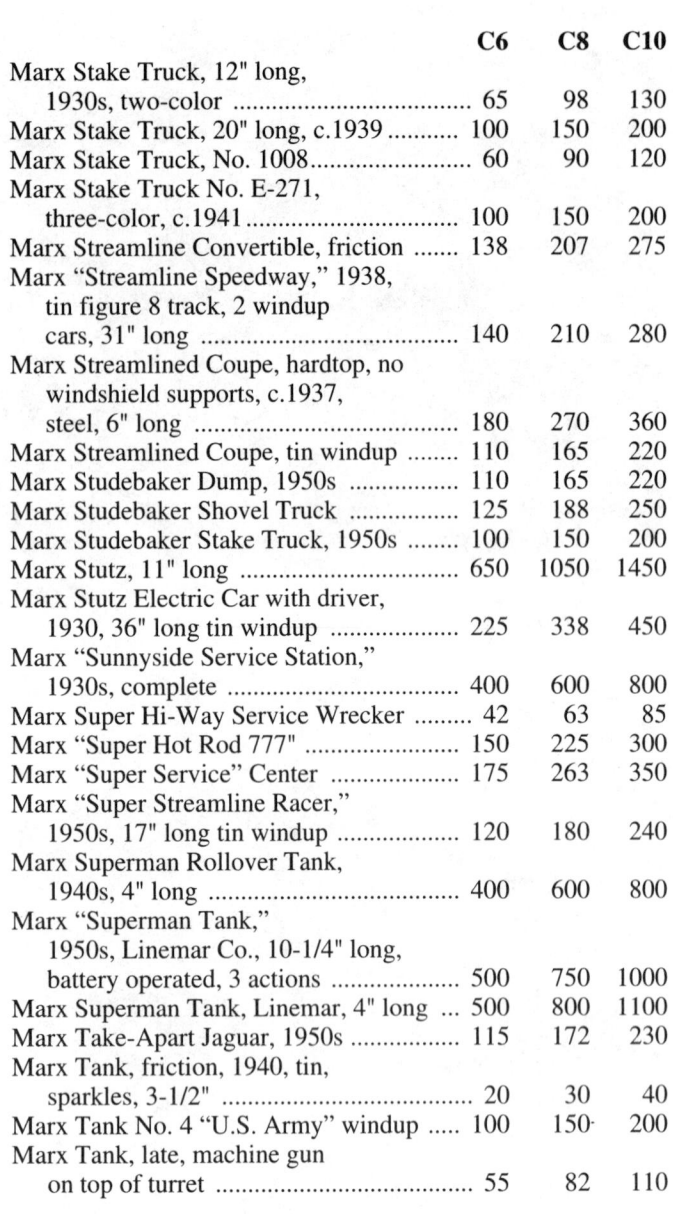

Marx Tip Over Motorcycle. Photo by Bob Smith.

Marx "Toy Town Express Van Lines Deluxe Service" truck. Courtesy Don Hultzman. Photo by Ron Chojnacki.

Marx Tricky Taxi. Photo by William G. Floyd.

Marx Turnover Tank No. 3. Photo by Max Heiss.

Marx Untouchables Touring Car. Photo by Gary Linden.

Marx "Toyland Farm Products" truck, c.1931, with box of 12 wooden milk bottles, 10-1/2" long. Photo by Bob Smith.

Marx "Tricky Tax" variation.

Marx Untouchables Rolls Royce. Photo by Gary Linden.

Marx "U.S.A. Mobile Artillery." Photo by Bill Holt.

	C6	C8	C10
Marx Tank No. 3, 2 machine guns or cannon on top of roof (no turret), tin windup	80	120	160
Marx Tank, 392-U.S. Tank Division, plastic & metal windup	22	33	45
Marx "Tank 392-U.S. Tank Division," 1950s battery operated, 9-1/2" long, 3 actions	60	90	120
Marx Tank Truck, c.1940, 4-1/2" long	80	120	160
Marx Tank Truck, 6" long	42	63	85
Marx Taxi Hauler, 2 cabs, c.1940	150	225	300
Marx Telephone Repair Unit, 30 pieces	275	415	550
Marx Telephone Truck, 11" long, plastic	75	100	175
Marx "Thimble-Drome Racer No. 1," plastic windup, 6" long, c.1950s	35	52	70
Marx "Thrifty Stores" Stake Truck, c.1940	160	240	320
Marx Tip Over Motorcycle, tin windup, 8" long, c.1933	225	375	500
Marx Tow Truck, 11" long, c.1941	65	98	130
Marx "Toy Town Express Van Lines Deluxe Service" Truck	100	150	200
Marx Toyland Dairy	135	202	270
Marx "Toyland Farm Products" Truck, tin windup, 10-1/2" long, c1931, 12 wooden bottles	500	675	1000
Marx Tractor, 1920s tin windup	60	90	120
Marx Tractor, early 1940s tin windup	50	75	100
Marx Tractor, plastic	20	30	40
Marx Track & Trailer set, 1930s, similar to climbing tractor set, but with rounded and radiator front and copper finish metal. Tin plow attaches to front, silver metal trailer attaches to rear; has tin, copper finish and "balloon" tires, windup	160	240	320
Earlier version, no balloon tires	125	188	250
Marx Tractor and Trailer, 16-1/2" long, c.1950s tin windup	95	138	190
Marx Tractor Service, 1940s, tractor, cardboard garage box, 3 pieces of farm equipment	225	338	450
Marx Tri-City Express Truck	150	225	300
Marx "Tricky Motorcycle," 1930s, 4-1/4" long, non-fail action with windup	90	135	180
Marx "Tricky Taxi," friction, 4-1/2" long	60	90	120
Marx "Tricky Taxi," 1940s, 4-1/2" long tin windup	78	117	155
Marx Tricky Tommy Big Brain Tractor, battery-op.	62	93	125
Marx Truck w/Trailer, c.1940, 19" overall	88	132	175
Marx Trucking Terminal	90	135	180
Marx Turn Over Tank No. 3 tin windup	70	105	140
Marx Uncle Wiggily Crazy Car, tin windup	500	800	1100
Marx Universal Bus Terminal, 12" long	95	142	190
Marx "Univeral Gas Service Station," 1940s, 6-1/2" high, base 12" long	138	208	275
Marx Untouchables Rolls-Royce, tin friction, 5-1/4"	42	63	85
Marx Untouchables Touring Car, tin friction	35	52	70
Marx UPS Truck, plastic, 10" long	100	150	200
Marx "U.S.A. Mobile Artillery" Truck	55	80	115
Marx "U.S. Air Force" Truck, cloth top	92	138	185
Marx "U.S. Air Force" Searchlight Truck	88	132	175
Marx "U.S. Army" Searchlight Trailer	30	45	60
Marx U.S. Army Troop Transport, plastic, 6" long	15	22	30
Marx "U.S. Army" Truck, plastic, 6-1/2" long	12	18	25
Marx "U.S. Army" Truck, 4-1/2" long, c.1940	100	150	200
Marx "U.S. Army" Truck with horns, cloth top, 18-1/2" long	80	120	160
Marx "U.S. Army" Truck, late, canvas cover, plastic cab	60	90	120
Marx "U.S. Army Truck," 1920s Mack, cloth cover, 10" long windup	90	135	180
Marx "U.S. Army Truck," cloth top, late	72	108	145

Marx "U.S. Army" Searchlight Trailer. Photo by Calvin L. Chaussee.

Marx U.S. Army Troop Transport, plastic, 6" long. Photo by Ron Fink.

Marx U.S. Army Truck, plastic, 6-1/2" long. Photo by Ron Fink.

Marx "U.S. Army" Truck, plastic, 6-1/2" long. Photo by Ron Fink.

Marx "U.S. Army" Truck, 4-1/2" long. MacNary Collection. Photo: RLM.

Marx "U.S. Army" Truck with horns, cloth top, 18-1/2" long. Photo by Joe and Sharon Freed.

Marx "U.S. Mail" truck, 9-1/2" long. Courtesy Phillips NY.

Marx War Tank, as seen in the November 1932 Butler Bros. catalog.

Marx "USA 41573147" Army Truck, 40. Photo by Bill Kaufman.

Marx "Westgate Service Plaza"; value in Good $75. Photo by Ron Fink.

	C6	C8	C10
Marx "U.S. Army 5th Div." Truck with canopy, c. late 1950s	80	120	160
Marx "U.S. Mail" Truck, 9-1/2" long tin windup	250	350	475
Marx "U.S. Mail" Truck, 12-1/2" long	45	68	90
Marx "U.S. Mail" Truck, 14" long	100	150	200
Marx "U.S. Mail" Truck, 24" long, late	200	300	400
Marx "U.S. Mobile Guided Missile Squadron" Truck	180	270	360
Marx "U.S. Tank Co. No. 4," 1931 windup, 5-1/4"	60	90	120
Marx "USA 4153147" Army Truck, c.1952, 13-3/4" long	100	150	200
Marx Utility Service Truck w/trailer	155	233	310
Marx "Volunteer Fire Department" Tin Garage, with 1950s "Chief FD" car	130	195	260
Marx Wacky Taxi tin windup	75	112	150
Marx Walt Disney Television Car, 1950s, 7-1/2" long	225	325	500
Marx War Tank, 5-1/4" long tin windup	68	102	135
Marx Wards Service Station	138	205	275
Marx Western Auto, 25" long, trailer truck	60	90	120
Marx Whoopee Car, laughing cows on wheels, driver looks like cowboy, 1929, tin wind-up	312	468	625
Marx Whoopee Car, "Yale-Princeton" pennants on wheels, tin windup	225	338	450

	C6	C8	C10
Marx "Whoopee Car with Flappers," 7-1/2" long tin windup	100	150	200
Marx Willys Jeep, steel, c.1940, 12" long, hood opens, windshield folds down	60	90	120
Marx Willys Jeep & Trailer, c.1940s, 22" long	100	150	200
Marx Willys Jeepster, plastic windup	75	112	150
Marx Willys Steel Jeep, 11" long, c.1946-67. Hood opens, windshield folds down; metal, rubber or plastic wheels	40	80	150
with electric headlights	50	70	250
and with mechanical or electric horn	60	100	300
with removable fabric top (military), optional figure	70	150	400
Marx "Woodie" Sedan, tin litho windup, 11" long	100	150	200
Marx "Woodie" Sedan, tin litho windup, 6-3/4"	48	72	95
Marx Woolworth's Trailer Truck, c.1960s	200	300	400
Marx Wreckage Service Truck, tin, battery lights	75	112	150
Marx Wrecker, 4" long, c.1941	27	41	55
Marx Wrecker, 4-1/2" long, c.1940	60	90	120
Marx Wrecker, 6" long, c.1940	42	63	95
Marx Wrecker, 10" long, 1920s	100	150	200
Marx Wrecker No. T-16, c.1930s	150	225	300
Marx Wrecker, plastic	40	60	80

Marx Whoopee Car, laughing cows on wheels. Courtesy Bill Bertoia Auctions. Photo by Jeanne Bertoia.

Marx Whoopie Car, "Yale-Princeton" pennants, with original box. Courtesy Bill Bertoia Auctions. Photo by Jeanne Bertoia.

Marx Willys Jeep, steel, c.1940. Photo by Calvin L. Chaussee.

Marx Willys steel jeep, 11" long. Photo by Richard Jansen.

	C6	C8	C10
Marx "Yellow Cab," first Marx plastic car, 4" long. Original has "MADE IN U.S.A." under roof. (1990s reissue has Marx emblem)	27	41	55
Marx "Yellow Cab-LMN 52," 1940s, 6-1/2" long tin windup	162	245	325

Marx "Yellow Cab"—Marx's first plastic car. The original has "Made in U.S.A." on the underside of the roof. The 1990s reissue bears a Marx emblem. Caption and photo courtesy Bob and Alice Wagner.

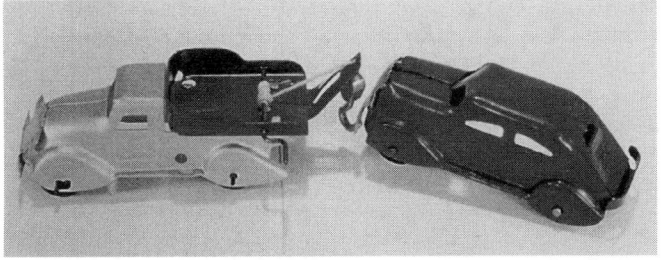

Marx. L to R: Wrecker, 4-1/2" long, Sedan, 4-1/2" long. Mac-Nary Collection. Photo: RLM.

MASON & PARKER

	C6	C8	C10
Mason & Parker (Winchendon, Mass.) Baby Auto, 1907, 7" long	450	700	1000
Mason & Parker Truck w/cloth top, wooden, c.WWII	20	30	40

	C6	C8	C10
Mason & Parker Truck w/log load, wooden, c.WWII	20	30	40

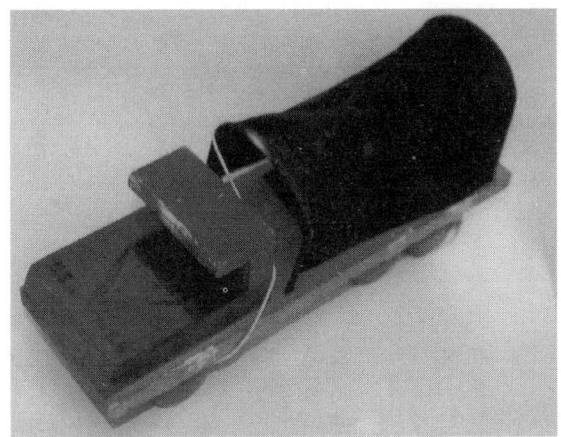

Mason & Parker truck with cloth top, wooden, c.WWII. Photo by Jack Matthews.

Mason & Parker truck with log load, wooden, c.WWII. Photo by Jack Matthews.

MATCHBOX

by Mark McManus

Matchbox Toys grew out of a company begun in 1947 by two former unrelated Navy friends, Leslie Smith and Rodney Smith. Manufacturing toys was not even planned at this point. On June 19, 1947, the two partners combined portions of their first names, and the name Lesney was born. In 1948, Lesney Products produced its first toy, a 4-1/2 inch Aveling Barford Road Roller. Encouraged by the brisk sales, three other toys were produced that year: a 4-1/2 inch Caterpillar Bulldozer, a 3-1/8 inch Caterpillar Tractor, and a 3-3/4 inch Cement Mixer. Value on these rare early Lesney toys today ranges up to $1,000. It was decided to package the toys in a matchbox-type box, and thereafter the toys would be known as "Matchbox."

These small vehicles quickly became very popular, and all other toy lines were discontinued. These first small vehicles had metal wheels, but these were quickly changed to plastic. These type wheels are now known to collectors as "Regular" wheels, not to be confused with the "Superfast" wheels that were introduced in 1969. It is not uncommon to find slight color and style variations for the same vehicle. These variations were often due to paint or part shortages, and these variations are now highly sought-after by collectors. Nineteen fifty-six saw the introduction of the "Models of Yesteryear" line. The king-size line was first developed and marketed in 1957 and was known as Major Packs. Matchbox toys were first marketed in the United States in 1958; by the early 1960s, they became a household standard. 1993 marked the 40th anniversary of Matchbox toys, and these small vehicles are rapidly gaining popularity and value among collectors. Listed are all of the basic models and some important variations.

Mark B. McManus lives in Boonville, New York, with his wife Suzanne and son Turner. Mark and Suzanne own and operate an AmeriSpec Home Inspection Service franchise in Northern New York. Mark is an avid miniature vehicle collector and specializes in Matchbox vehicles. He currently owns several hundred Matchbox vehicles. He also owns numerous Tonka vehicles, several GI Joes and their accessories, as well as many miscellaneous items.

Prices are for mint in box, since that is how most collectible Matchboxes are sold.

	MIB
No. 1 Diesel Road Roller, 1953	183
No. 1 Aveling Barford Road Roller, 1964	28
No. 1 Mercedes-Benz Lorry, 1968	17
No. 1 Mod Rod, 1971	13
No. 1 Dodge Challenger, 1976	10
No. 2 Dumper, 1953	110
No. 2 Muir-Hill Dumper, 1962	22
No. 2 Mercedes Trailer, 1968	14
No. 2 Hot Rod Jeep, 1971	13
No. 3 Cement Mixer, 1953	55
No. 3 Bedford Ton Tipper, 1961	82
No. 3 Mercedes-Benz Ambulance, 1968	20
No. 3 Monteverdi Hai, 1973	12
No. 3 Porsche Turbo, 1978	15
No. 4 Tractor, 1954	100
No. 4 Triumph Motorcycle and sidecar, 1959	100

	MIB
No. 4 Stake Truck, 1967	17
No. 4 Gruesome Twosome, 1971	7
No. 4 Pontiac Firebird, 1976	7
No. 4 '57 Chevy, 1981	6
No. 5 London Bus, 1954	30
No. 5 Lotus Europea Sports Car, 1969	17
No. 5 Seafire, 1976	6
No. 5 U.S. Mail Truck, 1981	12
No. 6 Quarry Truck, 1955	100
No. 6 Euclid 10-wheel Quarry, 1964	55
No. 6 Ford Pick up, 1969	19
No. 6 Mercedes Tourer, 1974	11
No. 7 Ford Anglia, 1961	27
No. 7 Ford Refuse Truck, 1967	17
No. 7 Hairy Hustler, 1971	13
No. 7 VW Golf, 1976	5
No. 8 Caterpillar Tractor, 1955	135
No. 8 Ford Mustang Fastback, 1966	28

Matchbox No. 9 Merryweather Marquis Fire Truck. Courtesy Gary Linden.

Matchbox No. 12 Land Rover. Courtesy Gary Linden.

	MIB
No. 8 Wildcat Dragster, 1971	17
No. 8 De Tomaso Pantera, 1975	8
No. 9 Dennis Fire Engine, 1955	110
No. 9 Merryweather Marquis Fire Engine, 1959	39
No. 9 Boat & Trailer, 1967	17
No. 9 Javelin, 1972	11
No. 9 Ford Escort RS200, 1978	8
No. 10 Mechanical Horse & Trailer, 1955	122
No. 10 Sugar Container Truck, 1961	93
No. 10 Pipe Truck, 1967	17
No. 10 Piston Popper, 1973	18
No. 10 Plymouth 'Gran Fury' Police Car, 1980	10
No. 11 Petrol Tanker (Esso decal), 1955	103
No. 11 Jumbo Crane (Taylor), 1964	22
No. 11 Scaffolding Truck (Mercedes), 1969	17
No. 11 Flying Bug, 1972	16
No. 11 Car Transporter, 1977	10
No. 12 Land Rover, 1953	22
No. 12 Safari Land Rover, 1965	36
No. 12 Setra Coach, 1971	11
No. 12 Big Bull, 1975	8
No. 12 Citroen CX, 1981	8
No. 13 Bedford Wreck Truck, 1955	85
No. 13 Thames Wreck Truck (MB Garages), 1959	103
No. 13 Dodge Wreck Truck (BP Label), 1961	33
No. 13 Baja Buggy, 1971	14
No. 13 Snorkel Fire Engine, 1977	6
No. 14 Daimler Ambulance, 1955	93
No. 14 Bedford Lomas Ambulance, 1962	22
No. 14 Grifo Sports Car, 1968	17
No. 14 Mini Ha Ha, 1975	10
No. 15 Prime Mover, 1955	55
No. 15 Dennis Refuse Truck, 1963	50
No. 15 Volkswagen 1500 Saloon, 1968	25
No. 15 Fork Lift Truck, 1972	11
No. 16 Low-Loading Trailer, 6 wheels, 1955	57
No. 16 Low-Loading Trailer, 8 wheels, 1955	55
No. 16 Scammel Mountaineer Dump with Plow, 1961	31
No. 16 Case Tractor Bulldozer, 1969	33
No. 16 Badger, 1974	11

	MIB
No. 16 Pontiac, 1981	3
No. 17 Bedford Removal Van, 1955	137
No. 17 Austin Taxi, 1960	99
No. 17 18-Wheel Tipper "Hoveringham," 1964	22
No. 17 Horse Box "Ergomatic Cab," 1969	17
No. 17 Londoner, 1973	13
No. 18 Caterpillar Bulldozer, 1955	66
No. 18 Field Car, 1969	17
No. 18 Hondarora, 1975	10
No. 19 MG Midget Sports Car, 1955	104

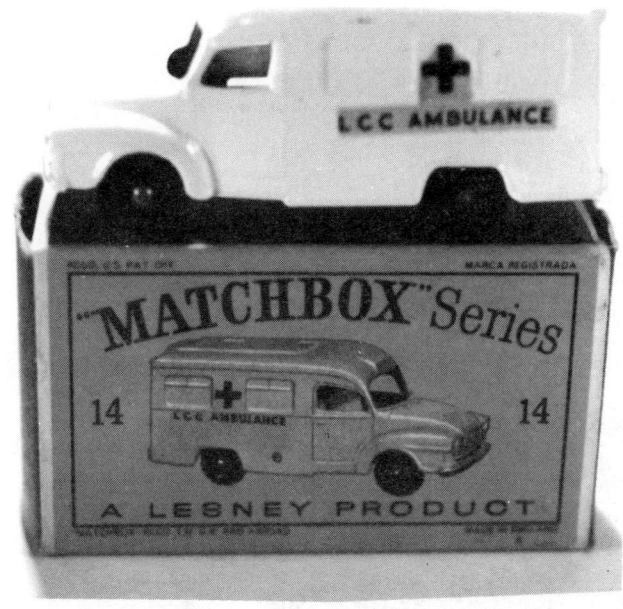

Matchbox No. 14 Bedford Lomas Ambulance. Courtesy Gary Linden.

Matchbox No. 19 MGA, Sports Car. Courtesy Gary Linden.

Matchbox No. 25 Bedford "Dunlop" Van. Courtesy Gary Linden.

	MIB
No. 19 MGA Sports Car, 1959	33
No. 19 Aston-Martin F.I., 1961	93
No. 19 Lotus Racing Car, 1965	17
No. 19 Road Dragster, 1971	11
No. 19 Cement Truck, 1976	10
No. 20 E.R.F. Lorry Truck, 1955	88
No. 20 Taxi Cab (Chevrolet Impala), 1965	25
No. 20 Lamborghini Marzel, 1969	11
No. 20 Police Patrol, 1975	8
No. 21 Long Distance Coach "London To Glasgow," 1955	104
No. 21 Commer Milk Truck, 1961	25
No. 21 Foden Concrete Truck, 1969	17
No. 21 Rod Roller, 1973	10
No. 22 Vauxhall Cresta, 1955	66
No. 22 Pontiac 'Grand Prix' Sports Coupe, 1964	30
No. 22 Freeman Inter-City Commuter, 1970	12
No. 22 Blaze Buster, 1975	10
No. 23 Caravan Trailer, 1956	17
No. 23 House Trailer Caravan, 1967	30
No. 23 Volkswagen Camper, 1970	17
No. 23 Atlas, 1975	8
No. 24 Excavator, 1956	30
No. 24 Rolls-Royce Silver Shadow, 1967	17
No. 24 Team 'Matchbox', 1973	11
No. 24 Diesel Shunter, 1979	8
No. 25 Bedford 'Dunlop' Van, 1956	66
No. 25 Volkswagen 1200 Sedan, 1958	103
No. 25 B.P. Tanker, 1960	20
No. 25 Ford Cortina G.T., 1968	17
No. 25 Mod Tractor, 1972	12
No. 25 Flat Car & Container, 1979	5
No. 26 Ready Mix Concrete Truck, 1956	55
No. 26 G.M.C. Tipper Truck, 1968	20
No. 26 Big Banger, 1972	11
No. 26 Site Dumper, 1976	8
No. 27 Bedford Low Loader, 1956	93
No. 27 Cadillac Sedan, 1960	104

	MIB
No. 27 Mercedes-Benz, 230SL, 1965	22
No. 27 Lamborghini Countach, 1974	10
No. 28 Bedford Compressor Truck, 1956	66
No. 28 Thames Compressor Truck, 1959	93
No. 28 Mark Ten Jaguar, 1964	25
No. 28 Mack Dump Truck, 1968	17
No. 28 Stoat, 1974	11
No. 28 Lincoln Continental, 1980	6
No. 29 Bedford Milk Delivery Van, 1956	55
No. 29 Austin A55 Cambridge, 1961	50
No. 29 Fire Pumper Truck, 1965	30
No. 29 Racing Mini, 1971	17
No. 29 Shovel Nose Tractor, 1976	7
No. 30 Ford Prefect with Towbar, 1956	83
No. 30 German Crane Truck, 1961	54
No. 30 Favin Crane, 8 wheel, 1965	22
No. 30 Beach Buggy, 1971	14
No. 30 Swamp Rat, 1977	6
No. 30 Articulated Truck, 1981	6
No. 31 Ford Customline Station Wagon, 1956	103
No. 31 Ford Fairlane Station Wagon, 1959	103
No. 31 Lincoln Continental, 1964	20
No. 31 Volks Dragon, 1971	17
No. 31 Caravan, 1977	5
No. 32 Jaguar, E Type	84
No. 32 Leyland Tanker, 1968	25
No. 32 Excavator, 1981	15
No. 33 Ford Zodiac MKII, 1956	93
No. 33 Ford Zephyr 6 MKIII, 1963	25
No. 33 Lamborghini Muira P400, 1969	13
No. 33 Datsun 126X, 1973	11
No. 33 Police Motorcyclist, 1977	12
No. 34 Volkswagen Microvan 'Matchbox' Express, 1956	66
No. 34 Volkswagen Camper, 1961	36
No. 34 Formula 1 Racing Car, 1971	13
No. 34 Vantastic, 1976	7
No. 34 Chevy Pro Stocker, 1981	8

Matchbox No. 28 Bedford Compressor Truck. Courtesy Gary Linden.

Matchbox No. 36 Lambretta Motorcycle with sidecar. Courtesy Gary Linden.

Matchbox No. 37 Coca-Cola Truck. Courtesy Gary Linden.

Matchbox No. 38 Darrier Refuse Collector. Courtesy Gary Linden.

Matchbox No. 42 "Bedford Evening News" Van. Courtesy Gary Linden.

Matchbox No. 46 Morris Minor 1000. Courtesy Gary Linden.

Matchbox No. 47 Trojan "Brooke Bond Tea" van. Courtesy Gary Linden.

	MIB
No. 35 Marschall Horse Box, 1956	71
No. 35 Sno-Trac Tractor, 1961	30
No. 35 Merryweather Marquis Fire Engine, 1970	20
No. 35 Fandango, 1975	17
No. 36 Austin A50 with Towbar, 1956	61
No. 36 Lambretta & Sidecar, 1960	71
No. 36 Opel Diplomat, 1966	20
No. 36 Hot Rod Draguar, 1971	17
No. 36 Formula 5000, 1975	7
No. 36 Refuse Truck, 1981	14
No. 37 Coca-Cola Truck, 1956	220
No. 37 Cattle Truck (Dodge), 1967	20
No. 37 Soopa Coopa, 1973	11
No. 37 Skip Truck, 1976	8
No. 38 Darrier Refuse Collector	93
No. 38 Vauxhall Estate, 1963	38
No. 38 Honda Motorcycle with Trailer, 1968	22
No. 38 Stingeroo, 1973	11
No. 38 Armored Jeep, 1976	16
No. 38 Camper, 1981	11
No. 39 Ford Zodiac Convertible, 1956	93
No. 39 Pontiac Convertible, 1962	62
No. 39 Ford Tractor, 1967	25
No. 39 Clipper, 1973	13
No. 39 Rolls-Royce Silver Shadow MKII	15
No. 40 Bedford 7 Ton Tipper, 1956	103
No. 40 Hay Trailer, 1967	20
No. 40 Leyland 'Royal Tiger' Coach/Long Distance, 1961	30
No. 40 Guildsman, 1971	11
No. 40 Horse Box, 1977	8
No. 41 'D' Type Jaguar Racing Car, 1956	110
No. 41 Ford G.T. 40 (Sports Racer), 1965	20
No. 41 Siva Spyder, 1972	11
No. 41 Ambulance, 1978	10
No. 42 Bedford 'Evening News' Van, 1956	71
No. 42 Studebaker Lark Wagonaire, 1965	19
No. 42 Iron Fairy Crane, 1969	54
No. 42 Tyre Fryer, 1972	16
No. 42 Container Truck, 1977	13

	MIB
No. 43 Hillman Minx, 1957	83
No. 43 Aveling-Barford Shovel, 1962	42
No. 43 Pony Trailer, 1968	20
No. 43 Dragon Wheels, 1972	11
No. 44 Rolls-Royce Silver Cloud, 1957	66
No. 44 Refrigerator Truck, GMC, 1967	20
No. 44 Boss Mustang, 1972	7
No. 44 Passenger Coach, 1978	14
No. 45 Vauxhall Victor, 1957	39
No. 45 Ford Corsair with Green Boat, 1959	22
No. 45 Ford Group Six, 1970	18
No. 45 BMW, 1976	8
No. 46 Morris Minor 1000, 1957	93
No. 46 Pickfords Removal Van, 1960	71
No. 46 Mercedes-Benz 300SE, 1968	18
No. 46 Stretcha Fetcha, 1972	11
No. 46 Ford Tractor, 1978	5
No. 47 Trojan 'Brooke Bond' Van, 1957	77
No. 47 Neilson Ice Cream Van, 1963	36
No. 47 DAF Tipper Container Truck, 1968	17
No. 47 Beach Hopper, 1973	14
No. 48 Sports Boat & Trailer, 1957	28
No. 48 Dodge Dumper Truck, 1967	24
No. 48 Pi-Eyed Piper, 1973	11
No. 48 Sambron Jack Lift, 1977	8
No. 49 Army Half Track MKIII, 1958	54
No. 49 Mercedes Unimog Truck, 1967	22
No. 49 Chop Suey, 1973	20
No. 49 Crane Truck, 1976	12
No. 50 Commer Pick-up Truck, 1958	83
No. 50 John Deere-Lanz Tractor, 1963	30
No. 50 Ford Kennel Truck, 1969	13
No. 50 Articulated Truck, 1973	9
No. 50 Harley-Davidson Motorcycle, 1981	6
No. 51 Albion Truck "Portland Cement," 1958	83
No. 51 Tipping Farm Trailer, 1963	20
No. 51 8 Wheel Tipper Truck, 1969	28
No. 51 Citroen SM, 1972	7
No. 51 Combine Harvester, 1979	6

Matchbox No. 49 Army Half Track MK III. Courtesy Gary Linden.

Matchbox No. 54 Army Saracen Personnel Carrier

	MIB
No. 52 Maserati 4 CLT, 1958	103
No. 52 BRM Racing Car, 1965	22
No. 52 Dodge Charger MKIII, 1970	11
No. 52 Police Launch, 1976	10
No. 53 Aston-Martin, DB2/4, 1959	93
No. 53 Mercedes-Benz 220SE, 1968	42
No. 53 Ford Zodiac MKIV, 1968	17
No. 53 Tanzara, 1972	13
No. 53 C.J. 6 Jeep, 1977	8
No. 54 Army Saracen Personnel Carrier, 1959	55
No. 54 Cadillac Ambulance, 1965	24
No. 54 Ford Capri, 1971	11
No. 54 Personnel Carrier, 1976	11
No. 54 Mobile Home, 1981	10
No. 55 D.U.K.W. (Army Amphibian), 1959	71
No. 55 Ford Police Car, 1963	32

	MIB
No. 55 Mercury Parkland Police Car, 1969	13
No. 55 Mercury Police Car (Station Wagon), 1970	22
No. 55 Hell Raiser, 1975	13
No. 55 Ford Cortina, 1980	6
No. 56 London Trolley Bus, 1959	93
No. 56 Fiat 1500, 1965	18
No. 56 BMC 1800 Pininfarina, 1970	11
No. 56 Hi Trailer, 1975	11
No. 56 Mercedes 450SEL, 1980	8
No. 57 Wolseley 1500, 1959	66
No. 57 Chevrolet Impala, 1966	84
No. 57 Eccles Caravan, 1970	33

Matchbox No. 56 Fiat 1500

Matchbox No. 55 Ford Police Car

Matchbox No. 59 Ford "Singer" Van. Courtesy Gary Linden.

Matchbox No. 60 Morris Omnitruck J-2 pick-up. Courtesy Gary Linden.

	MIB
No. 57 Wild Life Truck, 1973	14
No. 58 British European Airways Coach, 1959	93
No. 58 Drott Excavator, 1963	66
No. 58 DAF Girder Truck, 1968	17
No. 58 Woosh-N-Push, 1972	13
No. 58 Faun Dumper, 1976	8
No. 59 Ford 'Singer', Van, 1959	110
No. 59 Ford Fairlane Fire Car, 1964	30
No. 59 Fire Chief Car, 1966	16
No. 59 Planet Scout, 1975	11

	MIB
No. 59 Porsche 928, 1981	8
No. 60 Morris Omnitruck J2 Pick up	72
No. 60 Truck with Site Office, 1967	18
No. 60 Lotus Super Seven, 1971	14
No. 60 Holden Pick up, 1977	8
No. 61 Military Scout Car (Ferret), 1959	72
No. 61 Alvis Stalwart, 1967	42
No. 61 Blue Shark, 1971	7
No. 61 Wreck Truck, 1978	6
No. 62 General Army Lorry, 1959	83
No. 62 TV Service Van, 1964	36
No. 62 Mercury Cougar, 1969	18
No. 62 Rat Rod Dragster, 1971	13
No. 62 Renault 17TL, 1974	13
No. 62 Chevrolet Corvette, 1980	8
No. 63 Army Ambulance, 1959	42
No. 63 Airport Fire Fighting Crash Tender, 1964	49
No. 63 Dodge Crane Truck, 1968	18
No. 63 Freeway Gas Tanker, 1973	11
No. 64 Scammell Army Wreck Truck, 1959	93
No. 64 MG 1100, 1966	18
No. 64 Slingshot Dragster, 1971	18
No. 64 Fire Chief Car, 1976	14
No. 64 Caterpillar Tractor, 1981	8
No. 65 Jaguar 3.4 Litre Saloon, 1959	83
No. 65 Claas Combine Harvester, 1968	18
No. 65 Saab Sonnet, 1973	11
No. 65 Airport Coach, 1977	20
No. 66 Citroen DS19, 1959	83
No. 66 Harley-Davidson Motorcycle & Sidecar, 1963	143
No. 66 Greyhound Bus, 1967	18
No. 66 Mazda RX500, 1972	11
No. 66 Ford Transit, 1977	8
No. 67 'Saladin' Armored Car, 1959	33
No. 67 Volkswagen 1600 T.L., 1968	18

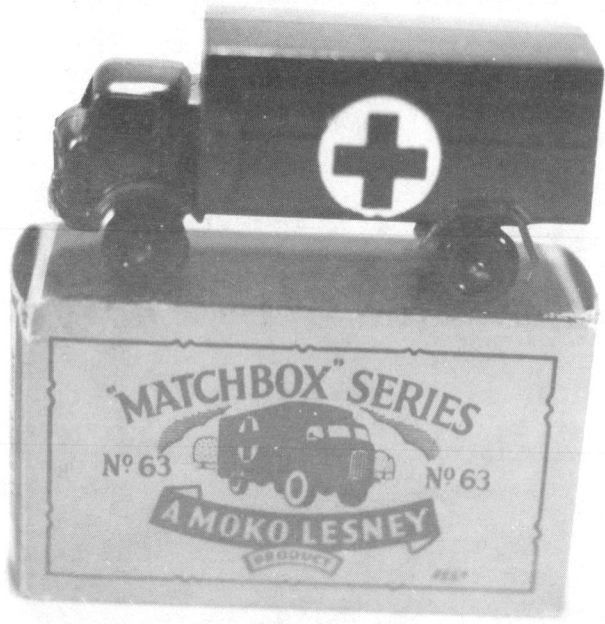

Matchbox No. 63 Army Ambulance. Courtesy Gary Linden.

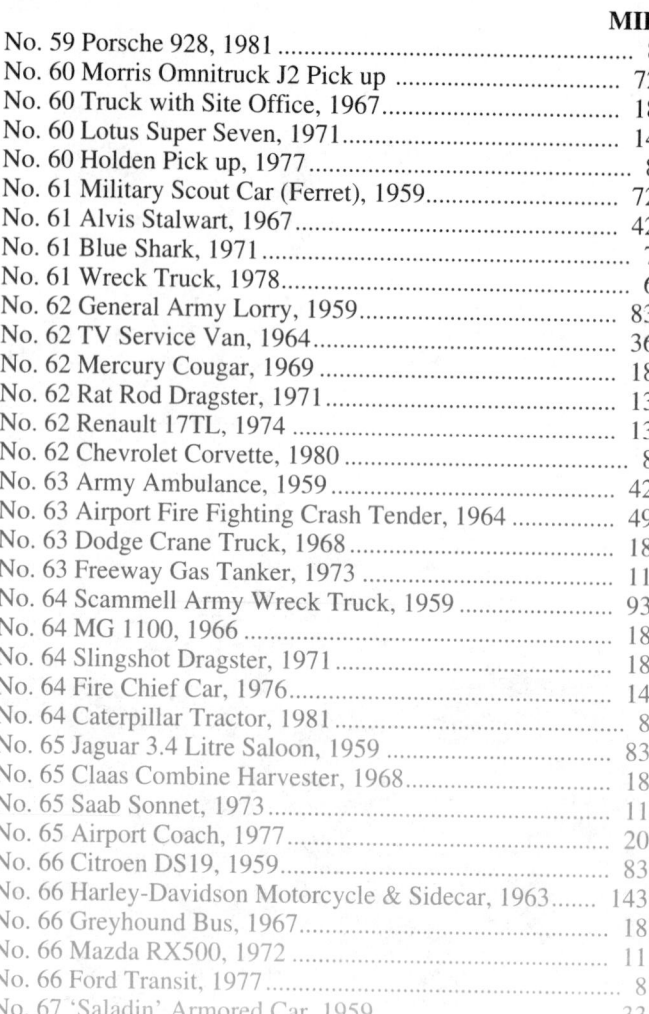

Matchbox No. 64 Scammel Army Wreck Truck. Courtesy Gary Linden.

Matchbox No. 68 Army Austin MK II Radio Truck. Courtesy Gary Linden.

	MIB
No. 67 Hot Rocker, 1973	11
No. 67 Datsun 260Z, 1978	8
No. 68 Army Austin MKII Radio Truck, 1959	61
No. 68 Mercedes Coach, 1965	18
No. 68 Porsche 910, 1970	17
No. 68 Cosmobile, 1975	15
No. 68 Chevrolet Van, 1980	8
No. 69 Commer 30 Cwt. Van 'Nestle's', 1959	110
No. 69 Hatra Tractor Shovel, 1965	42
No. 69 Rolls-Royce Silver Shadow, 1970	17
No. 69 Turbo Fury, 1973	11
No. 69 Wells Fargo Security, 1978	8
No. 70 Ford Thames Estate Car, 1959	46
No. 70 Atkinson Grit-Spreading Truck, 1965	16
No. 70 Dodge Dragster, 1971	17
No. 70 S.P. Gun, 1977	8
No. 70 Ferrari, 1981	8
No. 71 Army Water Truck, 1959	93
No. 71 Jeep Pickup Truck, 1964	67
No. 71 Ford Heavy Wreck Truck, 1968	44
No. 71 Cattle Truck, 1976	11
No. 72 Fordson Tractor (Power Major), 1959	71
No. 72 Standard Jeep, 1967	19
No. 72 Bomag Road Roller, 1980	7
No. 73 RAF 10-Ton Pressure Refueler Tanker, 1959	93
No. 73 Ferrari Racing Car, 1963	36
No. 73 Mercury Station Wagon (Commuter), 1969	18
No. 73 Weasel, 1974	11
No. 73 Model "A" Ford, 1981	8
No. 74 Mobile Refreshment Bar (Canteen), 1959	88
No. 74 Daimler Bus, 1966	24
No. 74 Toe Joe, 1972	7
No. 74 Cougar Villager, 1978	8
No. 75 Ford Thunderbird, 1959	110
No. 75 Ferrari Berlinetta, 1965	18
No. 75 Alfa Carabo, 1971	11

	MIB
Y-1 1936 Jaguar SS 100, 1977	17
Y-2 1911 "B" Type London Bus, 1955	90
Y-2 1911 Renault 2-Seater, 1963	36
Y-2 Prince Henry Vauxhall, 1970	21
Y-3 1907 London "E" Class Tramcar, 1955	120
Y-3 1910 Benz Limousine, 1965	50
Y-3 1934 Riley MPH, 1972	20
Y-4 Sentinel Steam Wagon, 1955	120
Y-4 1909 Opel Coupe, 1966	30
Y-4 1930 Duesenberg Model J, 1976	10
Y-5 1929 LeMans Bentley, 1955	77
Y-5 1929 Supercharged 4:1/2 Litre Bentley, 1960	30
Y-5 1907 Peugeot, 1968	33
Y-5 1927 Talbot Van, 1978	12
Y-6 1916 A.E.C. "Y" type Lorry Truck, 1955	72
Y-6 1926 Type "35" Bugatti, 1961	89
Y-6 1913 Cadillac, 1967	33
Y-6 1920 Rolls-Royce Fire Engine, 1978	14
Y-7 1914 4-Ton Leyland, 1955	130

Matchbox No. 69 Commer 30 CWT. Van "Nestle's." Courtesy Gary Linden.

Matchbox No. 73 RAF 10 ton Pressure Refueler Tanker. Courtesy Gary Linden.

Matchbox Y-5 Talbot Van. Courtesy Gary Linden.

	MIB
Y-7 1913 Mercer Raceabout Sportcar, 1961	16
Y-7 1912 Rolls-Royce, 1967	48
Y-8 1926 Morris Cowley "Bullnose," 1955	66
Y-8 1914 Sunbeam Motorcycle with Sidecar, 1962	113
Y-8 1914 Stutz Roadster, 1968	36
Y-8 1945 MGTC Sports Car, 1978	11
Y-9 1924 Fowler "Big Lion" Showman Engine, 1955	180
Y-9 1912 Simplex, 1967	54
Y-10 1908 Grand Prix Mercedes Racing Car, 1957	30
Y-10 1928 Mercedes-Benz, 36/220, 1963	54
Y-10 1906 Rolls-Royce Silver Cloud, 1968	18
Y-11 1920 Aveling & Porter Steam Roller, 1957	93
Y-11 1912 Packard Landaulet, 1963	42
Y-11 1938 Lagonda Drophead Coupe, 1972	19
Y-12 1899 Horse-Bus (London), 1957	99
Y-12 1909 Thomas Flyabout, 1967	42
Y-12 1912 Model "T" Ford, 1979	15
Y-13 1911 Daimler, 1965	60

	MIB
Y-13 1918 Crossley Truck, 1972	22
Y-14 1911 Maxwell Roadster, 1965	27
Y-14 1931 Stutz Bearcat, 1972	15
Y-15 1907 Rolls-Royce "Silver Ghost," 1960	48
Y-15 1930 Packard Victoria, 1969	16
Y-16 1904 Spyker Veteran Automobile, 1961	48
Y-16 1928 Mercedes SS, 1971	19
Y-17 1938 Hispano Suiza, 1972	19
Y-18 1937 Cord 812, 1979	19
Y-19 1935 Auburn 851, 1980	21
Y-20 1938 Mercedes 540K, 1981	17
Y-21 1929 Woody Wagon, 1981	11
Y-22 Model A Van	10

Matchbox Y-6 1913 Cadillac. Courtesy Gary Linden.

Matchbox Y-12 1912 Model T Ford. Courtesy Gary Linden.

Matchbox Y-14, 1931 Stutz Bearcat. Courtesy Gary Linden.

Matchbox Mobile Action Command; value in C6, C8, C10: $5, $10, $20. Photo by Gary Linden.

MATTEL'S HOT WHEELS

(1968-1979)

by Ron Smith

Whoda thunkit? But these little under-a-buck gems are the fastest-selling toys at flea markets and toy shows. It all started in 1968 when Mattel issued the original 16 metallic-colored toy cars. Today, most toy discount stores will have at least a 4-foot section of space devoted to this fast-turnover line of toy vehicles. Listed are issues from 1968 to 1979 (the red-line era).

These are the most sought after by toy collectors, especially if they are still in their original blister package (C-10). Most are found, however, in used condition (C-6).

Note: Asterisk denotes re-release with some probable change in color.

	C6	C8	C10
HW 1, A-OK	3	6	12
HW 2, Alive 55*	20	40	100
HW 3, Ambulance	8	15	30
HW 4, American Victory*	4	6	15
HW 5, American Hauler	4	8	20
HW 6, American Tipper	4	8	20
HW 7, AMX/2	10	20	35
HW 8, Army Funny Car	4	6	15
HW 9, Auburn 852	2	5	10
HW 10, AW Shoot	3	8	15
HW 11, Backwoods Bomb*	8	15	35
HW 12, Baja Breaker	2	5	10
HW 13, Baja Bruiser	4	10	30
HW 14, Beatnik Bandit	2	6	15
HW 15, Boss Hoss*	15	40	85
HW 16, Brabham Repco F1	3	6	15

	C6	C8	C10
HW 17, Breakaway Bucket	4	12	28
HW 18, Bubble Gunner	2	4	8
HW 19, Bugeye	3	10	25
HW 20, Buzz Off	10	30	75
HW 21, Bye Focal	10	20	60
HW 22, Bywayman	2	5	10
HW 23, Carabo	10	15	30
HW 24, California Cruisin'	3	6	10
HW 25, Captain America*	3	6	15
HW 26, Cement Mixer	6	12	30
HW 27, Chaparral 2G	2	4	10
HW 28, Chevy Monza 2+2	5	12	25
HW 29, Chevy 1957	3	5	15
HW 30, Chiefs Special 442	25	40	75
HW 31, Classic Cord	45	65	125
HW 32, Classic Nomad	8	12	50

L to R: HW7, HW115, HW114. Photo by Ron Smith.

L to R: HW19, HW136, HW109. Photo by Ron Smith.

L to R: HW34, HW31, HW33. Photo by Ron Smith.

L to R: HW36, HW32, HW35. Photo by Ron Smith.

L to R: HW41, HW42, HW46. Photo by Ron Smith.

L to R: HW48, HW50, HW45. Photo by Ron Smith.

	C6	C8	C10		C6	C8	C10
HW 33, Classic 31 Woody	6	10	20	HW 51, Custom T-Bird	10	20	45
HW 34, Classic 32 Ford Vicky	6	10	20	HW 52, Custom Volkswagen	8	15	35
HW 35, Classic 57 Bird	6	10	20	HW 53, Deora	12	25	45
HW 36, Classic 36 Ford Coupe	6	12	25	HW 54, Doozie '31	2	4	8
HW 37, Cockney Cab	8	15	40	HW 55, Double Header	12	30	55
HW 38, Continental MKIII	8	12	25	HW 56, Double Vision	12	25	50
HW 39, Cool One*	8	15	30	HW 57, Dumpin' A	2	4	10
HW 40, Corvette Stingray	10	18	30	HW 58, Dumptruck	10	20	30
HW 41, Custom AMX	10	20	40	HW 59, Dune Daddy	8	15	40
HW 42, Custom Barracuda	15	40	65	HW 60, Elray Special	8	15	45
HW 43, Custom Camaro	15	40	65	HW 61, Emergency Squad	4	8	20
HW 44, Custom Charger	20	45	65	HW 62, Evil Weevil	8	20	35
HW 45, Custom Corvette	10	20	60	HW 63, Exploder	20	50	100
HW 46, Custom Cougar	10	20	60	HW 64, Ferrari 312P ***	4	10	15
HW 47, Custom Eldorado	10	20	40	HW 65, Ferrari 512S	8	20	60
HW 48, Custom Firebird	10	20	40	HW 66, Fire-Chief Cruiser	4	10	20
HW 49, Custom Fleetside	12	18	35	HW 67, Fire Chaser	2	4	10
HW 50, Custom Mustang	10	20	60	HW 68, Fire Eater	2	4	10

L to R: HW49, HW176, HW53. Photo by Ron Smith.

L to R: HW51, HW44, HW38. Photo by Ron Smith.

L to R: HW64, HW112, HW141. Photo by Ron Smith.

L to R: HW-83, HW215, HW20. Photo by Ron Smith.

L to R: HW85, HW15, HW100. Photo by Ron Smith.

L to R: HW90, HW136, HW159B. Photo by Ron Smith.

L to R: HW138, HW133, HW66. Photo by Ron Smith.

	C6	C8	C10
HW 69, Fire Engine	8	20	35
HW 70, Flat Out 442	2	3	6
HW 71, Ford J Car	2	3	10
HW 72, Ford MK IV	2	4	10
HW 73, Formula P.A.C.K.*	2	6	16
HW 74, Formula 5000	2	3	10
HW 75, Fuel Tanker	25	40	55
HW 76, Funny Money**	10	15	30
HW 77, GMC Motorhome	2	4	8
HW 78, Grasshopper*	8	20	40
HW 79, Greased Gremlin	2	6	10
HW 80, Gremlin Grinder	6	12	35
HW 81, Gun Bucket	2	6	14
HW 82, Gun Slinger	2	6	20
HW 83, Hairy Hauler	4	10	25
HW 84, Hare Splitter	2	4	8
HW 85, Heavy Chevy ***	6	15	35
HW 86, Hi-Tail Hauler '56	2	5	20
HW 87, Hiway Patrol	3	8	15
HW 88, Hiway Robber	12	25	50
HW 89, Hot Bird	2	5	10
HW 90, Hot Heap	3	8	20
HW 91, Human Torch	2	5	10
HW 92, Ice T**	4	12	30
HW 93, Indy Eagle	2	5	15
HW 94, Inferno	6	15	30
HW 95, Inside Story	2	3	5
HW 96, Jack Rabbit Special	2	6	15
HW 97, Jaguar XJS	2	4	8
HW 98, Jet Threat	4	10	25
HW 99, Jet Threat II	4	10	25
HW 100, King Kuda*	6	12	30
HW 101, Khaki Kooler	6	10	20
HW 102, Large Charge*	5	10	25
HW 103, Letter Getter	2	5	10
HW 104, Lickety Six	3	6	12
HW 105, Light My Firebird	8	15	26
HW 106, Lola GT 70	2	4	10
HW 107, Lotus Turbine	2	3	10
HW 108, Lowdown*	5	12	25
HW 109, Mantis	3	6	10
HW 110, Maserati Mistral	4	10	30
HW 111, Maxi Taxi 442	15	22	35
HW 112, MC Laren M6A	2	3	8
HW 113, Mercedes-Benz C 111	5	10	25

	C6	C8	C10
HW 114, Mercedes-Benz 280 SL	4	9	17
HW 115, Mighty Maverick XXX	10	20	35
HW 116, Mod Quad	3	6	15
HW 117, Mongoose Funny Car	15	20	50
HW 118, Mongoose Dragster	15	25	40
HW 119, Monte Carlo Stocker*	8	12	25
HW 120, Moto Cross	9	15	35
HW 121, Moto Cross Van	8	12	35
HW 122, Moving Van	9	15	30
HW 123, Mustang Stocker ****	20	30	75
HW 124, Mutt Mobile	10	18	40
HW 125, Neet Streeter	3	6	15
HW 126, Nitty Gritty Kitty	12	20	30
HW 127, Noodle Head	9	15	30
HW 128, Odd Job	20	30	90
HW 129, Odd Rod*	8	12	25
HW 130, Olds 442	75	125	250
HW 131, Open Fire	40	60	90
HW 132, P-911*	3	8	15
HW 133, Paddy Wagon*	3	8	15
HW 134, Packin Pacer	2	4	8
HW 135, Paramedic	3	8	15
HW 136, Peepin Bomb	2	6	12
HW 137, Poison Pinto	3	8	15
HW 138, Police Cruiser	20	40	90
HW 139, Police Cruiser 442	30	40	55
HW 140, Pit Crew Car	30	45	65
HW 141, Porsche 917	2	6	12
HW 142, Power Pad	4	15	30
HW 143, Prowler*	20	40	90
HW 144, Python	2	3	10
HW 145, Race Bait 308	2	3	5
HW 146, Racer Rig	30	45	65
HW 147, Ramblin' Wrecker	5	10	30
HW 148, Ranger Rig	6	12	30
HW 149, Rash 1	8	20	40
HW 150, Rear Engine Mongoose (drag)	50	70	125
HW 151, Rear Engine Mongoose (funny)	50	70	125
HW 152, Rear Engine Snake (drag)	50	70	125
HW 153, Rear Engine Snake (funny)	50	70	125
HW 154, Red Baron*	4	8	10
HW 155, Road King Truck	50	70	100
HW 156, Rock Buster	4	8	16
HW 157, Rocket Bye Baby	5	10	30
HW 158, Rodger Dodger	6	12	50

L to R: HW144, HW14, HW160. Photo by Ron Smith.

L to R: HW170, HW173, HW203. Photo by Ron Smith.

L to R: HW171, HW27, HW93. Photo by Ron Smith.

L to R: HW175, HW163, HW76. Photo by Ron Smith.

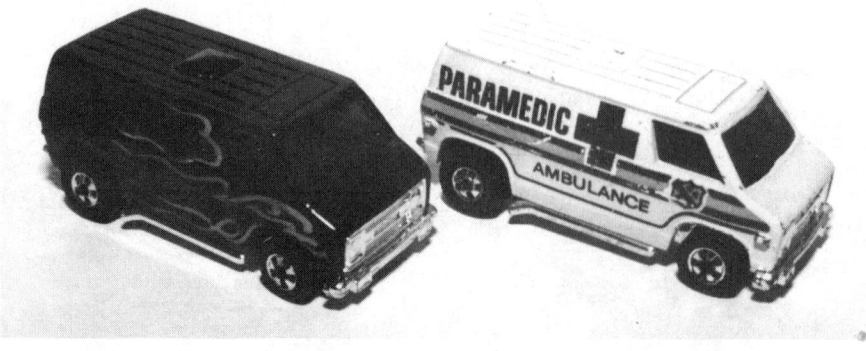

L to R: HW195, HW135. Photo by Ron Smith.

	C6	C8	C10		C6	C8	C10
HW 159, Royal Flash	2	3	6	HW 189, Street Eater	5	10	40
HW 159B, Rolls-Royce Silver Shadow	6	14	30	HW 190, Street Rodder	2	4	15
HW 160, Sand Crab	3	6	10	HW 191, Street Snorter	12	25	50
HW 161, Sand Drifter	6	12	22	HW 192, Strip Teaser	8	15	40
HW 162, Sand Witch	15	40	80	HW 193, Sugar Caddy	6	12	25
HW 163, S' Cool Bus	40	60	85	HW 194, Super-fine Turbine	75	90	125
HW 164, S' Cooper	30	40	55	HW 195, Super Van*	10	20	30
HW 165, Science Fiction	2	3	5	HW 196, S.W.A.T. Van	8	15	30
HW 166, Sea Sider	20	30	50	HW 197, Sweet 16	9	18	35
HW 167, Second Wind	6	12	15	HW 198, Swinging, Wing*	3	7	14
HW 168, Show Hoss II*	30	150	300	HW 199, T-4-2	8	15	30
HW 169, Show Off	8	20	40	HW 200, T-Bird 57	2	3	6
HW 170, Short Order	10	20	40	HW 201, T-Totaller	4	8	15
HW 171, Shelby Turbine	5	10	20	HW 202, Team Hauler	15	30	60
HW 172, Six Shooter	8	15	30	HW 203, The Demon	4	8	15
HW 173, Silhouette	2	4	10	HW 204, The Hood	5	10	20
HW 174, Side Kick	5	10	45	HW 205, The Incredible Hulk*	4	8	10
HW 175, Sir Rodney Roadster	6	12	40	HW 206, The Thing	4	8	15
HW 176, Sky Show Fleetside	50	100	200	HW 207, Thor	4	8	15
HW 177, Snake	40	60	125	HW 208, TNT Bird	5	10	20
HW 178, Snake Dragster	30	40	75	HW 209, Top Eliminator*	9	18	40
HW 179, Snorkel	30	40	50	HW 210, Torero	4	8	15
HW 180, Space Van	6	12	25	HW 211, Torino Stocker*	7	15	25
HW 181, Spacer Racer	2	4	7	HW 212, Tough Customer	2	5	10
HW 182, Special Deliveries	10	20	30	HW 213, Tow Truck	6	12	25
HW 183, Spider-Man*	6	10	15	HW 214, Tri Baby	5	10	20
HW 184, Splittin Image	3	6	10	HW 215, Turbo Fire	2	3	6
HW 185, Spoiler Sport	2	4	8	HW 216, Twin Mill	2	4	10
HW 186, Staff Car 442	100	300	500	HW 217, Twin Mill II	2	4	10
HW 187, Stagefright	3	6	9	HW 218, Up Front 924	2	3	6
HW 188, Steamroller	8	18	27	HW 219, Volkswagen	8	15	30

L to R: HW198, HW184, HW198. Photo by Ron Smith.

L to R: HW208, HW105, HW126. Photo by Ron Smith.

	C6	C8	C10		C6	C8	C10
HW 220, VW Beach Bomb	8	15	50	HW 225, What 4	10	20	50
HW 221, Vega Bomb	8	15	60	HW 226, Whipped Creamer	5	10	20
HW 222, Vetty Funny	6	8	12	HW 227, Winnipeg	12	25	60
HW 223, Warpath	4	8	20	HW 228, Z Whiz	4	8	15
HW 224, Waste Wagon	10	20	50				

Punched-hole blister card.
5¾" x 6"

NEW! HOT WHEELS ASSORTMENT
NO. 1 #A6221

12 each of 8 metal cars, shown at the
left, on set-up wire rack display with
header card. 96 total cars plus laminated
Collector's Catalog.
Std. Pack: 1 ea. (1 carton)   Wt: 14 Lbs.

NEW! HOT WHEELS ASSORTMENT
NO. 2 #A6222

12 each of 8 metal cars, shown at the
right, on set-up wire rack display with
header card. 96 total cars.
Std. Pack: 1 ea. (1 carton)   Wt: 12 Lbs.

NEW! HOT WHEELS BASIC
ASSORTMENT NO. 1 #A6231

Same contents as #A6221, without wire
rack and Collector's Catalog.
Std. Pack: 1 ea. (1 carton)   Wt: 7 Lbs.

NEW! HOT WHEELS BASIC
ASSORTMENT NO. 2 #A6232

Same contents as #A6222, without wire
rack
Std. Pack: 1 ea. (1 carton)   Wt: 7 Lbs.

A page from Mattel's initial 1968 "Hot Wheels" catalog.

L to R: HW216, HW23, HW154. Photo by Ron Smith.

L to R: HW19, HW136, HW109. Photo by Ron Smith.

MECCANO CARS

by Gates Willard

The Meccano Company closed its doors at the Liverpool, England, factory on Nov. 30, 1979. It was a sad ending to the great company founded by Frank Hornby early in the twentieth century. His construction sets had become very popular by the time the first specialized Meccano car constructor appeared in time for Christmas in 1932. The largest of the three cars to be made, it was later dubbed the No. 2 Motor Car Constructor Outfit. In 1933, the smaller No. 1 outfit became available at a much lower price. At about the same time, an accessory electric lighting set was made available for the No. 2 car only. The two-seater sports car (sometimes called the non-constructional car) probably appeared in 1934. It is in scale with the No. 1 constructor and has the same wheels, but it is nondemountable and was sold fully assembled. The two constructional cars were marketed in the USA, but the two-seater sports car was imported in very small numbers, if at all. In any case, it is rare in the United States and scarce in England. Meccano cars went out of production forever in 1940. A wooden garage was made, but few were sold. A beautiful miniature Kaye Oil can, made of copper and brass, is a much-sought-after accessory.

The French Meccano Factory also manufactured both car constructor sets, and these are identified by decals stating that they were made in France. Earlier models appear to be the same as their English counterparts, but the tires of the French No. 1 car can be marked Hutchinson, instead of Dunlop. Later French No. 1 cars continued to have demountable tires on stamped steel wheels, while the English No. 1 cars changed to solid-rubber wheels with metal discs on the outside only. The last French No. 1 cars retained the original chassis and wheels, but all of the sheet metal and radiators were revised to create a more modern appearance.

Recognizing that a complete construction set in a large box could be a bit formidable for a youngster whose manual dexterity, reading ability, and/or availability of funds might be limited, Meccano produced some lower-priced, factory-assembled constructional cars in both sizes. The box was big enough only for one assembled car, with no extra alternative pieces. Individually boxed assembled cars are identical to those sold in the larger sets. They were not very popular, and individually boxed constructor cars are rare today.

Why is no value guide possible for Meccano toys? Very few are changing hands in the 1990s, and not enough data exists to develop a reliable and useful listing of values.

How to identify approximately when an English Meccano car was made (note that over the years, parts can get substituted and moved around):

English No. 1 Meccano Car Constructor
Early (1933 to 1934): Demountable rubber tires on stamped steel wheels; yellow opaque headlight lenses, large oval decal (hood).

Later (1934 to 1940): Solid-rubber wheels with metal discs; translucent gray headlight lenses, small round decal (hood).

Colors:
Fenders: yellow/Body: green
Fenders: cream/Body: blue
Fenders: red/Body: cream
Fenders: red/Body: black
Fenders: blue/Body: red

English No. 2 Meccano Car Constructor
Early (1932 to 1933): Soft alloy wheels; Dunlop tires; rubber spare tire; no holes in seat or dashboard; tall handbrake lever; opaque yellow headlight lenses; split-pin steering mechanism assembly; large oval decal (rear body sections); smaller box.

Colors: All had cream fenders. Body was painted red, blue, or green. (Note from O' Brien: This set was auctioned in 1995 in excellent condition for $990.)

Later (1933 to 1940): Hard die-cast wheels (very subject to metal fatigue); Dunlop (more commonly) or Firestone tires; soft alloy cast metal tire cover; holes in seat and dashboard for figure and switch for lighting set; short handbrake lever; gray translucent headlight lenses; simplified steering assembly; round decal (rear body sections); larger box.

Colors:
Fenders: yellow/Body: green
Fenders: cream/Body: blue
Fenders: red/Body: cream
Fenders: red/Body: black
Fenders: blue/Body: red

Two-Seater Sports Car
Early: Opaque yellow headlight lenses; colors—same as No. 1 and No. 2 constructor cars (two-tone) except yellow-green and red-black combinations were not made; picture on box lid shows a red car with cream fenders, but the reverse of this combination was actually used; all had hand-painted black running boards.

Late: Translucent gray headlamp lenses; colors—the last cars were painted single colors—all blue with slightly darker blue wheel discs and all red with maroon wheel discs; hand painting of running boards black was phased out, cost savings passed on to the buyer, prices were slightly reduced; no picture label on box lid.

Left: Late French No. 1 Car; Right: Late English No. 1 Car. Courtesy Gates Willard. Photo by E.W. Willard.

Left: Late French No. 1 Car; Right: Late English No. 1 Car. Courtesy Gates Willard. Photo by E.W. Willard.

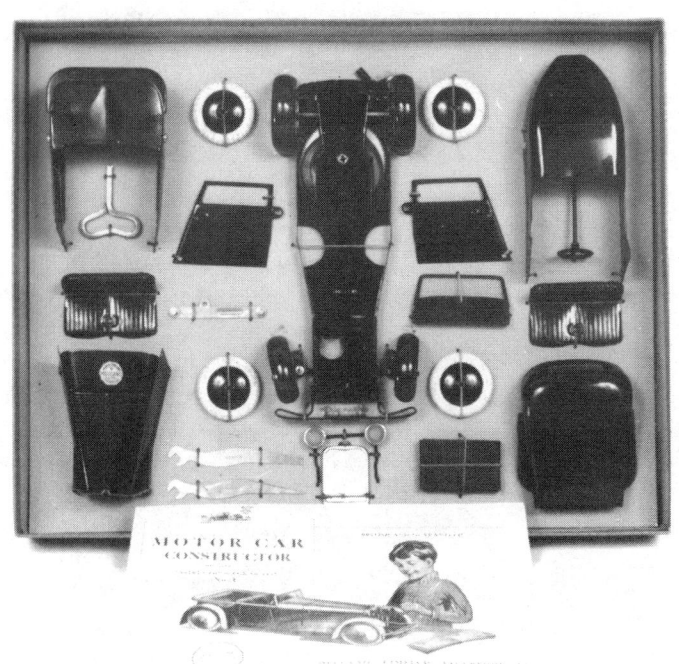

Five ways of assembling the English No. 1 Car; in front of original box. Photo by E.W. Willard. Courtesy Gates Willard.

Later (1939-40) No. 1 Car Constructor as purchased in the store. (Never out of its box.) Photo by E.W. Willard. Courtesy Gates Willard.

Left: Early (1933) No. 1 Car; Right: Later (1933-40) No. 1 Car. Courtesy Gates Willard. Photo by E.W. Willard.

Factory-assembled No. 1 Constructional Car with original box. Courtesy Gates Willard. Photo by E.W. Willard.

Meccano, left: Early (1932) No. 2 Constructor Car; Right: Later (1933-40) No. 2 Constructor Car. Courtesy Gates Willard. Photo by E.W. Willard.

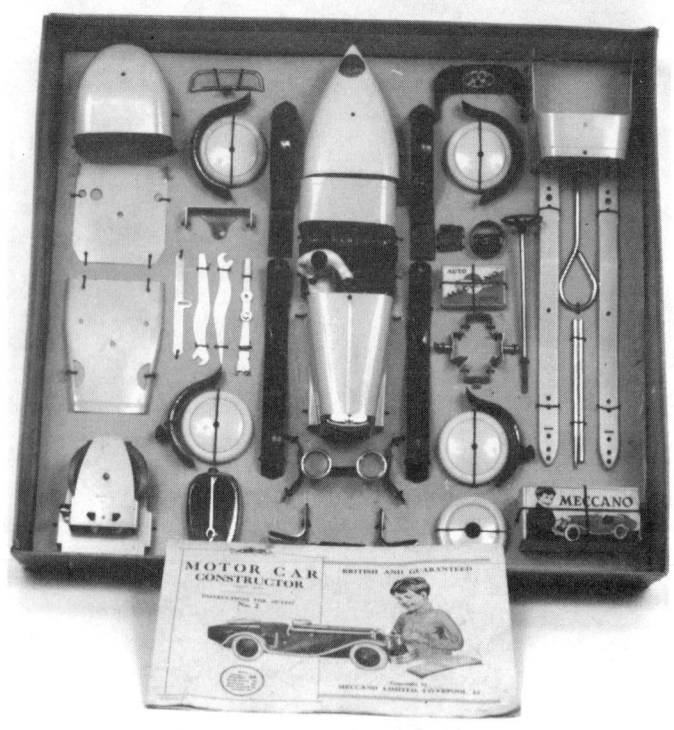

No. 2 Car Constructor shown as purchased at the store. Courtesy Gates Willard. Photo by E.W. Willard.

No. 2 Car assembled and placed on a store display stand; original box in background. Courtesy Gates Willard. Photo by E.W. Willard.

Left: Early (1932) No. 2 Constructor Car; Right: Late (1933-40) No. 2 Constructor Car. Courtesy Gates Willard. Photo by E.W. Willard.

Left: Miniature K (oil can) can be compared with a real one; Center: Electric Lighting Set with instructions; No. 2 Car is present to give concept of scale. Courtesy Gates Willard. Photo by E.W. Willard.

Tires for No. 2 Car, left Firestone, right Dunlop (more common). Courtesy Gates Willard. Photo by E.W. Willard.

Left: Early two-seater Sports Car with box; Right: Later two-seater Sports Car with box, picture label discontinued. Courtesy Gates Willard Photo by E.W. Willard.

A December, 1936 ad in Meccano Magazine *for the Meccano two-seater Sports Car. Courtesy Gates Willard.*

Size Comparison of No. 1 and No. 2 Constructor Cars. Courtesy Gates Willard. Photo by E.W. Willard.

Left: No. 1 Constructor Car. Right: 2-seater Sports Car (non-constructional). Courtesy Gates Willard. Photo by E.W. Willard.

September, 1935 Meccano Magazine. *Courtesy Gates Willard.*

METAL CAST PRODUCTS COMPANY

By Fred Maxwell, Slushmold *Contributing Editor*

Metal Cast Products, a reorganization c. 1925 of toy soldier and novelty company S. Sachs, made hand-operated slushcasting molds for small businesses and hobbyists—what some have called the home-casting industry. Since identical molds were sold to many, we cannot identify the actual makers, unless they engraved their names on their products. One who did was Fred Green Toys, whose name is found prominently on its toys. Metal Cast offered full-support services to its customers, including marketing, printing, publishing, and parts. A variety of wheels may be found on its ve-

hicles: including Tootsietoy-like metal disk wheels, metal spoke wheels, wood wheels with rubber tires, and white or black rubber wheels.

We see many home-cast lead soldiers (see O'Brien's *Collecting American Made Toy Soldiers Ed. 3*) and novelties, but the production of toy vehicles has not left us many. Perhaps it was the Great Depression, perhaps it was the lack of identity; demand today seems weak. However, collectors of the unusual should find many collectibles; most of those I have seen were well designed and professionally finished.

	C6	C8	C10
Metal Cast Van Truck, #01-02, COE, cab, semi-trailer moving van. Trailer also found in a "FRED GREEN" VERSION, 6"	20	30	40
Metal Cast Tank Truck, #01-03, same COE cab, semi-fuel tanker. My version is 5-3/4", "FRED GREEN TOYS," "Made in U.S.A.," 6"	20	30	40
Metal Cast Open Rack Truck, #01-04, COE cab, stake semi-trailer, 6"	8	12	16
Metal Cast War Tank, #39, early heavy Sherman Tank, 4"	33	49	66
Metal Cast Cadillac Sedan, #40, 2-door, 5-1/4" long	No Price Found		
Metal Cast Cadillac Sedan, #40, second version, 2-door, 5-3/4	No Price Found		
Metal Cast Packard Convertible, #41, 2-door, top down, 5-1/4"	10	15	20
Metal Cast Packard Convertible, #41, second version, 5-3/4"	No Price Found		
Metal Cast Dump Truck, #42	No Price Found		
Metal Cast Dump Truck, #43, COE unique chassis w/activating mechanism, 5-1/4"	No Price Found		
Metal Cast Sedan #44, postwar, 6"	No Price Found		
Metal Cast Packard Convertible #45, 6"	No Price Found		

	C6	C8	C10
Metal Cast War Tank, #55. Early WWI type w/side turrets	No Price Found		

Metal Cast Products, Top row: No. 01-02; Middle row: No. 01-03; Bottom row: No. 40. Photo by Perry Eichor.

Metal Cast War Tank No. 39. From a Metal Cast catalog.

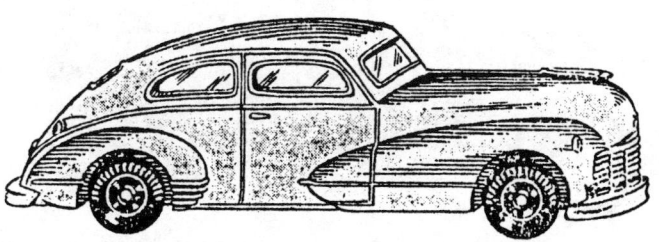

Metal Cast Cadillac Sedan #40, second version.

	C6	C8	C10
Metal Cast Streamline Sedan, #60, DeSoto? Airflow, 6 open windows, smooth grille, rubber tires, 4"	10	15	20
Metal Cast Sport Coupe, #60. Vee grille Graham (?), from 3-piece mold. Very similar to Kansas Toy's #75	No Price Found		
Metal Cast Fire Engine, #61, hook and ladder truck, crew of 2, 4-1/2"	6	10	14
Metal Cast Racer, #62, Bluebird type, blunt-nosed, V-8, record car, driver, 4-1/2"	No Price Found		
Metal Cast Coupe #63, convertible, 2 open windows, sidemounts, trunk	No Price Found		
Metal Cast Truck, #64, Dodge?, stake-body, 1920s, 2 OW, 4-1/4"	No Price Found		

	C6	C8	C10
Metal Cast Fire Engine, #65, Steam pumper w/water cannon, driver, 4"	No Price Found		
Metal Cast Fire Engine, no #, similar to #65 w/o water cannon, 3-7/8"	6	10	14
Metal Cast Racer, #92, large Indy type with bulging radiator, no driver, torpedo tail	No Price Found		
Metal Cast Greyhound Bus, no #	No Price Found		
Metal Cast Limousine, no #	No Price Found		
Metal Cast No. 01-02 Van Truck, 6" long, in 1949 catalog	No Price Found		
Metal Cast No. 01-03 Tank Truck, 6" long, in 1949 catalog, L molds	No Price Found		
Metal Cast No. 01-04 Open Rack Truck, 6" long, in 1949 catalog, 2 molds	No Price Found		

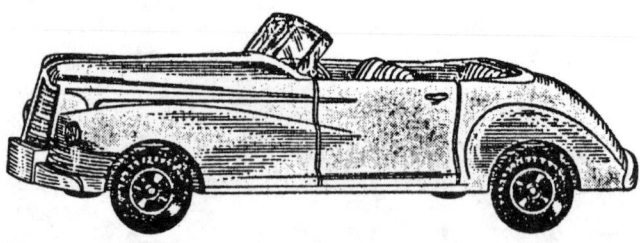

Metal Cast Packard Convertible No. 41, second version; from a Metal Cast catalog.

Metal Cast Dump Truck No. 42

Metal Cast Sport Coupe #60; from a Metal Cast catalog.

Metal Cast No. 61

Metal Cast No. 65

Metal Cast Racer #92. Courtesy Bob Ackerly.

Want to produce the Latest?
—HERE THEY ARE—
This year's fastest selling Wheel Toys!

The First Scale Models of Trailer-Trucks on the market. The newest in Sedans and Convertibles. Accurate in every detail. Fascinating Toys and attractive for Model Railway layouts, etc.

A LEADING LINE WITH ALL TOY AND NOVELTY DEALERS — DEPARTMENT AND CHAIN STORES.

No. 44 SEDAN
6 Inches Long
Bronze castingform
for hollow casting **$75.00**

No. 01-02 VAN TRUCK
6 Inches Long

Bronze form No. 01
for hollow casting
CAB OVER ENGINE
TRACTOR **$50.00**

Bronze form No. 02 for hollow casting
VAN TRAILER UNIT **$50.00**

No. 45 CONVERTIBLE
6 Inches Long
Bronze castingform
for hollow casting **$95.00**
(Includes mould for casting windshield which is easily assembled to casting.)

No. 01-04 OPEN RACK TRUCK
6 Inches Long

Bronze form No. 01
for hollow casting CAB
OVER ENGINE
TRACTOR **$50.00**

Bronze form No. 04
for hollow casting
RACK BODY
TRAILER UNIT **$50.00**

No. 01-03 TANK TRUCK
6 Inches Long
Bronze form No. 01
for hollow casting
CAB OVER ENGINE
TRACTOR **$50.00**
Bronze form No. 03 for hollow casting
TANK TRAILER UNIT **$50.00**

NOTE:—As the same Cab-Over-Engine Tractor is used for all Trailer Sets, only one No. 01 form is needed for manufacturing all three.
Trailer Trucks sell separately or in Sets
(See attached price list.)

Castings come from moulds with axle holes and rubber wheels are easily assembled by simply slipping over standard nails. A new exclusive method eliminates need of spreading or crimping axles.
Wheels supplied manufacturers at $ . . . . per thousand.

METAL CAST PRODUCTS CO.
1696 BOSTON ROAD
NEW YORK 60, N. Y.

Copyrighted 1949

A page from a 1949 Metal Cast catalog.

Metal Cast Products, Top row: Greyhound Bus, No. 62; Middle row: No. 40 Limousine, No. 60; Bottom row: No. 64. Photo by Perry Eichor.

METAL MASTERS

(listing by Dave Leopard)

	C6	C8	C10		C6	C8	C10
MM01 Roadster, c.1938, 7" long	25	38	50	MM09 Station Wagon, c.1940, 8-1/2" long, ambulance version	45	55	70
MM02 Bus, c.1938, 7-1/4" long	42	63	85				
MM03 Pickup Truck, c.1938, 7" long	25	38	50	MM10 Tow Truck, c.1940, 10" long, "ABC Towing Service"	50	75	100
MM04 Fire Truck version of Pickup, c.1938, 7" long	37	56	75	MM11 Tow Truck, c.1940, 10" long, windup motor	52	78	105
MM05 Tow Truck version of Pickup, c.1938, 7" long	30	40	50	MM12 Firetruck, c.1940, 10" long, removable ladders	50	60	75
MM06 Jeep, c.1947, 5-1/2" long	20	25	30				
MM07 Station Wagon, c.1940, 8-1/2" long	40	50	65	MM13 Firetruck, c.1940, 10" long, ladders, windup motors	60	90	120
MM08 Station Wagon, c.1940, 8-1/2" long, windup motor	45	55	70	MM14 Tractor w/driver, 5" long	55	82	110

METALCRAFT

Metalcraft, of St. Louis, Missouri, began producing its pressed-steel trucks in 1931. About a million were sold, most as "advertising toys." In 1937, defeated by the Depression, Metalcraft shuttered. According to a collector-researcher, Al Korte was the designer of all of the firm's trucks and worked there from 1931 to 1936.

	C6	C8	C10		C6	C8	C10
Metalcraft BFG Wrecker	300	450	600	Metalcraft Coca-Cola Truck, 10 bottles, 10-1/2" long, 1930s	350	525	700
Metalcraft "Bunte Candies" 12" truck	250	350	500				
Metalcraft "Buster Brown Shoes"	300	450	600	Metalcraft Coca-Cola Truck, 12" long, 10 bottles, late 1930s, long nose, stamped metal	450	675	900
Metalcraft "Clover Farm Stores"	450	675	900				
Metalcraft Coca-Cola Truck, 11" long, pressed steel, rubber tires, c. late 1920s-early 1930s, 10 bottles in rack, "Every Bottle Sterilized"	400	600	900	Metalcraft Coca-Cola Truck, c.1928, with bottles in racks	438	655	875
				Metalcraft CW Coffee Dump Truck, 10-3/4" long	300	475	600

Metalcraft Coca-Cola Truck, late 1930s, 12" long. Courtesy Richard L. MacNary.

Metalcraft "Clover Farm Stores." Photo by Bob Smith.

Metalcraft Coca-Cola Truck, 11" long. Courtesy Wilkinson Collection, Detroit Antique Toy Museum.

Metalcraft CW Coffee Dump Truck. Photo by Orville C. Britton.

Metalcraft "Decker's Iowana," sweet heart grill. Photo by Bob Smith.

Metalcraft, L to R: Coca-Cola truck, "Heinz" Truck. Courtesy Phillips NY.

	C6	C8	C10
Metalcraft CW Coffee Wrecker	350	525	700
Metalcraft "Deckers Iowana"	500	700	1000
Metalcraft Delivery Truck Van, 11" long, steel	200	300	450
Metalcraft Dump Truck, 24" long, electric headlights	200	300	450
Metalcraft Esso Stake Truck with barrels, 12" long	500	700	1100
Metalcraft "Goodrich Silvertown Tires" Wrecker, with 3 spare tires	275	415	550
Metalcraft Hardy's Salt Truck	200	300	400
Metalcraft "Heinz" Truck, c.1932 "Baked Beans, Bottled Vinegar," "Rice Flakes," 12" long	275	375	575
Metalcraft "Ice" Truck	245	368	490
Metalcraft "Kroger Food Express," 11" long	300	450	600
Metalcraft "Krug Bakery" truck	450	675	935

	C6	C8	C10
Metalcraft "Leslie Vacuum Packed Coffee"	425	638	850
Metalcraft "Machinery Hauling"	500	700	900
Metalcraft "Meadow Gold Butter" Truck, 13" long, battery lights	400	600	900
Metalcraft "Plee-zing Quality Products" Delivery Van, 11" long, c.1928	300	450	600
Metalcraft "Pure Oil Co." tanker, 14-3/4", elec. lights	500	700	1000
Metalcraft "Sand-Gravel" Dump	175	263	500
Metalcraft "Shell Motor Oil" Truck, includes 8 oil drums	400	675	900
Metalcraft "St. Louis" Truck, 11" long, c.1930	175	263	350
Metalcraft Steam Shovel	115	172	230
Metalcraft "Sunshine Biscuits" Truck	275	363	550
Metalcraft "Towing & Repairs"	250	375	500
Metalcraft "Toy Town Grocery"	275	363	550

Metalcraft "Machinery Hauling." Photo by Calvin L. Chaussee.

Metalcraft "Meadow Gold Butter." Photo by Bob Smith.

Metalcraft "Plee-Zing Quality Products" Delivery Van, 11" long, c.1928. Photo by Bob Smith.

Metalcraft "Pure Oil Co.," sweet heart grill. Photo by Bob Smith.

Metalcraft "Sand-Gravel" dump. Photo by Bob Smith.

Metalcraft "Shell Motor Oil" with eight oil drums. Photo by Bob Smith.

Heavy Gauge Steel Toy Trucks—2 Styles

Metalcraft, L to R: "Shell Motor Oil" and "Goodrich Silvertown Tires" trucks as shown in the October 1932 Butler Bros. catalog.

Metalcraft "Waldorf Lager," sweet heart grill. Photo by Bob Smith.

Metalcraft Steam Shovel. Photo by Calvin L. Chaussee.

	C6	C8	C10
Metalcraft "Waldorf Lager"	400	600	900
Metalcraft "Weatherbird Shoes"	245	375	490
Metalcraft "Werks Tag Soap" Truck	300	450	600

	C6	C8	C10
Metalcraft "Weston's English Biscuits" Truck	250	375	500
Metalcraft "White King Express" Truck, 12" long	258	385	515

METALGRAF COMPANY

(Milan, Italy)

By Bob Smith

Metalgraf Company manufactured toys from 1920 until 1939. It is still in business today, but has not produced toys for many years. A Metalgraf car is seldom found offered for sale. They are considered rare and are especially hard to find in the United States.

	C6	C8	C10
Metalgraf Touring Car, Gray/black litho, c/w motor, steering, 10" long, c.1922	1200	1750	2600

Metalgraf Touring Car, c.1922, 10" long. Photo by Bob Smith.

METTOY

(Great Britain)

	C6	C8	C10
Mettoy Bus, streamlined, windup, 7-1/4"	95	140	190
Mettoy Citroen Sedan, 11"	188	282	375
Mettoy Clown on Motorcycle, 7-1/4" long	550	800	1210
Mettoy Coupe	400	600	800
Mettoy Motorcycle, c.1940	425	638	850
Mettoy Motorcycle No. 49, tin windup, 8"	262	393	525
Mettoy Racer, "7", 5" long	750	1400	1800
Mettoy Rolls Royce, 14" long	500	800	1200
Mettoy Sedan, 14" long, c.1930	300	450	600
Mettoy Steam Roller, clockwork	100	150	200
Mettoy Tractor, tin windup, 8" long	55	83	110

MIDGETOY

Midgetoy was created in 1946 by brothers Alvin and Earl Herdklotz, who, from 1943, as A&E Tool and Gauge Co., had produced precision tooling for defense. Their intention with Midgetoy was to produce low cost die-cast vehicles that were sturdy and precisely detailed. Midgetoys run from 2 inches to 9 inches in length and were an immediate hit with five & tens, and later, at discount chains such as Wal-Mart. There were about 200 different models and 100 full-time employees. Midgetoy stopped producing toys in 1981.

Army Vehicles

	C6	C8	C10
Midgetoy Sherman Tank, late 40s, 4"	14	21	28
Midgetoy Self-Propelled Artillery, late 1940s, 4"	12	18	25
Midgetoy Half Track, late 1940s, 4-3/4"	12	18	25
Midgetoy Self-Propelled Artillery, 1957, 6"	14	21	28
Midgetoy Fuel Tank Truck, 1954, 4-1/2"	11	16	22
Midgetoy U.S.A. Jeep, 1950, 2-3/4"	7	11	15
Midgetoy U.S.A. Jeep, 1950, 1-1/2"	5	8	10
Midgetoy Howitzer, late 1940s, 3"	7	11	15
Midgetoy Staff Car, 1950s, 4-1/2"	12	18	25
Midgetoy Utility Trailer, 1940s, 1-1/2"	6	9	12
Midgetoy Army Bus, 1950s, 3-1/2"	10	15	20
Midgetoy American LaFrance Fire Truck, 6" long, 1957........................	16	24	32
Midgetoy Boat and Trailer, 1949, 2-3/4"	7	10	15
Midgetoy Cadillac Ambulance, 1971, red/white, 3" long	7	11	15

Some Military Vehicles by Midgetoy, Rockford, IL (Tootsietoy 1-1/2" soldier for scale).
L to R - Back row: Turreted Assault Gun, Truck towing Field-piece, Half-track towing trailer, Van, Sherman Tank, Tracked Assault Gun.
Front row: Firetruck, Tank-Truck, tiny Jeep, Jeep, Staff Car, Ambulance, Modern Jeep.
Note: All but van & ambulance (same casting) imprinted with manufacturer's name. Photo by Ed Poole.

Midgetoy 6" Self-Propelled Artillery. Photo by Thomas G. Nefos, National Toy Connection.

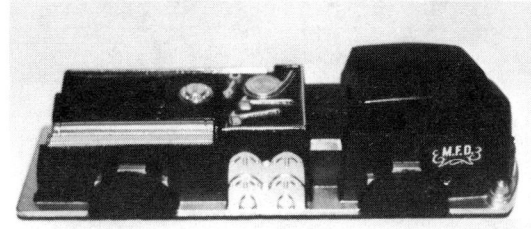

Midgetoy American LaFrance Fire Truck, 1957. Photo by Thomas G. Nefos, National Toy Connection.

Midgetoy 6" Oil Tank Truck, 1957. Photo by Thomas G. Nefos, National Toy Connection.

Midgetoy Scenic Cruiser Bus-Midgetoy Bus Lines, 1955. Photo by Thomas G. Nefos, National Toy Connection.

Midgetoy Semi-Auto Transporter with MG and Mustang, 1962. Photo by Thomas G. Nefos, National Toy Connection.

Midgetoy Semi-Tanker, 1963. Photo by Thomas G. Nefos, National Toy Connection.

	C6	C8	C10
Midgetoy Cadillac Convertible, 1949, green, 3-1/2"	10	15	20
Midgetoy Ford Mark IV, 1971, blue, 2-1/2"	7	11	15
Midgetoy Ford Mustang w/tow hook, 1970, orange, 2-1/2"	7	11	15
Midgetoy Ford Torino, 1971, green, 2-1/2"	7	10	14
Midgetoy Ford Torino, "Fire Chief," 1971, red, 2-1/2"	7	10	14
Midgetoy Ford Torino Police Car, 1971 white, 2-1/2"	7	10	14
Midgetoy Indy Car and Towing Trailer, late 40s, car 2", trailer 2-1/2"	10	15	20

	C6	C8	C10
Midgetoy Jeep, 1950s, red, 1-1/2"	5	8	10
Midgetoy Oil Tank Truck, "Midgetoy Oil Co.," 1957, 6" long	17	26	35
Midgetoy Scenic Cruiser Bus-Midgetoy Bus Lines, 1955, blue, 3-1/2"	9	13	18
Midgetoy Semi-Auto Transporter with MG & Mustang, 9", 1962	30	45	60
Midgetoy Semi-Tanker, 9", 1963	15	22	30
Midgetoy Streamline Car, 3-1/2"	7	10	14
Midgetoy Sunbeam Racer-Utah Salt Flats, 1950, 3-1/2"	10	15	20
Midgetoy Trailways Bus, 6", 1957	16	24	32

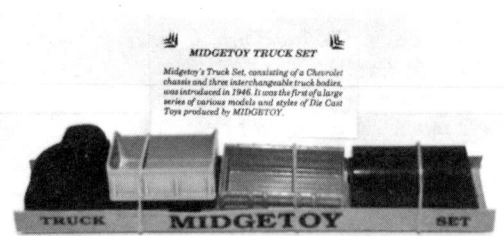

Midgetoy Truck Set, Chevrolet chassis with three interchangeable bodies, 1946; value in mint $45. Photo by Thomas G. Nefos, National Toy Connection.

The top layer of a Midgetoy salesman's sample box. Courtesy Thomas G. Nefos, National Toy Connection.

MID-WEST METAL NOVELTY MANUFACTURING COMPANY

Another "Orphan" dime-store toy maker is found.

By Fred Maxwell, Slushmold Contributing Editor, assisted by Ferd Zegel and John West.

In the late 1920s, the U.S. auto industry, led by Ford, was not only booming but dominating global production, and auto toys were keeping up with their prototypes. We focus on three companies that had developed a thriving slushmold toy business: C.A.W. Novelty Co., Mid-West Metal Novelty Co., and Kansas Toy and Novelty Co. These were in small northern Kansas towns, Clay Center and Clifton, only a few miles apart. These toy makers had other things in common: they loved racers, they all used metal-disc wheels and black-painted "tires," they tended to follow the lead of Tootsietoy, and they left almost no paper trail.

This lack of a paper trail accounts for the difficulty toy historians have had identifying some excellent models and toys. The above clues suggest that Mid-West was C.E. Stevenson's business title. Stevenson,

an active businessman, was at the center of all this. In 1923, he started casting toys at home. In 1925, he joined Western Diecasting of Clay Center, probably as an outside salesman. Shortly after Kansas Toy started, he contracted to furnish molds to them. He may also have sold master patterns and those prepainted wheels to C.A.W. and Kansas Toy, for all these were probably made in the foundry of Western Diecasting. Our sole surviving newsclip on Mid-West in a 1929 *Toys and Novelties* magazine shows a deluxe (five-window) coupe, a fairly exact copy of the Tootsie Buick, but with those Kansas black-painted "tires."

But what else did Mid-West make? Over the years we have found a group of auto toys with a family resemblance: Tootsie copies or look-a-likes, Tootsie wheels, including those distinctive lug boltheads, metal-disc wheels with a suggested rim between wheel and tire (see photos MV3, MV4), but most important, several versions of that Buick coupe seen in *Toys and Novelties*. The most likely maker was Stevenson, before he moved on to a larger city in 1931 and founded Lincoln (Nebraska) White Metal Works, with which he thrived for years, despite the Great Depression.

These Mid-West (?) toys are rarely seen today. If found, they should be low-priced.

	C6	C8	C10
MW1 Large Coupe, no lamps, large die-cast?, 5 "grooved" solid windows, disc wheels w/"lug bolts" HG, HO, VL, 3-1/2"	No Price Found		
MW2 Yellow Taxicab, no lamps, door handles, 7 "grooved" solid windows, MDW w/rims but no bolts, HG, HO VOL, 2-3/4" long. Other versions with driver & passenger embossed on front windows, other windows open	No Price Found		

	C6	C8	C10
MW3 Buick Coupe, no lamps, disc wheels, 5 "grooved" solid windows, HG, HO, VL, sidemounts, 3 variations 4 open windows; 5 smooth windows; MDW w/ "lug bolts," 3"	12	18	25
MW4 Midget Racer, driver crouched & hunched over steering wheel, torpedo tail, small disc wheels w/ "lug bolts," HG, HO, VL, variation: narrower body and large wheels (the postwar (Barclay?)) "M & L" reproduction is more often found, 2-3/4".	No Price Found		

Midwest, L to R: MW2, MW1. Photo by Fred Maxwell.

Midwest, MW3, two versions. Photo by Fred Maxwell.

Midwest, MW2, two versions. Photo by Fred Maxwell.

Midwest, top to bottom: two versions of MW4, MW5. Photo by Fred Maxwell.

C6   C8   C10

MW5 Large Racer, basically similiar to
    above but boattailed w/medium sized
    disc wheels, 3-5/8" .... No Price Found
MW6 Large Truck. AC Mack, gas tank ahead of
    windshield, V6, screen louvers, full-sized
    solid "stake" body with open rear (for
    pouring). Unique slushmold design with
    solid, curved pan, 3-1/4" .... No Price Found
MW7 Large Roadster, Buick or Packard,
    long hood, top up, HG, HO, VL, door
    handles & hinges, RM, rear bumper.
    Variation: 2 colors, 3 solid windows,
    different, painted disc wheels, 3-5/8" ...... No Price Found
MW8 Touring Car, Ford T, driver & lady
    passenger w/muff, top down, no
    lamps, plain grille, HO, VL, door
    handles, disc wheels, 3-1/8" .... No Price Found
MW9 Touring Car, top up, no seats,
    HG, HO, VL, RM, side lamps, door
    handles, disc wheels, 3-1/8" .... No Price Found
MW10 Bus, Yellow Coach?, high,
    school-bus body, no doors, 13 solid
    grooved windows, HG, RM, painted
    disc wheels, 3-3/4" .... No Price Found
MW11 Town Car, chauffeur, long hood,
    HG, HO, VL, L/I, 3 colors, 5 solid
    windows, grooved, door handles &
    hinges, disc wheels, 3-5/8" .... No Price Found

C6   C8   C10

MW12 Bus, overland/safety, no lamps,
    no doors, no spares, HG, HO, 10 open
    windows, disc wheels (same bus later
    reissued by Stevenson at Lincoln
    White Metal Works), 3-1/2" .... No Price Found
MW13 Sedan, 2-door, Ford A, finely
    detailed screen grille, headlamps and
    fenders (made with a 3-piece mold,
    a Stevenson specialty), VL, WSV, 4 open
    windows, door handles & hinges,
    painted disc wheels, 2-3/4" .... No Price Found
MW14 Sedan?, Buick, same finely detailed
    front-end as above, "B" cast on grille,
    HO, VL, side lamps, WSV, 6 open
    windows, door-hinges, RM, painted
    wheels (a similar car has been
    attributed to Barclay Mfg.), 3-1/16" .... No Price Found
MW15 (Midwest?) Coupe, Ford A.
    There are rumors of this companion
    to MW13 (it is likely that Fords and
    Buicks were issued in sets of 3 due
    to their 3-piece mold grilles) .... No Price Found

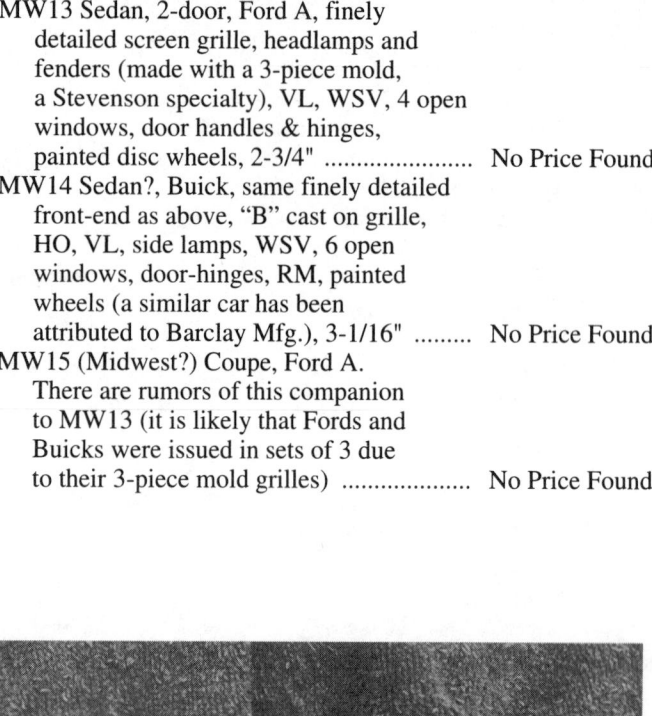

Midwest, L to R: MW9, MW8. Photo by Fred Maxwell.

Midwest, top: MW7. Bottom, L to R: MW7, MW11. Photo by Fred Maxwell.

Midwest, L to R: Unlisted, MW13. Photo by Fred Maxwell.

Midwest? Slush Ford, 3-1/2" Tootsie copy? Coupe. Photo by Fred Maxwell.

Are these Midwest? Photo by Fred Maxwell.

Midwest? Tootsie copy of a Mack Truck. Photo by Fred Maxwell.

The only known mention of Mid-West as shown in the August 1929 Toys & Novelties *magazine.*

NEW LINE OF CAST TOYS

Of particular interest to jobbers and quantity buyers will be the announcement of the three new attractively colored cast metal toys which are being offered by

the Mid-West Metal Novelty Manufacturing Co. of Clay Center, Kan.

This manufacturer of novelties and art castings has instituted a new finish process enabling them to use lacquers which do not chip. Also by the use of plenty of metal, strength is obtained and breakage avoided. Each one of their toys, including the coupe illustrated here, moves on its own wheels and the toys are packed securely and neatly three colors to each carton. A wide variety of these colors is offered from which choice may be made. Cartons contain either half gross or gross.

These toys retail at popular prices and are particularly interesting as 10 cents to $1 merchandise.

MILITARY VEHICLES

(IDs and Miscellaneous)

1/24 scale metal identification models WWII (Manoil 3-1/4" GI included for scale).
Back row - L to R: Amphibian Tractor, 105mm S.P. (illegible) M7", Half-trak car. M2.
Front row: Jeep (some of these movable wheel versions are also marked "Dale"), "4X4 Ton Truck-Jeep" (fixed wheel version), "Cletrac" (bulldozer).
Photo by Ed Poole.

1/36 Scale Metal Identification Model WWII German (Jones 54mm soldier included for scale).
L to R - Back row: "Ger. Light Med. Tank L.T.3.5," "Praga" Ger. Tank 8 ton T.N.H.P. Ex. (Czech), "Ger. Light Med. Tank C.K.V.D.8.H."
Front row: "German Light Amphibian Tank C.K.D.F.4.H.E.," "Ger. Light Arm. car Horch 1936 SD:K 223," "Ger. Heavy 8 wheeled armor car." Photo by Ed Poole.

1/36 Scale Metal Identification models - WWII British (Britains 54mm "Tommy" included for scale).
L to R - Back row: "Infantry Tank MKIV Comet NY" (Churchill Tank), "Humber MKII Comet NY" (armoured car), "Cruiser MKV" (Convenanter Tank), "UK Cruiser MKVI Crusader Comet NY" "Universal Carrier" (Bren Gun).
Front row: "Universal Carrier" (Bren Gun Carrier), "MKIII UK Cruiser Comet NY" (Valentine Tank), "UK Infantry Tank MKIIA Comet NY" (Matilda II Tank), "MKI Daimler Comet NY" (armoured car), "Carden Loyd Carrier."
Photo by Ed Poole.

1/36 Scale Metal Identification models (cont'd) - WWII Japanese (Britains Ltd. 54mm Soldier included for scale). Decals not original.
L to R - Back row: "Japanese Medium Tank - Cometal," "Japanese Cruiser Tank - Cometal," "Japanese Heavy Medium Tank - Cometal."
Front row: "Japanese Amphibian Tank," "Japanese 1938 Tankette," "Japanese L.M. Tank M2595 Comet," "Japan. Tankette M2592 - 1932 Comet." Photo by Ed Poole.

1/36 Scale Metal Identification Models (cont'd) WWII German (Jones 54mm Soldier included for scale).
L to R - Back row: "Ger. Light Tank P.Z.K.W.1 Maybach 1936," "Ger Light Tank (P) Z.K.1 Command Tank," "Ger. Light Tank PZ:KW:2," "Ger. Light Med. Tank PZ.KW3. Type 'C'." Photo by Ed Poole.

1/36 Scale Metal Identification Models (cont'd) WWII U.S. (Britains Ltd. GI included for scale) L to R - Back row: "Heavy Tank M-6," "Med. Tank, M4-2" (Turret Revolves), "Med. Tank M-4," "Med. Tank M-3."
Front row: "Light Tank M-3," "Light Tank M-3" (turret revolves), "3" Gun Car. M-5," "105 MM Howitzer Motor T32 My M7 Priest M-7." Photo by Ed Poole.

1/36 Scale Metal Identification Models - WWII U.S. (cont'd) (Britains Ltd. GI included for scale).
L to R - Back row: "Half TRK Car M2,"
"Half TRK pers. car - M3," "75 MM Gun Car. M-3 Half Track Car M2" (decal not original but AAF Acceptance tag dated "Jul 3 1946" is), "Scout Car M-3 A-1."
Front row: "Armoured Car T-17,"
"Duck" (1/48th scale), "37MM Gun Car. M6."
Photo by Ed Poole.

Movable Wheel Versions of 1/36 Scale Metal identification Models - WWII U.S. (Britains Ltd. 54mm GI included for scale).
L to R - Back row: "Med. Tank M4,"
"General Sherman" (turret rotates),
"105 MM Howitzer Motor T32 M7 Priest M7."
Front row: "Armored Car T-17 Dale model Co. Chicago,"
"75 MM Gun Car M3 Dale - Model Co. Chicago,"
"Stuart M5" (Company Name & City imprinted on hubs' of wheeled vehicles - other data on hulls).
Photo by Ed Poole.

Some contemporary Russian die-casts (Dinky 30mm soldier included for scale).
L to R - Back row: 76mm Gun, T34-85 Tank & 100mm Gun in 1/43 scale by UEHA (?).
Front row: T34 Tank by ?, Two YA3-469 Cars in 1/43 scale by Schelano B CCCP.
Photo by Ed Poole.

Some Military Vehicles by Miscellaneous British manufacturers (Skybird 30mm soldier included for scale).
L to R - Back row: Lone Star Bren Gun Carrier towing Gun, Skybirds Artillery Tractor towing Howitzer, Tri-ang Mini-Toys Jeep, Lledo Days Gone Ambulance.
Front Row: Charbens Armoured Car, Crescent Armoured Car towing Limber & Gun Corgi Major, International 6x6 Truck, Corgi Toys Hong Kong King Tiger Tank, Lone Star Jeep. Photo by Ed Poole.

Die-cast Military Vehicles from Various Countries (Starlux soldiers shown are 30mm tall). L to R - Back row: "Henschel Bau J 1926 Made in W. Germany" (maker unknown), Mercedes Benz 1937 Cabriolet Feuhrerwagen and Fiat Antocarro Militaire 1914 by RIO (Italy), Military truck, Rader Truck and Ambulance by TEKNO (Denmark). Front row: Liasson Car by Brumm (Italy), "Dodge 6X6 Made in France (marked FJ within a geared wheel), three tanks by Play Art (Hong Kong): Tiger I, Panther, and Sherman; Two jeeps - front by Play Art and behind by Fun Ho! (New Zealand), Zylmex "King Tiger" (Hong Kong). Photo by Ed Poole.

Miniature metal military vehicles as Souvenirs (Heyde 50mm soldier included for scale). L to R - Back row: Renault Tank Inkwells - "G.B.W. 1919..Carton Steel Company" (Turret hinges back to uncover inkpot), "G.B.W. 1919. Renault Constructeur" (Turret Cupola unstoppers; piece repainted & gun replaced), "Depose S.R. Tour Eiffel" (Turret hinges to left) (Like Mignot but lacks recessed wheels). Front row: Ashtray Decorations Fourth tank from left bears soldered plaque, "State Capital Columbus Ohio." Photo by Ed Poole.

1/108 Scale Metal Identification Models - WWII British. Numbering is that of the manufacturer Comet/Authenticast, but a Denzil Skinner model is substituted for number 5012. Authenticast GI by Holger Eriksson is 23mm tall. L to R - Back row: 5000 Convenanter IV, 5001 Churchill MKV, 5002 Universal Carrier, 5003 Humber Armoured Car, 5004 Carden Loyd Carrier. Middle row: 5005 Valentine, 5006 Matilda, 5007 Crusader, 5009 Cromwell. Front row: 5008 Daimler Armoured Car, 5010 Churchill MKVII, 5011 Sherman VC 5012 Centurion. Photo by Ed Poole.

Miscellaneous small metal AFVs (Comet 20mm GI included for scale). L to R - Back row: HR Products WWI Rhomboidal and Renault FT tanks, Quality Castings Desert War 2018 Stuart "Honey," 2019 MKVI light tank and 2020 Cruiser MK IV. Front row: Denzil Skinner (England): British tank Series BZ Centurion, B25 Vickers MKVI, and MKII Medium, British Armoured Car Series Bll Daimler, B23 Rolls Royce, and Armoured Truck (number unknown). Photo by Ed Poole.

Miscellaneous small metal AFVs (cont'd) (Comet 20mm GI included for scale).
L to R - Back row: Crescent (England) Russian Tank, British Cruiser Tank and Humber Armoured Car, Daimler Ambulance and tank by unknown makers. Front: Series by Unknown Maker - Patton Tank, Sherman Tank, Armored Car, Tank, and Amphibian; U.S. Markings by imprinted "JAPAN." Photo by Ed Poole.

Miscellaneous small die-cast military vehicles (Comet 20mm GI included for scale).
L to R - Back row: Mattel "Hot Wheels Gun Bucket," Corgi Junior (England) Daimler Scout Car, Lesney "Matchbox Rolamatics" No. 73 Weasel, Sherman Tank (made in Hong Kong, pencil sharpener aft!). Front row: Efsi (Holland) T-Ford 1919 Ambulance, Budgie Toy (England) Tank Transporter, 25pdr Gun Howitzer (maker unknown). Photo by Ed Poole.

This Dale 1/36 ID model bought in an Army "PX" post WWII; mailing label already attached to box to send home as souvenir. Photo by Ed Poole.

Prime Mover (after Barclay) and Howitzer (after Tootsietoy) from Junior Caster Model No. E45; homecast. Courtesy Ron Eccles. Photo by Ed Poole.

Lledo (U.K.): Three Battle of Britain
50th Anniversary Commemorative sets;
vehicles each about 8cm in length.
Photo by Ed Poole.

Homecastings from Ever-Ready Mould No. ML21 (American
Craft Manufacturing Company, Chicago), "Big Bertha in Action," Gun barrel 11.5cm long. Photo by Ed Poole.

Arnold (Germany) Jeep with Five and Dime Corps troops and
mascot; Jeep 17cm long. Photo by Ed Poole.

Five and Dime Corps HQ troops with Tri-ang Jeep
(England), 16cm long. Photo by Ed Poole.

Military Vehicles

MINIATURE VEHICLE CASTINGS INC.

Though these appear to be toys from the 1930s, they were first produced in 1985. The models were carved and cast by owner Robert E. Wagner. Made of die-cast lead from silicone molds, they were sold for $21 apiece and at least 3,500 have been sold. Some are beginning to appear at toy shops and on dealer lists. The average length is about 4-1/2 inches and the New Jersey firm's name is visible (sometimes dimly) on a piece of tin soldered to the bottom. The toys today seem to sell at slightly more than double their original price.

Following is a list of Miniature Vehicle Castings: 1937 Ford 2-door Sedan, 1938 Ford Standard Sedan Delivery, 1934 Olds 2-door Humpback, 1936 Olds 4-door Humpback, 1937 Hudson Terraplane 2-door, 1938 Dodge Step Van, 1937 Plymouth 5 window Coupe, 1937 Dodge 2-door Humpback, 1938 Plymouth 2-door Sedan, 1941 Ford COE Truck (flatbed or dump), 1935 Hudson 2-door Sedan, 1937 Studebaker 3-window Coupe, 1936 Plymouth 4-door Sedan, 1936 Plymouth 4-door Taxi, 1935 Pontiac 3-window Coupe, 1940 Dodge 2-door Sedan, 1939 Dodge 2-door Sedan, 1941 Divco Milk Truck (Sunrise Dairy). In 1993, Wagner was planning four new cars, to differ somewhat from the preceding in wheels, tires, and frame, so that the new series could be told from the old: 1934 Dodge 2-door Sedan, 1935 Pontiac 2-door Sedan, 1936 Plymouth Pickup and 1938 Hudson Coupe.

Miniature Vehicles Castings, L to R: 1937 Hudson Terraplane, 1935 Hudson. Courtesy Bob and Alice Wagner.

Miniature Vehicle Castings, L to R: 1938 Plymouth two-door Sedan, 1937 Plymouth Coupe, 5 windows, 1937 Dodge two-door Humpback. Courtesy Bob and Alice Wagner.

Miniature Vehicle Castings, L to R: 1934 Olds, 1936 Olds. Courtesy Bob and Alice Wagner.

Miniature Vehicle Castings, L to R: 1941 Ford C.O.E. Truck, 1937 Studebaker three-window Coupe, 1936 Plymouth Taxi. Courtesy Bob and Alice Wagner.

Miniature Vehicle Castings 1938 Dodge Step Van. Courtesy Bob and Alice Wagner.

MINIC (PRE-WAR TRI-ANG MINIC)

by Gates Willard

Established by George Lines in the 1870s, the original Lines company of England made wooden rocking horses. Brother Joseph joined the firm and ultimately bought out George's share. After WWI, three of Joseph's sons formed a company called Lines Bros., Ltd. and its logo was a triangle...made up of three lines! Later, its products came to be known as Tri-ang Toys. By the mid 1930s, the company was making prams, cycles, pedal cars, stamped steel trucks, wooden toys, doll houses, and many other kinds of playthings.

In 1935, the Tri-ang Minic Miniature Clockwork Vehicles were introduced. Only 14 models were available that first year. Three inches to 7 inches in length, they were robustly made of heavier gauge steel than that used by competing German manufacturers. They had brightly plated radiators and wheels. The trucks and some of the cars even had plated fenders. Painting was done by a dipping and baking process with runs, as well as thick and thin areas, but the finishes were durable. Subtle shades of red, blue, green, beige, orange and yellow, plus black and chrome were tastefully combined to make some unusually attractive color schemes. The road vehicles had white rubber tires and each Minic came boxed with a stamped steel key and a little color folding catalogue inside the box.

The first Minics must have sold well, for in 1936 many new types were added and a few had electric lights. A miniature Shell gasoline can appeared on the left running board of most cars and trucks. By early September 1939, England was at war and the Shell can had been deleted. The white tires were replaced with black, and the plated trunk rack on the ordinary cars was replaced by a decal number plate and a plain rear bumper. Since 1935, many new models were added and none discontinued. The factory claimed that more than 70 types were available. However, by 1940, some vehicles were painted in army camouflage, while others, such as the electric lighted types, were phased out. The non-military vehicles had some parts chemically blackened instead of plated. Steering wheels were later attached with miniature split pins instead of being pressed onto a brass column.

After hostilities ended, Minics were rushed back into production. The British economy required exports, and large quantities of Minics were sent to the United States, which was starved for metal toys. Minics seem to have been available in many areas of this country, whereas there had been very few outlets before the war. The first post-war Minics often had left-over pre-war parts and boxes. Stronger colors were used (mostly bright red, dark blue, and shades of green) and the quality of finish was below the pre-war standard. Tooling was wearing out and the stampings often lacked definition. In time, quite a few new types and variations were produced before the company ceased operations in the 1970s.

In addition to the vehicles, various garages, service stations, and even a fire station were made pre-war and post-war. The numbering system used below was instituted about 1938 to 1939. In general, the lower the number, the cheaper the item. However, new toys announced 1939 to 1940 were tacked on to the end of the existing list (65M-79M). Some of this last group were never put into production before toy manufacturing ended during WWII.

Why is there no value guide for pre-war Minic toys? Very few are changing hands in the 1990s and not enough data exists to develop a reliable and useful listing of values.

Use this numerical reference for the numbers appearing in the listings, usually preceding the year introduced.

1. Scarce: Fewer than 100 known.
2. Rare: Fewer than 50 known.
3. None made after WWII.
4. Made only 1939-40.
5. Headlights, radiator, bumper stamped in one piece (same for cars and trucks).
6. Small number made post-war. New tooling for radiator, matte-black baseplate.
7. Headlights riveted to bar held in place by radiator. Most post-war headlights are soldered to bar.
8. No front bumper (pre-war only).
9. No decals first year made (1935).
10. Cataloged but never made.
11. Cataloged pre-war but not made until post-war.
12. Painted glossy dark green. Light tank can also be grey.
13. Electric headlamps.
14. A special issue (not numbered) Brockhouse promotional made about 1937. Rare. Reportedly only 100 made.
15. Actually had 10 wheels.
16. Number on box is 70M.
17. Number on box is 71M.
18. Number on box is 75M.
19. Rare in colors other than dark blue.

Gates Willard became a toy collector at the age of nine, but gave away his carefully preserved collection when he was married in 1952. About 1965 he met an adult automotive toy collector and became motivated to build a second collection. He's still working on it. From 1946-89 he owned restored real cars, but nowadays it's toys only. "They require little maintenance, they don't break down, and it is possible to own many at a time." He has a B.A. and M.S. in geology and had a career in that field before becoming a science teacher, assistant principal, and principal of a public school from which he retired in 1983.

Gates Willard with a Tri-ang Minic Double-Deck Bus, February 1, 1941.

1M Ford Saloon (Sedan), 1936
1MCF Ford Saloon, Camouflaged 1, 3, 4, 1940
2M Ford Light Van, 1936
3M Ford Royal Mail Van, 1936
4M Sports Saloon (2 window Sedan) 3, 5, 6?, 1935
5M Limousine (3 window Sedan) 3, 5, 6, 1935
6M Cabriolet (Coupe) 5, 6?, 1935
7M Town Coupe (Town Car) 5, 6, 1935
8M Open Touring Car, 5, 6, 1935
9M Streamline Saloon (Airflow Sedan), 1935
10M Delivery Lorry (Pickup Truck) 5, 1935
11M Tractor 7, 1935
11MCF Tractor, Camouflaged 2, 3, 1940
12M Learner's Car 1, 5, 1936
13M Racing Car, 1936
14M Streamline Sports, 1935
15M Petrol Tank Lorry (Oil Tanker) 5, 1936
15MCF Petrol Tank Lorry, camouflaged 1, 3, 5, 1940
16M Caravan, Non Electric (House Trailer), 1937
17M Vauxhall Tourer, 7, 1937
18M Vauxhall Town Coupe, 7, 1937
19M Vauxhall Cabriolet, 7, 1937
19MCF Vauxhall Cabriolet, camouflaged, 1, 3, 7, 1940
20M Light Tank 3, 12, 1935
20MCF Light Tank, camouflaged 2, 3, 1940
21M Transport Van, 5, 9, 1935
21MCF Transport Van, camouflaged 1, 3, 5, 1940
22M Carter Paterson Van, 5, 1936
23M Tip Lorry (Dump Truck) 5, 1936

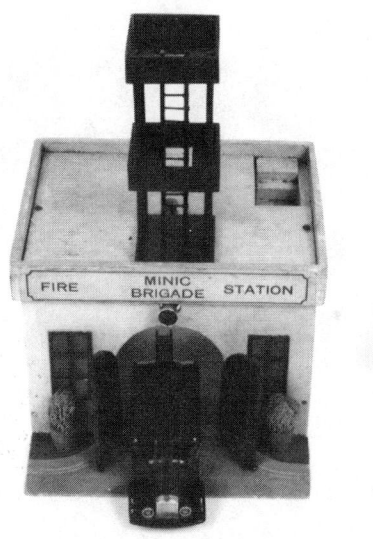

1E   *00*
Minic, L to R: Fire Station, small 00 Service Station. Courtesy Gates Willard. Photo by E.W. Willard.

2M   *3M*   *1M*   *1MCF*
Courtesy Gates Willard. Photo by E.W. Willard.

4M   5M

Courtesy Gates Willard. Photo by E.W. Willard.

12M   13M

Courtesy Gates Willard. Photo by E.W. Willard.

*Courtesy Gates Willard.
Photo by E.W. Willard.*

7M   6M   8M

15M   78M   31M   79M

Minic, L to R: Tanker, Wartime Pool Tanker, Mechanical Horse and Fuel Oil Tanker, Wartime Pool Articulated Tanker. Courtesy Gates Willard. Photo by E.W. Willard.

*Mini, L to R: Camouflaged
Tanker, Camouflaged Light Tank,
Light Tank. Courtesy Gates
Willard. Photo by E.W. Willard.*

15MCF   20M   20MCF

*Courtesy Gates Willard.
Photo by E.W. Willard.*

17M   18M   19M   19MCF

Minic (Pre-war Tri-ang Minic)

Minic, L to R: Late Pre-War car with plain bumper and number plate; earlier car with luggage rack and Shell can. Courtesy Gates Willard. Photo by E.W. Willard.

18M   8M

21M   22M   21M   21MCF

Minic Vans, L to R: 1936-38 type with Shell can, Carter Paterson, early wartime with black radiator and black tires, Camou-flaged Van. Courtesy Gates Willard. Photo by E.W. Willard.

24MCF   24M

Minic Luton Vans, L to R: Camouflaged and Civilian version. Courtesy Gates Willard. Photo by E.W. Willard.

25M   40M

Minic, Rear, L to R: Lorry with cases, Mechanical Horse and Trailer with cases; Front, L to R: Lorry, Tip Lorry. Courtesy Gates Willard. Photo by E.W. Willard.

10M   23M

Minic (Pre-war Tri-ang Minic)  437

24M Luton Transport Van (Moving Van) 5, 1396
24MCF Luton Van, camouflaged 3, 1940
25M Delivery Lorry with cases, 5, 1936
26M Tractor and trailer with cases, 1936
27M, 28M - Numbers not used
29M Traffic Control Car (Police Car), 7, 1938
30M Mechanical Horse and Pantechnicon 5, 9, 14, 1935
31M Mechanical Horse and Fuel Oil Tanker, 5, 1936
32M Dust Cart (Garbage Truck), 5, 1396
33M Steam Roller, 1935
34M Tourer with Passengers, 1, 3, 5, 1937
35M Rolls Tourer, Non-electric, 1, 7, 8, 1937
36M Daimler Tourer, Non-electric, 1, 7, 1937
37M Bentley Tourer, Non-electric, 1, 7, 1938

38M Caravan Set (Limousine and Non-electric caravan), 2, 1937
39M Taxi, 19, 1938
40M Mechanical Horse and Trailer with cases 1, 5, 1936
41ME Caravan with electric light 1, 3, 1937
42M Rolls Sedanca, Non-electric, 1, 7, 8, 1937
43M Daimler Sedanca, Non-electric 1, 7, 1937
44M Traction Engine, 1, 1938
45M Bentley Sunshine Saloon, (Sunroof Sedan), Non-electric, 2, 7, 1938
46M Daimler Sunshine Saloon, non-electric, 2, 7, 1938
47M Rolls Sunshine Saloon, Non-electric 2, 7, 1938
48M Breakdown Lorry (Wrecker Truck), 5, 1936
48MCF Breakdown Lorry, Camouflaged 2, 3, 5, 1940
49ME Searchlight Lorry, 3, 5, 1936
49MECF Searchlight Lorry, camouflaged 2, 3, 5, 1940
50ME Rolls Sedanca, Electric, 2, 3, 8, 13, 1936
51ME Daimler Sedanca, Electric, 2, 3, 13, 1937
52M Single Deck Bus, Red, 1936

30M   Not numbered
Minic Mechanical Horse and Pantechnicon, Left: typical 1936-38
version; Right: rare Brockhouse promotional. Courtesy Gates
Willard. Photo by E.W. Willard.

32M   Set 54M (with 44M)
Courtesy Gates Willard. Photo by E.W. Willard.

Minic, L to R: Steam Roller, Camouflaged Tractor, Tractor and
Trailer with cases. Courtesy Gates Willard. Photo by E.W. Willard.

33M   11MCF   Set 26M (with 11M)

35M   36M   37M   55ME
Minic, L to R: Four Tourers - Rolls, Daimler, and Bentley, non-electric (electric versions never made),
and electric-lighted Bentley Tourer. Note that Battery Box displaces the rear seat. Courtesy Gates Wil-
lard. Photo by E.W. Willard.

Left: Set 38M: 5M, 16M   Right: Set same; 34M, 41ME
Courtesy Gates Willard. Photo by E.W. Willard.

47M (56ME if electric lights)   45M (57ME if electric lights)
46M (58ME if electric lights)
Minic non-electric Sunshine Saloons, L to R: Rolls, Daimler,
and Bentley. Courtesy Gates Willard. Photo by E.W. Willard.

| 48M | 48MCF | 49ME | 49MECF |

Minic, L to R: Breakdown Lorry, Camouflaged Breakdown Lorry, Searchlight Lorry, Camouflaged Searchlight Lorry; note
original Ever Ready battery for Electric Searchlight. Courtesy Gates Willard. Photo by E.W. Willard.

| 50ME | 51ME | 42M | 43M |

Minic, Four Sedancas: The Rolls and Daimler on left have electric lights. The Rolls and Daimler on
the right are non-electric. Bentley Sedancas were never made. Courtesy Gates Willard. Photo by
E.W. Willard.

53M Single Deck Bus, Green, 1936
54M Traction Engine and Trailer, 2, 1939
55ME Bentley Tourer, Electric, (production probably delayed) 2, 3, 13, 1938
56ME Rolls Sunshine Saloon, Electric, 2, 3, 13, 1938
57ME Bentley Sunshine Saloon Electric, 2, 3, 13, 1938
58ME Daimler Sunshine Saloon Electric, 2, 3, 13, 1938

59ME Caravan Set, tourer with passengers and caravan with electric light, 2, 3, 1937
60M Double Deck Bus, red, 1935
61M Double Deck Bus, green, 2, 3, 1935
62ME Fire Engine, 13, 1936
63M No. 1 Presentation Set, 2, 3, 1937
64M No. 2 Presentation Set, 2, 3, 1937

50ME   51ME   42M   43M

Minic: The two Sedancas on the left have electric lights; the battery is inside the opening trunk. A turn screw operated the lamps. The two cars on the right are non-electric and there is no separate trunk lid. All Post-War Rolls, Bentleys, and Daimlers have an opening trunk, but they are non-electric. Courtesy Gates Willard. Photo by E.W. Willard.

56ME   51ME   55ME   47M   43M   37M

Courtesy Gates Willard. Photo by E.W. Willard.

60M (Red)   52M(Red)
61M (Green)   53M (Green)

Minic, L to R: Double-Deck Bus, Single-Deck Bus; produced in red and beige or two-tone green All four were separately numbered in the trade catalog. Courtesy Gates Willard. Photo by E.W. Willard.

62ME   39M   29M

Minic, L to R: Fire Engine with electric headlamps and attachments (hoses are in an opening compartment), Taxi, and Traffic Control Car. Courtesy Gates Willard. Photo by E.W. Willard.

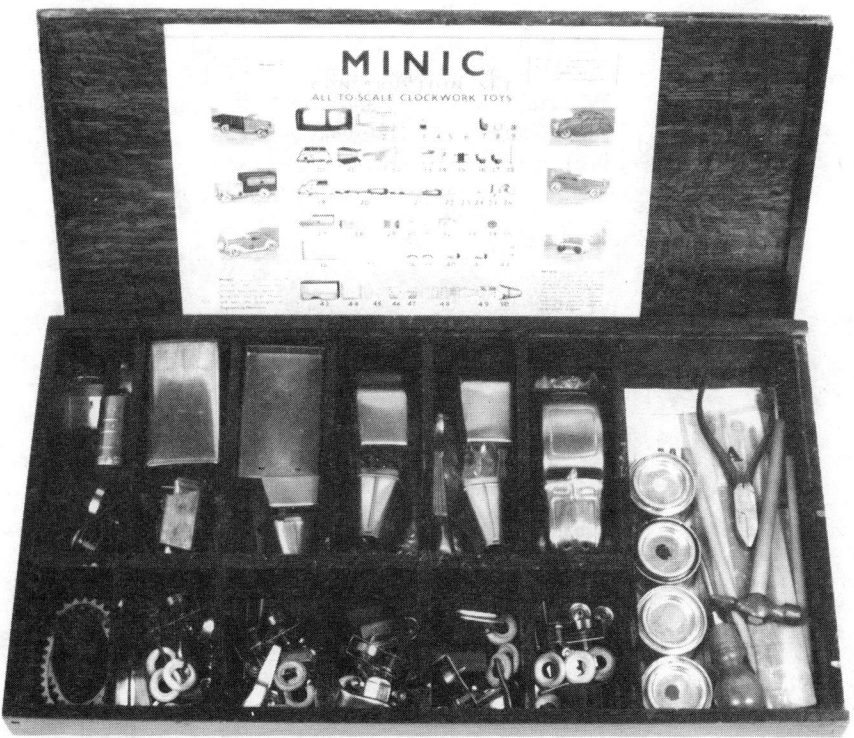

65M

Minic Construction Set: Everything needed to assemble and paint six vehicles. Courtesy Gates Willard. Photo by E.W. Willard.

Minic, late Pre-War issues, L to R: Farm Lorry, Timber Lorry, Mechanical Horse and Lorry with barrels. Courtesy Gates Willard. Photo by E.W. Willard.

67M   68M   72M

69M   69MCF   66M   66MCF

Minic, L to R: Canvas Tilt Lorry, Camouflaged Canvas Tilt Lorry, 6-wheel Army Lorry, Camouflaged 6-wheel Army Lorry. Courtesy Gates Willard. Photo by E.W. Willard.

65M Construction Set 2, 3, 1936
66M Six Wheel Army Lorry 1, 3, 5, 12, 15, 1939
66MCF Six Wheel Army Lorry, Camouflaged, 1, 3, 4, 5, 1940
67M Farm Lorry, 2, 3, 4, 5, 1939
68M Timber Lorry, 2, 5, 1939
69M Canvas Tilt Lorry (Enclosed Army Truck) 2, 3, 4, 5, 12, 15, 1939

69MCF Canvas Tilt Lorry, Camouflaged 3, 4, 5, 15, 1940
(70M) (Coal Lorry NOT MADE), 10, 1939
71M Mechanical Horse and Milk Trailer, 2, 5, 16, 1939
72M Mechanical Horse and Lorry with Barrels, 2, 5, 17, 1939
(73M) (Cable Lorry) (Pre-war, Not Made), 11, 1939
74M Log Lorry, 2, 5, 18, 1939
(75M) (Ambulance (Pre-war, Not Made), 11, 1939

71M   72M
Minic late Pre-War issues, L to R: Mechanical Horse and Milk Tanker, Log Lorry. Courtesy Gates Willard. Photo by E.W. Willard.

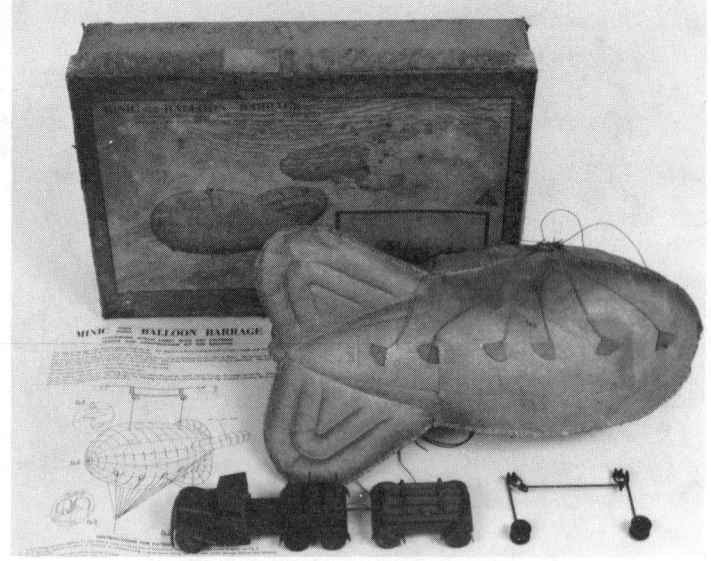

76M
Minic Balloon Barrage. Courtesy Gates Willard. Photo by E.W. Willard.

Minic electric-lighted Sunshine Saloons, L to R: Rolls, Daimler, Bentley. Courtesy Gates Willard. Photo by E.W. Willard.

Minic, L: Streamline Saloon; R: Streamline Sports. Courtesy Gates Willard. Photo by E.W. Willard.

Postwar Tri-ang Minic (U.K.) M101 Armoured Car (16cm long) with Box. One of the 15 vehicles in the Advanced Airfield Maintenance Wing and Armoured Brigade Headquarters Squadron Series. Photo by Ed Poole.

Minic (Pre-war Tri-ang Minic)

LOOKS LIKE A REAL ROAD DOESN'T IT?

Though it's difficult to believe, the traffic jam in this photograph is actually made up of MINIC scale model clockwork toys.

This unique clockwork series will contain almost every vehicle to be seen on the roads. Each model is true to scale so that the bus is exactly the right amount larger than the lorry and the limousine in the right proportion to the open tourer.

These MINIC vehicles are wonderfully built and have reliable long-running clockwork; they are most reasonably priced too, the smaller ones costing only 1/- each. They have a front wheel drive, so that they will run on carpet and can be used in any room.

Start collecting your road full now.

MINIC scale model LIMOUSINE
Strong construction, with powerful long-running clockwork motor. Colours: Dark Green, plated guards; Ivory, Red guards; New Blue, Ivory guards. Radiator and bumpers plated, also wheels, with rubber tyres. Length, 4¼ in.   Price 1/—

MINIC scale model STREAMLINE CLOSED.
Strong construction, with powerful long-running clockwork motor. Colours: Red, Ivory, New Blue. Plated bumpers, radiator, also wheels, with rubber tyres. Length, 5 in.   Price 1/—

MINIC scale model STREAMLINE OPEN.
Strong construction, with powerful long-running clockwork motor. Colours: Ivory, Red hood; Red, Ivory hood; or Light Green, Ivory hood. Plated radiator, bumpers, also wheels, with rubber tyres. Length, 5 in.   Price 1/—

MINIC scale model SPORTS SALOON.
Strong construction, with powerful long-running clockwork motor. Colours: Ivory, New Blue, Primrose, with plated mudguards, radiator, bumpers, also wheels, with rubber tyres. Length, 4¼ in.   Price 1/—

MINIC scale model TOWN COUPÉ.
Strong construction, with powerful long-running clockwork motor. Colours: New Blue, plated guards; Light Brown, Black mudguards; or Ivory, Red mudguards. Plated radiator, bumpers, also wheels, with rubber tyres. Length, 4¼ in.   Price 1/—

MINIC scale model TRACTOR.
Strong construction, with powerful long-running clockwork mechanism. Colours: Green with Red wheels, or Red with Green wheels. Length, 3 in.   Price 1/—

MINIC scale model CABRIOLET.
Strong construction, with powerful long-running clockwork motor. Colours: Ivory and Green with plated mudguards, or Red with Ivory mudguards. Radiator, bumpers, plated, also wheels, with rubber tyres. Length, 4¼ in.   Price 1/—

MINIC scale model OPEN SPORTS TOURER.
Strong construction, with powerful long-running clockwork motor. Colours: Green, plated mudguards, Ivory hood; Red, Ivory mudguards and hood; Ivory, Red mudguards and hood. Plated bumpers, radiator, also wheels, with rubber tyres. Length, 4¼ in.   Price 1/—

MINIC
Regd. Trade Mark

CLOCKWORK TOYS ALL TO SCALE
Obtainable from all good Toy Shops and Stores
Made by Lines Bros. Ltd., Tri-ang Works, Merton, S.W.19

The first Minic advertisement. Courtesy Gates Willard.

MINIC Regd. Trade Mark

ALL TO SCALE CLOCKWORK TOYS

Almost every type of vehicle on the road represented; some with ELECTRIC LIGHTS. Strongly constructed and fitted with powerful, long-running mechanism, they will run anywhere, EVEN ON THE CARPET. Each model is beautifully finished in a variety of colours, and packed singly in an attractive box.

MINIC Ford £100 Saloon
LENGTH 3¼ ins.   Price 6d.

MINIC Racing Car
LENGTH 5¼ ins.   Price 1/-

MINIC Luton Transport Van
LENGTH 5¼ ins.   Price 1/6

MINIC Breakdown Lorry
with Mechanical Crane
LENGTH 5¼ ins.   Price 3/6

MINIC Mechanical Horse and
Fuel Oil Trailer
LENGTH 7 ins.   Price 2/-

MINIC Dust Cart
LENGTH 5¼ ins.   Price 2/-

MINIC Steam Roller
LENGTH 5¼ ins.   Price 1/6

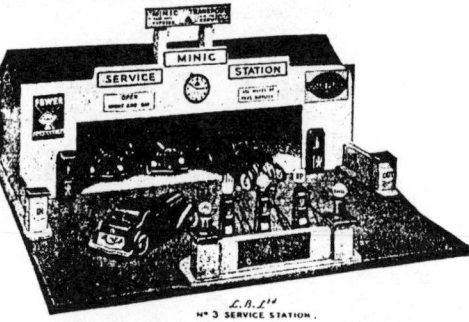

MINIC Service Station No. 3
Realistic design, imitation red tiled roof with sign, three large petrol pumps, one large oil cabinet, two electric lights and battery, dummy clock face and other signs. LENGTH 16 ins. 7/6
Other models 1/6, 3/11, 5/-, 15/-, 25/-

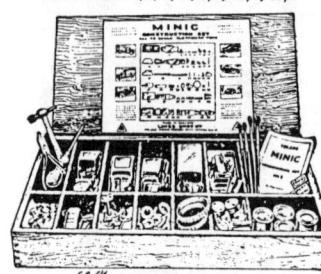

MINIC Contruction Set No. 1
A complete set of parts for making six types of MINIC all to scale clockwork models. All parts, including powerful clockwork motor units, are made with precision tools and machines. Full instructions and tools are included in each set which is packed in a handsome oak finished cabinet 18 ins. x 9¾ ins. x 2¼ ins.
PRICE 15/-

MINIC Caravan Trailer.
LENGTH 4¼ ins.
COMPLETE WITH ELECTRIC LIGHT AND BATTERY 3/6
CAR NOT INCLUDED, BUT CAN BE OBTAINED PRICE 1/-

There are thirty-four models to choose from; some with **ELECTRIC LIGHTS.**

Ask your dealer to show you the complete range, also the MINIC Service Stations.

TRI-ANG TOYS
OBTAINABLE AT ALL GOOD TOY SHOPS AND STORES

MINIC Light Tank
LENGTH 3¼ ins.   Price 1/6

MINIC Streamline Saloon
LENGTH 5 ins.   Price 1/-

MINIC Petrol Tank Lorry
LENGTH 5¼ ins.   Price 1/-

MINIC Searchlight Lorry
with Electric Searchlight and
Battery
LENGTH 5¼ ins.   Price 3/6

MINIC Single Deck Bus
LENGTH 7¼ ins.
Price 3/6. Red or green.

MINIC Lorry with cases
LENGTH 5¼ ins.   Price 1/6

MINIC Tip Lorry
LENGTH 5¼ ins.   Price 1/3

Made in England by

LINES BROS. LTD., Tri-ang Works, Morden Rd., London, S.W.19

The Minic line was getting more sophisticated. Courtesy Gates Willard.

76M Balloon Barrage Wagon and Trailer production delayed until 1940 made in camouflage only. Should have been numbered 76MCF, 2, 3, 4

77M Double Deck Trolley Bus (Not Made), 10, 1939
78M Pool Tanker, 2, 3, 4, 5, 1940
79M Mechanical Horse and Pool Tanker, 2, 3, 4, 5, 1940
NOTE: Post-war versions of foregoing averaged $95-$225 each in mint in 1996.

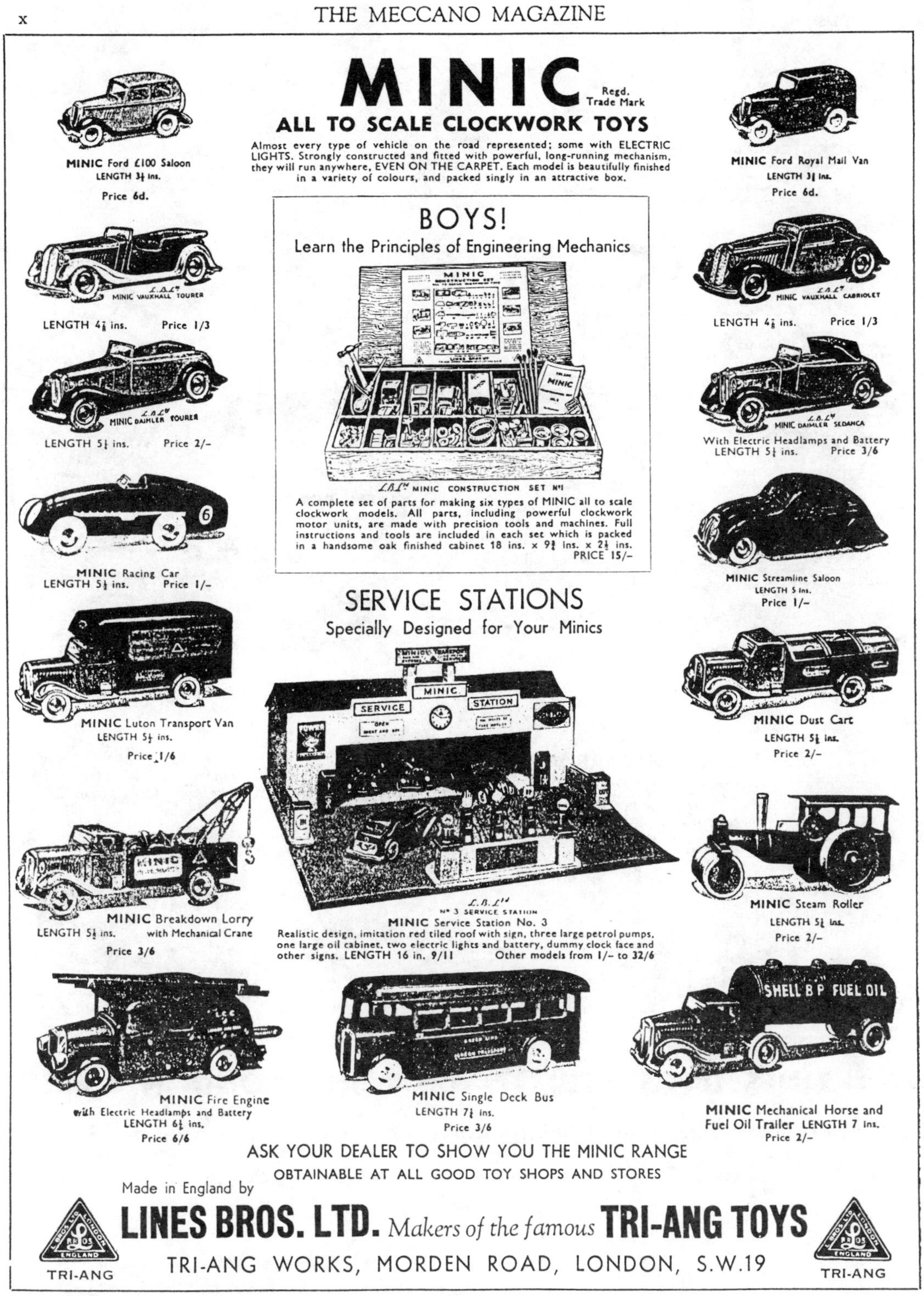

Sept. 1937 Meccano Magazine. *Courtesy Gates Willard.*

Minic (Pre-war Tri-ang Minic)  445

TRI-ANG
TOYS

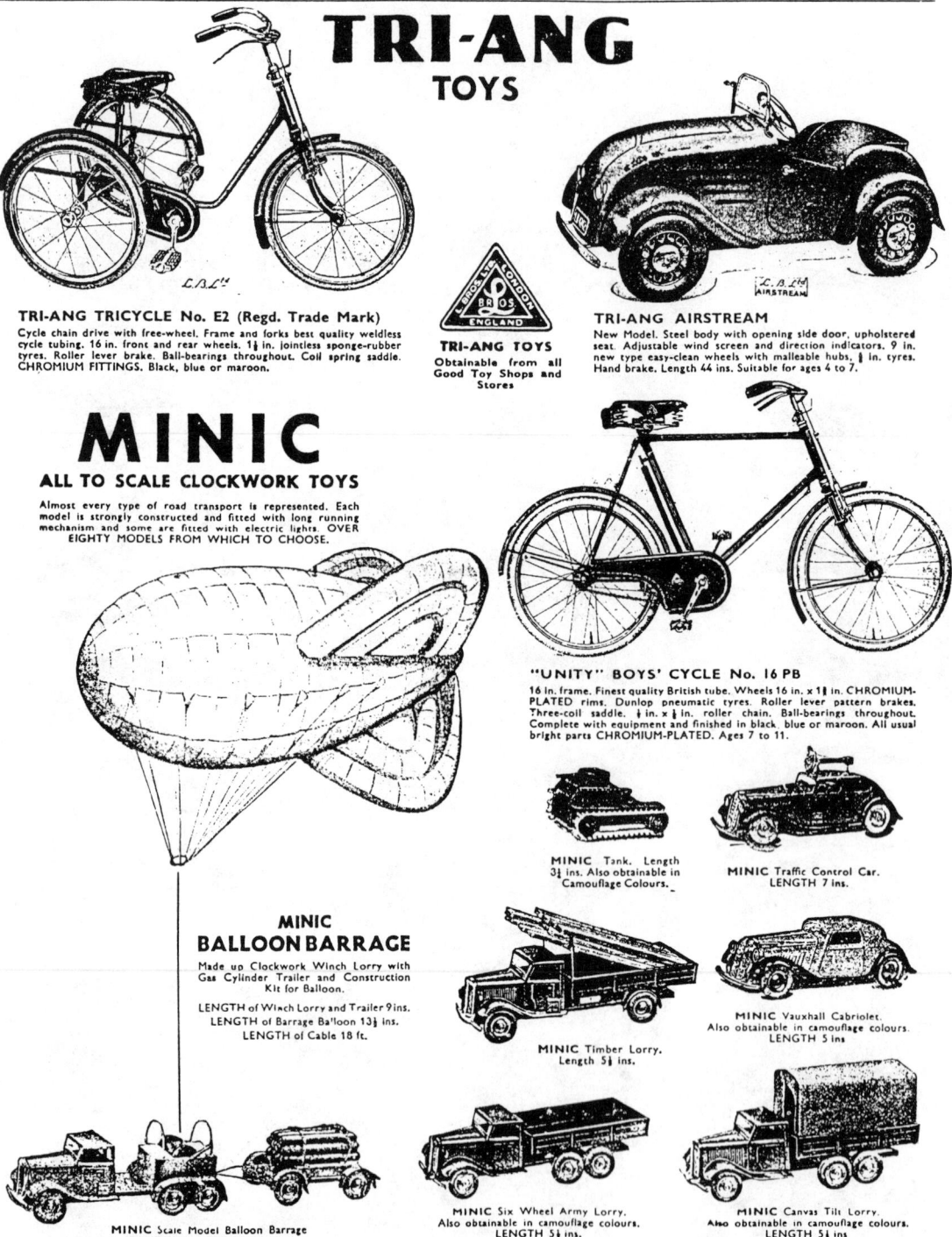

TRI-ANG TRICYCLE No. E2 (Regd. Trade Mark)
Cycle chain drive with free-wheel. Frame and forks best quality weldless cycle tubing. 16 in. front and rear wheels. 1⅛ in. jointless sponge-rubber tyres. Roller lever brake. Ball-bearings throughout. Coil spring saddle. CHROMIUM FITTINGS. Black, blue or maroon.

TRI-ANG TOYS
Obtainable from all Good Toy Shops and Stores

TRI-ANG AIRSTREAM
New Model. Steel body with opening side door, upholstered seat. Adjustable wind screen and direction indicators. 9 in. new type easy-clean wheels with malleable hubs, ⅝ in. tyres. Hand brake. Length 44 ins. Suitable for ages 4 to 7.

MINIC
ALL TO SCALE CLOCKWORK TOYS

Almost every type of road transport is represented. Each model is strongly constructed and fitted with long running mechanism and some are fitted with electric lights. OVER EIGHTY MODELS FROM WHICH TO CHOOSE.

"UNITY" BOYS' CYCLE No. 16 PB
16 in. frame. Finest quality British tube. Wheels 16 in. x 1⅜ in. CHROMIUM-PLATED rims. Dunlop pneumatic tyres. Roller lever pattern brakes. Three-coil saddle. ⅜ in. x ⅛ in. roller chain. Ball-bearings throughout. Complete with equipment and finished in black, blue or maroon. All usual bright parts CHROMIUM-PLATED. Ages 7 to 11.

MINIC BALLOON BARRAGE
Made up Clockwork Winch Lorry with Gas Cylinder Trailer and Construction Kit for Balloon.
LENGTH of Winch Lorry and Trailer 9 ins.
LENGTH of Barrage Balloon 13½ ins.
LENGTH of Cable 18 ft.

MINIC Tank. Length 3½ ins. Also obtainable in Camouflage Colours.

MINIC Traffic Control Car. LENGTH 7 ins.

MINIC Timber Lorry. Length 5½ ins.

MINIC Vauxhall Cabriolet. Also obtainable in camouflage colours. LENGTH 5 ins.

MINIC Scale Model Balloon Barrage

MINIC Six Wheel Army Lorry. Also obtainable in camouflage colours. LENGTH 5½ ins.

MINIC Canvas Tilt Lorry. Also obtainable in camouflage colours. LENGTH 5½ ins.

Made by LINES BROS. LTD., Tri-ang Works, LONDON S.W.19

At Last - The Balloon Barrage! England had been at war for a year. Courtesy Gates Willard.

Some Pre-War Minic boxes. Every Minic was sold with a box that also contained a folding color catalog and a steel key (as shown in front of the boxes). Courtesy Gates Willard. Photo by E.W. Willard.

MITTEN

	C6	C8	C10
Mitten Dunlop Stake Truck, 16" long	100	150	200

MODERN TOYS (MT)

	C6	C8	C10
Modern Toys (MT) Convertible, 9" long ...	125	188	250
Modern Toys Mobilgas Tanker	80	120	160
Modern Toys Stunt Car, No. 27, battery-op	35	52	70
Modern Toys Tin Lizzie, windup	No Price Found		

Modern Toys Tin Lizzie. Photo by Tim Oei.

MOHAWK

	C6	C8	C10
Mohawk Toy Blue Bird Taxi, windup, 6" long	188	282	375
Mohawk Toy "Metropolitan Groceries", tin windup, 6" long	170	255	340
Mohawk Toy "Yellow Taxi"	275	363	550

MOKO TOYS

(Moses Kohnstam, Furth, Germany, 1875-1959)

by Bob Smith

Moses Kohnstam not only manufactured toys, he also ran a large wholesale house and had his toys made to order by toy companies such as Guntermann, Distler, and Fischer. He became a distributor for Gama, Tippco, Levy, Carette, and other companies. Most special-order toys carried the "MOKO" logo. Moses died in 1912, leaving the business to his sons, Willi and Emil. His other son, Julius, had opened a branch office in England before 1900. The company was shut down in 1933, as were many other Jewish businesses in Germany before WWII. Emil fled to England, while Willi stayed in Germany. Willi died one year later. Emil joined his brother Julius tol help run the English firm. Julius died in 1935. The MOKO Company survived, however, and is still in business today.

Moko Six-Cylinder Limousine, c.1927, 9-1/2" long

	C6	C8	C10
Moko Flying Police Squad, C/W Motor, battery searchlight, 10" long	1100	2000	2700
Moko Six-Cylinder Limousine. Green/black, 9-1/2" long, c/w motor runs car in forward & reverse, as pistons on top of engine move up & down. Also has opening doors and hood. c.1927	700	950	1600
"Moko" Kohnstam Four-Cylinder Sedan. Green/black, 8" long, smaller version of above car, c.1928	500	750	1150
Moko Motorcycle & Rider, tin clockwork, 8-1/2" long	1500	2700	4000
Moko Motorcycle & Rider, spring action, 7-1/2" long	1200	2100	2800

Moko Motorcycle & Rider, tin clockwork, 8-1/2" long. Courtesy Bill Bertoia Auctions. Photo by Jeanne Bertoia.

Moko Motorcycle & Rider, spring action, 7-1/2" long. Courtesy Bill Bertoia Auctions. Photo by Jeanne Bertoia.

MORMAC

(Cleveland, Ohio)

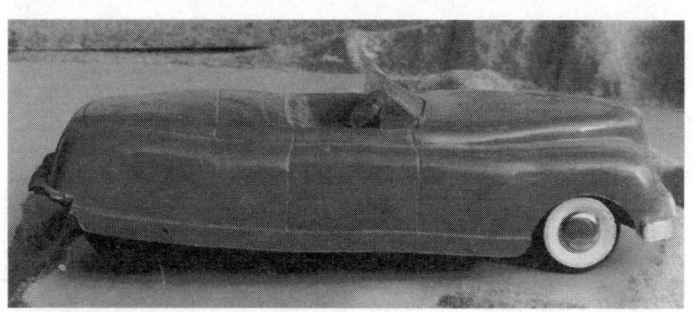

	C6	C8	C10
Mormac convertible, plastic, 9-3/4" long	30	45	60

Mormac Convertible, plastic, 9-3/4" long. Photo by Ron Fink.

MOXIE

	C6	C8	C10
"Moxie" Horse car (based on the actual promotional vehicle) tin litho, 8" long ..	338	507	675

"Moxie" Horse Car. Courtesy Sotheby's NY.

M.P.C.

	C6	C8	C10		C6	C8	C10
MPC Dump Truck, 7-1/4" long	11	16	22	MPC Firewagon, 3 figures, 10 accessories	12	18	25

MURRAY

	C6	C8	C10
Murray Buick Pedal Car, 1949	1500	2700	4600
Murray Camaro Pedal Car, 1968	88	132	175
Murray Champion Pedal Car	500	850	1150
Murray Clipper Pedal Car	550	900	1200
Murray Comet Pedal Car, 1956	800	1400	2000
Murray Country Squire Station Wagon Pedal Car, 1955.........................	325	488	650
Murray Earth Mover Pedal Car, 1959........	550	850	1200
Murray "Fire Chief" Pedal Car	500	800	1100
Murray "Fire" Truck Pedal Car	200	300	400
Murray Golden Wildcat, 1961, Pedal Car	425	635	850
Murray Pace Car, 1959, Pedal Car	500	800	1100
Murray Pontiac Station Wagon, 1948 Pedal Car	950	1500	2200
Murray Racer No. 8, 1960 Pedal Car	215	322	430
Murray Radio Sports Car, 1959	480	720	960
Murray Speedway Pace Car, 1959	500	800	1100
Murray Suburban Pedal Car, 1950.............	550	850	1200
Murray Super Wildcat Pedal Car, 1961	350	525	700
Murray Tee Bird Pedal Car, 1961	140	210	280
Murray Tractor Pedal Car, c.1950	400	600	800

NEFF-MOON TOY COMPANY

Neff-Moon, of Sandusky, Ohio, was owned by William Moon and Charles Neff. Production of its pressed steel toys began in 1923. The firm, which seems to have been located above a grocery, was apparently an early victim of the Depression.

	C6	C8	C10
Neff-Moon Groceries Van	175	262	350
Neff-Moon Sedan, 12" long	500	800	1100
Neff-Moon Sedan Delivery Truck	350	525	700
Neff-Moon Taxi, 12" long	350	525	700
Neff-Moon Tow Truck, 16", c.1925	200	300	400
Neff-Moon No. 14 Set, "10 Toys in 1"	500	750	1040

Neff-Moon Coupe; no price found. Photo by Don Hultzman.

Neff-Moon Dump Truck; no price found. Photo by Don Hultzman.

Neff-Moon "Emergency" Truck; no price found. Photo by Don Hultzman.

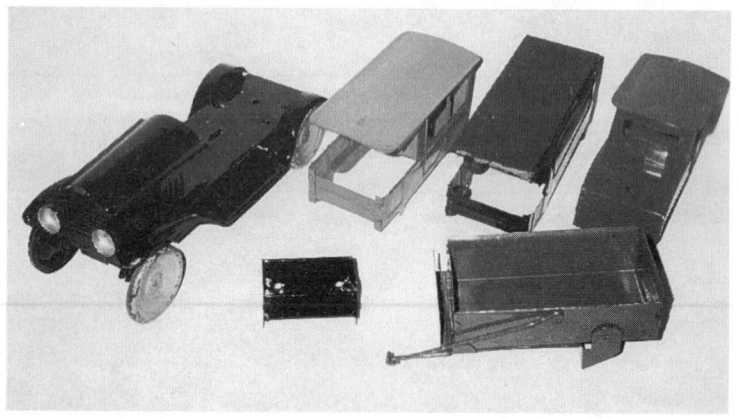

Neff-Moon made "Convertible Auto Sets" and "Interchangeable Toys." Here's one example; no price found. Photo by Don Hultzman.

Neff-Moon Sedan (?). Photo by Don Hultzman.

NIFTY

	C6	C8	C10
Nifty Bus, Double Decker, tin windup, 9" long	800	1400	2200
Nifty "Skidoodle" tin windup	1800	2900	4000
Nifty "Speedy Felix" Felix the Cat car	425	635	850
Nifty Truck, Automatic Tilter, w/driver, 9-1/2" long	600	950	1350

Nifty "Skidoodle." Courtesy PB84.

Nifty "Speedy Felix." Courtesy Phillips NY.

NOMA

	C6	C8	C10
Noma Car & Trailer, 1940s	65	98	130
Noma Low Boy, wooden	100	150	200
Noma Steam Shovel, wooden	90	135	180
Noma Tank, wooden, WWII	30	45	60
Noma Truck, wooden, 1940s	45	68	90

Noma Tank, wooden. That's a 4-inch wooden peg sticking out of the top (reason unknown). Photo by Jack Matthews.

NORTH & JUDD

Research by collector C.B.C. Lee suggests that this company, located at the time in New Britain, Conneticut, made cast-iron toys for only one year, probably 1930, for S.H. Kress. Its original designs appear to have been marked with the company's name, but its toys for the most part are unmarked. The company is still in business, making quality hardware.

	C6	C8	C10
Austin Convertible, open top, marked "North & Judd"	No Price Found		
Austin Sedan, 2-door, marked "North & Judd"	No Price Found		
Bus, looks like Dent, 4.667" long	No Price Found		
Ford Model A Coupe, looks like Arcade, length of left cab 1.528", has driver in window, trunk at rear	No Price Found		
Ford Model T Stake Truck, like Arcade's, but marked "Anchor Truck Co." (an anchor is North & Judd's trademark), 8-3/4" long	1500	2500	4200
Motorcycle Cop, like Hubley's "Cop," separate nickeled driver is held by mushrooms at front of handle-bars and on driver's feet	No Price Found		

	C6	C8	C10
Semi-Trailer Stake Truck, marked "North & Judd"	No Price Found		
Tractor, looks like Arcade, but has nickeled driver, 2.988" long	No Price Found		

North & Judd Ford Model T stake truck. Courtesy Sotheby's New York.

North & Judd semi-trailer stake truck. Photo by Terry Sells.

NOSCO PLASTICS

Nosco Plastics was located in Erie, Pennsylvania. It made a variety of plastic toys, including several planes and trains. Some of its toys appear in a 1952-53 *Toy Year Book*. In 1954 its address in Erie was 17th and Cascade Street..

	C6	C8	C10
Nosco Ace Racer, 8" long, No. 6390	60	100	160
Nosco Bus, "Nosco Lines"	No Price Found		
Nosco Cop-Cycle 5-1/2" long, friction. No. 6357	75	125	225
Nosco Doodle-Bug, No. 6381, 9-1/2" long windup	88	132	175
Nosco Fire Truck No. 6386, 7-1/2" long	No Price Found		
Nosco Hot'See Hot Rod, No. 6490, 10-1/4" long, friction	80	120	160
Nosco Pokey Joe Fire Pumper, No. 6430, 10-1/2" long	No Price Found		
Nosco Roaring Roadster, 8" long	90	135	180
Nosco Station Wagon	No Price Found		
Nosco Vizy Vee Stockar Racer, No. 6565, 9-1/4" long	70	110	180

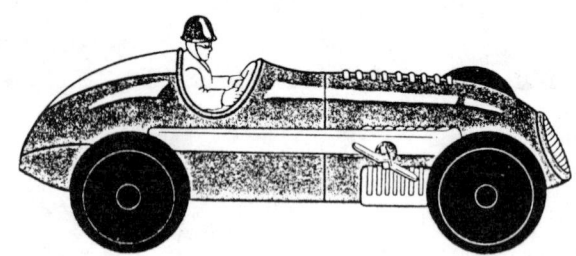

Nosco Ace Racer

Nosco Cop-Cycle. Photo by Terry Sells.

Nosco Doodle-Bug. Photo by Terry Sells.

Nosco Fire Truck

Nosco Hot' See Hot Rod. Photo by Terry Sells.

Nosco Pokey Joe

Nosco Station Wagon & Bus

Nosco Vizy Vee. Courtesy Bob and Alice Wagner.

NYLINT

The Nylint Tool and Manufacturing Company was formed in 1937 by Bernard C. Klint and David Nyberg (thus its name) in Rockford, Illinois. Toy production began in the spring of 1946. Since 1951, the firm has concentrated on the production of heavy-duty scale reproductions, in steel, of earth-moving equipment and over-the-road trucks. Jeff L. Hubbard provided part of the following list.

	C6	C8	C10
Nylint No. 600 Amazing Car, 1946-49, windup, 13-3/4" long	100	150	200
Nylint No. 700 Lift Truck (fork lift), 1947-49, windup	75	112	150
Nylint No. 800 Scootcycle, 1948-50, windup, 7-1/4" long	200	300	400
Nylint No. 1000 Deliverall, 1948-51, windup, 10" long	300	450	600
Nylint No. 1100 Elgin Street Sweeper, 1950-52, windup, 8-1/4" long	250	375	500

Nylint (1951-52) No. 1300 Tournarocker. Courtesy Thomas G. Nefos, Federal Shipping Network.

Nylint 1951-52 No. 1600 Payloader. Courtesy Continental Hobby House.

Nylint 1955 No. 2000 Speed Swing. Courtesy Thomas G. Nefos, Federal Shipping Network.

	C6	C8	C10
Nylint No. 1200 Pumpmobile, 1950-52, windup, 8-5/8" long	125	188	250
Nylint No. 1300 Tournarocker, 1951-52, open tractor w/driver, 18" long	62	93	125
Nylint No. 1300 Tournarocker, 1953-57, closed cab, no driver, 18" long	105	158	210
Nylint No. 1400 Road Grader, 1951, small wheels, 19-1/4" long	65	98	130
Nylint No. 1400 Road Grader, 1952-58, larger wheels	70	105	140
100 Nylint No. 1500 Tournahopper, 1951-56, 22-1/2" long	175	263	350
Nylint No. 1600 Payloader, 1951-54, red-colored, 18" long	75	112	150
Nylint No. 1600 Payloader, 1955, tan	125	188	250
Nylint No. 1600 Payloader, 1956-57, light green	100	150	200
Nylint No. 1600 Payloader, 1958, dark green and before year was out yellow (add 20% to yellow price)	100	150	200
Nylint No. 1700 Tournahauler, 1953-56, 30-1/4" long	70	105	140
Nylint No. 1800 Traveloader, 1953-55, 30" long	113	170	225
Nylint No. 1900 Tournatractor, 1954-55, 14-3/4" long	150	225	300

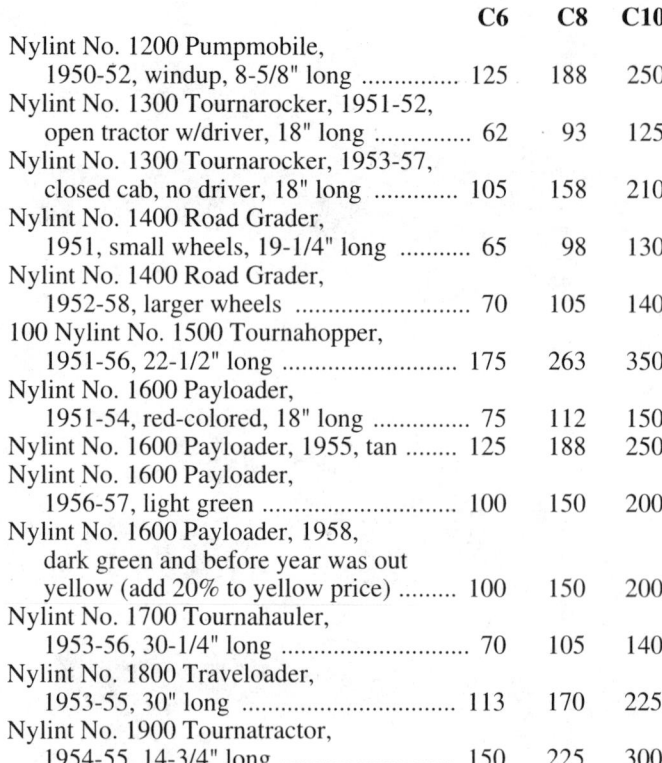

Nylint 1953-54 No. 1800 Traveloader. Courtesy Thomas G. Nefos, Federal Shipping Network.

Nylint 1955 No. 2200 Michigan Shovel.

	C6	C8	C10
Nylint No. 2000 Speed Swing, 1955-58, 19" long	100	150	200
Nylint No. 2100 Tournadozer, 1956-59, 20" long	110	165	220
Nylint No. 2200 Michigan Shovel, 1955-65, 31-1/2" long	78	117	155
Nylint No. 2300 Elgin Street Sweeper, 1956-57, Battery-operated version, closed cab	120	180	240
Nylint No. 2400 Electronic Cannon, 1956, has no radar antenna	100	150	200
As above, has radar antenna, 22-1/2" long	88	132	175
Nylint No. 2500 Telescoping Crane, 1957-60, 27" long	125	188	250
Nylint No. 2600 Missile Launcher, 1957-60, 31-1/2" long	125	188	250
Nylint No. 2700 Uranium Hauler, 1958-59. 22-1/2" long	125	188	250
Nylint No. 2800 Guided Missile Carrier, first version (1958), nose cone of missile doesn't fire, 15-1/2" long	150	225	300
Nylint No. 2800 Guided Missile Carrier, later (through 1960), cone of missile fires	75	112	150

	C6	C8	C10
Nylint No. 2900 Jack Hammer, 1958-60, 19-1/2" long, with box	150	225	300
Nylint No. 3000 Grader-Loader, 1959-61, 23-3/4" long	92	138	185
Nylint No. 3100 Payloader Tractor Shovel, 1959-61, 17-5/8" long	100	150	200
Nylint No. 3200 Power & Light Lineman Truck, 1959-61, 35-3/4" long	150	225	300
Nylint No. 3300 Power & Light Posthole Digger, 1959-61, 35-3/4" long	150	225	300
Nylint No. 3400 Highway Emergency Unit, 1959-63, 18-5/8" long	72	108	145
Nylint No. 3500 Countdown Rocket Launcher, 1959-61, 21" long	125	188	250
Nylint No. 3600 Ford Rapid Delivery, 18-1/4" long	163	245	325
Nylint No. 3700 Street Sprinkler Truck, 18" long	140	210	280
Nylint No. 3800 Ford Sales & Service, 13-5/8" long	140	210	280
Nylint No. 3900 Ford Platform Tilt Truck, 15-3/4" long	125	188	250
Nylint No. 4000 Ford Speedway Truck w/Racer, 24-3/4" long	122	185	250
Nylint No. 4100 Ford Pickup & U-Haul Box Trailer	110	165	220

Nylint 1956 No. 2400 Electric Cannon. Calvin L. Chaussee.

Nylint 1958 No. 2800 Guided Missile Carrier. Photo by Calvin L. Chaussee.

Nylint No. 8411, 1975, U-Haul Truck. Courtesy Thomas G. Nefos, Federal Shipping Network.

Nylint No. 4300 (Ford) U-Haul Rental Fleet. Courtesy Thomas G. Nefos, National Toy Connection.

	C6	C8	C10
Nylint No. 4200 Bulldozer, 14" long	65	98	130
Nylint No. 4300 Ford U-Haul Rental Fleet, 3 pieces	175	263	350
Nylint No. 4400 Camper on Pickup, 13-1/2" long	70	105	140
Nylint No. 4500 Ranch Truck, 14" long	75	112	150
Nylint No. 4600 Construction 4-Wheel Platform Dump, 15-3/4" long	88	132	175
Nylint No. 4700 Happy Acres Truck w/horses, 14" long	65	98	130
Nylint No. 4800 U-Haul Trailer, 8" long	50	75	120
Nylint No. 4900 U-Haul Trailer, 9" long	50	75	100
Nylint No. 5000 Dump Truck w/Cement Mixer, 20-1/2" long	125	188	250
Nylint No. 5100 Dump Truck, 13-1/2"	75	112	150
Nylint No. 5200 Pickup Truck (Econoline), 11-1/4" long	80	120	160
Nylint No. 5300 Custom Camper on above, 12-1/2" long	75	112	150
Nylint No. 5400 Custom Camper on above w/boat, 23-1/2" long	120	180	240
Nylint No. 5500 Pepsi Truck, 16-1/2"	125	188	250
Nylint No. 5800 Ford Econoline Van, 12" long	72	105	145

	C6	C8	C10
Nylint No. 6000 American Oil Emergency Truck, 11-1/4" long	100	150	200
Nylint No. 6200 Kennel Truck w/dogs, 11-1/2" long	88	132	175
Nylint No. 6300 Horse Van, 23-1/2"	78	117	155
Nylint No. 6600 Mobile Home, Semi type, 30" long, 1964	125	188	250
Nylint No. 6700 Ambulance, 12" long	100	150	200
Nylint No. 6800 Jalopy, 9-5/8" long	30	45	60
Nylint No. 6900 Airport Courtesy Van, "Holiday Inn," 12" long	275	332	550
Nylint No. 7100 Fun on Farm Econoline Truck, 29 pcs., 11-1/4" long ..	87	130	175
Nylint No. 7300 Army Ambulance, 12" long	60	90	120
Nylint No. 7900 Road Grader, 15" long	62	93	125
Nylint No. 8000 Pony Farm Van, 7 pcs set, 11-1/4" long	135	198	270
Nylint No. 8100 Suburban Fire Pumper, 12-1/2" long	100	150	200
Nylint No. 8200 Bronco, 12-1/2" long	75	112	150
Nylint No. 8300 Texaco Service Van, 12" long	150	225	300

Nylint 1961 No. 4500 Truck. (Chase & Sanborn version.) Courtesy Thomas G. Nefos, Federal Shipping Network.

Nylint 1962 No. 5500 "Pepsi" Truck, Ford Cab-Over, 1962?, 16-1/2" long. Photo by Bob Smith.

Nylint Truck No. 6000 American Oil Emergency. Photo by Bob Smith.

Nylint Ford Cab-Over Tow Truck, 17" long. Photo by Bob Smith.

	C6	C8	C10
Nylint No. 8400 U-Haul Cube Van, 1965, 22" long	87	130	175
Nylint No. 8410 Ford U-Haul Truck & Trailer, 1974, 22" long	75	112	150
Nylint No. 8411 U-Haul Truck, Chevy	75	112	150
No date known			
Nylint Austin Western Crane	125	188	250
Nylint Brinks Truck	48	72	95

	C6	C8	C10
Nylint Chase & Sanborn, stake sides	100	140	200
Nylint Fire Truck (1970) 20" long	27	41	55
Nylint Ford Cab-over Tow Truck, 17" long	95	143	190
Nylint Harley Davidson Tanker, 25" long	100	150	200
Nylint Hot Rod and Trailer	60	90	120
Nylint Jungle Wagon	100	150	200
Nylint 4125 Rhino Pickup	22	33	45

OH BOY

(Kiddies Metal Toys Inc., Plainfield, N.J.)

By Bob Smith

Kiddies Metal Toys established its business before 1920. In the early 1920s, the company hired Louis Emmets, a skilled lithographer. Emmets was previously employed by J. Chein & Co. He brought with him a vast knowledge of lithography. (In 1929, Emmets left Kiddies Metal Toy Co. and started his own company, the Emmets Toy Co.) In 1925, Kiddie Metal Toys began a line of large light pressed-steel vehicles. These trucks ranged in length from 19 inches to 27 inches. The gauge of metal used on the Oh Boy trucks was the same gauge metal that Chein used on its Hercules Trucks. Other similarities in these trucks, such as the body style and wheel types used, show a strong resemblance between the two toys. Some collectors believe that Louis Emmets brought this strong influence with him from J. Chein & Co. The Oh Boy toys, however, were finished with enamel paint, while Chein used lithography on the Hercules vehicles. Another peculiarity of the Oh Boy toys was the installing of decals on only one side. Kiddies Metal Toys, Inc. closed its doors in 1931, after going through tough times from the Depression.

*Some information was cited from *The Collectors Guide To American Transportation Toys* by Joe & Sharon Freed, 1995.

	C6	C8	C10
Oh Boy No. 100 "Dump Truck," black/gray, 19" long, with or without decals, c.1926	400	600	850
Oh Boy No. 100 "Dump Truck," same as above truck except black/red or all black	350	550	800
Oh Boy No. 105 "Bus," blue, 19-1/2" long, c.1926	600	1100	1600
Oh Boy "No. 110" Racer, red, 19" long, c.1926	800	1300	2000
Oh Boy No. 115 "Ice" Truck, 19-1/2" long, green, c.1926	400	650	900
Oh Boy No. 120 "Delivery Truck," open cab, stake sides, black/red, 19" long, c.1927	350	750	1050
Oh Boy "Delivery Truck," same as No. 120 except for closed cab	400	800	1100
Oh Boy No. 125 "Wrecker" Truck, black/red, 19" long, c.1926	400	1050	1550
Oh Boy No. 130 "Hook & Ladder" Truck, red, 21" long, c.1926	650	850	1150
Oh Boy No. 135 "Fire Engine," red w/copper plated boiler and hand rails, 19" long, c.1926	700	1050	1550
Oh Boy No. 135 "Fire Engine," same as above truck except w/orange boiler and hand rails	550	750	1050
Oh Boy No. 140 "Fire Patrol" Truck, red, 23" long, c.1926	350	950	1450

Oh Boy No. 100. Photo by Bob Smith.

Oh Boy No. 100, except black/red. Photo by Bob Smith.

Oh Boy "No. 110." Photo by Bob Smith.

Oh Boy No. 125. Photo by Bob Smith.

Oh Boy No. 130. Photo by Bob Smith.

Oh Boy No. 135. Photo by Bob Smith.

Oh Boy No. 140. Photo by Bob Smith.

Oh Boy No. 205. Photo by Bob Smith.

Oh Boy No. 205 "American Express Truck." Photo by Bob Smith.

Oh Boy No. 210. Photo by Bob Smith.

OH BOY

(Kiddies Metal Toys Inc., Plainfield, New Jersey)

$8.25 Doz "OH BOY" STEEL PULL TOYS

Sturdily constructed of heavy gauge metal, bright enamel finishes.
All with disc wheels and imitation balloon tires. Each in box.

1F2474—(Mfrs 100) Dump truck, 19½x7½x6½, red with black trim, crank for raising body, ½ doz. in pkg. ..... Doz **$8.25**

1F2486—(Mfrs 125) Wrecker, 19x7x6¼, orange with black trim, ⅓ doz. in pkg. Doz **$8.25**

1F2479—(Mfrs 115) Ice truck, 19½x7x6½, green chassis and body, stenciled "ice," ½ doz. in pkg. Doz **$8.25**

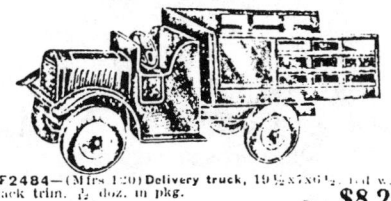
1F2484—(Mfrs 120) Delivery truck, 19½x7x6½, red with black trim, ½ doz. in pkg. Doz **$8.25**

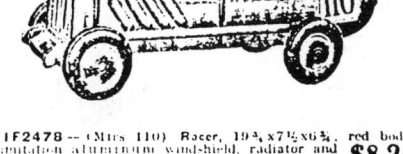
1F2478—(Mfrs 110) Racer, 19¾x7½x6¾, red body, imitation aluminum windshield, radiator and hood, ½ doz. in pkg. ..... Doz **$8.25**

1F2476—(Mfrs 105) Bus, 19½x7x6½, blue with black, pink and yellow trim, ½ doz. in pkg. Doz **$8.25**

1F2487—(Mfrs 130) Fire truck, 21x7x6½, red body, aerial and 2 orange side ladders, lever for raising aerial ladder, ½ doz. in pkg. Doz **$8.25**

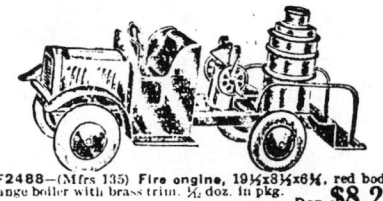
1F2488—(Mfrs 135) Fire engine, 19½x8½x6¾, red body, orange boiler with brass trim. ½ doz. in pkg. Doz **$8.25**

Oh Boy toys, as shown on a page from a circa 1928 Butler Bros. catalog; manufacturer's numbers in parentheses.

	C6	C8	C10
Oh Boy No. 200 "Auto Steam Shovel," c.1927, 4-wheel chassis w/vertical boiler, red/black, 23" long		No Price Found	
Oh Boy "Auto Shovel Truck," 27" long, red/black, same unit as No. 200 except mounted on open cab truck chassis		No Price Found	

	C6	C8	C10
Oh Boy No. 205 "American Express Truck" c.1927, 22" long, green	800	1250	2000
Oh Boy No. 209 "Mail Truck," c.1927, same as American Express Truck except painted olive green	800	1250	2000
Oh Boy No. 210 "Moving Van," c.1927, black/red, 22" long	800	1250	2000

OHIO ART

Ohio Art was started in October 1908, by a dentist, H.S. Winzeler. Originally, its intent was to make metal picture frames (thus, its name), but in 1917, the firm bought C.E. Carter (Erie Toy Plant) and began producing metal toys, including a climbing monkey on a string for Ferdinand Strauss. Winzeler later sold the plant to Louis Marx, but continued making tin toys, while Marx, according to Ohio Art history, used the former Carter plant as the foundation of his own company. Ohio Art is still making toys in Bryan, Ohio.

	C6	C8	C10
Ohio Art "Tank Bank" No. 15, 1941	78	117	155
Ohio Art "Traffic Control," 1950s, tin windup cars, 3-1/2" long, base 19x13"	40	60	80

Tank Bank. Photo by Don Hultzman.

OHLSSON & RICE

(Los Angeles)

	C6	C8	C10		C6	C8	C10
Ohlsson & Rice No. 76, gas-powered racer, 049 motor, recoil starter	500	750	1075	Ohlsson & Rice Midget Racer, aluminum body, rubber tires, c.1940s	260	375	575
				Ohlsson & Rice Pusher Racer, 11" long	270	455	540

OROBR TOY WORKS

(Brandenburg, Germany, 1900-1922)

by Bob Smith

Orobr Toy Works was founded by three partners, Neil, Muller, and Blechschmidt. The company produced numerous lower-end toy vehicles, many of which were made for the U.S. market. Even though a large amount of toy vehicles are found with the Orobr mark, there is not much information in print about the company. Orobr made some toys that do carry a fair value, and they make a nice accent to any collection.

Orobr Bus	500	800	1100
Orobr Double-Decker Bus, 9-1/2" long windup	312	468	625
Orobr Double-Decker Bus, 6" long, c.1915, windup	205	308	410
Orobr Express Wagon, 6" long windup, 1920s	288	432	575
Orobr Limousine, c.1910, open front cab, luggage rack on top, cw motor, 5-1/2" long	250	375	500

No. 24 Orobr Six Window Mercedes Pullman Limousine. Three tone green/red/white litho. 9-1/2" long, electric lights, c/w motor, 4 opening doors, driver, c.1920	800	1300	1700
Orobr Steam Roller, tin windup, 6" long	140	210	280
No. 25 Orobr Touring Car. Red/gray, 8-3/4" long, c/w motor, fold down rear seats, c.1918	400	600	800
No. 26 Orobr Model T Ford Sedan. Black, 6" long, c/w motor. c.1920s. Add $200 for color	182	275	365
No. 27 Orobr Model T Ford Sedan. Black, 7-3/4" long, c/w motor, full interior, c.1920s	475	675	900
No. 28 Orobr Model T Ford Touring Car. Black/gray, 7-3/4" long, c/w motor, c.1920s	550	750	1000
Orobr Taxi, 6" long, tin	275	363	550

Orobr No. 24 Six-Window Mercedes Pullman Limousine, 9-1/2" long. Photo by Bob Smith.

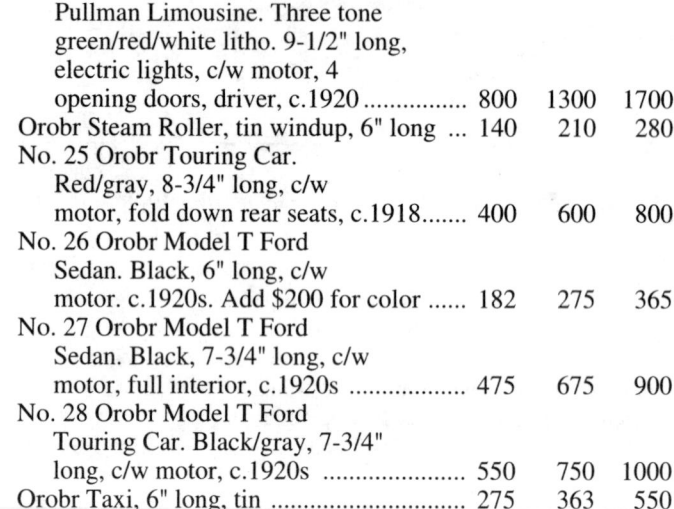

Orobr No. 25 Touring Car, c.1918, 8-3/4" long. Photo by Bob Smith.

Orobr, Top: No. 26 Model T Ford Sedan, 6" long; Bottom, L to R: No. 27 Model T Ford Sedan, 7-3/4" long, No. 28 Model T Ford Touring Car, 7-3/4" long. Photo by Bob Smith.

PAGCO

	C6	C8	C10
Pagco Racer with motor, 11" long	70	105	140

PARKER BROS.

Parker Bros. Toy Town Garage,
   3 litho tin penny cars,
   paper litho garage, c.1910...................... 600   900   1200

Parker Bros. Toy Town Garage.
Courtesy Heinz Muller,
Continental Hobby House.

PAYA (SPAIN)

	C6	C8	C10
Paya Chrysler Airflow Sedan, tin litho, c/w motor, 13" long	312	468	625
Paya Coupe, handpainted and stenciled, c/w motor, doors open, 13" long	1000	1750	2500

Paya Limousine, handpainted and
   stenciled, lights work,
   c/w motor, 19" long ....
	750	1300	1750

Paya Motorcycle & Rider tin windup, 10-1/2" long	312	468	625
Paya Sedan, steel, doors open, battery lights, 19" long	500	850	1200

Paya Motorcycle & Rider, tin windup, 10-1/2" long. Courtesy Bill Bertoia Auctions. Photo by Jeanne Bertoia.

PAYTON

(New York, NY)

	C6	C8	C10		C6	C8	C10
Payton Bulldozer, soft plastic	12	18	25	Payton Tiger Tank No. 411...........................	20	30	40
Payton Cement Mixer	12	18	25	Payton Tow Truck	12	18	25

No. 878 — TOW TRUCK
Polyethylene bag with header.
TO RETAIL AT 98¢
PKD.: 2 dozen to a shipping carton
WT.: 12 lbs.

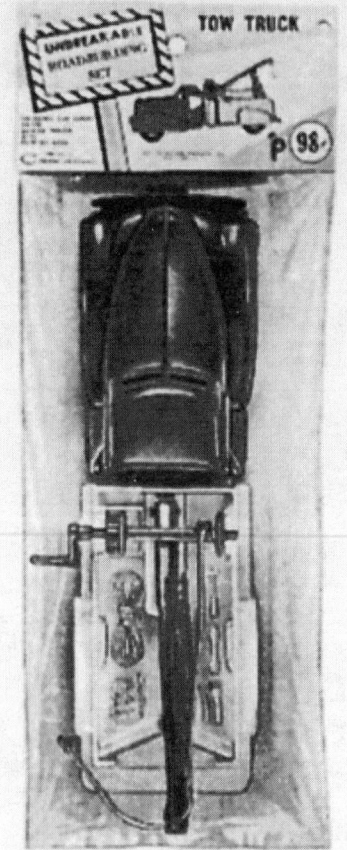

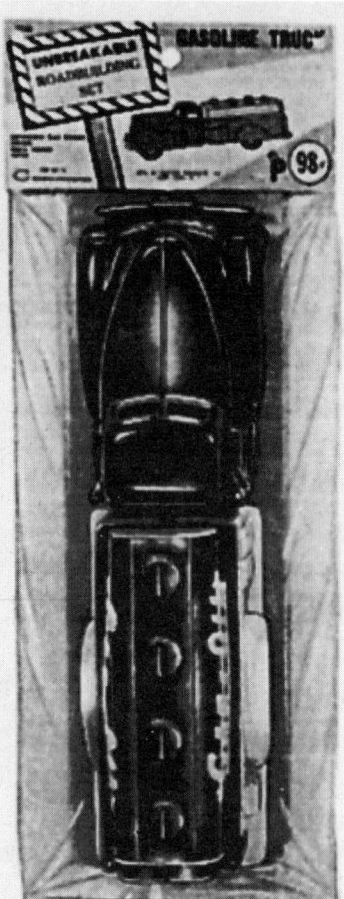

No. 876 — CEMENT MIXER, GAS TRUCK ASSORTMENT
Polyethylene bag with header.   **TO RETAIL AT 98¢**
PKD.: 2 dozen to a shipping carton   WT.: 12 lbs.

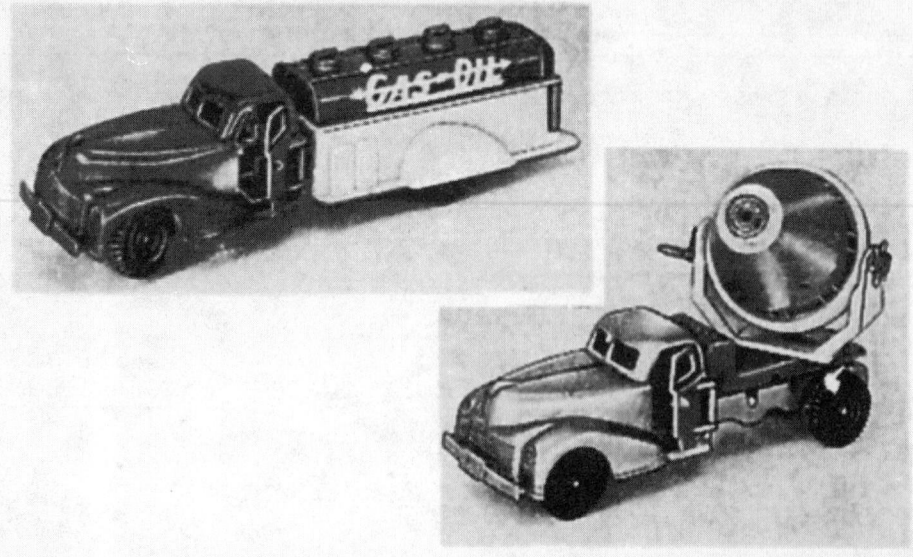

A Payton flyer for some of its vehicles.

PERFECT RUBBER CO.

(Mansfield, Ohio)

	C6	C8	C10
Perfect Rubber Co. 1935			
Slantback Sedan, 3-3/4"	35	52	70

Perfect Rubber Company 1935 slantback sedan, 3-3/4" (Pontiac premium). Courtesy Dave Leopard, from his book Rubber Toy Vehicles.

PETER-MAR TOYS

by Mary Gaeta

Ralph Lohr was the owner of Peter Products Manufacturing, Muscatine, Iowa. He was an entrepreneur, artist, and musician. He operated a music store in the early 1920s. In 1941, he started manufacturing wooden kitchen items, such as clothes racks, stools, ladders, and ironing boards. When WWII broke out, lumber was limited to government contracts, and Lohr was faced with closing his business. It was then that he found he could purchase scrap lumber from government contractors, and he started to design toys. The first of these were military vehicles. Farm toys were very popular, so he began making tractors, hay racks, trailers, and wagons. These toys were very much in demand and continued to be much sought-after. Other toys were Noah's Ark, Humpty Dumpty, Lucky Dog, Village Smitty, Old Woman in a Shoe, trolley cars, Carousel, and Ferris Wheel.

Lohr had a son, Peter; his colleague, Clifford Hakes, had a daughter, Mary—hence the name Peter-Mar was chosen for the toys. After more than 50 years, these toys are still popular and very much sought-after. When these toys are found in antique stores, the prices for arks in Mint condition are $300. The Village Smitty, a pound-a-peg-type toy, has been sold for as much as $65. These toys are well constructed and durable. Peter Mar's address was 708 E. Fourth Street.

	C6	C8	C10
Peter-Mar Hay Wagon	42	63	85
Peter-Mar Jeep, wood	No Price Found		
Peter-Mar Milk Wagon	42	63	85
Peter-Mar Tractor, wood	90	135	180
Peter-Mar Trailer, wood	67	100	135

Mary Gaeta is a lifetime resident of Muscatine, Iowa. She graduated from Saint Mathias School and Muscatine Community College. She has been active in family business, has enjoyed a life long interest in antiques, and has managed an antique consignment business for many years.

All kinds of {sales, eye-appeal, play-value, safety-value} *Power!*

PETER-MAR TOYS SELL THEMSELVES - *It's the craftsmanship!*

These attractive toys are not a substitute made necessary by wartime restrictions — these are quality toys that will have a ready market in peacetime as well. These well-built miniature farm toys are made by experienced craftsmen. They are doweled and glued — they are attractively designed and finished — they are made from

selected, well-seasoned woods. Special lubricated, hardwood axles.

Peter-Mar Toys have Eye Appeal — Safety Appeal — Play Value — All of which adds up to more SALES POWER for you. A sample order will convince you that Peter-Mar Toys . . . SELL THEMSELVES !

HAY RACK (removable platform)____10 inches high — 21 inches long.

TRACTOR _____ 8 inches high — 12 inches long.

An original Peter-Mar flyer. Courtesy of Mary Gaeta.

	PINARD		
	(France)		

	C6	C8	C10
Pinard Cannon Truck, c.WWI, searchlight on grill, 13" long	475	713	950

Pinard Cannon Truck, c.WWI, searchlight on grill, 13" long. Courtesy Bill Bertoia Auctions. Photo by Jeanne Bertoia.

PLAS-TEX: See "Aerocar"

PLASTICRAFT

	C6	C8	C10		C6	C8	C10
Plasticraft Jeep, articulating driver, plastic, 4"	5	8	10	Plasticraft Truck, plastic	6	9	12

PLASTICVILLE

	C6	C8	C10		
Plasticville Gas Station	4	6	8	Plasticville Sedan	No Price Found

PLAYBOY

	C6	C8	C10		C6	C8	C10
Playboy Delivery Truck, "Playboy Trucking Co." 21" long	225	338	450	Playboy "Intercity Bus," 23-1/2" long, cream color	300	450	600
Playboy Dump Truck, 22" long	150	225	300	Playboy Tow Truck, "Playboy Trucking Co.," white, 22" long	250	400	650

Playboy Delivery Truck, "Playboy Trucking Co." Photo by Calvin L. Chaussee.

Playboy Tow Truck "Playboy Trucking Co." tow truck, white, 22" long, c.1930s. Photo by Bob Smith

PLAYWOOD PLASTICS

This was a WWII-era company that employed wood composition. It was a subsidiary of Transogram, and its factory was at 133 Floyd St., Brooklyn, New York.

	C6	C8	C10
Playwood 407? "Dispatch Rider on Cycle"	7	11	15
Playwood 407?a As above, round base, head higher	7	11	15
Playwood 438 or 436? Motorcyclist, leather-type helmet (probably post-WWII)	No Price Found		

Playwood Plastics, L to R: 438 or 436?, 407?a

PRECISION PLASTICS

	C6	C8	C10
Precision Plastics Station Wagon, plastic windup, 7" long	55	82	110

Precision Plastics Station Wagons. Photo by Dave Leopard.

PREMIER
(Brooklyn)

	C6	C8	C10
Premier Station Wagon No. 52, plastic, 4-3/4" long	15	22	30

Premier Station Wagon No. 52, plastic, 4-3/4" long. Photo by Ron Fink.

PREMIER
(Japan)

Premier Heavy Tank No. 144 30	45	60

PRESSMAN

Pressman Ambulance, plastic 45	68	90

PROCESSED PLASTIC

Processed Plastic Army Tank 37	56	75

	C6	C8	C10
Processed Plastic Army Wrecker, 9" long, c.1950s	35	52	70
Processed Plastic Wrecker, 9" long	25	38	50

PROMOTIONALS

by Ron Smith

Promos are very accurately-produced reproductions of the full-size cars sitting on your car dealer's show room floor. They are almost always produced in 1/25th scale plastic or pot metal. Most of the pot metal (like a lead dimestore soldier) were discontinued by the very early 1950s. Molded in factory colors, they were sold to car dealers, who passed them out to the children of customers, so that Junior could have one just like Dad. This price guide deals mostly with those produced up to 1972. They are still being made today, but in reduced numbers. In recent years, as few as 3 or 4 different models were produced, whereas in the mid 1960s, as many as 50 different models were produced. The most popular full-size cars are usually the popular promo. The most dominant manufacturers were AMT (Aluminum Model Toys), BAN (Banthrico), JH (JoHan Models), MC (Master Caster), MPC (Model Products Corp.), NP (National Products), PM (Product Miniatures), and SMP (Scale Model Products).

When using this guide, remember that sometimes even mint in the original box may not get you the C10 price. The plastic of the 1950s and early 1960s had a tendency to warp and each car had a specific place where warp occurred. In addition, the plating on the grille or bumpers might be flaking or dull. Something as small as a missing hood ornament or a cracked vent window post can reduce your C10 to a C6.

	C6	C8	C10
AMX 2-door hardtop, 1969 JH	18	27	54
AMX 2-door hardtop, 1970 JH	18	36	63
Aero Willys 4-door Sedan, 1953 BIR	72	153	306
Aerocar convertible, 1953 GLA	36	72	144
Barracuda 2-door fastback, 1965 AMT	18	45	90
Barracuda 2-door fastback, 1966 AMT	18	36	72
Barracuda 2-door hardtop, 1967 AMT	18	36	72
Barracuda 2-door hardtop, 1968 MPC	36	72	135
Barracuda 2-door hardtop, 1969 MPC	27	45	100
Barracuda 2-door hardtop, 1970 MPC	63	135	260
Barracuda 2-door hardtop, 1971 MPC	81	162	325
Buick 4-door Sedan, 1947 NP	36	72	145
Buick 4-door Sedan, 1948 NP	27	63	125
Buick Sedan, 1950 NP	27	54	108
Buick 4-door Sedan, 1952 BAN	27	54	108
Buick Sedan, 1953 BAN	27	45	100
Buick 2-door hardtop, 1954 BAN	18	36	80
Buick Skylark Convertible, 1954 AMT	36	72	135
Buick 4-door Sedan, 1954 AMT	18	36	80
Buick 2-door hardtop, 1955 BAN	18	36	72
Buick 4-door Sedan, 1955 AMT	18	36	63
Buick Convertible, 1955 AMT	18	36	72
Buick 4-door hardtop, 1956 BAN	27	45	90
Buick Roadmaster 4-door hardtop, 1956 AMT	18	36	72
Buick Century Convertible, 1956 AMT	27	54	108
Buick Roadmaster Convertible, 1957 AMT	27	54	108
Buick Roadmaster 2-door hardtop, 1957 AMT	27	54	108
Buick Roadmaster Convertible, 1958 AMT	18	45	90
Buick Roadmaster 2-door hardtop, 1958 AMT	18	45	90
Buick Invicta Convertible, 1959 AMT	18	45	80
Buick Invicta 2-door hardtop, 1959 AMT	18	36	72
Buick Invicta 2 door hardtop, 1960 AMT	27	54	108
Buick Invicta Convertible, 1960 AMT	27	54	108
Buick Special Station Wagon, 1961 AMT	18	27	63
Buick Invicta Convertible, 1961 AMT	27	54	108

	C6	C8	C10
Buick Invicta 2 door hardtop, 1961 AMT	18	36	81
Buick Electra 225 Convertible, 1962 AMT	27	45	90
Buick Special Station Wagon, 1962 AMT	9	27	54
Buick Electra 225 2-door hardtop, 1962 AMT	18	45	90
Buick Electra 225 2-door hardtop, 1963 AMT	18	45	90
Buick Riviera 2-door hardtop, 1963 AMT	27	63	125
Buick Electra 225 Convertible, 1963 AMT	27	63	115
Buick Wildcat 2-door hardtop, 1964 AMT	54	108	215
Buick Riviera 2-door hardtop, 1964 AMT	18	45	90
Buick Riviera 2-door hardtop, 1965 AMT	45	81	160
Buick Wildcat Convertible, 1965 AMT	54	108	215
Buick Wildcat 2-door hardtop, 1965 AMT	54	117	235
Buick Skylark 2-door hardtop, 1966 AMT	36	81	160
Buick Wildcat 2-door hardtop, 1966 AMT	18	36	72
Buick Riviera 2-door hardtop, 1966 AMT	18	27	65
Buick Riviera 2-door hardtop, 1967 AMT	18	27	55
Buick Riviera 2-door hardtop, 1968 AMT	27	45	100
Buick Riviera 2-door hardtop, 1969 AMT	18	36	72
Buick Wildcat 2-door hardtop, 1969 AMT	9	27	55
Buick Wildcat 2-door hardtop, 1970 AMT	9	18	35
Cadillac 4-door Sedan, 1952 BAN	27	54	110
Cadillac 4-door Sedan, 1954 BAN	27	54	115
Cadillac 2-door hardtop, 1955 AMT	18	45	90
Cadillac 4-door Sedan, 1955 BAN	36	63	125
Cadillac Eldorado, 2-door hardtop, 1956 BAN	27	63	125
Cadillac 62, 2-door hardtop, 1956 AMT	18	36	72
Cadillac 60 S, 4-door Sedan, 1958 JH	9	27	54
Cadillac Fleetwood, 4-door, 1959 JH	18	36	80
Cadillac Fleetwood, 4-door hardtop, 1960 JH	18	45	80
Cadillac Fleetwood, 4-door hardtop, 1961 JH	18	36	80
Cadillac Fleetwood, 4-door hardtop, 1962 JH	18	45	80
Cadillac Convertible, 1963 JH	9	27	55
Cadillac 2-door hardtop, 1963 JH	9	27	55
Cadillac Convertible, 1964 JH	18	36	72
Cadillac 2-door hardtop, 1964 JH	18	36	72

	C6	C8	C10
Cadillac 2-door hardtop, 1965 JH	18	36	72
Cadillac Convertible, 1965 JH	18	36	72
Cadillac 2-door hardtop, 1966 JH	18	36	72
Cadillac Convertible, 1966 JH	18	36	80
Cadillac Eldorado, 2-door hardtop, 1967 JH	18	36	72
Cadillac 2-door hardtop, 1967 JH	18	27	65
Cadillac Convertible, 1967 JH	18	36	72
Cadillac Convertible, 1968 JH	9	18	45
Cadillac 2-door hardtop, 1968 JH	9	18	45
Cadillac Eldorado, 2-door hardtop, 1968 JH	9	27	45
Cadillac 2-door hardtop, 1969 JH	9	27	45
Cadillac Eldorado, 2-door hardtop, 1969 JH	9	27	45
Cadillac 2-door hardtop, 1970 JH	9	18	35
Cadillac Eldorado, 2-door hardtop, 1970 JH	18	27	55
Cadillac Eldorado, 2-door hardtop, 1971 JH	9	27	55
Cadillac Eldorado, 2-door hardtop, 1972 JH	9	18	36
Camaro Convertible, 1967 AMT	36	72	135
Camaro Convertible pace, 1967 AMT	117	225	450
Camaro 2-door hardtop, 1967 AMT	36	72	155
Camaro Convertible, 1968 MPC	45	81	170
Camaro Convertible, 1969 AMT	36	81	160
Camaro Convertible pace, 1969 AMT	72	144	290
Camaro 2-door hardtop, 1969 AMT	36	72	145
Camaro 2-door hardtop, 1970 AMT	27	54	110
Camaro 2-door hardtop, 1971 MPC	18	36	72
Camaro 2-door hardtop, 1972 MPC	18	45	80
Chevelle Station Wagon, 1964 AMT	18	36	80
Chevelle 2-door hardtop, 1964 AMT	27	45	100
Chevelle Malibu Station Wagon, 1965 AMT	27	45	90
Chevelle Malibu SS, 2-door hardtop, 1965 AMT	18	36	72
Chevelle 2-door hardtop, 1969 AMT	27	54	115
Chevelle Convertible, 1969 AMT	36	72	145
Chevelle SS Convertible, 1970 AMT	27	63	125
Chevelle SS 2-door hardtop, 1970 AMT	27	63	125
Chevelle 2-door hardtop, 1971 MPC	18	45	90
Chevelle SS 2-door hardtop, 1972 MPC	18	45	90
Chevrolet Fleetline 2-door, 1947 NP	36	72	145
Chevrolet Fleetline 2-door, 1948 NP	36	72	145
Chevrolet Styline 4-door Sedan, 1949 BAN	27	63	125
Chevrolet Convertible, 1949 BAN	36	81	160
Chevrolet Fleetline 2-door, 1949 BAN	36	72	145
Chevrolet Fleetline 4-door, 1949 BAN	36	72	145
Chevrolet Styline 2-door, 1949 BAN	27	63	125
Chevrolet 2-door Coupe, 1949 BAN	54	117	235
Chevrolet 2-door Coupe, 1950 BAN	27	63	115
Chevrolet Bel Air 2-door hardtop, 1950 BAN	27	63	125
Chevrolet Convertible, 1950 BAN	36	72	145
Chevrolet Fleetline 4-door, 1950 BAN	27	63	115
Chevrolet Styline 4-door Sedan, 1950 BAN	27	54	110
Chevrolet Styline 2-door Sedan, 1950 BAN	27	54	110
Chevrolet Fleetline 2-door, 1950 BAN	36	63	135

Chevrolet Styline 4 dr. Sedan, 1951. Photo by Ron Smith.

	C6	C8	C10
Chevrolet Styline 4-door Sedan, 1951 PMC	27	63	125
Chevrolet convertible, 1951 PMC	54	108	215
Chevrolet Bel Air 2-door hardtop, 1951 PMC	27	63	125
Chevrolet Styline 2-door Sedan, 1951 PMC	27	63	125
Chevrolet 2-door Coupe, 1951 PMC	27	63	115
Chevrolet Fleetline 2-door, 1951 PMC	36	72	145
Chevrolet Fleetline 4-door, 1951 PMC	36	72	155
Chevrolet Styline 2-door Sedan, 1952 PMC	36	63	135
Chevrolet Styline 4-door Sedan, 1952 PMC	27	63	115
Chevrolet Fleetline 2-door, 1952 PMC	36	72	145
Chevrolet 2-door Coupe, 1952 PMC	36	63	135
Chevrolet convertible, 1952 PMC	54	108	215
Chevrolet Bel Air 2-door hardtop, 1952 PMC	27	63	115
Chevrolet 210 2-door Sedan, 1953 PMC	27	54	115
Chevrolet Bel Air 4-door Sedan, 1953 PMC	27	54	110
Chevrolet 150 4-door Sedan, 1953 PMC	27	54	115
Chevrolet Bel Air 2-door hardtop, 1953 PMC	27	63	125
Chevrolet Bel Air 2-door Sedan, 1953 PMC	27	63	115
Chevrolet 210 4-door Sedan, 1953 PMC	27	54	110
Chevrolet 150 2-door Sedan, 1953 PMC	27	54	115
Chevrolet Convertible, 1953 PMC	36	72	145
Chevrolet Bel Air 2-door hardtop, 1954 PMC	36	72	145
Chevrolet 210 4-door Sedan, 1954 PMC	27	54	110
Chevrolet Bel Air Convertible, 1954 PMC	36	72	145
Chevrolet 210 2-door Sedan, 1954 PMC	36	72	145
Chevrolet Bel Air 2-door Sedan, 1954 PMC	27	63	125
Chevrolet 150 2-door Sedan, 1954 PMC	36	72	145
Chevrolet Bel Air 4-door Sedan, 1954 PMC	36	63	125
Chevrolet 150 4-door Sedan, 1954 PMC	36	72	145
Chevrolet 2-door hardtop, 1955 PMC	27	63	125
Chevrolet 4-door sedan, 1955 PMC	27	63	125
Chevrolet 2-door hardtop, 1955 BAN	36	63	135

	C6	C8	C10
Chevrolet 4-door hardtop, 1956 PMC	27	63	125
Chevrolet Cameo Pickup, 1956 PMC	36	63	125
Chevrolet 4-door Sedan, 1956 PMC	27	63	115
Chevrolet 2-door hardtop, 1956 PMC	27	54	100
Chevrolet Station Wagon, 1956 PMC	18	45	80
Chevrolet 2-door hardtop, 1956 BAN	36	63	125
Chevrolet Station Wagon, 1957 SMP	27	63	115
Chevrolet 4-door hardtop, 1957 PMC	27	54	115
Chevrolet 2-door hardtop, 1957 SMP	27	63	125
Chevrolet Convertible, 1957 SMP	36	63	125
Chevrolet Pickup, 1957 PMC	27	54	115
Chevrolet 2-door hardtop, 1958 AMT	27	54	110
Chevrolet Convertible, 1958 AMT	27	54	110
Chevrolet Station Wagon, 1958 PMC	18	45	80
Chevrolet 4-door hardtop, 1958 PMC	18	36	72
Chevrolet Pickup, 1958 AMT	36	81	160
Chevrolet Pickup, 1959 PMC	36	81	155
Chevrolet Station Wagon, 1959 SMP	18	36	80
Chevrolet Convertible, 1959 SMP	27	63	125
Chevrolet 2-door hardtop, 1959 SMP	18	36	72
Chevrolet Pickup, 1960 SMP	45	81	160
Chevrolet Impala 2-door hardtop, 1960 SMP	18	27	65
Chevrolet Impala 4-door hardtop, 1960 SMP	27	54	110
Chevrolet El Camino Pickup, 1960 AMT	27	54	110

Chevrolet El Camino Pick-Up, 1960. Photo by Ron Smith.

Chevrolet Nomad Station Wagon, 1960 SMP	18	36	80
Chevrolet Impala Convertible, 1960 SMP	27	54	100
Chevrolet Impala Convertible, 1961 AMT	45	90	180
Chevrolet Impala 4-door hardtop, 1961 AMT	54	108	215
Chevrolet Apache Pickup, 1961 AMT	36	72	145
Chevrolet Pickup, 1962 AMT	54	108	215
Chevrolet Impala Convertible, 1962 AMT	45	90	180
Chevrolet Impala 2-door hardtop, 1962 AMT	63	135	270
Chevrolet Impala Convertible, 1963 AMT	63	126	260
Chevrolet Impala 2-door hardtop, 1963 AMT	45	90	190

Chevrolet Impala 2 dr. HT, 1963. Photo by Ron Smith.

	C6	C8	C10
Chevrolet Pickup, 1963 AMT	54	117	235
Chevrolet El Camino Pickup, 1964 AMT	27	63	115
Chevrolet Impala Convertible, 1964 AMT	36	63	135
Chevrolet Impala 2-door hardtop, 1964 AMT	36	63	125
Chevrolet Fleetside Pickup, 1965 AMT	36	72	145
Chevrolet El Camino Pickup, 1965 AMT	36	63	125
Chevrolet Impala SS 2-door hardtop, 1965 AMT	27	54	100
Chevrolet Impala SS Convertible, 1965 AMT	27	63	125
Chevrolet Impala SS Budget Rent-A-Car, 1966 AMT	36	72	145
Chevrolet Impala SS 2-door hardtop, 1966 AMT	27	54	115
Chevrolet Impala Convertible, 1966 AMT	27	54	110
Chevrolet Fleetside Pickup, 1966 AMT	45	81	170
Chevrolet Impala 2-door hardtop, 1967 AMT	27	63	115
Chevrolet Fleetside Pickup, 1967 AMT	27	63	115
Chevrolet Impala Convertible, 1967 AMT	36	63	125
Chevrolet Impala 2-door hardtop, 1968 MPC	27	63	115
Chevrolet Fleetside Pickup, 1968 MPC	27	54	110
Chevrolet Impala Convertible, 1968 MPC	36	72	155
Chevrolet Impala Convertible, 1969 AMT	18	36	72
Chevrolet Fleetside Pickup, 1969 AMT	27	63	125
Chevrolet Impala 2-door hardtop, 1969 AMT	18	36	72
Chevrolet Impala Convertible, 1970 AMT	18	36	72
Chevrolet Impala 2-door hardtop, 1970 AMT	18	36	65
Chevrolet Monte Carlo 2-door hardtop, 1970 AMT	18	36	72
Chevrolet Fleetside Pickup, 1970 AMT	27	63	115
Chevrolet Fleetside Pickup, 1971 MPC	27	45	100
Chevrolet Monte Carlo 2-door hardtop, 1971 AMT	27	54	100
Chevrolet Impala 2-door hardtop, 1971 MPC	18	36	80
Chevrolet Impala Convertible, 1971 MPC	18	36	80
Chevrolet Impala 2-door hardtop, 1972 MPC	18	27	65
Chevrolet Monte Carlo 2-door hardtop, 1972 MPC	18	45	90
Chevrolet Fleetside Pickup, 1972 MPC	27	45	90

	C6	C8	C10
Chevrolet Nova 2-door hardtop, 1962 AMT	36	81	160
Chevrolet Nova Convertible, 1962 AMT	27	54	110
Chevrolet Nova Convertible, 1963 AMT	45	90	190
Chevrolet Nova Station Wagon, 1963 AMT	18	36	80
Chevrolet Nova 2-door hardtop, 1963 AMT	27	54	110
Chevrolet 11 2-door hardtop, 1965 AMT	27	54	100
Chrysler 2-door hardtop, 1953 BAN	27	45	90
Chrysler 4-door hardtop, 1957 JH	18	27	54
Chrysler New Yorker 4-door 1958 JH	18	36	72
Chrysler New Yorker 4-door hardtop, 1959 JH	9	27	54
Chrysler New Yorker 2-door hardtop, 1960 JH	9	27	54
Chrysler New Yorker 2-door hardtop, 1961 JH	9	27	54
Chrysler 300 Convertible, 1962 JH	18	36	80
Chrysler 300 2-door hardtop, 1962 JH	18	36	80
Chrysler 300 Convertible Pace, 1963 JH	63	126	250
Chrysler 300 Convertible, 1963 JH	36	63	135
Chrysler 300 2-door hardtop, 1963 JH	27	54	115
Chrysler Convertible, 1964 JH	36	63	135
Chrysler Turbine 2-door hardtop, 1964 JH	9	27	55
Chrysler 2-door hardtop, 1964 JH	18	36	72
Chrysler 300 Convertible, 1965 JH	27	63	125
Chrysler 300 2-door hardtop, 1965 JH	45	90	190
Chrysler 300 Convertible, 1966 JH	18	36	72
Chrysler 300 2-door hardtop, 1966 JH	36	72	145
Chrysler 300 2-door hardtop, 1967 JH	9	18	36
Chrysler 300 Convertible, 1967 JH	9	18	45
Chrysler 300 Convertible, 1968 JH	9	27	45
Chrysler 300 2-door hardtop, 1968 JH	9	18	45
Chrysler 4-door Sedan, 1950 BAN	27	54	110
Chrysler 4-door Sedan, 1948 NP	18	36	80
Chrysler 4-door Sedan, 1954 BAN	27	45	90
Comet 4-door Sedan, 1960 AMT	9	18	36
Comet 2-door Sedan, 1961 AMT	9	18	45
Comet 2-door Sedan, 1962 AMT	9	27	55
Comet Convertible, 1963 AMT	9	27	55
Comet 2-door hardtop, 1964 AMT	54	117	235
Comet Cyclone GT pace car (white), 1966 AMT	45	81	170
Comet Cyclone GT pace car (red), 1966 AMT	45	90	170
Comet 2-door Sedan, 1971 JH	9	18	27
Continental Mark II 2-door hardtop, 1956 AMT	36	72	135

	C6	C8	C10
Continental Mark II 2-door hardtop, 1957 AMT	36	72	135
Continental MK III 4-door hardtop, 1958 AMT	9	27	54
Continental MK IV Convertible, 1959 AMT	18	36	63
Continental MK IV 2-door hardtop, 1959 AMT	18	36	63
Continental MK V 2-door hardtop, 1960 AMT	9	18	45
Continental MK V Convertible, 1960 AMT	9	27	45
Continental Convertible, 1961 AMT	18	36	72
Continental 4-door Sedan, 1961 AMT	18	36	72
Continental 4-door Convertible, 1962 AMT	27	54	100
Continental 4-door Sedan, 1962 AMT	25	54	100
Continental 4-door Sedan, 1963 AMT	18	27	55
Continental 4-door Convertible, 1963 AMT	18	27	63
Continental 4-door Sedan, 1964 AMT	36	81	160
Continental 4-door Convertible, 1964 AMT	18	36	80
Continental 4-door Convertible, 1965 AMT	9	18	35
Continental 4-door Sedan, 1965 AMT	27	45	90
Continental 4-door Sedan, 1966 AMT	18	45	80
Continental 4-door Sedan, 1967 AMT	18	45	90
Continental 4-door Sedan, 1968 AMT	9	18	45
Corvair 4-door Sedan, 1960 AMT	18	36	72
Corvair Monza Coupe, 1961 AMT	18	36	80
Corvair 700 4-door Sedan, 1961 AMT	18	45	80
Corvair Monza 2-door hardtop, 1962 AMT	45	90	180
Corvair Monza 2-door hardtop, 1963 AMT	27	54	110
Corvair Monza Convertible, 1963 AMT	27	63	115
Corvair Monza 2-door hardtop, 1964 AMT	36	81	155
Corvair Monza Convertible, 1964 AMT	36	81	155
Corvair Corsa Convertible, 1965 AMT	27	63	115
Corvair Corsa 2-door hardtop, 1965 AMT	36	72	145
Corvair Corsa Convertible, 1966 AMT	18	27	65
Corvair Corsa 2-door hardtop, 1966 AMT	27	63	125
Corvair Monza 2-door hardtop, 1967 AMT	27	54	110
Corvette Convertible (orig.), 1954 BAN	18	45	90
Corvette Convertible, 1954 PMC	99	198	395
Corvette Convertible, 1958 AMT	81	162	325
Corvette Convertible, 1959 AMT	72	153	305
Corvette Convertible, 1960 AMT	99	198	395
Corvette Convertible w/hardtop, 1961 AMT	54	108	215
Corvette Convertible, 1961 SMP	135	270	540
Corvette Convertible, 1962 AMT	135	270	540
Corvette Sting Ray Convertible, 1963 AMT	63	135	270
Corvette Sting Ray Coupe, 1963 AMT	135	270	550
Corvette Sting Ray Coupe, 1964 AMT	108	225	450
Corvette Sting Ray Convertible, 1964 AMT	117	234	475
Corvette Sting Ray Coupe, 1965 AMT	126	252	505
Corvette Sting Ray Convertible, 1965 AMT	117	234	470

Continental MK III 4 dr. HT, 1958. Photo by Ron Smith.

	C6	C8	C10
Corvette Sting Ray Coupe, 1966 AMT	198	396	790
Corvette Sting Ray Convertible, 1966 AMT	207	414	830
Corvette Sting Ray Coupe, 1967 AMT	225	459	920
Corvette Sting Ray Convertible, 1967 AMT	202	396	790
Corvette Sting Ray Convertible, 1968 MPC	90	180	360
Corvette Sting Ray Coupe, 1968 MPC	18	45	90
Corvette Sting Ray Convertible, 1969 AMT	90	180	360
Corvette Sting Ray Coupe, 1969 AMT	135	270	540
Corvette Sting Ray Coupe, 1970 AMT	81	162	315
Corvette Sting Ray Convertible, 1970 AMT	81	171	340
Corvette Sting Ray Coupe, 1971 MPC	90	180	360
Corvette Sting Ray Coupe, 1972 MPC	81	162	325
Cougar 2-door hardtop, 1968 AMT	9	27	54
DeSoto Sedan, 1948 NP	18	36	72
DeSoto 4-door Sedan, 1955 JH	18	27	54
DeSoto 4-door 1956 JH	18	27	63
DeSoto Sportsman 4-door hardtop, 1957 JH	18	36	72
DeSoto Fireflight 4-door hardtop, 1958 JH	18	27	54
DeSoto Fireflight 4-door hardtop, 1959 JH	9	27	54
DeSoto Adventurer 2-door hardtop, 1960 JH	18	27	54
Diamond T Semi-Truck, 1956 PMC	18	36	81
Diamond T Dump Truck, 1956 PMC	18	36	72
Divco Milk Truck, 1951 AMT	63	117	235
Dodge 4-door Sedan, 1948 NP	18	45	90
Dodge Pickup, 1950 NP	27	63	115
Dodge Stake Truck, 1950 NP	27	54	115
Dodge 4-door Sedan, 1950 BAN	18	45	90
Dodge 4-door Sedan, 1951 BAN	18	45	80
Dodge 4-door Sedan, 1953 BAN	18	45	90
Dodge 4-door Sedan, 1954 BAN	18	36	80
Dodge Lancer 2-door hardtop, 1955 BAN	18	27	65
Dodge Lancer 4-door hardtop, 1956 AMT	27	45	90
Dodge Custom Royal 2-door hardtop, 1958 JH	18	27	54
Dodge Custom Royal 2-door hardtop, 1959 JH	9	27	54
Dodge Phoenix 2-door hardtop, 1960 JH	18	36	63
Dodge Phoenix 2-door hardtop, 1961 JH	18	27	63
Dodge Police Car, 1961 JH	18	45	90
Dodge Dart 2-door hardtop, 1962 JH	9	27	54
Dodge Dart Police Car, 1962 JH	54	108	215
Dodge Dart Convertible, 1962 JH	18	27	65
Dodge Polara Convertible, 1963 JH	18	36	72
Dodge Polara 2-door hardtop, 1963 JH	27	45	90
Dodge Polara 2-door hardtop, 1964 JH	27	45	90
Dodge Polara convertible, 1964 JH	27	45	100
Dodge Custom 880 convertible, 1965 MPC	36	72	145
Dodge Monaco 2-door hardtop, 1965 MPC	27	63	115
Dodge Coronet 500 2-door hardtop, 1965 MPC	45	90	190
Dodge Coronet 500 convertible, 1965 MPC	36	81	160
Dodge Charger 2-door hardtop, 1966 MPC	36	72	145
Dodge Polara 500 convertible, 1966 MPC	36	72	145
Dodge Monaco 500 2-door hardtop, 1966 MPC	36	63	135
Dodge Charger 2-door hardtop, 1967 MPC	45	81	170
Dodge Charger 2-door hardtop, 1968 MPC	63	126	245
Dodge Coronet 2-door hardtop, 1968 MPC	54	117	235
Dodge Charger R/T 2-door hardtop, 1969 MPC	54	99	205
Dodge Coronet Convertible, 1969 MPC	45	99	200
Dodge Coronet 2-door hardtop, 1969 MPC	45	90	190
Dodge Challenger 2-door hardtop, 1970 MPC	54	108	215
Dodge Charger RT 2-door hardtop, 1970 MPC	45	99	200
Dodge Charger 2-door hardtop, 1971 MPC	63	126	240
Dodge Challenger 2-door hardtop, 1971 MPC	45	90	180
Dodge Challenger 2-door hardtop, 1972 MPC	27	63	115
Dodge Charger 2-door hardtop, 1972 MPC	27	54	115
Edsel Convertible, 1958 AMT	45	90	170

Edsel Convertible, 1958. Photo by Ron Smith.

	C6	C8	C10
Edsel 2-door hardtop, 1958 AMT	45	81	170
Edsel Corsair Convertible, 1959 AMT	36	81	160
Edsel Corsair 2-door hardtop, 1959 AMT	36	72	155
Edsel Ranger Convertible, 1960 AMT	27	63	115
Edsel Ranger 2-door hardtop, 1960 AMT	27	54	110
Euclid Quarry Dump Truck, 1950 PM	18	45	90
Euclid Dump Truck, 1958 BAN	18	27	55
Euclid Dump Truck, 1965 BAN	9	27	55
F-85 Station Wagon, 1961 JH	9	18	35
F-85 Convertible, 1964 JH	27	54	110
F-85 2-door hardtop, 1964 JH	27	54	110
F-85 Cutlass Convertible, 1962 JH	18	36	65
F-85 Cutlass 2-door Sedan, 1962 JH	18	27	55
F-85 442 2-door hardtop, 1968 JH	18	36	70
Fairlane 2-door Sedan, 1962 AMT	18	27	65
Fairlane 2-door hardtop, 1963 AMT	18	36	72
Fairlane 500 2-door hardtop, 1964 AMT	18	36	80
Fairlane 2-door hardtop, 1965 AMT	18	27	65
Fairlane 2-door hardtop, 1966 AMT	27	54	100
Fairlane Cobra 2-door hardtop, 1970 AMT	9	27	55
Falcon 2-door Sedan, 1960 AMT	18	27	55
Falcon Ranchero Pickup, 1961 SMP	18	36	65
Falcon 2-door Sedan, 1961 AMT	9	18	45
Falcon Futura 2-door Sedan, 1962 AMT	9	18	45
Falcon Convertible, 1963 AMT	27	54	110

	C6	C8	C10
Falcon Sprint Convertible, 1964 AMT	18	36	80
Falcon Sprint 2-door hardtop, 1964 AMT	18	36	72
Falcon Convertible, 1965 AMT	18	27	65
Falcon 2-door hardtop, 1965 AMT	18	36	72
Falcon Futura 2-door 1966 AMT	18	36	72
Falcon 2-door hardtop, 1969 AMT	9	18	35
Firebird Convertible, 1967 MPC	36	72	145
Firebird 2-door hardtop, 1967 MPC	18	36	70
Firebird Convertible, 1968 MPC	54	108	215
Firebird 2-door hardtop, 1968 MPC	36	81	150
Firebird Convertible, 1969 MPC	27	63	115
Firebird 2-door hardtop, 1969 MPC	27	63	115
Firebird 2-door hardtop, 1970 MPC	18	45	90
Firebird 400 2-door hardtop, 1971 MPC	18	27	65
Firebird 400 2-door hardtop, 1972 MPC	18	36	65
Ford 4-door Sedan, 1948 AMT	27	54	110
Ford 2-door Sedan, 1948 MC	27	54	110
Ford 4-door Sedan, 1950 BAN	27	54	140
Ford Pickup, 1950 NP	36	72	145
Ford 2-door Sedan, 1950 MC	27	63	125
Ford 4-door Sedan, 1950 AMT	18	36	72
Ford Stake Truck, 1951 NP	18	36	72
Ford Pickup, 1951 NP	18	45	90
Ford 4-door Sedan, 1951 AMT	18	36	72
Ford Panel Truck, 1951 NP	18	36	80
Ford 4-door Sedan, 1953 BAN	18	45	90
Ford 4-door Sedan, 1953 AMT	18	36	72
Ford Pickup, 1953 BAN	36	72	145
Ford 4-door Sedan, 1954 AMT	18	36	72
Ford Convertible, 1954 AMT	18	45	90
Ford Station Wagon, 1955 PMC	27	45	90
Ford Station Wagon, 1956 PMC	18	45	80
Ford 4-door Sedan, 1956 AMT	27	54	110
Ford Station Wagon, 1957 PMC	18	36	72
Ford Station Wagon, 1958 PMC	18	36	72
Ford Station Wagon, 1959 AMT	18	36	72
Ford Station Wagon, 1960 HUB	18	36	72
Ford Pickup, 1960 AMT	27	63	115
Ford Station Wagon, 1961 HUB	18	36	72
Ford Station Wagon, 1962 HUB	18	36	72
Ford Custom 4-door Sedan, 1952 AMT	18	36	65
Ford Pace Car Convertible, 1953 AMT	63	135	260
Ford Sunliner Convertible, 1955 AMT	36	72	145
Ford Victoria 2-door hardtop, 1955 BAN	18	45	90
Ford Victoria 4-door Sedan, 1955 BAN	27	54	110
Ford Sunliner Convertible, 1956 AMT	18	36	72
Ford Victoria 4-door Sedan, 1956 AMT	18	36	80
Ford Fairlane Convertible, 1957 AMT	27	45	100
Ford Custom 300 2-door Sedan, 1957 AMT	63	126	250
Ford Fairlane 2-door hardtop, 1957 AMT	18	45	80
Ford Fairlane Convertible, 1958 AMT	27	54	100
Ford Fairlane 2-door hardtop, 1958 AMT	18	27	65
Ford Galaxie Convertible, 1959 AMT	27	45	90
Ford Galaxie 2-door hardtop, 1959 AMT	18	45	90
Ford Ranchero Pickup, 1959 PMC	18	36	65
Ford Galaxie 4-door hardtop, 1960 AMT	18	36	72
Ford Starliner hardtop, 1960 AMT	18	45	80
Ford Sunliner Convertible, 1960 AMT	18	45	90
Ford Fairlane 4-door Sedan, 1960 HUB	18	36	65
Ford Fairlane 4-door Sedan, 1961 HUB	18	36	65
Ford Starliner hardtop, 1961 AMT	18	36	72
Ford F-100 Pickup, 1961 AMT	36	63	135
Ford Galaxie 2-door hardtop, 1961 AMT	18	36	65
Ford, Sunliner Convertible, 1961 AMT	18	45	90
Ford F-100 Pickup, 1962 AMT	27	54	100
Ford Galaxie 2-door hardtop, 1962 AMT	18	45	80
Ford Galaxie Convertible, 1962 AMT	27	45	100
Ford Galaxie 2-door hardtop, 1963 AMT	18	36	65
Ford Galaxie Convertible, 1963 AMT	18	36	65
Ford Galaxie 500XL 2-door hardtop, 1964 AMT	18	36	80
Ford Galaxie 500XL Convertible, 1964 AMT	18	36	80
Ford Cobra Roadster, 1964 AMT	10	30	50
Ford Galaxie Convertible, 1965 AMT	18	27	55
Ford Galaxie 2-door hardtop, 1965 AMT	9	27	55
Ford Galaxie 500 2-door hardtop, 1966 AMT	18	36	65
Ford Galaxie 500 Convertible, 1966 AMT	18	36	65
Ford Galaxie 2-door hardtop, 1967 AMT	18	27	55
Ford Galaxie 2-door hardtop, 1968 AMT	18	27	65
Ford LTD 2-door hardtop, 1969 AMT	18	27	55
Ford Torino 2-door hardtop, 1969 AMT	27	54	110
Ford Torino Cobra hardtop, 1969 AMT	18	36	80
Ford LTD 4-door hardtop, 1970 AMT	18	27	55
Ford Grand Torino 2-door hardtop, 1972 JH	9	18	45
GMC Pickup, 1950 NP	27	45	100
GMC Dump Truck, 1950 NP	27	45	100
Henry J 2-door Sedan, 1951 AMT	36	72	135
Hornet 2-door Sedan, 1970 JH	9	18	35
Hudson 4-door Sedan, 1948 MC	45	90	180
Hudson Sedan, 1950 MC	36	72	145
Hudson 4-door Sedan, 1951 MC	27	54	110
Imperial Convertible, 1958 AMT	18	36	80
Imperial 2-door hardtop, 1958 AMT	18	36	80

Imperial 2 dr. HT, 1958. Photo by Ron Smith.

	C6	C8	C10
Imperial Convertible, 1959 SMP	18	36	72
Imperial 2-door hardtop, 1959 SMP	18	36	72
Imperial Convertible, 1960 SMP	9	27	55
Imperial 2-door hardtop, 1960 SMP	9	27	55
Imperial 2-door hardtop, 1961 AMT	36	63	125
Imperial Convertible, 1961 AMT	27	45	90
Imperial Convertible, 1962 AMT	18	36	70
Imperial 2-door hardtop, 1962 ATM	18	36	70
Imperial 2-door hardtop, 1963 AMT	45	90	180
Imperial Convertible, 1963 ATM	18	36	72
Imperial Crown 2-door hardtop, 1964 AMT	45	90	180
Imperial Convertible, 1964 AMT	45	90	180
Imperial 2-door hardtop, 1965 AMT	18	36	72

	C6	C8	C10
Imperial Convertible, 1965 AMT	45	90	180
Imperial Convertible, 1966 AMT	54	108	225
Imperial 2-door hardtop, 1966 AMT	54	108	215
Imperial 2-door hardtop, 1967 AMT	36	63	135
Imperial 2-door hardtop, 1968 JH	9	18	45
International Pickup, 1947 PMC	45	90	170
International Telephone Truck, 1947 NP	27	63	125
International Pickup, 1950 PMC	36	63	135
International Semi-Truck, 1951 PMC	27	45	100
International Pickup, 1951 PMC	36	72	145
International Dump Truck, 1951 PMC	27	54	110
International Stake Truck, 1951 PMC	27	54	115
International Semi (plain), 1953 PMC	18	45	80
International Stake Truck, 1953 PMC	18	45	90
International Semi "Mayflower," 1953 PMC	18	36	72
International Dump Truck, 1953 PMC	18	45	90
International Tilt Cab Semi, 1955 PMC	18	36	65
International Pickup, 1956 PMC	18	36	80

International Pickup, 1956. Photo by Ron Smith.

	C6	C8	C10
International Pickup, 1957 PMC	18	45	90
International 4-door Sedan, 1958 PMC	9	18	45
International Dump Truck, 1958 PMC	9	18	35
International Scout Convertible, 1965 ESK	18	27	65
Javelin 2-door hardtop, 1968 JH	9	27	55
Javelin 2-door hardtop, 1969 JH	9	27	55
Javelin 2-door hardtop, 1970 JH	18	27	65
Javelin/AMX 2-door hardtop, 1971 JH	9	27	45
Javelin/AMX 2-door hardtop, 1972 JH	9	18	35
Jeep Station Wagon, 1950 AUT	36	81	160
Kaiser 4-door Sedan, 1953 BAN	72	144	290
Lincoln Cosmopolitan 4-door sedan, 1950	99	198	395
Lincoln 4-door Sedan, 1951 BAN	27	45	90
Lincoln 4-door Sedan, 1953 BAN	18	45	90
Lincoln 2-door hardtop, 1954 BAN	18	45	80
Mack Tanker Truck, 1950 NP	27	55	110
Maverick 2-door Sedan, 1969 JH	9	18	35
Mercedes 300 SL Coupe, 1958 HUB	18	36	72
Mercedes 300 SL Convertible, 1958 HUB	18	45	80
Mercury 4-door Sedan, 1951 BAN	27	54	110
Mercury 4-door Sedan, 1953 BAN	18	45	90
Mercury 2-door hardtop, 1954 BAN	18	45	80
Mercury 2-door hardtop, 1955 BAN	27	54	115
Mercury Park Lane 2-door. hardtop, 1959 AMT	18	36	72
Mercury Park Lane Convertible, 1959 AMT	18	36	65
Mercury Park Lane 2-door hardtop, 1960 AMT	18	36	72
Mercury Park Lane Convertible, 1960 AMT	18	36	72
Mercury Monterey Convertible, 1961 AMT	18	45	90
Mercury Monterey 2-door hardtop, 1961 AMT	11	18	45
Mercury Monterey 2-door hardtop, 1962 AMT	27	63	115
Mercury Monterey Convertible, 1962 AMT	27	63	125
Mercury Monterey Convertible, 1963 AMT	18	36	72
Mercury Monterey 2-door hardtop, 1963 AMT	18	36	72
Mercury Park Lane Convertible, 1964 AMT	18	45	80
Mercury Park Lane 2-door hardtop, 1964 AMT	18	27	65
Mercury Breezeway 2-door hardtop, 1964 AMT	18	36	72
Mercury Park Lane 2-door hardtop, 1965 AMT	9	18	45
Mercury Park Lane 2-door hardtop, 1966 AMT	9	27	55
Meteor Custom 2-door Sedan, 1962 AMT	36	72	145
Meteor 2-door hardtop, 1963 AMT	27	54	110
Metro panel trk. (sgl.), 1952 PMC	18	27	55
Metro panel trk. (dbl.), 1952 PMC	18	27	65
Metropolitan Convertible, 1958 HUB	63	135	270
Metropolitan 2-door hardtop, 1958 HUB	63	126	250
Mustang 2-door hardtop, 1964 AMT	27	54	100
Mustang Convertible Pace, 1964 AMT	45	90	180
Mustang 2-door Convertible, 1964 AMT	27	54	110
Mustang Convertible, 1965 AMT	27	45	90
Mustang 2-door Fastback, 1965 AMT	27	45	90
Mustang 2-door hardtop, 1965 AMT	18	36	72
Mustang 2 + 2 2-door hardtop, 1966 AMT	45	99	200
Mustang 2-door hardtop, 1966 AMT	27	54	110
Mustang Convertible, 1966 AMT	18	45	80
Mustang 2 + 2 2-door hardtop, 1967 AMT	54	99	200
Mustang Mach I 2-door Fastback, 1969 AMT	54	108	220
Mustang Mach I 2-door Fastback, 1971 AMT	36	72	145
Mustang Mach I 2-door hardtop, 1972 AMT	27	54	110
Nash 4-door Sedan, 1950 NP	18	36	65
Nash 4-door Sedan, 1953 PMC	18	45	90
Nash 4-door Sedan, 1954 PMC	27	45	90
Nash Golden Airflight 4-door, 1952 PMC	27	45	90
Oldsmobile 4-door Sedan, 1953 BAN	27	45	90
Oldsmobile 2-door hardtop, 1954 BAN	18	36	80
Oldsmobile 2-door hardtop, 1955 BAN	18	36	80
Oldsmobile 4-door hardtop, 1956 JH	18	36	70
Oldsmobile 98 4-door hardtop, 1957 JH	18	45	80
Oldsmobile 4-door hardtop, 1958 JH	18	27	55
Oldsmobile 98 4-door hardtop, 1959 JH	18	36	72
Oldsmobile 98 2-door hardtop 1960 JH	9	27	55
Oldsmobile 88 4-door. hardtop, 1961 JH	18	27	65
Oldsmobile Starfire Convertible, 1962 JH	18	36	72
Oldsmobile 88 4-door hardtop, 1962 JH	18	36	80
Oldsmobile Starfire Convertible, 1963 JH	8	27	54
Oldsmobile Starfire 2-door hardtop, 1963 JH	8	27	54

	C6	C8	C10
Oldsmobile 88 2-door hardtop, 1965 AMT	18	45	90
Oldsmobile 88 Convertible, 1965 AMT	27	45	100
Oldsmobile Toronado 2-door hardtop, 1966 JH	9	27	55
Oldsmobile Toronado 2-door hardtop, 1969 JH	9	27	55
Oldsmobile 442 2-door hardtop, 1969 JH	18	36	72
Oldsmobile Toronado 2-door hardtop, 1970 JH	9	18	35
Oldsmobile 442 2-door hardtop, 1970 JH	18	36	65
Oldsmobile 442 2-door hardtop, 1971 JH	18	36	65
Oldsmobile Toronado 2-door hardtop, 1971 JH	18	27	65
Oldsmobile Toronado 2-door hardtop, 1972 JH	9	18	35
Opel Sedan, 1959 PMC	9	18	35
Opel GT 1900 Coupe, 1969 AMT	18	36	80
Packard Convertible, 1948 MC	27	54	110
Packard Henesey Ambulance, 1951 AMT	63	135	270
Packard 4-door Sedan, 1953 BAN	36	63	125
Packard 4-door Sedan, 1954 BAN	27	54	110
Pinto 2-door Sedan, 1971 AMT	9	18	25
Pinto Runabout 2-door Sedan, 1972 AMT	9	18	25
Plymouth Sedan, 1948 NP	27	54	110
Plymouth 4-door Sedan, 1950 AMT	18	36	80
Plymouth 4-door Taxi, 1953 PMC	18	36	80
Plymouth 4-door Sedan, 1953 BAN	27	54	110
Plymouth 4-door Sedan, 1953 PMC	18	36	72
Plymouth Station Wagon, 1954 PMC	27	54	100
Plymouth 4-door Sedan, 1954 PMC	18	36	72
Plymouth Sedan, 1955 BAN	18	45	80
Plymouth 4-door Sedan, 1955 JH	18	45	90
Plymouth Belevedere 4-door, 1956 JH	18	36	80
Plymouth 2-door Sedan, 1956 BAN	18	45	80
Plymouth Belvedere 2-door hardtop, 1957 JH	18	36	72
Plymouth Taxi, 1957 JH	36	63	135
Plymouth Fury 2-door hardtop, 1958 JH	27	54	110
Plymouth Belvedere 2-door hardtop, 1958 JH	9	27	55
Plymouth Taxi, 1958 JH	36	63	135
Plymouth Fury 2-door hardtop, 1959 JH	18	36	72
Plymouth Fury Taxi, 1959 JH	9	27	55
Plymouth Fury 2-door hardtop, 1960 JH	18	36	65
Plymouth Fury Taxi, 1960 JH	27	63	125
Plymouth Station Wagon, 1960 JH	9	27	55
Plymouth Fury 2-door hardtop, 1961 JH	18	36	80
Plymouth Taxi, 1961 JH	27	63	125
Plymouth Police Car, 1961 JH	18	45	90
Plymouth Fury Convertible, 1963 JH	18	36	80
Plymouth Fury 2-door hardtop, 1963 JH	18	45	90
Plymouth Fury Convertible, 1964 JH	18	36	72
Plymouth 2-door hardtop, 1964 JH	27	63	125
Plymouth Fury III Convertible Pace, 1965 JH	54	117	235
Plymouth Fury III driver's training, 1965 JH	18	36	80
Plymouth Fury III 2-door hardtop, 1965 JH	27	54	110
Plymouth Fury III Convertible, 1965 JH	27	63	125
Plymouth Fury III Convertible, 1966 JH	18	36	72
Plymouth Fury III Driver's Training, 1966 JH	27	45	100
Plymouth Fury III 2-door hardtop, 1966 JH	18	36	72
Plymouth Fury 2-door hardtop, 1967 JH	9	27	55
Plymouth Fury Convertible, 1967 JH	18	27	55
Plymouth Fury III Convertible, 1968 JH	18	27	55
Plymouth Fury III 2-door hardtop, 1968 JH	9	27	45
Plymouth GTX 2-door hardtop, 1969 JH	18	36	80
Plymouth GTX 2-door hardtop, 1970 JH	18	45	90
Plymouth Duster 2-door hardtop, 1971 MPC	18	45	90
Plymouth Roadrunner 2-door hardtop, 1971 MPC	27	63	125
Plymouth Roadrunner 2-door hardtop, 1972 MPC	27	54	110
Plymouth Duster, 1972 MPC	27	54	110
Plymouth "Cuda" 2-door hardtop, 1972 MPC	45	80	160
Plymouth Fury Police Car, 1962 JH	36	72	145
Plymouth Fury Taxi, 1962 JH	45	99	200
Plymouth Fury 2-door hardtop, 1962 JH	27	45	90
Plymouth Fury Convertible, 1962 JH	27	45	100
Pontiac 4-door Sedan, 1947 NP	36	63	135
Pontiac 4-door Sedan, 1948 NP	27	63	115
Pontiac 4-door Sedan, 1951 AMT	18	36	72
Pontiac 4-door Sedan, 1952 AMT	18	45	90
Pontiac 2-door Sedan, 1953 AMT	18	45	90
Pontiac Sedan, 1953 BAN	27	45	90
Pontiac 2-door Sedan, 1954 AMT	18	36	80
Pontiac Sedan, 1955 BAN	18	36	72
Pontiac 4-door Sedan, 1955 JH	18	36	72
Pontiac 2-door Sedan, 1955 JH	18	36	72
Pontiac 4-door hardtop, 1956 JH	18	36	72
Pontiac Star Chief 4-door hardtop, 1957 AMT	27	63	125
Pontiac Star Chief Convertible, 1957 AMT	36	81	160
Pontiac Bonneville Convertible, 1958 AMT	27	63	125
Pontiac Bonneville 2-door hardtop, 1958 AMT	18	36	72
Pontiac Bonneville Convertible, 1959 AMT	18	36	80
Pontiac Bonneville 2-door hardtop, 1959 AMT	27	54	100
Pontiac Bonneville 2-door. hardtop, 1960 AMT	18	36	72
Pontiac Bonneville Convertible, 1960 AMT	18	36	72
Pontiac Bonneville 2-door hardtop, 1961 AMT	27	54	110
Pontiac Bonneville Convertible, 1961 AMT	27	54	110
Pontiac Bonneville 2-door hardtop, 1962 AMT	36	72	155
Pontiac Bonneville Convertible, 1962 AMT	63	126	250
Pontiac Bonneville Convertible, 1963 AMT	36	72	145
Pontiac Bonneville 2-door hardtop, 1963 AMT	27	45	90
Pontiac Bonneville 2-door hardtop, 1964 AMT	27	54	115
Pontiac Bonneville 2-door hardtop, 1964 AMT	36	63	125

	C6	C8	C10
Pontiac Bonneville			
Convertible, 1964 AMT	36	63	135
Pontiac Grand Prix			
2-door hardtop, 1965 AMT	36	72	145
Pontiac Bonneville			
Convertible, 1965 AMT	36	63	135
Pontiac Bonneville			
2-door hardtop, 1965 AMT	36	72	145
Pontiac Bonneville			
Convertible, 1966 MPC	36	63	125
Pontiac Bonneville			
2-door hardtop, 1966 MPC	36	72	145
Pontiac Bonneville			
Convertible, 1967 MPC	27	54	110
Pontiac Bonneville			
2-door hardtop, 1967 MPC	27	54	110
Pontiac Bonneville			
2-door hardtop, 1968 MPC	18	36	70
Pontiac Bonneville			
Convertible, 1968 MPC	27	45	100
Pontiac Bonneville			
2-door hardtop, 1969 MPC	18	36	72
Pontiac Grand Prix			
2-door hardtop, 1969 MPC	18	36	72
Pontiac Bonneville			
Convertible, 1969 MPC	18	36	72
Pontiac Grand Prix			
2-door hardtop, 1970 MPC	18	36	72
Pontiac Bonneville			
2-door hardtop, 1970 MPC	9	27	55
Pontiac Bonneville			
2-door hardtop, 1970 MPC	18	36	65
Pontiac GTO 2-door hardtop, 1970 MPC	27	45	100
Pontiac GTO 2-door hardtop, 1971 MPC	18	45	90
Pontiac Grand Prix			
2-door hardtop, 1971 MPC	18	36	65
Pontiac GTO 2-door hardtop, 1972 MPC	18	45	90
Pontiac Grand Prix			
2-door hardtop, 1972 MPC	18	36	72
Rambler Convertible, 1951 NP	27	54	110
Rambler 2-door hardtop, 1952 BAN	27	54	100
Rambler Sedan, 1953 BAN	18	45	90
Rambler 2-door hardtop, 1954 BAN	27	63	125
Rambler Station Wagon, 1959 JH	9	27	45
Rambler Station Wagon, 1960 JH	9	27	55
Rambler American 2-door Sedan, 1961 JH	9	18	36
Rambler Cross			
Country Station Wagon, 1961 JH	9	27	55
Rambler Unit Construction Demo, 1961 JH	9	18	36
Rambler Classic 4-door Sedan, 1962 JH	9	18	45
Rambler American 2-door Sedan, 1962 JH	9	18	36
Rambler American Convertible, 1962 JH	9	18	45
Rambler Classic Station Wagon, 1962 JH	9	18	45
Rambler Classic Station Wagon, 1963 JH	9	27	45
Rambler Classic 4-door Sedan, 1963 JH	9	27	55
Rambler American Convertible, 1963 JH	9	27	45
Rambler Classic Station Wagon, 1964 JH	9	18	35
Rambler Classic 4-door Sedan, 1964 JH	9	18	35
Rambler American Convertible, 1964 JH	9	18	35
Rambler American			
2-door hardtop, 1964 JH	9	18	45
Rambler Classic 4-door Sedan, 1965 JH	9	18	36
Rambler Marlin 2-door Fastback, 1965 JH	18	27	65
Rambler Classic Convertible, 1965 JH	9	18	45
Rambler Marlin 2-door Fastback, 1966 JH	18	36	72
Rambler American Convertible, 1966 JH	9	18	45
Rambler American			
2-door hardtop, 1966 JH	9	27	45
Rambler Ambassador			
2-door hardtop, 1966 JH	9	27	45
Rambler Ambassador			
2-door hardtop, 1967 JH	9	18	35
Rambler Ambassador Convertible, 1967 JH	9	18	35
Rambler Ambassador Convertible, 1968 JH	9	18	35
Rambler Ambassador			
2-door hardtop, 1968 JH	9	18	35
Rambler Ambassador			
2-door hardtop, 1969 JH	9	18	35
Rambler C.C. Station Wagon, 1966 JH	9	18	45
Rambler Dauphine 4-door, 1958 HUB	9	18	35
Rambler Rolls Royce Silver Ghost			
4-door sedan, 1958 HUB	18	36	72
Studebaker 2-door Sedan, 1947 NP	36	72	145
Studebaker 2-door Sedan, 1948 NP	27	63	115
Studebaker Stake Truck, 1950 NP	81	162	325
Studebaker 2-door Sedan, 1950 AMT	27	54	100
Studebaker 2-door Sedan, 1951 AMT	27	54	110
Studebaker 2-door Sedan, 1952 AMT	18	45	90
Studebaker Starliner Coupe, 1953 BAN	18	45	80
Studebaker Starliner Coupe, 1953 AMT	18	45	80
Studebaker Starliner Coupe, 1954 AMT	18	45	90
Studebaker 2-door hardtop, 1955 AMT	18	36	72
Studebaker Golden			
Hawk 2-door, 1956 AMT	18	45	80
Studebaker Lark 2-door hardtop, 1959 JH	9	27	55
Studebaker Lark 2-door hardtop, 1960 JH	9	27	55
Studebaker Lark 2-door hardtop, 1961 JH	9	27	55
Studebaker Lark Convertible, 1962 JH	18	27	65
Studebaker Lark 2-door hardtop, 1962 JH	18	27	65
Tempest 4-door Sedan, 1961 AMT	18	27	65
Tempest LeMans			
2-door sedan, 1962 AMT	18	36	65
Tempest LeMans Convertible, 1962 AMT	18	36	72
Tempest LeMans Convertible, 1963 AMT	27	63	115
Tempest LeMans			
2-door Sedan, 1963 AMT	36	63	125
Tempest LeMans			
2-door hardtop, 1964 AMT	27	54	115
Tempest GTO 2-door hardtop, 1964 AMT	18	27	55
Tempest LeMans Convertible, 1964 AMT	27	54	110
Tempest GTO 2-door hardtop, 1965 AMT	63	135	270
Tempest GTO Convertible, 1965 AMT	63	135	270
Tempest GTO 2-door hardtop, 1966 MPC	72	144	290
Tempest GTO Convertible, 1966 MPC	54	117	235
Tempest GTO 2-door hardtop, 1967 MPC	63	126	250
Tempest GTO Convertible, 1967 MPC	63	126	260
Tempest GTO Convertible, 1968 MPC	36	81	160
Tempest GTO 2-door hardtop, 1968 MPC	18	36	80
Tempest GTO 2-door hardtop, 1969 MPC	36	81	160
Tempest GTO Convertible, 1969 MPC	45	90	180
Thunderbird Convertible, 1956 AMT	36	72	150
Thunderbird Convertible, 1954 AMT	27	54	110
Thunderbird Convertible, 1955 AMT	36	72	145
Thunderbird Convertible, 1957 AMT	36	63	125

	C6	C8	C10
Thunderbird 2-door hardtop, 1958 AMT	18	36	72
Thunderbird Convertible, 1959 AMT	18	36	72
Thunderbird 2-door hardtop, 1959 AMT	18	36	72
Thunderbird 2-door hardtop, 1960 AMT	18	36	72
Thunderbird Convertible, 1960 AMT	18	45	90
Thunderbird Convertible, 1961 AMT	27	63	126
Thunderbird 2-door hardtop, 1961 AMT	18	45	90
Thunderbird 2-door hardtop, 1962 AMT	27	54	110
Thunderbird Convertible, 1962 AMT	45	109	190
Thunderbird 2-door hardtop, 1963 AMT	18	36	72
Thunderbird Convertible, 1963 AMT	45	90	190
Thunderbird 2-door hardtop, 1964 AMT	18	36	72
Thunderbird Convertible, 1964 AMT	27	54	110
Thunderbird 2-door hardtop, 1965 AMT	18	36	65
Thunderbird Convertible, 1965 AMT	18	36	70
Thunderbird Convertible, 1966 AMT	18	27	65
Thunderbird 2-door hardtop, 1966 AMT	18	27	55
Thunderbird 2-door hardtop, 1967 AMT	9	27	55
Thunderbird 2-door hardtop, 1968 AMT	9	18	45
Thunderbird 2-door hardtop, 1969 AMT	9	27	55
Thunderbird 2-door hardtop, 1970 AMT	9	27	55
Thunderbird 2-door hardtop, 1971 AMT	9	27	55
Torino Cobra 2-door hardtop, 1971 AMT	9	27	55
Triumph TR-3A hardtop, 1958 HUB	9	18	45
Triumph TR-3A Convertible, 1958 HUB	9	18	45
Valiant 4-door Sedan, 1960 AMT	9	18	45
Valiant 4-door Sedan, 1961 AMT	9	18	45
Valiant 2-door hardtop, 1961 AMT	9	18	35
Valiant Signet 800 2-door hardtop, 1962 AMT	27	63	115
Valiant Signet 800 2-door hardtop, 1963 AMT	9	27	55
Valiant Signet 200 2-door hardtop, 1964 AMT	36	72	145
Valiant 2-door hardtop, 1965 AMT	18	27	65
Valiant 2-door hardtop, 1966 AMT	81	162	325
Vega Hatchback 2-door hardtop, 1971 MPC	9	18	25
Valiant Hatchback 2-door, 1972 MPC	9	18	25
Volkswagen Karmann Ghia Convertible, 1959 PM	9	18	35
Volkswagen Sedan, 1959 PM	9	18	25
White C.O.E. Truck, 1950 NP	45	90	180
Willys Jeep FC Pickup, 1961 AUT	27	45	90
Willys Jeep FC Stake Truck w/plow, 1961 AUT	27	54	110
Willys Jeep "Jolly," 1961 AUT	18	45	90
Willys Jeep Stake Truck, 1961 AUT	27	45	100
Willys Jeepster, 1968 MPC	9	18	25
Willys 3/4-ton Army Truck, 1969 BAN	18	36	72

PYRO

(1939-1969)

by Terry Sells

Pyro is probably best known for its plastic model kits produced in the 1950s and 1960s, but it did produce a nice line of toy vehicles in the 1950s. The originals of these were probably military vehicles made around the time of the Korean War. There were two sizes of vehicles, molded in khaki, olive drab, and gray (for Navy and Marine) plastic. They were heat-stamped with stars and other identifying marks. Lionel used the large Pyro military vehicles as loads for its Navy and Marine trains. The loads were all gray and had no figures glued in place. After the war came the inevitable decline in sales of war toys. The vehicles were issued in civilian roles (i.e., Horse Transport) and specialty roles (i.e., Coca-Cola Truck). Pyro also produced a wide range of toys and trinkets for Planters Peanuts.

Specialty advertising issued included at least one political truck: an "Elect Marvin Griffin for Governor--Get On The Griffin Bandwagon" truck. Griffin was governor of Georgia from 1954 to 1958. Military sets continued in production into the mid- to late 1950s. A 1956 Pyro advertisement in *Toys & Novelties* magazine declared: "Military Toys Are Hot Again!" The ad pictured boxed military sets C-242, C-243, and C-244. Toys gradually faded behind Pyro's growing line of model kits. The company went out of business in 1969. It was located in Pyro Park, Union City, New Jersey. At its height, it had 400 employees.

Terry Sells was born and raised in the Atlanta area. He is a graphic artist who works with music and entertainment accounts. He cartoons for fun and collects all manner of plastic and celluloid toys. He started collecting in 1972, when his wife innocently gave him a toy car for his birthday. He mostly collects toys from the 1945-1960 period. His wife, Patti, shares his interest in toys and also collects Disney and children's books. They have two "daughters," Birdie and Jinkie.

	C6	C8	C10
Pyro Army Tank P-1020	30	45	60
Pyro Balloon Racer, 3-1/2"	12	18	25
Pyro Bulldozer, front loader	35	70	100
Pyro Canteen Truck	30	45	60
Pyro City Bottling Truck, 4"	11	16	22
Pyro "City Builders" Truck, 5-1/2" long	No Price Found		

Pyro "City Builders" truck, 5-1/2." Photo by Terry Sells.

Pyro "Coca-Cola" truck, 5-1/2". Photo by Terry Sells.

Pyro "Design-A-Car" set, builds 14 models. Photo by Terry Sells.

Pyro "Elect Marvin Griffin Governor," "Get On The Griffin Bandwagon" truck, 5-1/2". Photo by Terry Sells.

Pyro "Ice & Coal" truck, 5-1/2". Photo by Terry Sells.

Pyro "Mr. Peanut's Peanut Wagon," 5-1/2". Photo by Terry Sells.

Pyro "Planter's Peanuts" semi w/trailer, 5-1/2". Photo by Terry Sells.

Pyro "Planters Peanuts" stake truck, semi, 5-1/2". Photo by Terry Sells.

	C6	C8	C10
Pyro "Coca-Cola" Truck, 5-1/2" long	75	112	150
Pyro "Design-A-Car" set, builds 14 models, with box	35	52	70
Pyro "Elect Marvin Griffin Governor," "Get On The Griffin Bandwagon" Truck, 5-1/2" long		No Price Found	
Pyro Express Truck, 1950s	15	22	30
Pyro Ford, 1932 No. C-295...........................	5	8	10
Pyro F7U Cutlass, 6" long	15	22	30
Pyro "Ice & Coal" Truck, 5-1/2" long		No Price Found	
Pyro Lumber Loader	20	35	50
Pyro Lunch Wagon Truck, 5-1/2"	18	27	37
Pyro "Mr. Peanut's Peanut Wagon," 5-1/2" long		No Price Found	
Pyro Mobile Anti-Aircraft Truck, P-1015	48	72	95
Pyro Mobile Radar Truck, P-957.................	48	72	95

	C6	C8	C10
Pyro Mobile Searchlight Truck, P-958	48	72	95
Pyro Mobile Sound Truck, P-956	48	72	95
Pyro Motorcycle	32	48	65
Pyro "Planters Peanuts" semi w/trailer, 5-1/2" long		No Price Found	
Pyro "Planters Peanuts" Stake Truck, semi, 5-1/2" long		No Price Found	
Pyro "Pyro Ranch Horse Transport," 5-1/2" long		No Price Found	
Pyro Race Car, 3-1/2" long	10	15	21
Pyro Race Car, 4" long	20	30	40
Pyro Range Patrol Truck, 5" long	15	22	30
Pyro Road Roller	12	18	25
Pyro 6 U.S. Army Mobile Units Set		No Price Found	
Pyro Soap Box Supersonic Racer, 4-3/4"	75	112	150
Pyro Soldier Transport, P-955	20	30	40

Pyro toys, as advertised in a December, 1951 Woolworth's comic book catalog.

	C6	C8	C10
Pyro Steam Roller	12	18	25
Pyro 21-piece U.S. Army Set	17	26	35
Pyro Twin 40-mm Mobile Gun, P-1087	48	72	95
Pyro U.S. Army Ambulance	12	18	24
Pyro "U.S. Army" Truck	9	13	19

	C6	C8	C10
Pyro U.S. Army Stake			
Trailer Truck, 5-1/2" long	10	15	20
Pyro "U.S.M.C." Truck	10	15	20
Pyro "U.S. Navy" Truck	10	15	20

Pyro "Pyro Ranch Horse Transport," 5-1/2". Photo by Terry Sells.

Pyro 21-piece U.S. Army Set; value, mint in box $45. Courtesy Harvey K. Rainess.

RAINBOW

(Butler, Pa.)

The following list, with its codings, was compiled by David Leopard. Vehicles are broken down by types.

	C6	C8	C10
RA01 '35 Oldsmobile Coupe, 3-3/4" long ...	35	40	55
RA02 '35 Oldsmobile			
4-door Sedan, 3-1/4" long	35	40	55
RA03 '35 Oldsmobile			
4-door Sedan, 5" long	50	60	75
RT01 '35 Studebaker (?)			
Stake Side Pickup, 5-1/4" long	35	45	55
RR01 Open Racer, tapered tail, 4" long	30	40	50
RR02 Open Racer, tapered tail, 5" long	No Price Found		

Rainbow RA01. Courtesy Dave Leopard from his book Rubber Toy Vehicles.

Rainbow, L to R: RA03, RA02. Courtesy Dave Leopard from his book Rubber Toy Vehicles.

Rainbow RT01. Courtesy Dave Leopard from his book Rubber Toy Vehicles.

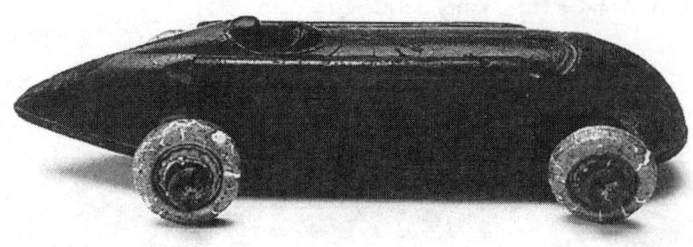

Rainbow RR01. Courtesy Dave Leopard from his book Rubber Toy Vehicles.

RALSTOY

(Ralston Toy and Novelty Company)

by Fred Maxwell and Ferd Zegel with Assistance of Alice Shooter and the Ralston Archives

Ralston Toy & Novelty Co. was founded in July 1939 to manufacture slushmold toys and novelties. It was formed—by Dr. Felix Despecher, former mayor of Ralston, Nebraska, A.M. Erickson, and Henry C. Nestor—to acquire the assets of Best Toy Co. of Manhattan, Kansas, and the surviving molds of Kansas Toy Co. of Clifton, Kansas. These assets included the temporary services of John M. Best, his molder Conrad Morsch, and about 140 molds from these pioneering slushmold toy-vehicle companies. The new enterprise was located in a building formerly occupied by the American Legion at 7632 Burlington St. This continued a low-cost toy line familiar to collectors since Kansas Toy was founded in 1923.

With the death of its founder, Despecher, about a year later, the young company was forced into reorganization. Paul Massey, a lawyer, reorganized the company, but had to give up production of potmetals soon thereafter, due to the war's need for lead. To survive, he turned to making wooden toys, including a replica of the famous Army Jeep, of which about 2 million copies were sold through the dimestores, mainly Woolworth and Kresge. Other wooden toys included an Army tank, a Navy PT boat, and a (rumored) DUKW amphibious landing craft. These toys were completely made in Ralston, except for Jeep wheels, which were made in Omaha by blind workers (when war-time labor became short, handicapped workers were hired).

After the war the company turned to die-casting toys and novelties. As the business expanded it moved to 5707 S. 77th St., where it is today producing a well-known line of promotional trucks under Art Massey. But the post-war history is for other researchers. By now, the history of those migrating molds "with the numbers" is getting confusing. Although market values will depend on other factors than the actual makers, we will mention some clues to assist collectors. Ralstoy did label a few of its toys. They liked bottom pans, introduced by Best to increase rigidity of these fragile toys; this provided a surface to emboss "Ralstoy" and "Made in USA." Military olive-drab colors reflected the growing war consciousness. Wheels are not a good clue, even when the latest fad, black rubber wheels, were used.

Ralstoy probably reproduced many pieces from its acquired molds, but there is no practical way to know who made them when they are not labeled. (See "Best Toy Co." and "Kansas Toy Co." in this book.) The toys described below are mostly new issues.

	C6	C8	C10
RAV1 Dump Truck, "42," 3-3/8". International? COE, 2 open windows (OW), hinged tin dump body. Different casting than Kansas Toy Dump Truck #42.	No Price Found		
RAV2 Tractor, "48," 3" "Caterpillar" tractor, "Whoopee," driver in different color, grooved wood 3/4" wheels with rubber tracks on Kansas Toy body	No Price Found		
RAV3 Army tank, "74," 2-1/4". "US Army," 2 gun turret. Entirely different tank than Kansas Toy #74	13	20	26
RAV4 Tanker Truck, "No. 102," 6-3/4". "Ralstoy" International ? sleeper cab, 3-3/8", 2 OW, vertical grille with "Gasoline" semi-trailer, "No. 102," 4", 4 tanks 4 storage compartments, Ralstoy cab found in commercial finish or military O.D. Trailer was Best Toy	14	21	28

Ralstoy, Top: RAV4; Middle: RAV2A, RAV2B metal wheels; Bottom: Ralstoy field gun. Photo by Perry Eichor.

Ralstoy, L to R - Top: RAV5 - Transporter with tank #74, Cannon #34, Aircraft #32 ?; Middle: RAV6 - Anti-aircraft unit, RAV8 - Railway? Cannon; Bottom: RAV7 - Tank #107, Cannon. Photo by Ed Poole.

Ralstoy RAV7. Courtesy K. Warren Mitchell.

Ralstoy RAV11. Photo by Ed Poole.

Ralstoy RAV12. Photo by Fred Maxwell.

	C6	C8	C10
RAV5 Large Transporter, 9". "Ralstoy" cab unit in RAV4 above, steel semi-trailer with #74 tank, #34 muzzle-loading cannon and #32 aircraft, olive drab color. Not known if Ralstoy issued them as a set	20	45	60
RAV6 Large Gun Truck, 5-5/8". "US Army Anti-aircraft Unit," 3 axle carrier, AA gun, searchlight and crew of 3	28	42	56
RAV7 Army Tank, "107," 3-1/8". "US Army," wood grooved 3/4" tracklaying wheels, 2-gun turret, larger version of #74 above. Also version w/black rubber wheels, and an unnumbered version	13	20	26
RAV8 & RA9 (not vehicles).			
RAV10 Army Jeep. Wooden, 5-1/8", WWII issue, "Ralstoy," "78 HR1," white star on hood, white grille & headlamps, no steering wheel, rearmount spare. Crude, assembled with nails. Also a metal version, details not available	20	30	40
RAV11 Army Tank. Wooden, "USA W356," "Ralstoy" on bottom, WWII issue	37	56	75

	C6	C8	C10
RAV12 Large Sedan, "2R," 5-5/8". Die-cast, Cadillac?, "Ralstoy," "Made in USA," 4 open vent windows, divided open windshield, 3 open rear windows, burnished white metal, long fenders, rear-wheel skirts, bumper guards, black rubber wheels. Early post-war issue?	No Price Found		
RAV13 Fire-rescue Truck, c.6". Die-cast, streamlined, with ladder cast on roof, 6 open windows, tandem rear axles with wheel skirts. Same vintage as RAV12.......	No Price Found		
RAV14 Indy Racer, 3-3/4". Slanted grille, removable tin hood, torpedo tail. Earlier attributed to Craftoy, it is now known to be a different casting. Since it is also found with large white rubber wheels (not shown in our photo) it is more likely Ralstoy	No Price Found		
Ralstoy Ford Tractor, 1948, with trailer, 9" overall	30	45	60
Ralstoy Mayflower Moving Van, 8-1/2" long	15	22	30
Ralstoy Phillips 66 Tanker	37	56	75

RANGER STEEL CO.

	C6	C8	C10
Ranger Steel Co. (Roslyn Hts., NY) No. 450 Cross Country Turnpike, two windup racers, etc.	85	128	170

RANLITE

by Gates Willard

Whatever happened to Automobiles (Geographical) Limited of Halifax, Yorkshire, England? Except for the Ranlite Toys made from 1931 to 1932, there is no information about the company and what else it may have manufactured. The only advertising known is in the December 1931 issue of the *Meccano Magazine*. It is possible that the company was yet another Depression casualty. Ranlite toys were quite expensive for their time, and it is unlikely that they were a marketing success. Certainly, very few have survived.

Complex in design, these were quite different from other toys made in the 1930s. Bodies and wheels were molded in "Ranlite," which was similar to Bakelite, a hard and brittle plastic commonly used to make control knobs and radio cases. The chassis and fenders of the two cars were stamped out of heavy-gauge steel. The large clockwork motor powered the rear axle. The front wheels were steerable. At extra cost, a remote-cable control kit was available so that the vehicle could be wound up and steered around obstacles. Wheels could be removed and re-installed with the small hub-nut wrench provided. The hollow Dunlop "Semi Pneumatic" tires were demountable. The boxes were made of heavy cardboard, but the maroon paper covering tends to fade badly.

Two popular English saloons (sedans) were modeled rather realistically. Body and chassis are identical for the Singer and the Austin, but the radiator and hood are unique to each. The Austin has more wire spokes per wheel than the Singer. Both cars have a sliding sunroof. Upper and lower body sections were cast separately, which allowed for variations in color schemes. The Austin has a rear-mounted spare wheel and luggage rack, but no bumpers. The Austin name appears on a diagonal bar across the radiator, and the bonnet (hood) has vertical louvers. The Singer has a small letter "s" at the top front of the radiator, and the bonnet louvers are horizontal. The Singer has double-bar spring-steel bumpers front and rear, resulting in a total length of 10-3/4 inches, whereas the bumperless Austin is 10 inches long. Of the two cars, the Singer is scarcer. The foldaway key wind is permanently attached underneath so the body is not spoiled by having a visible key hole. No headlamps were fitted. The die-cast key wind, differential gears and front axle are subject to metal fatigue, which has often destroyed them.

The Golden Arrow racing car is 16-1/2 inches long and it is a beautifully proportioned model of the famous Seagrave Record Car. Except for the tires, it does not share parts with the two passenger cars. The key is separate and not attached to the motor. It has steerable front wheels and a remote-control cable was also available at extra cost.

The petrol (gasoline) pump is made of Bakelite. It has a flexible hose made of a tightly coiled spring and is a good model of a contemporary English Hammond pump. There is no value guide to (or for) Ranlite toys, since few are changing hands in the 1990s and not enough data exists to develop a reliable and useful listing of values.

Ranlite Austin with original box; sunroof is in open position. Courtesy Gates Willard. Photo by E.W. Willard.

Ranlite, L to R: Singer, Austin, with Hammond Petrol Pump in between. Courtesy Gates Willard. Photo by E.W. Willard.

Ranlite, L to R: Singer, Austin. Courtesy Gates Willard. Photo by E.W. Willard.

Ranlite Singer with original box and catalog; the sunroof is closed. Courtesy Gates Willard. Photo by E.W. Willard.

Ranlite Golden Arrow Racing Car with original box and key and advertising brochure. Courtesy Gates Willard. Photo by E.W. Willard.

Underside of Ranlite Singer; at left: Hub Nut Wrench and Envelope. Courtesy Gates Willard. Photo by E.W. Willard.

The only known Ranlite ad, from December, 1931 Meccano Magazine. *Courtesy Gates Willard.*

RANLITE SERIES

A.G.L. PRODUCTIONS—SEASON 1931.

GOLDEN ARROW RACING CAR.—A replica in Ranlite material of this world-famous Racing Car, 16½ in long, operated by strong clockwork mechanism, having semi-pneumatic tyres, detachable wheels and stub axles may be obtained ready assembled or as a Constructional Set, comprising a complete set of components with fully illustrated assembly instructions for building the model. No special tools required. Neatly boxed, price **27/6** for either type.

Made in three standard colours: Red, Mahogany and Walnut.

AUSTIN AND SINGER SALOON CARS. The only scale models of these renowned cars are in the Ranlite Series, and are by far the most attractive toy ever produced. The models are driven by strong clockwork mechanism, having machine cut gears, folding winding key, sliding sunshine roof, semi-pneumatic tyres, detachable wheels and stub axles, and are in appearance exactly like the real car. The body work being of Ranlite, the colours are both rich and permanent. The chassis is heavily enamelled, whilst metal fittings are plated. Austin models are provided with a folding luggage carrier; Singer models with front and rear bumpers. Models may be obtained either ready assembled or as Constructional Sets, comprising a complete set of components with fully illustrated assembly instructions for building your own model. No special tools required. Neatly boxed, priced **35/-** for either type.

Made in four standard colours: Black, Maroon, Green and Black, Yellow and Black.

RADIATORS. Separate Radiators of the Austin and Singer type conforming to the official designs may be obtained in any of the following colours: Black, Green, Maroon, and Yellow, ready for fitting to existing cars. Price **3/6** each.

WHEELS. Sets of five wheels, complete with semi-pneumatic tyres of the Austin and Singer types, may be obtained in any of the following colours: Black, Green, Maroon, and Yellow, ready for fitting to existing cars. Price **5/-** per set.

HAMMOND PETROL PUMP. RANLITE Models of Hammond Petrol Pumps are correct in detail and proportion, and are made in three standard colours: Red, Green, and Yellow. Price **2/6** each, boxed complete.

A.G.L. PATENT REMOTE CONTROL. A unique feature of Ranlite Toys is that they can be readily fitted with the A.G.L. Patent Remote Control thereby enabling the cars to be steered by hand when in motion, in any desired direction. The control in the form of Bowden Wire, has a cable 4 ft. 6 in. long, and is complete with moulded handle and heavily plated fitting. The controls can be easily fitted to existing cars without the aid of any special tools. Price complete with full instructions for fitting, **7/6** each. Please state whether Saloon or Racing Car Control is required.

BRITISH MANUFACTURE

A reprint of a Ranlite catalog page. Courtesy Gates Willard.

REALISTIC

by Dave Leopard

Realistic toys were made by Freeport Toys Mfg. Co., in Freeport, Illinois, during the late 1940s and early 1950s. It used some original Arcade molds to produce cast-aluminum vehicles. Realistic seemed to specialize in buses and produced varieties of both Greyhound and Trailways buses. Its bus models were often sold as souvenirs at bus terminals.

	C6	C8	C10
RV1 1939 Studebaker			
President Yellow Cab, 8-1/4 in	60	75	100
RV2 Greyhound Bus,			
Silversides, 8-3/4 in, No. 101	60	75	100
RV3 Trailways Bus, 9-1/4", No. 301	88	132	175

	C6	C8	C10
RV4 Trailways Bus, 8-3/4 in	88	132	175
RV5 Flex "Clipper" Bus, No. 201	No Price Found		
RV6 Racer, No. 401, 5-1/2" long	No Price Found		
RV7 Hook & Ladder			
Truck, No. 501, 8-1/2" long	No Price Found		

A Realistic ad in the August, 1947 Toys & Novelties *magazine, p. 68. Courtesy Dick MacNary.*

REHRBERGER

	C6	C8	C10
Rehrberger "David" Moving Van, c.1924, 7-1/4" long	2000	3500	5000

Rehrberger "David" Moving Van, c.1924, 7-1/4" long. Courtesy Bill Bertoia Auctions. Photo by Jeanne Bertoia.

RELIABLE
(Toronto, Canada)

	C6	C8	C10
Reliable Bus, 6-1/4" long, plastic	No Price Found		
Reliable "Curbside Delivery" Van, 10-3/4" long, plastic	62	93	125
Reliable Delivery Truck, plastic, 1950s, 4-1/2"	25	38	50
Reliable Lowboy w/crane, 6-1/2" long, plastic	No Price Found		

	C6	C8	C10
Reliable Pickup Truck, plastic, 1950s, 4-1/2" long	25	38	50
Reliable Sedan, plastic, 1950s, 4-1/2"	25	38	50

	C6	C8	C10
Reliable Super Deluxe Mechanical Sedan, windup, 6" long, plastic	50	75	100
Reliable Tow Truck, 10-1/2" long	31	46	62
Reliable Tractor-Trailer, 6-1/4" long, plastic			No Price Found

Reliable Bus, 6-1/4" long. Photo by Terry Sells.

Reliable Lowboy w/Crane, 6-1/2" long. Photo by Terry Sells.

Reliable Tractor-Trailer, 6-1/4" long. Photo by Terry Sells.

Reliable Super Deluxe Mechanical Sedan, wind-up, 6" long. Photo by Terry Sells.

RELIANCE MOLDED PLASTICS, INC.

(335 Barton St., Pawtucket, R.I)

Reliance Indian Scout Motorcycle, movable handlebars, revolving wheels, plastic, sold for 29¢ c.1948.......... No Price Found

Reliance Indian Scout

REMCO

(Harrison, N.J.)

Remco Electronic Mobile Loudspeaker & Signal System

	C6	C8	C10
Remco Barney's Auto Factory, builds convertible **or** sedan, w/box	160	240	320
Remco Bulldog Tank	72	108	145
Remco Electronic Mobile Loudspeaker & Signal System, 24" long, 1955	50	75	100
Remco Flying Dutchman Antique Car	48	72	95
Remco Mr. Kelly's Car Wash, 1960s	65	98	130
Remco "Movieland Drive-In Theatre," battery-operated, 1959, 14" long, includes 6 small cars, ad cards, filmstrips	80	120	160
Remco Old-Timer Convertible, 22" long	50	75	100
Remco Shark Racer	55	82	110
Remco Tiger Joe Tank, 1959	110	165	220
Remco Tricky School Bus, 1968	35	52	70
Remco Tru-Smoke Diesel Dump Truck, 1969	20	30	40
Remco U-Drive Auto w/driver	36	54	72

RENWAL

Accounts vary as to whether Renwal Manufacturing Company was founded in 1939 by Irving Rosenblum or Irving Lawner. What is indisputable is that Lawner spelled backward is Renwal. The firm seems to have begun as a manufacturer of a glass knife. A plastic knife replaced it and presumably led to the manufacture of plastic toys, which went on sale at least as early as August 1945. Its initial line consisted of WWII airplanes and doll house furniture. Vehicles were probably introduced in late 1946 or 1947 (the earliest known Renwal catalog is from 1948). The firm's early ads proclaimed it was "Famous for toys and houseware products."

In 1945, Renwal's showroom and factory were at 902 Broadway, New York City. An additional showroom at 200 Fifth Avenue seems to have been given up by 1946. In 1950, Renwal moved to Toyland Park, Mineola, New York. It seems to have remained there until the end (1970s). When it went out of business, its tooling was sold to Chein, which in turn sold it to Revell. (Years in parentheses indicate the earliest known year of production.)

	C6	C8	C10
No. 23 Motorcycle & Side Car with Passenger, 5-1/4" long. Handlebars steer (1949)	50	75	100
No. 39 Convertible Sedan with Driver, 6-1/2" long, doors open, top slides back, trunk opens (1948)	30	45	60
No. 46 Coal Truck with Driver, 7-1/2" long, doors open, body raises (1948)	50	75	100

Renwal No. 23. Photo by Terry Sells.

Renwal No. 39. Photo by Terry Sells.

	C6	C8	C10

No. 48 Transport Truck
with Driver, 10-3/4" long,
doors open, body swings (1948) 75   100   125

No. 49 Gasoline Truck
with Driver, 7-3/4" long, doors
open, tank holds water (1948) 50   75   100

	C6	C8	C10

No. 49 Like above, but top
reads "Super-X," working faucet
inside rear door (1950) 50   75   100

No. 50 Dump Truck with Driver,
7-1/2" long, doors open, body
raises (1948), "Sand-Gravel" 62   93   125

Renwal No. 46. Photo by Terry Sells.

Renwal No. 48. Courtesy Bob and Alice Wagner.

Renwal No. 49. Courtesy Bob and Alice Wagner.

Renwal No. 49, "Super-X" version. Collection of Bob and Alice Wagner.

Renwal No. 50. Photo by Terry Sells.

Renwal 57. Courtesy Bob and Alice Wagner.

Renwal, rear, No. 58; Front, L to R: No. 150, No. 88. Photo by Terry Sells.

	C6	C8	C10
No. 56 Cement Mixer Truck, 7-1/4" long, mixer revolves, rear cap comes off, tank raises (1948)	75	112	150
No. 57 Fire Truck with Three Fireman, 7" long, 8" high when ladder extended (1948)	48	72	95

	C6	C8	C10
No. 58 Racing Car, 6-3/8" long, marked "Speed King" (1948)	30	50	70
No. 59 Sedan, 4-1/4" long (1948)	6	9	13
No. 60 Coupe, 4-1/4" long (1948)	6	9	13
No. 61 Racer, 4-3/16" long (1948)	12	18	25
No. 62 Truck (pick-up), 4-1/4" long (1948)	5	8	10
No. 79 Auto Carrier Truck with Driver, 4 autos, 13" long, cab turns, doors open, elevator raises cars for upper level (1949)	50	100	175
No. 86 Steam Shovel Truck with Truck Driver and Steam Shovel Operator, 19" long. Doors open, cab swings, shovel can be raised, lowered, extended via handle on side of cab (1949)	45	68	90
No. 88 Racer, 4-3/8" long (1950)	14	21	27
No. 90 2-door Sedan with Driver, 6-1/2" long, doors and trunk open (1949)	45	60	95
No. 91 Taxicab with Driver, 6-1/2" long, cab doors and trunk open (1949)	42	63	85

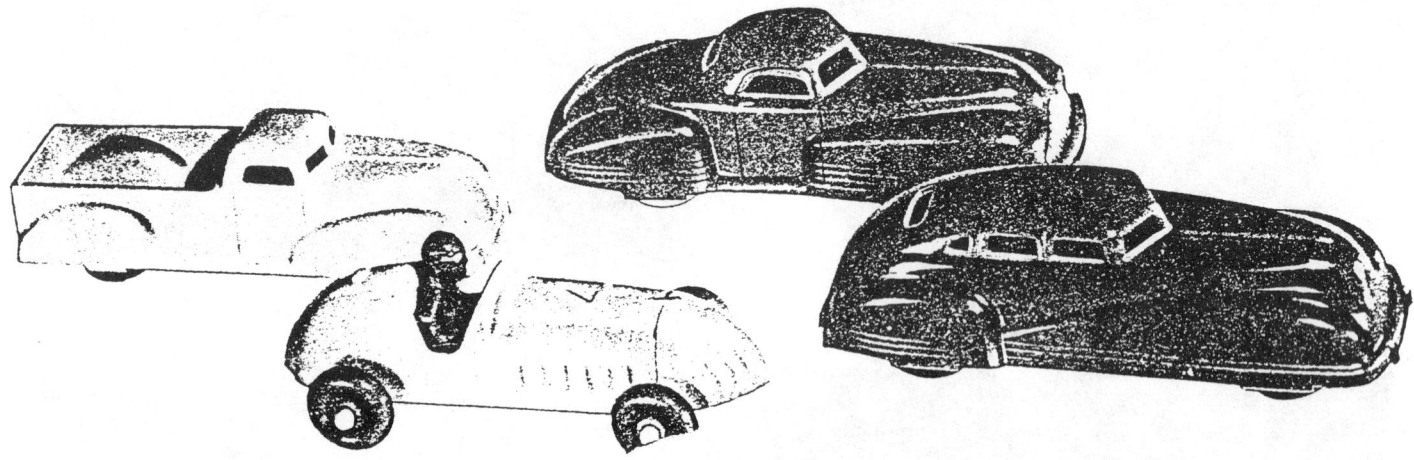

Renwal, Top to Bottom: No. 62, No. 60, No. 61, No. 59. Amended from ad brochure c.1948 courtesy Islyn Thomas.

Renwal No. 79. Courtesy Bob and Alice Wagner.

Renwal No. 86. Photo by Terry Sells.

	C6	C8	C10
No. 92 Plastic Garage, 6-1/2" long (1949)	50	75	100
No. 93 Panel Truck, "Delivery," 4-1/4" long (1949)	12	18	25
No. 94 Gasoline Truck, "Gasoline," 4-1/4" long (1949)	12	18	25
No. 99 Stake Wagon (8-3/8" long), gates removable, tongue hinged (1950)	No Price Found		
No. 101 Stake Truck with Driver, 7-3/4" long, doors open, gates removable (1950)	No Price Found		
No. 102 Coupe, 4-1/4" long (1950)	8	10	15
No. 103 Sedan, 4-1/4" long (1950)	8	10	15
No. 104 Convertible, 4-1/4" long (1950)	10	15	20
No. 105 Fire Engine, 4-1/4" long, with ladder (1950)	10	12	20
No. 106 Friction Motor Convertible with Driver, 9-1/2" long (1950)	50	75	150

	C6	C8	C10
No. 107 Speed King Friction Motor Racer with Driver, 10-1/4" long (1950)	No Price Found		
No. 110 Auto Jack, base 3-3/4" long. Raises cars 1-1/2" (1950)	5	8	10
No. 113 Friction Motor Fire Truck with Driver and two Firemen, 11-1/2" long, 16" high when ladder extended. Has water tank, pump, unwinding hose, nozzle with water release, siren, gear-controlled ladder (1950)	No Price Found		
No. 123 School Bus, 4-7/16" long, new in 1950	7	11	15
No. 124 City Bus, 4-7/16" long, new in 1950	14	21	28
No. 126 Hook & Ladder Truck with Drivers. 15-3/4" long, 16" high when ladder extended. Cab turns, doors open, rear wheels turn (1950)	60	80	100

Renwal No. 90. Courtesy Bob and Alice Wagner.

Renwal No. 91. Courtesy Bob and Alice Wagner.

Renwal No. 92. Photo by Dave Leopard.

Renwal 106. Courtesy Bob and Alice Wagner.

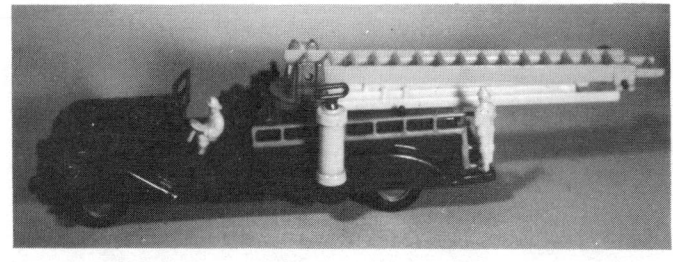

Renwal No. 113. Photo by Terry Sells.

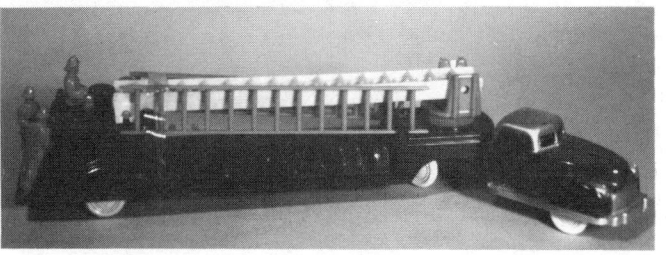

Renwal No. 126. Photo by Terry Sells.

	C6	C8	C10

No. 131 Cement Mixer, 9-7/8" long, Crank turns mixer, mixer revolves, tilts. Can be filled & emptied. Doors open (1951) 50 70 90

No. 132 Gasoline Truck, 12" long, "Gas Oil," rear and cab doors open. Tank can be filled & emptied through plastic hose, which folds up inside rear doors (1951) ... No Price Found

No. 133 Heavy Duty Tow Truck with Driver, 11" long. Adjustable crane, windlass clicks, doors open (1951) 50 70 90

No. 134 Heavy Duty Dump Truck with Driver, 10-7/8" long, crank operates hoist, cab doors & tailgate open (1951) .. 50 70 90

No. 135 Heavy Duty Coal Truck with Driver, 10-3/4" long, crank operates hoist, load divider, unloading chute, cab doors open (1951) 50 70 90

No. 143 Sedan, 3-1/8" long, new in 1950 .... 9 14 18

No. 144 Coupe, 3-1/16" long, new in 1950 .... 7 11 15

No. 145 Fire Truck, 3-1/4" long, new in 1950 .... 7 15 15

No. 146 Hook & Ladder, 3-1/4" long, new in 1950 .... 7 10 15

No. 147 Convertible, 3-1/8" long, new in 1950 .... 6 12 13

No. 148 Gasoline Truck, 3-1/8" long, new in 1950 .... 6 9 12

No. 149 Pickup Truck, 3-3/16" long, new in 1950 .... 7 10 15

No. 150 Racer, 3-1/4" long, new in 1950...... 17 26 35

No. 151 Fire Chief Coupe, 4-1/4" long (1950) .... No Price Found

No. 152 Police Coupe 4-1/4" long (1950) 12 18 24

	C6	C8	C10

No. 153 Taxi, 4-1/4" long (1950) 10 15 21

No. 167 Fire Truck Builder Kit (1953), truck 7" long. Has ladder, hose reel, crank, firemen, driver .... No Price Found

No. 168 Auto-Boat (1954), 6-1/2" long, auto on one side, boat on other 20 30 50

No. 173 Speedway Racer, 9-1/2" long (1953) with driver 85 128 170

No. 174 Cadillac Convertible with Driver, 5-1/2" long, top goes up and down (1953) 20 30 50

No. 175 Motorcycle with Sidecar Construction Kit (1953), cycle 5-1/4" long ..... No Price Found

No. 176 2-door Sedan Construction Kit (1953), 6-1/2" long with driver and spare wheel; doors &trunk open .... No Price Found

No. 177 Taxicab Construction Kit (1953), cab 6-1/2" long, with driver, spare; doors & trunk open 35 52 70

No. 178 Fire Truck, 15" long (1953), ladder extends to 16", turns, 2 firemen ..... No Price Found

No. 179 Fire Truck, 7-1/2" long, 2 firemen, 8" high with ladder up (1953) .. 30 45 60

No. 186 Tractor, 5-1/4" long with driver (1953) .... No Price Found

No. 187 Tractor & Trailer (1953), tractor is No. 186........................... No Price Found

No. 188 Motorcycle Cop, 9" long (1953) 50 75 100

No. 189 Motorcycle Cop. Same as No. 188 but 3-3/4" long (1953) .... No Price Found

Renwal No. 132. Photo by Terry Sells.

Renwal No. 174. Photo by Terry Sells.

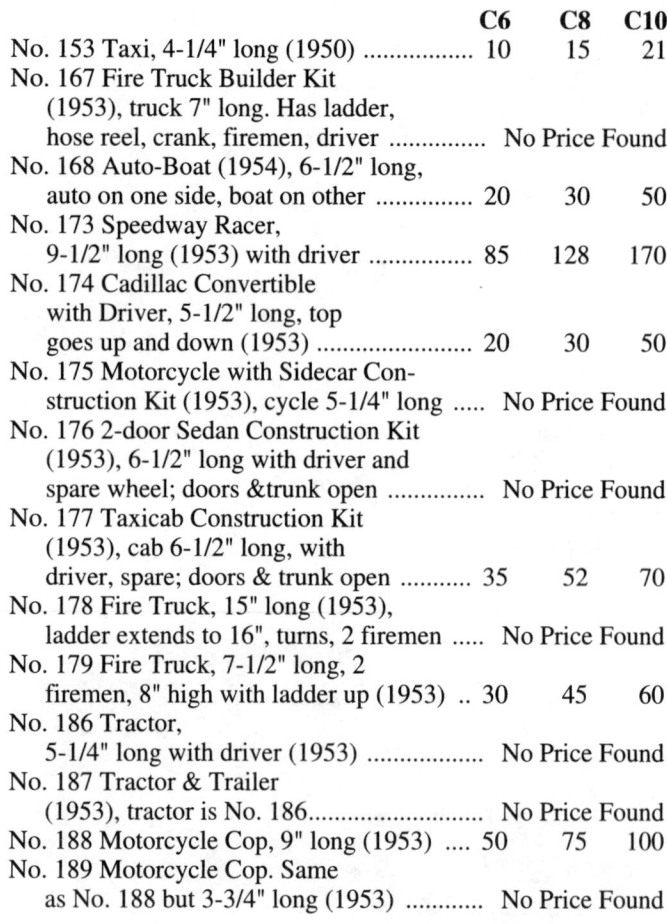

Renwal No. 135. Photo by Terry Sells.

Renwal No. 188. Photo by Gary Linden.

Renwal No. 189. Photo by Terry Sells.

	C6	C8	C10
No. 191 Trailer Truck with Load of 2 Boats, 13-1/4" long (1953)	No Price Found		
No. 192 Trailer Truck with 8 Logs, 13-1/4" long (1953)	No Price Found		
No. 195 Two-Car Garage with 2 Cars (1954), 4-1/8" x 3-5/8" x 2-1/4", doors open	12	18	25
No. 196 Pick-up Truck, 11" long (1953)	No Price Found		
No. 201 Old Fashioned Car, 8-1/2" long. Open top, with driver (1954)	No Price Found		
No. 206 Convertible (1952), like No. 106, but no motor	No Price Found		
No. 207 Racer (1952), like No. 107, but no motor	90	135	180
No. 210 Take-Apart Hot Rod (1954), 10-1/2" long	No Price Found		
No. 213 Fire Engine (1952), like No. 113, but no motor	No Price Found		
No. 216 Champion Racer, 10-3/8" long, friction motor (1954), dome over driver, siren	No Price Found		
No. 218 Toytown Service Garage Set (1955), 7 x 5 x 2-7/8", five 3-1/4" cars	No Price Found		
No. 220 Take-Apart Racer, 10-1/2" long (1954)	No Price Found		
No. 221 Coal Truck Kit, truck 7-1/2" long (1954)	No Price Found		
No. 222 Dump Truck Kit (1954), truck 7-1/2" long	No Price Found		
No. 223 Transport Kit (1954), truck 10-3/4" long	No Price Found		
No. 224 Gasoline Truck Kit (1954), truck 7-3/4" long	No Price Found		
No. 226 Cement Mixer Kit (1954), truck 7-1/4" long	No Price Found		
No. 235 Motorized Fuel Truck (1954), 7-1/2" long, friction, driver, doors open, body raises, rear door opens to slide out chute	No Price Found		
No. 236 Motorized Sand Truck (1954), 7-1/2" long, friction, doors open, body raises, rear gate opens	No Price Found		
No. 237 Motorized Tank Truck (1954), 7-3/4" long, friction, doors open, tank cap opens for filling, rear door opens to faucet	No Price Found		

	C6	C8	C10
No. 238 Motorized Ready-Mix Concrete Truck (1954), 7-1/8" long, friction, driver. Doors open, mixer revolves as truck moves, raises, rear cap comes off	No Price Found		
No. 239 Motorized Moving Van (1954), 10-5/8" long, friction, driver; cab, trailer doors open	No Price Found		
No. 243 Racer, 9-1/2" long (1954), with driver	No Price Found		
No. 248 Motorized Fire Truck with Siren (1955), 15" long, friction, driver, 2 firemen, ladder extends to 16"	No Price Found		
No. 259 Engine Running Racer (1955), 10-1/2" long, transparent engine block shows action	No Price Found		
No. 260 TV Mobile (1956). Truck, camera, spotlight, microphone, cable. "Renwal-TV" on side	75	112	150
No. 270 Steam Shovel Construction Kit (1953), truck 8-1/8" long	No Price Found		
No. 271 Hook & Ladder Construction Kit (1953), truck 15-3/4" long, 2 drivers, firemen	No Price Found		
No. 284 U.S. Army Tank	3	5	7
No. 301 Customized Service Truck (1964), 1/32 scale	No Price Found		
No. 313 Motorized Pumper Fire Truck with Siren and Extension Ladder (1955), 11-1/2" long, friction, throws water through plastic hose. Driver, 2 firemen	No Price Found		
No. 329 Gasoline Truck, soft plastic, 6"	8	12	16
No. 621 Truck (1951), 4-1/4" long, same as No. 62	No Price Found		
No. 813 Visible Auto. Chassis over 3 feet long. c.early 1960s	No Price Found		
No. 2039 Convertible with Driver, 6-1/2" long (1952), same as No. 39, but has "simulated chrome trim"	32	48	65
No. 2057 Fire Truck (1952). Same as No. 57, but with "simulated chrome trim"	48	72	95
No. 2061 Racer (1952). Same as No. 61, but with "simulated chrome trim"	No Price Found		
No. 2088 Racer (1952). Same as No. 88, but with chrome trim	No Price Found		
No. 2090 Sedan, with driver, 6-1/2" long (1952). Same as No. 90, but with "simulated chrome trim"	No Price Found		
No. 2091 Taxicab (1952). Same as No. 91, but with "simulated chrome trim"	60	90	120
No. 2093 Delivery Truck (1952). Same as No. 93, but with chrome trim	10	15	20
No. 2094 Gasoline Truck (1952). Same as No. 94, but with chrome trim	10	15	20
No. 2102 Coupe (1952). Same as No. 102, but with chrome trim	10	15	20
No. 2103 Sedan (1952). Same as No. 103, but with chrome trim	10	15	20
No. 2104 Convertible (1952). Same as No. 104, but with chrome trim	10	15	20
No. 2621 Truck (1952). Same as No. 62, but with chrome trim	10	15	20
No. 8001 Ferrari Racer, metal (1955), 9-1/4" long, motorized	100	150	200

HIGH GLOSS INFRA-RED BAKED ENAMEL
FINISHES...safe, non-toxic!

8007 Sedan

8009 Racer

AN INFINITE CAPACITY FOR TAKING PAINS . . . that's what goes into your finished Renwal toy . . . from careful polishing of dies before they are hardened to the final application of enamel to a casting. Your customers will show their appreciation by buying the WORLD'S FINEST TOYS . . . toys by Renwal!

8015 Convertible

8013 Jeep

8012 Hot Rod

FINEST FINISHES ON ANY METAL TOYS . . . . ON WORLD'S FINEST TOYS BY *Renwal*

A page from a 1955 Renwal catalog.

	C6	C8	C10
No. 8002 Maserati Racer, metal (1955), 9-1/4" long, motorized	No Price Found		
No. 8003 Pontiac Convertible, metal (1955), 8-1/4" long, motorized	60	90	120
No. 8004 Plymouth Convertible, metal (1955), 7-7/8" long, motorized	No Price Found		
No. 8005 Chevrolet Sedan, metal (1955), 7-7/8" long, motorized	No Price Found		
No. 8006 Ford Sedan, metal (1955), 7-7/8" long, motorized	No Price Found		
No. 8007 Sedan, metal (1955), 6" long	No Price Found		
No. 8008 Gasoline Truck, metal (1955), 6" long	27	41	55
No. 8009 Racer, metal (1955), 7" long	No Price Found		
No. 8010 Delivery Truck, metal (1955), 6" long	40	50	70
No. 8011 Pickup Truck, metal (1955), 6" long	30	45	60
No. 8012 Hot Rod, metal(1955), 6-1/2" long	No Price Found		
No. 8013 Jeep, metal (1955), 5-5/8" long	No Price Found		
No. 8014 Fire Truck, metal (1955), 6" long	No Price Found		
No. 8015 Convertible, metal (1955), 6" long	35	52	70
No. 8028 Citroen, metal (1955), 6" long	No Price Found		
No. 8029 Porsche, metal (1955), 5-3/4" long	No Price Found		
No. 8030 Pegasa, metal (1955), 6" long	No Price Found		
No. 8031 Lancia, metal (1955), 6" long	No Price Found		
No. 8032 Rolls Royce, metal (1955), 6-1/8" long	No Price Found		

	C6	C8	C10
No. 8033 Jaguar, metal (1955), 6-1/8" long	No Price Found		
No. 8034 MG, metal (1955), 6" long	No Price Found		
No. 8035 Mercedes-Benz, metal (1955), 5-7/8" long	No Price Found		
No. 8036 Kaiser-Darrin, metal (1955), 6-1/8" long	No Price Found		
No. 8037 Austin-Healey, metal (1955), 6" long	No Price Found		
No. 8853 3-1/2" metal replicas of Renwal's plastic convertible, sedan, coupe, pick-up truck, gasoline truck, fire truck, hook & ladder, racer (1955)	No Price Found		
No. 8854 4-1/4" to 4-1/2" metal replicas of Renwal's plastic convertible, coupe gasoline truck, city bus (1955)	No Price Found		

Renwal No. 8008. Photo by Terry Sells.

REPUBLIC TOOL PRODUCTS CO.

(Dayton, Ohio 1922-32)

by Bob Smith

Charles Black received a patent for a unique cover to protect the friction mechanism from dirt and moisture. The patent date, Nov. 1, 1921, is stamped on this cover, which sits between the rear wheels of their "Republic Toy" cars and trucks. Black had been employed at the Dayton Toy Works until 1922, when he left the company to form a partnership with Elijah Miller, another ex-Dayton employee. The company ceased making "Republic Toys" in 1932. Although Republic toys were produced for a mere ten years, they have become an important part of American toy manufacturing history.

	C6	C8	C10
Republic Bus, 28" long, 1920s	450	600	900
Republic Cargo Truck, friction drive, green, 13" long, c.1922	275	400	600
Republic Chemical Truck	170	255	340
Republic Coupe	275	400	600
Republic/Dayton Racer. Operates on large spring-wind motor cranked from front of car. Gray/Blue/Red, 11" long, c.1910 or 1922	300	450	650
Republic Ladder Truck, 24" long, friction	250	375	500

Republic Cargo Truck, friction drive, 13" long, c.1922. Photo by Bob Smith.

	C6	C8	C10
Republic Ladder Truck, 17" long, c.1920s	250	350	475
Republic Limousine, friction drive, blue, c.1922, 11" long	250	375	525
Republic Momentum Dump Truck, pat. 11/1/21, driver, 20" long	300	450	600

	C6	C8	C10
Republic Roadster, friction drive, red, 11" long, c.1922	225	350	500
Republic Taxi Cab with Driver, sheet-metal, friction, c.1926	275	400	550

Republic Limousine, friction drive, c.1922, 11" long. Photo by Bob Smith.

Republic/Dayton Racer, spring-wind, c.1910 or 1922, 11" long. Photo by Bob Smith.

Republic Roadster, friction drive, c.1922, 11" long. Photo by Bob Smith.

REUHL PRODUCTS, INC.

(2609 Monroe St., Madison, Wis.)

	C6	C8	C10
Reuhl Caterpillar D-7, T-4000	345	515	690
Reuhl Caterpillar Grader No. 12	800	1300	1800
Reuhl Caterpillar Ripper	125	188	250
Reuhl Caterpillar Scraper No. 70, 16" long, plastic, S-4500	325	488	650
Reuhl Cedar Rapids Rock Crusher	600	950	1330
Reuhl Cedar Rapids Paver	75	112	150

	C6	C8	C10
Reuhl DW-10	600	1000	1400
Reuhl Farmall Cub T-3000, 1950, 6-1/4" long			No Price Found
Reuhl Lorain Shovel	700	1200	1700
Reuhl Massey Harris Combine	250	375	500
Reuhl Massey Tractor w/loader No. 44	375	562	750

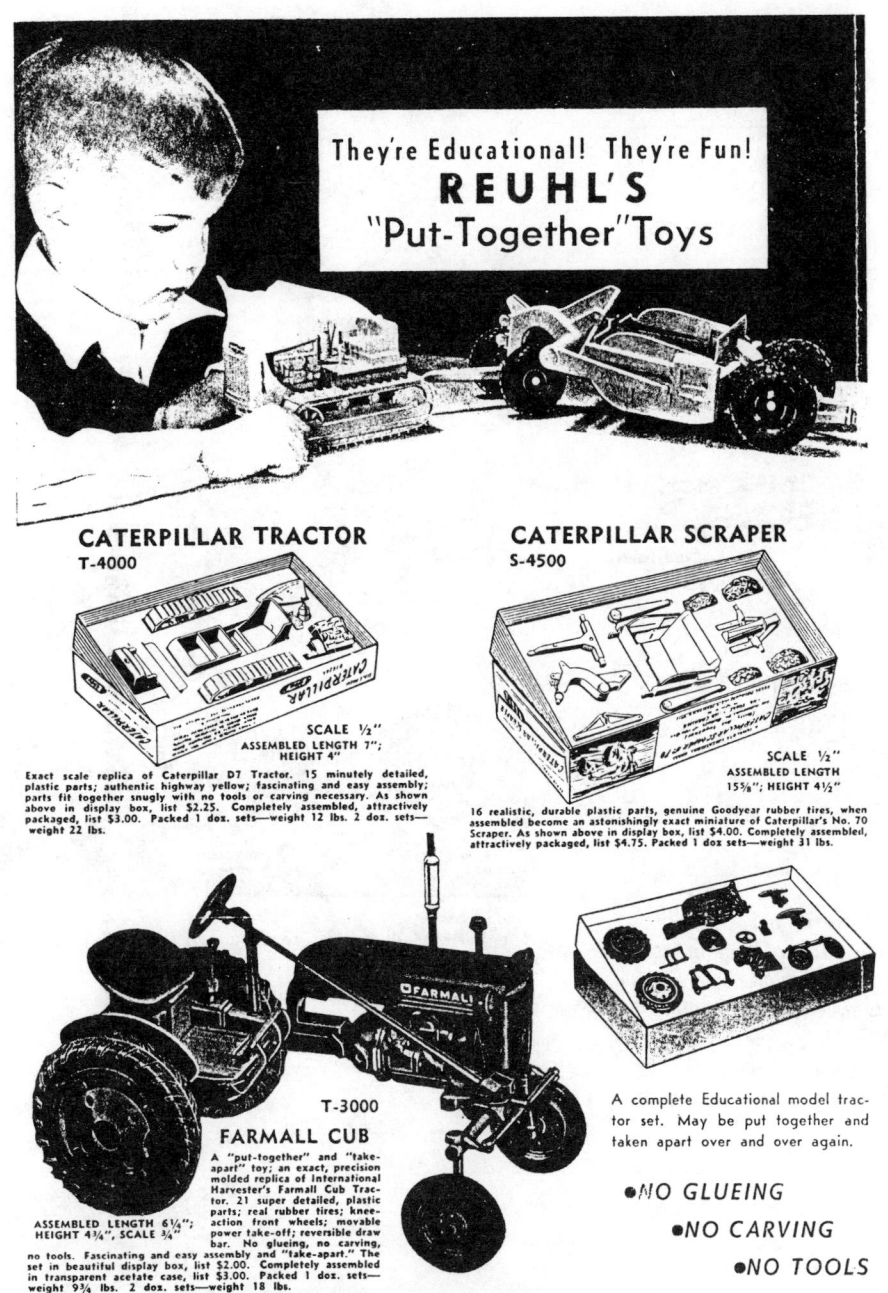

A Reuhl flyer from Jan. 1950. Courtesy Ray Funk.

REVELL

Revell seems to have begun in 1951 and soon produced more cars a year than Ford, General Motors, and Chrysler put together. Located in Venice, California, the firm was founded by Lewis H. Glaser.

	C6	C8	C10		C6	C8	C10
Revell Backfiring Hot Rod	42	63	85	Revell Jr. Mechanic Gift Set	No Price Found		
Revell Caterpillar Tractor & Wagon	60	90	120	Revell Plumbing Service Truck w/tools	67	100	135
Revell Grader, 12" long	45	68	90	Revell Police Motorcycle w/Sirens	17	26	35
Revell Maxwell Auto, c.1950-51	37	56	75	Revell Prestige Auto Carrier, two cars	135	202	270

Revell Back-Firing Ford: Constructed of durable plastic, this is an authentic replica of the famous 1917 model "T" Closed Coupe. It runs along freely as a pull toy and when the trigger is squeezed, the engine backfires with a loud BANG! The clever metal backfiring mechanism takes any standard roll of caps. $3. Toy Yearbook, 1952-53.

Revell Antique Autos, as shown in the Toy Yearbook from 1953-54.

Revell Maxwell Auto: This seems to have been Revell's first toy. Courtesy Charles D. Richards.

RICH TOY

	C6	C8	C10
Rich Toy National Biscuit Company truck w/2 trailers, wood, wooden Nabisco boxes	800	1400	2200

	C6	C8	C10
Rich Toy Texaco Gas Station, 16" x 22"	205	308	410

RICHARD APPEL

	C6	C8	C10
Richard Appel (New York)			
Victory Tank, wooden, WWII	22	33	45

Richard Appel Victory Tank with original box. Photo by Jack Matthews.

RICHARD TOYS

Richard Toys "Heavy			
Transport," 32" long Ridem, steel	225	338	450

RICHMOND

Richmond Dump Truck, steel, 12" long	48	72	95

RICO CO.

(Spain)

Rico Bonnet Bus,			
c.1940s, tin windup, 6-1/4" long	262	393	525
Rico BMW, 1930s, 13"	800	1400	2200
Rico "Silver Bullet"			
racer, driver, windup, 11" long	300	450	600
Rico Streamline Car,			
c.1935 tin windup, 7-3/4" long	262	393	525
Rico "Tom and Jerry Car," 1960s,			
13" long, battery operated, 3 actions	262	393	525
Roberts Refuse Dump Truck, 1950s	68	102	135
Roberts U-Ride-It Fire			
Rescue Van, 21" long	175	263	350
"Robot Bus" - see Woodhaven.			
"Rocket" Pedal Car	450	675	900
Roi-Tan Cigars promotional			
car w/pic of Sophie Tucker	130	195	260

Rico Tom and Jerry Car. Courtesy Don Hultzman. Photo by Ron Chojnacki.

ROSS TOOL AND MANUFACTURING CO.

(All Plastic)

List by David M. Leopard

	C6	C8	C10
(RO1) Ladder Truck, 4.75 in., plastic	12	15	18
(RO2) Mack Dump Truck, 4.25 in	15	18	20
(RO3) Mack Moving Van, 4.65 in.	15	18	20
(RO4) Mack Gasoline Truck, 4.65 in.	15	18	20
(RO5) Racer, 4 in., plastic	10	12	14

	C6	C8	C10
(RO6) Racer, several varieties, approx. 3 in. plastic	6	8	10
(RO7) Hot Rod, 5 in., plastic	15	18	20
(RO8) Convertible, 3 in., with woman and dog	6	8	10
(RO9) Hose Truck, 3 in., plastic	6	8	10

Ross R01. Photo by Dave Leopard.

Ross R05. Photo by Dave Leopard.

Ross R06 small racers. Photo by Dave Leopard.

Ross R07. Photo by Dave Leopard.

Ross R08. Photo by Dave Leopard.

Ross R09. Photo by Dave Leopard.

RSA

(Spain)

	C6	C8	C10
RSA Motorcycle, driver, 6-1/2" long	225	338	450
RSA Motorcycle, driver, rider, tin windup, 9" long	700	1100	1500
RSA Motorcycle, sidecar, driver, rider, tin windup, 10" long	1200	2000	3400

RSA, L to R: Motorcycle, sidecar, Motorcycle, driver, rider. Courtesy Bill Bertoia Auctions. Photo by Jeanne Bertoia.

RUBBER VEHICLES

Unknown Manufacturers

The following list, with its codings, was compiled by Dave Leopard. Vehicles are broken down by types. The gaps in the numbering indicate vehicles that have been identified since the list was made up.

	C6	C8	C10
UA06 '35 DeSoto 4-door Airflow Sedan, 5" long	50	75	100
UA07 '35 Chrysler 4-door Airflow Sedan, rear spare, 4-3/4" long, ad on roof	No Price Found		

	C6	C8	C10
UA08 '35 Chrysler 2-door Airflow Sedan, 5-1/8" long	50	75	100
UA08A '35 Plymouth 4-door Sedan, 4-7/8" long	No Price Found		

Rubber Vehicles UA06 (Leopard's UA01). Courtesy Dave Leopard from his book Rubber Toy Vehicles.

Rubber Vehicles UA07 (Leopard's UA03). Courtesy Dave Leopard from his book Rubber Toy Vehicles.

Rubber Vehicles UA08 (Leopard's UA02). Courtesy Dave Leopard from his book Rubber Toy Vehicles.

Rubber Vehicles UA08A (Leopard's UA04). Courtesy Dave Leopard from his book Rubber Toy Vehicles.

Rubber Vehicles UA09 (Leopard's UA05). Courtesy Dave Leopard from his book Rubber Toy Vehicles.

Rubber Vehicles UA10 (Leopard's UA06). Courtesy Dave Leopard from his book Rubber Toy Vehicles.

Rubber Vehicles UA12 (Leopard's UA07). Courtesy Dave Leopard from his book Rubber Toy Vehicles.

Rubber Vehicles UA11. Photo by Dave Leopard.

Rubber Vehicles UR02. Courtesy Dave Leopard from his book Rubber Toy Vehicles.

Rubber Vehicles UR01. Courtesy Dave Leopard from his book Rubber Toy Vehicles.

Rubber Vehicles UR03. Courtesy Dave Leopard from his book Rubber Toy Vehicles.

	C6	C8	C10
UA09 '36 Plymouth 4-door Trunkback Sedan, 4-7/8" long	75	112	150
UA10 '37 Plymouth 4-door Trunkback Sedan, 4-7/8" long	75	112	150
UA11 '46 Nash, 2-door Fastback Sedan, hollow, molded tires, 4" long	12	18	25
UA12, c. '35 LaFayette (?) Sedan, fastback, solid, w/tires, 4" long ...	30	40	50

	C6	C8	C10
UT04 '34 Dodge Rack Truck, 4-7/8" long	No Price Found		
UR01 Open Racer, left side Header pipes, solid rubber, 3-1/2" long	No Price Found		
UR02 Open Racer, V-8, solid, large tires on wood hubs, 4" long	No Price Found		
UR03 Open Racer, solid, rubber tires on wood hubs, 6" long	No Price Found		

SAUNDERS TOOL & DIE CO.

(Aurora, Ill.)

	C6	C8	C10
Saunders Bump & Dump Truck, 10-3/4" long	40	60	80
Saunders Convertible, plastic windup, 10-1/4" long	48	72	95
Saunders "Fire Chief" car windup, 10" long	42	63	85
Saunders Fire Truck, 12" long windup, plastic	45	68	90
Saunders Frazer Convertible, plastic windup	75	112	150
Saunders Hot Rod, 7" long friction	34	51	68
Saunders Jaguar, 8" long	40	100	150
Saunders Ladder Truck	55	82	110

	C6	C8	C10
Saunders Marvelous Mike, 1950s battery operated, 17" long, four actions	118	177	235
Saunders Military Police Car, 9" long friction	No Price Found		
Saunders "Nu-Style" Sportster Convertible	50	75	100
Saunders Packard Convertible, 1947, 10-1/2" long	62	93	125
Saunders Police Car	27	41	55
Saunders Police Rescue Car	48	72	95
Saunders Race Car windup, 8" long	42	63	85
Saunders Race Car	16	24	32

Saunders Convertible, plastic windup, 10-3/4" long. Photo by Ron Fink.

Saunders "Fire Chief." Courtesy Continental Auctions.

Saunders Marvelous Mike. Photo by Don Hultzman.

Saunders Military Police Car. Photo by Terry Sells.

	C6	C8	C10
Saunders Sand Dump Truck	55	82	110
Saunders Searchlight Truck	85	128	170
Saunders Sedan, windup	42	63	85
Saunders Semi Trailer, 16" long, 1960s	88	132	175
Saunders Semi Van	32	48	65
Saunders Stock Car Racer with removable hood, friction, 8" long	60	125	175
Saunders Super Battle Tank, 8" long	27	41	55
Saunders Super Motor Bus	55	82	110
Saunders Super Searchlight Fire Truck, battery, bulb, on/off switch, 12" long	No Price Found		

Saunders, L to R: Hot Rod, Stock Car Racer. Courtesy Bob and Alice Wagner.

SAVOYE PEWTER TOY COMPANY

Savoye was incorporated August 1930. In 1931, Savoye Pewter Toy Co., manufacturer of "pewter toys" (pewter was often the word used for lead alloy or pot-metal) was listed in a directory at 69 Paterson Plank Road in North Bergen, New Jersey, with 6 male and 3 female employees. The names of the owners may have been Selma and Joseph Wigh. In 1934, at the same address, the workforce was 7 males and 2 females. Slush-mold toys were probably its only product. Savoye was in the 1936 phonebook and out of the February 1937 directory. Collectors identify vehicle toys as Savoye if they have a somewhat coarse appearance, heavy slushmold body, and white rubber tires on oversized red wooden hubs that are smooth on the outside surface (no axle showing); but whether this is simply lore is not known at present. The son of one of the owners of Tommy Toy Co. thinks some Savoye-looking vehicles were made by Tommy Toy. If so, it's possible Savoye sold its molds to nearby Tommy Toy.

The following was contributed by Fred Maxwell: Those big red hubs and rubber tires are consistent with industry styles of the early 1930s, but the style of some of the vehicles is from an earlier era (see SA17 and SA19, whose metal wheels suggest an earlier beginning of the Savoye-Tommy Toy-Barclay dynasty).

	C6	C8	C10
SA1 Roadster, 3-1/2". Driver, open rumble seat, silver vertical grille, (VG, reminiscent of Tootsietoy Graham), vertical louvers (VL)	No Price Found		
SA2 Roadster, 3-1/2". Similar to above; different casting	No Price Found		
SA3 Coupe, 3-3/8". 2 open windows (OW), silver VG, (Graham like), VL	20	30	40

	C6	C8	C10
SA4 ? Coupe, 3-3/8". Similar to above (Savoye or copy ?). Slanted louvers, fantasy grille and large black rubber wheels (original ?)	14	21	28
SA5 Van, 3-1/4". "Milk Grade A," 2 OW, sidemounts (SM)	20	30	40
SA6 Van, 4". "Police Patrol," policeman on rear step, 6 OW, gilt trim, SM	24	36	48
SA6A Like above, solid windows	24	36	48

Savoye, Top, L to R: SA1, SA2. Bottom, L to R: SA7, SA3. Photo by Fred Maxwell.

Savoye SA5. Photo by Al Lane.

	C6	C8	C10
SA7 Bus, 4-3/4". Heavy 5th Ave. sight-seeing bus, open overhanging upper deck, 12 OW, gilt or silver trim	62	93	125
SA8 Bus, 3-3/8". Cross-country bus, partial upper deck, 12 OW, rear-mount spare	20	30	40
SA9 Bus, 7-1/2". Tour bus; Mack cab, 3-1/2", 2 OW; "Motor Coach," 5-1/4", dual-axle semi-trailer, 12 OW, gilt trim, also came with single axle	No Price Found		
SA10 Truck, 4-3/8". Heavy "Beer Truck," 6 wood barrels set in cast depressions	40	60	80
SA10A Like above, Dump	No Price Found		
SA11 Truck, 4-1/2". Stake body	12	18	24

	C6	C8	C10
SA12 Truck, 5-3/4". Stake body, hinged tailgate w/chains	No Price Found		
SA13 Truck, c.4". Tow truck, SA3 - like coupe cab, chain & hook on crane	No Price Found		
SA14 Truck, 5-3/4". Heavy tow truck, oversized crane, wire hook	No Price Found		
SA15 Fire Truck, 4-1/4". Driver and steersman w/high style gilt helmets, bell on hood, 2 ladders (glued on), oversized wheel wells, oversized tires	No Price Found		
SA16 Fire Truck, 3-3/4". Driver & fireman w/high style gilt helmets, 2 detachable ladders on high rack, oversized wheel wells, oversized tires	No Price Found		

Savoye, L to R: SA7, SA18, SA20. Photo by Craig A. Clark.

Savoye SA8 with window variation. Photo by Albert W. Lane.

Savoye SA9. Photo by Fred Maxwell.

Savoye, Top: SA10, SA15; Middle: SA7, SA6; Bottom: SA14, SA12. Photo by Fred Maxwell.

Savoye SA13. Photo by Craig A. Clark.

Savoye SA15, SA16.

Savoye SA17?. Photo by Fred Maxwell.

Savoye SA18 at right, next to the similar Barclay tractor. Notice the backward bulge to the rear wheel housing on the Savoye. Photo by Bill Conover.

Savoye SA19?. Photo by Fred Maxwell.

Savoye SA20. Courtesy Ferd Zegel.

SA22 Pickup Truck

Savoye SA21. Photo by Bill Conover.

SA24 Racer

SA23 Moving Van

Savoye SA25, SA6, SA6 w/ Barclay wheels. Courtesy Ferd Zegel.

	C6	C8	C10

SA17 ? Fire Engine, 3-3/4". Steam pumper, driver & fireman w/high style gilt helmets, large 10-spoke metal wheels. An early Savoye ? in the style of fire trucks above; large wheels would explain over-sized wheel wells in SA15 & SA16 above .... No Price Found

SA18 Tractor, 2-3/4". Caterpillar? tractor w/stack 10 15 20

SA19 ? Tractor, 3". Same as above w/large 10 spoke metal wheels. An early Savoye ? (same casting as Tommy Toy but longer wheelbase than Barclay #7) ..... No Price Found

SA20 Tank Car Set, 10-1/4". Tow cab shorter version of SA13, 3-1/4"; 2 tank cars 3-1/2", "Oil" "Cap. 80000" (RR type). Not known whether Savoye sold these as a set; no known Savoye train, either 40 60 80

SA21 Gun Truck, 3-1/4". Army, driver & gunner. (smooth gear under gun barrel distinguishes it from similar gun trucks) .... No Price Found

SA22 Pickup Truck 20 30 40

SA23 "Moving Van," 3-7/8", six wheels ... 105 158 210

SA24 Racer 4-1/4" long, driver and co-pilot .... No Price Found

SA24A Like above, but one driver .... No Price Found

SA25 "Ambulance" (same as the Tommy Toy, who probably bought the molds) 16 24 32

SA26 Open Convertible with Driver in Cap (just like Tommy Toy's TTV7; probably from the same mold) 10 15 20

SA27 "Coal" Truck, 4-3/8", dump body on chassis similar to SA10 but open windshield, driver & steering wheel .... No Price Found

Savoye SA26. Photo by Al Lane.

Savoye SA10B, SA27. Courtesy Ferd Zegel.

SCHIEBLE TOY & NOVELTY CO.

(Dayton, Ohio, c.1909-1931)

by Bob Smith

William E. Schieble was a partner in D.P. Clark & Co. for nearly 10 years. In 1909, after some disagreements with Clark, he broke up the partnership and became the sole owner. At this time, Schieble changed the name of the company to "Schieble Toy & Novelty." Things went well during the 1920s, but, as did many manufacturing companies, Schieble declared bankruptcy, in 1931.

Schieble Fire Engine Pumper, flywheel drive, c.1917, 11-3/4" long. Photo by Bob Smith.

Schieble Fire Truck, flywheel drive, 11-1/2" long, c.1917. Photo by Bob Smith.

	C6	C8	C10
Schieble Armored Car	300	450	600
Schieble Bus, 1920s, No. 110	375	562	750
Schieble Cannon Truck	400	600	800
Schieble Coupe, 18" long	350	500	675
Schieble Delivery Truck	382	573	765
Schieble Fire Engine Pumper, flywheel drive, red/gold, 11-3/4" long, c.1917	300	425	625
Schieble Fire Engine Pumper, 1920s, 20" long, working light	362	545	725
Schieble Fire Ladder Truck, 1920s, 20" long	325	487	650
Schieble Fire Ladder Truck, flywheel drive, white/red, 21-1/2" long, c.1909, small driver	375	475	625

	C6	C8	C10
Schieble Fire Ladder Truck, flywheel drive, white/red, 21-1/2" long, c.1909, large driver	400	550	775
Schieble Fire Truck, flywheel drive, red/gold, 11-1/2" long, c.1917	275	400	600
Schieble Mack Semi Dump Truck, 22" long, c.1925 (Chein lookalike)	325	575	825
Schieble Packard Express Truck	400	600	800
Schieble Pickup Truck	325	475	625
Schieble Roadster, 13" long	165	248	330
Schieble Roadster, 18-1/4" long, spare tire on back	350	525	700
Schieble Sedan, 17" long	400	600	800
Schieble Tank, WWI type	300	450	600
Schieble Touring Car, 14" long, c.1909	300	450	600
Schieble Wrecker	500	850	1300

Schieble, L to R: large driver, small driver; both are Fire Ladder Trucks with flywheel drive, 21-1/2" long, c.1909. Photo by Bob Smith.

Schieble Mack Semi Dump Truck, 22" long, c.1925. Photo by Bob Smith.

SCHOENHUT

	C6	C8	C10
Schoenhut "Every Boy Auto Build 5 in 1 Toy," wood set to build, boxed	45	67	90
Schoenhut Stutz Racer, 10" long	150	250	350

SCHUCO

by Don Hultzman

Schuco was founded in 1912 by Heinrich Muller and Herr Schreyer, which was later called Schreyer and Co., and adopted the name "Schuco" as its trademark. Schuco toys, noted for their ingenious mechanisms, were produced in the 1930s into the 1950s, and marked either "Germany" or "U.S. Zone Germany." Other markings are reissues.

	C6	C8	C10
"Akustico 2002," 1940s, 5-1/2" long	87	130	175
"Anno 2000," 1940s, 5-1/2" long	80	120	160
Buick No. 5311, 9" long	200	300	400
"Cadillac DeVille Convertible 5505," 1960s, 11" long, plastic	80	120	160
"Dalli 1011," 1950s, 6-1/2" long, tin car & plastic driver	112	168	225
"Elektro Ingenico 5311," 1950s, 8-1/2" long, remote control	250	382	510
"Examico 4001," 1950s, 6" long, 5 speed BMW	165	248	330
Fernlenk Auto No. 3000	92	138	185
"Fex 1111," 1950s, 6" long	90	135	180

Schuco Examico 4001. Courtesy Don Hultzman. Photo by Ron Chojnacki.

	C6	C8	C10
"Fx-Atmos," almost 2" long, c.late 1950s-early 60s	No Price Found		
"Gas Station 3054," 1950s, 8" long	60	90	120
"Grand Prix Racer 1070," 1950s, 6" long	65	98	130
"Jaguar 1250," 1940s, 5-1/2" long	160	240	320
"Lasto 3042," 1950s, 4-1/2" long truck	60	90	120
"Magico Auto 2008," 1950s, 5-1/2" long, responds to blowing	300	450	600
"Magico Car and Garage," 1950s, 6" long	120	180	240
"Mercedes 190SL, 2095," 1950s, 8" long	170	255	340
"Mercedes TYP SSK 1928," 1950s, 4" long	100	150	200

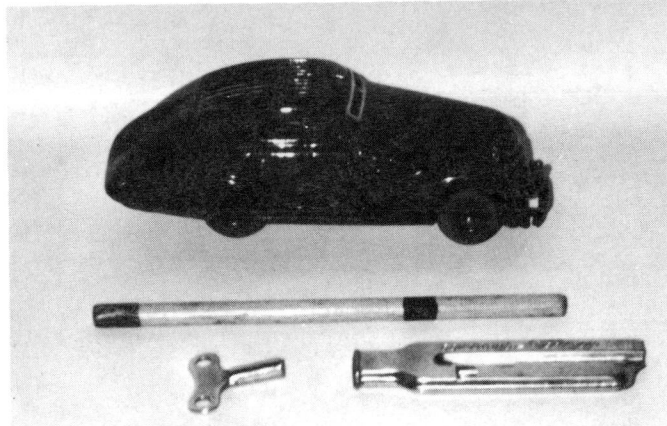

Schuco Magico Auto 2008. Photo by Don Hultzman.

Schuco Micro Racer 1040. Photo by Don Hultzman.

	C6	C8	C10
"Mercer Auto 1225," 1950s, 7-1/2" long	75	112	150
"Micro Racer 101," 1950s, 3-1/2" long, Porsche style	90	135	180
"Micro Racer 102," 1950s, 3-1/2" long, Indy style	90	135	180
"Micro Racer 104," 1950s, 3-1/2" long, Indy style	90	135	180
"Micro Racer 1036," 1950s, 4-1/2" long	100	150	200
"Micro Racer 1040," 1950s, 4" long	75	105	145
"Micro Racer 1041," 1950s, 4" long	72	112	150
"Micro Racer 1042," 1950s, 4" long	100	150	200
"Micro Racer 1043," 1950s, 4" long	75	112	150
"Micro Racer '57 Ford 1045," 1950s, 4" long	80	120	160
"Micro Racer Alpha Romeo 1048," 1950s, 4" long	90	135	180
"Micro Racer Go Kart 1035," 1950s, 4" long	100	150	200
"Micro Racer Hotrod 1036," 1950s, 4" long	90	135	180
"Micro Racer - Mercedes Benz 1038," 1950s, 4" long	100	150	200
"Micro Racer - Mercedes Benz 1044," 1950s, 4" long	110	165	220
"Micro Racer Mercer 1036/1," 1950s, 4" long	100	150	200
"Micro Racer Porsche 1047," 1950s, 4" long	110	165	220
"Micro Racer Rally 1034," 1950s, 10'6" long - 8 three lane tracks	60	90	120
"Micro Racer Stake Truck 1049," 1950s, 4" long	90	135	180
"Micro Racer Volkswagen 1046," 1950s, 4" long	90	135	180
"Micro Racer Volkswagen Polizei 1039," 1950s, 4" long	100	150	200
"Mirakocar 1001," 1950s, 4-1/2" long, non-fall action	72	108	145
"Monkey Car," 1930s, 6" long, orange-black, smiling monkey	1400	2100	2800

Schuco Motodrill Clown 1007. Photo by Don Hultzman.

	C6	C8	C10
"Motodrill Clown 1007," 1950s, 5" long Motorcycle, composition head	1000	1500	2000
"Mystery Car 1010," 1950s, 5-1/2" long, non-fall action	90	135	180
"Radio 4012," 1950s, 6" long, musical car	238	355	475
"Station Car 3118," 1950s, 4-1/2" long	60	90	120

	C6	C8	C10
"Studio Racer 1050," 1950s, 5-1/2" long, includes tools	125	188	250
"Synchromatic 5700," 1950s, 11" long - resembles Packard Hawk	500	750	1000
"Telesteering 3000 Limo," 1950s, 4" long	72	105	145
"Varianto 3010," 1950s, tin cars are 4-1/2" long, two car playset	100	150	200
"Varianto 3010 Super," 1950s, service station with two 4-1/2" tin cars	170	225	340
"Varianto 3041 Limo," 1950s, 4" long	50	75	100
"Varianto 3064," 1950s, 8" long, all plastic	30	45	60
"Varianto Box 3010/30," (tin garage and 3041 Limo, 1950s, 4-1/2" long	110	165	220
"Varianto Bus 3044," 1950s, 4" long	70	105	140
"Varianto Electro 3112," 1950s, 4" long truck	60	90	120
"Varianto Electro 3112u," 1950s, 4-1/2" long truck	60	90	120
"Varianto Lasto," No. 3042, 1950s, 4-1/4" long truck	80	120	160

Schuco Studio Racer 1050. Photo by Don Hultzman.

SCIENTIFIC

	C6	C8	C10
Scientific Forklift	67	100	135

SEIBERLING RUBBER

Compiled by Dave Leopard

	C6	C8	C10
GA01 '35 Ford 2-door Slantback Sedan, 5" long	40	50	65
GA02 '35 Ford 2-door Slantback Sedan, 4" long	30	40	50

Seiberling, L to R: GA01, GA02. Courtesy Dave Leopard, from his book Rubber Toy Vehicles.

SHARRON

by Dave Leopard

Sharron toys are die-cast aluminum, with two-piece construction similar to cast-iron vehicles from the 1930s. Sharron toys were made for a brief time at the Eastern Mennonite College in Harrisonburg, Virginia, during the Depression era. The molds were designed by a craftsman from Hubley, and the toys were made at the school from melted-down scrap aluminum. The toys are not marked in any way, but the originals bore a small paper tag that read "Indestructable Aluminum Toys." Manufacture of the toys was part of the work-study program at the school, and it apparently landed some large orders with chain stores. Julian Thomas now owns the plates, which produced eight of the smaller cars in one pouring.

	C6	C8	C10
SV1 1933 Pierce-Arrow			
Silver Arrow, 6" long	125	175	225
SV2 1934 Rohr, 5" long	100	150	200
SV3 Open Racer, 6" long.	75	100	125
SV4 Trolley Car		No Price Found	

Sharron SV-2 (with mold). Photo by Perry Eichor. Courtesy Dave Leopard.

SHERWOOD TOY CO.

(New York)

	C6	C8	C10
Roy Rogers "Nellybelle,"			
Pedal Car, 1954......................................	800	1400	2000

SKIPPY

Skippy Pedal Car, 54" long (American National ?), Chrysler Airflow; 1936. Asking price in 1992, $25,000.

SKOGLUND & OLSON

	C6	C8	C10
Skoglund & Olson Bugatti Racer,			
1929-30, cast-iron, 7-1/2" long	2000	3500	5500
Skoglund & Olson Bus, 10-1/2" long	850	1400	2200

	C6	C8	C10
Skoglund & Olson "Central			
Garage" Wrecker, 11-1/4" long	800	1350	2000

Skoglund & Olson Bus. Courtesy James S. Maxwell Jr./Virginia Caputo.

Skoglund & Olson "Central Garage" wrecker, 11-1/4" long. Courtesy Bill Bertoia Auctions. Photo by Jeanne Bertoia.

	C6	C8	C10
Skoglund & Olson Tank Truck, 10-1/2" long	1000	1900	2600

Skoglund & Olson Tank Truck, 10-1/2" long. Courtesy Bill Bertoia Auctions. Photo by Jeanne Bertoia.

SLIK-TOYS See "Lansing Slik-Toys"

SMITH-MILLER (SMITTY)

Smith-Miller (later, Miller-Ironson) of Santa Monica, California, was founded in 1945. The firm's plan was to produce, in two price ranges, duplicates of trucks and tractors in cast metal and aluminum. The lower-priced items weren't exact replicas, but the higher-priced items were. The prices were extremely high for the day: $6.95 to $27.85 (for an aerial ladder truck). According to Smitty expert Ray Funk, the trucks had one terrible flaw—their wheels, which were "simple and poorly produced." Despite this flaw, Smith-Miller-Ironsons are highly collectible, and custom reproductions are being made by Fred Thompson. The original firm closed its doors in 1954. (Thanks to Dennis C. Bellesfield for his help on this section.)

	C6	C8	C10
Smitty (Smith-Miller) No. 201-L Lumber Truck, 60 boards, 6 wheel, 14" long	230	345	460
Smitty No. 202-M Material Truck, 3 barrels, 3 cases, 18 boards, 4 wheels, 14" long	450	675	900
Smitty No. 203-H Heinz Grocery Truck, 6 wheels, 14" long	237	355	475
Smitty No. 204-A Arden Milk Truck, 12 milk cans, 4 cases, 4 wheels, 14" long	250	350	500
Smitty No. 205-P Oil Truck, 4 drums, 6 wheels, 14" long	275	415	550
Smitty No. 206-C Coca-Cola Truck, 16 Coca-Cola cases, 4 wheels, 14" long	450	675	900
Smitty No. 208-B Bekins Vanliner, 14 wheels, 22-1/2" long	325	488	650
Smitty No. 209-T Timber Giant, 3 logs, 14 wheels, 23-1/2" long	162	243	325

	C6	C8	C10
Smitty No. 210-S Stake Truck, 14 wheels, 23-1/2" long	250	375	500
Smitty No. 211-L Sunkist Special, 14 wheels, 23-1/2" long	250	350	500
Smitty No. 212-R Red Ball, 14 wheels, 23-1/2" long	250	350	500
Smitty No. 301-W GMC Wrecker, 4 wheeler	250	350	500
Smitty No. 302-M GMC Materials Truck, 4 barrels, 3 timbers	250	350	500
Smitty No. 303-R GMC Rack Truck, 6 wheels	250	350	500
Smitty No. 304-K GMC Kraft Foods, 4 wheels	275	375	550
Smitty No. 305-T GMC Triton Oil, 3 drums	175	263	350
Smitty No. 306-C GMC Coca-Cola, 4 wheels, 16 Coke cases	450	675	900
Smitty No. 307-L GMC Redwood Logger Tractor-Trailer, 3 logs	500	800	1100
Smitty No. 308-V GMC Lyon Van Lines Tractor-Trailer, 14 wheels	375	575	800
Smitty No. 309-S GMC Super Cargo Tractor- Trailer, 14 wheels, ten barrels	250	350	500
Smitty No. 310-H GMC Hi-Way Freighter Tractor-Trailer, 14 wheels	250	350	500
Smitty No. 311-E GMC Silver Streak Express Tractor Trailer, 14 wheels	212	318	425
Smitty No. 312-P GMC Pacific Intermountain Express ("P.I.E.") Tractor Trailer	300	450	600
Smitty No. 401 Tow Truck, 15" long	250	350	500
Smitty No. 402 Dump Truck, 11-1/2" long	250	350	500

Smitty No. 206-C Coca-Cola Truck. Photo by Dick MacNary.

Smitty No. 311-E GMC "Silver Streak," 14 wheels. Photo by Bob Smith.

Smitty No. 312-P GMC Pacific Intermountain Express ("P.I.E."). Photo by Calvin L. Chaussee.

402—Dump

Heavy duty earth-mover, with extra sturdy dump body. Load is discharged through self-operating tail-gate, by rack and pinion. Length 11½"

$9.95

401—Tow Truck

The vital emergency truck for righting "wrong-turners" or recovering ditched toy trucks. With crane, rope and "wrecker" hook. Length 15"

$7.95

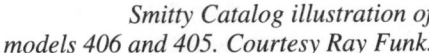

Smitty Catalog illustrations of Models 402 and 401. Courtesy Ray Funk.

Smitty No. 404-T "B" Mack Lumber & Trailer, 12 wheels. Courtesy Bob and Alice Wagner.

405—Silver Streak

The glittering glamour truck, with 14 rubber-tired wheels, plenty of toy-load and weight capacity for rugged action-play. A happy combination of bigness and beauty. Length 28"

$15.95

406—Bekins Van

Authentic model of the nationally famous furniture hauler. Big enough to move a double doll house full of toy furniture! Easy loading through full opening door. Length 29"

$16.95

Smitty Catalog illustration of models 406 and 405. Courtesy Ray Funk.

10th Anniversary SMITH-MILLER toy trucks for 1954

SMITH-MILLER Famous Trucks in Miniature have established a ten-year tradition of sturdy playability and authentic scale model design. Here are toy trucks, accurately patterned after the real giants of the highway, that give youngsters the "realism" they so greatly desire. From metal construction to brilliant durable colors, a SMITH-MILLER Truck is built like a truck in authenticity and wear.

407—Searchlight

A single handsomely designed unit with new Mack Truck cab and brilliant color scheme. Tilting-turning off-on searchlight. A four star play-value. Length 16½" (batt. not incl.)

$16.95

403—Scoop Dump

Just the thing for construction-minded kids. Scoops up gravel, sand or rocks and loads itself! A sand-pile sensation. Length 14"

$12.95

409—P·I·E

The big freight carrier that dominates the junior highway. Polished aluminum body, new cab-top air horn. I.C.C. riding lights. Length 29"

$19.95

Smitty Catalog illustrations of models 407, 403, and 409. Courtesy Ray Funk.

Smitty Catalog illustrations of models 408, 404, and 404T. Courtesy Ray Funk.

	C6	C8	C10
Smitty No. 403 Scoop Dump, 14" long	275	325	550
Smitty No. 404 Lumber Truck, 19" long ...	375	560	750
Smitty No. 404T Lumber Trailer, 17" long	200	300	400

Smitty Catalog illustration of Model 410. Courtesy Ray Funk.

Smitty No. 401-W GMC Wrecker. Photo by Calvin L. Chaussee.

Smitty #409 Pacific Intermountain Express. Photo by Ray Funk.

	C6	C8	C10
Smitty No. 405 Silver Streak 6-wheel tractor, 28" long	170	255	340
Smitty No. 406 Bekins Van, 29" long, six-wheel tractor and four-wheel trailer	325	495	650
Smitty No. 407 Searchlight Truck, 18-1/2" long, "Hollywood Film ad"	300	500	775
Smitty No. 408 Blue Diamond 10-wheel Dump Truck, 18-1/2" long	650	1100	1600
Smitty No. 409 Pacific Intermountain Express (P.I.E.) six-wheel tractor semi with eight wheel aluminum trailer, 29" long	500	750	1000
Smitty No. 410 Aerial Ladder Semi, six-wheel tractor and four-wheel trailer, 36" long, "SMFD"	432	648	865
Smitty No. 401-W GMC Wrecker, 6 wheels	350	525	700
Smitty No. 402-M GMC Material Truck, 4 barrels, 2 timbers	250	350	500
Smitty No. 403-R GMC Rack Truck, 6 wheels	125	188	250
Smitty No. 404-B GMC Bank of America, lock and key, 4 wheels	200	300	400
Smitty No. 405-T GMC Triton Oil, 6 wheels, 3 drums	250	350	500
Smitty No. 406-L GMC Lumber Tractor-Trailer, 14 wheels, eight timbers	250	350	500
Smitty No. 407-V GMC Lyon Van Tractor-Trailer, 10 wheels	350	500	700
Smitty No. 408-H GMC Machinery Hauler, 13 wheels, "Fruehauf"	300	450	600
Smitty No. 409-G GMC Mobilgas Tanker, 14 wheels, 2 hoses	270	405	540

Smitty No. 402-M GMC Material Truck. Photo by Calvin L. Chaussee.

Smitty No. 404-B GMC Bank of America Truck. Photo by Calvin L. Chaussee.

Smitty No. 407-V GMC Lyon Van Lines Tractor Trailer, 10 wheels. Photo by Bob Smith.

Smitty No. 409G GMC Mobilgas Tanker. Photo by Tim Oei.

Smitty No. 412-P GMC P.I.E., 14 wheels. Photo by Bob Smith.

Smitty "B" Mack Orange Dump, 10 wheels. Photo by Tim Oei.

Smitty GMC "Drive-O" Steerable Dump, 6 wheels. Photo by Bob Smith.

Smitty GMC Machinery Hauler. Courtesy Ray Funk.

	C6	C8	C10
Smitty No. 410-F GMC Trans-Continental Tractor-Trailer, 14 wheels, "Trans- Continental Freighter"	250	350	500
Smitty No. 411-E GMC Silver Streak Tractor-Trailer, 14 wheels	185	280	375
Smitty No. 412-P GMC P.I.E. 14 wheels	250	375	500
Smitty "B" Mack "Associated Truck Lines," 14 wheels	No Price Found		
Smitty "B" Mack Jr. Fire Truck, warning light, battery-operated, 4 wheels	400	650	950
Smitty "B" Mack Orange Dump, 10 wheels	750	1350	1800
Smitty "B" Mack P.I.E., 18 wheels	400	625	850
Smitty Chevy Bekins Van, 14 wheels, plain tires, hubcaps	300	400	600
Smitty Chevy Coca-Cola, 4 wheels, plain tires, early	425	638	850
Smitty Chevy Flatbed Tractor-Trailer, 14 wheels, unpainted wood trailer, plain tires, hubcaps, early	200	300	450
Smitty Chevy "Ice" Truck, c.1945	250	375	500
Smitty Chevy Milk Truck, 4 wheels, plain tires, hubcaps, early, 1945-46	200	300	450
Smitty Ford Bekins Van, 14 wheeler, plain tires, hubs. Earliest Smitty?, 1944	250	350	450

	C6	C8	C10
Smitty Ford Coca-Cola, 4 wheels, wood soda cases, 1944	600	1000	1400
Smitty GMC Be Mac 14 wheel T-Trailer, 1949	165	250	370
Smitty GMC Coca-Cola Truck, 24 plastic bottles in 6 cases, 4 wheels, 1954-55	425	675	925
Smitty GMC "Drive-O" Steerable Dump, 6 wheels, cable with hand control, 1949	225	350	525
Smitty GMC Dump Truck, 1950-53, 6 wheels	185	280	370
Smitty GMC "Furniture Mart" Pickup, 4 wheels, 1953	250	350	500
Smitty GMC Heinz Grocery Truck	250	350	500
Smitty GMC Machinery Hauler, 10 wheels	200	300	450
Smitty GMC Marshall Field & Company Tractor-Trailer, 10 wheel T-Trailer	300	450	600
Smitty GMC Peoples First National Bank and Trust Company Armored Truck; lock and key, 1951	225	400	525
Smitty GMC Rexall Drug, 4 wheels	275	415	550
Smitty GMC Searchlight Truck, "Hollywood Film Ad" with trailer, 1953	550	900	1300
Smitty GMC "U.S. Treasury" Truck Armored Truck, with lock and key, 1952	250	375	500
Smitty "L" Mack Aerial Ladder, "SMFD," 8 wheels	440	660	880

Smitty GMC Searchlight Truck, "Hollywood Film-Ad," with trailer. Photo by Bob Smith.

Smitty "L" Mack Aerial Ladder Truck, "SMFD." Photo by Bob Smith.

Smitty "L" Mack Army Materials Truck, 7-piece cargo load, 10 wheel. Photo by Bob Smith.

Smitty "L" Mack Army Personnel Carrier, 10 wheels. Photo by Bob Smith.

Smitty "L" Mack Material Truck, minus 2 barrels, 6 timbers. Courtesy R.F. Sapita.

Smitty "L" Mack Merchandise Van, 6 wheels. Photo by Ray Funk.

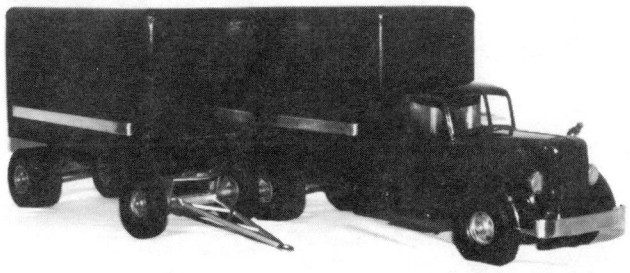

Smitty "L" Mack Merchandise Van & Trailer, 12 wheels. Photo by Bob Smith.

Smitty MIC Aerial Ladder. Courtesy Ray Funk.

A—House Trailer & Car. Die-cast extruded aluminum trailer has open-close doors and a removable top. Interior is luxuriously furnished. Car is a replica of a popular make modern hard-top convertible. 15" long and finished in smooth ivory and chrome. Overall length 42". **$29.95*.**
B—Liftomatic. Automatic lift tail gate is activated by a hydraulic cylinder and closes at top to protect load of barrels (included). Cab has full 45-degree steering ability. Doors open and close. 19¾" long. **$17.95*.** (Also recommended: Tow Truck, $14.95; Hydraulic Dump, $17.95*; Freuhauf, $19.95*.)

* *Prices Approximate—See Page 8½*

MILLER-IRONSON TOYS are designed and built to exemplify perfection. Their unusual play features give them distinction which is positively unique.

Smitty, Top: MIC House Trailer and MIC Lincoln Capri; Bottom: MIC Lift Gate Truck (Liftomatic). From Toy Yearbook, *1953-54.*

	C6	C8	C10
Smitty "L" Mack Army Materials Truck, 3 barrels, 2 boards, 1 large crate, 1 small, 10 wheels	460	690	925
Smitty "L" Mack Army Personnel Carrier, 10 wheels	460	690	925
Smitty "L" Mack Bekins Van, all white, 10 wheels	750	1100	1500
Smitty "L" Mack Blue Diamond Dump, 10 wheels	800	1300	1800
Smitty "L" Mack International Paper Co., 10 wheels	500	800	1100
Smitty "L" Mack Lyon Van, 6 wheels	450	675	900
Smitty "L" Mack Material Truck, 2 barrels, 6 timbers, 6 wheels	350	550	750
Smitty "L" Mack Merchandise Van, 6 wheels	375	575	800
Smitty "L" Mack Merchandise Van & Trailer, 12 wheels	850	1400	2000
Smitty "L" Mack Mobile Tandem Tanker, 12 wheels	800	1300	1800
Smitty "L" Mack Orange Hydraulic Dump, 10 wheels	450	650	950
Smitty "L" Mack Orange Material Truck, 10 wheels, 3 barrels, 2 boards, one large crate, one small	450	750	1000
Smitty "L" Mack P.I.E., 14 wheel	450	800	1050
Smitty "L" Mack "Sibley's" Van, 6 wheels (rare)	600	900	1500
Smitty "L" Mack Tandem Timber, 6 wheel, 18 or 24 timbers (varies)	420	630	840

	C6	C8	C10
Smitty "L" Mack Telephone Truck, 6 wheels	600	1000	1400
Smitty "L" Mack West Coast Transport, 6 wheel	800	1300	1800
Smitty MIC Aerial Ladder	375	562	750
Smitty MIC "Fruehauf Road Star" Tractor-Trailer, 14 wheels	300	450	625
Smitty MIC House Trailer	280	420	560
Smitty MIC Hydraulic Dump, 10 wheels	500	850	1250
Smitty MIC Lift Gate Truck, 6 wheels, 2 barrels	500	800	1100
Smitty MIC Lincoln Capri (for MIC House Trailer), steerable	425	638	850
Smitty MIC Lumber Truck, 6 wheels, 9 timbers	600	1000	1450
Smitty MIC P.I.E. Tractor-Trailer, 14 wheels	600	1000	1400
Smitty MIC "Teamsters" Hydraulic Dump, 10 wheels	650	1000	1500
Smitty MIC "Teamsters" Tow Truck, 6 wheels	800	1400	1800
Smitty MIC "Teamsters" Tractor-Trailer, 14 wheels	750	1100	1700
Smitty MIC Tow Truck, "Official Tow Car," 6 wheels	500	800	1200
Smitty MIC Tow Truck, 6 wheels, unpainted, polished	400	575	825
Smitty MIC Tractor-Trailer, polished aluminum trailer, no decals, 14 wheels	375	600	850

Smitty MIC Lift Gate Truck, 6 wheels. Photo by Bob Smith.

Smitty MIC Tow Truck "Official Tow Car," 6 wheels. Photo by Bob Smith.

Early Smith-Miller trucks, as seen in the July, 1946 Toys & Novelties. Courtesy Dick MacNary.

SOLIDO

(France)

Solido's military line seems to sell for between $45 to $65, in Mint condition. The following list is of their civilian line, as sold mint in box.

	MIB			MIB
12 Peugeot 104	20	24 Porsche Carrera RS		25
14 Matra Simco	35	25 BMW 2.0 CSL		35
15 Lola T820	30	26 Ford Capri Rallye		30
16 Ferrari Daytona	30	27 Lancia Startos		30
17 Gulf Mirage	30	28 BMW 2002		35
18 Porsche Can Am	50	29 Citroen CX2200		25
20 Alpine Renault A441	20	30 Renault 30		35
22 Renault 12 Station Wagon	20	31 Delage D8 120 '39		20
		35 Duesenberg '31 Conv		25
		37 Renault 17TS Rally du Maros		25
		38 Gulf LeMans		35
		39 Simca 1308 Hatchback		20
		40 Peugeot 604 Sedan		25

Solido 40th Anniversary (1984) Gift Set "A" consists of Tigre Tank, M3 Halftrack, M20 Scout Car, M10 Tank Destroyer; value mint in box $200. Courtesy Harvey K. Rainess.

Early "Solido" Military Model and Box (M-20 U.S. Armored Car in French markings); Crewman is a 30mm Starlux, also made in France. Photo by Ed Poole.

Solido (France) Military Vehicles (Starlux 30mm Soldier at left and Britains Ltd. 54mm Gunner at right included for scale). L to R, back row: 200 Combat Car M20, 202 Patton Tank, 203 Renault 4X4 truck, 204 Antiaircraft Gun; Front row: 205 105mm Howitzer, 206 250mm Howitzer, 207 Russian PT-76 Tank. Photo by Ed Poole.

Late "Solido" Military Models and Box (253 "General Lee" U.S. Tank and, on right, 245 GMC 6X6 U.S. truck): Decals were supplied and left to buyers' imagination where to apply. Officer is French Starlux 30mm tall. Photo by Ed Poole.

Solido Vehicles (Starlux 30mm GIs included for scale). L to R, Back row: 242 Dodge 6X6 truck, 244 Half-Track M-3, 245 GMC 6X6 M-34 Truck, 252 M7BI "Priest" Assault Gun. Front row: 253 General Lee Tank, 253 Jeep & Trailer, GMC Truck (?) Air Compressor and Dodge Ambulance (numbers unknown). Photo by Ed Poole.

*Solido Vehicles (cont'd); Starlux 30mm soldiers included for scale.
L to R, Back row: 222 Tiger Tank, 226 German Armored Car (radio aerial missing), 231 Sherman Tank, 232 M10 Tank Destroyer; Front row: Renault R35 Tank, 234 Somua S35 Tank, 237 Panzer IV Tank, 241 German Half-Track. Photo by Ed Poole.*

SONICON

	C6	C8	C10
"Sonicon Bus," Japanese, 13", battery operated	288	432	575

SONNY

	C6	C8	C10
Sonny Army Truck, 27" long, open cab	500	850	1250
Sonny Dump, 26-1/2" long	600	900	1400
Sonny Moving Van	400	700	1000
Sonny Parcel Post Van	700	1200	1900
Sonny Police Patrol Paddy Wagon	600	900	1400
Sonny "Railway Express Co." Truck, 26" long, c.1920s	800	1200	2000

	C6	C8	C10
Sonny "USA 1120" Anti-Aircraft Truck, 24" long	600	925	1450
Sonny "US 1120" Artillery Truck, 26" long	325	480	650

Sonny Dump, 26-1/2" long. Courtesy Joe and Sharon Freed.

Sonny "Railway Express Co." truck, 26" long, c. 1920s. Photo by Bob Smith.

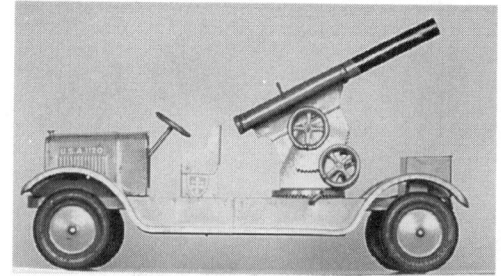

Sonny "USA 1120" Anti-Aircraft Truck. Courtesy Bill Bertoia Auctions. Photo by Jeanne Bertoia.

Sonny Trucks, as shown in a 1928 Butler Bros. catalog.

STANLEY & COX

	C6	C8	C10
Stanley & Cox Tank, wooden, c.WWII	32	48	65

Stanley & Cox Tank, wooden, with original box. Photo by Jack Matthews.

STANLEY WORKS

	C6	C8	C10
Stanlo Coupe, c.1920s, build-it, 5-1/2"	85	128	170

STAR BRAND

	C6	C8	C10
"Star Brand Shoes Are Better," racing car "The Winner," tin litho. 8-1/2" long	650	1050	1500

"Star Brand Shoes Are Better" Racing Car. Courtesy Sotheby's NY.

STEELCRAFT
Murray-Ohio Co.

	C6	C8	C10
Steelcraft Army Truck, Mack, c.1930, 22" long	650	1000	1450
Steelcraft Army Truck, Mack, c.1930, 26" long	375	562	750
Steelcraft "Bloomingdale's" Delivery Truck, 25" long	450	650	900
Steelcraft Buick Pedal Car, c.early 1930s, 46" long	2000	4500	8000
Steelcraft Cadillac Pedal Car, c.1930s, 38" long	2500	4500	9000
Steelcraft Cadillac Pedal Car, 1926	1500	2500	5000

	C6	C8	C10
Steelcraft "City Delivery" Truck, 19" long	287	421	575
Steelcraft "City Fire Dept." Ladder Truck, early	500	800	1200
Steelcraft "City Ice Co." Mack Truck, 24" long	375	562	750
Steelcraft "City Ice Cream Co."	250	375	500
Steelcraft "City Milk Co.," 18" long	400	600	800
Steelcraft Coca-Cola Truck, 12 bottles on side	400	600	800
Steelcraft "Cream Crest" Truck, 18" long	270	405	540

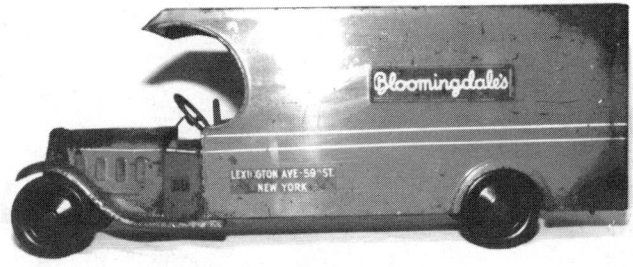

Steelcraft "Bloomingdale's" Delivery Truck, c.1930s, 25" long. Photo by Bob Smith.

Steelcraft "City Fire Dept." Ladder Truck, early. Photo by Tim Oei.

Steelcraft "City Ice Co." Mack Truck, as shown in a September, 1934 Butler Bros. catalog.

Steelcraft "Cream Crest" Truck, 18" long. Photo by Bob Smith.

Steelcraft Lincoln Pedal Car, 46" long (restored in photo). Courtesy Sotheby's New York.

	C6	C8	C10
Steelcraft Dump Truck, 23" long, early 1930s	261	392	522
Steelcraft Dump Truck, 24" long, c.early 30s	135	203	270
Steelcraft Dump Truck, Airflow	1500	2500	3500
Steelcraft Dump Truck, Mack, 26" long	450	700	1000
Steelcraft Dump Truck, Mack, 20" long, 1930s	150	225	300
Steelcraft Dump Truck Pedal Car, 62" long	2000	4000	6600
Steelcraft Fire Truck, 25" long	750	1100	1500
Steelcraft Fire Hook & Ladder, Airflow pedal truck	1600	2700	3800
Steelcraft Ford Pedal Car, 1930, 30" long	650	1100	1650
Steelcraft "Fro-Joy" Ice Cream Truck, c.1930s	350	525	700
Steelcraft GMC Scissor Dump Truck, 26" long	550	850	1400
Steelcraft GMC Trailer Truck	1200	2000	2800
Steelcraft Inter City, 24" long	500	800	1100
Steelcraft Lincoln Pedal Car, 46" long	1500	2500	4000
Steelcraft Lincoln Zephyr, 1941 pedal car	1400	2500	4000
Steelcraft Little Jim Fire Truck	600	900	1200
Steelcraft "Little Jim" Mack Dump Truck, red/black, c.1928 (Little Jims were sold by J.C. Penney's)	600	900	1400

	C6	C8	C10
Steelcraft Mack Ladder Truck, 26" long	450	675	900
Steelcraft Mack "Moving Van," c.1920s	No Price Found		
Steelcraft Mack Pedal Car Dump Truck, 44" long	700	1100	1500
Steelcraft Mack Police Patrol, 25" long	1400	2500	4000
Steelcraft Mandrel Bus Van	1100	1800	2400
Steelcraft Marion Steam Shovel	200	300	400
Steelcraft Model T Roadster Pedal Car, 50" long, Lic. #65-287	450	675	900
Steelcraft "New York Trucking Co.," 23-1/4" long, headlights work, 1930s	800	1100	1400
Steelcraft Racer Pedal Car, 1941	800	1300	1800
Steelcraft Railway Express Truck, 26" long	1100	1600	2600
Steelcraft Richfield Oil Tanker	800	1300	1800
Steelcraft Road Roller, 16-1/2" long	238	357	475
Steelcraft Roadster Pedal Car, c.1920s, 38" long	1800	2900	4500
Steelcraft "Sheffield Farms" Truck, 1930s, 21" long	500	800	1300
Steelcraft Shell Motor Oil Truck with oil barrels	300	450	600
Steelcraft Steam Shovel, 26" long	225	338	450
Steelcraft Tank Truck, sheet metal, 25-1/2" long	650	1100	1500
Steelcraft "U.S. Mail," 27-1/4" long, c.1928	1150	1725	2300
Steelcraft Van	450	700	1000

Steelcraft "Little Jim" Mack Dump Truck, sold by J.C. Penny's Dept. Store, c.1928. Photo by Bob Smith.

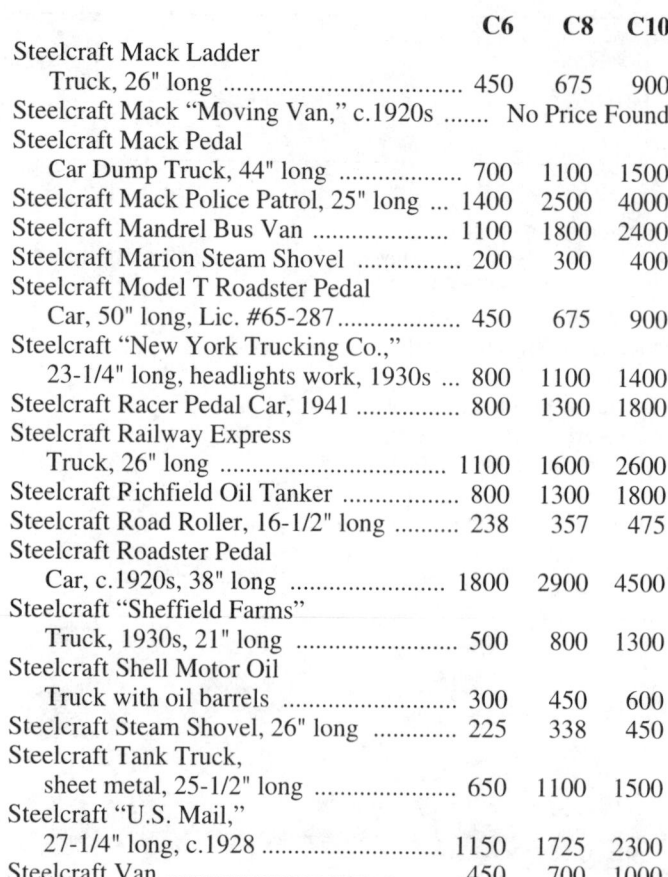

Steelcraft Mack "Moving Van." Photo by Tim Oei.

Steelcraft "New York Trucking Co.," 23-1/4" long. Photo by John Gibson.

Steelcraft Road Roller, 16-1/2" long; from a November, 1932 Butler Bros. catalog.

Steelcraft "Sheffield Farms" truck, 1930s, 21" long. Courtesy Bill Bertoia Auctions. Photo by Jeanne Bertoia.

Steelcraft Tank Truck, sheet metal, 25-1/2" long. Courtesy Bill Bertoia Auctions. Photo by Jeanne Bertoia.

Steelcraft "U.S. Mail." Photo by Calvin L. Chaussee.

Steelcraft Pontiac pedal car, 1935, 36" long. Courtesy Sotheby's New York.

Mfrs 100

2F-5804—1/12 doz. in box............△☆Doz **$8.10**
Dump truck, 23¾x6¼ in., lt. green & yellow, 3 in. double wheels, real dumping mechanism.

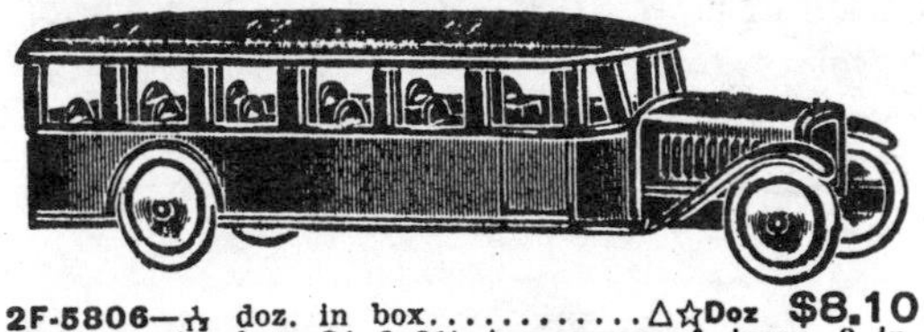

2F-5806—1/12 doz. in box............△☆Doz **$8.10**
Cross country bus, 24x6x6¼ in., maroon & ivory, 3 in. double wheels.

2F-5807—1/12 doz. in box................Doz **$8.10**
Fire truck, 21x6¼ in., brilliant red, 3 in. double wheels, 2 ladders.

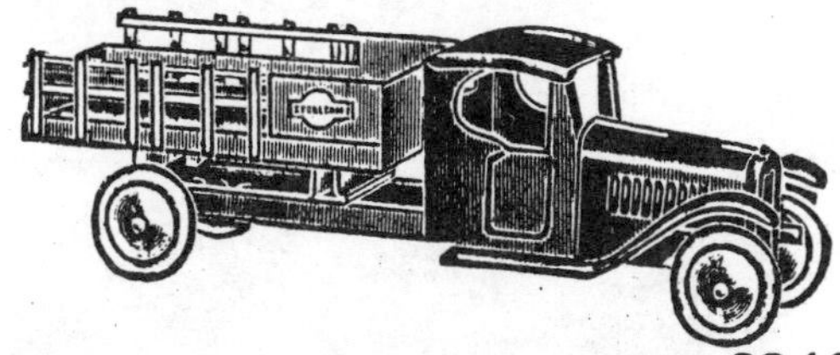

2F-5805—1/12 doz. in box............△☆Doz **$8.10**
Stake body truck, 22½x6¼ in., blue & yellow, 3 in. double wheels.

2F0-5817—1/12 doz. in box, 7 lbs........Doz **$10.50**
"Sheffield" milk truck, 21¾x6¼ in., red & ivory, 3⅛ in. rubber wheels, miniature milk cans.

Steelcraft vehicles, as shown in an October, 1932 Butler Bros. catalog.

	C6	C8	C10
Convertible, c.1950s, 12" long Kaiser-Nash type, plastic, push down to operate	300	450	600

Steer O Toys (Chicago) Convertible, c.1950s, 12" long. Photo by Tim Oei.

STRAUSS

Ferdinand Strauss was an immigrant from Alsace. He began as a toy importer in the early 1900s. By 1914, he had four New York toy shops. When war disrupted imports of toys, he began manufacturing them. In 1918, he was located in East Rutherford, New Jersey, with 50 employees. Eventually Strauss was known as "The Founder of the Mechanical Toy Industry in America." Strauss seems to have been wholly or partially out of business in the late 1920s, and then resumed, turning out wind-ups and other toys until at least 1941-42. He is also famous for having given employment to the very young Louis Marx.

	C6	C8	C10
Strauss Big Show Circus Truck	1500	2250	3000
Strauss "Big-Show Circus," c.1925, tin windup, 9" long, containing lion and tamer, more in cage, no engine compartment	800	1500	2100
Strauss "Bus Deluxe," 1920s, 12" long	1000	1800	2500
Strauss Check-A-Cab	450	675	900
Strauss Circus Wagon, containing lion and tamer, 8-1/2" long, no engine compartment	800	1500	2100
Strauss Circus Wagon, 10" long, has engine compartment	1250	1875	2500
Strauss "Green Racer," 8-1/2" long windup, c.1920s	200	300	550
Strauss "Haul Away Truck" No. 22, dump body	240	360	480
Strauss Hooligans Hack	300	450	600
Strauss "Interstate Bus" Double Decker, tin windup, 10-1/2" long	375	600	850
Strauss "Jitney Bus" No. 66, 10" long, tin windup, c.1921................	300	550	750
Strauss "Kraka Jack Car," 1920s, 5-1/2" long	150	225	300
Strauss "Leaping Lena" tin windup, 8" long	400	600	800
Strauss "Long Haulage Truck"	350	525	700

Strauss "Big-Show Circus" wagon. Photo by Bob Smith.

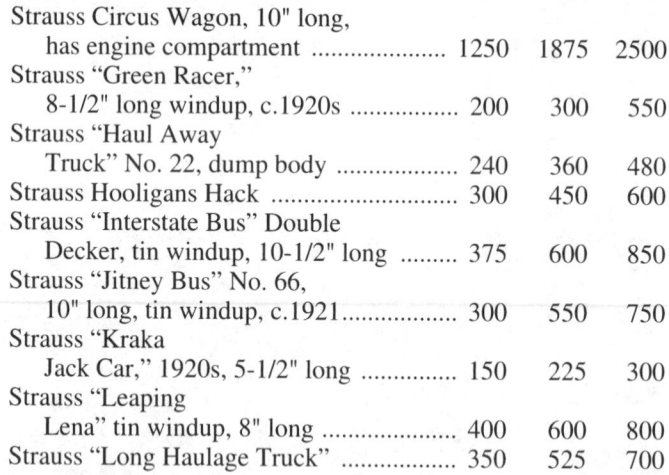

Strauss "Green Racer." Photo by Bob Smith.

Strauss "Interstate Bus." Photo by Bob Smith.

Strauss "Jitney Bus." Photo by Bob Smith.

Strauss "Leaping Lena." Photo by Bob Smith.

Strauss Racer No. 21. Photo by Bob Smith.

Strauss "Red Flash Racer." Photo by Bob Smith.

Strauss "Yell-O Taxi." Photo by Bob Smith.

	C6	C8	C10
Strauss "Old Jalopy, The,"			
4 college kids	100	150	200
Strauss Racer			
No. 21, tin windup, c.1923	200	350	550
Strauss Racer "Red Flash Racer," 9-1/2"			
long, windshield, tin windup, c.1919	250	400	600
Strauss "Red Star Van"	400	600	800
Strauss "Reo" Racer, tin windup	225	338	450
Strauss "Standard Oil Truck 73"	325	488	650

	C6	C8	C10
Strauss "Timber King" Log Truck,			
driver, windup, 1920s, 18" long	235	355	470
Strauss "Trikauto," No. 53	188	282	375
Strauss "Water Sprinkler" Truck	450	675	900
Strauss "What's It?" Car,			
No. 53, 1925, 9-1/2" long	600	900	1200
Strauss "Yell-o Taxi"			
No. 59, 8-1/2" long	425	750	950

STROMBECKER

(Moline, Illinois)

Strombecker Wooden Truck Hauler. Photo by Perry R. Eichor. No price found.

Strombecker: The Truck Hauler's cab used as a wrecker, thus finally explaining what the Eye and String were used for. Photo by Perry R. Eichor.

STRUCTO

Structo, of Freeport, Illinois, was founded in 1908 by three men: brothers Louis and Edward Strohacker and C.C. Thompson. They initially manufactured Erector Construction Kits. About 1919, they started making toy vehicles. In 1935, J.G. Cokey bought a majority of the business. When he died in 1975, the toy patents and designs were taken over by the Ertl Company. (Numbered Structos are found at the end of this listing.)

	C6	C8	C10
Structo Aerial Ladder Truck, 33" long	188	282	375
Structo American Airlines "Sky Chief" Box Van	92	138	185
Structo Army Ambulance No. 416, 17" long	175	263	350
Structo Army Searchlight Cannon	88	132	175
Structo Army Tank No. 4120	60	90	120
Structo Army Tank, like 4120 but lights up, winds up, 13" long	150	225	300
Structo Army Truck w/canvas top, 17" long	200	300	400

	C6	C8	C10
Structo Army Truck with canvas top, 21" long	155	233	310
Structo Army Truck with canvas top, 18" long, 1920s	350	525	700
Structo Army Van, 17-1/2" long, pressed steel and canvas, No. 415	170	255	340
Structo Auto Haul-Away w/cars	70	105	140
Structo Auto Transport, 1950s	92	138	185
Structo "Ballantine beer & ale" Truck, 1950s	500	750	1000
Structo Barrel Truck, windup	135	202	270
Structo Bearcat Speedster, No. 10, 1919	400	600	800
Structo Cadillac, metal, 6-1/2" long	25	38	50
Structo Camper with cloth top, 12" long	55	82	110
Structo Caterpillar Tractor with Trailer, heavy spring clockwork motor, steel treads, No. 46	200	300	400

Structo Army Truck with canvas top, 18" long, 1920s. Photo by Calvin L. Chaussee.

Structo "Ballantine beer & ale" truck. Photo by Tim Oei.

Structo Bearcat Speedster No. 10, 1919. Photo by Tim Oei.

Structo Cadillacs, metal, each 6-1/2" long. Photo by Ron Fink.

"Structo Cattle Farms" Truck, 22" long. Photo by Calvin L. Chaussee.

Structo Dump Truck, 20" long, 1930s. Photo by Calvin L. Chaussee.

Structo Dump Truck, 19" long, 1940s. Photo by Calvin L. Chaussee.

Structo Dump Truck, open cab, 18" long, 1920s, levers on each side of cab. Photo by Calvin L. Chaussee.

Structo Dump Truck, 14" long, 1959. Photo by Calvin L. Chaussee.

	C6	C8	C10
"Structo Cattle Farms" Truck, 22" long	80	120	160
Structo Cement Mixer, 20" long, c.1950s	90	135	180
Structo "City of Toyland" Garbage Truck, 1948, 21" long	112	168	245
Structo City of Toyland Utility Truck	120	180	240
Structo Cletrac Crawler, wind-up	212	318	425
Structo Communications Center Truck, 21" long	175	263	350
"Structo Construction Company" Truck, 1950s	68	102	135
Structo Corvair Pickup	30	45	60
Structo Coupe, convertible, 1920s	160	240	320
Structo Delivery Truck, tin electric lights	150	225	300
Structo Diamond T Hook & Ladder	190	285	380
Structo Diamond T Machinery Hauler & Shovel, c.1940	188	282	375
Structo Diamond T Semi, 1940s	265	398	530
Structo Dump Truck, 21" long, c.1930s	200	300	400
Structo Dump Truck, 20" long, 1930s	150	225	300
Structo Dump Truck, 19" long, 1940s	55	82	110
Structo Dump Truck, 18" long, open cab, 1920s, levers on each side of cab, No. 405	250	375	500
Structo Dump Truck, 14" long, 1959	50	75	100
Structo Dump Truck, metal, 8-1/2" long	40	60	80
Structo Dump Truck, 1950s	100	150	200

	C6	C8	C10
Structo Earth Mover	60	90	120
Structo Fire Dept. Emergency Patrol Truck, red bubble light, 12" long, 1950s	55	82	110
Structo Freeport Motor Express	70	105	140
Structo Garbage Truck, 21" long	75	112	150
Structo Gasoline Truck No. 912, 1950s, 13" long	75	112	150
Structo Grader, 18" long	75	112	150
Structo Guided Missile Launcher, No. 906, 13" long, with wood & vinyl missiles	70	105	140
Structo Hi-Lift Bulldozer	40	60	80
Structo Hi-Way Maintenance Truck	70	105	140
Structo Hi-Way Transport Tandem, c.1920s	412	618	825
Structo Hi-Way Transport, 2 trailers, 1940	325	488	650
Structo Hook & Ladder Fire Truck, early	262	394	525
Structo Hook & Ladder Fire Truck, No. 251, 1939	185	278	370
Structo Horse Van, 1966, 22" long	65	98	130
Structo Hydraulic Dump Truck, 1960s	48	72	95
Structo Ladder Truck, 1950s	200	300	400
Structo Ladder Truck, 1938	450	675	900
Structo Livestock Truck, 1960s	32	48	65
Structo Loboy & Shovel	200	300	400
Structo Log Truck, 11" long, 1950s	70	105	140
Structo "Mail Truck," 1928	288	432	575
Structo Machinery Hauler	150	225	300
Structo Mechanical Dumper, 1940s, 19-1/2" long			No Price Found

Structo Dump Truck, metal, 8-1/2" long. Photo by Ron Fink.

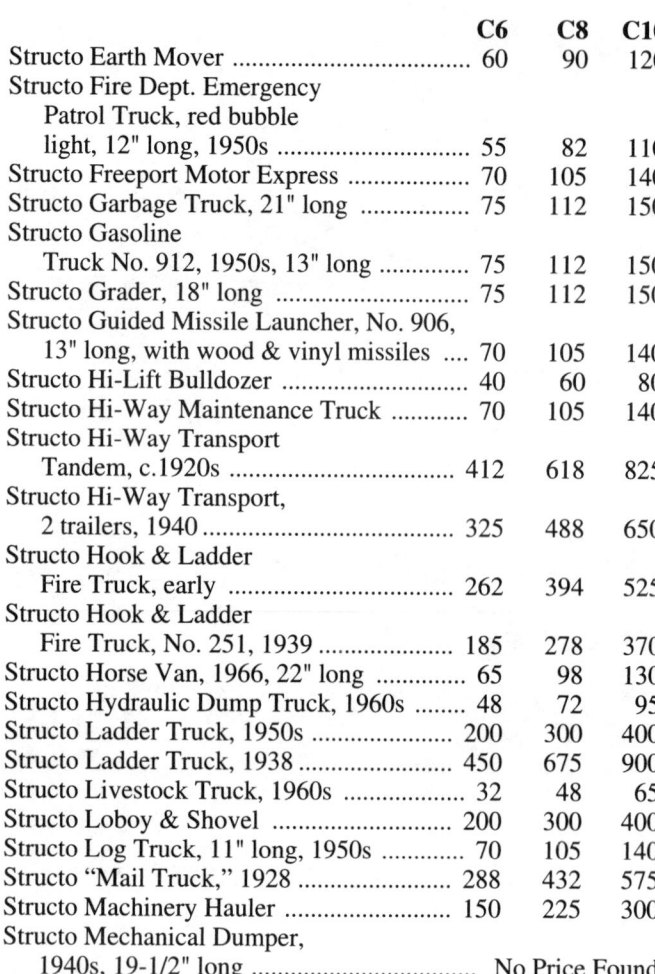

Structo Machinery Hauler. Photo by Calvin L. Chaussee.

Structo Mechanical Dumper, 1940s, 19-1/2" long. Courtesy Harvey K. Rainess.

"Structo Package Delivery" Truck, 12" long. Photo by Calvin L. Chaussee.

Structo Pick-Up Truck, 17" long, 1940s. Photo by Calvin L. Chaussee.

Structo Pickup Trucks, metal, each 6" long. Photo by Ron Fink.

Structo "Police Patrol" Truck No. 426. Photo by Thomas G. Nefos, National Toy Connection.

Structo "Pumper," 22" long, 1920s. Courtesy Bill Bertoia Auctions. Photo by Jeanne Bertoia.

"Structo Ready-Mix" Cement Truck, 14" long. Photo by Calvin L. Chaussee.

"Structo Ready-Mix" Concrete Truck, c.1960s. Photo by Bob Smith.

"Structo Rocker," 23-1/2" long. Photo by Calvin L. Chaussee.

	C6	C8	C10
Structo Mobile Communication Center	150	225	300
Structo Mobile Crane, Ford Cabover	88	132	175
Structo Motor Dispatch Tandem, 1929	450	675	900
Structo Motor Dispatch Trailer Truck, 24", c.early 30s	475	713	950
Structo Moving Van, 16" long, open cab, c.1929, No. 427	175	265	350
Structo North American Van Lines	100	150	200
"Structo Package Delivery" Truck, 12" long	85	128	170
Structo "Parcel Service"	85	128	170
Structo Pickup Truck, 17" long, 1940s	130	195	260
Structo Pickup Truck, metal, 6" long	32	48	65
Structo Piledriver, 13" high	175	263	350
Structo Police Patrol Truck, 17" long, No. 426	250	375	500
Structo "Popeye" Truck, early	1700	2800	4200
Structo Pumper, 1950s, 19"	106	159	212
Structo Pumper, 1938	265	398	530
Structo "Pumper," 22" long, 1920s	500	800	1200
Structo Ramp Truck	90	135	180
Structo "Ready-Mix" Cement Truck, 14" long	100	150	200
"Structo Ready-Mix" Concrete Truck, c.1960s	100	150	200
Structo Renault Tank, clockwork, green with red turret	260	390	520
Structo Road Builder Set, c.1950s	100	150	200
Structo Roadster, 16" long, 1920s, clockwork	600	1000	1400
"Structo Rocker," 23-1/2" long	90	135	180
Structo Sand Loader, 12" high, c.1928	100	150	200
Structo Sand Loader, c.1962	40	60	80
"Structo Sanitation Dept." Garbage Truck, c.1960s, 17" long	105	158	210
Structo Searchlight Truck, truck metal, light and generator plastic, uses batteries, has rubber tires	62	93	125
Structo Speedster, 1920s	400	600	800
Structo Stake Truck, lights work, 21" long, 1930s	212	318	425
Structo Steam Shovel, 9-1/2" long, 1920s	200	300	400
Structo Steam Shovel, 14"x11"	45	68	90
Structo Steam Shovel, 16"	58	88	115
Structo Steam Shovel, 21"x18"	95	138	190
Structo Steel Hauler, cast cab	110	165	220
Structo Steer-O-Matic Turbine Wrecker	75	112	150
Structo Tank, #48, 11" long	225	338	450
Structo Tank, olive drab with orange turret, ten metal wheels, 12-1/2" long	300	450	600
"Structo Telephone Co.," 12" long, c.1948	67	101	135
Structo Texaco Tanker, 25" long	50	75	100
Structo Tow Truck, early	200	300	400

"Structo Sanitation Dept." Garbage Truck, c.1960s. Photo by Bob Smith.

Structo Tank, No. 48, 11" long. Courtesy Mapes Auctioneers & Appraisers.

Structo Tank, olive drab with orange turret, ten metal wheels, 12-1/2" long. Courtesy Joe and Sharon Freed.

"Structo Telephone Co." Photo by Bill Kaufman.

	C6	C8	C10
Structo "Toyland Construction Company" elevated dump, 12" long	150	225	300
Structo "Toyland Garage" Wrecker	80	120	160
Structo Toyland Oil Co.	175	263	350
Structo Toyland Tow Truck	120	180	240
Structo Tractor, early windup, 2 trailers, overall 20"	162	243	325
Structo Tractor, 8-1/2" long with cast iron driver, early, caterpillar type	275	415	550
Structo Track Loader	37	56	75
Structo Trailer Truck, 24" long, early	600	1000	1400
Structo "Transcontinental Express," c.1950s, plastic & metal	120	180	240
Structo Truck Assortment No. 317: Dump Truck, blue, Stake truck, Lumber truck. Each 9" long, 3-1/2" wide, 3-1/2" tall. Heavy gauge metal, rubber wheels, original box folds to form garage. 1920s. Price per set	150	225	300
Structo U.S. Air Force Jeep Ridem, 26"	110	165	220
Structo U.S. Air Force Truck	115	172	230

	C6	C8	C10
Structo U.S. Army Road Grader	45	68	90
Structo "U.S. Hi-Way Maintenance Service Truck"	100	150	200
Structo U.S. Mail Delivery Truck, 17" long, No. 428	225	338	450
Structo Van Lines, 20" long, 1960s	45	68	90
Structo Vista Horse Van, 22" long, 4 horses, 1966	50	75	100
Structo Whippet Tank, 12" long, heavy spring clockwork motor, enameled green, red and black, may read "Patented 1920," on sale in 1929, No. 48	200	300	400
Structo Yuba Tractor, copyright 1924	450	675	900
Structo No. 340 End Loader	95	143	190
Structo No. 601 Motor Express Stake Truck, early 1950s	55	82	110
Structo No. 603 Package Delivery, early 1950s	80	120	160
Structo No. 605 Shovel Dump, early 1950s	150	225	300
Structo No. 607 Machinery Truck, early 1950s	170	255	340
Structo No. 609 Barrel Truck, early 1950s	140	210	280
Structo No. 700 Transport Trailer, early 1950s	150	225	300
Structo No. 702 Steel Cargo Trailer, early to mid-1950s	90	135	180
Structo No. 704 Overland Freight Trailer, early 1950s	140	210	280

Structo "Toyland Construction Company" elevated dump, 12" long. Photo by Calvin L. Chaussee.

Structo "Transcontinental Express," c.1950s, plastic & metal. Courtesy Harvey K. Rainess.

Structo "U.S. Hi-Way Maintenance Service Truck." Courtesy Thomas G. Nefos, National Toy Connection.

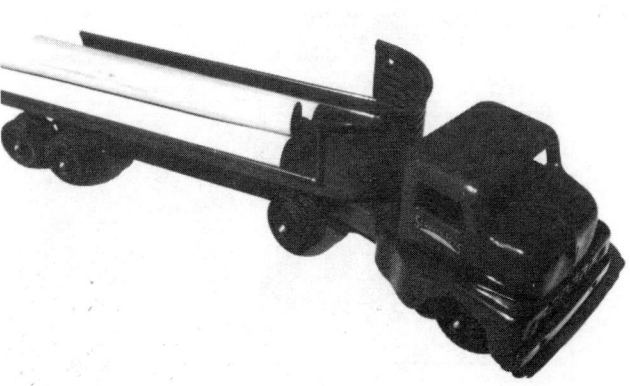

Structo 940 Log Truck. Courtesy Thomas G. Nefos, National Toy Connection.

"STRUCTO" HEAVY DUTY STEEL TOYS

"Built to last a playtime age"....the finest line of heavy duty steel toys for the money. Details of construction faithfully carried out make them perfect models of REAL THINGS. Made of heavy automobile pressed steel, spot-welded (not put together with lugs). Auto enamel finish.

Strongest Steel Toys Made ....for the Money!

Here are typical features that make STRUC-TO Toys so remarkably durable.

Heavier!

BUILT like the real things. Heavier gauge steel than is used in any similar toys of comparative price. Gears, axles, chains, etc, are fully in keeping with the heavy gauge steel bodies.

Spot Welded!

NO LUGS — All joints are electrically spot welded, fusing the two metals into one solid connection. As many as 121 welds are made on one toy.

Proof!

SO STRONG are STRUCTO toys that many boys ride them as coasters. This practice is not recommended but it proves the remarkable strength of STRUCTO construction.

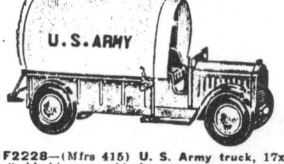

1F2228—(Mfrs 415) U. S. Army truck, 17x 6x9, khaki, removable heavy canvas top with uprights, drop tail gate with latch. 1 in pkg....................Each **$1.15**

1F2222 — (Mfrs 416) Ambulance, 17x10x9, khaki, inside seats, canvas drop side, rear step with railing. 1 in box. Each **$1.15**

1F2241—(Mfrs 111) Giant grab bucket, 19x 7x17½, red & black, revolving engine house, crank lever automatically opens and closes bucket. 1 in box. Each **$1.35**

1F2253—(Mfrs 421) Air mail transport, extreme length 24 in., 12½x5½ tractor with 4 wheels, 11 x5 van trailer with 2 wheels and latticed sides, khaki, airplane decoration, drop tail gate. 1 in box. Each **$1.35**

1F2244 — (Mfrs 420) Motor dispatch, extreme length 24 in., 14½x5½ tractor with 4 wheels, 11 x5 van trailer with 2 wheels, blue, airplane decoration, drop tail gate. 1 in box. Each **$1.35**

DOLLAR WONDERS $8.50 Doz YOUR CHOICE

4 DOZ. OR MORE ALIKE OR ASSTD. $8.00 Doz

1F2225—(Mfrs 407) Fire patrol, 18x6x5¾, red, side seats, rear step and hand rails, brass bell. ½ doz in pkg....Doz **$8.50**

1F2227—(Mfrs 410) Moving van, 17 x 6 x 6¾, yellow, drop tail gate with chains. ½ doz. in box......Doz **$8.50**

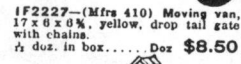

1F2226 — (Mfrs 411) U. S. Mail truck, 17x6x6¾, green, openwork sides, drop tail gate with chains. ½ doz. in box. Doz **$8.50**

1F2251—(Mfrs 405) Dump truck, 17½x6x6, red, levers raise and lower body, 90 degree (dumping action) swing. ½ doz. in pkg......Doz **$8.50**

1F2239—(Mfrs 409) Police patrol, 17x6x6¾, blue, inside seats, rear step and handle rails. ½ doz. in pkg......Doz **$8.50**

1F2240—(Mfrs 408) Speed wagon, 17x6x6, green, drop tail gate with chain and latch. ½ doz. in pkg......Doz **$8.50**

1F2234—(Mfrs 65) Steam shovel, 18¾ x6x13, red & black, revolving engine house, crank lever automatically opens and closes bucket. ½ doz. in box. Doz **$8.50**

1F2237—(Mfrs 122) Pile driver, 8x4 platform, red & black, 12½ in. tower, revolving engine house, copper finish crank, wood pulleys. ½ doz. in box. Doz **$8.50**

1F2238 — (Mfrs 66) Grab bucket crane, 14x6x15, red & black, revolving engine house, crank lever automatically opens and closes bucket. ½ doz. in box. Doz **$8.50**

1F2243—(Mfrs 406) Hook & ladder, 24x6x 7¾, red, reel with imitation hose and brass nozzle, brass bell, 4-section 6 ft. extension ladder. 1 in box. Each **$1.35**

1F2242—(Mfrs 110) Giant steam shovel, 22¾ x7x15½, red & black, revolving engine house, crank lever automatically opens and closes bucket. 1 in box. Each **$1.35**

1F2245—(Mfrs 48) Whippet war tank, 12 in. long, 3-color, strong wheel geared spring motor propels tank under its own power, "safety" brake keeps spring from winding too tight. 1 in box........Each **$2.00**

1F2246—(Mfrs 44) Tractor & trailer, 17x4½ x5, 3-color enameled, steel geared spring, speed control lever. 1 in box. Each **$2.00**

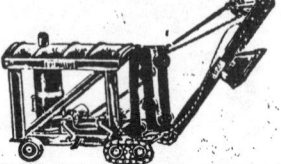

1F2252—(Mfrs 57) Excavator, extreme length 29 in., yellow, blue and black, 12x5½ platform, 15 in. derrick with shovel, 8 in. donkey engine, two 4 in. wood pulleys with chains and crank handles, steel link chain tread, 7 distinct operating features. 1 in box. Each **$3.30**

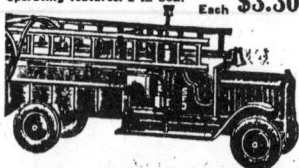

1F2229—(Mfrs 449) Pumping fire engine, 21 x6x8, red body, 4-section, 6 ft. black enameled extension ladder, brass bell, radiator, hub and tank caps, pump, 8 in. yellow water tank, 4½ in. hose with brass nozzle, gilt rail with rear step. Pump action will shoot stream of water 30 ft. 1 in carton. Each **$3.35**

72 Inches Long

1F2249—(Mfrs 56) Dump truck, sand hopper, conveyor & loader, 3-color enameled, 72 in. long, 17 in. high, 10 in. wide, collects and dumps sand into hopper, moves it by conveyor to bins to be screened and separated, very heavy construction, patented steel link chain and dumping device. 1 in carton.................................Each **$3.35**

BUTLER BROTHERS ST LOUIS

81

Structo Toys as shown in a 1929 Butler Bros. Christmas catalog.

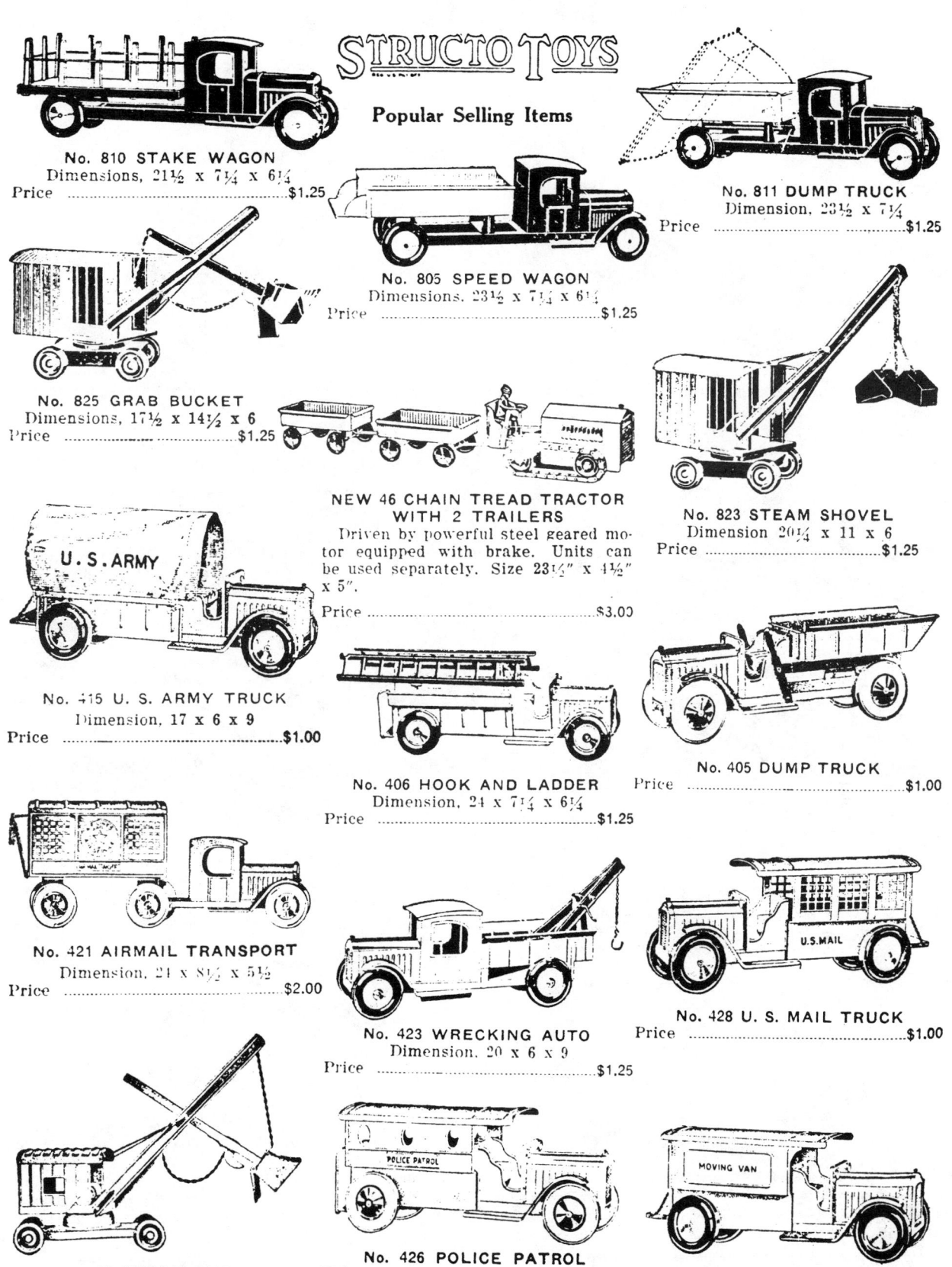

STRUCTO TOYS

Popular Selling Items

No. 810 STAKE WAGON
Dimensions, 21½ x 7¼ x 6¼
Price $1.25

No. 805 SPEED WAGON
Dimensions, 23½ x 7¼ x 6¼
Price $1.25

No. 811 DUMP TRUCK
Dimension, 23½ x 7¼
Price $1.25

No. 825 GRAB BUCKET
Dimensions, 17½ x 14½ x 6
Price $1.25

**NEW 46 CHAIN TREAD TRACTOR
WITH 2 TRAILERS**
Driven by powerful steel geared motor equipped with brake. Units can be used separately. Size 23½" x 4½" x 5".
Price $3.00

No. 823 STEAM SHOVEL
Dimension 20¼ x 11 x 6
Price $1.25

No. 415 U. S. ARMY TRUCK
Dimension, 17 x 6 x 9
Price $1.00

No. 406 HOOK AND LADDER
Dimension, 24 x 7¼ x 6¼
Price $1.25

No. 405 DUMP TRUCK
Price $1.00

No. 421 AIRMAIL TRANSPORT
Dimension, 21 x 8½ x 5½
Price $2.00

No. 423 WRECKING AUTO
Dimension, 20 x 6 x 9
Price $1.25

No. 428 U. S. MAIL TRUCK
Price $1.00

No. 65 STEAM SHOVEL
Price $1.00

No. 426 POLICE PATROL
Price $1.00

No. 427 MOVING VAN
Price $1.00

Structo, circa the early 1930s.

STRUCTO TOYS

The following features are your assurance of their salability:

Solid Rubber Wheels

Plated Hub Caps

Front Bumpers

Two-Time Enamel Finish

Packed in individual corrugated shipping cartons

No. 4122—STRUCTO SAND ELEVATOR AND BIN. Size of elevator 15x5⅜-x16 inches high. Bin is 6x4¼x11¼ inches high. Both pieces made of steel finished in yellow and green. 9 buckets are fastened to the steel chains which is operated by means of a crank. Bin is fitted with hinged gate...Per Doz. $16.00

No. 4124—STRUCTO WRECKER. Extreme length 21¼ inches. Made of heavy steel finished in bright enamel. Truck is fitted with removable crane which is operated by crank and steel chain. Complete with tool box...Per Doz. $16.00

No. 4125—STRUCTO STAKE TRUCK. Length 21¾ inches. Made of heavy sheet steel finished in a combination red and yellow enamel. Stakes are removable to add to its play value.....................Per Doz. $16.00

No. 4126—STRUCTO AERIAL FIRE TRUCK. Length 29½ inches. This sturdy steel toy finished in a combination red and yellow features an automatic coupling mechanism and is fitted with a large bell. Complete with three 18 inch extension ladders...................Per Doz. $24.00

No. 4127—STRUCTO STAKE TRUCK. Length 25 inches. Sturdily made of sheet steel finished in combination red and white enamel. Features an automatic coupling mechanism. The trailer body is fitted with removable stakes and panels...Per Doz. $24.00

No. 4128—STRUCTO TRUCK AND STEAM SHOVEL. Size when in operation, 32 inches long. Truck size 22½ inches long. Steam shovel 21 inches long. Truck is equipped with removable loading skid, crank and steel chain winding mechanism which is controlled by a ratchet and dog. Steam shovel fitted with automatic opening shovel......Per Doz. $36.00

No. 4129—STRUCTO HI-WAY TRANSPORT. Extreme length 30½ inches. This big, sturdy transport is fitted with automatic coupling mechanism hinged tail gate with steel chain lock and the heavy gauge top is removable for added play value. Finished in two-tone blue and yellow. Per doz. $36.00

No. 4130—STRUCTO THREE-PIECE TRANSPORT UNIT. Truck is 15¾ inches long, Van Trailer is 19½ inches long and the Delivery Trailer is 12¼ inches long. The complete unit is made of heavy steel finished in red and white. Truck is equipped with automatic coupling device. Van Trailer has drop tail gate and steel chain lock. Panel and stakes are removable from delivery trailer.........................Per Doz. $42.00

No. 4131—STRUCTO PUMPING FIRE ENGINE. Extreme length 26 inches. A bright red pumper with plenty of action. It is fitted with a real pressure pump which throws a stream of water 25 feet. Water tank with a capacity of 1½ quarts, 2 ft. fire hose with real brass nozzle, hose reel for winding hose, two 15 inch extension ladders, fire extinguishers and two fire axes. When truck is in motion, gong rings automatically. Per doz. $48.00

PRICES SUBJECT TO CHANGE WITHOUT NOTICE

Structo Toys as shown in a 1940-41 L. Gould catalog.

	C6	C8	C10
Structo No. 704 Grain Trailer, early and mid-1950s (replaced Freight Trailer)	100	150	200
Structo No. 706 Auto Transport Trailer, sold 1953-54, with cars	110	165	220
Structo No. 708 Cattle Trailer	65	98	130
Structo No. 811 Barrel Truck windup, early 1950s	600	900	1200

	C6	C8	C10
Structo No. 822 Wrecker Truck, windup, early-mid 1950s	68	102	135
Structo 844 Hi-Lift Dump, windup, early 1950s	85	128	170
Structo 866 Gasoline Truck, windup, early 1950s	260	390	520
Structo 902 Aerial Ladder Truck	100	150	200
Structo 940 Log Truck	120	180	240

STURDIBILT

	C6	C8	C10
Sturdibilt Logging Truck (Oregon)	325	510	650

STURDITOY

The Sturdy Corporation of Providence and Pawtucket, Rhode Island, manufactured its steel toy trucks from about 1929 to 1933.

	C6	C8	C10
Sturditoy Ambulance, 26" long, open cab, c.1926	2000	3500	5000
Sturditoy American LaFrance Water Tower Fire Truck, 34"	1000	1800	2750
Sturditoy American Railway Express Truck, c.1920s, 26" long	1000	1500	2200
Sturditoy Armored Truck, 24" long	2200	3700	5500
Sturditoy Coal Dump Truck, 1920s, 25" long	1200	2000	2900

	C6	C8	C10
Sturditoy Coal Truck, 26" long	1400	2300	3200
Sturditoy Coal Truck, high-sided, 27" long	1400	2350	3300
Sturditoy Dairy Truck, 34" long	1700	3000	4200
Sturditoy Dairy Truck, 25" long	600	1000	1400
Sturditoy Delivery Truck, 1920s, 26" long	1200	2000	3500
Sturditoy Dump Truck, 1920s, 25" long	800	1300	1800
Sturditoy Dump Truck, 1920s, 26-1/2" long	500	800	1200

Sturditoy Coal Dump Truck, 1920s. Photo by Tim Oei.

Sturditoy Coal Truck, 1920s, 25" long. Courtesy Bill Bertoia Auctions. Photo by Jeanne Bertoia.

Sturditoy Dairy Truck, 34" long. Courtesy Bill Bertoia Auctions. Photo by Jeanne Bertoia.

"Sturditoy Oil Company" tanker. Photo by Tim Oei.

	C6	C8	C10
Sturditoy Huckster Truck, 27" long	450	700	1000
"Sturditoy Oil Company" Tanker, 27" long	1100	1800	2500
Sturditoy Police Patrol, 26" long	1100	1800	2500
Sturditoy Pumper, 26" long, c.1930	1100	1800	2500
Sturditoy Sand & Gravel Truck	900	1600	2000
Sturditoy Side Dump, 26-1/2" long	1100	1800	2530
Sturditoy Steam Shovel, 26" long	162	243	325
Sturditoy Tanker, 15" long	2000	3500	7500

	C6	C8	C10
Sturditoy Traveling Store 26" long	1800	2900	4200
"Sturditoy Trucking Co.," 24" long	1150	1800	2600
Sturditoy "U.S. Army" Truck, 26" long	550	850	1300
Sturditoy U.S. Mail Screenside Truck	1200	2000	2725
Sturditoy "Wells Fargo" Armored Truck, 24" long, c.1927	900	1700	2500
Sturditoy Water Tower	1500	2500	3500
Sturditoy Wrecker, 30" long	1000	1650	2750

Sturditoy Pumper, 26" long, c.1930. Courtesy Bill Bertoia Auctions. Photo by Jeanne Bertoia.

Sturditoy Police Patrol. Photo by Calvin L. Chaussee.

Sturditoy Oil Tanker, 27" long (truck in photo restored). Courtesy Bill Bertoia Auctions. Photo by Jeanne Bertoia.

Sturditoy Traveling Store, 26" long. Courtesy Bill Bertoia Auctions. Photo by Jeanne Bertoia.

Sturditoy "U.S. Army" truck (canvas replaced). Photo by Tim Oei.

Sturditoy Wrecker, 30" long (tow line & hook missing in photo). Courtesy Bill Bertoia Auctions. Photo by Jeanne Bertoia.

SUN RUBBER

Sun Rubber of Barberton, Ohio, was founded in 1923. Toymaking started in 1924 and autos were introduced in April, 1935. The owner was Tom W. Smith Jr. (List by Dave Leopard).

	C6	C8	C10
SA01 Coupe, external exhaust pipes, from 1936, 4" long, No. 515	20	30	40
SA02 '34 DeSoto Airflow, 4-door sedan, 4" long, No. 500	20	30	40
SA03 '40 Dodge, 4-door Sedan, 4-1/2" long No. 12001	20	30	40

	C6	C8	C10
SA04 c.1936 "Teardrop" Sedan, 5-1/2" long, No. 1010 (1936)	25	35	55
SA05 Art Deco Housetrailer, fits SA04, 4-3/8" long, No. 1025	50	75	100
SA06 Town Car, Brewster type limo, exposed driver, 5-3/8" long, No. 1015	25	45	65
SA07 Station Wagon, woody, mid-30s. 3-3/4" long, No. 12007	20	30	40
ST01 Pickup Truck, stake sides, streamlined, 4-1/2" long, No. 510	22	33	45
ST02 Open Truck, stake sides, streamlined (White?), 5 -1/4" long, No. 1005	25	38	50
ST03 Tractor/trailer, one-piece, 3 axles, futuristic, 5-1/8" long, No. 12013	20	30	40
ST04 Open Truck, futuristic, 4-1/2" long, No. 12003	21	31	42

Sun Rubber SA01, in postwar (two-toned) and prewar (solid color) versions. Courtesy Dave Leopard from his book Rubber Toy Vehicles.

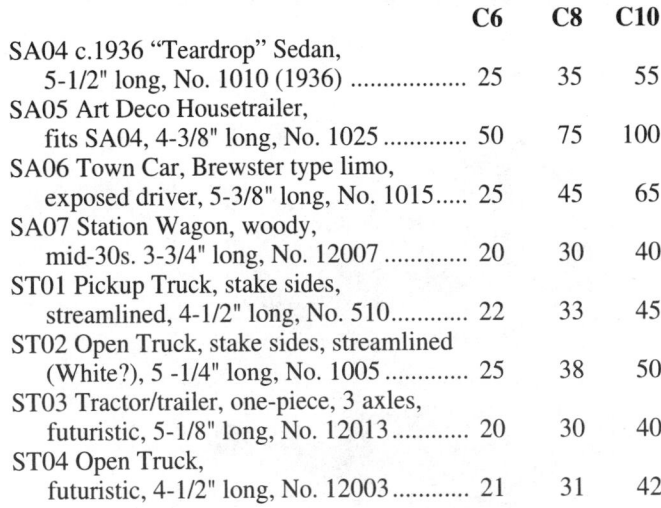

Sun Rubber SA02. Courtesy Dave Leopard from his book Rubber Toy Vehicles.

Sun Rubber SA03. Courtesy Dave Leopard from his book Rubber Toy Vehicles.

Sun Rubber SA04. Photo by Dave Leopard.

Sun Rubber SA05. Courtesy Dave Leopard from his book Rubber Toy Vehicles.

 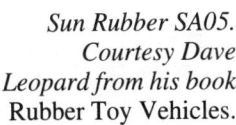

Sun Rubber SA06. Photo by K. Warren Mitchell.

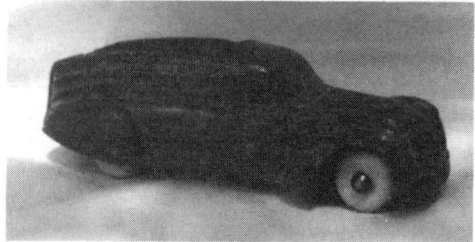

Sun Rubber ST01. Photo by Dave Leopard.

Sun Rubber SA07 in its civilian (left) and military versions. Courtesy Dave Leopard from his book Rubber Toy Vehicles.

Sun Rubber ST02. Courtesy Dave Leopard from his book Rubber Toy Vehicles.

Sun Rubber ST03. Courtesy Dave Leopard from his book Rubber Toy Vehicles.

Sun Rubber, L to R: ST04, ST05. Photo by Dave Leopard.

Sun Rubber ST07 (Leopard's ST06). Courtesy Dave Leopard from his book Rubber Toy Vehicles.

Sun Rubber, L to R: ST08 (Leopard's ST07), ST08A. Courtesy Dave Leopard from his book Rubber Toy Vehicles.

Sun Rubber, L to R: ST08A, ST04A. Photo by Ed Poole.

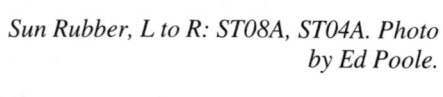

	C6	C8	C10
ST04A as above, "U.S. Army"	20	30	40
ST05 Open "Master" Truck, futuristic, 5-5/8" long, No. 12111	22	33	45
ST06 Unused.			
ST07 '36 White Bus, streamlined, 4-1/4" long, No. 520 (1936)	35	52	70
ST08 Ambulance, c.late 1930s, 3-3/4" long, No. 12006	20	30	40
ST08A Ambulance, military paint	21	31	42
SR01 Open Racer, 2 drivers, 4-3/8" long, No. 505 (1936)	20	30	40
SR02 Open Racer, full fenders on rear, 6 -1/2" long, No. 1000 (1936)	30	45	60

	C6	C8	C10
SR03 Open Racer, boat tail, "Super" racer, 6-3/4" long, No. 12012	25	40	55
SM01 Tank, revolving turret and gunner, 6" long, No. 12015 (1946)	50	75	100
SM02 Scout Car, 4 gunners, 6-3/4" long, No. 12014 (1946), with or without front winch (made both ways)	25	38	50
SD01 Mickey Mouse and Donald Duck Fire Truck, No. 12017	75	112	150
SD02 Mickey Mouse Tractor No. 12020	65	98	130
SD03 Donald Duck Roadster, with Pluto	80	120	160
SD04 Donald Duck Tractor	112	188	225

Sun Rubber SR01. Courtesy Dave Leopard from his book Rubber Toy Vehicles.

Sun Rubber SR02. Courtesy Dave Leopard from his book Rubber Toy Vehicles.

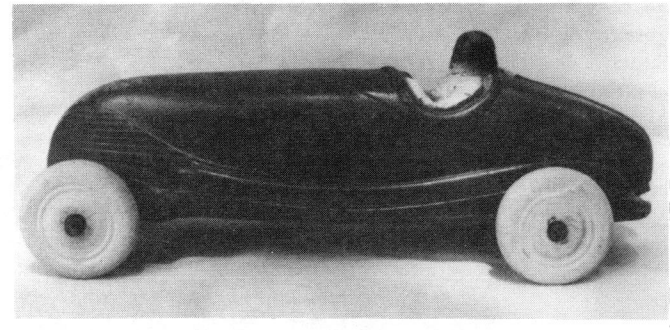

Sun Rubber SR03. Photo by Dave Leopard.

Sun Rubber, L to R: SM02, SM01. Photo by Ed Poole.

Sun Rubber SD01

Sun Rubber SD02

Sun Rubber SD03. Photo by Dave Leopard.

	C6	C8	C10
Superior Circus Truck	88	132	175
Superior Dump Truck	40	60	80
Superior "Fire Chief" Car, w/driver	32	48	65
Superior Service Station, metal, 1950s	188	282	375

Superior Service Station; value in Good $65. Photo by Ron Fink.

Superior "Garage Entrance" Service Station; value in Good $100. Photo by Ron Fink.

Superior "Sales Service" station; value in Good $150. Photo by Ron Fink.

TCO

(Germany)

Policeman on Motorcycle, tin litho windup, 11" long	185	278	370

TECHNOFIX

(US Zone, Germany)

	C6	C8	C10
Technofix Racer Motorcycle			
No. 4, 7" long tin windup	125	175	250
Technofix Racer Motorcycle			
No. 15, 7" long tin windup	125	175	250

Technofix Racer Motorcycles, L to R:
No. 15, No. 4. Photo by Kent M. Comstock.

TED TOYS

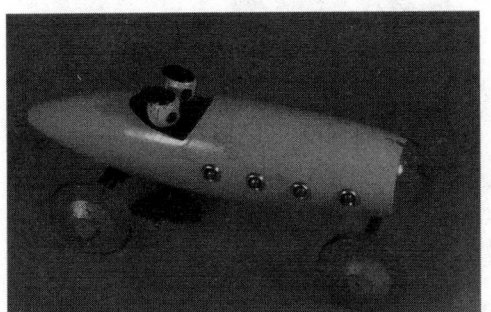

	C6	C8	C10
Racer, wood, 2 riders, pull toy	125	188	250

Ted Toys Racer, wood, two riders,
pull toy. Photo by Perry R. Eichor.

THIMBLE DROME

	C6	C8	C10
Thimble Drome(Roy			
Cox) Champion Racer	288	432	575
Thimble Drome Prop Rod	68	102	135
Thimble Drome Racer, pusher	170	255	340
Thimble Drome Racer No. 25....................	188	282	375
Thimble Drome Racer with engine	275	363	550
Thimble Drome Special wind-up	400	600	800
Thimble Drome			
Special No. 2 Pusher, 8" long	138	205	275
Thimble Drome			
Special No. 28, w/motor	275	413	550
Thimble Drome No. 81	225	338	450

Advertisement for Thimble Drome

Roy Cox
THIMBLE DROME
Race Car

304-CT THIMBLE DROME CHAMPION
TETHER MODEL. ... CHAMPION
Racer, equipped ...
and Ten Feet of C... Each

THIMBLE DROME DE LUXE
... sational Seller, Chrome Ex...
... Polished Disc Wheels...
... Rubber Tires, & Color Combina...
... contrasting numerals.
L 8" W 4" H 3"
Individually Boxed. 1 lb. Each

THIMBLE DROME STANDARD. Same
... Aluminum Body and Detail less
... Solid Colors instead of 2...
... tion.
L 8" W 4" H 3"
Individually Boxed. 1 lb. Each

Advertisement for Thimble Drome

THOMAS TOYS

Thomas Toys was owned from first to last by Islyn Thomas, (5/27/12-), who founded the company in 1944, after leaving his post as general manager of the Ideal Toy Company. According to Thomas, its first toys—jeeps, planes, and vinyl dolls—were produced that year. The firm was located from first to last at 80 Clinton St., Newark, New Jersey. It made only toys, and at its peak had 350 employees. It was also tied to Acme, in the sense that Acme's Ben Shapiro was a financial partner, and Thomas made up toys at his request with the Acme imprint substituted for that of Thomas. When Thomas sent the author his company's order sheets, some were printed in Acme's name, with Thomas indicating in handwriting to the author that they were Thomas', as well. In addition, on at least one Thomas page, "Acme" can be clearly seen on the hoods of two trucks. Acme and Thomas sometimes, perhaps always, shared the same catalog art. Sometimes, but not always, even their order numbers coincided.

The company's molds, and perhaps some of its sculpting, were provided by Richard Koegl (perhaps Koegel), whose Koegl stampworks were in Newark. Sculpting of some of Thomas' finer-detailed toys, such as its lines of small babies, dolls, and civilians, were done by a "Mr. Kaiser." In 1960, Thomas, aware of the impending impact of new, low-priced Japanese imports, sold out to Banner Plastics. Thomas then became an international plastics consultant, which remains his profession.

Thomas was made a member of the Plastics Hall of Fame in 1977 (the presentation made by President Ford). He was also made an Officer of the British Empire by Queen Elizabeth. He had served as chief engineer for the plastic parts in the Spitfire's Merlin engine (which was made in the United States) and in the immediate post-war period, heading Thomas Engineering Company, he had helped restore the ravaged European community by setting up a number of companies in England and the continent. One of these was the toy company Popular Playthings in Wales, of which he was half-owner for a while. This was founded in 1945 and continues in business today. Thomas is also the author of the books *Our Welsh Heritage, Injection Molding of Plastics* (Reinhold Publishing Corp.) and many technical articles.

The following listing was prepared by the author from the order sheets Islyn Thomas sent him. It is not necessarily complete. Thomas had at least three different numbering systems over the years, with the same items having their numbers changed as time went on. All of the items have been listed in numerical order, with an alphabetical code preceding them where it applies. Those with a "TMC" preceding the number appear to be the earliest, those with a "T" next, and those without a code the latest. Where toys appeared on dated sheets, the date is given in parentheses.

Islyn Thomas

	C6	C8	C10
TMC-9 Streamlined Truck, 5" long (1949)	10	12	14
TMC-10 Jeep, 4-1/4" long (1949)	15	20	27
TMC-10 Jeep & Driver, driver is khaki soldier, jeep red, blue or green	12	14	16
TMC-13 Trailer, 4" long, for jeep (1949)	4	6	8
TMC-17 Same as T-17			
T-17 Streamlined Buick Sedan, 4-5/16" long, appears in 1949 as TMC-17 and in 1947 Acme catalog sheet	16	19	22
T-18 Wrecker, 5" long	25	35	45
No. 18 Same as TMC-9, listed in 1955 as No. 18			
TMC-19 Airline Limousine, 4-1/2" long (1949)	15	20	27
No. 19 Jeep & Trailer, 8-3/8" long, with yellow driver in GI helmet (1954)	14	16	18
No. 19 Jeep & Trailer, 8-3/8" long, yellow civilian driver, otherwise same as above	14	16	18
No. 24 Sport Convertible & Sedan, each 4-1/4" long (1955), set consists of numbers 77 and 77S.	20	24	28
TMC-25 Limousine (TMC-19) & Trailer (TMC-40), 6-3/4" long, (1949)	25	30	36
No. 25 Sedan w/Canoe & Polyethylene House Trailer, overall length 9-1/2" (1955)	30	35	40

	C6	C8	C10
No. 26 Truck Wrecker, 5" long	35	40	45
No. 30 Coupe & House Trailer, 8-1/4" long	20	22	24
TMC-32 Dump Truck, 5" long (also in 1947 Acme order sheet)	12	14	16
TMC-40 Utility Trailer, 2-1/2" long (1949) ...	6	8	10
No. 40 Texaco Gas Truck, 4" long	15	20	25
No. 41 Delivery Truck, 4" long	15	18	20
No. 43 Esso Gas Truck (Acme's 1947 numbering. Doesn't turn up in known Thomas order sheets, but presumably was sold by Thomas Toys)	No Price Found		
TMC-51 Jeep (TMC-10) and Trailer (TMC-13), (1949), 8-1/2" long	14	16	18
TMC-53 Truck (TMC-9) & Trailer (TMC-13), (1949), 9" long overall	14	16	18
T-66 Same as No. 67			
No. 67 Police-Fire Chief Radio Car, each 4-1/2" long, price per each	15	20	27
No. 72 Plastic Motorcycle & Rider, 4" long	35	45	55
No. 74 Merry-Go-Round Truck, 4-3/4" long	20	25	30
No. 77 Convertible Coupe & Driver, 4-1/2" long (1953, 1954)	9	11	13
No. 77C Same as No. 77. Sold with or without driver under the same number			
No. 77S Streamlined Sedan, 4-1/2" long	11	13	15
T-79 Convertible Coupe (or Sedan), 4-1/2" long (Same as No. 77 and No. 77S)			
T-89, Same as No. 74			
No. 107 Military Policeman & Motorcycle (with detachable Policeman), 4" long	20	25	30

No. 107 Military Policeman & Motorcycle
(with detachable Policeman)

	C6	C8	C10
T-110 Same as No. 168, but plated	No Price Found		
T-114 Road Roller (Self Winding), 4-1/2" long, with ivory driver (1953)	No Price Found		
No. 125 Same as No. 168, but plated	No Price Found		
No. 126 Same as T-114			
No. 128 Taxi, 4-1/2" long (1953)	22	33	45
No. 131 Car & House Trailer, overall length 9-1/2"	25	30	35
No. 132 Truck & Racer, 4" long	No Price Found		

	C6	C8	C10
No. 134 Same as No. 257			
No. 135 Repair Truck (with detachable ladder), (1953), 4" long	15	20	27
No. 139 Same as T-148			
T-140 Same as No. 131			
T-141 Same as No. 132			
T-144 Same as No. 257			
T-145 Same as No. 135 (both 1953)			
T-148 Tow Truck, 4" long, 1953	8	10	12
No. 148 Truck & Air Compressor, 8-1/2" long	14	16	18
T-152 (1953) Same as No. 148			
No. 160 International Racer, 5" long (1955), sold with & without driver, same number	30	35	40
No. 162 Servi-Car (Driver not included), 4-1/2" long	25	30	35
No. 168 Solo Motorcycle (Driver not included), 4" long	20	25	30
No. 170 Motorcycle & Sidecar with passenger, 4" long (yellow girl passenger, no driver)	No Price Found		
T-171 Same as No. 162			
T-174 Large Tow Truck, 5-1/2" long	12	14	16
No. 175-6 Police & Fire Chief Radio Cars, each 4-1/2" long, price per each	11	13	15
No. 177 Large Tow Truck, 5-1/2" long	12	14	16
T-179 Motorcycle, 4" long	20	25	30
No. 183 Army Jeep and Trailer (with Driver) 8-3/4" long	14	16	18
No. 184-5 Army Radar & Tow Trucks, each 4" long (may be the same as T-192/3) price per each	16	20	24
No. 188 Military Police Jeep w/3 MPs (1955, 1956), 4-1/4" long	11	13	15
No. 189 Maintenance Truck, 5-1/2" long, with detachable ladders	No Price Found		
T-192/3 Army Radar & Tow Trucks, each 4" long, olive drab (may be the same as No. 184-5)	No Price Found		
No. 196 Army Road Roller (self-winding) 4-1/2" long	No Price Found		
T-205 Army Jeep & Driver. Same as T-10, but all khaki	No Price Found		
T-209 Same as No. 189 (1953)			
T-209 Army Maintenance Truck (with detachable ladders), 5-1/2" long, olive drab (crane may differ from No. 189's) ...	No Price Found		
No. 212 Plated Two-Tone Racer with Driver, 5" long (same No. 160 except top half is Special Silver Metal Plated)	No Price Found		
T-215 Army Road Roller (same as No. 196)			
No. 222 Mobile Searchlight Unit, 15-1/2" overall length, uses batteries	100	120	140
No. 222 Mobile Searchlight Unit with Friction Motor, overall length 15-1/2", uses batteries (1954). Same number as above, but also slight variations	55	65	75
T-223 Same as No. 77 (both in 1953)			
No. 234 Gas & Delivery Trucks with Trailers, overall length 6-1/4", per each	14	16	18
No. 237 Motorcycle & Side-Car, 4" long (1955) same as No. 170, but no passenger	No Price Found		

	C6	C8	C10

T-242 Same as non-friction-motor
No. 222

No. 245 Limousine & Trailer
w/luggage & rack, assembly kit (1955) .... No Price Found

No. 254 Polyethylene TV Truck
w/ladder, 4" long (1955) .... No Price Found

No. 257 Polyethylene
Sound Truck, 4" long, (1955) 30   35   40

No. 261 Vespa Motor Scooter, 4" long (1955)   No Price Found

No. 267 Truck & Polyethylene
Trailer, 6-1/4" long overall (1955) .... No Price Found

No. 289 Jet Hot Rod,
5-1/2" long (1955) .... No Price Found

No. 299 Searchlight Truck w/Friction
Motor Assembly Kit (1955) .... No Price Found

No. 303 Ferguson Tractor
Assembly Kit (1955) .... No Price Found

No. 334 Electronic Airport Traffic
Control Set (1956), contains plane,
"Flash" Truck with Signal Light,
"Radar" Truck with Signal Buzzer,
remote control Morse Code Unit .... No Price Found

No. 360 Indianapolis Speed Race,
2 racers with drivers, spring-action
mechanism, (1956) .... No Price Found

No. 369 Radar Signal Set-4 radar
vehicles (1956) .... No Price Found

No. 449 Lumberyard Express,
trailer has retractable wheels .... No Price Found

No. 457 Jet Car .... No Price Found

Thomas Toys No. 457 Jet Car. Courtesy Islyn Thomas.

	C6	C8	C10

No. 519 Sport Car Transport, 23-1/2" long
when boxed, four sports cars included
from Jaguar, Mercedes-Benz, Thunderbird,
Alfa Romeo, Talbot, Corvette .... No Price Found

No. 520 Overland Express
Van, 21-5/8" when boxed .... No Price Found

No. 521 Cabin Cruiser and Trailer, 22-7/8" long
when boxed, 56 put-together parts .... No Price Found

No. 522 Jeep & Horse Trailer Set,
18-7/8" long when boxed, includes
doll family, pet, table, and bench .... No Price Found

No. 524 Animal Transport, 21-1/8" long
when boxed. No animals included .... No Price Found

No. 545 Speed Boat, Jeep & Trailer,
with boat driver. Outboard motor is
rubber-band propelled .... No Price Found

No. 558 Auto and Horse
Trailer, 7-1/2" long bagged .... No Price Found

No. 566 Military Set. Jeep,
Howitzer, 4 Soldiers .... No Price Found

No. 572 Assorted 6" Sport
Cars. Pkg. 5-1/8"x9" .... No Price Found

No. 576 International Sport Cars, same
as No. 581, except packed 3 dozen in plain box

No. 579 Authentic 8" Jeep. Spare tire,
moveable windshield, no driver .... No Price Found

No. 580 8" Jeep and Driver,
moveable windshield, spare tire .... No Price Found

No. 581 Chest of Sport Cars. Contains
6 Dozen "All-Poly Cars" in 6 styles:
Jaguar, Mercedes-Benz, Thunderbird,
Talbot, Corvette, Alfa Romeo .... No Price Found

No. 592 Stake Trailer Truck,
24-1/2" long when bagged
(probably the same as No. 524) .... No Price Found

No. 597 Van Trailer Truck,
24-1/2" long when bagged .... No Price Found

No. 604 Same as T-114.

No. 607 Auto Transport, 24-1/2" long
when bagged. Trailer loaded with
any four of these Sports Cars;
Jaguar, Mercedes-Benz, Thunderbird,
Alfa Romeo, Talbot, Corvette .... No Price Found

No. 614 Assortment of 8" Authentic
All-Poly Ack-Ack & Searchlight
Jeeps, Price per each 8   10   12

No. 635 Sight-Seeing Bus .... No Price Found

No. 638 Same as No. 25, but in blister pack

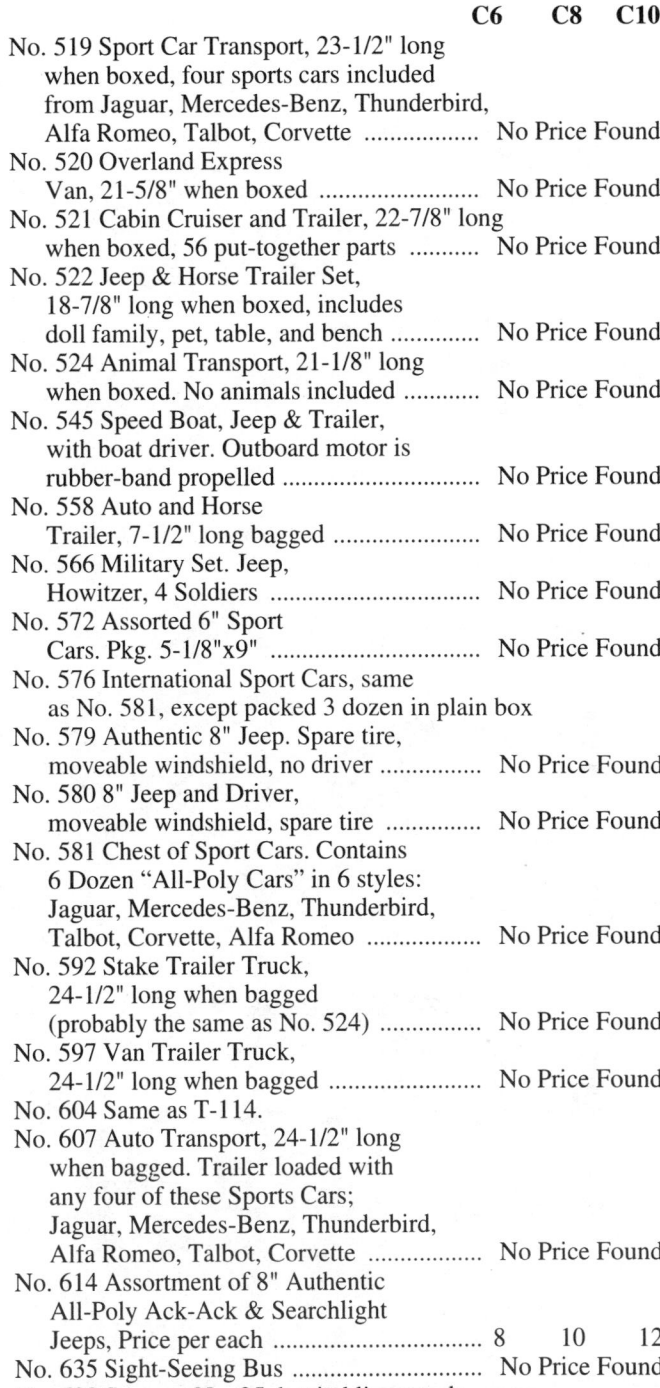

No. 566 Military Set

T-18 Wrecker, 5" long, 2-1/8" wide, 2-3/8" high

No. 26 Truck Wrecker

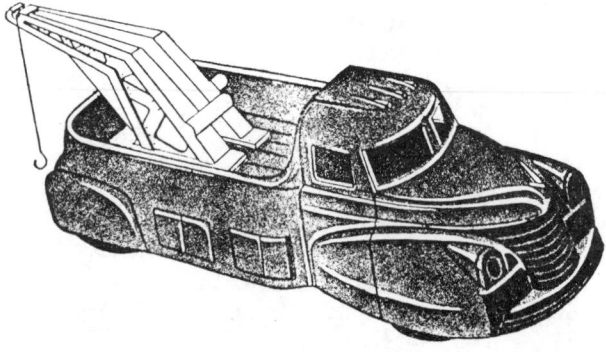

T-148 Tow Truck

No. 177 Large Tow Truck

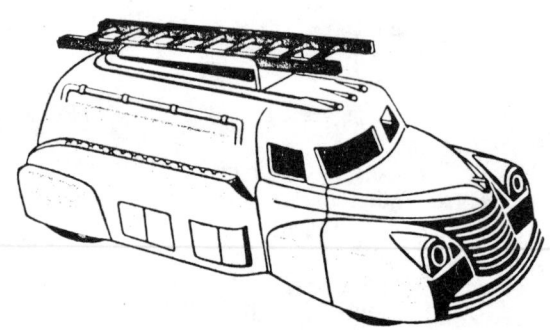

No. 135 Repair Truck

No. 189 Maintenance Truck (with detachable ladders)

No. 449

No. 25 Sedan w/Canoe & Polyethylene House Trailer

No. 30 Coupe & House Trailer

No. 131 Car & House Trailer

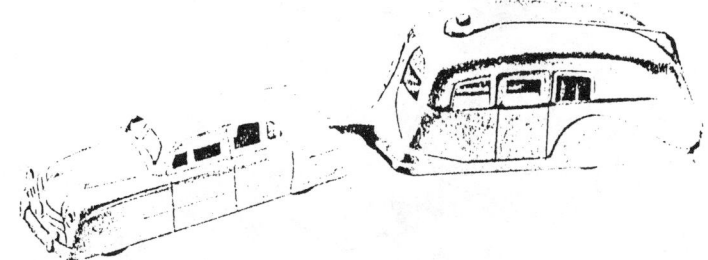

T-140 Car & House Trailer

No. 245 Limousine & Trailer
w/luggage & rack (Boxed)

No. 558

No. 522 Jeep and House Trailer Set

No. 72 Plastic Motorcycle & Rider

No. 107 Motorcycle & Policeman

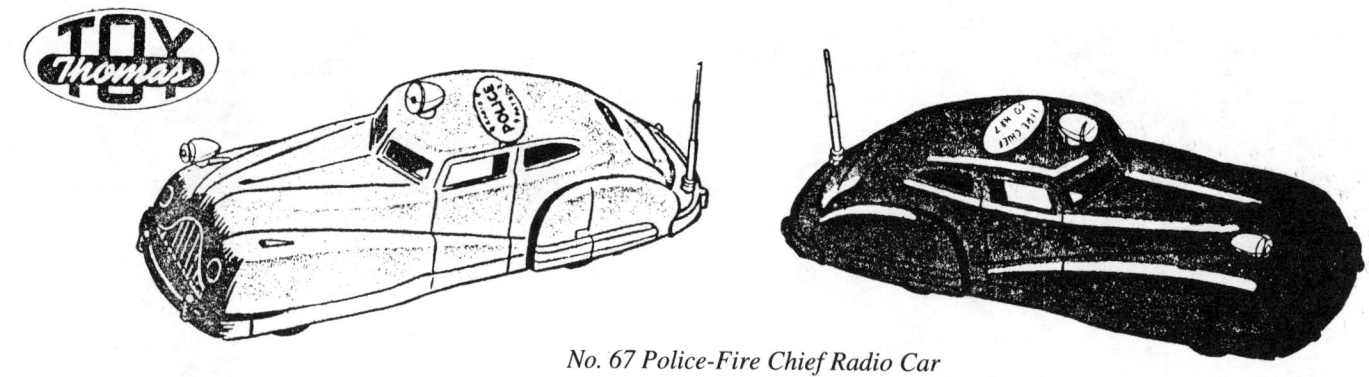

No. 67 Police-Fire Chief Radio Car

No. 128 Taxi

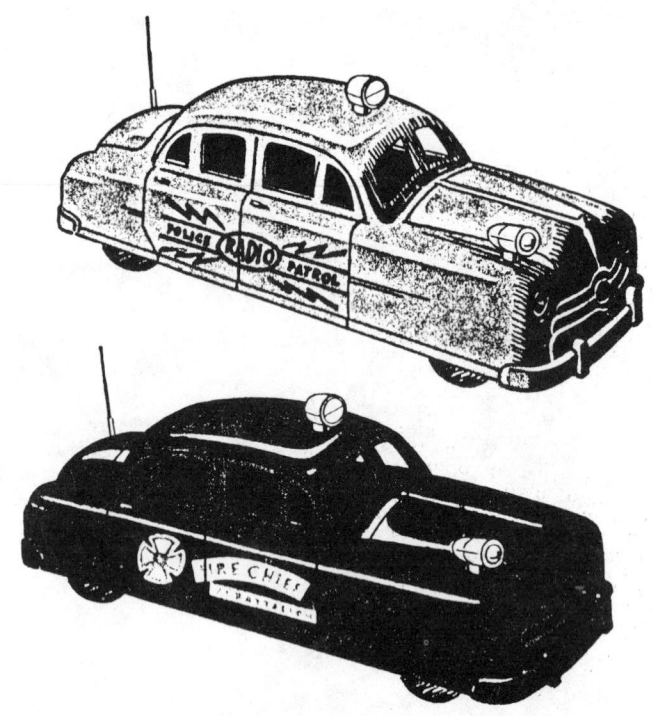

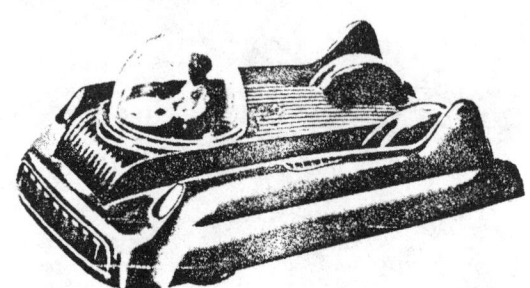

No. 289 Jet Hot Rod

No. 175-6 Police & Fire Chief Radio Cars (50% each model)

No. 572

No. 576

T-114 Road Roller

No. 303 Ferguson Tractor (Boxed)

No. 545 Speed Boat, Jeep & Trailer

No. 635

T-10 Jeep & Driver

No. 183 Army Jeep and Trailer (with driver)

No. 74 Merry-Go-Round Truck

No. 162 Servi-Car (Driver not included)

No. 170 Motorcycle & Sidecar with passenger
4" long, 3-1/2" wide, 2" high. Asst Colors: Metallic Silver and
Blue, Red with Yellow Wheels and Yellow Girl Passenger

No. 261 Vespa Motor Scooter

No. 132 Truck & Racer

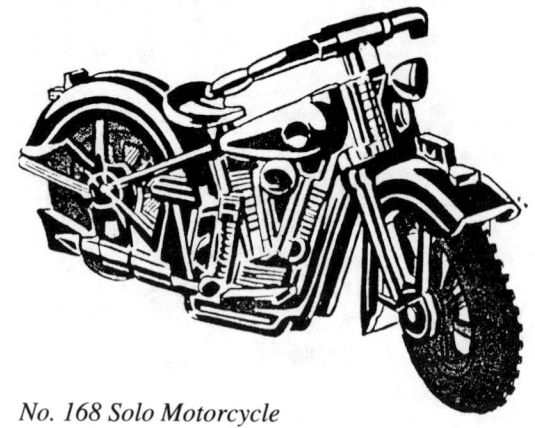

No. 168 Solo Motorcycle

T-179 Motorcycle

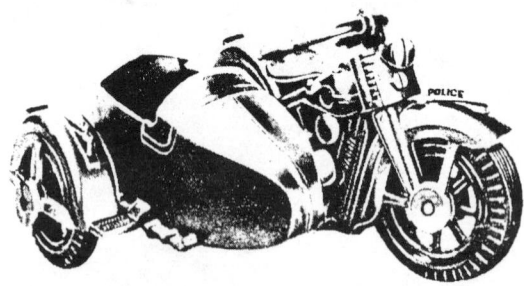

No. 237 Motorcycle & Sidecar

No. 160 International Racer & Driver

No. 267 Truck & Polyethylene Trailer

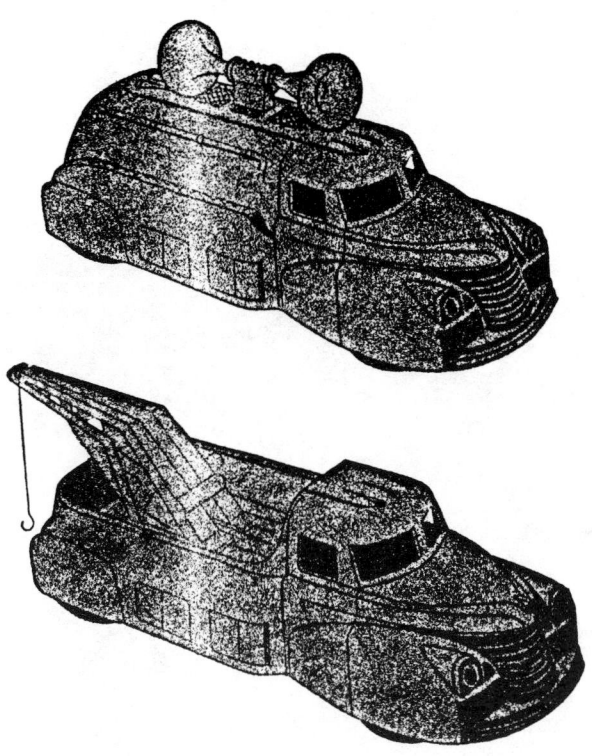

No. 188 Military Police Jeep w/3 MPs

No. 184-5 Army Radar & tow trucks

No. 189 Army Maintenance Truck (with detachable ladders)

T-192/3 Army Radar & Tow Trucks

No. 196 Army Road Roller (Self-Winding)

T-209 Army Maintenance Truck (with detachable ladders).

No. 222 Mobile Searchlight Unit (Boxed)

No. 22 Mobile Searchlight Unit with Friction Motor (Boxed)

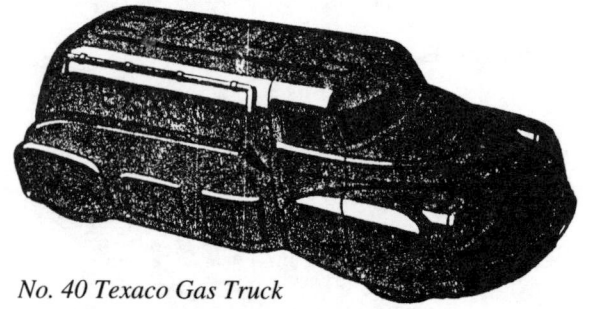

No. 40 Texaco Gas Truck

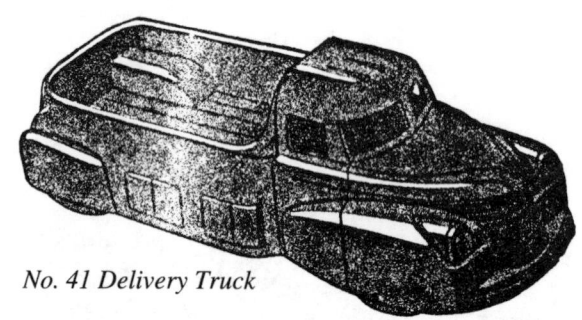

No. 41 Delivery Truck

No. 257 Polyethylene Stound Truck

**No. 579
Authentic 8″ Jeep
Bulk**
- Assorted Red and Blue
- All-Poly Jeep with Realistic Plastic Wheels on Free-Running Steel Axles
- Spare Tire and Movable Windshield

Retail .... **59¢**

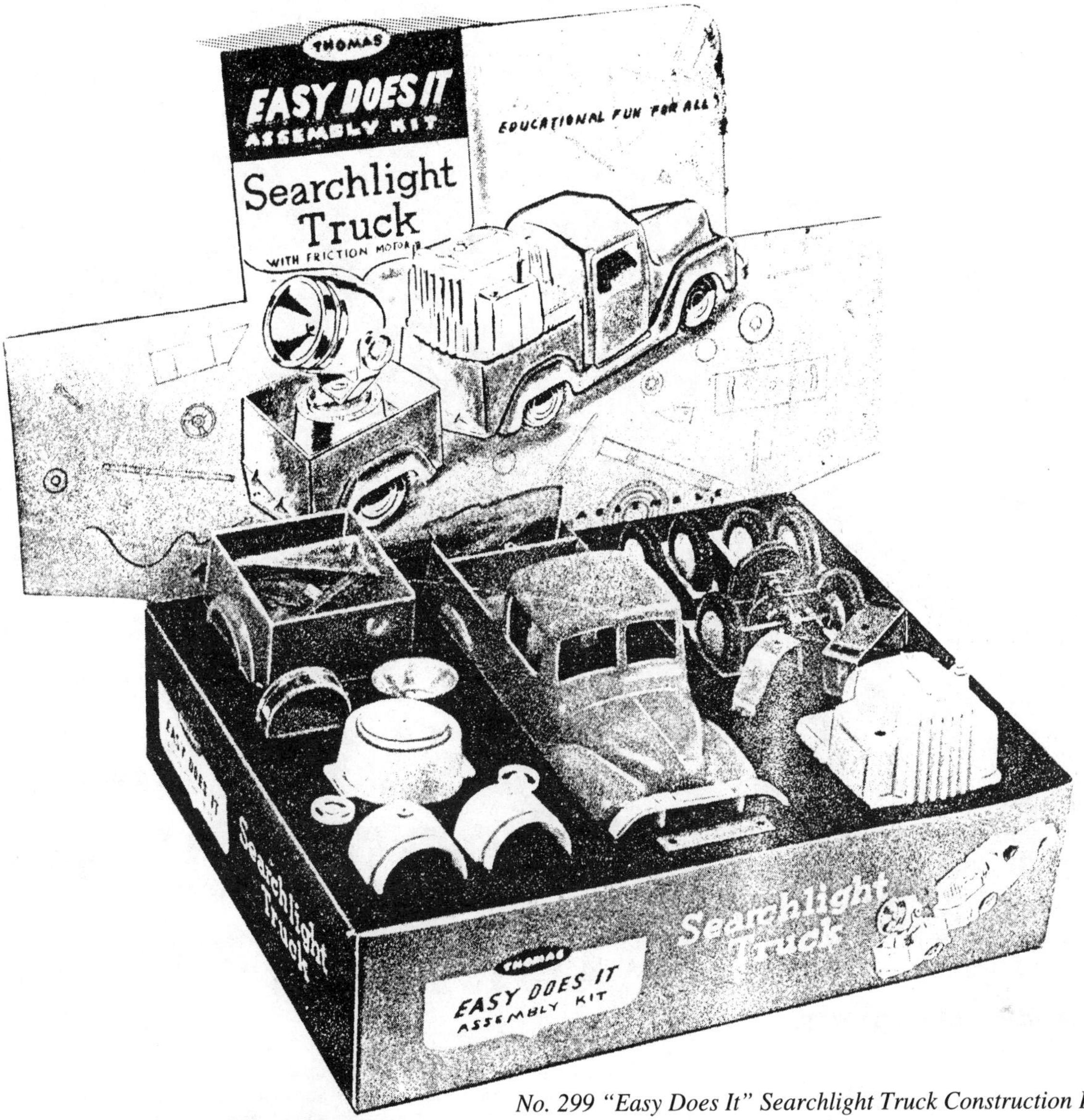

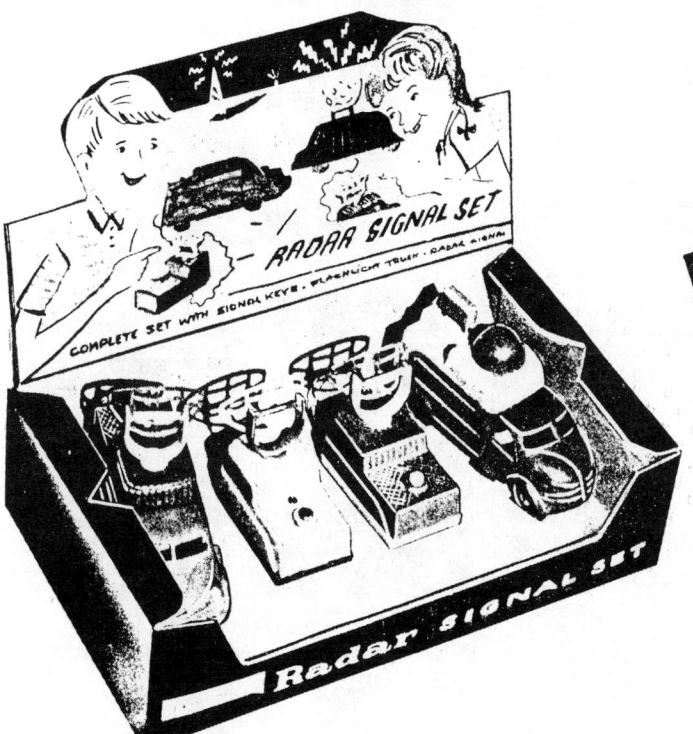

No. 299 "Easy Does It" Searchlight Truck Construction Kit

NEW !

RADAR SIGNAL SET
(Boxed)
Item No. 369
Size: 12" x 7" x 3" overall
Packed: 1 dozen to carton
Weight: 10 bs.   I
Suggested retail: $1.98

Inspired by America's Playtime "Pilots"

SUGGESTED $2⁹⁸ RETAIL

- BIG 13" SUPER CONSTELLA-TION with both Signal Light Flasher and Code Buzzer.
- "FLASHER" TRUCK WITH SIGNAL LIGHT.
- "RADAR" TRUCK WITH SIGNAL BUZZER.
- BATTERY POWERED REMOTE CONTROL UNIT.
- INTERNATIONAL MORSE CODE.

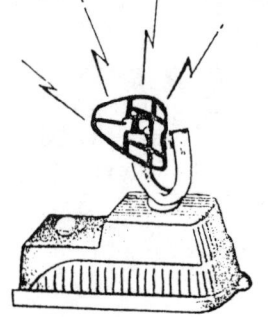

THOMAS' ELECTRONIC AIRPORT TRAFFIC CONTROL SET

Here's an intriguing new action toy by THOMAS that's really different. There may be other toy planes, but only THOMAS' Replica of the Lockheed Super Constellation has electronic code signalling "flashing" light and "radar" buzzer.

There may be other "communication" trucks, but only THOMAS' mobile units have electronic code "flashing" light and "radar signalling buzzer.

And to top it off — nobody but THOMAS has a battery powered remote control unit for secret code communication between plane and trucks.

Yes, this new item, another THOMAS educational toy for children 4 to 12, is extraordinary in ACTION . . . PLAY APPEAL . . . and VALUE.

ORDER NOW! ITEM NO. 334

(Boxed)
SIZE: 12" x 19" x 2½" overall
PACKED: 1 dozen to carton
WEIGHT: 25 lbs.

It's a THOMAS Toy!

MARK OF QUALITY

THOMAS
MANUFACTURING CORP.
80 CLINTON STREET, NEWARK 5, N. J.
Showroom: 200 Fifth Avenue, New York 10, N. Y.

Export Sales Agents: GUITERMAN COMPANY INC.
35 S. William Street, New York 4, New York, U.S.A.

No. 334

PUSH THE BUTTON **SEE WHO WINS THE RACE!**

POWERFUL SPRING ACTION MECHANISM

INDIANAPOLIS
SPEED RACE
WITH AUTOMATIC STARTER

69¢

THOMAS MANUFACTURING CORP. NEWARK

No. 360

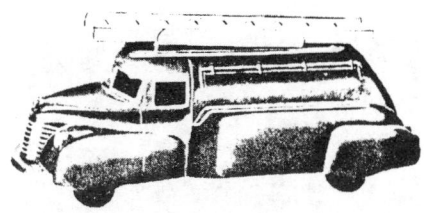

No. 254 Polyethylene TV Truck w/ladder

No. 580
8" Jeep and Driver
Bagged with Header
Pkg.: 4¼" x 11"
● Assorted Red and Blue Poly Jeeps with Driver at Wheel
● Plastic Wheels on Free-Running Steel Axles
● Spare Tire on Back of Jeep
● Movable Windshield
Retail .... 69¢

No. 614
Assortment of 8" Authentic All-Poly Ack-Ack & Searchlight Jeeps
Bagged with Header — Pkg.: 4½" x 4½" x 11"
● Movable Windshield
● Spare Tire Attached
● Black Poly Wheels on Free-Running Steel Axles
● Guns and Searchlight Swivel and Elevate
● Realistic Lens in Searchlight
● 2 Action Soldiers
● 1 Doz. Each Style — 75% Flaming Red and 25% Thomas Blue to the 2 Doz. Carton
Retail .... 98¢

Thomas Toys   557

No. 520

No. 524

No. 519

No. 521

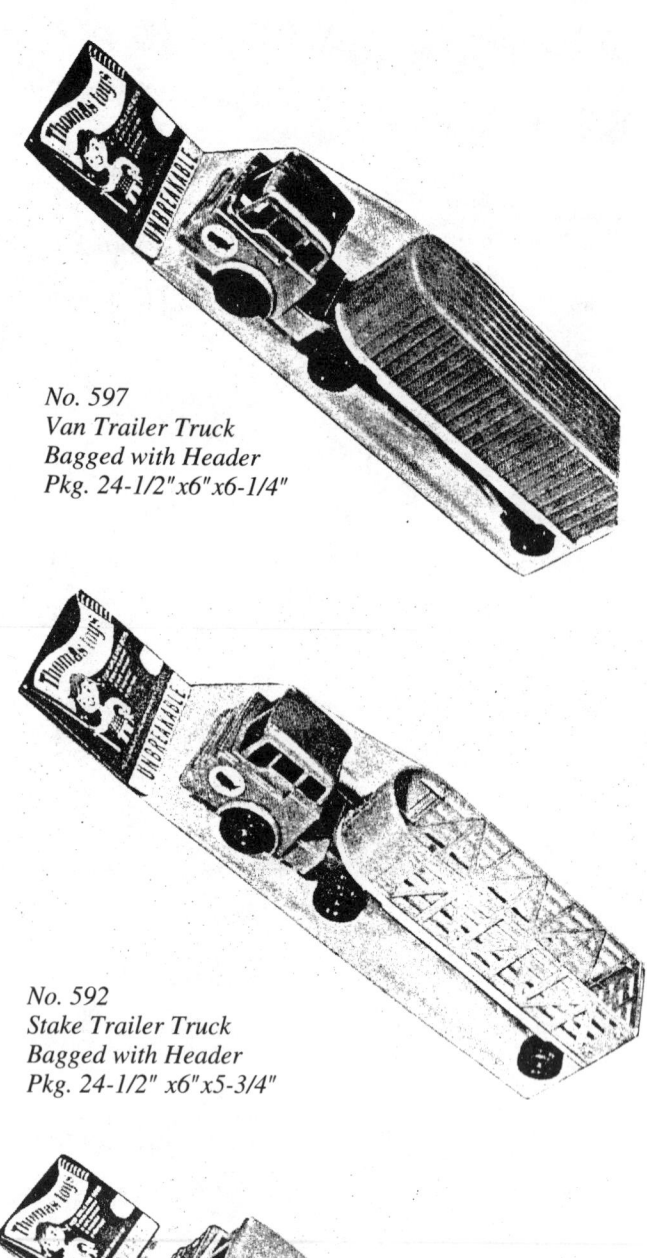

No. 597
Van Trailer Truck
Bagged with Header
Pkg. 24-1/2"x6"x6-1/4"

No. 592
Stake Trailer Truck
Bagged with Header
Pkg. 24-1/2" x6"x5-3/4"

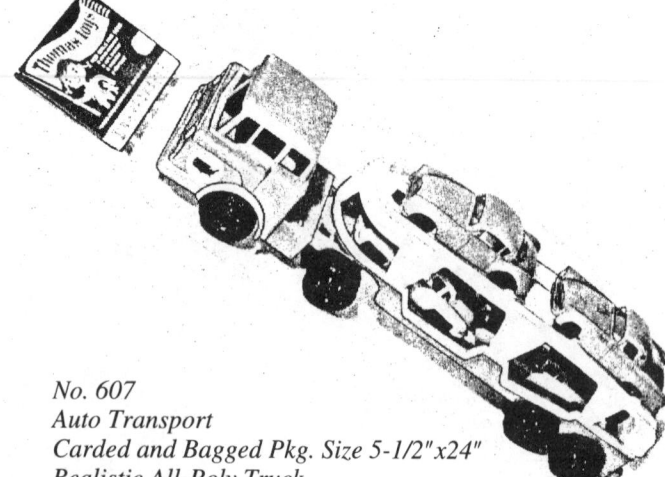

No. 607
Auto Transport
Carded and Bagged Pkg. Size 5-1/2"x24"
Realistic All-Poly Truck
Huge All-Poly (Tu-Tone) Trailer

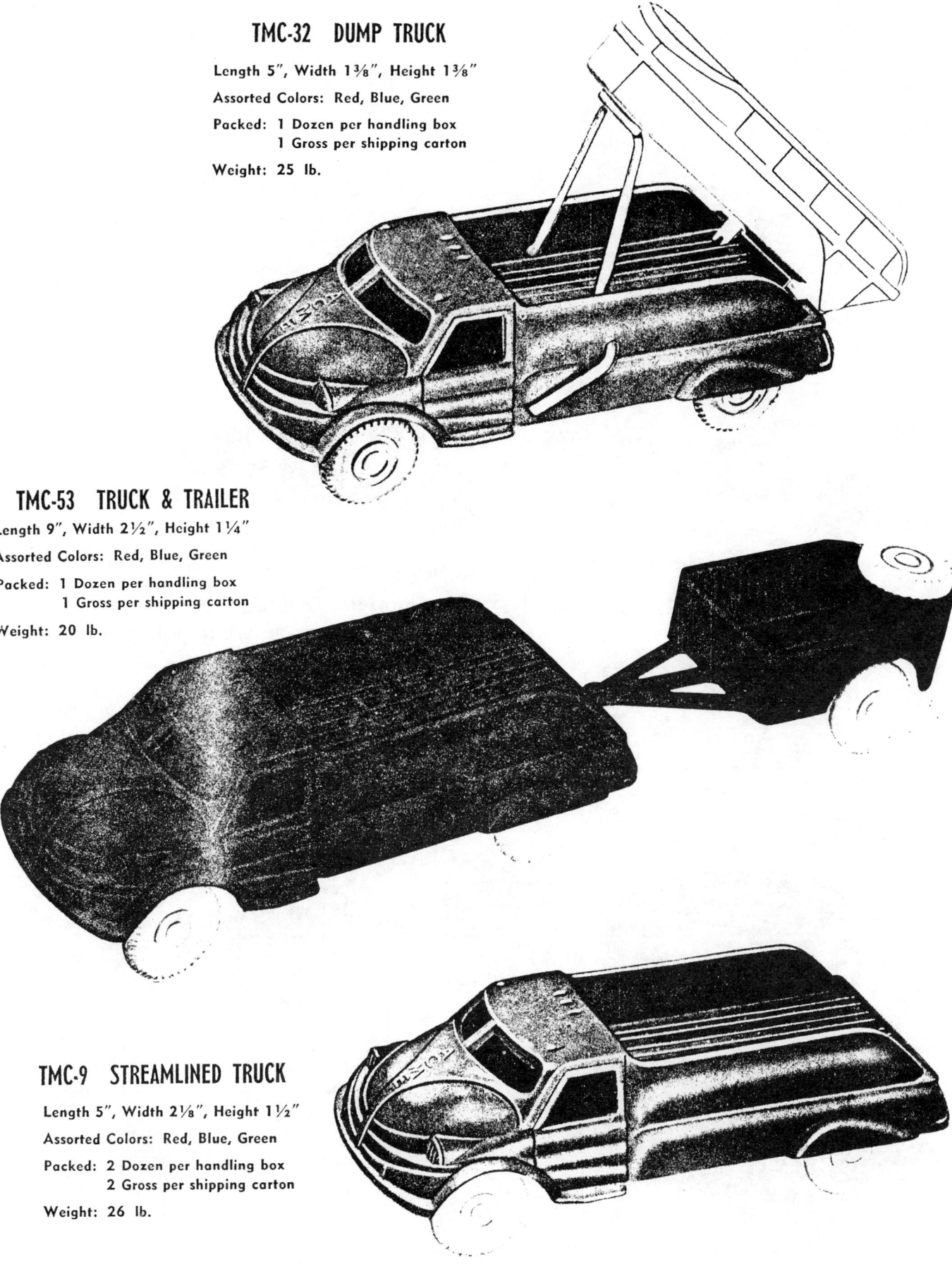

TMC-32 DUMP TRUCK

Length 5", Width 1⅜", Height 1⅜"

Assorted Colors: Red, Blue, Green

Packed: 1 Dozen per handling box
1 Gross per shipping carton

Weight: 25 lb.

TMC-53 TRUCK & TRAILER

Length 9", Width 2½", Height 1¼"

Assorted Colors: Red, Blue, Green

Packed: 1 Dozen per handling box
1 Gross per shipping carton

Weight: 20 lb.

TMC-9 STREAMLINED TRUCK

Length 5", Width 2⅛", Height 1½"

Assorted Colors: Red, Blue, Green

Packed: 2 Dozen per handling box
2 Gross per shipping carton

Weight: 26 lb.

This is a Thomas Toys order sheet, but note the "Acme" marking on the hoods.

T-17 STREAMLINED BUICK SEDAN

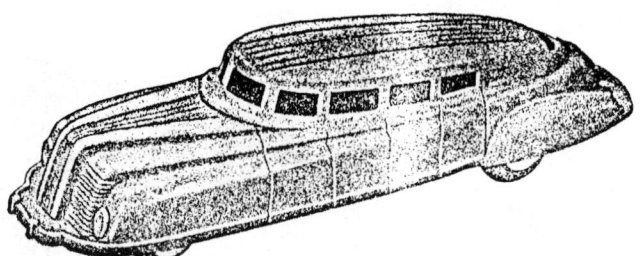

TMC-19 AIRLINE LIMOUSINE

No. 19 JEEP & TRAILER (with Driver)

No. 19 JEEP & TRAILER (with Driver)

THE **Tommy-Car Line** for '49 | 4 smart models—2 utility trailers—sold individually and in combination units

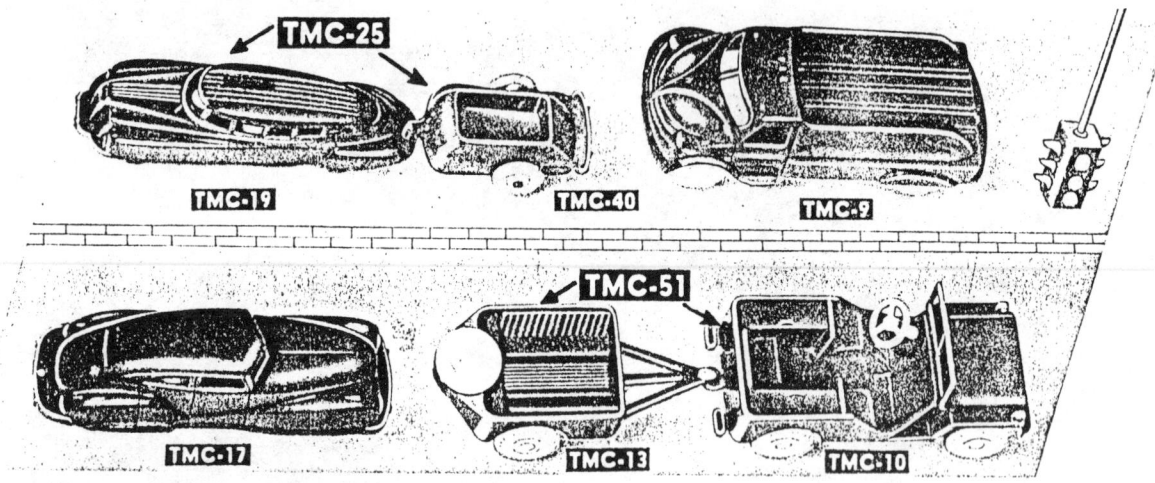

No. 77 CONVERTIBLE COUPE & DRIVER

No. 77S STREAMLINED SEDAN

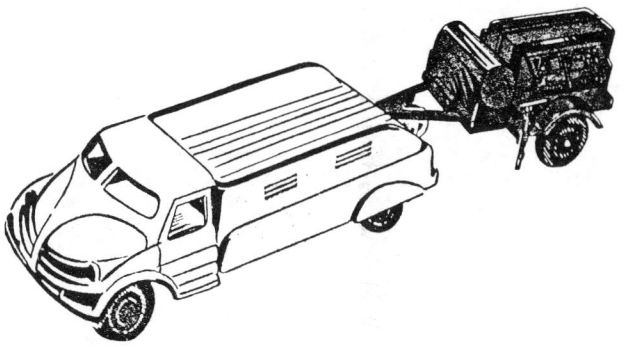

No. 148 Truck & Air Compressor

No. 234 Gas & Delivery Trucks with trailers

TIMMEE			
	C6	C8	C10
Army Tow Truck, hard plastic, 9" long	12	18	25

TIMPO			
Delivery Van, friction, 4" long	100	150	200

TIP-TOP TOYS

By Fred Maxwell, Contributing Editor,
Assisted by Nelson Adams and Ferd Zegel

C.B.C. Lee had one of the best post-war collections of these quality toys and he was one of the first to publicize the line. In an earlier magazine article, he called them "diecast," not "slushmold," as were (or are) most I have seen with "A TIP-TOP TOY" embossed on the ceiling. There are a few slush clones and some with die-made interiors, but with parting lines and minor flash on their lower edges, such as coupe TTT11.

Lee's article referred to a "Tip-Toy Co., San Francisco" box. The accompanying "1930 TOY WORLD" ads show "G.H. Curry Mfg. Co., Los Angeles" These ads also show toys #155 and 140 originally made by Kansas Toy and C.A. Wood. Was Curry the maker and Tip-Top the distributor or what?

Tip-Top toys were realistic, crisply detailed, and often unique. Wheels were metal discs or "wires" or Tootsietoy-like with lugbolts, metal hubs with rubber tires, and rubber wheels. This progression helps us to date the issues. Windshields and windows were open. With exceptions noted below cars and trucks were without bumpers.

		C6	C8	C10
TTTV1 Coupe, 3-1/8", 1923				
Dodge? sidemounts, 4 windows		16	24	32
TTTV2 Tanker Truck, 3-1/2".				
Diecast, "Gasoline," 2 filler caps	No Price Found			

TTTV1. Courtesy Ferd Zegel.

TTTV2, TTTV3a. Photo by Dave Leopard.

	C6	**C8**	**C10**

TTTV3a Pickup Truck, 3-1/4". Diecast,
"Tow Car," openwork handrails 16   24   32

TTTV3b Same as above
with solid-cast handrails .... No Price Found

TTTV3c Trailer for above,
2", 2 wheel dolly with shaft .... No Price Found

TTTV4 Pickup Truck,
3-1/4", hinged tailgate .... No Price Found

TTTV5 Overland Bus,
3-3/8", die-cast, 13 windows .... No Price Found

TTTV6 Coupe,
3-3/16", die-cast, rearmount tire .... No Price Found

TTTV7a Coupe, 3-1/4". Diecast,
streamlined, 1935 Huppmobile? with

	C6	**C8**	**C10**

realistic front end (forward fenders,
setback grille, large louvers,
bumpers, rearmount, tow loop) .... No Price Found

TTTV7b Travel Trailer
for above, 3-5/8". Die-cast, "Airstream"
type, 8 windows, right-side door .... No Price Found

TTTV8 Tanker Truck,
2-11/16". Diecast, 3 fillers .... No Price Found

TTTV9 Tanker Truck. Small,
with bumpers.? No details.
Has anyone seen it? .... No Price Found

TTTV10 Panel Truck,
2-1/8". "Parcel Delivery" .... No Price Found

TTTV2, TTTV19. Courtesy Ferd Zegel.

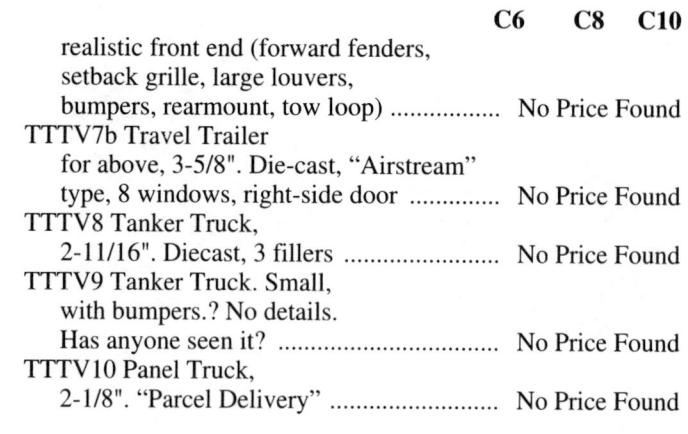

TTTV3a w/2ea TTTV3c. Courtesy Ferd Zegel.

TTTV4, TTTV10. Courtesy Ferd Zegel.

TTTV5. Courtesy Ferd Zegel.

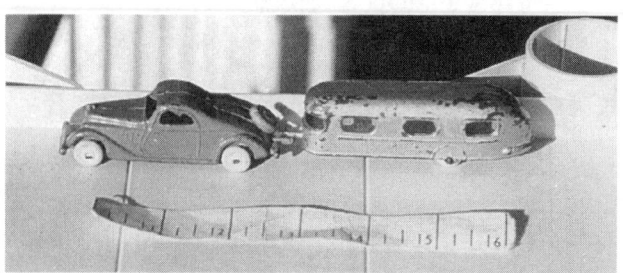

TTTV7a, TTTV7b. Courtesy Ferd Zegel.

TTTV8, TTTV19, TTTV2. Courtesy Ferd Zegel.

TTTV11, TTTV18. Courtesy Ferd Zegel.

TTTV13a. Courtesy Ferd Zegel.

TTTV11 Sport coupe #145, 2-1/8".
Die-made "TipTop Toy," under-dash
ventilator door, landau irons. Shows
parting-line & lower edge flash. (Note:
My only TTT. I said they were rare) .... No Price Found

TTTV12 Small Sedan,
2-1/4". 1933 Studebaker? .... No Price Found

TTTV13a Stake Truck, 4-5/8". 4 or
6-wheel versions, body separately
cast and fastened to chassis .... No Price Found

TTTV13b Stake Truck, 5-1/4".
Larger version of above, 6 wheels .... No Price Found

TTTV14 Airflow sedan. 6 windows,
bumpers. Has anyone seen one lately? ..... No Price Found

TTTV15 Airflow. Shorter 1934, similar to
1936 Tootsietoy, rearmount. Why no
details from Lee on these? They were hot
stuff from Detroit and most toymakers issued
them. Another case of Chrysler being
difficult about publishing rights? .... No Price Found

TTTV16 Ambulance? "A rumor" said Lee,
but plausible. Most toymakers had one .... No Price Found

TTTV17 Coupe. 3-5/8". Early, high-topped,
4 windows, short rearend. Photo by Lee and
"based on 1923 Dodge" but I have seen
a closer Dodge?--see TTV1 above .... No Price Found

TTTV18 Coupe, 3-1/4". Die-cast, cast rearmount.
(Looks like Tootsietoy copy) .... No Price Found

TTTV24,
TTTV20.
Courtesy
Ferd
Zegel.

TTTV25, TTTV26, TTTV27. Courtesy Ferd Zegel.

The undersides: TTTV25, TTTV26, TTTV27. Courtesy Ferd Zegel.

TTTV19 Tanker Truck,
3-1/4". Die-cast, 3 filler caps .... No Price Found

TTTV20 Midget racer, 1-7/8". Die-cast, easily
confused with slush Barclay #53 or CAWV12b.

TTTV21 Racer, 3". Die-cast, slanted vee grille,
round V8 ports, driver.

TTTV22 Racer, 3-1/2". Die-cast, rounded grille,
strapped hood, short tail.

TTTV22, TTTV21. Courtesy Ferd Zegel.

TTTV23 Racer, 4". Die-cast, strapped "16" hood,
right exhaust. (On the tracks, famous as "Old 16").

TTTV24 Racer, 3". Die-cast, Miller-like, driver, torpedo tail, 6
cylinder right exhaust.

TTTV25 Racer, c.4" Die-cast, slanted vee grille, strapped hood,
left exhaust, boattail. (similar to TTTV21).

TTTV26 Racer, c.3 1/4". Die-cast, squarish grille, left exhaust,
driver, boattail.

TTTV27 Record racer, c.4". Die-cast, Bluebird, rear fin.

There must be a few more out there, but so far nothing to explain Tip-Top's numbering system, which reached #165
by 1930.

Parcel
Delivery
(on side)

NO. 25 TIP-TOP TOY ASSORTMENT
Cash in on this
The Biggest Two Bit Value This Year
Five Wheel Toys in a Four Color Box
To Retail at
25c
Manufactured by
G. H. CURRY MFG. CO.
1266 So. Eastman St.
Los Angeles, Calif.

*Ad for Tip-Top Toys in the November, 1930
Toy World magazine—note that G.H. Curry
advertises itself as the manufacturer. Courtesy
Fred Maxwell.*

A November, 1930 Toy World ad showing Tip-Top Toys. Courtesy Fred Maxwell.

TIPP (TIPP & CO., TIPPCO)

by Jack Matthews

Tipp's history is interesting. Founded in 1912 and named after an early director/employee(?), Miss Tipp, its ultimate owner, Phillip Ullman, was forced to flee from Germany in 1933 for political and religious reasons. He went to England, where he founded Mettoy, eventually returning to Germany and recovering his company following the war. Tipp's military vehicles and overall production are clearly not up to the quality standards of Lineol and Elastolin and current prices reflect that fact. However, some of its pieces are particularly well-crafted, such as the Hitler Mercedes car. In the United States, Tipp tinplate pieces turn up at shows far more often, with its small Prime Mover being the most popular. Tipp military pieces sell for about a third that of Lineol and Hausser. Prices for Tipp military vehicles can be found as part of their photo captions.

	C6	C8	C10
Tipp Aerial Ladder Fire Truck, early	350	525	700
Tipp Club Sedan, 1933, tin litho, electric head lights, c/w motor, rear trunk opens, 17" long	500	800	1150

Tipp & Co. Club Sedan, 1933. Courtesy Bill Bertoia Auctions. Photo by Jeanne Bertoia.

	C6	C8	C10
Tipp "8 Cylinder Sedan," 12" long, c.1930	550	900	1300
Tipp Motorcycle & Rider, 6-1/2" high	285	418	570
Tipp Police Motorcycle, 11" long, battery headlight & friction	550	950	1300
Tipp "Provincial Omnibus Co." Bus	1500	2900	4500
Tipp Santa Driving Roadster tin windup, approx. 13", tree lights up	3500	5500	9500
Tipp "Silver Racer" windup motorcycle, 7-1/2" long	500	750	1000
Tipp Stake Truck, c.1930, 10" long, windup	135	198	270
Tipper Fire Ladder Truck	400	600	800

Tipp Santa Driving Roadster tin windup. Courtesy Bill Bertoia Auctions. Photo by Jeanne Bertoia.

Tipp "Silver Racer." Courtesy Kent M. Comstock.

Tipp No. 162 with baggage cart; value as shown $450. Photo by Jack Matthews.

Tipp No. 162/175; value as shown $500. Photo by Jack Matthews.

Tipp No. 164 early large Sedan with British crew (rare); value as shown $1,750. Photo by Jack Matthews.

Tipp No. 169/240 Towing 88mm; value as shown $650. Photo by Jack Matthews.

Tipp No. 169/274; value as shown $700. Photo by Jack Matthews.

Tipp No. 169/71; value as shown $600. Photo by Jack Matthews.

Tipp No. 169/72/171 with cleated cannon wheels; value as shown $600. Photo by Jack Matthews.

Tipp No. 162/167 Field Kitchen; value as shown $450. Photo by Jack Matthews.

Tipp No. 162/174; value as shown $450. Photo by Jack Matthews.

Tipp No. 164 (rare); value as shown $550. Photo by Jack Matthews.

Tipp No. 170/175 Wheeled Mortar; value as shown $600. Photo by Jack Matthews.

Tipp No. 176 Anti-Aircraft Truck; value as shown $950. Photo by Jack Matthews.

Tipp No. 181/4 Pioneer Auto (rare); value as shown $950. Photo by Jack Matthews.

Tipp No. 181/4 Military Pioneer Auto; value as shown $600. Photo by Jack Matthews.

Tipp No. 184 Military Lastwagon, early camouflage and top (rare); value as shown $1,800. Photo by Jack Matthews.

Tipp No. 194 Panzer Spahwagen, rare; value as shown $175. Photo by Jack Matthews.

Tipp No. 197, early: An accurate shot at the shield stops the clockwork-running mechanism; value as shown $175. Photo by Jack Matthews.

Tipp No. 204 early tank (rare); value as shown $650. Photo by Jack Matthews.

Tipp No. 208 Tank; value as shown $750. Photo by Jack Matthews.

Tipp No. 217 Tracked Prime Mover; value as shown $900. Photo by Jack Matthews.

Tipp No. 217 Tracked Prime Mover: Camouflaged, British crew; value as shown $1,050. Photo by Jack Matthews.

Tipp No. 934 Fuhrer Wagon (very rare); value as shown $3,500. Photo by Jack Matthews.

Tipp No. 934 Fuhrer Wagon (very rare, in tan); value as shown $4000. Photo by Jack Matthews.

A Tipp large scenic box; it held various toys. Photo by Jack Matthews.

Tipp Armored Car, early (very rare); value as shown $1,500. Photo by Jack Matthews.

Tipp Military Sedan; value as shown $600. Photo by Jack Matthews.

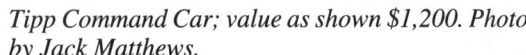

Tipp Command Car; value as shown $1,200. Photo by Jack Matthews.

Tipp Electric Tank, camouflaged (very rare); value as shown $2,000. Photo by Jack Matthews.

TOLEDO METAL WHEEL COMPANY

("Blue Streak")

The Toledo Metal Wheel Company was located in Toledo, Ohio, during at least the early and late 1920s. It manufactured a large range of pedal cars, as well as toy trucks. Its trade name for its products was "Blue Streak."

	C6	C8	C10
Toledo No. 45 "Bull Dog" Truck, 26" long, open cab	500	1000	1500
Toledo No. 46 "Bull Dog" Dump Truck, 26-1/2" long	600	1000	1475
Toledo No. 47 "Bull Dog" Sprinkler Truck, 27-1/2" long	600	1100	1510
Toledo No. 48 "Bull Dog" Moving Van, 26" long	550	1050	1550
Toledo No. 50 "Bull Dog" Coal Truck, 25" long	800	1350	1875

	C6	C8	C10
Toledo "De Luxe" pedal car, 54" long	2500	5000	7500
Toledo Fire Chief Pedal Car, for sale in 1992 for $10,000			
Toledo Fire Pumper Car, red-painted, 59" long	1250	1875	2500
Toledo Pedal Car, 46" long	1200	2200	3300
Toledo White Dump Truck Pedal Car, 68"	5000	9000	14,750

TOMMY TOY

Tommy Toy, 131 Palisade Ave., Union City, New Jersey, had its first sale on Nov. 13, 1935. Its principal owners were Dr. Albert Greene and Charles E. Weldon. It seems to have gone out of business sometime between August 1938 and May 1939.

The following vehicles have been identified by Charles E. Weldon Jr., son of one of the owners of Tommy Toy. He is sure these are Tommy Toy, but admits there is always a chance he could be mistaken on some. Certainly, the Cannon Truck, aside from the hubs, looks just like Barclay's, which was produced in the same years. Some others resemble Metal Cast, Savoye, and other companies' vehicles. However, since slush molds did tend to change hands, production of a vehicle by one company would not preclude later manufacture of the same toy by another company. American Alloy is known to have produced copies of Tommy Toy's soldiers, using new molds. The only vehicle known to bear the Tommy Toy trademark is the 810 Cord (TTV8).

	C6	C8	C10
TTV1 Aerial Ladder Truck (like Savoye), late 20s type	20	30	40
TTV2 Airflow type auto (like Kansas Toy), c.1935	32	48	65
TTV3 "Ambulance," late 20s--early 30s type	16	24	32
TTV 4 "Beer truck" with wooden barrels, late 1930s	14	21	28
TTV5 Cannon Truck, mid-30s (like Barclay; Barclay's had wooden hubs)	17	25	34
TTV6 Convertible, no driver, mid-late 30s	8	12	16
TTV7 Convertible with driver, mid-late 30s, 1935 Oldsmobile	10	15	20
TTV8 Cord, 810 (1935)	40	60	80
TTV9 "Delivery Deluxe" Delivery Truck (like Savoye), late 30s	18	27	36
TTV10 Double-Decker Bus, closed top, early 30s	16	24	32

Tommy Toy TTV8. Photo by Perry R. Eichor.

L to R, Top: TTV18, TTV17, TTV14, TTV16.
Bottom: TTV10, TTV11, TTV12.

TTV19

L to R, Top: TTV20, TTV5, TTV7, TTV21.
Bottom: TTV4, TTV18, TTV6.

L to R: TTV23, TTV22, TTV3

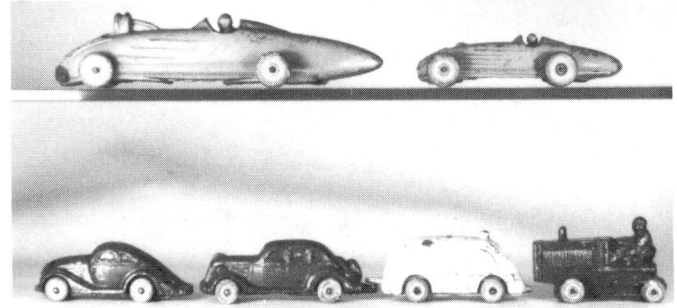

L to R, Top: TTV27, TTV28.
Bottom: TTV2, TTV30, TTV32.

	C6	C8	C10
TTV11 Double-Decker Bus, open top, extended hood (like Savoye), late 1920s	35	52	70
TTV12 Double-Decker Bus, open top, no hood (like Barclay), late 1930s	16	24	32
TTV13 Dump Truck, late 1930s (resembles Kansas Toy, Best Toy, Manhattan Toys)	16	24	32
TTV14 "General Trucking" late 30s	12	18	25
TTV15 Ladder Truck, mid 30s	20	30	40
TTV16 "Milk" Truck, late 1930s	20	30	40
TTV17 "Milk Truck," grilled window c.late 1930s	20	30	40
TTV18 "Milk Truck," smooth window, c.late 30s	20	30	40
TTV19 "Motorcoach" mid-30s (like Savoye)	No Price Found		

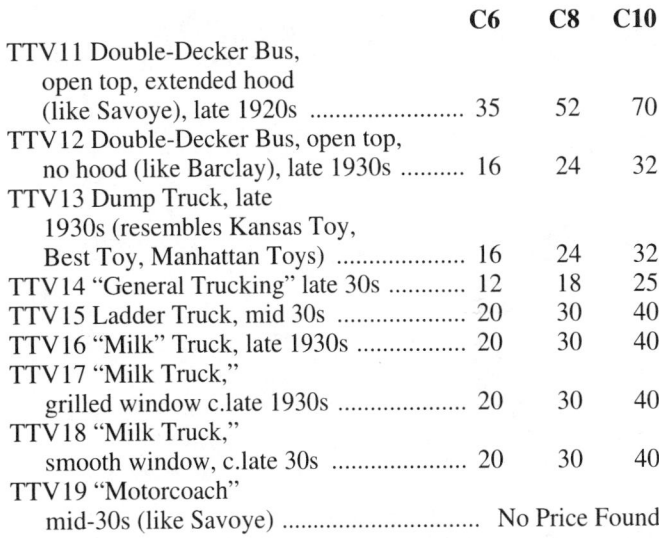

L to R, Top: TTV24, TTV1, TTV15.
Bottom: TTV25, TTV26.

Tommy Toy "Tourist"—TTV30. Photo by Perry Eichor.

	C6	C8	C10
TTV20 "Oil" tanker, "Cap 80,000" (like Metal Cast, which has different capacity number), 1930s, attaches to Tommy Toy Towing Car Coupe	8	12	16

L to R, Top: TTV31, TTV33, TTV13.
Bottom: TTV9, TTV29, TTV30.

	C6	C8	C10
TTV21 "Packard," coupe, mid-30s	17	26	35
TTV22 "Police Patrol," open windows, late 20s-early 30s type	70	105	140
TTV23 "Police Patrol," solid windows, late 20s-early 30s type	35	52	70
TTV24 Pumper, mid 1930's	12	18	25
TTV25 Pumper, large, red hubs, late 30s	11	16	22
TTV26 Pumper, small, late 30s	8	12	16
TTV27 Racing Car, large, c.mid 30s	16	24	32
TTV28 Racing Car, small, c.mid 30s	12	18	25
TTV29 Sedan, 4-door, c.1935	17	26	35
TTV30 Sedan towing "Tourist" Trailer, c.1936-1937	20	30	40
TTV31 Towing Car Coupe (like Savoye), early 30s type	16	24	32
TTV32 Tractor	12	18	25
TTV33 Wrecker, late 1930s	10	15	20

TONKA

By Don and Barb DeSalle

Tonka toys began production in the basement of a small schoolhouse in Mound, Minnesota, a suburb of Minneapolis. Mound Metalcraft Company was founded by Lynn E. Baker, Avery Crounse, and Alvin Tesch. During the first year of production, the tooling for a steam shovel was purchased from the L.E. Streeter Company. Mound Metalcraft refined the tooling and produced the first two Tonka toys for 1947, the #100 steam shovel and the #150 crane and clam. The crane and steam shovel were displayed at the New York Toy Show in 1947 and were well received. The small staff of employees manufactured a total of 37,000 of the two metal toys.

In 1948, Mound Metalcraft produced the #200 power lift and trailer. In 1949 began the production of the cab over trucks. Nineteen fifty-four marked the introduction of the "round-fendered cab" Ford trucks. In 1958, the "square-fendered cab" trucks were introduced. Trucks produced after 1961 are referred to as "generic," because they no longer resemble any particular truck.

Don and Barb DeSalle, authors of the book
Collector's Guide to Tonka Toys. *The DeSalles are avid Tonka collectors.*

1947

Tonka No. 100 Steam Shovel, 20-3/4" long	135	202	270
Tonka No. 150 Crane and Clam, 24" long	88	132	175

1948

Tonka No. 200 Lift Truck and Cart	100	150	300

1949

Tonka No. 100 Steam Shovel Deluxe, 22" long	100	150	200
Tonka No. 120 Tractor and Carry-All Trailer with No. 50 Steam Shovel	155	280	350

Tonka No. 120 Tractor and Carry-All Trailer with No. 50 Steam Shovel (very early type with rubber tracks in large set box). Photo by Tim Oei.

	C6	C8	C10
Tonka No. 125 Tractor & Carry-All Trailer with No. 100 Steam Shovel	150	250	350
Tonka No. 130 Tractor-Carry-All Trailer, 30-1/2" long	100	150	250
Tonka No. 140 "Tonka Toy Transport Van," 22-1/4" long	150	225	300
Tonka No. 170 Tractor & Carry-All Trailer with No. 150 Crane & Clam	200	300	400
Tonka No. 180 Dump Truck, 12" long	100	150	240

	C6	C8	C10
Tonka No. 190 Loading Tractor, 10-1/2" long		No Price Found	
Tonka No. 250 WreckerTruck, 12-1/2" long	100	150	250

1950

	C6	C8	C10
Tonka No. 145 Steel Carrier Semi, 22" long	125	188	250
Tonka No. 175 Utility Hauler, 12" long	100	150	200

Tonka 1949 No. 140 "Tonka Toy Transport" Van. Photo by Calvin L. Chaussee.

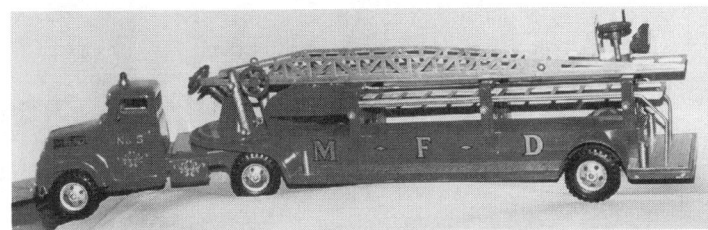

Tonka 1954 No. 700 Aerial Ladder. Courtesy Harvey K. Rainess.

Tonka 1954 Steel Carrier Truck. Courtesy Continental Hobby House.

Tonka 1952-on Grain Hauler. Courtesy Harvey K. Rainess.

Tonka, 1954, No. 750. Photo by Mark McManus.

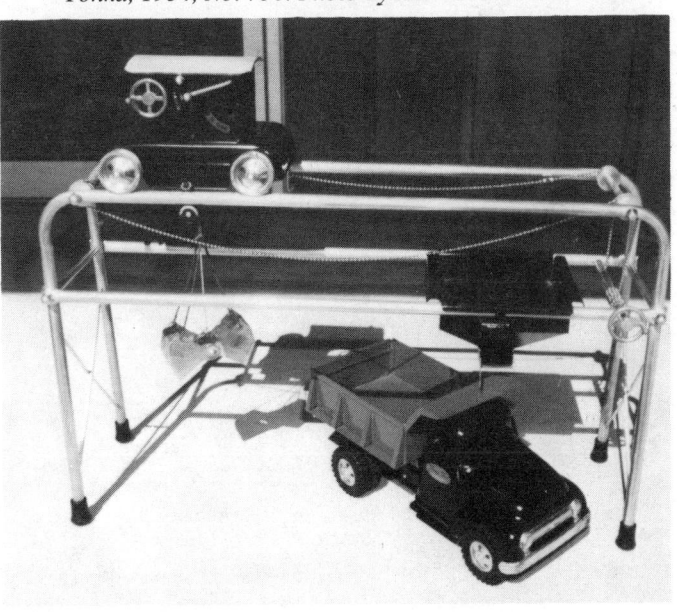

Tonka 1955 No. 992 Aerial Sand Loader Set. Courtesy Thomas G. Nefos, Federal Shipping Network.

Tonka 1955 Dump Truck. Courtesy Thomas G. Nefos, Federal Shipping Network.

	C6	C8	C10
Tonka No. 185 "Express" Truck, 13-1/2" long		No Price Found	
Tonka No. 400 Allied Van Lines Semi, 23-1/2" long	175	260	350

1952

	C6	C8	C10
Tonka No. 500 Livestock Hauler Semi, 22-1/4" long	90	155	250
Tonka No. 550 Grain Hauler Semi, 22-1/4" long	125	188	250

1953

	C6	C8	C10
Tonka No. 575 Logger Semi, 22-1/4" long	125	188	250
Tonka No. 575 Logger Semi, wood flat bed	125	150	250
Tonka No. 600 Road Grader, 17" long	50	75	100
Tonka No. 650 Green Giant Transport Semi, 22-1/4" long	150	225	350
Tonka Wrecker	110	150	250
Tonka No. 675 Trailer Fleet Set, two tractors (five interchangeable trailers), per set	350	580	775

1954

(Newer Style Trucks--Rounded Fenders)

	C6	C8	C10
Tonka No. 700 Aerial Ladder Semi Fire Truck, 32-1/2" long	175	260	450
Tonka No. 725 Star Kist Van, 14-1/2" long	250	375	750
Tonka No. 750 Carnation Milk Step Van, 11-3/4" long	200	300	400
Tonka No. 750 Parcel Delivery Van, 11-3/4" long	200	300	400
Tonka No. 145 Steel Carrier Truck	90	135	280
Tonka Wrecker	90	200	400
Tonka Utility Truck	112	175	325
Tonka No. 775 Road Builder Set-5 pc.-Road Grader (Semi T&T Crane and Dump Truck)	350	525	900

1955

	C6	C8	C10
Tonka No. 725 Minute Maid Orange Juice Van	275	450	750
Tonka No. 750 Carnation Milk Delivery Van	150	275	400
Tonka No. 880 Pick-up Truck	125	280	450
Tonka 0850 Lumber Truck, 6-wheel	175	260	400

	C6	C8	C10
Tonka No. 0860 Stake Truck, 6-wheel	175	260	400
Tonka Allied Van Lines	100	200	400
Tonka Dump	70	105	240
Tonka Freighter	90	135	280
Tonka Hook & Ladder	100	300	450
Tonka Livestock Truck	110	165	220
Tonka Loboy & Shovel	150	225	300
Tonka Rescue Van	100	250	450
Tonka No. 65 Trailer, Stake Side	30	45	60
Tonka No. 600 Grader	40	80	100
Tonka No. 992 Aerial Sand Loader Set, Loader & Dump Truck	175	325	475

1956

	C6	C8	C10
Tonka No. 120 Shovel & Carry-All (Loboy), 33" long total	188	280	475
Tonka No. 180 Dump Truck, 13" long	60	90	120
Tonka No. 600 Road Grader, 17" long	45	80	100
Tonka No. 700 Aerial Ladder, 32-1/2" long	150	300	450
Tonka No. 880 Pickup Truck, 13-3/4" long	100	250	450
Tonka No. 950 Pumper, 17" long	150	275	350
Tonka No. 960 Wrecker	100	200	450
Tonka No. 980 Hi-Way Dump Truck, 13" long	130	180	265
Tonka No. 991 Farm Stake Truck, 13" long	80	120	260
Tonka No. 996 Wrecker (white color) (AAA) 12" long	390	525	700
Tonka No. 998 Lumber Truck, 18-3/4" long	130	195	260
Tonka Rescue Squad Van, 11-3/4" long	225	335	450
Tonka Green Giant Semi Reefer	155	250	400

1957

	C6	C8	C10
Tonka Aerial Ladder Truck	200	300	400
Tonka Big Mike Dual Hydraulic Dump Truck, 14" long	325	488	750
Tonka Farm Stake Truck	190	275	380
Tonka Gasoline Truck, 15" long	350	525	700
Tonka Hook & Ladder	150	225	300
Tonka Parcel Delivery Van, 12" long	200	300	400

Tonka Fire Truck Set, c.1957: Rescue Squad Ladder Truck, Pumper, Hydrant; value in C6, C8, C10: $400, 625, 850. Photo by Bob Smith.

Tonka, 1956, No. 950. Photo by Mark McManus.

	C6	C8	C10
Tonka Pickup w/Stake Trailer, 20-1/2" long	100	150	300
Stake Trailer alone	30	45	75
Tonka Stock Rack Truck with Animals, 16-1/4" long	175	300	500
Tonka 3-in-1 Hi-way Service Truck, w/2 snowblades, 13" long	200	300	500
Tonka Thunderbird Express Semi, 24" long	150	250	350
Tonka Wrecker	100	200	450

1958 Next Generation Cars

	C6	C8	C10
Tonka No. 02 Pickup Truck	60	90	120
Tonka No. 03 Utility Truck	92	138	185
Tonka No. 04 Farm Stake Truck	65	98	130
Tonka No. 05 Sportsman Pickup with Topper, 12-3/4" long	70	125	300
Tonka No. 06 Dump Truck	80	120	160
Tonka No. 12 Road Grader	75	112	150
Tonka No. 18 Wrecker Truck	100	150	250
Tonka No. 20 Hydraulic Dump Truck	132	198	265
Tonka No. 28 Pickup with Stake Trailer & Animal	100	150	200
Tonka No. 29 Sportsman Truck with Box Trailer	150	225	300
Tonka No. 32 Stock Rack Truck	112	168	225
Tonka No. 33 "Gasoline" Truck, hinged back door, hose & nozzle	250	400	600
Tonka No. 34 Deluxe Sportsman with Boat Trailer, 22-3/4" long	150	225	450
Tonka No. 35 Farm Stake with 2-Horse Trailer, 21-3/4" long	125	188	250
Tonka No. 36 Livestock Van	175	263	350
Tonka No. 37 Thunderbird Express	150	250	450
Tonka No. 39 Nationwide Moving Van, 24-1/4" long	250	375	500
Tonka No. 41 Hi-Way Service Truck	70	105	140
Tonka No. 43 Shovel & Carry-All Trailer	190	275	380
Tonka No. 45 Big Mike Dual Hydraulic Dump Truck w/Snow Plow	275	475	700
Tonka No. 46 Suburban Pumper	175	260	350
Tonka No. 48 Hydraulic Aerial Ladder	100	250	350

1959

	C6	C8	C10
Tonka No. 01 Service Truck, 12-3/4" long	75	150	250
Tonka No. 05 Sportsman	75	150	250
Tonka No. 14 Dragline, 20" long	75	175	275

	C6	C8	C10
Tonka No. 16 Air Express	150	225	300
Tonka No. 22 Deluxe Sportsman	150	225	300
Tonka No. 30 Tandem Platform Stake, 28-1/4" long	140	250	400
Tandem No. 36 Tandem Air Express, with trailer, 24-3/4" long	225	450	700
Tandem No. 40 Car Carrier	100	200	300
Tandem No. 41 Boat Transport, 38" long	150	300	500
Tandem No. 42 Hydraulic Land Rover, 15" long	350	525	700
Tonka No. 44 Dragline & Trailer, 26-1/4" long	112	168	225
Tonka Sanitary Truck (Square back)	350	500	700

1960

(Two Center Ribs on Truck Cabs Replaced by One Rib)

	C6	C8	C10
Tonka No. 01 Service Truck	75	150	250
Tonka No. 02 Pickup	60	100	175
Tonka No. 04 Farm Stake Truck	50	715	225
Tonka No. 05 Sportsman	75	175	250
Tonka No. 06 Dump Truck	55	82	110
Tonka No. 08 Logger	150	225	300
Tonka No. 18 Wrecker, white sidewalls	85	150	270
Tonka No. 20 Hydraulic Dump	45	75	100
Tonka No. 22 Deluxe Sportsman	70	150	300
Tonka No. 28 Pickup & Trailer	100	150	200
Tonka No. 35 Farm Stake & Horse Trailer	125	188	250
Tonka No. 37 Thunderbird Express	150	250	450
Tonka No. 40 Car Carrier	75	125	250
Tonka No. 41 Boat Transport, 38" long	150	250	350
Tonka No. 46 Suburban Pumper	100	150	200
Tonka No. 48 Aerial Ladder	125	188	250
Tonka No. 100 Bulldozer, 8-7/8" long, (plated roller wheels only in 1960)	40	60	80
Tonka No. 105 Rescue Squad, 13-3/4" long	90	150	250
Tonka No. 110 Fisherman Pick-up with Sportsman, cover, 14" long	50	75	100
Tonka No. 115 Power Boom Loader (1960 only), 18-1/2" long	225	450	650
Tonka No. 120 Cement Mixer, 15-1/2" long	100	150	200
Tonka No. 125 Lowboy and Bulldozer, 26-1/4" long	190	275	380

Tonka 1958 No. 46 Suburban Pumper with hydrant. Courtesy Harvey K. Rainess.

Tonka 1960 No. 01 Service Truck. Photo by Calvin L. Chaussee.

	C6	C8	C10
Tonka No. 130 Deluxe Fisherman (also new boat & trailer)	150	225	300
Tonka No. 135 Mobile Dragline	100	150	250
Tonka No. 140 Sanitary Truck	250	350	500
Tonka No. 145 Tanker (first Tonka with major use of plastic), 28" long	100	250	350
Tonka "Jolly Green Giant" Special, white, green stake racks	175	250	350
Tonka "Standard" Oil Company Wrecker Special	200	400	600

1961

("T" Eliminated in Grill's Center)

	C6	C8	C10
Tonka No. 02 Pickup	60	90	120
Tonka No. 04 Farm Stake	85	125	170
Tonka No. 05 Sportsman	85	125	230
Tonka No. 06 Dump	55	82	110
Tonka No. 12 Road Grader, yellow	50	75	100
Tonka No. 14 Dragline, yellow	62	93	125
Tonka No. 18 Wrecker	100	150	200
Tonka No. 20 Hydraulic Dump	75	112	150
Tonka No. 22 Deluxe Sportman	100	200	350
Tonka No. 35 Farm Stake Truck & Horse Trailer	70	105	140
Tonka No. 39 Allied Van	120	200	300
Tonka No. 40 Car Carrier	100	150	250
Tonka No. 41 Boat Transport Truck	150	300	450
Tonka No. 48 Aerial Ladder	125	188	250
Tonka No. 116 Dump Truck with Sandloader, 23-1/4" long total	80	120	260
Tonka No. 117 Boat Service Truck (1961 only)	75	150	250
Tonka No. 118 Giant Dozer, 12-1/2" long	50	100	150
Tonka No. 120 Cement Mixer	100	150	200
Tonka No. 130 Deluxe Fisherman	100	250	350
Tonka No. 134 Grading Service Truck, Trailer & Bulldozer, 25-1/2" long total	100	150	250
Tonka No. 135 Mobile Dragline	100	200	350
Tonka No. 136 Houseboat Set, 29" long total	200	400	500
Tonka No. 140 Sanitary Truck	400	700	1000
Tonka No. 142 Mobile Clam, 27-1/4" long	100	150	200
Tonka No. 145 Tanker	100	150	250

Tonka 1961 No. 140 Sanitary Truck: According to research by Patrick O'Neil, this truck is extremely rare because it was discontinued, according to a retired Tonka executive, in early March of 1961 because of an "unfortunate accident." Photo by Patrick O'Neil.

1962

(New Tonka logo; Tonka above wavy line, Mound, Minnesota below)

	C6	C8	C10
Tonka No. 200 Jeep Dispatcher, 9-3/4" long	40	60	80
Tonka No. 201 "Serv-I-Car," 9-1/8" long	50	75	100
Tonka No. 249 Jeep Universal	25	50	75
Tonka No. 250 Tractor, 8-5/8" long	50	75	100
Tonka No. 300 Bulldozer	50	75	100
Tonka No. 301 Utility Dump, 12-1/2" long (revised Golf Club Tractor, 1961 only)	100	150	200
Tonka No. 302 Pickup	35	50	100
Tonka No. 308 Stake Pickup, 12-5/8" long	50	75	100
Tonka No. 350 Jeep Surrey, fringe top, 10-1/2" long	50	75	100
Tonka No. 402 "Loader," yellow & green	40	60	80
Tonka No. 404 Farm Stake Truck	50	75	100
Tonka No. 405 Sportsman	55	82	110
Tonka No. 406 Dump Truck	60	90	120
Tonka No. 410 "Jet Delivery" Truck, 14" long (1962 only)	100	150	250
Tonka No. 420 Airlines Luggage Service, 16-5/8" long	100	150	200
Tonka No. 512 Road Grader	45	68	90
Tonka No. 514 Dragline	150	225	300
Tonka No. 516 Jeep Runabout, trailer, boat, 25-5/8" long, total	75	112	150
Tonka No. 518 Wrecker	45	75	125
Tonka No. 520 Hydraulic Dump	60	90	120
Tonka No. 524 Dozer Packer, 18-1/4" long total, Packer has 11 tires, sold only in 1962	75	150	200
Tonka No. 528 Pickup & Trailer	50	75	100
Tonka No. 530 Camper, 14" long	50	100	150
Tonka No. 616 Dump Truck & Sand Loader	70	105	140
Tonka No. 618 Giant Dozer	100	150	200
Tonka No. 620 Cement Mixer	85	150	200
Tonka No. 735 Farm Stake & Horse Trailer	50	75	125
Tonka No. 739 Allied Van	112	168	225
Tonka No. 834 Grading Service Truck	70	100	150
Tonka No. 840 Car Carrier	100	150	200
Tonka No. 926 Pumper Truck	100	150	200
Tonka No. 942 Mobile Clam	80	150	220
Tonka No. 1348 Aerial Ladder	100	150	250

1963

(Faceted headlights introduced)

	C6	C8	C10
Tonka No. 50 Mini-Tonka Jeep pickup, 9-1/4" long	35	52	70
Tonka No. 56 Mini-Tonka Stake Truck, 9-1/4" long	35	52	70

Tonka 1961 No. 145 Tanker. Courtesy Harvey K. Rainess.

	C6	C8	C10
Tonka No. 60 Mini-Tonka Dump, 9-3/4" long	75	112	150
Tonka No. 68 Mini-Tonka Wrecker, 9-1/2" long	30	45	60
Tonka No. 70 Mini-Tonka Camper, 9-5/8" long	75	112	150
Tonka No. 200 Jeep Dispatcher	No Price Found		
Tonka No. 201 "Servi-I-Car"	55	82	110
Tonka No. 250 Tractor, yellow with red seat	75	112	150
Tonka No. 251 Military Jeep Universal, 10-1/2" long	25	38	50
Tonka No. 300 Bulldozer	55	82	110
Tonka No. 302 Pickup	35	52	70
Tonka No. 308 Stake Pickup	35	52	70
Tonka No. 350 Jeep Surrey	50	75	100
Tonka No. 352 Loader	40	60	80
Tonka No. 354 Style-Side Pickup, 14" long	40	60	80
Tonka No. 404 Farm Stake Truck	60	90	120
Tonka No. 406 Dump Truck	45	68	90
Tonka No. 422 Back Hoe, 17-1/8" long	65	98	130
Tonka No. 425 Jeep Pumper, 10-3/4" long	80	120	160
Tonka No. 512 Road Grader, red clearance lights	No Price Found		
Tonka No. 514 Dragline	60	90	120
Tonka No. 516 Jeep Runabout, trailer & boat	60	90	120
Tonka No. 518 Wrecker	25	38	50
Tonka No. 520 Hydraulic Dump Truck	45	68	90
Tonka No. 522 Style-Side Pickup & Stake Trailer, 22-3/4" long total	No Price Found		
Tonka No. 524 Dozer Packer, yellow	200	300	400
Tonka No. 530 Camper	25	38	50
Tonka No. 534 Trencher, 18-1/4" long	32	48	65
Tonka No. 536 Giant Dozer	112	168	225
Tonka No. 616 Dump Truck & Sand Loader, yellow	67	100	135
Tonka No. 620 Cement Mixer	75	112	150
Tonka No. 625 Stake Pickup & Horse Trailer, 21-3/4" long overall	100	150	200
Tonka No. 640 Ramp Hoist, 19 1/4" long, red & white	175	300	450
Tonka No. 720 Terminal Train, 33-5/8" long, total, 15 suitcases	105	158	210

	C6	C8	C10
Tonka No. 739 Allied Van	118	175	235
Tonka No. 840 Car Carrier	42	63	85
Tonka No. 926 Pumper	60	90	120
Tonka No. 942 Mobile Clam	75	112	150
Tonka No. 1001 Trencher & LoBoy, 28-1/2" long total	75	112	150
Tonka No. 1348 Aerial Ladder Truck	100	150	200
Tonka No. 2100 Airport Service Set	150	225	300

1964
(Futuristic Cab introduced)

	C6	C8	C10
Tonka No. 77 Mini-Tonka Mixer, 9" long	50	75	100
Tonka No. 86 Mini-Tonka Van, 16" long	36	54	72
Tonka No. 90 Mini-Tonka Livestock Van, 16" long	50	75	100
Tonka No. 96 Mini-Tonka Carrier, 18-1/2" long, 2 cars	50	75	150
Tonka No. 250 Military Tractor, black seat	55	70	100
Tonka No. 251 Military Jeep Universal	35	55	75
Tonka No. 304 Jeep Commander, canvas top, 10-1/2" long	30	45	60
Tonka No. 315 Dump Truck, 13-1/2" long	40	60	90
Tonka No. 375 Jeep Wrecker, 11" long	50	75	150
Tonka No. 380 Troop Carrier, 14" long	70	120	175
Tonka No. 384 Military Jeep & Box Trailer, 19-3/8" overall	50	75	150
Tonka No. 404 Stake Truck, red	70	120	170
Tonka No. 425 Jeep Pumper, black steering wheel	100	150	250
Tonka No. 504 Stake Pickup & Trailer, 21-5/8" long	50	75	100
Tonka No. 525 Jeep & Horse Trailer, 19-1/4" long total, 2 horses	45	68	90
Tonka No. 616 Dump Truck & Sandloader, orange & yellow	75	125	175
Tonka No. 640 Ramp Hoist, park green & white, very rare	200	350	600
Tonka No. 739 Allied Van Lines, black knob on door	75	125	175
Tonka No. 900 Mighty Tonka Dump Truck (Most Popular Tonka of all: 9,655, 000 sold between 1964 & 1983)	65	98	130
Tonka No. 942 Mobile Clam, yellow	50	75	100
Tonka No. 998 Aerial Ladder, 2 auxiliary ladders	50	75	100

Tonka 1968 No. 2252 Air Force Jeep; value in mint $45. Photo by Calvin L. Chaussee.

Tonka 1968 No. 2435 Jeep Wrecker & Plow; value in Mint $100. Photo by Calvin L. Chaussee.

TOOTSIETOY

By John Gibson

Tootsietoy began in 1876, as Dowst & Company, publishers of the *National Laundry Journal*. Using the "Linotype" machine purchased at the 1893 World's Fair, Samuel Dowst began turning out die-cast novelties and eventually toys. His first significant success occurred with the production of a small limousine. The Tootsietoy trade name was registered in 1924; in 1926, the company was sold to Nathan Shure, who merged it with his Cosmo Toy and Novelty Company. With the acquisition of the Strombecker Company in 1961, the company was renamed to Strombecker and is still in business today, producing toy cap guns, die-cast and plastic vehicles, wood pre-school toys, plastic action figures, Easter-egg dyes, and other novelties.

BIOGRAPHY: John Gibson has always been a collector of sorts, including antique firearms, Arts & Crafts Movement, Art Nouveau, Art Deco, advertising tins, vintage posters, and pin-up art. While antique hunting in 1989, he discovered a mint, boxed set of Deluxe Grahams and has been actively involved with Tootsietoys ever since. He also repairs and restores them for fellow collectors. Born in Montpelier, Vermont, he graduated from the University of Wisconsin and is self-employed in the Washington D.C. area. He is currently researching and writing a pre-war book on Tootsietoys.

PRE-WAR TOOTSIETOYS

	C6	C8	C10
4528 Limousine	24	32	40
4570 Ford, Model T, Open Tourer	33	50	65
4610 Ford Model T Pickup Truck	30	50	70
4629 (Yellow Cab) Sedan	15	23	30
4630 (Federal) "Grocery" Delivery Van	38	57	75
4631 (Federal) "Bakery" Delivery Van	50	80	105
4632 (Federal) "Market" Delivery Van	35	60	75

	C6	C8	C10
4633 (Federal) "Laundry" Delivery Van	35	60	75
4634 (Federal) "Milk" Delivery Van	36	48	60
4635 (Federal) "Florist" Delivery Van	135	180	225
4636 Buick Coupe	23	34	45
4638 Mack Stake Truck	23	34	45
4639 Mack Coal Truck	23	34	45
4640 Mack Tank Truck	23	34	45
4641 Buick Touring Car	28	42	55
4642 Long Range Cannon	13	18	25
4643 Mack Anti-Aircraft Gun	25	38	50
4644 Mack Searchlight Truck	27	41	55
4645 Mack "US Mail - Airmail Service"	38	57	75
4646 Caterpillar tractor, original treads only	27	41	55
4647 Renault tank, original treads only	23	34	45
4648 Steamroller	90	120	150
4651 Fageol safety coach	27	41	44
4652 Fire Engine - hook and ladder	30	45	60
4653 Fire Engine - water tower	48	64	80
4654 Farm Tractor	35	53	70
4655 Ford, Model A Coupe	20	30	40
4656 Buick Coupe in tinplate garage	60	90	150
4657 Buick Sedan in tinplate garage	60	90	150
4658 Mack Insurance Patrol in tinplate garage	100	150	200
4665 Ford Model A Sedan	20	30	40
4666 Bluebird I Daytona record car	23	34	45
4670 Mack Tractor and two semi-trailers, "A&P," "American Express"	115	170	225
4680 "Overland Bus Lines"	45	65	85
23 Racer with driver intact	45	68	90
190 Mack auto transport with 3 Buicks	111	148	195

Tootsietoy No. 4630 "Store Name" Federal Delivery Van (1924); Emil Kraus, State at 18th, an Erie, PA store. Collection & Photo John Gibson.

Tootsietoy No. 4635 "Florist" Delivery Van, issued 1924. Collection & Photo John Gibson.

Tootsietoy No. 04638. Courtesy Phillips NY.

Tootsietoy No. 4657 Tinplate Garage with No. 103 Buick Sedan. Collection & Photo John Gibson.

Tootsietoy, L to R: 4665, 5655, unnumbered "U.S. Mail" (sold only in sets), 0716 "Doodlebug." Courtesy Phillips New York

Tootsietoy, L to R: 4670, 4680, 4651, 4634. Courtesy Phillips NY.

Tootsietoy No. 4670 Mack A&P Trailer Truck, 1929. Collection & Photo John Gibson.

Tootsietoy No. 4680 "Overland Bus," issued 1929 (later Diesteel wheels). Collection & Photo by John Gibson.

Tootsietoy No. 6105 Cadillac Touring Car from Tootsietoy GM series (1927). Collection & Photo John Gibson.

Tootsietoy No. 6-06 "No Name" Delivery Truck (1933), often called "Screenside" (GM series). Collection & Photo John Gibson.

Tootsietoy No. 801 Mack Stake Truck, 1933. Collection & Photo John Gibson.

Tootsietoy 0192. Courtesy Phillips NY.

	C6	C8	C10
190 Mack auto transport with 4 Buicks	150	200	250
191 Contractors tipper set	114	152	190
5101 Andy Gump Roadster, standard	175	265	350
5101 Andy Gump Roadster, articulated	225	340	450
5102 Uncle Walt Roadster, standard	175	265	350
5102 Uncle Walt Roadster, articulated	225	340	450
5103 Smitty Motorcycle, standard	175	265	350
5103 Smitty Motorcycle, articulated	225	340	450
5104 Moon Mullins Police Wagon, standard	175	265	350
5104 Moon Mullins Police Wagon, articulated	225	340	450
5105 Kayo Ice Wagon, standard	150	225	300
5105 Kayo Ice Wagon, articulated	185	285	375
5106 Uncle Willie Rowboat, standard	135	210	275
5106 Uncle Willie Rowboat, articulated	175	265	350
6001 Buick Roadster, GM series	30	45	60
6002 Buick Coupe, GM series	28	41	55
6003 Buick Brougham, GM series	28	41	55
6004 Buick Sedan, GM series	28	41	55
6005 Buick Touring car, GM series	50	75	100
6006 Buick Screenside Delivery Truck, GM series	35	53	70
6101 Cadillac Roadster, GM series	40	60	80
6102 Cadillac Coupe, GM series	40	60	80
6103 Cadillac Brougham, GM series	40	60	80
6104 Cadillac Sedan, GM series	40	60	80
6105 Cadillac Touring car, GM series	48	71	95
6106 Cadillac Screenside Delivery truck, GM series	48	71	95
6201 Chevrolet Roadster, GM series	38	55	75
6202 Chevrolet Coupe, GM series	33	50	65
6203 Chevrolet Brougham, GM series	33	50	65
6204 Chevrolet sedan, GM series	33	50	65
6205 Chevrolet Touring car, GM series	55	83	110
6206 Chevrolet Screenside Delivery Truck, GM series	35	53	70
6301 Oldsmobile Roadster, GM series	38	55	75
6302 Oldsmobile Coupe, GM series	35	53	70
6303 Oldsmobile Brougham, GM series	35	53	70
6304 Oldsmobile Sedan, GM series	35	53	70
6305 Oldsmobile Touring car, GM series	55	83	110
6306 Oldsmobile Screenside Delivery Truck, GM series	45	68	90
6-01 "No Name" Roadster, GM series	55	83	110
6-02 "No Name" Coupe, GM series	55	83	110
6-03 "No Name" Brougham, GM series	55	83	110
6-04 "No Name" Sedan, GM series	55	83	110
6-05 "No Name" Touring Car, GM series	75	113	150

	C6	C8	C10
6-06 "No Name" Screenside Delivery Truck, GM series	65	95	125
--- Ford Model A Van marked "U.S. Mail," sold only in sets	38	56	75
4654 Farm Tractor for Army Field Battery Set No. 5071	58	86	115
--- Box Trailer and Roadscraper Raker, sold only in boxed set Farm Tractor No. 7003	135	205	275
6665 Ford Model A Sedan	25	38	50
101 Buick Coupe	10	15	20
102 Buick Roadster	13	19	25
103 Buick Sedan	10	15	20
104 Mack Insurance Patrol	23	34	45
105 Mack Tank Truck	28	41	55
108 Caterpillar Tractor, original treads only	23	34	45
109 Ford Pickup Truck	20	30	40
110 Bluebird Daytona record car	28	41	55
0192 Mack Tootsietoy Dairy, 1-piece cab, 3 trailers	111	148	185
0192 Mack Tootsie Toy Dairy, 2-piece cab, 3 trailers	115	165	225
0198 Mack Auto Transport, 1-piece cab, 3 '35 Fords	150	225	300
0198 Mack Auto Transport, 2-piece cab, 3 '34 Fords	215	320	425
0801 Mack "Express" Stake Semi-trailer, 1-piece cab	55	80	105
0801 Mack "Express" Stake Semi-trailer, 2-piece cab	63	95	125
0802 Mack "Domaco" Tank Semi-trailer, 1-piece cab	60	90	120
0802 Mack "Domaco" Tank Semi-trailer, 2-piece cab	65	98	130
0803 Mack "Long Distance Hauling" Semi-trailer	111	148	185
0804 Mack "City Fuel" Coal Truck, 10-wheel	114	152	190
0804 Mack "City Fuel" Coal Truck, 4-wheel	125	187	250
0805 Mack "Tootsietoy Dairy" Semi-trailer Truck	70	105	140
0806 Graham Wrecker	75	113	150
0807 Delivery Motorcycle adapted from 5103	175	260	350
0808 Graham "Tootsietoy Dairy"	75	113	150
0809 Graham Ambulance	75	113	150
--- Graham "Commercial Tire & Supply"	112	168	225

Tootsietoy No. 802 Mack "Domaco" Oil Trailer (1933). Collection & Photo John Gibson.

Tootsietoy 803 Mack "Long Distance Hauling" semi-trailer, "Century of Progress" issue. John Gibson Collection.

Tootsietoy No. 804 "City Fuel Co." 100mm 10-wheel version, issued 1933, in catalog 1933-35. Courtesy The Graham Werkes.

Tootsietoy No. 0804 "City Fuel Co." rarer 4-wheel version - issued 1936, in catalog 1936-38. Courtesy The Graham Werkes.

Tootsietoy No. 805 Dairy Trailer, 1933. Collection & Photo John Gibson.

Tootsietoy 0806. Courtesy Phillips NY.

Tootsietoy unnumbered Graham "Commercial Tire & Supply Co." Van, issued 1935 Collection & Photo John Gibson.

Tootsietoy No. 716 Doodlebug, issued 1935 and patterned after Briggs prototype sedan. Collection & Photo John Gibson.

Tootsietoy No. 6015 Lincoln Zephyr (1937): This was a revised version of the #716 Doodlebug, issued with or without a windup motor. Collection & Photo John Gibson.

Tootsietoy No. 113 1935 Ford Wrecker. Collection & Photo John Gibson.

Tootsietoy No. 1009 "Shell" Oil Tanker, 1938. Collection & Photo John Gibson.

	C6	C8	C10
0810 Mack "Railway Express Co." Truck with "Wrigley's Gum" ad, 1-piece cab ...	70	105	140
0810 Mack "Railway Express Co." Truck with "Wrigley's Gum" ad, 2-piece cab ...	75	115	150
0511 Graham Roadster, 5-wheel	83	125	165
0512 Graham Coupe, 5-wheel	72	110	145
0513 Graham Sedan, 5-wheel	72	110	145
0514 Graham Convertible Coupe, 5-wheel ..	80	120	160
0515 Graham Convertible Sedan, 5-wheel ..	80	120	160
0516 Graham Town Car, 5-wheel	88	130	175
0611 Graham Roadster, 6-wheel	83	125	165
0612 Graham Coupe, 6-wheel	72	110	145
0613 Graham Sedan, 6-wheel	72	110	145
0614 Graham Convertible Coupe, 6-wheel ..	80	120	160
0615 Graham Convertible Sedan, 6-wheel ..	80	120	160
0616 Graham Towncar, 6-wheel	75	113	150
--- Graham Roadster, 4-wheel, Bild-A-Car .	88	130	175
--- Graham Coupe, 4-wheel, Bild-A-Car	65	98	130
--- Graham sedan, 4-wheel, Bild-A-Car	65	98	130
0712 LaSalle Coupe	133	200	265
0713 LaSalle Sedan	133	200	265
0714 LaSalle Convertible Coupe	143	214	285
0715 LaSalle Convertible Sedan	143	214	285
0716 Briggs Lincoln prototype, "Doodlebug"	60	90	125
6015 Lincoln Zephyr (plain version)	165	245	325
6015 Lincoln Zephyr (windup)	240	365	485
6016 Lincoln Wrecker (plain version)	275	415	550
6016 Lincoln Wrecker (windup)	350	525	700
0111 1934 Ford V8 sedan	30	45	60
0111 1935 Ford V8 sedan	15	23	30
0112 1934 Ford V8 Coupe	33	49	65
0112 1935 Ford V8 Coupe	18	26	35
0113 1934 Ford V8 Wrecker	38	56	75
0113 1935 Ford V8 Wrecker	33	49	65
0114 1934 Ford V8 Convertible Coupe	40	60	80
0114 1935 Ford V8 Convertible Coupe	30	45	60
0115 1934 Ford V8 Convertible Sedan	40	60	80
0115 1935 Ford V8 Convertible Sedan	30	45	60
0116 Ford V8 Roadster	23	34	45
--- 1935 Ford V8 Roadster Fire Chief's Car	50	75	100
0117 Zephyr Railcar	38	56	75
0118 DeSoto Airflow Sedan	23	34	45
0120 Oil Tank Truck	23	34	45
0121 Ford Pickup Truck	18	26	35
0123 Ford "Special Delivery" Camelback Van	25	38	50
0123 Ford "Wieboldt's" Camelback Van ..	145	215	285

	C6	C8	C10
0123 Ford "Lewis's" Camelback Van	135	205	275
0123 Ford "Miller & Rhoads" Camelback Van	145	215	285
0123 Ford "McLeans" Camelback Van	145	215	285
0123 Ford "Shepards" Camelback Van	145	215	285
180 Lincoln Zephyr & Roamer House Trailer without windup motor ...	435	655	875
180 Lincoln Zephyr & Roamer House Trailer with windup motor	515	775	1035
187 Mack Auto Transport with up-tilted trailer & 3 vehicles	275	415	550
4634 Army Supply Truck	33	49	65
4635 Armored Car	33	49	65
1006 "Standard" Oil Truck	55	80	110
1007 "Sinclair" Oil Truck	55	80	110
1008 "Texaco" Oil Truck	55	80	110
1009 "Shell" Oil Truck	60	90	120
1010 "Wrigley" Box Van	55	80	110
1011 "Massey-Ferguson" Farm Tractor	200	300	400
1016 Auburn Roadster, jumbo torpedo-single color	23	34	45
1016 Auburn Roadster, jumbo torpedo-two tone	36	48	60
1017 Coupe, jumbo torpedo-single color	20	30	40
1017 Coupe, jumbo torpedo-two tone	30	40	50
1018 Sedan, jumbo torpedo-single color	23	34	45
1019 Pickup Truck, jumbo torpedo-single color	23	34	45
1019 Pickup Truck, jumbo torpedo-two tone	23	34	45
1026 Cross Country Bus, jumbo torpedo-fully skirted	30	45	60
1027 Wrecker, jumbo torpedo-single color .	23	34	45
1027 Wrecker, jumbo torpedo-two tone	36	48	60
1040 Fire Engine, Hook & Ladder	35	50	70
1041 Fire Engine, Hose Car	35	55	75
1042 Fire Engine, Insurance Patrol, open end	30	45	60
1042 Fire Engine, Insurance Patrol w/single ladder & rear fireman	38	56	75
1043 No. 111 Ford Sedan & small House Trailer	35	53	70
1044 Roamer House Trailer w/door & tin bottom	270	360	450
1045 Greyhound Deluxe Bus-open front fenders & tin bottom	55	83	110
1045 Greyhound Deluxe Bus-open front fenders	35	50	70
--- TransAmerica Bus (sold only in sets)	90	130	175

Tootsietoy No. 1010 Wrigley's truck, 114mm long, issued 1940, reissued post war 4." Courtesy The Graham Werkes.

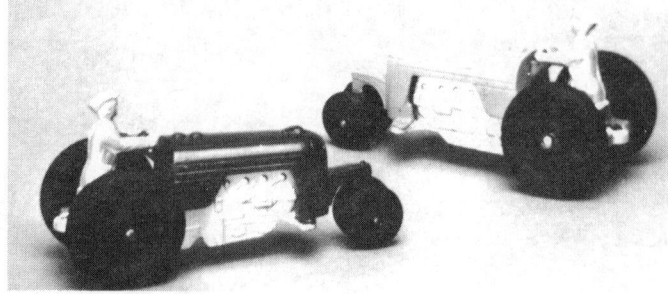

Tootsietoy No. 1011 Massey-Ferguson farm tractors in only known colors: green/silver and red/silver. Issued in 1941; 4" long, considered rare. Courtesy The Graham Werkes.

Tootsietoy No. 1040 Hook & Ladder, issued 1937, in catalog 1937-41, 139mm. Courtesy The Graham Werkes.

Tootsietoy No. 1046 Station Wagon, issued 1940, reissued postwar, 113 mm. Courtesy The Graham Werkes.

Tootsietoy No. 1044 Roamer Trailer, 1937. Collection & Photo John Gibson.

	C6	C8	C10
1046 Station Wagon	43	64	85
230 LaSalle Sedan	15	20	30
231 Coupe	15	20	30
232 Open Touring Coupe	15	20	30
233 Boattail Roadster	15	20	30
234 Box Van	15	20	30
235 Oil Tank Truck	13	18	25
236 Fire Engine, Hook & Ladder	20	30	40
237 Fire Engine, Insurance Patrol	15	25	35
238 Fire Engine, Hose Wagon	20	30	40
239 Station Wagon	20	30	40

Miniature Vehicles

510 Midget Assortment Boxed Set (8-piece)	75	100	150
510 Midget Assortment Boxed Set (10-piece)	90	130	175
610 Midget Assortment Boxed Set (12-piece)	100	150	200

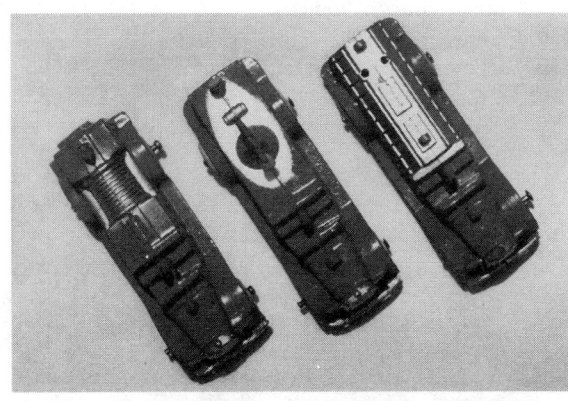

Tootsietoy Firetrucks resembling Macks, Left to Right: No. 237 Insurance Patrol, No. 238 Hose Car, No. 236 Hook & Ladder (all issued 1940 and reissued postwar w/black tires). Collection & Photo John Gibson.

	C6	C8	C10
1628 Bus	6	9	12
1629 Wrecker	7	10	14
1630 Racer	5	7	10
1631 DeSoto Airflow sedan	5	7	10
1632 Zephyr Railcar	7	10	14
1634 Firetruck	7	10	14
1635 Delivery Van	6	9	12
1635 Delivery Van (Ambulance)	7	10	14
1666 Army Tank	4	6	8
1667 Armored Car	5	7	10

IMPROVED 1933 "TOOTSIETOYS"

Modeled after 1933 autos with the latest streamline bodies. Some with rubber tires.

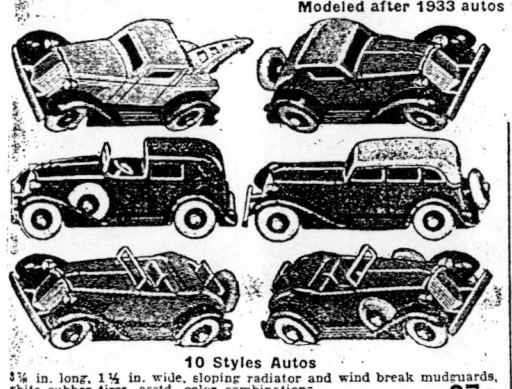

10 Styles Autos

3¼ in. long, 1¼ in. wide, sloping radiator and wind break mudguards, white rubber tires, asstd. color combinations.
2F-6316—10 in box .... Box **67c**

2F-6301

2F-6302

2F-6311

Comic Strip Figures

2F-6300—Moon Mullins
2F-6301—Kayo
2F-6302—Uncle Willie and Mamie
Aver. 3½ in. long, asstd. color combinations, action figures. 1 doz in box.

2F-6305—Andy Gump
2F-6307—Uncle Walt
2F-6311—Smitty and Herby

2F-6305

Doz **80c**

Aeroplanes

Tri-Motor—4 in. long, 5¼ in. wing spread, 3 propellers, white rubber tires, asstd. aluminum, yellow and red. Each in box.
2F-6313—1 doz. in carton .... Doz **84c**

Tootsietoys shown in the April, 1933 Butler Bros. catalog.

	C6	C8	C10

Post-War

	C6	C8	C10
1954 American LaFrance Pumper, 3" long	10	15	20
Atomic Cannon/155mm Howitzer 5-1/4" long	100	150	200
1956 Austin Healy 100-6, 4-passenger Roadster, 6" long	20	30	40
1955 Austin Healy 100-6 unassembled kit, 6" long	150	225	300
1954 Buick Century Estate Wagon, 6" long	18	26	35
1951 Buick LeSabre Experimental Roadster, 6" long	23	34	45
1949 Buick Roadmaster, 4-door Sedan, 6" long	25	38	50
1956 Caterpillar Roadscraper, 6" long	18	26	35
1950 Chevrolet Ambulance, 4" long	13	19	25
1955 Chevrolet BelAir, 4-door Sedan, 3" long	10	15	20

	C6	C8	C10
1956 Chevrolet Cameo Pickup, 4" long	13	19	25
1947 Chevrolet Coupe, 4" long	13	19	25
1950 Chevrolet Deluxe Panel Truck, 4" long	13	19	25
1950 Chevrolet Deluxe Panel Truck, 3" long	10	15	20
1960 Chevrolet El Camino w/camper/boat, 6" long	50	75	100
1960 Chevrolet El Camino, 6" long	18	26	35
1950 Chevrolet Fleetline, 2-door Fastback Sedan, 3" long	10	15	20
1959 Chevrolet Semi Cab only	63	94	125
w/"Mobile" Trailer*	80	120	160
w/Hook & Ladder*	93	139	185
w/Log Trailer*	75	113	150
w/3 Boat Trailer*	78	116	155
w/3 Car Transport*	78	116	155
w/Army Flatbed*	80	120	160
w/Dean Van Lines*	75	113	150
1953 Chrysler New Yorker 4-door Sedan, 6" long	18	26	35
1942 Chrysler Thunderbolt Experimental Roadster, 6" long	23	34	45
1941 Chrysler Windsor Convertible, 4" long	14	21	28
1950 Chrysler Windsor Convertible, 6" long	66	88	110
1960 Chrysler Windsor Convertible, 4" long	13	19	25
w/"Mobile" Trailer*	80	120	160
w/Hook & Ladder*	93	139	185
w/Log Trailer*	75	113	150
w/3 Boat Trailer*	78	116	155
w/3 Car Transport*	78	116	155
w/Army Flatbed*	80	120	160
w/"Dean Van Lines"*	75	113	150

Tootsietoy (Postwar) 1947 Futuristic-Looking Pickup Truck (commonly called "Hudson"; never identified by Tootsietoy, sold only in boxed sets). Collection & Photo John Gibson.

Tootsietoy 1948 Buick Super Estate Wagon, open grille (postwar). Collection & Photo John Gibson.

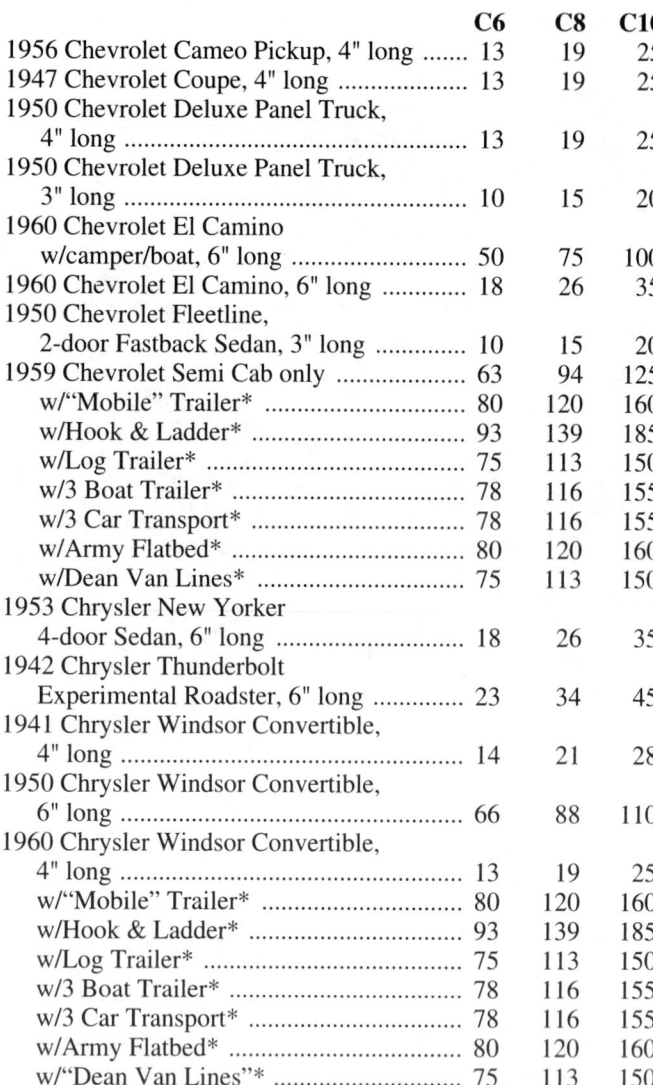

Tootsietoy Chrysler Thunderbolt experimental roadsters. Photo by Gerald F. Slack.

Tootsietoy Dodge D100 Panel Truck from 1956 and a No. 1008 Texaco Oil Truck (1939-41). Courtesy Mapes Auctioneers.

	C6	C8	C10
1953 Chrysler New Yorker 4-door Sedan, 6" long	18	26	35
1942 Chrysler Thunderbolt Experimental Roadster, 6" long	23	34	45
1941 Chrysler Windsor Convertible, 4" long	14	21	28
1950 Chrysler Windsor Convertible, 6" long	66	88	110
1960 Chrysler Windsor Convertible, 4" long	13	19	25
1954-55 Corvette Roadster, 4" long	13	19	25
1956 Dodge D100 Panel Truck, 6" long	20	30	40
1950 Dodge Pickup Truck, 4" long	13	19	25
1956 Ferrari Racer, 6" long	28	41	55
1931 Ford B Hot Rod, 3"	8	11	15
1947 Futuristic-Looking Pickup Truck (commonly called Hudson)	37	56	75
1949 Ford Custom Convertible, 3" long	11	16	22
1949 Ford Custom, 4-door Sedan, 3" long	11	16	22
1955 Ford Customline V8 2-door Sedan, 3" long	11	16	22
1962 Ford Econoline Pickup, 6" long	15	23	30
1949 Ford F1 Pickup, 3"	8	11	15
1949 Ford F6 Oil Tanker, 6" long	30	45	60
1949 Ford F6 Oil Tanker, 4" long	10	15	20
1949 Ford F6 Stake Truck (Pickup), 4" long	13	19	25
1957 Ford F100 Styleside Pickup w/rear window, 3" long	8	11	15
1957 Ford F100 Styleside Pick-up w/o rear window, 3" long	8	11	15
1956 Ford F600 Army Gun Truck, 6" long	18	26	35
1955 Ford F600 Stake Truck w/tin cover, 6" long	60	90	120
1957 Ford Fairlane 500 Convertible, 3" long	8	11	15
1960 Ford Falcon, 2-door Sedan, 3" long	8	11	15
1956 Ford Farm Tractor, 6"	25	38	50
1960 Ford LTD, 2-door Hardtop, 4" long	13	19	25
1952 Ford Mainline, 4-door Sedan, 3" long	8	11	15
1954 Ford Ranch Wagon, 4"	13	19	25
1954 Ford Ranch Wagon, 3"	8	11	15
1940 Ford Special Deluxe Convertible, 6" long	28	41	55
1940 Ford V8 Hot Rod, 6"	18	26	35
1948 GMC 3751 Greyhound Bus, 6" long	23	34	45
1957 Greyhound Sceni-Cruiser Bus, 6" long	23	34	45
1040 Hook & Ladder, 4"	18	26	35
1041 Hose Car, 4" long	18	26	35
1941 International K1 Panel Truck, 4" long	20	30	40
1946 International K11 Oil Tanker, 6" long	18	26	35
1960 International Metro Step Van, 6" long	88	131	175
1955 International RC180, 6" long w/Rocket Launcher, Army version	60	90	120
w/Grain Trailer	30	50	65
w/Oil Tanker, no decals	30	50	65
w/Moving Van	30	50	65
w/Boat Transport	30	45	60
w/Car Transport	30	45	60
w/Gooseneck Trailer	25	38	50
1957 Jaguar type D, 3"	8	11	15
1954 Jaguar XK120 Roadster, 3" long	10	15	20
1956 Jaguar XK140 Coupe, 6" long	18	26	35
1950 Jeep CJ3, Army version, 3" long	8	11	15

Tootsietoy Jeep CJ3, 1950, 3." Photo by Ed Poole.

	C6	C8	C10
1950 Jeep CJ3, Civilian version, 3" long	8	11	15
1950 Jeep CJ3, Army version, 4" long	13	19	25
1950 Jeep CJ3, Civilian version, 4" long	13	19	25
1960 Jeep CJ5, Civilian version, 6" long	18	26	35
1960 Jeep CJ5, Army version, 6" long	18	26	35
1960 Jeep CJ5, Snowplow version, 6" long	38	56	75
1947 Jeepster, 3" long	9	14	18
1947 Kaiser Sedan, 6" long	20	30	40
1956 Lancia Racer, 6" long	38	56	75
1952 Lincoln Capri, 2-door Hardtop, 6" long	18	26	35
1955 Mack B Line Cement Mixer, 6" long	20	30	40
1955 Mack B Line Hook & Ladder, 6" long	38	56	75
1955 Mack B Line Moving Van (w/o doors) 6" long	43	64	85
1955 Mack B Line Moving Van (w/doors), 6" long	60	90	120
1955 Mack B Line Log Trailer, 6" long	43	64	85
1955 Mack B Line Oil Tanker, 6" long	23	34	45
1955 Mack B Line Open Stake Truck, 6" long	63	94	125
1947 Mack L Line Dump Truck, 6" long	18	26	35
1947 Mack L Line Fire Pumper, 6" long	43	64	85
1947 Mack L Line Fire (ladder) Trailer, 6" long	43	64	85
1947 Mack L Line Log Truck, 6" long	43	64	85
1947 Mack L Line Moving Van, 6" long	25	38	50
1947 Mack L Line Closed Side Stake, 6" long	20	30	40
1947 Mack L Line Stake Trailer, 6" long	63	94	125
1947 Mack L Line "Tootsietoys Coast to Coast," 6"	43	64	85
1947 Mack L Line Tow Truck, 6" long	20	30	40
1956 Mercedes 190SL, 6"	18	26	35
1955 Mercedes 300SL Gullwing (doors intact), 9" long	150	225	300
1952 Mercury Custom Sedan, 4-door, 4" long	13	19	25
1949 Mercury Fire Chief Car, 4" long	14	21	28
1949 Mercury Sedan, 4-door, 4" long	13	19	25
Metro Van, HO Series	8	11	15
1954 MG TF Roadster, 6"	21	32	42
1954 MG TF Roadster, 3"	10	15	20
1954 Nash Metropolitan Convertible, 3" long	30	45	60
1947 Offenhauser Hill Climber Racer, 3" long	9	13	18
1949 Oldsmobile 88 Convertible, 4" long	15	23	30

	C6	C8	C10
1959 Oldsmobile Dynamic 88 Convertible, 6" long	13	19	25
1955 Oldsmobile 98 Holiday, 2-door hardtop, 4" long	13	19	25
1955 Oldsmobile 98 Holiday, 4-door hardtop, Army version, 4"	13	19	25
1956 Packard Patrician, 4-door Sedan, 6" long	18	26	35
1957 Plymouth Belvedere 2-door hardtop, 3" long	8	11	15
1950 Plymouth Special Deluxe, 4-door Sedan, 3" long	8	11	15
1950 Pontiac Chieftan Deluxe Coupe Sedan, 4" long	13	19	25
1950 Pontiac Chieftan Fire Chief Coupe Sedan, 4" long	18	26	35
1955 Pontiac Safari Station Wagon, (#895), 9" long	100	150	200

	C6	C8	C10
1959 Pontiac Star Chief, 4-door Sedan, 4" long	13	19	25
1956 Porsche Spyder Roadster, 6" long	18	26	35
1960 Rambler Super Cross Country Station Wagon, 4" long	15	23	30
School Bus, HO series	10	15	20
1947 Studebaker Champion, 5-window Coupe, 3" long	25	38	50
1960 Studebaker Lark Convertible, 3" long	8	11	15
1955 Thunderbird Coupe, 4" long	11	17	22
1955 Thunderbird Coupe, 3" long	8	11	15
1956 Triumph TR3 Roadster, 3" long	9	14	18
1950 Twin Coach Bus, 3"	23	34	45
1960 Volkswagen Beetle, 6" long	18	26	35
1960 Volkswagen Beetle, 3" long	5	8	10
1941 White Army Half Track, 4" long	18	26	35

An early Tootsietoy boxtop.

TOY FOUNDERS

	C6	C8	C10
Toy Founders Kaiser Convertible, 1947, windup, 11" long	175	263	350
Toy Founders "Kar Kit," clockwork, car 11" long, makes 3 types	175	263	350

TRAILER CO.

(Los Angeles)

	C6	C8	C10
Traveleer Land Coach Traveler, 1927	180	270	360

TRU-SCALE INTERNATIONAL TRUCKS

by Bob Smith

Early in the 1940s, Joseph Carter founded the Carter Machine Company. After WWII, Carter began to manufacture a line of toys. At first, Carter's toy line mainly consisted of International and John Deere farm tractors and implements. In the 1950s, Carter began his new line of 1/16th scale trucks under the "Tru-Scale" trademark. He felt that the International truck model would be the best choice, because International had been building trucks since 1907. The first Tru-Scale model was in the "S" series. This was the model then in production by the International Truck Company. The models marked with the "I.H." logo on the doors were sold by International Harvester outlets only. Any models marked "Tru-Scale" on the doors would have been sold through other retail outlets.

As the International Truck Co. re-designed its body style, Carter would follow this design with its comparable model. While thought of as a toy, one must consider the fine detail and workmanship that went into the Tru-Scale models. Its paint colors were correct, the grille styling and fender lines followed the real truck body lines, and they were very well detailed for a pressed-steel toy.

After the "S" series, the "A" series, "B" series, and "C" series trucks followed, in respective order. The models were made as pick-up trucks, service trucks with tool boxes, dump trucks with single or dual axle, semi-tractor trailer trucks with open or enclosed trailers, and also as grain trucks. The dump trucks came with either a hydraulic cylinder or manual control, depending on which model or year it was produced. The later "C" series came with plastic windows and white-wall tires with full hubcaps. Another feature was the finger-tip steering that worked by applying pressure on the front of the cab to steer the front wheels. Tru-Scale also produced some Private Label trucks, such as Ryerson Steel and Yale Trucking.

In 1971, Carter Tru-Scale sold the business to Ertl, which used parts of the Tru-Scale line for the new Ertl die-cast International "Loadster" series. Ertl did not continue with the Tru-Scale line of International trucks.

	C6	C8	C10
No. 1 Tru-Scale "S" series International Service Truck, green/white, c.1953	175	300	450
No. 2 Tru-Scale "A" series International Service Truck, red/white, c.1957	175	300	450
No. 2a Tru-Scale "S" series International Pickup Truck, light blue/white,. c.1953.	125	225	350
No. 3 Tru-Scale "B" series International Service Truck, red/white, c.1959	125	250	375
No. 4 Tru-Scale "C" series International Service Truck, orange/white, w/w tires, windshield, c.1961	150	250	375
No. 5 Tru-Scale "A" series International Pickup Truck, red/cream, c.1957	150	250	375
No. 6 Tru-Scale "C" series International Pick up Truck, red/white, T/S decal, c.1961	150	250	375
No. 6a Tru-Scale "C" series International Pickup Truck blue/white, I/H decal, c.1961	100	175	275
No. 7 Tru-Scale "A" series International Grain truck, blue, I.H decal, c.1957	150	250	375
No. 7a Tru-Scale "B" series International Grain Truck, green, I/H decal, c.1959	100	175	275
No. 8 Tru-Scale "S" series International 10-wheel Hydraulic Dump Truck, orange/white, c.1953	175	275	400

Tru-Scale No. 1. Photo by Bob Smith.

Tru-Scale, Top to Bottom: No. 2, No. 2a. Photo by Bob Smith.

Tru-Scale No. 3. Photo by Bob Smith.

Tru-Scale No. #4. Photo by Bob Smith.

Tru-Scale No. 5. Photo by Bob Smith.

Tru-Scale, Top to Bottom: No. 6, No. 6a. Photo by Bob Smith.

Tru-Scale No. 7. Photo by Bob Smith.

Tru-Scale No. 7a. Photo by Bob Smith.

Tru-Scale International Trucks

	C6	C8	C10

No. 9 Tru-Scale "A" series
International 10-wheel Hydraulic
Dump Truck, orange. c.1957 .... 175 275 400

No. 10 Tru-Scale "B" series 6-wheel
Manual Dump Truck, orange, c.1959 .... 150 250 375

No. 11 Tru-Scale "B" series 10-wheel
Hydraulic Dump Truck, orange, c.1959 125 200 300

No. 12 Tru-Scale "C" series 6-wheel
International Dump truck,
red/white, c.1961 .... 125 200 300

	C6	C8	C10

No. 13 Tru-Scale "B" series Semi-Tractor
& Van Trailer, red/white, c.1959 .... 250 350 500

No. 14 Tru-Scale "C" series Semi-Tractor
& Van Trailer, green/ white,
"Yale Trucking," c.1961 .... 275 400 550

No. 15 Tru-Scale "B" series
Semi-Tractor Hydraulic Dump Truck,
dark red, c.1959 .... 125 225 350

No. 15a Tru-Scale "C" series Semi-Tractor
Stake Truck, red/yellow,
"Ryerson Steel," c.1961 .... 150 250 375

No. 16 Tru-Scale/Ertl, Ertl Int'l.
Fleetstar Cab w/Tru-Scale Dump
Trailer, white/green, c.1971,
"Anderson Payload" 150 275 400

No. 16a Tru-Scale International "C" series
Semi-Tractor Hydraulic Dump Truck,
orange/yellow, c.1961 .... 125 225 350

Tru-Scale No. 8. Photo by Bob Smith.

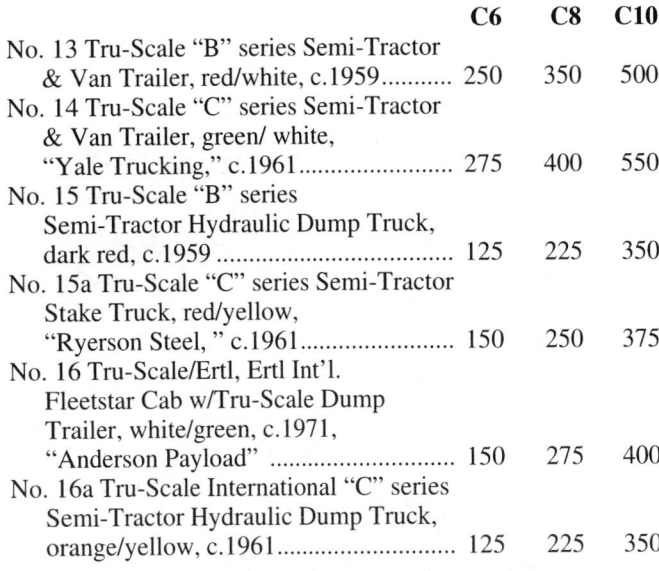

Tru-Scale No. 9. Photo by Bob Smith.

Tru-Scale No. 10. Photo by Bob Smith.

Tru-Scale No. 11. Photo by Bob Smith.

Tru-Scale No. 12. Photo by Bob Smith.

Tru-Scale No. 13. (Model in photo restored.) Photo by Bob Smith.

Tru-Scale No. 14. Photo by Bob Smith.

Tru-Scale, Top to Bottom: No. 15, No. 15a. Photo by Bob Smith.

*Tru-Scale, Top to Bottom: No. 16, No. 16a.
Photo by Bob Smith.*

TRU-TOY

	C6	C8	C10
Tru-Toy Steer-O-Car, 13" long	112	168	225

TRUMODEL See "Kelmet"

TURNER, JOHN C.

By Bob Smith

John Turner began in the trade working first with D.P. Clark and later with the Schieble Toy Co. He went off on his own in 1915. Within two years, he was producing a line of friction cars. In 1925, he was issued a patent for a new flywheel design made of metal disks, giving the appearance of large flat washers fitted together. The Turner flywheel is noticeably different from other manufacturers' mechanisms. Turner was located in Dayton and Wapkoneta, Ohio, from about 1915 into the 1940s.

Turner Ahrens Fox Ladder Truck, 15", 1920	500	750	1080
Turner Ahrens Fox Pumper, 16" long	650	1100	1600
Turner Bulldog Mack closed cab Dump Truck, red and green steel, 23" long	400	600	800
Turner Car Hauler	225	338	450
Turner Crane Truck, 22" long	300	450	600
Turner Delivery Van, 12-1/2" long, c.1920s	900	1500	2200
Turner Dump, friction, 15-1/2" long, c., early 1930s	240	360	480
Turner Dump, 17" long, 1930s.	200	300	400
Turner Dump, 22" long, C-Cab	400	600	800

	C6	C8	C10
Turner Dump, 26" long	250	375	500
Turner Dump, 28" long, Dodge	100	150	200
Turner Fire Engine Pumper, 15" long	750	1400	1800
Turner Fire Engine Pumper, 26" long, early	550	800	1200
Turner Garage, pressed steel, 21" long, 15" wide	150	225	300
Turner Hook & Ladder, 15" long, c.1930s	225	338	450
Turner Intercity Bus	500	750	1000
Turner Ladder Truck, 1940	235	353	470
Turner Limousine	2000	3500	5000
Turner Lincoln Sedan, 26" long	2000	3500	5000

	C6	C8	C10
Turner Mack Dump, 23" long	350	525	700
Turner Mack Ladder Truck	250	375	500
Turner "Overland Bus," pressed steel	No Price Found		
Turner Packard Racer, 1924, 26" long	800	1400	2000
Turner Packard Roadster, 16-1/2" long, 1920s	600	950	1300

	C6	C8	C10
Turner Packard (?) Roadster, 26" long, friction	900	1500	2200
Turner Panel Truck, early, 13" long	250	375	500
Turner Speedster, 1920s, 17" long, c. late 1920s, early 1930s	500	750	1000
Turner Stake Truck, deco style	130	195	260
Turner Stake Truck, C-Cab, 22" long	188	282	375
Turner Steam Shovel, 14" long	68	102	135
Turner Tow Truck, 20", elec. lights	130	195	260
Turner Water Truck, copper tank	150	225	300
Turner "Yellow Taxicab," flywheel drive, orange/black, 9-3/4" long, four riders, c.1927................................	312	468	625

Turner Crane Truck, 22" long. Photo by Calvin L. Chaussee.

Turner Dump, 26" long. Photo by Calvin L. Chaussee.

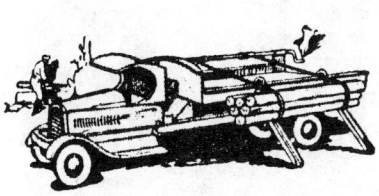

Turner trucks, as shown in the June, 1931 Toys and Novelties *magazine.*

Turner, John C. 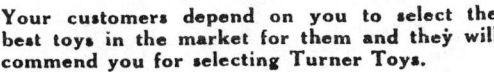 589

Turner "Overland Bus." Courtesy James Apthorpe.

Turner "Yellow Taxicab" (note passengers). Photo by Bob Smith.

UNIQUE ART MFG. CO.

Unique Art Mfg. Co. was in business from 1916, when it introduced its Merry Juggler and Charlie Chaplin. In 1931, it was located at Waverly and Peshine Avenues in Newark, New Jersey. Its president was Wm. Marbe, and there were 28 male employees (no females listed). In 1934, employees numbered 110 male and 165 female (same address). In a 1946-47 directory the address was 200 Waverly Avenue, Newark, and the president was Samuel Burger (this last name may be incorrect; the handwriting in my notes is hard to read). Employees were equally divided: 125 male and 125 female. Unique was still manufacturing toys, mainly windups, in 1952. Little else is known about the company, except that Louis Marx bought it at some date.

	C6	C8	C10
Unique Artie the Clown in his Crazy Car ..	300	450	600
Unique "Capitol Hill Racer," 1930s, 17-1/2" long with 2" tin racing car	100	150	200
Unique "Daredevil Motor Cop," 8-1/2" long, 1940s	500	750	1000
Unique "G.I. Joe and His Jouncing Jeep," post WWII, 7"	165	247	330

	C6	C8	C10
Unique Krazy Kar, new in 1921	300	450	600
Unique "Lincoln Tunnel," moving vehicles, cop, 1935, 24" long	275	363	550
Unique "Motorcycle Cop," 1930s, 9" long	220	330	440
Unique Rodeo Joe Crazy Car	158	235	315
Unique "Rollover Motorcycle Cop," 1935 .	200	300	400

Unique "Daredevil Motor Cop." Courtesy Kent M. Comstock.

Unique G.I. Joe & His Jouncing Jeep. Courtesy Mapes Auctioneers.

UNKNOWNS

These are vehicles whose manufacturer has yet to be established.

Plastic old-time car (Renwal?), large number "1" underneath, 6" long; value in this condition $25. Photo by Ron Fink.

Wooden Tank, c.WWII; value as shown $80. Photo by Jack Matthews.

"US W57" wooden tank, c. WWII; value as shown $35. Photo by Jack Matthews.

Composition Jeep (possibly by M. A. Henry Co.); value as shown $40. Photo by Jack Matthews.

WWII-era cardboard vehicles; value as shown $15 each. Photo by Jack Matthews.

Cardboard Tank, c. WWII, possibly by D.A. Pachter Company; value as shown $30. Photo by Jack Matthews.

Bronzed slush metal souvenir tanks, L to R: M12, M13, M14 (the tank at right was attached to an ashtray), 2" to 4" long; no price found. Photo by Ed Poole.

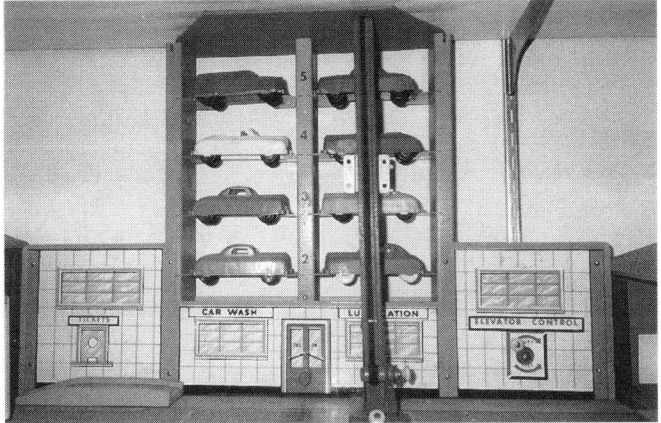

"Car Wash Lubrication Elevator Control" (possibly Keystone); value in Good $125. Photo by Ron Fink.

"Complete Car Service Washing-Greasing" service station (probably De Luxe); value in Good $100. Photo by Ron Fink.

"Firestone Complete Car Service - De Luxe Laundry" (very rare); value in Good $300. Photo by Ron Fink.

"Texaco Service You Can Trust" service station; value in Good $50. Photo by Ron Fink.

Germany, Horseless Carriage, tin litho, clockwork motor, driver & passenger, c.1903, 6" long; prices in C6, C8, C10: $700, 1200, 1800. Photo by Bob Smith.

Germany, Vis-a-Vis, tin litho, clockwork motor, steering, rubber tires, c.1900, 6-1/2" long (possibly Carette and marketed by MOKO); prices in C6, C8, C10: $1700, 2200, 2800. Photo by Bob Smith.

Germany, white hand-painted tin, clockwork motor, hand brake, doors open, rubber tires, lamps, cast seats. c.1911, 9" long (possibly Carette); prices in C6, C8, C10: $1450, 2200, 3000. Photo by Bob Smith.

Mack Trucks and a fire engine by an unknown maker (possibly Greyshaw of Georgia, Inc. c.1940s-50s), plastic, 4-1/2" long; values in C6, C8, C10: $6, 15, 25. Photo and caption courtesy Bob and Alice Wagner.

Germany, tin litho, green, gray, red, clockwork motor, rear doors open, c.1915, 9" long (possibly Carette); prices in C6, C8, C10: $1300, 1800, 2400. Photo by Bob Smith.

Unusual 30s steel coupe; no price found. Photo by Calvin L. Chaussee.

German Bulldog Macks, c.1950s, 7" long; value of each in C6, C8, C10: $15, 25, 50. Courtesy Bob and Alice Wagner.

Renault FT tank, slush-cast, 3" long; value about $25 in mint. Photo by Ed Poole.

L to R: Wooden "Ambulance" and "Supply Co. 123rd Field Artillery" truck; almost certainly Strombecker c.1932. Courtesy Roger Johnson and Charles Breslow.

Three 3-1/2" to 4" long composition tanks; no price found.
Top: MI1.
Bottom, L to R: MI2, MI3. Photo by Ed Poole.

Scale model autos!

No. 2473

Ford Sedan has accurate detail, really astonishing down to the last touch. In HO scale. Various colors. Carton – 36 assorted. List, each . . . . **10¢**

No. 2474

Ford Pickup is another Varney plastic triumph. Rolls freely. Great on train layouts. Assorted colors. List, ea...**10¢**

No. 2475

Ford Panel Truck, like the above, comes 36 to the carton, assorted colors. Really ingenious HO models. List, ea... **10¢**

	C6	C8	C10
Varney No. 2473 Ford Sedan, HO scale			No Price Found
Varney No. 2474 Ford Pickup			No Price Found
Varney No. 2475 Ford Panel Truck, HO Scale			No Price Found

Varney Scale Models, as advertised in the May, 1954 Hobby Merchandiser.

VICEROY

(Canada)

According to collector-author Dave Leopard, Viceroy had several locations and specialized in rubber and vinyl toys and dolls. Some were authorized versions of Sun Rubber Toys.

	C6	C8	C10
VR01 Open Racer, Sun Rubber type, 6-1/2"	30	45	60
VR02 Open Racer, 4-1/2"	22	33	45
VD02 Donald Duck Roadster, 6-2/3"	62	93	125
VD06 Donald Duck Tractor, 4-3/4"	62	93	125

Viceroy VR02 (both). Courtesy Dave Leopard from his book Rubber Toy Vehicles.

Viceroy VR01. Courtesy Dave Leopard from his book Rubber Toy Vehicles.

Viceroy VD02. Courtesy Dave Leopard from his book Rubber Toy Vehicles.

Viceroy VD06. Courtesy Dave Leopard from his book Rubber Toy Vehicles.

VIKING

(Ohio)

	C6	C8	C10
Viking Dump Truck, 27" long	550	850	1300

VINDEX

Vindex of Belvidere, Illinois, was in business as a toymaker from about 1928 to 1932. Its products were cast iron. Vindex was a division of National Sewing Machine Co.

	C6	C8	C10
Vindex Case Model L Tractor, 6-1/2" long	500	750	1030
Vindex Case 3 Bottom Tractor Plow, 10-1/4" long, auctioned 1994, near mint, for $3700			
Vindex Coast to Coast Bus, cast iron, c.1930, 12" long	1250	1875	2500
Vindex Combine	850	1500	2300
Vindex Hay Loader, Case, 9" long, auctioned 1994, excellent for, $5200			

	C6	C8	C10
Vindex "John Deere" Thresher, 15" long	1500	2800	3900
Vindex John Deere Tractor, Model D, 6-1/2" long	950	1700	2600
Vindex John Deere 3-bottom Tractor Plow, 9" long, auctioned 1996, pristine, for $2420			
Vindex John Deere Van Brunt Drill, 9-3/4" long, auctioned 1994, near mint, for $2900			

Vindex Motorcycles list by M. Comstock

	C6	C8	C10
(VM1) Motorcycle with detachable cop, "Henderson," 9", red or green	1000	1500	2500
(VM2) Motorcycle with sidecar, 2 detachable cops "Henderson," 9", red or green	1200	1800	3000
(VM3) Motorcycle with Package Truck, "Henderson PDQ Delivery" with detachable blue rider, 9", red or green	1800	2500	3500

Vindex Case 3 Bottom Plow, 10-1/4" long. Courtesy Bill Bertoia Auctions. Photo by Jeanne Bertoia.

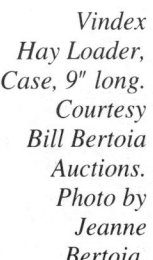

Vindex Coast to Coast Bus, 12" long. Courtesy Bill Bertoia Auctions. Photo by Jeanne Bertoia.

Vindex Hay Loader, Case, 9" long. Courtesy Bill Bertoia Auctions. Photo by Jeanne Bertoia.

	C6	C8	C10
Vindex Oldsmobile Sedan, 1929, 8" long	3000	5500	10,000
Vindex Packard Club Sedan, 1929, auctioned 1994, near mint, for $26,000			
Vindex "P&H" power shovel, cast-iron, 12" (17" extended), wheels in Caterpillar base, handle revolves rig ..	2500	5500	8000
Vindex Pickup Truck, cast-iron, 7-1/2" long	300	450	600
Vindex Pontiac Coupe, 7-3/4"	800	1400	1900
Vindex Racer, cast-iron, "2," 11-1/2" long, c.1920s	900	1400	2100

Vindex VM1. Photo by Kent M. Comstock.

Vindex 3-Bottom Tractor Plow, 9" long. Courtesy Bill Bertoia Auctions. Photo by Jeanne Bertoia.

Vindex John Deere Van Brunt Drill, 9-3/4" long. Courtesy Bill Bertoia Auctions. Photo by Jeanne Bertoia.

Vindex "P&H" Power Shovel. Courtesy Bill Bertoia Auctions. Photo by Jeanne Bertoia.

Vindex Motorcycle VM2, rider missing. Courtesy Bill Bertoia Auctions. Photo by Jeanne Bertoia.

Vindex Motorcycle VM3. Courtesy Bill Bertoia Auctions. Photo by Jeanne Bertoia.

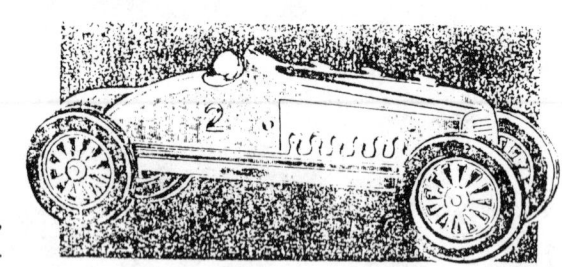

Vindex Racer, cast iron, "2" from a c.1932 Vindex catalog.

WALKER & STEWART

	C6	C8	C10		C6	C8	C10
Walker & Stewart Mack Box Van, cast-iron, 5-1/2" long	95	153	190	Walker & Stewart Mack Open Bed Truck, cast-iron, 5-1/2" long	95	153	190

WANNATOY

	C6	C8	C10		C6	C8	C10
Wannatoy Cadillac, 9" long, plastic	7	11	15	Wannatoy Delivery Truck, 4" long	5	8	10
Wannatoy Convertible, 6" long	7	11	15	Wannatoy Fire Truck, ladder, 5"	9	14	18

	C6	C8	C10
Wannatoy Gas/Oil Truck, 5"	17	26	35
Wannatoy Race Car, 2-3/4"	5	8	10
Wannatoy sedan, 3-1/2" bubble top	11	16	22
Wannatoy Tank Truck, 5" long	7	11	14
Wannatoy Tow Motor w/trailer	7	11	14
Wannatoy Tractor w/Scoop, 4"	17	26	35
Wannatoy Woodie Jeep, 3-1/2"	14	21	28

Wannatoy Woodie Jeep.
Photo by Dave Leopard.

WARREN

Warren, of New York City, was a toy soldier company, owned by John Warren Jr., from about 1936 to 1939. Its two vehicles were conversions of toys made by Kenton and are of particular interest to toy soldier collectors.

	C6	C8	C10
Warren (W173) Scout Car	300	450	600
Warren (W174) Staff Car	300	450	600

Warren, L to R: W173, 174. Courtesy Phillips NY.

WEEDEN

Weeden was founded in 1882 by William N. Weeden, in New Bedford, Massachusetts. In 1884, he invented his first toy steam engine. His toys included engines, vehicles, and boats. Weeden toys were produced into at least the 1940s.

	C6	C8	C10
Weeden Auto, live steam, 8-3/4", early	1500	3000	4500
Weeden Steam Fire Pumper	1200	2000	3000
Weeden Steam Road Roller, 1920s, 7" long, brass, tin, cast iron, steam toy fired by alcohol	250	375	500
Weeden Steam Tractor, 9"	250	375	500

Weeden Auto, Live Steam,
8-3/4" long, early. Courtesy Sotheby's NY.

WELLMADE DOLL & TOY CO.

	C6	C8	C10
Wellmade Doll & Toy			
Co. Jeep, composition, 7-1/2" long	37	56	75

	C6	C8	C10
Wellmade Doll & Toy Co.			
Jeep, composition, 3-1/2" long			No Price Found

The 7-1/2" long composition jeep is by New York's Wellmade Doll & Toy Co. The 3-1/2" copy appears to be by New York's M.A. Henry, which made a similar 8" version. Photo by Ed Poole.

A variation of Wellmade Doll & Toy Company's Jeep, 7-1/2" long (possibly by the same firm or by M.A. Henry); no price found. Photo by Ed Poole.

WELLS

(England)

	C6	C8	C10
Wells (England) Dump Truck,			
1930s, tin windup, 12"	275	415	550
Wells Rolls Royce limo, 9" long	130	195	260
Wells, Touring Sedan,			
tin windup, 11" long	312	468	625

WEN-MAC

	C6	C8	C10
Wen-Mac Automite Racer, plastic, 9" long	60	90	120
Wen-Mac Go Cart, gas operated	90	135	180
Wen-Mac Mustang, 13"	75	112	150
Wen-Mac Texaco Fire Pumper	60	90	120
Wen-Mac Texaco Tanker	42	64	85

WESTERN TOY CO.

	C6	C8	C10
Western Toy Co.			
Jeep Pedal Car, aluminum	375	562	750

WILKINS TOY COMPANY

Wilkins, of Keene, New Hampshire, was begun by James S. Wilkins as the Triumph Wringer Company. But the tiny model Wilkins produced to promote his product proved so intriguing to prospective customers and their children that requests for them poured in. The real thing was quickly forgotten as Wilkins turned to toy making. Its toys were generally cast iron and steel. The firm was acquired in 1894 by Kingsbury, which is still in business, though now as a tool and die maker.

	C6	C8	C10
Wilkins Aerial Ladder Truck, 1910, 18", windup	300	450	600
Wilkins Automobile Racer, silver, clock-work motor, light stamped steel, 10" long, c.1905	750	1100	1700
Wilkins Dray, driver, barrels, tiller	400	600	800
Wilkins Hook & Ladder, early, 26" long	No Price Found		
Wilkins Fire Pumper, c.1924, driver, clock-work, 9-1/2"	225	338	450
Wilkins Fire Pumper, c.1924, driver, 11" long	550	850	1200
Wilkins Hook & Ladder, early, 14-1/2" long	600	900	1250
Wilkins Hook & Ladder Open Truck, steel, windup motor, 9-1/4" long	175	250	325

	C6	C8	C10
Wilkins Ladder Truck, 15" long, windup, early	450	695	925
Wilkins Motor Truck Wagon, 13" long, 18 barrels, driver, 13" long ...	300	450	600
Wilkins "Panama" Dump Truck, gray, c.1919, 14" long, light stamped steel, clock-work motor (also made as Kingsbury in 1923, different wheels, same value)	400	600	800
Wilkins Runabout, 1911, with driver	650	1000	1500
Wilkins Tractor, 8-1/2" long	165	248	330
Wilkins Tractor & Trailer, 17" long	225	338	450
Wilkins Truck, open cab, 11" long, very early, clock-work	450	675	900

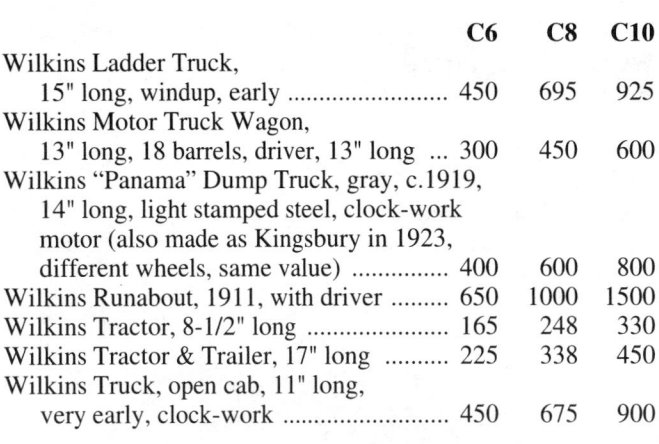

Wilkins Aerial Ladder Truck, c.1910, 18" long. Courtesy Phillips NY.

Wilkins Automobile Racer, 10" long. Photo by Bob Smith.

Wilkins Hook and Ladder open truck, steel, windup motor, 9-1/4" long. Courtesy Phillips NY.

Wilkins "Panama" Dump Truck, clockwork, c.1919, 14" long. Photo by Bob Smith.

A.C. WILLIAMS

A.C. Williams was founded in 1886 when Adam Clark Williams (1848-1932) bought the J.W. Williams Company from his father. After a fire, the firm moved in 1893 from Chagrin Falls, Ohio, to Ravenna. Toy production began about this time. Small cast iron toys were Williams' specialty, with banks, cars, and aircraft predominant. A.C. Williams retired in 1919, but the firm continued to make toys until 1938, after which it continued in business in a non-toys capacity. Williams marked few, if any, of its toys. Two clues to an A.C. Williams toy are turned steel hubs and starred axle peens

	C6	C8	C10
Williams Austin for Car Carrier	85	128	170
Williams Auto Bank, early, 6" long	275	413	550
Williams Bus, 5" long	75	112	150
Williams Bus, Twin Coach, 1936, 8-1/4" long	325	488	650
Williams "C.to C. Co." Stake Truck, 7" long, 2-piece	275	415	550
Williams Car Carrier, with 3 Austins, 12-1/2" long, 1920	385	575	770

	C6	C8	C10
Williams "Coast to Coast Cartage Co." Stake Trailer Truck, 10-1/8" long	180	270	360
Williams Coupe, 3" long, 2-piece body, 1936	90	135	180
Williams Coupe, 3-1/2" long	48	75	95
Williams Coupe, 4-1/2" long	100	150	200
Williams Coupe, 6" long, 1928	118	177	235
Williams Coupe, Rumble Seat, 6-3/4" long, side mounts, 1930	175	263	350
Williams Coupe, 7" long, 1930s	500	800	1100
Williams Delivery Van, 8" long	350	525	700
Williams Doctor's Coupe, w/curtains, 5" long	225	338	450
Williams Dump Truck, 7" long	112	168	225
Williams Express Truck, Model T, 7" long	188	282	375
Williams Fire Pumper, 5" long, interchangeable	80	120	160
Williams Ford Opera Coupe, 5" long	165	248	330
Williams four-casting nickeled radiator car, approx. 4" long	75	112	150
Williams Grader, 6" long	212	318	425
Williams Hook & Ladder, 7-1/2" long	150	225	300

Williams "Coast to Coast Cartage Co." stake trailer truck. Photo by Bill Kaufman.

Williams Coupe, 6" long, 1928. Photo by Rod Carnahan.

Williams Coupe, rumble seat, 6-3/4" long. Photo by Chic Gast.

Williams Lincoln Touring Car, 9-1/4" long. Courtesy Bill Bertoia Auctions. Photo by Jeanne Bertoia.

Williams Machinery Hauler, 3 lowboy trailers, roadscraper, roadroller, tractor, 28-5/8" long. Courtesy Bill Bertoia Auctions. Photo by Jeanne Bertoia.

Williams Mack Stake Truck, 3-1/2" long. (1932 ad).

Williams Racer, 2 passengers, 7-1/8" long. Photo by Tim Oei.

Williams Sedan, 4-1/2", 2-piece. Courtesy Mapes Auctions.

	C6	C8	C10
Williams Laundry Truck, 8" long	400	600	800
Williams Lincoln Touring Car, 7" long	200	300	400
Williams Lincoln Touring car, 9-1/4" long	475	715	950
Williams Lincoln Touring Coupe, 8-3/4" long	550	850	1200
Williams Machinery Hauler, 3 Lowboy Trailers, Roadscraper, Roadroller, Tractor, overall length 28-5/8" long ...	1500	2700	4200
Williams Mack Gas Tank Truck, 3-3/4" long	45	68	90
Williams Mack Gas Tank Truck, 5-1/8" long	102	153	205
Williams Mack Gas Tank Truck, 7-1/4" long	140	210	280
Williams Mack Stake Truck, 3-1/2" long	45	68	90
Williams Mack Stake Truck, 4-1/4" long	80	120	160
Williams Mack Stake Truck, 5-1/8" long ..	112	170	225
Williams Mack Stake Truck, 7" long	375	565	750
Williams Mack Stake Truck, 8-1/2" long ..	200	300	400
Williams Mack Truck, 3-1/2" long	45	68	90
Williams Mack Truck, 4-3/4" long	55	82	110
Williams Mack Truck, 6-3/4" long	100	150	200
Williams Model T Express Truck, 7-1/4" long	230	345	460
Williams Model T Coupe, 6" long	125	187	250
Williams "Moving & Storage" Truck, 3-1/2" long	112	168	225

	C6	C8	C10
Williams Open Bed Truck, 8" long	115	172	230
Williams Phaeton, driver, lady passenger, open, 12" long, c.1921		No Price Found	
Williams Racer, 8-1/2" long, driver, tail fin	250	375	500
Williams Racer, 7-1/8" long, 2 passengers	375	562	750
Williams Racer, 6-1/2" long, boat-tailed ...	125	188	250
Williams Racer, 5-1/2" long, two-man, c.1934	150	225	300
Williams Sedan, approx. 3-1/2" long, c.1920s	200	300	400
Williams Sedan, 4" long, c.1920..................	68	102	135
Williams Sedan, 4-1/2" long, 2-piece	115	172	230
Williams Sedan, 5" long	110	165	220
Williams Sedan, 6-1/2" long	165	248	330
Williams Sedan, c.1930, cast-iron, 6-1/2" long, streamlined rear fender	225	337	450
Williams Sedan, 6-3/4" long, c.1931, cast-iron, interchangeable body	313	470	625
Williams Steamroller, 5-1/2", 1930s	75	112	150

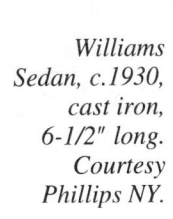

Williams Sedan, c.1930, cast iron, 6-1/2" long. Courtesy Phillips NY.

Williams Tank, 4" long. Photo by Ed Poole.

Williams Touring Car, c.1917, 11-3/4" long, two riders not pictured. Photo by Bob Smith.

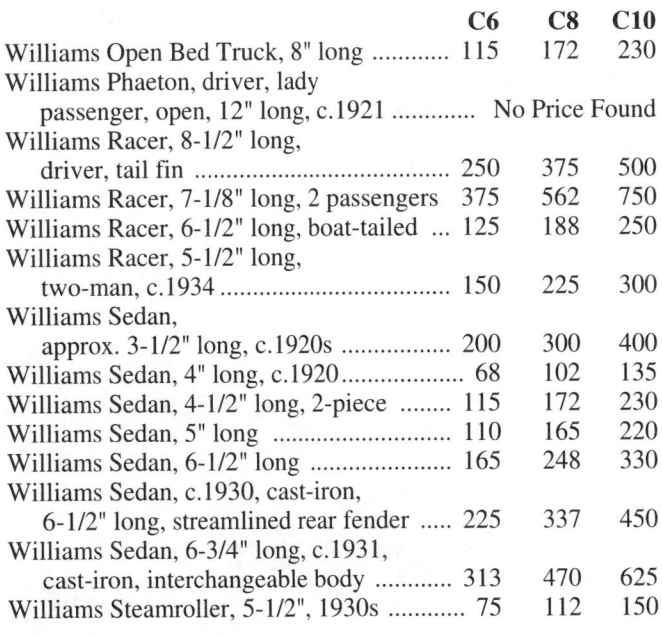

1F-2833— 3¾ In. Racer

1F-2834— 3½ In. Bus

1F-2838— 8½ In. Dump Car Trailer

1F-2866— 4 In. Wrecker

1F-2839— 8¾ In. Austin Coupe

1F-2867— 3⅝ In. Roadster

1F-2831— 3¾ In. Fire Engine

1F-2868— 3⅝ In. Coupe

1F-2836— 8½ In. Mack Truck

1F-2869— 3¾ In. Moving Van

A.C. Williams vehicles, as shown in the November, 1932 Butler Bros. catalog; each sold for a dime.

	C6	C8	C10
Williams Streamline Sedan, 8" long	500	800	1200
Williams Studebaker, c.1933-34, approx. 4" long, two-tone sedan	110	165	220
Williams Tank, 4" long	67	101	135
Williams Taxi, 5-1/4", 1920s	165	248	330
Williams Touring Car, 7" long	425	638	850

	C6	C8	C10
Williams Touring Car, 9-1/2" long, cast-iron	362	443	725
Williams Touring Car, c.1917, 11-3/4" long, with two riders	550	900	1300
Williams Tractor w/driver, 5"	100	150	200
Williams Wrecker, 5" long	85	128	170
Williams Wrecker, 6-1/2" long	250	375	500
Williams Wrecker, 7-3/4" long	375	562	750

S. S. Kresge Co.   **TOY LIST**   Sheet No. **2**

The A. C. Williams Co.   20c   Feb. 15, 1933

Ravenna, Ohio

No. 17-T-R—SEDAN
Patent No. 1,877,661
Red, Blue, Green and Yellow Bodies
Red, Blue Green and Black Chassis
Bodies interchangeable on Chassis
with 1 spring
Rubber Tired Wheels
Wt. about 24 oz. 3 doz. in case
Shipping wt. about 210 ℔ per gross

No. 18-T-R—TRUCK
Patent No. 1,877,661
Red, Blue, Green and Yellow Bodies
Red, Blue Green and Black Chassis
Bodies interchangeable on No. 17-T
Chassis
Rubber Tired Wheels
Wt. about 24 oz. 3 doz. in case
Shipping wt. about 240 ℔ per gross

No. 23-T-R—MACK TRUCK
Patent No. 1,877,661
Red, Blue. Green and Yellow Bodies
Red, Blue Green and Black Chassis
Bodies interchangeable on No. 17-T
Chassis
Rubber Tired Wheels
Wt. about 25¼ oz. 3 doz. in case
Shipping wt. about 240 ℔ per gross

No. 3068½-R—DUMP TRAY TRUCK
Red Chassis. Green Dump Tray
Rubber Tired Wheels
Wt. about 18 oz. 4 doz. in case
Shipping wt. about 150 ℔ per gross

No. 28-T-R—RACER
Red, Blue, Green and Yellow Bodies
Nickeled Man
Rubber Tired Wheels
Wt. about 20 oz. 4 doz. in case
Shipping wt. about 200 ℔ per gross

No. 27-T-R—MOTOR CYCLE
Blue Enamel Only
Rubber Tired Wheels
Wt. about 22 oz. 3 doz. in case
Shipping wt. about 210 ℔ per gross

No. 7067-R—GASOLINE TANK TRUCK
Red, Blue, Green and Yellow Bodies
Rubber Tired Wheels
Wt. about 24½ oz. 3 doz in case
Shipping wt. about 264 ℔ per gross

No. 8867½-R—FIRE ENGINE
Red Enamel. Gold and Aluminum
decorations
Rubber Tired Wheels
Wt. about 20 oz. 3 doz. in case
Shipping wt. about 204 ℔ per gross

No. 9067-R—HOOK and LADDER
Red Enamel. Gold and Aluminum
decorations
Rubber Tired Wheels
Wt. about 20½ oz. 3 doz. in case
Shipping wt. about 220 ℔ per gross

(over)

A.C. Williams vehicles, as shown on Kresge's February 15, 1933 sheet.

WOLVERINE

Wolverine, of Pittsburgh, Pennsylvania was founded in 1903 by B.F. Bain. The company got its name from Bain's Michigan hometown. In later years, Wolverine became a subsidiary of Spang Industries. In 1970, it moved to Boonville, Arkansas. The "Sandy Andy," in all its variations, was probably Wolverine's most successful and famous toy. The firm's name is now Today's Kids.

	C6	C8	C10
Wolverine "Autolift," 1930s, 10-1/4" high, includes 2-1/2" tin car and four sections of track	150	225	300
Wolverine Caterpillar Tractor w/trailer, c.1930, windup, 20"	305	458	610
Wolverine "Coke" Coal Truck	88	132	175
Wolverine Dump Truck, 12" long, white	55	82	110
"Wolverine Express Bus," 14" long, "Mystery Motor"	100	150	200
Wolverine "Fire Dept." Truck	90	135	180
Wolverine "Loop-A-Loop," 1930s, 19" long, includes small car No. 30	125	188	250
Wolverine Magic Auto Race, 1940s, 2 cars	37	56	75
Wolverine Motorcycle Rabbit, 1930s, 9-1/2" long	90	135	180

	C6	C8	C10
Wolverine "Mystery Car," 13" long	138	205	275
Wolverine "Mystery Car" and Trailer, press down to make car move, c.1953	218	327	435
Wolverine Sky View Taxi	115	172	230
Wolverine Speeding Bus "5 Via Main St." tin litho, driver and occupants, 14" long, "19302," press down on rear to move	105	158	210
Wolverine "Sunny Andy" Tank, 14" long	130	195	260
Wolverine Taxi, 13" long, tin	180	270	360
Wolverine "U.S.A. Transport" Army Truck	150	225	300
Wolverine "U.S. Army" Staff Car, 12" long	130	195	260
Wolverine "White Mustang" Dump Truck, 14" long	75	112	150
Wolverine White Stake Truck	102	153	205

Wolverine Mystery Car & Trailer. Photo by Calvin L. Chaussee.

Wolverine "Sunny Andy Tank" from a December, 1929 Butler Bros. catalog.

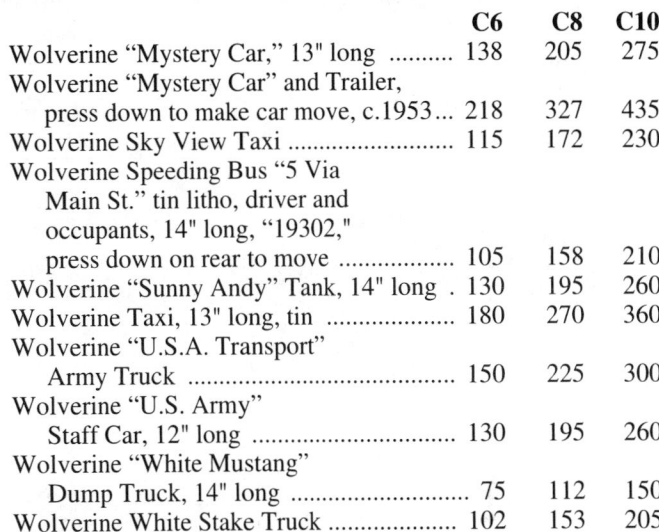

Wolverine "U.S.A. Transport" army truck. Photo by Terry Sells.

WOOD COMMODITIES CORP.

Wood Commodities Jeep, wooden. Photo by Jack Matthews.

This seems to be another version of Wood Commodities' Jeep. Photo by Perry R. Eichor.

	C6	C8	C10
Wood Commodities Corp.			
(New York) Jeep, wooden, WWII	40	60	80
Wood Commodities Tank, wooden, WWII .	25	38	50

Wood Commodities Tank, wooden.
Photo by Jack Matthews.

WOOD PRODUCTS CORP.

	C6	C8	C10
Wood Products Corp. Jeep,			
steel, 10-1/2" long	60	80	100

Wood Products Corp. Jeep.
Photo by Richard Jansen.

WOODHAVEN

Research by John Monteleone has established that in the 1930s, Herman Joerger bought Animate Toy and, about the same time, Ranger Toys. He sold the business to his son, Herman Jr., who, in turn, sold it to his son, Kurt, the present owner. The firm made toys until at least 1939. It was located in Woodhaven, New York. Now called Woodhaven Telesis Corporation, it makes sheet-metal parts to order

	C6	C8	C10
Woodhaven Animate			
Climbing Tractor, tin windup	125	188	250
Woodhaven "Robot			
Bus," tin litho, 14" long	58	87	115

Woodhaven Animate Climbing Tractor,
tin windup. Courtesy John Monteleone.

WYANDOTTE

(All Metal Products)

by Brian Seligman

Wyandotte Toys began in the fall of 1921, when William Schmidt and George Stallings decided that instead of making steel parts for the automobile industry, they would make toys. All Metal Products initially became well known for its large line of toy guns, rifles, and water pistols, but also would be increasingly known for pressed-steel vehicles and airplanes, mechanical toys and games, target sets, musical tops, doll carriages, and other sturdy toys for boys and girls to spend hours of good and safe fun.

Arthur Edwards bought into the growing company and became its president and general manager, running the company until his death in 1932. He was succeeded by his son C. Lee Edwards. By the mid 1930s, Wyandotte Toys was a major mid-price contender in the toy business. It was not unusual for Wyandotte to issue different sizes of the same toy. One might find the same stake truck in four sizes, ranging from 4-1/2 inches to 15 inches. Additionally, the baked enamel toys came in many colors and color combinations, with special color runs for the Easter holiday. Lithographed toys also figured prominently, and with the Wyandotte Circus #503 truck and trailer of 1936, it reached the pinnacle of lithography.

During WWII, Wyandotte made clips for the M-1 rifle and was able to offer a reduced toy line of all-wood toys, but it would not be until after the war that it would get back to major toy production. In April 1947 longtime employee William Wenner was elected president. In 1950, Wyandotte bought Hafner Manufacturing Company, with the thought of increasing market penetration by marketing its toy train line. In 1951, C. Lee Edwards, Mary Reberdy, and the estate of his late father, sold their interests to a new set of owners. The new directors hoped to reorganize the company successfully. It was during this time one plant was moved to Martin's Ferry, Ohio, another to Pequa, Ohio, and one to the Mc-Cord Corporation for its gasket division.

The year 1955 saw both C. Lee Edwards and William Wenner retiring and selling their stock that was acquired as part of the 1951 reorganization. The company was also undergoing financial problems at the time. It has been reported that Louis Marx, of Marx Toys, to assume a larger market share for his own company, purchased some of the Wyandotte and Haffner toy lines and sent them to his Mexican operations. All Metal Products (Wyandotte Toys) filed for bankruptcy Nov. 6, 1956, thereby closing this chapter in toy history. (Except where noted, all photos by Brian Seligman.)

Brian Seligman was first introduced to collecting by his mother, an antique collector/dealer in Vermont. He thought that nothing was better than going to an old farm estate auction until, in 1989, he picked up his first toy, a Steelcraft riding road roller, because it looked "neat." He was hooked. Originally, he started with large pressed steel pieces, such as Buddy L and Keystone, but, as he was drawn deeper and deeper into the hobby, he began to pick up many of the more reasonably priced examples of pressed steel, Marx, Girard, and Wyandotte. What has now transpired is a growing collection of Wyandotte vehicles and airplanes. By no means an expert, Seligman is currently trying to fill in the spaces of his collection, as well as acquiring as much research material to further knowledge of Wyandotte. A series of articles entitled "why not Wyandotte?" has been running in U.S. Toy Collector Magazine. Seligman is a real estate developer in South Florida, has a wife, three kids, one dog, five box turtles, a house, two cars, and a mortgage.

Abbreviations

brt: black rubber tires	bpw: black plastic wheels
bww: black wood wheels	eww: embossed wood wheels
lmw: litho metal wheels	pmw: pressed-steel wheels
wrt: white rubber tires	www: white wood wheels
yww: yellow wood wheels	e/l: electric lights
trk: truck	" :" lettering on vehicle

Some words of explanation:

1. "(wy__)" signifies a log number for a toy in my collection. If there is no number, I do not have that specific piece or have decided not to include in this edition.

2. "[#?]" at the end of a description signifies lack of company originated model number. If you know of a number not listed, send it to me and I will add it to the list for the next edition.

3. I am often asked to describe the differences in shapes and styles of various Wyandotte pieces. In this edition, I created a list of names and abbreviations that I hope are helpful in making descriptions easier. The abbreviations are found after the "WY__" designation. I am suggesting the following:

Air Speed/flat grille: AS/F	Open Eye: OE
Air Speed/convex grille: AS/C	Plastic: PL
Army Wood: AW	Rocket Racer: RR
Boat Tail Racer: BT	Rounded Windshield: RW
Cab Over: CO	Rooster Comb: RC
Checker Board: CB	Shaded Windshield: SW
Convertible: CV	Slanted Grille: SG
Cord: CD	Sleepy Eye: SE
Cord & Trailer: CDT	Soap Box: SB
La Salle: LS	Speedster: SP
La Salle & Trailer: LST	Sportsman Convertible: SPC
Long Nose: LN	Square Cab: SC
Long Nose & Trailer: LNT	Toy Town: TT
Open Cab: OC	Wide Face: WF

4. Values listed are estimates only and should be used ONLY as a guide. Prices vary due to availability and condition of toys. As to pricing, the West Coast is usually higher than the East Coast, while the Midwest is usually lower than the East Coast. What you, the collector, offer to pay and eventually pay, is the true value. Offer or pay only what you feel a piece is worth. Don't be afraid about walking away from a toy, these toys are not one of a kind and eventually another one will pop up. Beware of "Col-

lector Lust," or you will end up with some nasty high-priced toys that someday you will wonder, "what made me buy this toy?" Happy hunting!!

TRUCKS

ARMY

	C6	C8	C10
(wy__) - 9-1/2" - AW - 1941/42 - bww - "Army Supply" - all wood construction - [214]	35	50	90
(wy__) - 11-3/4" - LN - 1941 - brt - "Army Supply Corp." - canvas cloth top - [433]	45	75	105
(wy327) - 17-1/2" - LN - 1941 - brt - "Army Engineer Corp. No. 42" - canvas cloth top - [#?]	60	90	130
(wy__) - 21" - LN - 1940-41 - brt - "Army Corps," canvas cloth top - [1006]	65	95	135
(wy__) - 21" - LN - 1941 - brt - "Engineers Corp. USA" - [#?]	65	95	135

AUTO TRANSPORT

	C6	C8	C10
(wy__) - 8-3/4" - CO - 1950s - brt - plastic cab/metal trailer - four plastic cars - [#?]	20	30	55
(wy__) - 9-3/8" - CO - 1940s/50s four plastic cars - [#?]	30	40	65
(wy__) - 10" - CO - 1952 - brt - plastic cab & litho trailer - "#455"" - "Auto Transport" - [#?]	35	50	75

	C6	C8	C10
(wy093) - 10-1/4" - CO - 1952 - brt - plastic cab - "Wyandotte" or "Auto Transport" on the side - [455]	50	70	145
(wy318) - 12-5/8" - OE - 1953 - brt - litho cab & trailer - four Cars - "Transmobile Jr." - "Transcontinental Auto Freight Lines" - "I.C.C. 2034/LT. WT. 6800/CAPY 9000" - [#?]	50	70	145
(wy__) - SW - 19" - 1932 - yww - orange cab & trailer with three vehicles - [#?]	65	150	250
(wy186) - SW - 21-5/8" - 1932 - yww - orange cab & trailer with four vehicles - [#?]	75	160	260
(wy__) - SW - 21-5/8" - 1932 - yww - green cab & black trailer with four vehicles - electric lights - [#?]	85	175	300
(wy_) - 22" - CO - 1952/53 - pmw - red/yellow litho cab/red and yellow trailer with four "Cadillac" cars and ramp - "AUTO TRANSPORT" - [#?]	55	75	135
(wy_) - 22-1/2" - CO - 1956/57 - brt - litho cab & trailer - "Car o van" - [#?]	45	70	105
(wy_) - 23" - OE - 1954 - brt/red plastic hubs - litho cab w/rear toolbox & five tools - four cars w/ramp - "Car o van" - [#?]	50	65	125

BAGGAGE TRUCK

	C6	C8	C10
(wy320) - 11-1/2" - SG - 1953 - bmw - "Baggage" - [#?]	40	60	75
(wy_) - 11-3/4" - LN - 1941 - brt - "Baggage" - with freight Cart - [#?]	45	75	105

WY327

Auto Transport, WY93. Courtesy Brian Seligman.

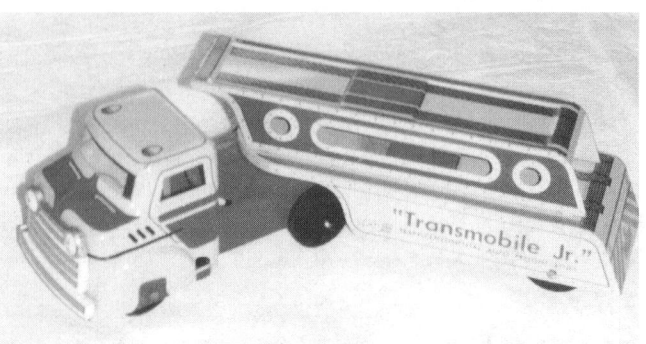

WY318

WY186

WY320

	C6	C8	C10
BANK TRUCK (also called bus bank)			
(wy019) - 6-3/8" - RC - 1936/40 - bww - green/red/orange - four portholes on each side - rear hatch with coin slot & key - [#375]	40	60	85

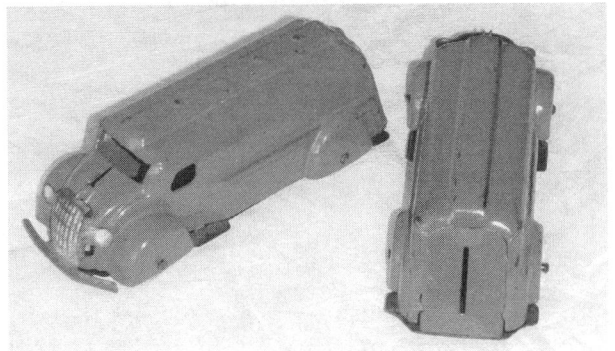

WY019, two views.

BUS
(wy020) - 6-3/8" - RC - 1936/40 - bww or wrt - green/red/orange/yellow- 8 windows each side & rear panel w/two windows and embossed spare tire - [377] 40   60   85

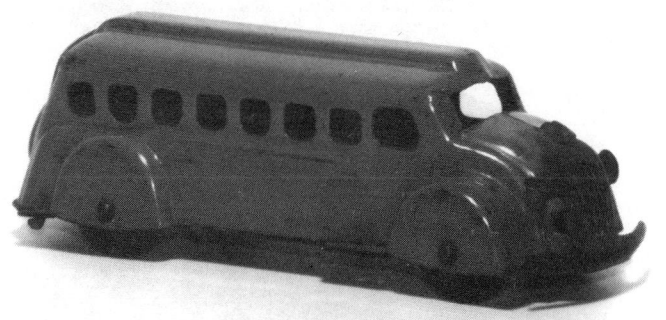

Bus WY20. Courtesy Brian Seligman.

(wy060) - 6-3/8" - CO - 1939 - bww - blue - same window & rear panel design as #371, but different nose & grille design - [#233] 40   60   85

	C6	C8	C10
(wy_) - 21" - CO - 1938 - bww - roof rack & rear door - [1002]	90	135	200
(wy_) - 21" - CO - 1939/40 - bww - no roof rack - rear door - "Coast to Coast Bus Line" - [#1002 Heavy Duty Motor Bus]	90	135	200
(wy_) - 21" - CO - 1941 - brt - no roof rack - rear door - "Coast to Coast Bus Line" - [1002]	90	135	200

Bus WY60. Courtesy Brian Seligman.

CEMENT TRUCK
(wy_) - 5" - CO - 1940/50 - brt - "Cement Mixer/Sell/Rent" - may have had attached mixer - [#?] 20   40   55

CIRCUS TRUCK (two piece)
(wy063) - 19-1/4" - RN - 1936 - eww - red cab & litho double trailers with swing down rear ramps - "Greatest Show On Earth" - cardboard animals on metal stands - [#503] 200   750   1000

WY063

(wy0xx) - 19-1/4" - LN - 1941? - same as above except long nose style cab - very scarce - [#?] 250   850   1200

CONTRACTOR TRUCK
(wy_) - 11-1/4" - LN - 1941- bww - "Contractor Truck" - [434c] 45   70   105

DAIRY/MILK TRUCKS AND VANS
(wy276) - 4-7/8" - PL - 1952 - brt - yellow body & red frame - "Sunshine Dairy" - friction & plastic van body - [805] 20   35   50

Top to Bottom:
WY276 on
original box,
WY314

Left to Right: WY291, WY330

	C6	C8	C10
(wy_) - 11-1/2" - LN - 1939 - bww - with 2 milk bottles - [#349]	50	80	115
(wy_) - 11-1/2" - PL - 1952 - "Toy Town Delivery Service" - "Full Delivery/Pick Up" - opening rear door - [353]	50	75	110
(wy_) - 11-3/4" - LN - 1941 - brt - with 1 milk bottle - "Drink More Milk" - [431]	60	85	120
(wy_) - 12" - SN - 1949 - brt - "Sunshine Dairy" - 1 milk bottle - [#?]	50	90	110
(wy_) - 17-3/8" - LN - 1937/38 - brt/brt on hubs - [362]	55	80	115

DELIVERY (same body as 11-1/4" ambulances)

	C6	C8	C10
(wy357) 11-3/8" - LN - 1938/39 - bww, green/red/grey/yellow - "City Delivery" - [#345]	60	75	100

Wyandotte Delivery Van, 11" long. Photo by Bob Smith.

DUMP

	C6	C8	C10
(wy002) - 4-3/4" - SW - 1934/36 - wrt - green or red - [315]	40	65	80
(wy_)-5" - CO - late 1940s/50 - brt - [#?]	25	45	65
(wy336) - 5-5/8" - SW - 1932 - yww - [#?]	20	35	55
(wy003) - 6" - RC - 1934/37 - wrt - red/green/orange - [318]	40	65	80
(wy???) - 6" - LN - 1938 - bww - [318]	35	55	75

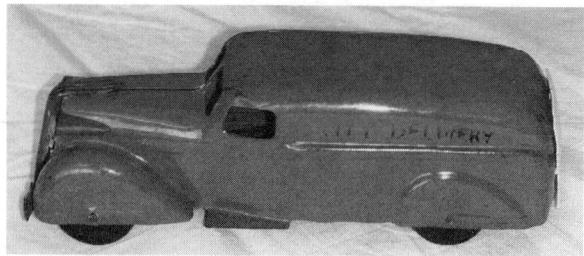

WY357

DELIVERY (cab and rear van body)

	C6	C8	C10
(wy330) - 6" - OE - 1954 - brt-litho cab & body - "Wyandotte Trucking" - "Speedy Delivery" - "New York Chicago San Francisco" - [#?]	25	50	75
(wy291) - 9-7/8" - OE - 1954 - brt - litho cab & body - "Express Delivery Service" "Local" "National" "I.C.C. 120 - Cap. 4500 - WT. 3250" - [#?]	35	60	85
(wy_) - 12" - SE - 1949 - brt - [#?]	30	55	70
(wy_) - 16" - LN - 1938 - brt/ws hub, spring motor with attached key - [382]	80	95	120
(wy_) - 16-3/8" - LN - 1938/39 - wd whls - [#?]	60	75	100

WY336

WY003

WY???

Dump Body, WY4. Courtesy Brian Seligman.

Dump Body, WY5. Courtesy Brian Seligman.

Dump Body, WY9. Courtesy Brian Seligman.

WY006

Dump Body, WY6. Courtesy Brian Seligman.

WY165

	C6	C8	C10
(wy009) - 6" - CO - 1939/41-bpw - [#222]	20	35	50
(wy005) - 7" - SW - 1933 - eww - [#?]	50	70	95
(wy004) - 7" - SW - 1934 - wrt - similar to #315 - [#?]	40	60	85
(wy006) - 10" - RC - 1934 - brt - electric lites or fake lights - [324]	40	60	85
(wy165) - 10-1/2" - SE/CB - 1953 - brt - "Wyandotte" - front scoop - [#?]	50	65	95
(wy_) - 11-1/4" - LN - 1938/41 - bww - with 5-1/4" - wheelbarrow - [343c]	60	80	100
(wy_) - 12" - CO - 1952 - mw - attached front end loader - lever action rear dump - plastic cab & chassis - litho body - "Sand" - [443]	30	45	60
(wy_) - 12" - SN - 1949 - bww - [#?]	40	55	70

	C6	C8	C10
(wy088) - 12-1/4" - LN - 1941 - bww - side lever/rear dumping action - with wheelbarrow - [#?]	45	60	75
(wy_) - 12-1/4" - CO - 1940/45 - bww/mw - [#?]	40	55	65
(wy037) - 12-3/4" - SW - 1934 - wrt/red hubs - [328]	65	85	115
(wy_) - 13-1/4 - AW - 1942 - bww- "Highway Dept. Dump" - all wood construction - [1009]	No Price Found		
(wy44) - 15" - SW - 1933/34 - wrt/red hubs - elec lights - [#?]	55	95	165
(wy51) - 15-1/4" - RC - 1934/37 - brt/red hubs - [353]	65	95	135
(wy_) - 16" - LN - 1938/39 bww - mechanical - attached key - shovel - [138]	65	95	135

Dump Body, WY37. Courtesy Brian Seligman.

Dump Body, WY44. Courtesy Brian Seligman.

Dump Body, WY51. Courtesy Brian Seligman.

Dump Body, "Arrow Truck Lines"; value in C6, C8, C10: $55, 95, 145. Photo by Bob Smith.

Dump Body, "Wyandotte Construction Co."; value in C6, C8, C10: $65, 105, 155. Photo by Bob Smith.

Dump Body, WY88. Courtesy Brian Seligman.

	C6	C8	C10

(wy_) - 16" - LN - 1938/39 -
   bww - with shovel - [360] 50 75 100
(wy_) - 17-3/8" - CO - 1939/47 -
   bww - side dump [391] 45 70 110
(wy_) - 20" - CO - 1952 - mw - plastic
   cab & metal dump body - [#?] ...... No Price Found
(wy_) - 21" - CO - 1938/41 -
   bww - with shovel - [#1001
   Heavy Duty Dump Truck] 65 105 135
(wy_) - 21" - CO - 1941 -
   brt/wd hubs - [#?] 45 70 110
(wy_) - 21" - CO - 1953/54 - brt -
   with 12" shovel - "Giant" - [#?] 60 75 115

DUMP (dual rear wood wheels)
(wy299) - 9-5/8" - SW -
   1931/32 - yww - side lever
   with slide track mechanism - [326] 60 80 95
(wy208) - 9-5/8" - SW -
   1931/32 - yww - side spring release
   mechanism - [326 later version] 60 80 95
(wy041) - 15-1/4" - SW - 1931/32 - yww
   - side spring release mechanism - [#?] ... 75 150 225

WY299

WY208

DUMP (Easter Style)
(wy_) - 6" - RC - 1937/38 - bww -
   pink cab & purple dump body with
   chicken stamped on sides - [E318] 40 60 75

	C6	C8	C10

EXPRESS (see tractor trailer)
FIRE TRUCK
(wy126) - 6" - OC - 1932 - wrt -
   red body/3 green ladders - [308r] 65 80 110

WY126

(wy_) - 6-1/4" - SC - 1952 - wpw -
   red/white ladders - all plastic - [#?] 20 35 70
(wy_) - 7-1/2" - SB - 1952 - brt -
   friction - siren & ladder - [156] 30 45 60
(wy294) - 10" - OC -
   1932/34 - wrt - red body with 3
   ladders - axle activated bell - [329] 65 90 110

WY294

(wy_) - 11" - CO - late 1940s/50s -
   brt - attached green ladder -
   "Wyandotte Fire Department" - "Fire
   Chief Hook and Ladder Truck" - [#?] 30 45 65
(wy_) - 11" - CO - 1952 - brt with
   bright metal hubs - plastic & steel-
   friction - siren & red flashing light-
   lever release ladder - [#?] 35 50 65
(wy_) - 11" - CO - 1952 - brt - hook and
   aerial ladder truck - plastic cab & metal
   litho trailer - "Hook & Ladder CO. No. 3"
   or "Wyandotte Fire Department" - rear
   plastic driver - [#?] 50 75 110
(wy_) - 11-3/4" - LN - 1941 - bww -
   bell - two 7-1/2" ladders - [428] 50 70 120
(wy_) - 12 - SN - 1949 - brt -
   2 or three ladders - [428] 45 70 100
(wy_) - 17-1/2" - LN - 1941 -
   bww - bell - two ladders - [366] 50 70 120

	C6	C8	C10

(wy_) - 20" - CO - 1952 - brt - plastic
  cab & metal litho trailer - mechanical -
  crank to raise ladder - [#?] 65   95   135

(wy309) - 27-1/2" - CO - 1940/41 -
  6 bww - "Hook and Ladder No. 10" - 29"
  expanding ladder-hood bell-[1004] 50   70   195

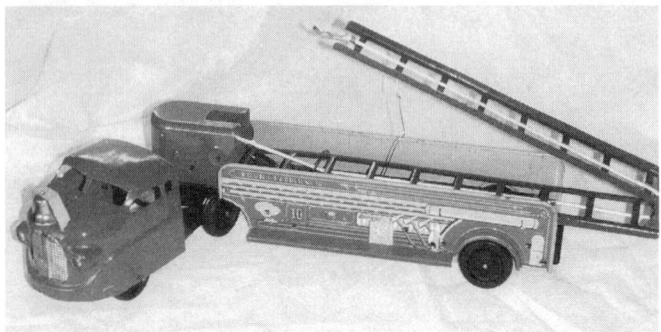

WY309

GARDENER'S TRUCK
(wy_) - 10" - CO/CB - 1953 -
  mw/brt - "Ferry's Seeds" - [#?] 50   75   110

GARBAGE TRUCK
(wy_) - 17" - CO - 1956/57 -
  brt - dump action & rear
  loading sliding gate - [332] 70   110   140

ICE TRUCK
(wy287) - SE - 10-1/4" -
  1954 - lmw - "Igloo Ice Company" -
  1 ice cube - 1 ice tong - [123] 50   75   110

WY287

(wy_) - 11-1/2" - LN - 1938/39 - bww -
  2 ice cubes & 1 ice tong - [#348] 45   70   120

(wy222) - 11-3/4" - LN - 1941 - brt -
  1 ice cube & 1 ice tong, "Toy Town
  Ice Co." - "Crystal Clear" - [432] 45   70   120

WY222

	C6	C8	C10

LUMBER TRUCK
(wy_) - 9-1/4" - CO - 1952 - brt -
  all plastic - 3 logs included - [176] 45   60   75

(wy_) - 11-1/2" - CO -
  1956/57 - brt - metal cab and
  trailer - 3 logs included - [#?] 50   75   135

MEDICAL TRUCK
(wy136) - 11-3/4" - LN - 1940/41 - bww -
  "Medical Corps"/Red Cross on side
  of canvas cloth top - [430] 70   100   135

WY136

OIL/GAS TANKER
(wy018) - 6-3/8" - RC - 1936/38 -
  wrt - 4 imitation top hatches &
  fold down rear hatch - [376] 20   35   65

Oil/Gas Tanker, WY18. Courtesy Brian Seligman.

(wy076) - 6-3/8" - RC - 1939 -
  bww - 4 imitation top hatches
  & fold down rear hatch - [225] 20   35   65

Oil/Gas Tanker, WY76. Courtesy Brian Seligman.

	C6	C8	C10

(wy021) - 10-1/2" - RC - 1935/36 -
  wrt - 4 imitation top hatches &
  fold down rear hatch - [330] 65   90   125

Oil/Gas Tanker, WY21. Courtesy Brian Seligman.

(wy082) - 10-1/2" - RC - 1937 -
  brt - 4 imitation top hatches &
  fold down rear hatch - [#?] 65   90   125

Oil/Gas Tanker, WY82. Courtesy Brian Seligman.

(wy_) - 21" - CO - 1939/40 - brt -
  rear fold down hatch - [#1003 -
  Heavy Duty Gas Truck] 60   90   125

PAINTING TRUCK
(wy317) - 10-1/4" - SE -
  brt - "Jiffy Painting - Decorating"
  "Quick Service" - 2 ladders - [#?] 50   75   110

WY317

RAILWAY EXPRESS TRUCK
(wy096) - 6-1/2" - CO -late
  1940s - brt - "Wyandotte Toys"
  & REA litho on each side - [#?] 35   50   65
(wy_) - 12-1/2" - CO - late 1940s/52 -
  brt - REA litho - [#?] 60   90   135

Railway Express, WY96. Courtesy Brian Seligman.

	C6	C8	C10

RIDING TRUCK
(wy057) - 16-1/4" -
  RC - 1935/36 - brt - [356] 50   75   135

Riding Truck, WY57. Courtesy Brian Seligman.

(wy_) - 32-1/2" - SC - 1952/56 -
  brt - fire truck with electric
  spot light & siren - [1704] 75   105   150
(wy_) - 32-1/2" - SC - 1956/57 - brt on
  metal wheels - "Towing Service
  Car" - wrecker boom with chain
  operated winch - [1705] 75   105   145

STAKE TRUCK
(wy045) - 4-5/8" -
  SW - 1934 - wrt - [314] 40   65   80

WY045

WY054

Stake Body, WY55. Courtesy Brian Seligman.

WY269

WY046

WY075

Stake Body, WY283. Courtesy Brian Seligman.

WY324

Stake Body, WY48. Courtesy Brian Seligman.

	C6	C8	C10
(wy_) - 5" - CO - late 1940s/50s - brt - [#?]	35	60	75
(wy054) - 5-5/8" - RC - 1934/37 - wrt & bww - [317]	40	55	75
(wy055) - 6" - CO - 1939/46 - brt & bpw - "Wyandotte Toys" embossed on driver's side of cab - [221]	20	35	50
(wy269) - 6" - LN - 1932/37 - wrt/bww - [317]	40	65	80
(wy046) - 6-3/8" - SW - 1934/35 - wrt - [317]	50	75	85
(wy075) - 9-5/8" - SW - 1931 - wrt or brt mounted on metal spoke whls - [325]-(non-spoke wheels) - [323]	60	85	175
(wy_) - 11-1/4" - LN - 1938 - mw - with 5-3/4" hand truck - [342c]	65	80	105
(wy283) - 11-3/4" - SE/CB - 1954 - brt - "Pickwick Pastures" "Livestock - Dairy Cows" - "Wyandotte"-[#?]	35	50	75

	C6	C8	C10
(wy_) - 12" - LN - 1938/39 - bww - with 5-3/4" hand truck - [342c]	65	75	105
(wy_) - 12" - SN - 1949 - mw - [#?]	55	75	115
(wy324) - 12" - SG - 1953 - bmw - [#?]	40	60	100
(wy048) - 12-1/8" - SW - 1935 - wrt/wrt on red hubs - [337]	75	150	220
(wy053) - 12-1/4" - LN - 1940/41 - bww - [#?]	50	75	95
(wy_) - 12-1/4" - CO - 1940/45 - mw - [#?]		No Price Found	
(wy043) - 15" - SW - 1933/34 - wd whls - elec lights - [352]	60	95	150
(wy049) - 15-1/4" - RC - 1934/37 - wrt brt mounted on red hubs - electric lights - [360]-(brt on red hubs - wy050)	75	105	150
(wy052) - 16" - LN - 1938/39 - or brt mounted on red hubs - hand truck - [#?]	60	95	135

Stake Body, WY53. Courtesy Brian Seligman.

Stake Body, WY43. Courtesy Brian Seligman.

Stake Body, WY49. Courtesy Brian Seligman.

Stake Body, WY50. Courtesy Brian Seligman.

Stake Body, WY52. Courtesy Brian Seligman.

Stake Body, "Wyandotte Truck Lines," plastic cab; value in C6, C8, C10: $85, 125, 175. Photo by Bob Smith.

	C6	C8	C10

(wy_) - 16" - LN - 1938/39 - wrt
mounted on wood hubs - mechanical
with attached key - [#380] 65   90   130

(wy_) - 21" - CO - 1939/40 - brt -
with hand truck - [#1000] 65   105   135

(wy_) - 21" - CO - 1941 - brt - mini
hand truck - "Express" - [#1000] 65   105   135

(wy_) - 23" - CO - 1952 - 6 brt - plastic
cab with metal litho grille & metal
trailer - "Wyandotte Truck Lines" -
rear spare tire - [#?] 90   135   165

STAKE TRUCK (dual rear wood wheels)

(wy047) - 9-3/8" -
SW - 1931/32 - yww - [#?] 50   75   105

WY047

(wy_) - 10" - RC -
1935/36 - wrt or brt - [#?] 55   80   110

(wyxxx) - 15" - SW -
1931/32 - yww - [#?] 60   85   115

WYXXX

STAKE TRUCK (Easter)

(wy188) - 6" - RC - 1937/38 -
bww - pink cab/light green bed -
rabbit stamped on side - [E317] 35   65   80

L to R: WY116, WY188.

	C6	C8	C10

(wy116) - 10" - RC - 1937/38 -
imw - pink cab/light green bed-
rabbit stamped on - [E325] 45   75   95

TELEVISION TRUCK

(wy314) - 4-7/8" - PL - 1954 -
brt - red body/yellow frame -
"Television Repair Service" - [803] 35   50   65

WY314

TOW TRUCK

(wy125) - 4-3/4" -
CO - late 1940s/50s - brt - [#?] 45   60   75

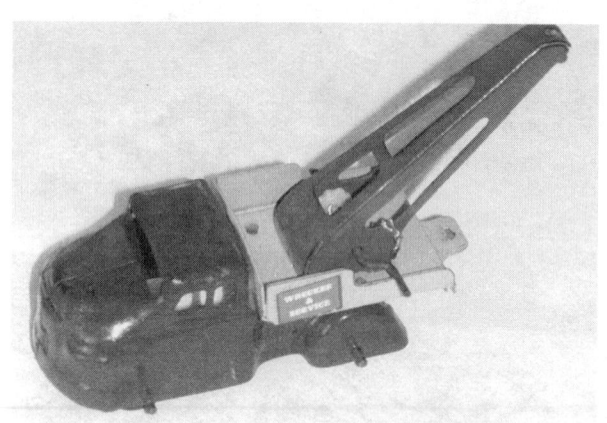

WY125

(wy308) - 9" - SE - 1953 - lmw -
"Wyandotte Automobile Society" -
"Towing & Repairs" - "Towing
Service Nite & Day" - rear crank
operated hoist - [#?] 45   70   95

WY308

	C6	C8	C10
(wy_) - 11-3/4 - LN - 1940/41 - bww - "Official Service Car" - rear hoist - [429]	50	90	130
(wy_) - 12" - SN - 1949 - brt - "Official Service Truck" - "W" in a dot - rear hoist - [429]	50	75	100
(wy_) - 12-1/4" - CO - 1940s - bww - rear hoist - [#?]	40	70	95
(wy_) - 13-7/8" - CO - 1956/7 - brt - "Towing - Day & Nite" - [#?]	45	65	90

Wyandotte "Dot Towing Service Nite/Day" radio-dispatched towcar; value in C6, C8, C10: $65, 105, 155. Photo by Bob Smith.

	C6	C8	C10
(wy_) - 15" - CO - 1953/54 - brt - "24 hr" - "Emergency" - "Auto Service" - "W" - with tools and spare tires - plastic cab - [1015]	65	105	145

Tow Truck Wyandotte "Emergency Auto Service," plastic cab, 15" long. Photo by Bob Smith.

	C6	C8	C10
(wy_) - 15" - CO - 1954 - brt on yellow plastic hubs - "Moto-Fix" - "Toolkit" - "Towcar" - "Towing-Repairs-Tire Change-Parts" - with tools and 2 spare tires - all metal construction - [#?]	105	135	150
(wy_) - 15" - CO - 1954/56 - brt - "Towing Service" - with tools and spare tires - roof mounted light - [#?]	65	105	145
(wy_) - 17-1/2" - LN - 1938 - brt - "Service + Wrecker" - "Toy Town Only 24 hr Service" - rear hoist - [365]	50	90	130

	C6	C8	C10
(wy_) - 22-1/2" - LN - 1940 - brt on wood hubs - "AAA Service" - rear hoist - [1005]	50	90	130
(wy_) - 22-1/2" - LN - 1941 - brt on wood hubs - "W" - rear hoist - [1005]	50	90	130

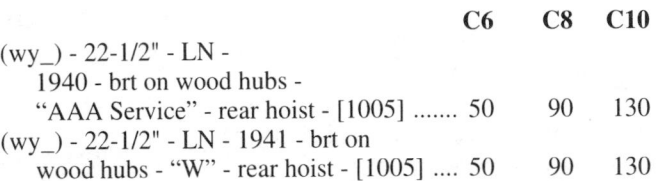

Wyandotte "Towing" truck, 14" long, value in C6, C8, C10: $60, 100, 150. Photo by Bob Smith.

TRACTOR TRAILERS (semis)

	C6	C8	C10
(wy095) - 7-3/4" - CO - 1953 - brt - "Wyandotte Van Lines" - "Coast To Coast" - "Moving Packaging Storage" - [#?]	50	70	105

Tractor (Semi) Trailer, WY95. Courtesy Brian Seligman.

	C6	C8	C10
(wy094) - 7-3/4" - CO - 1953 - brt - "Produce Van" - "Refrigerated Cargo" - "Coast To Coast" - [#?]	50	70	105

Tractor (Semi) Trailer, WY94. Courtesy Brian Seligman.

	C6	C8	C10
(wy_) - 8-1/2" - CO - 1953 - brt - "Valley Farms Livestock Produce" - [#?]	50	70	105
(wy_) - 9" - CO - 1952 - brt - plastic cab - [#?]	50	65	80
(wy_) - 9-1/4" - CO - 1952 - all plastic parts - removable side stake panels - [#?]	50	65	80
(wy_) - 15" - SN - 1949 - brt - "Wyandotte Van Lines" - [#?]	65	80	95
(wy_) - 17" - CO - 1952 - 6 brt - baggage truck with hand truck and baggage [#?]	70	90	110
(wy_) - 17" - CO - 1952/53 - pmw - side dump with shovel - [#?]	45	70	145
(wy_) - 17-3/8" - CO - 1939/41 - brt - "Highway Freight" - [#392]	55	80	115
(wy069) - 17-3/8" - CO - 1939/41 - brt - side dump - "Wyandotte Construction Co." - [#391]	65	95	140

Tractor (Semi) Trailer, WY69. Courtesy Brian Seligman.

	C6	C8	C10
(wy068) - 17-3/8" - CO - 1939/41 - brt - "Wyandotte Express Co" - [#390]	50	75	100

Tractor (Semi) Trailer, WY68. Courtesy Brian Seligman.

	C6	C8	C10
(wy_) - 17-1/2" - CO - 1950s -brt - "Green Valley Stock Ranch" - litho cab with "Wyandotte" and "W" in a dot on cab - [390]	80	95	120
(wy_) - 23" - CO - 1952/54 - 14 brt on red plastic hubs - "Wyandotte Van Lines" (also "Gambles") - retractable landing gear - double rear doors - [1850]	95	130	175
(wy_) - 23" - CO - 1952 - brt - plastic cab - "Deluxe Highway Express" - [#?]	65	80	105
(wy_) - 23" - CO - 1952 - brt - plastic cab - "Coast To Coast Truck Lines" - [#?]	85	110	145
(wy_) - 23" - CO - 1952 - brt/2 sets rear dual wheels - plastic cab & metal open trailer - removable chains and side pieces - [#?]	85	110	145

618 Wyandotte

	C6	C8	C10
(wy_) - 24" - CO - 1954 - 14 brt on die cast hubs - die cast cab and aluminum trailer - "Grey Van Lines" - "De Luxe Long Distance Moving" "Affiliated with Greyhound Lines" - (also comes in "Chun King Orient Express" and Allied Van Lines versions) - side and rear doors open - [6000]	90	150	225
(wy_) - 24" - CO - 1956/57 - brt - cattle truck - [#?]	70	90	115
(wy_) - 24-1/2" - CO - 1953 - brt on die cast hubs - removable stake panels - "Motor Freight Lines" - [#?]	75	100	125
(wy_) - 25" - CO - 1941 - 6 brt with wood hubs & metal inserts - 1941 - rear door with mounted spare tire - 3 front/2 rear reflectors - "Van Truck"-[#1500]	60	105	150
(wy_) - 25" - CO - 1941 - 6 brt with wood hub & metal inserts - 1941 - rear door with mounted spare tire - Mini tarpaulin-"Highway Freight"[1501]	60	105	150

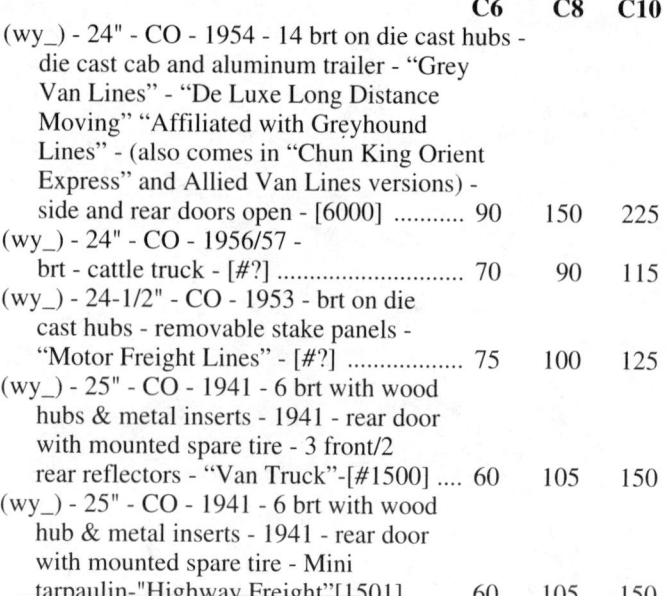

Tractor (Semi) Trailer, "Shady Glen Stock Ranch" cattle truck; value in C6, C8, C10: $70, 95, 140. Photo by Bob Smith.

CARS

	C6	C8	C10

ADVERTISING

	C6	C8	C10
(wy204) - 4-3/8 - LN - 1936/40 - www- "Take a ride with Sophie" "Sophie Tucker and her ROI - TAN show on the radio/C.B.S. Mon. Wed. Fri." on one side - "Roi-Tan Cigars/An auto a day is given away/a brand new 1939 Chevrolet" - on the other side - [#?]	130	195	260

WY204

	C6	**C8**	**C10**

AIR SPEED COUPES
(wy026) - 6" - AS/F - 1934/37 - wrt - [309]   70   85   100

Coupe, WY26. Courtesy Brian Seligman.

WY026 AS/F

(wy225) - 6" - AS/C -
    1934/37 - wrt - [309] 70   85   100

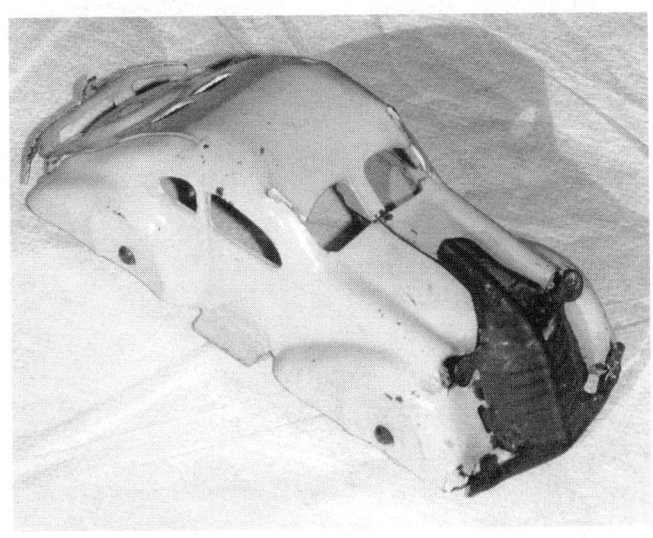

WY225 AS/C

	C6	**C8**	**C10**

AIR SPEED COUPE & TRAILER
(wy080) - 11-1/4" -
    AST - 1934 - wrt/brt - [341] 130   170   225

WY080

AMBULANCE
(wy_) - 6-3/8" - RC - 1938 - wrt - side
    ports - surface mounted grille - [#?] 40   65   80
(wy_) - 6-3/8" - RC - 1939 - bww - side
    ports - inset front grille - [#224] 35   50   75
(wy_) - 6-1/2" - LN -
    1952 - brt - friction - "Ambulance
    & Red Cross" - stretcher - [#?] 70   85   105
(wy_) - 9-1/2" - LN - 1952/53 - brt -
    red - "Fire Dept. Rescue Squad
    truck" - friction motor & siren -
    ("ambulance" - white - with
    stretcher - same look) - [#?] 35   50   75
(wy042) - 11-1/4" - LN - 1936/38 -
    bww - "Ambulance" - "Wyandotte
    Toys" - opening rear hatch - [#340] 65   85   105

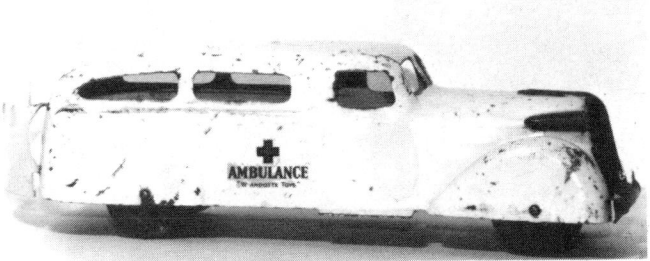

Ambulance, WY42. Courtesy Brian Seligman.

(wy_) - 11-1/4" - LN - 1939 -
    bww - "Ambulance" stamped -
    opening rear hatch - [#?] 65   85   105

ARMY
(wy_) - 9" - AW - 1942 - bww - "Jeep" -
    all wood - construction - [368] .... No Price Found

The jeep, armored car, and probably the ambulance, are WWII Wyandottes, cardboard; value as shown $10 each. Photo by Jack Matthews.

Top to Bottom: WY016, WY017, WY207

Boat Tail Racer, WY16. Courtesy Brian Seligman.

	C6	C8	C10
BOAT - TAIL RACER			
(wy016) - 5-7/8" - BT - 1933/34 - wrt - green/red - [310]	40	50	75
(wy017) - 8-5/8" - BT - 1934 - wrt - green/red - electric lights - [333]	60	95	125
(wy340) - 8-5/8" - BT - 1933 - yww - red - electric lights - [#?]	75	105	135
(wy207) - 10-1/4" - BT - 1934 - bww - red - elec lites - [#?]	95	120	150
CONVERTIBLES			
(wy029) - 4-3/8" - CV - 1936/40 - wrt/www - also part of the garage set-1938/40 - [102]	10	25	35

L To R: WY017, WY340

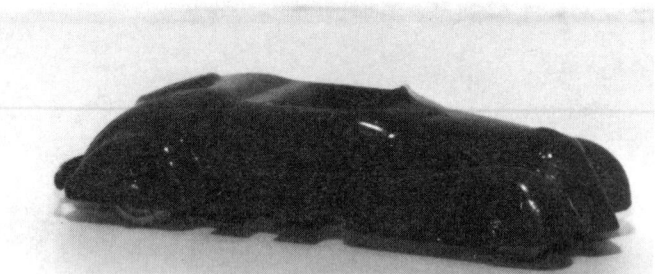

Convertible, WY29. Courtesy Brian Seligman.

Boat Tail Racer, WY17. Courtesy Brian Seligman.

WY029, two views

WY121

	C6	C8	C10
(wy121) - 12" - SPC - 1947/48 - brt - sportsman convertible - retractable top - woodie look sides - license plate WY650 - [650]- (with wind up motor - 651)	165	190	235
(wy166) - 12" - SPC - 1947/48 - brt - non woodie - plastic driver and windshield - attached key wind up - license plate WY 652 - [#?]	150	200	250

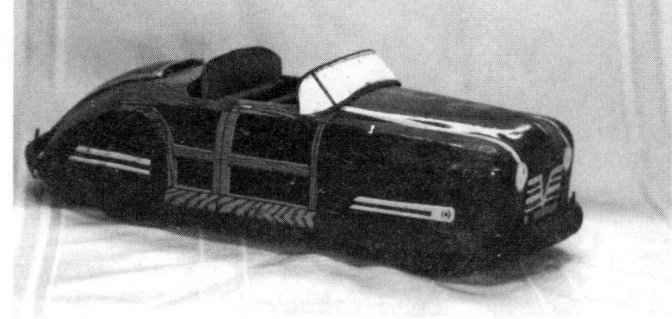

Woody Convertible. Photo by Calvin L. Chaussee.

WY166

CORD

	C6	C8	C10
(wy162) - 13-3/8" - 1936/37 - brt on wood hubs - "Zephyr" pull back wind up motor-[600]	125	350	550

WY162

	C6	C8	C10
(wy_) - CD - 13-3/8" - 1938/39 - bww - [#?]	75	275	425
(wy036) - CD - 13-3/8" - 1937 - bww - "Fire Dept" - wind up motor with attached key - hood mounted brass bell - [#?]	125	300	475

WY036

	C6	C8	C10
(wy_) - CD - 13-3/8" - 1938 - brt - "Fire Dept" - "Zephyr" motor - hood mounted brass bell - [#?]	125	300	425
(wy_) - CD - 17-1/4" - 1938/39 - brt - "Fire Dept" - brass bell - [#?]	100	300	525
(wy_) - CD - 17-3/8" - 1939-brt - "Fire Dept" - brass bell - wind up motor with attached key - [#384]	125	325	575

CORD AND TRAILER SET

	C6	C8	C10
(wy024) - 23-1/2" - CDT - 1938/39 - bww - rear opening trailer door - [#363]	100	300	450

Cord & Trailer Set, WY24. Courtesy Brian Seligman.

	C6	C8	C10
COUPES (2-DOOR)			
(wy086) - 4-3/8 - LN - 1936/40 - wrt or www - also with 2 car garage set - [103]	10	25	40

WY086, two views

Coupe, WY86. Courtesy Brian Seligman.

L to R: WY015, WY014

	C6	C8	C10
(wy014) - 4-1/2" - RW - 1934/36 - wrt - trunk mounted spare tire - [312]	35	50	70
(wy038) - 4-7/8" - SW - 1932 - yww - [#?]	60	75	90

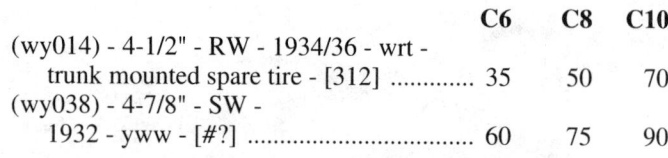

Coupe, WY38. Courtesy Brian Seligman.

L to R: WY059, WY058

	C6	C8	C10
(wy058) - 6-3/8 - RW - 1934 - eww "Circus type" - [#?]	35	50	70
(wy039) - 8-1/4" - SW - 1932 - yww - Rumble Seat - [#?]	55	95	135

Coupe, WY39. Courtesy Brian Seligman.

Coupe, WY40. Courtesy Brian Seligman.

	C6	C8	C10
(wy040) - 8-1/4" - SW - 1933 - wrt - electric lights - [#?]	55	100	135
(wy289) - 8-1/4" - SW - 1933 - wrt/red hubs - no light - [#?]	45	90	105

WY289

Coupe w/Trailer, WY27. Courtesy of Brian Seligman.

Coupe w/Trailer, WY90. Courtesy Brian Seligman.

	C6	C8	C10
(wy027) - 11-3/4", 1936/38, bww	No Price Found		
(wy090) - 11-3/4", 1936/38, wrt	No Price Found		

GARAGE SET

	C6	C8	C10
(wy193) - GS - 3-3/4" x 4-3/4" metal litho double door garage with a 4-3/8" coupe and convertible - 1938/39 - wrt - [501]	50	75	115

WY193

Garage Set, "2 Car Garage." Courtesy Brian Seligman.

LA SALLE (a.k.a. Land Cruiser)

	C6	C8	C10
(wy_) - 15" - LS - 1936/39 - wrt - [357]	65	125	190
(wy_) - 15" - LS - 1939 - wrt - hood opens - electric lights - [385]	75	130	210
(wy158) - 15" - LS - 1939 - brt or/wd hubs - hood opens - no electric lights - [#?]	65	110	190
(wy_) - 15-3/4" - LS - 1938 - brt - key attached spring motor - [383]	75	150	190

WY158

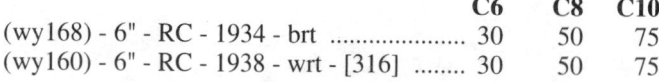

	C6	C8	C10
(wy168) - 6" - RC - 1934 - brt	30	50	75
(wy160) - 6" - RC - 1938 - wrt - [316]	30	50	75

LA SALLE WITH TRAVEL TRAILER

	C6	C8	C10
(wy022) - 26-1/2" - LS - 1936/38 - wrt- opening rear trailer door - [358]	145	275	425

WY344

(wy296) - 6" - CO - 1939/41 - bpw - touring sedan - [#220]	30	50	75

LaSalle & Trailer Set, WY22. Photo by Bob Smith.

ROCKET RACER

(wy061) - RR - 6-1/4" - 1935/36 - wrt or bww - wd rear wheel - [#319]	60	75	115

WY296

Rocket Racer, WY61. Courtesy Brian Seligman.

SEDANS (4-Door)

(wy015) - 4-1/2" - RW - 1934/37 - wrt - trunk mounted rear spare - [311]	35	50	70
(wy344) - 5" - SW - 1934 - bww - sometimes included with auto transport wy99 - [#?]	45	60	75

Sedan, WY59. Courtesy Brian Seligman.

WY059

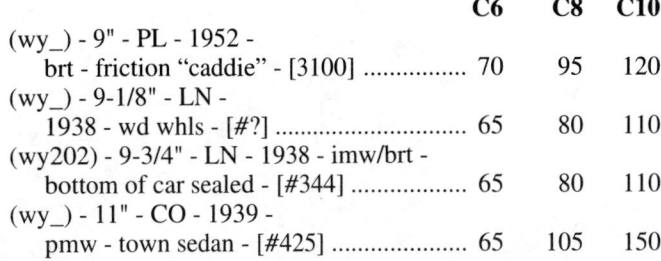

	C6	C8	C10
(wy_) - 9" - PL - 1952 - brt - friction "caddie" - [3100]	70	95	120
(wy_) - 9-1/8" - LN - 1938 - wd whls - [#?]	65	80	110
(wy202) - 9-3/4" - LN - 1938 - imw/brt - bottom of car sealed - [#344]	65	80	110
(wy_) - 11" - CO - 1939 - pmw - town sedan - [#425]	65	105	150

	C6	C8	C10
(wy059) - 6-1/4" - RW - 1934 - eww - [#?]	30	50	75
(wy033) - 9" - RC - 1934 - wrt - electric lights - [#?]	65	80	110

Top to Bottom: WY033, WY168

Sedan, WY33. Courtesy Brian Seligman.

L to R: WY202, WY160

WY033

Wyandotte Cadillac, plastic friction, 8-3/4" long (unlisted); value as shown $75. Photo by Ron Fink.

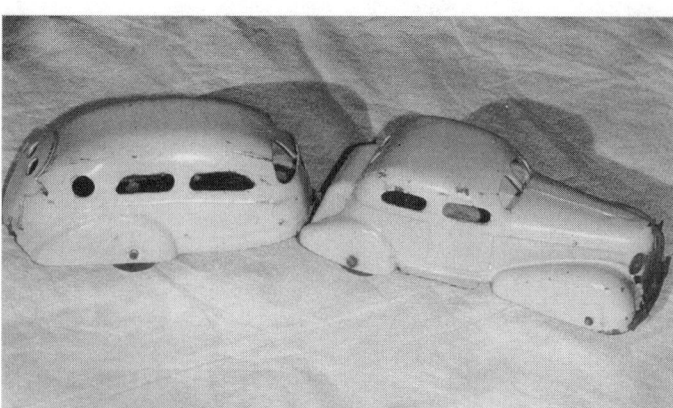

WY030

	C6	**C8**	**C10**

SEDAN WITH TRAVEL TRAILER
(wy030) - 11-3/4" - LN -
   1938 - wrt or bww - opening
   rear trailer door - [346] 60   105   145
(wy080) - 11-3/4, 1938, bww, #7625............. No Price Found

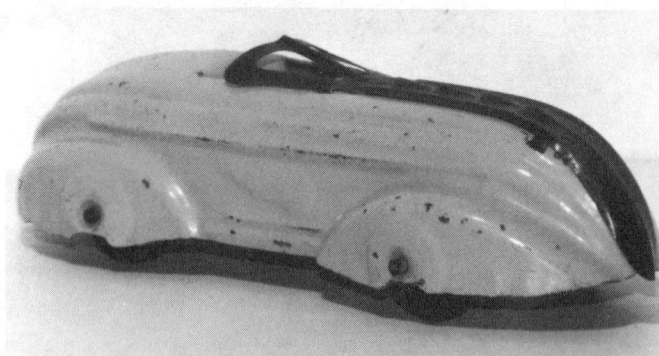

Sedan w/Trailer, WY80. Courtesy Brian Seligman.

SOAP BOX DERBY RACER
(wy161) - 6-1/4" - SB -
   1941 - brt - "Soap Box Derby"-
   "Thunderbird 226" - [226] 75   150   195

WY161

	C6	**C8**	**C10**

SPEEDSTER
(wy011) - 6-3/4" - SP-
   1937/38 - bww - w/litho driver
   and passenger-[378]-(wy012 -
   without people - same number) 40   60   100

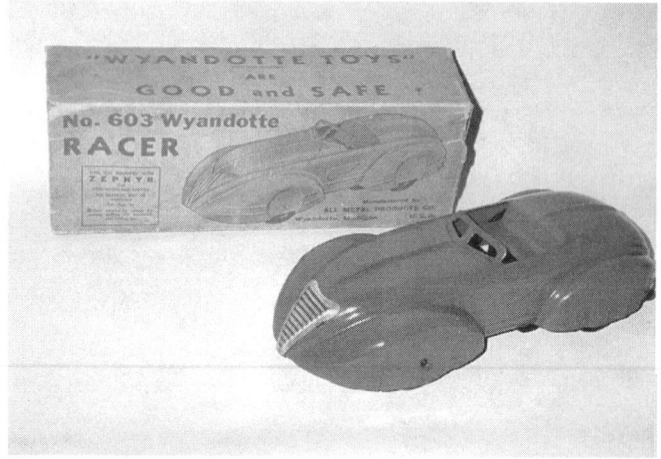

Speedster, WY11. Courtesy Brian Seligman.

(wy013) - 10" - SP - 1937 - bww -
   pull back spring motor - [603] 60   100   140

WY013. Photo by Don Hultzman.

Speedster, WY13. Courtesy Brian Seligman.

Speedster, WY12. Courtesy Brian Seligman.

	C6	C8	C10

(wy012) - 10" - SP - 1938 -
   bww - pull back spring motor -
   cord-like roof over cockpit - [#?] ....
	65	105	150

TOWN CAR (mistaken for Wyandotte but is Marx)

TOY TOWN-large scale
(wy_) - 21" - TT - 1941 - brt on wood
   hubs - estate station wagon -
   "woodie" sides - litho of family in
   windows - rear doors open - [1007] -
   (1009 has luggage rack on roof) 70   125   215
(wy_) - 21" - TT - 1941 - brt on wood hubs - grocer
   wagon - "Meats and Groceries," litho of driver
   in window, rear-doors open - [1008] 70   125   215

Toytown Estate Station Wagon, missing door. Photo by Calvin L. Chaussee.

CONSTRUCTION

STEAM SHOVEL
(wy167) - 7" x 4" body/12" boom/6-1/2"
   x 3-7/8 chassis - early 1950s - brt -
   "Wyandotte Construction Company" -
   also came with litho body and
   "Sturdy Construction" on side - [#?] 35   55 75

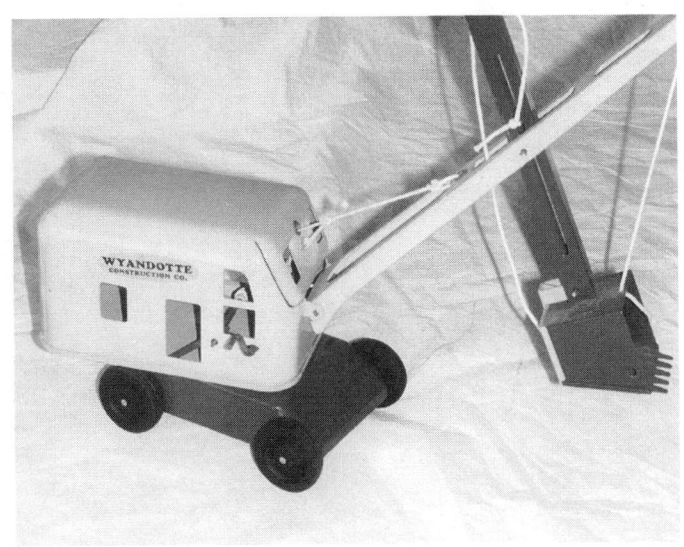

WY167

	C6	C8	C10

CATERPILLAR GRADER
(wy_) - 12" - 1952 - all plastic
   construction except for metal
   blade - black & yellow - [#?] ....
	60	80	100

CATERPILLAR SCRAPER
(wy_) - 12" - 1952 - all plastic
   construction except for metal
   blade - black & yellow-[#?] ....
	60	80	100

CATERPILAR WAGON (wy_) - 12" - 1952 - all plastic construction - black & yellow - [#?]	60	80	100

EARTH MOVER
(wy313) - 20-1/2" - CE -
   1952/53 - brt - orange - "Heavy
   Duty" - "Highway Engineers" - [#?] ......
	55	85	105

WY313

WY328

	C6	C8	C10

ROAD GRADER
(wy328) - 19" - 1952/53 - CE -
   brt - orange - "Power Grader" - [#?] 55   85   105

SAND LOADER AND CRANE
(wy110) - 5-1/2" high/3-3/4" base/20"
   reach - bww - red & green - ("super
   scoop shovel" - 401) - 7" high/5-1/2"
   square (sand hopper - 347) - 1938 -
   N/A -when 11-1/4" dump truck was
   added it was known as the
   "Highway Construction Set" [402] 50   80   100

	C6	C8	C10

SAND LOADER AND DUMP TRUCK
(wy290) - 10-3/4" truck - CO/CB - 1954/56 -
   brt and 10-5/8" tall Sand Loader w/string
   operated dump hoist - "Wyandotte"
   on side of truck - "Wyandotte
   Construction Company" on
   side of Sand Loader - [401] 85   125   190

WY290

Construction WY110. Courtesy Brian Seligman.

**TRUCK MOUNTED CLAM SHELL BUCKET STEAM
SHOVEL**
(wy_) - 14/21" - CO - 1952 - brt -
   plastic cab with litho grille - steel
   chassis & clam bucket - "Sturdy
   Construction" - [1012] 185   225   275

	C6	C8	C10

WINCH TRUCK and STEAM SHOVEL

Construction WY97. Courtesy Brian Seligman.

(wy_) - 7" - CO - late 1940s/50s - brt -
removable steam shovel - [#?] 65   80   90

(wy_) - 10" - CO - 1952 - brt - all plastic
- removable steam shovel - [#?] 60   75   80

(wy097) - 22" - CO - 1952 - brt -
removable crane - [1201] 80   100   125

(wy_) - 22-1/2" - OE - 1954 - brt on
red plastic hubs - tractor & flatbed with
treaded steam shovel - tool box
w/tools behind cab - [#?] 50   75   125

(wy333) - 23" - WF - 1949/53 - brt -
"Wyandotte Construction Co." on
side of removable crane - [#?] 85   105   135

YONE

(Japan)

Yone, Ford Falcon, wipers work 45   68   90

Yone, Monster Car tin windup,
c.1960s, monsters at windows 48   72   95

SOURCES

TOY SHOWS

There are hundreds of toy shows across the United States every year. The best way to find out about them is through such periodicals as *Antique Toy World* and *Toy Shop*. However, to get the novice started, here are a few of the more prominent shows:

ALLENTOWN, PA: November, 800-392-TOYS.
ROCHESTER, NY: June and November, Bob Smith (716) 377-8394, fax (716) 377-6019.
DALLAS: July, November, Don Maris, (817) 261-8745.
CHICAGO: April, June, October, (312) 725-0633.
NEW YORK and NEWARK, NJ: September, June, Bob Bostoff, (516) 791-4858.
DAYTON, OHIO: May, (513) 233-8381.
TOLEDO, OHIO: July, October, John Carlisle, Old Toyland Shows, Bewley Bldg., Rm. 409, Lockport, NY 14094.
ATLANTA: November, (404) 987-2773.
PASADENA. CA: January, (213) 656-1266.

PERIODICALS

There are many periodicals devoted wholly or partially to toys. The following are probably the most important to readers of this book. *Antique Toy World* tends to run articles and ads on the older vehicles, *Toy Shop* tends to run ads on the newer ones, and *U.S. Toy* concentrates, in text and ads, almost exclusively on vehicles.

American Toy Collector, bimonthly, $36 a year, DeSalle Promotions, Inc., 5106 Knollwood, Anderson, IN 46011.
Antique Toy World, monthly, $39.95 a year, P.O. Box 34509, Chicago, IL 60634.
National Toy Connection, bimonthly, $22.95 a year (sent first class), Ste. 2346, 779 E. Merritt Island Cswy., Merritt Island, FL 32952.
Toy Shop, biweekly, $26.95 a year, 700 E. State St., Iola, WI 54990.
U.S. Toy, Monthly, $21 a year, P.O. Box 4244 Missoula, MT 59801.

TOY REPAIRERS AND RESTORERS

There are a number of experts in this area. Some of them do it full-time and even have full-time employees. Most or all advertise in the publications above. But for the beginner, here are some of the leading names:

New Era Toy Restorations: pressed steel, (609) 397-2113.
Portell Restorations: pedal cars, (314) 937-8192.
Castings: Walter Allen, (508) 283-2988.
Decals: Bob Gerrity, (206) 941-6055.
Arnie Prince: cast iron, (209) 334-6101.
Paint & Rust Removal: (914) 359-1736 and (914) 937-3354.
Plastic Parts Reproductions: Toy Surgeon, 6528 Cedarbrook, New Albany, Ohio 43054.
Buddy L, etc. parts, accessories, decals, (215) 838-6505.
Don Hultzman: Repairs battery-operated and tin wind-ups, 5026 Sleepy Hollow Rd., Medina, Ohio 44256.
Tin Toy Works: missing parts and complete restorations, (215) 439-8268.
Julian Thomas: iron or tin repairs, wind-ups, decals, Thomas Toys, P.O. Box 405, Fenton, MI 48430. (Enclose SASE.)
Joe Freeman: Tin Toy Works, repairs, parts made for tin toys. 1313 N. 15th St. Allentown, PA 18102, (610) 439-8268.

SOME LEADING COLLECTORS & DEALERS

When writing to any of the following, please enclose a stamped, self-addressed envelope.

IAIN C. BAILLE
Lledo Collector
20 Chester St.
London, SW1X 7BL
England

BILL BERTOIA AUCTIONS
1881 Spring Road
Vineland, NJ 08360
(609) 692-1881, fax (609) 692-8697

BLYSTONE'S (Bill & Sue Blystone)
Leading dealer in collector books, especially toys
2132 Delaware Ave.
Pittsburgh, PA 15218
Phone: (412) 371-3511, fax: (412) 244-8028

JEFF BUB
Auctioneer, appraisals
1658 Barbara Dr.
Brunswick, OH 44212
(216) 225-1110

ROD CARNAHAN
Classic cast-iron toys, etc.
541 El Paso St.
Jacksonville, TX 75766

CHICAGO ANTIQUE TOY AUCTIONS
by JUST RIGHT, INC.
6582 R.F.D.
Long Grove, IL 60047
(708) 949-0059

KENT M. COMSTOCK
Motorcycles of every type
532 Pleasant St.
Ashland, Ohio 44805
(419) 289-3308

CONTINENTAL HOBBY HOUSE
Toys and trains, regular catalogs
P.O. Box 193
Sheboygan, WI 53082

DON COVIELLO
Collector and produces die-cast police-car replicas
Box 283
Purchase, NY 10577

BARB & DON DESALLE
Tonka, especially Private Label trucks
5106 Knollwood
Anderson, IN 45011
800-392-TOYS

ECCLES BROTHERS
Vehicles from original molds
Catalog: $3
R.R. 1, Box 253-D
Burlington, IA 52601

PERRY EICHOR
Vehicles, aircraft, literature
703 N. Almond Dr.
Simpsonville, SC 29681

JOE & SHARON FREED
Vehicles
6209 Sandy Forks Rd.
Raleigh, NC 27609

WAYNE FREESE
Sells many toy catalogs, originals and copies
1459 Dogwood
Chester Springs, PA 19425

RAY FUNK
Toy, bicycles
P.O. Box 5019
Upland, CA 91785

JOHN A. GIBSON
Strombecker-Tootsietoy historian
Tootsietoy restoration, parts and services
The Graham Werkes
P.O. Box 40054
Washington, DC 20016
(301) 767-0014, fax (301) 767-0098

HAKE'S AMERICANA & COLLECTIBLES

Mail Auctions
Sample catalog: $3
P.O. Box 1444N
York, PA 17405
(717) 848-1333

BILL HELLIE

ALL AMERICAN TOY COMPANY
American Toy Company parts and limited editions;
buy, sell, restore antique toys
540 Lancaster, S. E.
Salem, OR 97301
(503) 399-8609

JEFFREY L. HUBBARD

Doepke, Nylint, other construction toys, catalogs,
etc.
1770 4th St. South
Naples, FL 34102-7502

DON HULTZMAN

Tin wind-up and battery-operated, also repairs,
restorations
5026 Sleepy Hollow Road
Medina, OH 44256
(330) 225-2668

PEG & RICHARD JANSEN

Mostly pressed steel toys
6420 Weber Rd.
Denmark, WI 54208-9438
(920) 863-2906

WILLIAM KILBORN

Military Dinky, etc.
P.O. Box #614
St. Mary's, Ontario
N4X, 1B4 Canada

BILL LANGO

Barclay vehicles, animals and soldiers from original
and new molds; send for flyer
127 74th St.
North Bergen, NJ 07047

LLOYD L. LAUMANN

Tonka expert, sells copies of catalogs
6980 Co. Rd. 10, North
Waconia, MN 55387-9643

DAVID M. LEOPARD

Old toy cars and trucks
2507 Feather Run Trail
West Columbia, SC 29169-4915

GARY J. LINDEN

Marx and other plastic toys
P.O. Box 243
River Forest, IL 60305

RICHARD MacNARY

Coca-Cola vehicles
4727 Alpine Dr.
Lilburn, GA 30247

MAPES AUCTIONEERS & APPRAISERS

1600 Vestal Parkway West
Vestal, NY 13850
(607) 754-9193

JOHN D. (JACK) MATTHEWS

World War II toys, etc.
13 Bufflehead Dr.
Kiawah Island, SC 29455

FRED MAXWELL: COLLECTOR-RESEARCHER

Slush-mold cars, planes, novelties, literature, toys
4722 N. 33rd St.
Arlington, VA 22207

MARK B. McMANUS

Matchbox, Tonka, etc.
204 Post St.
Boonville, NY 13309
(315) 942-2185, fax (315) 942-5579

JOHN MURRAY

Fisher-Price
Box 29
Eden, NY 14057

National Automotive and Truck Museum of the United States (Includes museum of toy and model cars and trucks)
1000 Gordon M. Buehrig Place
Auburn, Indiana 46706
 (219) 925-9100

THOMAS G. NEFOS
Hess, investment-quality transportation toys
Publisher of *National Toy Connection*
National Toy Connection
779 East Merritt Island Cswy.
Merritt Island, Florida 32952-3516
800-704-1232

OEI ENTERPRISES, LTD.
Buys, sells, trades, restores old toys
241 Rowayton Ave.
Rowayton, CT 06853-1227
(203) 866-2470

EDWARD K. POOLE
1/36 scale ID vehicles and old wooden military vehicle kits
926 Terrace Mt. Drive
Austin, TX 78746

HARVEY K. RAINESS
Dealer in vehicles, tin, all soldiers
Rustic Ridge-N13
289 Mount Hope Ave.
Dover, NJ 07801
(201) 366-4677

LLOYD W. RALSTON
Auctions
173 Post Road
Fairfield, CT 06430
(203) 255-1233

VINCENT ROSA
Brooklins (sells the *Brooklin Book & Collector's Guide*)
Model Cars & Trains Unlimited
28 Arthur Ave.
Blue Point, NY 11715
(516) 363-2134

SECOND CHILDHOOD
Antique Toys
283 Bleecker St.
New York, NY

BRIAN SELIGMAN
Wyandotte, Marx, Girard
11004 SW 37th Manor
Davie, FL 33328
(954) 431-6942

SCOTT SMILES
Tin wind-ups, etc.
848 S. Atlantic Dr., E.
Lantana, FL 33462

BOB SMITH
Old Toys, buy, sell, trade, appraise
RATS Toy Shows
62 West Ave.
Fairport, NY 14450
(716) 377-8394, fax (716) 377-6019

RON SMITH
Tin, Hot Wheels, promos, die-cast cars, trucks, planes
33005 Arlesford
Solon, Ohio 44139
(216) 248-7066

FRED THOMPSON
New designs of Smitty vehicles
Smith-Miller Inc.
P.O. Box 139
Canoga Park, CA 91305

ROBERT & ALICE WAGNER
Toy vehicles of all types
58 S. Main St.
Wharton, NJ 07885

GATES WILLARD
1925-40 automotive toys
233 Manhasset Ave.
Manhasset, NY 11030

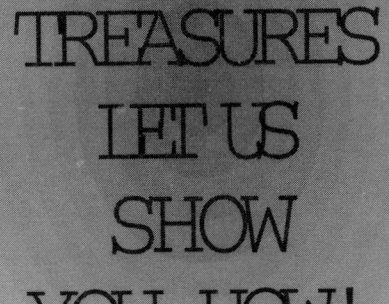

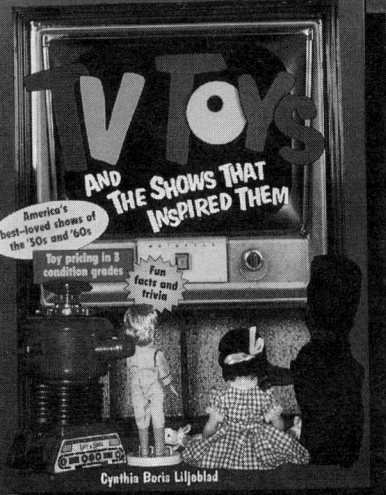

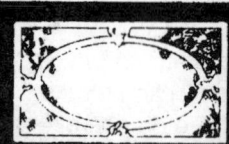